69
93
03
1
PROVIMI
VEAL
6

GO!

THE BETTENHAUSEN STORY

The Race Against A Dream

by Carl H. Hungness

Carl Hungness Publishing
Book Manufactory

Speedway, Indiana

Carl Hungness Publishing
P. O. Box 24308
Speedway, IN 46224

First Printing: December, 1982

Library of Congress Card No.82-84360
ISBN: 0-915088-33-9

Printed in the U.S.A. by
Carl Hungness Publishing

For my mother, Josephine.

"The Sins of The Fathers
Are Visited Upon The Sons"

Exodus 20:5

Acknowledgements

It is standard procedure for a race car driver to stand up at an awards banquet and thank his crew, his car owner and a multitude of sponsors who have aided his effort. Such is the case with this biography, but there are literally hundreds of owners, drivers, fans, mehcanics, sponsors, acquaintances and even some adversaries who have assisted me in the ten year compilation of this work. To list one and leave out another is unfair.

Thus it is impossible to print a list of contributors to the Bettenhausen story. Sometimes it took a couple of seasons to convince a man that his story or ancedote was important to this manuscript and through luck and perserverance I can honestly say that everyone I asked for assistance cooperated. Dusty files were opened to me and old negatives illuminated once again to recapture history. The writing of this book was a task that required outside assistance from its inception to completion.

Through the efforts of my own staff, Justyn Blackwell, Terri Gunn, Rick Whitt and Wilma Steffy I've been afforded the freedom to produce this manuscript. Also, a special thanks to Dr. Mary Rae for editing assistance. My sincere thanks to everyone, for without you the job would have been impossible one for me.

This Is A True Story.

Preface

The name is well-known only in some towns in the United States. Throughout the corn-belt, Pennsylvania, some parts of New York and out west in Arizona and California you mention the name Bettenhausen and our listener may say, "Yes, it rings a bell....what's he do?"

To the oval track automobile racing fans of the world the name has been recognizable for over forty years. But there are so many forms of automobile racing that each segment has its own heroes. The common grounds for anyone who considers themself an auto racing fan are the two most famous race tracks in the U.S.: The Daytona International Speedway and the race track located only a few miles from downtown Indianapolis, Indiana. The race track in Daytona Beach, Florida holds, among many other events, the Daytona 500. It is a race for a type of vehicle known as a Stock car. Simply, a Stock car is meant to resemble our everyday passenger vehicles.

The track at Indianapolis holds one race annually, the Indianapolis 500. Although the Indianapolis Motor Speedway is open during the entire month of May for practice and qualifying, its only event throughout the year is held near the end of the month. Over 400,000 spectators jam the 529 acre facility to make the Indy 500 the world's largest single-day sporting event. The first "500" was held in 1911 and except for the war years, the race has become not only an annual tradition, but a way of life to some of its participants and fans.

This is the story of one family, basically a farm family who tilled the Midwest soil, and their quest for one of their men to become victorious in the Indianapolis 500. There exists at the Indianapolis Motor Speedway, as well as at most any other automobile race in the world, an aura that has an addictive magnetism for some. To the casual fan or the uninformed, this addiction cannot be understood unless it is experienced. Shaking one's addiction to professional automobile racing has been likened to quitting heroin. Participants become so enamored with being involved with the auto racing scene, that better judgement is often cast aside. The participation reaches much farther than to those who merely drive the cars. Fans, photographers, writers, mechanics, racing promoters, sponsors all share the same feeling when they're at an automobile race.

The Indianapolis 500 is not only the world's most famous race, it is a convention for those dedicated to auto racing. Once the Indianapolis 500 has been run, where do the drivers go? To a dozen or more other race tracks that run the Indy cars.

How does a man qualify to become an Indianapolis 500 driver? It used to be said that he would serve an apprenticeship and become a journeyman in other types of vehicles with names like Sprint cars and Midgets.

Tony Bettenhausen became a journeyman driver and they called him The Tinley Park Express, in honor of his home town in Illinois of the same name. Tony Bettenhausen never did win the Indianapolis 500 and he died trying. He left behind three sons who would all attempt to accomplish what their father could not.

The sons have wives and families just as their father did. They are all verbal, intelligent human beings who do not have a death wish. They cry just like you and I. They do not believe that people come to automobile races to see someone get killed. They believe that the people in the grandstands want to see close competition, action. They know that the fan in the stands doesn't mind seeing a driver go through a horrendous crash, but they believe the fans want to see the car's occupant stand up and wave to the crowd after the accident as taken place.

On their way to becoming Indianapolis 500 drivers, they find that the monetary rewards are few and the risks are high. They consider themselves fortunate people because they are doing what they want to do in life. Sometimes. They know they're different. The sons of Tony Bettenhausen have worked a dozen hours a day to follow their seemingly predestined occupation but they have never considered it a job.

While making a profession out of a sport that may also be considered an enterprise, the Bettehausens have seen the curious come and look at them and wonder what it is, this fascination with cars that go around in a circle, that outlines their lives into such a seemingly narrow pattern. Yet the Bettenhausens know that all of the world's business, its leaders and followers may at sometime come into their way of life. The small, relatively insignificant sport of auto racing has within its confines all those who make up the rest of the population. Within the sport of speed they can experience love, marriage, death and business. They can find poetry and literature, experimentation and innovation. They can know the publicized joy of victory and agony of defeat.

For your reading enjoyment we suggest you take a moment and turn to page ix to familiarize yourself with terms that are used throughout the text. You'll find simple descriptions of four basic vehicles: Championship Indy car; Sprint Car; Midget and Stock Car.

Glossary

Automobile Racing consists of so very many forms that the casual fan or observer is easily confused. It may be broken down into many categories. This book is concerned with "Championship" (Indy car), "Midget" and "Sprint" car racing on a professional level.

Sports Car Racing: Just what the name implies. The vehicles range from stock-bodied production cars to highly sophisticated racing machines. Races held on road courses as opposed to oval tracks.

Drag Racing: Not mentioned at all in this book. Consists of two vehicles racing side-by-side for a distance of a quarter mile.

Stock Car Racing: Performed by vehicles that are supposed to resemble every day passenger cars. Most local oval tracks in the United States feature a form of Stock Car racing.

Championship Racing: Traditionally the cars that race at the Indianapolis 500 are called Championship cars. Considered the most exotic and sophisticated of all racing machines. Today these same cars run 12-15 other tracks, both oval and road course. (See Definitions)

Sprint Car Racing: Special vehicles designed to run mostly on half-mile and larger dirt and paved oval tracks. (See Definitions)

Midget Car Racing: Very similar to Sprint cars, slightly smaller. (See Definitions)

Formula I Racing: Very similar in appearance to Championship cars. Run on road courses only throughout the world.

Open-Cockpit/Open Wheel: When someone refers to an open-wheel or open cockpit car it may be anything but a stock car. An Indy car, Sprint, Midget, Dirt car are all open-wheel/open-cockpit cars. Traditionally had no driver protection, progressed to having a small roll bar behind the driver's head and in the early Seventies progressed to having a full roll cage assembly over the driver's head.

CHAMPIONSHIP INDY CAR

Sometimes simply called a Champ car, or an Indy car or a "Speedway" car. These are the cars that run not only in the Indianapolis 500, but 12-15 other races around the country on a circuit popularly titled: The Championship Trail. Considered the most sophisticated of all racing machinery. They race on tracks of one mile or more in length. They are powered mostly by turbo-charged V-8 engines.

SPRINT CAR

Considered to be the most lethal race car ever invented. Their power to weight ratio is awesome and it is usually agreed they have too much horsepower. They race mostly on half mile tracks, both dirt and pavement. In days gone by a good Sprint car driver would expect to be hired by an Indy 500 car owner.

MIDGET

Probably the most versatile of all race cars. The name is a mis-nomer, for they are full size racing vehicles that are capable of competing on a variety of tracks ranging from a tenth-mile indoor hockey rink sized track to a full mile track where the Indy cars run. Powered mostly by four-cylinder engines. They look like a Sprint car, only smaller. Traditionally, Indy 500 drivers would start their careers in Midgets and graduate to Sprint cars.

STOCK CARS

They look like modern-day passenger vehicles with their interiors gutted and replaced with a maze of roll bars. Gained their popularity in the Southern United States.

CHAMPIONSHIP DIRT CAR

Looks like a Sprint car, slightly larger. Races only on the old, traditional one-mile dirt tracks at places like DuQuoin and Springfield, Illinois; Syracuse, New York. Once upon a time most Indy 500 cars looked like this. They are a hold-over from a bygone age in racing that still survives on a limited basis.

Here are some of the people you will encounter in this book.

Melvin Eugene (Tony) Bettenhausen	Patriarch of the family. Born in 1916 in Tinley Park, Illinois. Started his auto racing career in 1937 and by 1950 was one of America's most popular and successful drivers. Was a two time national driving champion and considered one of the greatest dirt track drivers of all time. Had a life-long desire to win the Indianapolis 500.
Valerie Stephan	Wife of Tony Bettenhausen. Born Valerie Rice. Was twice married to Tony and is the mother of his four children. Re-married after his death to Webb Stephan.
Gary Bettenhausen	Eldest son of Tony Bettenhausen. Born 1941.
Merle Bettenhausen	Second son of Tony Bettenhausen. Born 1943.
Susan Anselmi	Daughter of Tony Bettenhausen. Born Susan Bettenhausen in 1945.
Tony Bettenhausen, Jr.	Youngest son of Tony Bettenhausen. Born 1951.
Dennis (Duke) Nalon	Tony Bettenhausen's early idol and later best friend.
Emil Andres	Tony's first friend in auto racing, lifelong acquaintance, early auto racing teacher to Tony.
Paul Russo	Race car driver, close friend of Tony's.
Henry Banks	Race car driver, close friend of Tony and his sons. Later in his life was Director of Competition of the United States Auto Club (USAC).
Murrell Belanger	Automobile dealer and race car owner who became a close family friend. Tony Bettenhausen drove Belanger's race cars, successfully, for many years.

Lindsey Hopkins	Southern gentleman, race car owner who has been active in the sport since before World War II. Friend of Tony Bettenhausen and his sons.
Bill Vukovich, Sr.	Two-time Indianapolis 500 winner sometimes called "The Mad-Russian" by the racing press. Quiet man, friend of Tony Bettenhausen's who was killed while attempting to win a third Indianapolis 500.
Billy Vukovich, Jr.	Son of Bill Vukovich, Sr. Closest friend to Gary Bettenhausen and also a professional race car driver.
Johnnie Parsons, Sr.	Close friend of Tony Bettenhausen, winner of the 1950 Indianapolis 500.
Johnny Parsons, Jr.	Son of Johnnie Parsons, Sr. Considered a chip off the old block. Close friend to the Bettenhausen sons.
Chris Economaki	Editor and publisher of the nation's most popular oval track auto racing newspaper, *National Speed Sport News.* A fan and writer since the Thirties. Has known virtually every famed race driver in America for the past 40 years. ABC commentator.
Larry Dickson	Gary Bettenhausen's arch rival in Sprint car racing. Considered one of the finest Sprint car drivers ever to appear in America. Close friend of Gary Bettenhausen.
Ernest Schlausky/Crocky Wright	A fan whose life-long desire it was to race in the Indianapolis 500. Has devoted his entire existence to following the sport.
Willie Davis	Gary Bettenhausen's Sprint car owner and mechanic. Davis has also devoted his entire life to automobile racing.
Roger Penske	One of the most successful car owners ever to appear at Indianapolis. Gary Bettenhausen drove for him.

Wavelyn Bettenhausen	Wife of Gary Bettenhausen. Mother of his twin sons Cary and Todd. Born Wavelyn Kent.
Leslie Bettenhausen	Wife of Merle Bettenhausen, mother of his two children Tracy and Ryan. Born Leslie Sauer.
Shirley McElreath Bettenhausen	Wife of Tony Bettenhausen, Jr. Mother of his daughter Bryn. Daughter of race car driver Jim McElreath and sister of James McElreath who was killed in a Sprint car accident.
Webb Stephan	Second husband of Valerie Bettenhausen, step-father to Tony Bettenhausen's sons. Had no connection with auto racing before meeting Valerie.
AAA	American Automobile Association. The premier auto racing sanctioning body from 1902-1955.
USAC	United States Auto Club: The club founded in late 1955 to carry on AAA's auto racing sanctioning activities.
CART	Championship Auto Racing Teams: Group of Indy car owners who split from USAC to sanction their own races. Sanction all Indy car races except the Indy 500 which USAC still controls.

Contents

1

I Can Do That

The new Ford was going at least sixty. Its driver smiled when he saw the red-read standing in the yard at the corner. Without letting off the gas he jerked the wheel to the left and began a slide onto Harlem Avenue. Eyes widening, the girl anticipated an accident. It'd tip over sure.

As he snapped the steering wheel all the way back to the right so the skinny tires were pointing in the direction of the slide, he looked out the window, grinned, and shouted, "Hi, Val."

She could see a rooster-tail of dirt flying from under the churning rear wheels, and in a second he was gone.

"His fancy driving and new car! Oh, that Bettenhausen boy! Who's he trying to impress?"

Tony had already gained a reputation around Tinley Park as a show-off, but a popular show-off. Blessed with a smile that tagged the kid a charmer, he was christened Melvin Eugene Bettenhausen. But he wasn't a horn-rimmed Melvin. He was cocky and feisty. Out on the family farm, he boxed every day with Frank Jackson, head of the hired hands. Frank would stand tall and shout, "I'm Jack Dempsey. Now who'll be Gene Tunney?"

"I'm Tunni!" Tony would boast. And thus the name stuck. He was good at pretending he was a tough guy. When the tough guy act didn't work, he'd hit out with the charm. That worked. And when he was caught digging ruts in the Tinley Park streets with the back wheels of his new Ford, or sliding around corners daredevil style, the town cop shook his head. "Melvin Eugene Bettenhausen" -- he said the name distinctly -- "Better slow down. Next time I'll tell Clarence."

Clarence was tough. Tony could usually talk his way out of almost any problem with Mom, but you couldn't bluff Clarence. He was probably more strict than Dad. What could Dad have been like anyway? Tony often wondered.

All he knew was a photograph -- tall, black hair, deep eyes -- dead at forty-eight -- kicked in the chest by a work horse. Christian H. Bettenhausen -- born on the farm his father had purchased when he migrated from Bremen, Germany. Dad had made the land pay, and Mom and Clarence sold corn and beans and milk enough to take care of the nine of them.

It hadn't been easy. Tony remembered Mom telling how, after the funeral, she had gathered the children around the kitchen table and prayed that God would guide them -- keep them together -- make them good. She named Clarence head of the family; it was his duty; he couldn't dodge it. He must guide his brothers and sisters, from Herbert to little Melvin.

The excitement of Chicago, only an hour's drive away, had not lured the Bettenhausen sons, even though they read the *Chicago Tribune* every day. Men were out of work everywhere. Soup lines formed four blocks long off State Street. But there was no Depression on the Bettenhausen farm -- good crops, chickens, hogs, cows.

Everyone had his chores. But Tony didn't take much pride in his. Yet by the time he was thirteen, he was the farm handyman. Clarence couldn't do without him. Tony had already learned to drive by the time he was a teenager and was fascinated by anything that had wheels on it. He liked to get his hands dirty with those things under the hoods of Model A Fords and tractors. Things that most people didn't know anything about. Let somebody else fix them when they didn't run. But not Tony. When they didn't start there was always a simple reason. Know what you were doing. And Tony always knew exactly what he was doing. All you had to do was ask him.

"I can fix it," he'd say. And he could usually back up his claims. When caught experimenting, he'd tell you he was going to make something work better.

"I don't know if you're just plain lazy or smart," Clarence told him after Tony had installed an electric pump on their hand-operated well.

"Try 'er now, Clarence." He wanted his brothers to be proud of him. They mustn't call him "Mama's Boy" and be jealous.

Once, when he was 15, someone was needed to drive the milk route around the neighboring farms. Each morning farmers left their cans in the small white milk houses out front for collection. Tony told Clarence he could handle the job if he could use the truck. Clarence warned him first, people would be depending on him, and so he would have to be reliable.

Tony never missed a morning. Clarence was proud and later put him to work driving a grain truck. The baby of the family showed that he also could do a hard day's work. If he wanted. But he wasn't much interested in the farm -- that was sure.

Once his work was over, Tony would take off for town. "What do you do there?" Clarence asked.

"Mess around," Tony replied.

Tony's adventures usually amounted to no more than an evening's drive with his buddies to neighboring towns. Sometimes they would go to Chicago where Tony could show off his new Ford. The new Fords had V-8 engines and the company heralded their innovation with an advertising slogan of "Move Over, There's A Ford Going By." That fit Tony's style.

"They're right," he told Clarence. "This thing is a lot faster than our old Model A. This V-8 engine's sure better."

Tony considered himself an automotive expert -- a veteran mechanic. He had been out of school three years now. Actually, how much could you learn about cars in school?

Tony and school never got along very well anyhow. So after he finished the eight grade, he didn't go back. High school was all the way into town: it wasn't worth the effort.

Tony's grade school had been right next door. A one-room, white-board building with a tall steeple and pointed roof. Going was kinda like doing the chores: it had to be done, but you didn't have to like it. A picture of a car, an airplane, a locomotive -- then the books became interesting. Then, you could imagine what it's like driving a car or flying a fighter plane, who wanted to know all that history stuff anyway?

He had to study about the War. Some of it was interesting. "Did you know that Captain Eddie Rickenbacker shot down 22 planes?" he asked Clarence.

"Why Melvin, I thought you didn't read."

"Oh, I like fellas who do something exciting. Now Cap'n Eddie . . . he was a race car driver too, you know."

Clarence liked the boy. He was sharp. When they would go to town, Tony delighted in identifying the different makes of cars they saw.

"That's a Pierce."

"How do you know?"

"Cause it's the only one that has the headlights right in the fenders."

Tony asked Clarence if he had ever seen a Rickenbacker car.

"Sure," Clarence told him. "They were really the first to have brakes on all four wheels."

Clarence was smart. Tony admired the way he farmed, but he

never talked about wanting to do anything else. Tony never talked about wanting to be a farmer. Clarence sometimes complained, "Aren't you ever going to grow up? Aren't you ever going to be anything?"

"Maybe I'll be like Cap'n Eddie."

Tony knew he'd have to be a pilot somewhere else. There sure wasn't much going on around Tinley Park. Once, near the turn of the century, a local resident named Goodall said that after his new aeroplane revolutionized travel, Tinley would be known as the aeronautical capital of the world. But the plane failed on its first flight. So the only thing that put the small dairy-farming community on the map was the great Rock Island Railroad. It did make a stop in Tinley. Not every town could say that. Local residents were proud and renamed their community (once called Bremen, then Yorktown) in honor of Charlie Tinley, a popular conductor on the great line.

A railroad station. A bunch of farms. And the North American Mushroom Company. All OK maybe, for Clarence and Mom and the kids, but Tony thought things were sorta dull day after day.

You had to make your own fun in Tinley Park. How could those people work in the fields, run stores, go to church, go to bed, week after week? They weren't caught up in Tony's bustling way of life.

So, early one Sunday afternoon he stopped by the house where the cute red-headed girl lived. He wasn't afraid of girls -- not by a longshot; they always liked him. But the red-head never gave him any encouragement.

When he'd seen Valerie Rice standing in her yard, he'd imagined she was waiting for him. But he knew she saw him as kinda dumb, trying to turn over his new car and making a fool out of himself. Yet he would always flash his best grin and wave. "Hi, Babe. I'm Tony Bettenhausen. Aren't you ever going to speak?" He'd even told his buddies in town, "That red-headed number on the corner's my girl, you know."

Now this Sunday he'd be bold. He wouldn't just smile. He'd take her driving. He rang the doorbell up on the porch of the white house. Valerie's grandmother came to the door.

"Hello. I'm Tony Bettenhausen and I'd like to take Val out for a ride. In my new car. Right there. Brand new '32 Ford." The words tumbled out.

Valerie was nowhere to be seen. She was inside with Maggie Lorentz, her best girlfriend, finishing the dishes, just as she always did at home. She hadn't heard Tony pull up because for this once he'd parked normal -- not pulled the emergency brake and skidded sideways.

"You've got a caller, Val," Grandma announced back to the kitchen, without emotion. "Melvin Bettenhausen says he'd like to take you -- you and Maggie for a ride in his new car."

"Oh, I didn't say anything about Maggie," Tony corrected. He stood by the screen looking into the hall.

"Melvin?" he thought. "How'd she find out I was Melvin. Nobody's called me that for a long time. She knows Mom, I suppose. Everybody does. Maybe she thinks I'm OK. I did comb my hair and shine my shoes. Probably it's the car, though. It is classy; shiny black with a red stripe and red wire wheels, chrome hubcaps."

"You want to go?" Grandma asked Valerie then looked him over. She seemed to approve. At least she didn't say he was the image of his father -- or some other crazy thing like that.

"Oh, yes," Val's voice came back from the kitchen.

"Sure," Maggie chimed in. Then Val appeared in the hall. Smiling, still holding the dishcloth. She'd heard what he said about Maggie.

For the the first time she was looking at Tony right up close. She was staring. He had two different eyes: one green, the other grey. Showing off again, she supposed. Anyway, going out with him would be better than doing dishes.

"Well, you just gonna stand there?" Tony broke the silence.

Grandma, however, answered with authority. "All right young man. But you drive carefully and don't . . ." She was going to add "and don't try any funny business." Then she realized Maggie would be kind of a chaperone.

The girls dashed inside to take off their aprons and get ready. They'd powder their noses and pretend they were adults. And never tell Tony they were only twelve years old.

The Ford waited out front -- a two-door sedan. Tony had wanted a coupe' but Mom had bought the car. She reasoned the bigger one was more practical, could hold more people.

It had two separate seats up front but you couldn't really get next to anybody. Tony didn't like that.

"You can have the whole back seat, Maggie," Tony said.

And they were on their way. Tony was himself again.

"I'll take you ladies for a ride on my yacht," Tony said as he pulled himself a little higher in the driver's seat.

The yacht was a rowboat that Tony paid a quarter to rent. After they climbed in, Tony told them he was the captain and a captain couldn't be caught rowing, now could he? Val rowed and dreamed a little. She sure liked him.

For the next couple of years Tony continued to drive one of Clarence's trucks. He set aside any thoughts he might have have had about leaving Tinley Park. He had a new car every year, Val, and money in his pocket. Life wasn't as exciting as he would have liked: He turned over his '34 Ford once and shrugged off the incident to "I hit a mud puddle." He knew he had it a lot better than some folks. Hardly a day went by that the *Tribune* didn't report the number of people out of work was at an all time high. When he was 19, he heard the Ford plant in Chicago was hiring and the pay was pretty good. Clarence was building a new house for himself right next door to the family homestead and was having a tough time financially. His trucking business was growing, but he didn't have enough work to keep Tony busy full time.

Tony realized Clarence was probably giving him work when Clarence needed it himself. A job at the Ford plant sounded like a good idea. It would be something different anyhow.

Tony proved to be a versatile worker. The foreman discovered that the new boy was quick. He could use him for nearly any job on the line. Tony liked the idea of impressing the new boss but confided to Val that there was probably something better to do than factory work. He continued to live at home and didn't complain to Clarence or Mom; they would tell him there was enough work right here on the farm to keep him busy.

Yet Tony kept looking for ways to get off the farm . . . especially for entertainment. One day he announced to Clarence, "Hey, there's a new thing in Chicago. It says here in the *Trib* that there's a new kind of automobile racing coming to town. Midget race cars. Why don't we go watch?"

Tony would always read the sports pages and looked close when they printed a picture of a race car. The cars he saw were single seat open-cockpit jobs with no fenders. They were narrow and sleek; as though you could add a double set of wings, a propeller and have yourself a bi-plane -- like the ones he used to see in his history books.

The picture in the *Tribune* excited Tony. "SEE THE MIDWEST'S GREATEST STARS."

"C'mon, let's go to Riverview and watch 'em race," he asked Clarence.

"I've been there. Too many people. Got too much work to do around here. You go." Clarence was busy sweeping.

Tony felt that Clarence never left the farm. He could go alone. Besides, Riverview was fun.

Chicagoland's permanent circus. Riverview's myriad of rides

and walkways promised unforgettable thrills and for a nickel you could ride high above the ground on George Ferris' huge revolving wheel or have your breath taken away on a roller coaster. Directly below the criss-crossed white boards that held the speedy little train some three stories high, there was a small oval cut into the earth. From the roller-coaster the little racing cars below looked like they would fit into your vest pocket. They made a loud buzzing. You could watch them only for a second or two and then your little train made a nose dive to the ground.

For most, Riverview was a special occasion place. It drew largely from Chicago's varied population and offered something different from the beach and the movies. It never had enough maintenance help to clean the general rubble left by its carefree clientele, and at best was slightly cleaner than Chicago's streets. Riverview Midget race spectators expected a carnival atmosphere. The announcer's name, "Twenty-Grand Steinbock" promised something out of the ordinary. Tony himself was expecting something exciting. Tony wished that Clarence was here with him. He worked so hard. The world consisted of a whole lot more than the cornfields of Tinley Park.

When Tony entered the grandstand there were about a dozen small cars circling the track. It didn't look like they were racing, maybe just warming up. They were short. Not shaped like the bumper cars you drove inside the amusement park nor much longer. The driver sat just ahead of the rear wheels, and the front wheels were much closer to you than in a passenger car. They looked like regular race cars, just a little smaller. Sorta cute. The dirt track wasn't very big either, not as big as the track around a football field.

A man on the front straight-away, dressed in a white shirt and tie, started waving the green flag at the oncoming cars. Several entered the first turn at the same time -- side by side. The drivers all turned left and started to slide. Then they jerked the wheel all the way back to the right so the front wheels were pointing in the direction of the slide.

"I can do that," Tony though. "I can do it."

Just a few laps later, the man waved the checkered flag. There wasn't any winner. Warm-ups had just ended.

A blaring voice came over the public address system: "Ladies and Gen-tul-mun! Welcome to Riverview! I'm Twenty-Grand Steinbock and I will be your host this evening for what will probably be the greatest thrills, chills, spills, and excitement you have ever seen. We will start qualifications for tonight's races in just a few minutes after the boys have had time to add fuel and make final adjustments to their cars that are so very important in Midget auto racing.''

Edward J. ''Twenty-Grand'' Steinbock had just informed the crowd of his presence. He was a race driver who never quite made it. He wound up in a full body cast after a ''little mis-calculation'' at Evanston in '32. He tried a comeback in '33, but he didn't fare much better. He landed upside down in a cornfield and scrambled his way to safety.

''Look at old Twenty-Grand go for that corn,'' one of his rescuers exclaimed.

Twenty-Grand was a Kentucky Derby winner and Steinbock figured the name was appropriate. He kept it.

''Tonight you will witness the closest form of auto racing competition ever invented!'' Twenty-Grand exclaimed. ''While we're waiting for the fellas, I'm going to give you a little bit about Midget auto racing so you can tell your friends and bring them here with you next week.

''Old Twenty-Grand has never really been accused of boasting, but he probably knows more about auto racing than anyone else in the whole world. I've been around racing all my life. Used to slide around corners in my baby carriage. I'm sure you all know that I was a driver from '24 to '32, but thought I oughta give the other fellas a chance to earn some of that prize money.''

Tony listened to Twenty-Grand. Everybody was listening. He knew what he was talking about.

Old Twenty-Grand did know. He remembered every driver's age, first ride, best race.

Twenty-Grand went on to explain that Midget auto racing was actually invented about 1915.

''They used to build cycle-cars back then. How many of you remember cycle-cars? Four wheel motorcycles with bodies on them. Well, they held a few races with the cycle-cars and some people called them Midget racers. But they weren't too popular. Then, four years ago in 1933, a group of fellas in Los Angeles got together with their home-made Midget racers and talked a promoter into holding a race for them. The rest is history.

''In 1934 the fabulous Gilmore Stadium was built especially for Midget auto racing at a cost of $150,000. Earl Gilmore of the Gilmore Oil Company built it -- and packed 'em in. Just like we're going to do here. You know they have 18,000 people at Gilmore every week.''

The announcer referred to the Midgets as ''baby Indy 500 cars.'' He said many of the cars here tonight were powered by motorcycle or outboard boat engines; some Midgets actually had scaled-down Offenhausers. The Offenhauser was the expensive engine used at Indianapolis.

Twenty-Grand was Tony's new teacher. He listened intently. Motorcycle engines. Offenhauser. He even called it an "Offy." Wonder what it looked like? Tony wanted to get closer to the cars. He didn't want the announcer to stop talking. He'd never listened to a teacher like him before.

The crowd was waiting for a time-trials. Tony didn't know what to expect. Maybe they had a bunch of short races that qualified you for one big race at the end of the night. The ad in the *Trib* had said, "20 Lap Feature Event."

Three men pushed a Midget out on the track. It was a pretty car. Shiny white. A red Number 2 painted on the hood and tail.

"Here comes the night's first qualifying attempt. The driver is big Wally Zale. He's from Chicago and . . ."

In short, choppy sentences Twenty-Grand reeled off Zale's life story while a truck pulled in front of the Number 2 Midget. Twenty-Grand made him sound fantastic. Was he reading all these facts? He sure knew a lot.

"Remember," the new teacher continued, "each driver will take two consecutive laps around the track. His best lap time will be recorded. You can mark it down in your program, too. You DID buy a program? If not, hurry up. You've still got a couple of minutes."

Tony spotted a vendor walking up the aisle. He gave the boy a nickel for a program.

"Now then, only the fastest 16 qualifiers will be allowed to run in the 20 lap Main Event. We have 22 cars on hand here tonight, so six of the boys will have to try their luck again next week."

The truck pulled Zale with a rope for a few feet and the miniature racer started buzzing along under its own power. Zale released the rope and going down the backstretch you could hear him open it up and he slid through the third and fourth turns completely sideways. The man with the white shirt and tie waved the green flag as he went by and Zale drove into the first turn just like he had in three and four. Tony could see him wrestling the wheel back and forth. As he came down the front straight, the starter waved the white flag. One lap to go. Zale crossed the finish line; next time around, and the checkered flag was being waved. He pulled off the track and revved the engine a couple of times.

That's all there was to it. Not very exciting. Tony liked it better when there were several cars on the track.

Twenty-Grand announced Zale's qualifying time. "He was consistent. Turned a 16.22 on the first lap and 16.25 on the second. First lap's fastest."

Tony wrote down the lap times next to Zale's name. He saw a Johnny Zale listed too. Maybe it was his brother. Soon the next car was out on the track. It wasn't nearly as pretty as Zale's. The driver spun completely around in the first turn and came to a stop near the guard rail. The truck had to be called to re-start him. His qualifying times were over seventeen seconds. He didn't look nearly as smooth as Zale. It sounded like he was on and off the gas pedal too much.

Now Tony knew what to expect. Green flag on the first lap, white flag and then the checkered. Twenty more cars came out to qualify and only one was faster than Zale. Teddy Duncan had turned a 16.20. There's not much difference between 16.20 and 16.22 Tony thought. That's less than an eye-blink! Three drivers had qualified with identical times of 16.22. Close competition!

After qualifying was over, Twenty-Grand said that the first heat race would be held in about five minutes. Everyone had time to visit the concession stand and buy a hot dog and a Coke. Tony saw another vendor hawking newspapers. Tony had never bought a newspaper in his life.

"Get your racin' news here. *National Auto Racing News*. Ten Cents. Read about the stars."

A racing newspaper? Tony gave the man a dime. The paper had pictures on the front and back covers but none inside. There weren't any big headlines inside either; they all looked the same. That didn't make any difference. Tony would read it from cover to cover. He wanted to learn more.

After the race was over, Tony couldn't wait to get home and let Clarence know all about it. Yes sir, he thought. Twenty-Grand had said to let your friends know and bring them back next week to the Midget races. He'd be there Sunday night sure . . . with or without Clarence.

"Boy, they're swell! Tony told Clarence the next morning. Clarence was already asleep by the time Tony got home. He had stopped for a hamburger after the race and had read every story in the *National Auto Racing News*. Tony would send in a dollar subscription blank to make sure he got a copy every week.

"They're not real small," he described to Clarence. "Just the right size. They really go, too. Some of them have motorcycle engines and some have out-boards. The really good ones have Offenhausers -- Those are the engines they use at Indianapolis, you know."

All the next week at supper Tony talked to Clarence about the

Midget races. Soon Clarence was stopping him. "You already told me that."

Val also provided an ear. Tony could tell her about the same incident two or three times over and she was always a good listener. They agreed some time back that they loved each other and knew what they wanted. Val was 16 now and Tony was 20; they should probably get married. Tony had a good job at the Ford plant and didn't really like living at the farm. Val said she was tired of doing all the housework for her parents and wanted a home of her own. For her and Tony.

Val's mother wanted her to join her profession. Be a hair-dresser. But Val said she didn't like the smell of burned hair. Her mother had a beauty shop in Chicago's Lithuanian section and used a hot Marcelle iron to curl hair. Val told her Mom she'd bet those women wouldn't wash their hair for months after getting a treatment. It looked all knotted up. She didn't want to be a hair-dresser. She wanted to marry Tony.

It was four years since that first Sunday afternoon drive and row-boat outing. Tony kept Val's weeks exciting. Otherwise, life went on in a dull routine of housekeeping; dishes and dusting and meals while her parents worked. Her father, Clyde Rice, was employed as a foreman on the Rock Island. He owed his soul, he would often complain, to the Rock Island . . .

As soon as Clyde was assigned to the Joliet territory, the family would have to move because the company said you had to live in the area you worked in. Still, it was a good job, and times were rough. Her mother Nan was happy, styling the most modish hair in town. Why wouldn't Valcric bccomc a hair-drcsscr? It was a fine profession -- steady, good money. But Val always gave the same answer. She had no intention of bending over basins and washing dirty heads. She expected something more glamorous.

And Tony did make her feel more glamorous and grown-up. Some other girls her age weren't even allowed dates. Tony appeared on Saturday nights with his self-assured airs and his shiny car -- a new one every year. Her parents said he seemed a bit too wild and a little too proud. (Her father repeatedly commented that the long hours at the Ford plant might humble him). Still, Val knew they called him "genial," "good natured," and "from a fine family." She would keep house for Tony. So, she filled the days mentally arranging her home -- her's and Tony's. Why couldn't they get married?

When she and Tony talked it over with her parents, they reminded both of them that marriage was a big step -- a big change in their way of life. They were too young; they had years yet.

Privately, alone with Val they asked if she *had* to get married.

No, she answered quietly. She just wanted to.

But did she know how people in Tinley Park would talk?

Oh yes. She guessed she knew the old gossips better than anybody. She didn't care.

And so it was with her parents consent that on April 10, 1937, Tony Bettenhausen took Valerie Rice for his wife. Tony was five months away from his twenty-first birthday. He rented a little white bungalow in town for his new bride. He was happy to be leaving the farm.

At last Val was free. There were a million tomorrows. Shopping, cooking, even cleaning -- all had become fun, all for "my Tony." On free afternoons -- now almost every afternoon was free -- she drove a brand new Ford coupe around town -- the latest in economy, equipped with a V-8 60 engine, designed, Tony explained, to increase mileage without sacrificing performance. Tony knew all about such things.

In a few weeks, though, Tony didn't share her happiness. He would come home from the Ford plant, his short, thick fingers nicked and sore. Val loved his strong, muscular hands. Like his eyes, they were out of the ordinary, strange -- full of deep lines as if they'd been soaked a long time in water. Now sometimes after work they were scarred and old scabs bled. Tony would explain that the assembly line jobs were too tedious, that he'd tackle any new job the foreman would give him. Val begged him not to be so aggressive, to be patient and less eager. He said she'd never understand about the Ford plant. And what could she know about how much he wanted to learn? Besides, she had her house. That was what she wanted. Take care of it.

All day long Val brooded on Tony. Even a drive in the new coupe in the spring sunshine didn't take the hurt away. She couldn't get the idea out of her mind--he was hardheaded; he was bossy; he was hurtful.

Perhaps Tony sensed Val's mood. They'd have a sort of honeymoon: they'd go to Indianapolis for the 500 on Memorial Day. It wasn't exactly Niagara, Val thought, but at least it would be different. She was right.

They spent the night before the event -- along with a few thousand other spectators, outside the track on 16th Street. Tony talked of nothing but the race, its cars and drivers.

"Someday, I'm going to drive here," Tony added slowly and positively.

All right. The new Mrs. Bettenhausen felt the soft mohair upholstery of the coupe. She was happy because Tony was happy, only why didn't he talk about the two of them? He never mentioned the new furniture; she'd ordered the pattern special and only after they could afford it. He wouldn't let her buy on credit.

They sat in the infield and saw little of the actual race. It was two and a half miles around the track, Tony explained, and you couldn't expect to see everything. He bought a program and became lost in its pages. All the way home he wanted to talk about the race; she wanted to sleep.

Marriage wasn't what she had imagined. A lonely, stupid house. A husband who bossed her around. She'd get a divorce.

She went to see the Chicago attorneys, Joseph H. and Norman Becker.

"Are you sure? You won't change your mind?" the older one asked her.

"No" Val answered immediately. "Not until Mister Tony Bettenhausen lets me think for myself. And he won't," she added flatly. "I do have a mind of my own."

"You're the youngest girl, you must realize, in all of Cook County ever to file for divorce," one of the attorneys said.

"People will talk, you know," the other added.

"OK. Let them talk. I don't care." Valerie's voice rose. "I won't be bossed."

The divorce went through.

After Val left, Tony moved back to the farm. Val went to live with her parents and withstood any gossip about "that Valerie Rice . . . divorced already." She never did get to see the new furniture they had put a deposit on.

Tony continued working at the Ford plant: All that money was too good to pass up. He even started a savings account. He had plans.

Each week he eagerly looked forward to the arrival of the *National Auto Racing News*. He had subscribed to the weekly publication the day after he saw his first Midget race. Midgets were definitely the big thing. Races were being held all over the country. In a few weeks Tony had become familiar with some of the names. Many of the drivers, he thought, were like a bunch of gypsies. Duke Nalon from Chicago was winning races in New York; Ronney Householder from Los Angeles was winning in Detroit; Wally Zale and Harry McQuinn, both from Chicago, were running in St. Paul, then down to Springfield, Illinois and in the same week back up to Milwaukee.

The *National Auto Racing News* didn't print many photos in its sixteen pages. Only a few on the front and back covers. Tony wondered what some of the drivers looked like. He hadn't been able to see their faces very well from his grandstand seat, but Twenty-Grand made them all sound like really special people. Brave. Strong. Even mean, he said.

But Tony knew that each of them weren't all that special. He remembered that one fellow he saw his first night at the races, kept spinning out. Didn't look good at all. He himself could do as well as some of the drivers he'd seen. And you didn't have to be real old to be a good race driver. The racing news told about Sam Hanks, only 22 years old and winning races in California.

Tony wanted to go to another Midget race, his fourth maybe. Get closer to the action this time. Be next to the cars. Meet some of the drivers. He had met a driver once, back when he was sixteen. It was in a gas station along Route 41. The man's name was Wilbur Shaw, a real professional. Tony didn't exactly have a long conversation with Shaw, but he did get to talk to him for a minute or two. Shaw was on his way to a race and Tony admired his race car while Shaw was getting gasoline. Real keen. He introduced himself and was surprised to see how friendly Shaw was. Shaw apologized for not staying longer. He was running late. Tony had already informed Shaw that he too, was probably going to drive a race car someday.

Now he thought about driving a Midget. They looked like just the right size. He could do it. That'd be just Jake, slidin' around corners and hollerin' back, "Now you guys catch me!"

He was dreaming. Three months ago when he'd gone to the races, they wouldn't even let him into the area where they kept all the cars. The guy at the gate told him he had to have a pass. A pit pass, for racin' people. Spectators sit in the grandstands, son.

Tony had to make friends with a race driver. Then he could get in. And he knew just who could help him.

A driver named Emil Andres who didn't live too far from Tinley Park. After Tony started talking about race cars, Clarence mentioned that Emil, who had already driven at Indianapolis once, was practically a neighbor. Matter of fact, he might even be a shoestring cousin.

Tony had driven past Andres' house several times since, but never had the nerve to knock. He didn't know exactly what he'd say. Now, however, he had a reason.

The next Sunday morning Tony was walking up to a new house again. This time, he jazzed the engine in his coupe a little before he shut it off.

"Hi, Mr. Andres?"

"Yes?"

"I'm Tony Bettenhausen and I want to be a race car driver. I know you'll help me, huh?''

Emil Andres didn't look him up and down the way Val's grandmother had. Emil didn't look serious. He started chuckling.

''So your name is Tony and you are going to be a race driver, eh?''

''Yup,'' Tony said confidently.

And I suppose you want me to take you to the races at Riverview tonight. Get you in?''

''Yeah. That'd be swell.''

There was no way that Emil was going to refuse. Tony's grin did it. Besides, hardly a night at the races went by without some kid telling Emil (and most other drivers) that he *too* would someday be a racing driver. It was almost a warning. Usually, though, the warning came from fans, under ten years old. This Tony Bettenhausen was all of five feet nine and looked like he weighed in at 165, maybe 175 pounds. Strong as an ox. This is one kid, Emil thought, that better not get near a race car. Looks like he's rarin' to go. Too wild. Probably kill himself.

Normally, Emil probably would have said he was busy at the races and wouldn't really have time. But he knew the Bettenhausen name and from the start he greeted Tony as a friend. Besides, he got a kick out of being called Mr. Andres by a fella only a few years younger. Sure enough, he thought. C'mon in.

Emil knew how Tony felt. Only a few years earlier, in 1932, Emil felt the same way. He wanted to be a racer, too. Getting started was the hard thing. You couldn't just walk up to a race car owner, although he and thousands of others had tried, and tell the man that you wanted to drive his car and you're sure you'll be a winner. The owners had heard that one.

''You want me to put *you* in this machine? Why do you know how much money I've got invested here? It's one of the best, if not *the* best, race car in the business. You're liable to wipe it out on the first lap. Then what have I got? A busted racer and probably a dead rookie.

''No, not this car, Sonny. You can always buy yourself one, you know.''

And so it went. Rookie after rookie asked owner after owner for a ride. The best personality in the world was no substitute for a season's worth of driving. Thus some rookies lied: ''Oh yeah, been running over East a lot,'' they'd tell a prospective owner.

Emil knew all that. Had Tony already been down the road of asking for a ride? It didn't matter. He liked him. He'd take him under his wing. At 24, Emil was the veteran. A Speedway driver. Ran there in '35.

By early afternoon Emil was ready to leave for the track. He usually waited till around four, but this Bettenhausen kid was wearing him out with questions. Of course he wanted to know all about last Wednesday night's accident. "How'd it happen? Didn't get hurt, did you?"

Tony was disappointed when he learned that Emil wasn't a real pro. He had figured the drivers, the good ones anyway, just raced. They didn't have to work. When he wasn't racing, Emil drove a delivery truck. Anyone who had driven in the Indianapolis 500, like Emil, Tony figured, was rich -- real rich!

Still, it was OK though, even if Emil wasn't exactly wealthy yet. Times were still tough for some people. Clarence had said that there were over 300 women sleeping in Grant and Lincoln parks in Chicago. Tony couldn't imagine anyone not having a place to sleep. Sometimes he'd see several men in the boxcars on the Rock Island. By their clothes you could tell they didn't work for the railroad. Guess some people didn't have *any* money.

* * *

Emil called Hello to the man in the little shack outside the pits and gave him fifty cents. Then he nodded toward Tony and said, "He's with me." Emil recalled Tony was beaming again. Tony had a pit pass.

The pits are considered a sacred place. No one ever said where the name stemmed from, although it probably had something to do with a six feet deep little trench at the service station where you pulled your car over. "Drive it over the pit," they'd say when the oil needed to be changed.

In the Indianapolis 500 a driver didn't make a tire and refueling stop, he made a pit stop. It was probably there, at Indy, the laws of the pits were cast forever:

1) You don't allow women in the pits; 2) You do not eat peanuts in the pits; 3) You do not wear green in the pits (and if you are foolish enough to paint your car that dreaded color you'll be cursed and probably doomed). 4) You wear white and show the spectators you are professionals; 5) You shouldn't smoke in the pits, but everybody does so you don't complain; 6) You don't drink beer in the pits . . . until after the race . . . then you don't mind if the place looks like a rum-runners' warehouse.

Tony wasn't wearing white, but the other men weren't either. He stuck close to Emil, who seemed to know everybody. As they walked around, Emil introduced Tony to several drivers. He met Ray Richards, Bert Knight, Ted Tetterton, Paul Russo (He'd read about Russo, who'd won a lot of races around Chicago). Finally,

Emil said he had to get ready and run warm-ups. Tony didn't need a guide. He had found a new home.

Qualifying for the night's races went just about the same way they had back in April for the first race Tony had attended. Three guys were all tied at 16.22 and Teddy Duncan beat them with a 16.20. Twenty-Grand went wild over Duncan, a newcomer with only about a month's experience.

The program consisted of four heat races, 12 laps each; two 15 lap consolation races and the 20 lap feature event.

Wally Zale drove his Montgomery Ward sponsored car to an easy win in the first heat. In the second heat, everyone thought he saw a man get killed. Carl Peterson and Joe Burany, who, Twenty-Grand said was a school teacher in Milwaukee, collided on the first lap with Burany doing several barrell rolls down the back-stretch. The race was stopped. It was quiet thru the pits. Burany was slumped over in his Midget, which had come to rest on its side. As several men ran to his aid he moved his head -- shook it a couple of times, and started crawling out of his injured racer. Then he raised his arm in a wave to the grandstands and there was an immediate round of applause. He had gambled and won.

The fans had shown they weren't the bloodthirsty bunch some newspaper writers had claimed. Sunday's flip added excitement to the already close competition, and the fans could tell and re-tell their friends that they were there, right on the scene. They were proud to see him walk away.

After they re-started the race, tough Harry McQuinn barged to the front and was never headed. Mechanics found it difficult to work on their cars: Spectators who had to go to the bathroom waited. Twenty-Grand had them right where he wanted. He had 'em believing that the single, most important event in the history of the world was probably going to take place right before their very eyes . . . right here on this crusty, hard, little fifth-mile oval at Riverview! When the heat race was over, one mechanic said, "Jesus, that guy can make a mountain out of a mole hill. A lousy old heat race, but you'd have though the Lord himself was driving out there. If he brings spectators in though, I guess that's all that counts."

Teddy Duncan and Paul Russo battled for the third heat and it wasn't settled until the last lap when Russo went wide. It looked like he slipped for just a second . . . less than that . . . and Duncan got by. One mistake -- and you're history.

Emil had a good starting position for the fourth heat, number one spot, inside on the front row, pole position. Race starter Bill Vandewater dropped the green flag and Emil led going into the first turn. He made it look easy, like he was out for a Sunday drive. Right behind him Shorty Sorensen and Cowboy O'Rourke were banging wheels with one another dueling for second place. They did it for twelve laps and many times it looked like they were both going to crash. They didn't and neither challenged Emil. He came into the pits and Tony was happy. He was with a winner.

There wasn't much time for celebration. Emil showed Tony that this racin' was serious business.

They had to get the car ready for the feature. Check to see that everything's tight. It's one thing to crash because you're just racing, but it's another to have something fall off the car and make you crash. That's unforgivable. Driver error's one thing -- that's his fault -- he did it to himself. But a mechanical failure, that's something else. It had been said that the mechanic who leaves a bolt loose, or a wheel not tight, should be shot. Or something worse. You just don't send a man out to risk his neck in a car that isn't ready to do battle.

They added fuel. It's not unforgivable to run out of fuel. That can't hurt anybody. You'll always remember the race that, "I had it won by a mile -- and ran outa gas." You laugh about that.

"You check the tires," Emil continued. Make a decision about the tires. Which kind should you run. Will the dirt stay moist and tacky so you can get a good bite on it, or will it turn pavement hard? You have to learn how to read a race track, kid. Very important. The best driver in the world can't go anywhere on the wrong set of tires. Check the oil. Clean the dirt out of the wheels. Too much dirt in the wheels makes them run out of balance -- makes the car shake. Check the brakes. They still work? Wipe the car off. And wait.

They talked a little about the Republic Steel Strike going on in South Chicago. There wasn't anything more that could be done to the car.

Tony blended into the atmosphere as another one of the boys. While Emil had given him a quick course in race car maintenance, Tony had watched and listened intently. The cars were exciting. The people were exciting. Everybody was friendly. They had all come to Riverview with the same goal: Win the race. And they were all there because that's precisely where they wanted to be. Just *being there* -- in the pits -- at nighttime, created a different feeling for things. Like nighttime baseball. Everything seems more life-like. Not like night at all. It's supposed to be dark, but in the pits it's just a little dark. And out there on the race track it's bright, like day. When the cars are on the track you can see them just right. Coming out of the corners, sometimes it seems as though they jump out from nowhere -- and are heading toward nowhere. The speed is multiplied. They aren't going nearly as fast as you think. The shadows make the diference maybe. There's no comparison between a day and a night race. You can actually get *scared* watching at night.

There was a race official walking through the pits with a clipboard. He stopped and reminded everyone where they started in the feature. He knew that a fella could get nervous enough to get in his car, be pushed off and suddenly realize that in his anxiety he forgot his starting position. He had enough other things to worry about. Everything tight? Boy, that was a hell of a ride that school teacher took. Don't know how he lived through that one.

Emil was starting the feature in sixth spot; third row outside position. He told Tony that if he was lucky maybe there'd be a little wheel banging going on up front and maybe he could drive right around all of 'em on the outside.

But it wasn't to be. Emil had a flat tire in three laps and had to pull back into the pits. Wally Zale had led from the beginning and won without incident. McQuinn had second wrapped up for 39 laps when he too had a flat, but wrestled the car around for third money.

Emil shrugged the incident off to bad luck and watched the feature with Tony. After the race was over, they strolled through the pits again. Everyone was re-running the race. Some had bad luck. Others blamed their cars. It was too hard to pass on this track, it had only one groove where you could really race. They don't put enough water on the track to make it tacky. Or they put on too much water and it was muddy on the outside.

There was beer and cigarettes. Crews were loading their cars. Some had trailers that matched the cars. Others had pick-up trucks and four or five men could hoist a Midget and load it in a matter of seconds.

"I want to see Wally Zale," Tony told Emil.

"What for?"

"I want to buy his Midget. I got the money with me," Tony said.

"I should have know, I guess," Emil replied.

Zale's pit was a popular one. He had just won the race. The car didn't look any different from when he had rolled it out on the track to start the feature. Everyone was talking to him -- looking at the car -- offering congratulations -- telling him how good he was and what a good car he had. It was the usual stuff. They all loved a winner. Where were they when he finished second?

"Wally, I want you to meet a friend of mine. This is Tony

Bettenhausen and he says he wants to buy your car."

Wally had seen more than one Tony come by. He had sold no less than four Midgets to eager kids in the last two years -- especially just after he had won a race. Zale was a mean six-footer who would have probably gotten out and carried the car around the track if it gave him any shit. Zale didn't settle for second when a little shoving or an added bit of bravery meant winning.

Zale was friendly. He couldn't tell a prospective buyer from a kid that just wanted to meet him, so he treated everyone alike. Except when he was drunk. Then he wasn't a very good salesman.

"You wanna drive it yourself?" Zale asked him.

Emil knew the answer and was a little surprised when Tony said, "Well, not right away. Maybe Emil'll drive it some. How much do you want for it?"

"I've got good equipment, you know," Zale said. "This one was built by Pop Dreyer in Indianapolis. He builds good race cars. It ain't a home-made job. It's got his engine in it too -- a Harley-eighty."

"I've got two hundred dollars -- right here."

"That's about four-hundred short," Zale told him.

"Well, I'll be back next week," Tony said. "Take good care of it till then."

They turned all the lights out and several crews were still hanging around, drinking a beer, not in a hurry to go anywhere. Now though, it seemed like nighttime. Like any other night. No magic anymore. Just a bunch of cars and guys in a big lot. Emil and Tony went home.

The very next day, Emil and Tony paid Walter a visit at his home.

"I've got the rest of the money," Tony told him.

"You've just bought yourself a race car," Zale said.

Tony had talked to Mom. He couldn't wait. He told her about all the good parts of owning a Midget. Especially *this* Midget. She should see Zale's winner. Why it'd probably win back what it cost in a couple of weeks. Mom smiled and said OK. Tony knew she always had a soft spot.

Two days later Emil and Tony were back at Riverview. They were racing there on Wednesday and Sunday now. Midgets were popular and race promotor Gerard Murray, as well as others around the country, were going to play them for all they were worth. Emil would drive and Tony would be mechanic. Wally had gone to St. Paul with Harry McQuinn, where they had previously found easy money. Zale had another Midget waiting for him.

Emil qualified well -- third quick. He was on the pole for the first heat race and couldn't have designed the race better if he'd tried. He set a new track record for twelve lap distance, erasing the old mark, held by Zale, by four full seconds! Tony was estatic. He knew they could do it!

Their luck in the feature was all bad. The drive chain came off just as Emil was challenging Paul Russo for the lead. Russo won the race in record time in a car that said "Finkl Outboard." He had clipped five seconds off the record.

Tony took the car home and told Emil he was going to fix it so the chain wouldn't come off anymore, make it a little faster, too. Don't worry about anything -- just be ready to drive again on Sunday night -- this time they'd win the feature.

On Saturday, Emil stopped by the farm to see if Tony was ready to go. He had warned him that he better make a diagram of how that thing comes apart -- he was liable to never get it together again. Tony had told him to quit worrying. He'd take care of everything.

The car was scattered all over the garage. On one side sat the frame with most of the body and all four wheels still attached. On the other, mostly dumped into a wheelbarrow, lay its engine. Greasy looking. Tony was sitting on the floor next to the single-wheeled tub.

"Got it all figured out," he smiled from his sitting position.

"Bettenhausen, the only thing you got figured out his how to get dirty. That car ain't going to race tomorrow night -- and from the looks of things, you'll be lucky if it ever sees a race track again. Why'd you have to take the engine apart -- it ran fine -- it was the chain, remember?"

Tony laughed. Then Emil laughed and shook his head. Pretty soon they were both greasy.

They didn't make the Sunday night race, and it was probably just as well. So far, the accidents that Tony had seen were all of a fairly minor nature. At least the drivers were able to talk afterwards. But on the Fourth of July, a big night at Riverview, with a little extra patriotism in the air, everyone was eager. Wally's brother Johnny, was trying to impress his successful counterpart and flipped wildly after a tangle with Teddy Duncan, his brother's young mechanic. He hit the outside guard rail and was thrown from the car. There were no restraint devices in a Midget -- most thought your chances were better if the car didn't land on top of you. He was taken to the hospital in critical condition by his brother and the regular medical attendants. Wally drove hell-bent-for-leather back to the track and finished fourth in the

A young Tony Bettenhausen in his first Midget race car. [*Harms. Coll.*]

feature. There wasn't much he could do for his brother -- might as well race.

Tony worked on the Midget all the next week and finally called Emil to help him come start it. He needed somebody to pull him and he wantd to show Emil that the thing would run all right.

First they pushed it. Then they pulled it. Tony'd shout, "Faster!" and they pushed it some more. No fire. Not a pop.

"You've got the ignition screwed up," Emil told him.

"Maybe you're right," Tony admitted. "But I can still fix it."

"Let's get Teddy Duncan down here. He's worked on this thing before," Emil suggested.

No one around the farm could offer any assistance. Clarence was intrigued with Tony's new Midget, but he couldn't offer mechanical help. And although the car didn't represent anything productive (like a good truck or tractor), Clarence was pleased to see Tony take such a full interest.

Teddy Duncan came by the farm, made one minor adjustment to the car's magneto and told Tony, "You just had 'er out of time. She'll start now."

Duncan was OK. They pushed the car a few feet and it popped to life. Sounded good, too. Wacka. Wacka. Tony could feel the power right there under his toe.

He and Teddy talked about the car for a long time afterwards. Duncan wanted to be a driver and spent all of his spare time helping Zale. You work around a winner and maybe you'll be one, too.

Duncan had the same problem as Tony. He wanted to drive, but who was going to give him a ride? He couldn't afford to buy a car, like Tony.

Tony promised Teddy that he could use his Midget sometime. Emil wouldn't always be free to drive -- especially if there was a Big Car race somewhere. The Big Cars paid better than the Midgets and who could pass up a chance to make some dough?

Riverview was rained out the last meet in July, the eighth time during the season. Emil and Tony were ready to run. Teddy Duncan was preparing for his ride, too. He had fixed another Midget with the agreement that he could drive it.

The next race at Riverview was a near copy of Tony and Emil's previous outing. Emil qualified well, won a heat race and had the chain fly off during the feature. Duncan made an appearance and finished fifth. It was only his third race. Emil was disappointed and said he'd probably have to go back to his old ride until the chain problem was fixed. The next week Duncan and Tony went to work on the car again. Duncan was anxious to continue racing. After his Riverview ride, he went to Springfield, Illinois, and was doing well in warm-ups until he hooked a rut on the small dirt track and flipped. He wasn't hurt, but the car would be out of action for a couple of weeks. He had to get back into action right away. The time would never be better. Some of the regular front-runners at Riverview had decided to leave Chicago.

"Let's go over East and bring some of that money back home -- like Nalon's doing," Harry McQuinn had said. "He's won six features out of six starts, you know."

Duncan and Tony figured that while some of the hotshoes were gone, their chances of winning right in their own backyard were pretty good.

The trio that went over East consisted of Paul Russo, Harry McQuinn and Shorty Sorensen (who both drove for the Marchese

Emil Andres

brothers from Milwaukee). McQuinn and Sorensen had gained reputations as rough drivers, blessed with top-notch equipment. And it wasn't beneath either of them, the racing papers had said, to do a little blocking to help one another out. They were a team on the track. Some of their competitors came up with more descriptive names.

Russo had already made a couple of trips to the East during the summer, but usually drove for an eastern car owner and was well liked wherever he ran.

The next Sunday night, August 15, Tony and Duncan made their assault on Riverview. They'd heard that Sorensen had won his first race at Freeport, Long Island and in doing so clipped twenty-three seconds off the track record. McQuinn placed third. The news traveled fast. The Easterners were referring to those Midwestern drivers as the Chicago Gang. Teddy and Tony were talking about their invasion of the East next summer. They'd get some of that prize money themselves; thousand dollars a night, total.

Duncan proved his ability by setting fifth fastest time at Riverview, taking a second in his heat race and finishing third in the feature. Tony's car ran fine all evening.

The following day they learned that Russo had won the Friday night race at Freeport, while Sorensen and McQuinn elected to run at Yellow Jacket in Philly. Sorensen won and McQuinn was second. Nalon took third.

Tony' pace was quickening now. He was becoming a part of the scene. Meeting new guys every week. Russo made a quick trip back to Chicago for a Big Car race, which Teddy and Tony went to watch. He told them about the Eastern scene: "I don't think they like those guys (Sorensen and McQuinn) too much - they're takin' all the marbles."

Duncan and Bettenhausen went back to Riverview on Sunday night and entered auto racing's echelon: They won the feature! After the race Tony exclaimed, "We got everything but the hot-dog stand."

Duncan had set fast time, won the first heat and out-raced veteran Cowboy O'Rourke in the 60-lap final event. So what if Zale, McQuinn and Sorensen weren't there, they had raced and won -- nobody handed them the victory.

On Monday afternoon the auto racing gossip news wire was working again. The Riverview racers learned that there was a sit-down at Long Branch, N. J. A group of drivers and owners refused to run unless McQuinn and Sorensen were barred from the track. Too rough, they said. The race promoter bowed to their wishes. Two nights later the same thing happened at Freeport: The Chicago Gang, or at least the roughest part of them, were being given the old bum's rush: Go back home. We won't race if you race. And if you see that Russo on your way, tell him he isn't welcome, either. Eastern racing's for Eastern guys. We don't need no Chicago guys comin' in here and screwin' things up.

Russo was on his way back to the East when he encountered McQuinn and Sorensen. "You may as well turn around, Paul. They aren't going to let you run," McQuinn told him.

Russo hadn't had trouble previously. He thanked them for their advice. But he wasn't going back to Chicago. Nalon was still running there and nobody was giving him a hard time, now were they?

Teddy and Tony were ecstatic. They were winners. They thought alike. We'll beat 'em even worse next week. What can we do to make the car better? Try some other pistons -- higher compression? Change the carburetor maybe?

The next Sunday put Duncan's name, and photograph, in the *National Auto Racing News* headlines. They won again. The story read:

> Chicago -- Ted Duncan, the former stoogie for Wally Zale and recently entered into Midget racing, won a thrilling feature at the Chicago Riverview meet Sunday night, August 29. This is two in a row for Duncan and he is now commanding the respect even from his former boss . . . he was driving the number 2 Harley owned by Tony Bettenhausen of Tinley Park, Ill.

McQuinn and Sorensen went back to Milwaukee and started

winning again. Russo paid Eastern car owner Mike Caruso a visit and told him he wanted to continue driving for him. Caruso convinced his fellow owners that it shouldn't make any difference where a driver comes from as long as he's driving an East coast based car, he should be allowed to race. They went back to Freeport and won their first night out.

Nalon, meanwhile, had gone to Nashville, Tennessee, on Labor Day to run a Big Car race which nearly ended his career. He recalled later that he thought it was going to be a bad day. Ted Horn, the 1936 National Driving Champion had arrived in Nashville with a new green Ford tow car. "Horn, you're either awfully brave or stupid," someone told him. "That green car ain't going to mean anything but trouble."

Then the Tadlock boys, Monk and Eldridge, brothers from Norfolk, Virginia, brought out some peanuts and offered them to Horn -- then to Nalon, and as soon as Duke turned his back one of the Tadlocks sneaked up and jammed a handful into his overalls pocket. Duke dumped them quickly.

Later, Nalon was leading the race with only five laps to go. His good friend Howdy Cox spun in the first turn and created a huge cloud of dust. Nalon slammed into Cox and was followed by Horn, Vern Orenduff and Carl Beal. Cox was killed and the other three were all injured, although none seriously. Thereafter, Nalon didn't have any use for the Tadlocks or peanuts. He'd go home to Chicago and recuperate. He had won enought Midget races to be crowned 1937 Eastern Champion.

From his hospital bed, Horn ordered his green tow car painted maroon.

The following week some 54 participants purchased a full page ad in the *National Auto Racing News* in memory of the popular Cox. The peanut jinx gained respect.

The activity in Chicago had wound down now, and everyone looked forward to the opening of the Armory and the indoor Midget racing season. Standing Room Only signs were often posted at the ticket office of the 124th Field Artillery Armory. All 8,000 available seats were sometimes taken a week in advance. Eager kids climbed into rafters to get a better vantage point. Nothing like indoor Midget racing. It's a mechanized rodeo. Duncan and Tony looked forward to these nights. They had a good car now, and sliding around the Armory's small track sounded great.

The Riverview season was over in October, but there were still a couple of races for the Big Cars at the Chicago Fairgrounds track. Tony and Teddy visited Nalon in his southside Chicago home and

Duke Nalon

Duke Nalon in 1937 photo. [IMS]

although Duke complained of some back pain, he said he'd be in good enough shape to run the next weekend. Tony liked Duke right away.

"Heard you guys been doin' OK with Zale's ole' Midget," Duke said.

Tony felt good that a famous racer like Duke Nalon had heard about him. Tony had heard plenty about "The Iron Duke." He was popular. He asked him if he could go to the Fairgrounds with him on Sunday and when Nalon said, "Sure, you can help in the pits," Tony was happy. Duke could teach him a lot, he thought.

Nalon was driving for car builder Pop Dreyer. Everyone respected Dreyer's cars, they were the best. Tony's Midget was a Dreyer, and they talked about it for awhile before the race.

Nalon didn't show any after effects from the Nashville accident

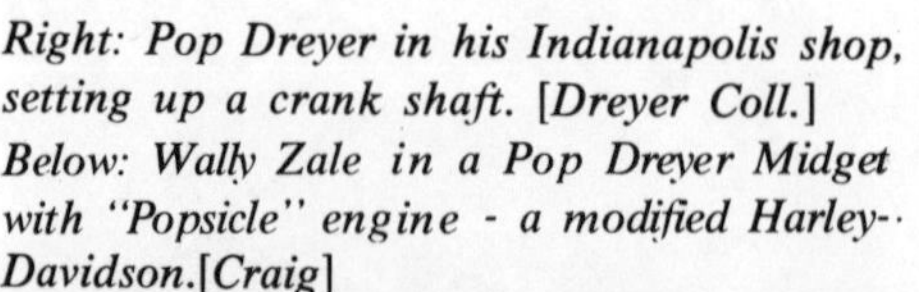

Right: Pop Dreyer in his Indianapolis shop, setting up a crank shaft. [*Dreyer Coll.*]
Below: Wally Zale in a Pop Dreyer Midget with "Popsicle" engine - a modified Harley-Davidson.[*Craig*]

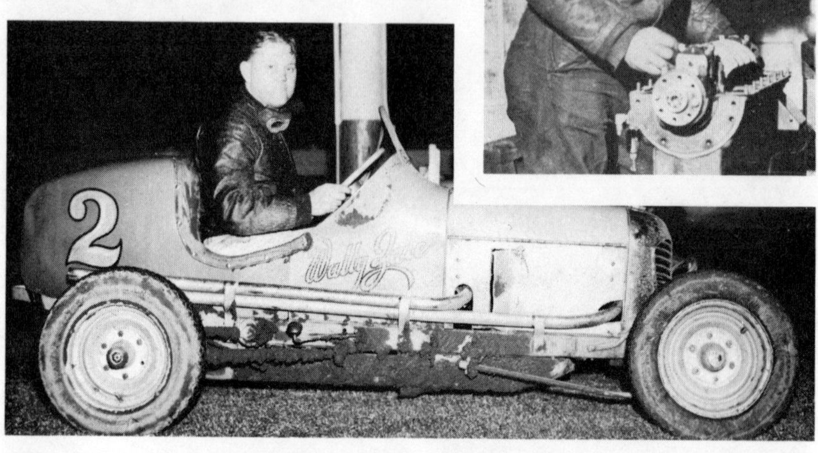

and won with the same car he had crashed in. Tony knew you had to be good to win a Big Car race. They were more respected than a Midget because you run Midgets on little tracks. Big Cars meant business. They looked harder to handle. Heavier. Lots of horsepower. You didn't want to get into trouble with them. You could be a goner in a hurry. They were louder. Plain mean.

But Nalon was a mestro. He handled a Dirt tracker like its was a Midget. No effort at all. He used the throttle to control his slides through the corners and didn't look like he was fighting the car all the time. Tony wanted to be just like Duke Nalon.

"Someday," Tony said after the race," "I'm gonna drive as good as you."

Nalon winked at him and said, "It isn't so hard once you get on to it."

Duke had invited him to help on the pit crew. Tony thought Duke would help him learn to drive a race car, too. Just being around Duke was something special. After the race, they all went and had steaks. Tony promised Nalon, "See you next week," and Duke had said, "Sure enough." Tony's hero liked him.

* * *

2

No, My Neck's Not Broke

"You guys going to have that Popsicle running?" Duke said as he walked by the Duncan and Bettenhausen pit.

It was the opening Armory race, a reunion for the Chicagoland racers. No pressure here, nothing but fun running indoors. Hardly anyone ever got hurt. There were hay bales around the inside of the corners and a regular guard rail on the outside, but you usually didn't go fast enough on the tenth-mile track to really take a flier. There was lots of action indoors. Since the track was narrow, it was hard to pass on the outside, so sometimes you just moved the guy in front out of the way. Hardly a lap went by when there wasn't some bumping from behind. The crowd loved it and when one of the chain reactions took place: Someone up front would spin out (or get turned sideways from the fella behind) and everyone behind him would have to take evasive action. Cars would climb over one another, some would stop completely, others went through the infield.

"Is it gonna run?" Tony quipped back to Nalon. "Why this little shaker hasn't failed us yet. You'll know it's OK when it goes by you."

Popsicle and shaker. The engine in Tony's car was originally from a Harley-Davidson motorcycle and Dreyer had figured out a few modifications. It had two cylinders jutting up in a 'V' shape vaguely resembling a split popsicle. But Harleys vibrated. More than vibrated: they shook. In a long race, badly enough to loosen nuts, bolts and the driver's teeth. It wasn't the perfect Midget engine. It wasn't an Offy.

Tony and Teddy did well indoors. They didn't win a feature, but they were always running for the money positions: the top four. After they'd run about five races, just making the feature event became an accomplishment. By December, 45 to 50 Midgets tried for the ten main-event starting spots.

The Midget Tony purchased from Wally Zale, 1937 photo. [*Craig*]

Emil was a favorite indoors. His younger brother Chuck had managed to buy a Midget, too, and although he didn't make the features, he was having a good time running the Class B events. Nalon and Russo along with McQuinn were considered the potential feature winners, but Duncan's consistency was putting him high up in the point standings.

Teddy liked driving Tony's Midget, but he knew Tony was getting anxious to drive it himself. And it looked like he was going to get his chance pretty soon. An Eastern car owner named George Pickenpack had asked Duncan to drive the new car that he was having Pop Dreyer build for him.

On December 12, Pickenpack arrived at the Armory and Teddy strolled over to Tony and said, "She's all yours tonight -- Pickenpack is here. Just go out there and put 'er to the wood. But don't bend 'er. I might have to drive again next week."

Duke, Emil, Russo and several others saw that Tony was actually going to drive. They surrounded him and offered their best wisecracks. Then they followed with some sound advice: Don't try to break the track record when you qualify. Just get the feel of the thing. Don't bend it -- or yourself.

Tony hadn't any intention of following the advice. After waiting six months, he'd win, of course. He'd been slidin' around corners all of his life. And running the Midget would be just like drivin' on the dirt roads -- only better. He knew all the procedures by heart, he'd been practicing them mentally over and over for months. You don't waste any time once they push you off to qualify. Soon as you come down the front stretch, they throw the green flag and you're on the clock. Next time around, they give you the white flag -- then the checkered and it's all over. You had to do your very best when qualifying. He wanted to make the feature for sure.

It wasn't as easy as he had imagined. Sitting inside and driving was a lot different from watching like he'd been doing. The first thing he noticed going down the back stretch was that the steering was quick -- you just barely moved the wheel and the car darted. All you had to do was touch the throttle pedal and the Midget lurched forward. Tony wanted to sort of idle around for a couple of laps and get the feel of things, but Duncan had already driven it in warm-ups and now it was time to quality.

Tony drove as hard as he could, but he wasn't happy with his run. He knew he didn't look smooth, but he went fast, he thought. It felt fast anyhow. But it wasn't fast enough to make the feature. When they announced his time, Tony was surprised that he hadn't gone faster. But he did go faster than a few of the other drivers -- and they had experience. His qualifying time put him in the Class B race, way in the back. He was to start on the inside of the fifth row. At least it was better than not starting at all like some of the others who missed the show completely. They had to wait until next week for another chance.

After his qualifying run, Teddy asked him what he thought. How'd he like it? It's different when you're actually out there driving one, isn't it?

Once again, several drivers offered advice for the Class B event. Just stay out of trouble and get the feel of things. He was starting far enough back that he could watch the other fellas in front of him and see how they did it. Running the B race was no disgrace they said. Why, look at Pete Romcevich, he's a hot dog and he's running the B race. Get behind him and follow. You'll learn something.

That was all good advice, for someone else maybe. Tony knew they were trying to help him, but he didn't want to just putt around and follow guys. He wanted to race!

There he was, on the inside of the fifth row when starter Bill Vandewater threw the green flag. He didn't drop back a single position in the first corner. He kept up with the pack. Going into the third turn, he passed the guy in front, went underneath him when the driver slipped just a little wide. Tony'd seen it done a dozen times. Scoot past him fast, before he had a chance to get back in the groove again. He did the same thing on the next lap -- passed another car. And then again. Everybody was having trouble driving too fast and slipping to the outside. Tony's Midget was sticking right where he pointed it. Each lap he was ducking inside somebody and passing them when they came off the corner. Now there was only one car in front. On the seventh lap Pete Romcevich slipped wide too. Tony was leading!

On the next lap he drove into the first turn too hard, got sideways. Would Romcevich pass him? He couldn't tell how far behind that Serbian was. Can't look. No rear-view mirror. He was sliding sideways and losing time. Romcevich could scoot under him and take back the lead. But he didn't. And as he was going down the backstretch, he saw Nalon an Emil standing in the infield. Emil was giving him a hand signal, like a fisherman describing the length of his catch. Nalon was a few feet farther down the track, almost on the racing surface itself. He was tapping the top of his head with his forefinger, as if to say, "Use your head dummy -- you got the lead -- now don't spin and lose it."

Tony slowed going into the next turn and still didn't know where Romcevich, or anybody else for that matter, was. He knew that if someone was going to pass him it'd have to be the hard way -- around the outside. Down the back chute again and there was Emil showing a good spread between his out-stretched arms. Must have a good lead Tony thought. There's Duke again, still tapping his finger on his head. Nalon was right close to the corner and Tony smiled to himself as he slowed and drove through smoothly. He shot down the front chute, Vandewater waved the checkered flag! He'd won. His first race! What happened to the white flag? Hadn't even seen it. No matter now . . . he'd won . . . from ninth place to the lead in seven laps!

Tony coasted into the pits and found a group waiting for him. They began patting him on the back, asking how he liked it, telling him he looked good. Someone warned, "We better watch out. He's liable to do that in the feature one of these days."

Tony ran a consolation race the following week and finished third. He won another consi, as they came to be called, the day after Christmas. He was learning the ropes of indoor racing in a hurry: He'd have to better his qualifying times so he could start running in the feature race.

Finally, in mid-January he qualified sixth fastest and was ready for the 100 lap main event. He wanted to win his ten lap heat race just to warm-up. Emil was starting on the pole and when the green flag was dropped he was the early leader. Tony and Jimmy Caris were fighting for second. Tony wanted to get up there next to Emil and give him a go. Then, Caris spun lightly in the third turn and

Tony had no alternative but to drive over his right rear wheel.

It happened quickly. Tony felt a bump as he hit Caris back tire and hoped he'd go right over it. Instead, his car shot straight up, as though launched from a teeter-totter. The crowd gasped and some stood and pointed at the gyrating machine as it started to descend toward the ground. It was rolling in mid-air. Doing a forward flip. Tony's head would touch first, then the 800 pound vehicle would mash it into the ground. His hands were frozen on the steering wheel. If he had let go he might have been thrown out of the car, and possibly, some drivers said, out of danger. They didn't wear safety belts to hold them in. Most didn't like the idea of the car landing on top of them.

While it appeared as though the car would land upside down, Tony had been going fast enought to make the small machine complete its ungainly front flip. When he landed it was with a slam -- on all four wheels. In ragdoll fashion, his head went forward and hit the wheel, then snapped backwards. He was still holding the wheel when attendants ran to his aid, but like the Milwaukee school teacher at Riverview, he shook his head a couple of times and said, "No, my neck's not broke. I'm OK."

Again, the crowd cheered as he climbed from his right side up car. It was on all four wheels all right, but didn't roll too easily. There'd be no feature event for Tony Bettenhausen that night. Several of the other drivers told him that running the feature wasn't important. You've just been upside down, Bettenhausen. You're a lucky boy.

Two weeks later Tony was back in action. In his first race that night he finished second behind Jimmy Caris. Later, he spun directly in front of Andres and Nalon, completely stopping them. It was only a heat race, not much money and he was both a little embarrassed and proud at the same time. He was racin' with the pros. Running indoors sure was fun. Duke and Emil weren't too upset by Tony's spin, but they let him know that people would start talking about him being a squirrely driver if he didn't keep it straight all around the track.

One of the people who had an opportunity to talk about Tony was the auto racing writer, H. B. Overstreet. But Overstreet wasn't likely to write anything derogatory. He had met Tony three months ago, in October, before Tony took his first Midget ride. The winning grin and enthusiasm impressed Oversteet too, and the *National Auto Racing News* writer always made it a point to stop by Tony's pit and talk awhile. Tony had noticed that there was a core of photographers and writers, the same ones, week after week, who covered the races. Sometimes they'd stand down in the

THE BERGEN HERALD

NATIONAL AUTO RACING NEWS

SUPER SPEED

AMERICAN SPEEDWAYS' PICTURE NEWSPAPER

RACING EDITION

VOL. XVII, NO. 12 | Entered as Second Class Matter Post Office, East Paterson, N. J. | EAST PATERSON, N. J. FEB. 24, 1938 | Published Every Thursday I.A. 8-1346 | PRICE TEN CENTS

PLANS ARE BEING LAID FOR DRIVERS' TRAINING SCHOOL

(Story Page 2)

COMING STARS—(at right), who have made outstanding records the past year under the tutelage of the well-known Emil Andres. Tony Bettenhausen, seated in the No. 2 Harley, and Chuck Andres in the Andres Elto. Chuck is a younger brother of Emil and Bettenhausen is a cousin. Both of these young drivers make tough for competition in the Chicago Armory and show promise of wonderful possibilities. Emil Andres is shown standing in center in leather jacket. Note neat appearance of the pit crew. Great interest is shown in the midget races at the Armory.

Staff Photo by Loren E. Tutell

MIDGET CHAMP—This is the first picture of Sam Hanks, at left, in his new car. The 1937 American Midget Racing Assn. champ shown seated in his new Offenhauser powered midget. Sam and his beautiful red speedster will be ready for the 1938 midget opener at Gilmore Stadium on Sun day, March 13. On that date a 100-lap afternoon classic will be held, featuring the leading midget [illegible] on the West Coast.. More new models on back page.

By Douthett Photos

Tony made the front page of the National Auto Racing News only months after he started driving.

corners, too close to the hay bales, and would have to scurry out of the way when a car spun to the infield. They were brave, or just plain stupid, he thought. Some of them had a few pretty dumb questions too, but Tony always made time for them. Besides, he liked to talk about his car.

When he was ready to take his first ride, a photographer named Loren Tutell introduced himself and asked if he minded having a picture taken. Tony didn't mind at all, in fact he felt flattered. Some drivers refused to have their photo taken before an event. Bad luck. Tutell lined up Tony, Chuck Andres in his new Midget along with Emil and some of the helpers behind them.

"Look here, you're a star," Emil told Tony, handing him the latest *National Auto Racing News.* "It says you've compiled an *outstanding* record. How come they didn't print a picture of you getting upside down?"

Tutell had submitted the photo the racing paper with one of his weekly batches that included some of Chicago's best known drivers. He couldn't explain why the editors gave Tony and Chuck front-page billing and a capition that read:

> Coming stars who have made outstanding records the past year under the tutelage of well-known Emil Andres are Tony Bettenhausen and Chuck Andres . . . they show promise of wonderful possibilities.

The bottom photo pictured Sam Hanks, the 1937 American Midget Racing Association champion and the West coast champ. Neither Tony nor Chuck had scored many actual points while racing in the Armory, but they both felt a certain amount of status by sharing such an important position with a star like Hanks. Everybody in the pits at the Armory kidded them about their new-found fame. Chuck and Tony talked about what they'd do for the outdoor season that would open in a couple of months. Chuck wanted to race at Riverview. Tony said he'd been talking to Nalon about going over East. That's where the money was. Racing every night over there.

What Tony didn't tell Chuck, or anyone else, was that he'd go anywhere to be with Duke. He was teriffic. Tony and Duke had already talked about it a little bit. They'd get a truck, Tony said, and become a racing team: Bettenhausen and Nalon, or Nalon and Bettenhausen, whichever fit on the truck door the best. Duke warned him that the competition was pretty rugged. No easy pickin's. "We can handle it," Tony said. Duke could drive the Midget until Tony got the feel of things. Then, maybe, he'd take a few rides himself. Besides, Duke had a Big Car ride over East and

Tony's new 1938 Ford truck that he and Duke Nalon hauled Bettenhausen's first Midget in.

wouldn't always have time to run the Midget so their plan was set. The summer would be good.

Nalon hoped so too. Popular and successful over East, he wanted to run at Indianapolis. To be a 500 driver -- that meant a lot. Tony understood that if Duke could get a ride for Indy he'd have to leave and come back to the Midwest. Someone else might have to drive the Midget. OK, no problem. Duncan had said he wanted to come over. Tony was ready to go. So was the truck.

"How do you like 'er?" Tony said as he pointed out the doorway of Nalon's house. "Brand new '38. Already had it lettered."

"You get top billing again," Nalon said. "But it looks pretty good. Where'd you get the money?"

"Never mind. Besides, I traded my coupe in."

Tony had bought a brand new 1938 Ford truck. Cream colored. He ordered it special, with a chrome grill, chrome hubcaps and beauty rings around the wheels. It was a stake bed job, the kind where you could lift off the sides to gain easy access to the platform that would carry the Midget. Tony had taken the new vehicle to a sign painter. TONY BETTENHAUSEN Duke Nalon MIDGET RACING TEAM Chicago was emblazoned on the door.

"Chicago, not Tinley Park," Tony explained. "Who'd ever heard of Tinley Park?"

Further back he had the painter install a big board on the bed with a large number 2 painted on it. The rig looked classy. Mom had helped a little with the truck purchase, but Tony wan't telling.

In early April of 1937 Tony, Duke and their Number 2 were headed for the East coast. The spirit was adventuresome. Why worry about an economic recession which had begun that fall? If they were successful there was a chance to pick up well over a hundred dollars a night. Not bad, considering you could buy a dozen doughnuts for a dime; three loaves of bread for a quarter or two pounds of peanut butter for twenty three cents.

As they headed East, Tony found out how Wally Zale had given Duke his first real chance. Duke couldn't afford to buy his own car but used to help out on Zale's pit crew. Once in a while Zale would let him warm-up. Duke was cautious, sort of idling around. Then one day at Chicago's Roby Speedway he got his chance. Zale's mechanic, Walter Galven, arrived with a new driver and a car he'd been rebuilding. Galven explained that the driver's father, a wealthy meat market owner, had purchased the car and he was supposed to help the rookie driver along. Zale and the officials were apprehensive. They consented to let the youngster warm-up and to suspend judgement until after they saw him perform.

"Zale's pretty mean you know," Duke told Tony as they headed across highway 40 toward the East.

"I know," Tony replied.

"Well anyway," Duke continued, "Soon as he found out about this kid he tagged him "Butcher Boy' and commented about bein' a rich kid. That poor devil was nervous as Hell. He got in the car, was pushed off and no sooner went into the first turn -- and spun. Then he came driving back up the front chute the wrong way.

"Everybody really scrambled to miss him," Duke said. "Boy, was that Zale hot! He went to the officials and told them there was no way they should allow the kid to race. He'd kill himself -- or somebody else for sure. The officials agreed, and that left the car open.

"We were all standing around, it" Duke went on, "When Galven said, 'Who can I get to drive it? and I popped up and said, 'I can.' "

"Right away one of the officials asked if anyone had ever seen me on the track?

"Then good old Zale said, 'Sure, he's been running out West. I'll vouch for him.' "

Tony quickly asked, "How'd you do?"

"I won," Nalon said, "But it wasn't all that great a drive. I just kept it between the fences and pretty soon all the hot-dogs dropped out and I was leading. It was pretty lucky, really."

When Nalon won a 100 mile event a couple of months later at the same track, he was on his way.

Their talk drifted to the Speedway. Of course Tony said he'd wanted to drive there someday. Duke had tried last May, but failed to qualify. He was working on a ride for the '38 race.

The newly-formed Bettenhausen and Nalon Racing Team found headquarters in Paterson, New Jersey at a place called "Gasoline Alley," a horseshoe shaped set of garages named after the garage area at the Indianapolis Motor Speedway. Its summertime occupants were mostly people like Duke and Tony: those invaders of the East, there for winning. Lots of the racers just hung around the place watching cars being serviced, rebuilt and readied for the next race. Everybody gathered for meals and beers right down the street at Willie Belmont's. Willie was a former prizefighter who could put up with the good-natured, general rowdiness and got along well with this seemingly homeless racing crowd.

Talk during the last week in March centered around the upcoming Midget racing schedule. New tracks were planned for Cedarhurst, up in Long Island and a board race track over at Nutley, New Jersey. The track at Nutley caused the most comment. It had started out life as a bicycle and motorcycle speedway. After five seasons, Joseph Meile, the wealthy builder of the track, decided to close it for lack of spectator interest. Then, promoter Jack Kochman, the Boy Wonder of Midget racing, contracted with Meile to present Midget races on the sixth-mile board surface.

At first, Meile argued that the track was too small, and the turns, banked at a full 45 degrees, were too steep. A man couldn't even walk up them. Kochman, however, held a practice session and convinced the owner. Meile was partially right -- the cars did go awfully fast. But no one was injured and soon Kochman had himself a race track.

Through Kochman's efforts, the opening event at Nutley on April 3 received a good deal of pre-race publicity. Packed grandstands became the site of a near panic when driver Ken Fowler crashed into the guard rail and continued into the crowd. Thirteen spectators were reported injured along with Fowler, who had a broken arm. Tony and Duke didn't run in the first race and there was speculation that there wouldn't be a second. The town council wanted to close the place down. Promoter Kochman convinced the mayor that a new guard rail, one that woldn't allow the cars to carom upwards, was the solution. The track was closed for two weeks while the new rail was installed. Soon Nutley was famous among the East coast racers. It was too fast, they said. Vern Orenduff had set quick time at the opening meet at just over nine seconds. Nine seconds.

While the new guard rail was being installed Duke and Tony went to Philly to run at the Yellow Jacket Speedway and then to the Bronx. They didn't win, but Duke earned them a few dollars.

NUTLEY - The Wooden Speedway

The board speedway at Nutley, New Jersey had the highest banks of any track in the country. The view below shows a part of the front-stretch that is relatively flat. The turns were banked at an amazing forty-five degrees. [*Harms Coll.*]

Duke was leading a heat race at Yellow Jacket when the drive chain flew off. Later he told Tony, "I took it easy in the feature because I thought that chain would go off again."

"Looks like *some* place," Duke said after they pulled into the Nutley track. "Look at those banks," Tony commented.

The banking in the turns was impressive. Not only the 45 degress, but the height. The top of each turn stood sixteen feet from the ground. You didn't have to be a professional to see how you could hurt yourself here. One slip on the bank and your car would tumble down into the infield.

"We'll give 'er a try," Duke said. "Can't make any promises about this place. Never tried anything like this before."

Duke adapted right away. He set third fastest qualifying time and finished second in his heat race. He was running second in the feature behind Red Redmond when the drive chain flew off again. He coasted into the pits and told Tony, "We'll never make any money like this. Gotta get that chain fixed."

Throughout the next week the same thing happened. Duke would qualify well, win a heat race and have chain trouble in the feature. When they went back to Nutley the following Sunday, car owner Mike Caruso walked up to the pair and said, "Things getting a little slim for you guys?"

"How could you tell?" Nalon answered in mock sarcasam.

"Why don't you drive my Offy tonight?" Caruso offered. "Make a few bucks til you get Tony's car straightened out."

Nalon thought it was a good idea. He didn't want to leave Tony, but they could use the money.

"Who's going to drive my car?" Tony asked.

"Why you could probably run it yourself," Duke said. "You did a pretty good job indoors." Duke didn't particularly want Tony to start his outdoor career at Nutley, but figured he'd miss the entire show in qualifying, so didn't give the matter much thought. He couldn't get into too much trouble out there all by himself.

"Gee you really think I can drive it here?" Tony asked.

"Why sure. Just don't go out there and try to set the world on fire. Remember, there's always another race."

"Hey Benski," the hoarse voice called. "You sure you know which direction to drive that thing?"

It was curly haired little Paul Russo. Already a star at Nutley, (he had won the first race) Russo was going to offer some more advice. He had been ribbing Tony for the past couple of weeks ever since Tony managed to get a ticket for driving the wrong way on a Pennsylvania highway. Tony and Duke were behind Russo in

Paul Russo

Wisecracking Paul Russo, one of Nutley's stars and Tony's pal. [*Harms Coll.*]

a long line of traffic when the impatient Bettenhausen said, "Watch this," and pulled across the road onto the shoulder of oncoming traffic. He was met by a highway patrolman.

"Listen," Russo continued, "Ya gotta keep turning left on a race track, Bettenhausen. Remember that. You don't wanna disgrace us Chicago guys, do you?"

Tony took the ribbing good-naturedly. Russo was OK. Always had a smile and a wisecrack. The little wop. He liked being a small guy.

Then just like before Tony's first indoor race, Paul told him, "Now you know that only eight guys make the feature here. Don't go out there and wrap that thing around one of them telephone poles that are supposed to keep us outa the grandstands. You're a long way from home. This thing's gotta feed ya for a couple more months."

It was like talking to a rock. Tony knew, Duke knew and Russo knew that Tony would go out and stand on it for all he was worth. He'd already convinced himself, indoors, that he could drive. Now he was going to be in the major leagues. Right at their toughest ballpark. He had to make the program. Russo'd never let him live it down if he had to put it on the truck right after qualifying. Besides, they didn't give you any money if you missed the show. Not to Tony Bettenhausen anyway. With Russo it was a different story. He had a deal. He got a hundred bucks a night just to show up. The crowd loved him. And promoter Kochman loved seeing those grandstands full. Maybe Tony'd get a deal when he was good too.

They pushed him off, and going down the backstretch he moved high so as to go through turns three and four full tilt. He'd seem it done before. He took the green flag and went into the first turn a split second later. Maybe it was just a little too fast. Or a bit erratic. He headed toward the new guard rail, almost saved it, but clipped the fence with the right rear tire. It was a glancing blow and he kept going without letting off as if to say, "Oops." He was a little more cautious in three and four and ended his first lap just like he began it. Through one and two once more, this time a little lower: down the backstretch and really nail'n' it through three and four. There's the checkered flag and it's all over. First turn again and up too high. Bang! Hit the fence with the right rear again. He coasted down the backchute and into the pits.

Nalon and Russo were waiting for him. "You got something against that first turn fence?" Russo asked. "You leave it alone and it'll leave you alone."

Tony hadn't made the feature, but he did go fast enough to run a heat and a consi. He was happy. Then the mood became serious when Chick Meyer spun slowly, headed up the banking into the rail and flipped on the way back down. He was tossed out of the car, but stood up almost immediately and waved to the crowd. They cheered.

Tony started on the pole in the third heat race and led the entire first lap. Then two guys passed him and he decided to follow them and maybe just learn how to drive this place. It sure was fast. A lap every nine seconds. You don't have much time to miss the guy in front of you if he makes a mistake. Tony finished third. Duke and Russo congratulated him for not crashing. Announcer Nat Kleinfield had said that Tony Bettenhausen looked good.

* * *

Up in the grandstands two young men were especially happy. Little Ernie Schlausky and his older buddy Gus Gerhardt. Ernie was 18 years old and Gussie was 23. When Ernie was 14 Gus took him to his first race, a motorcycle race at Tri-City Speedway and the youngest of the four Schlausky boys fell in love with the way the riders would broadslide through the cinder covered turns.

"I'm going to be a racer," Ernie told Gus.

"Me too," was the reply.

Over the next four years Ernie and Gus made it a point not to miss any motorcycle or Midget auto race in the area. Ernie's folks didn't think it was such a good idea for him to be hanging out with an older boy, especially one who looked so ragged all the time. Gus had long hair and a beard. He was a bad influence they said. But Ernie didn't think so. He used to ride his bicycle past Gus' house and see him working on his Model T Ford out in the yard. Finally one day he stopped and started talking about the car and what was being done to it. Soon Ernie was helping Gus work on the old Ford. Ernie wasn't very mechanically inclined, but he liked the way Gus treated him. He was a buddy. He didn't care what his parents said, he knew Gus was alright. He didn't smoke, or drink or curse he'd tell them. So what if he was older? Ernie was always a bit shy and it was nice to have someone who appreciated you.

After going to his first motorcycle race, Ernie decided that he'd be just like the star of the show, a man named Crocky Rawding. Rawding had won every event he entered at Tri-City and although he had no interest in motorcycles before attending the race, Ernest Schlausky decided that he'd be a motorcycle racer first, and then a car racer. And he owed it all to Gus. If it hadn't been for Gus he would have never gone to the races in the first place.

Soon Ernie lost interest in school. Who needed school when you could earn all that money racing? But they told him he had to stay in until he was 16, it was the law. He spent his last year in a vocational school, taking a machine shop course. But, he didn't like machinery very much. When he reached his 16th birthday he got a job down at Herman's grocery store, delivery boy. Then he moved up to clerk and used to wait for Mrs. Kushman to come in with her daughter Gene. Ernie thought Gene was beautiful, but was aftraid to say anything to her. Once in a while he'd write her a note and drop it in the grocery sack. He was good at writing notes, his teachers always told him he was good at writing in general and he should do more of it.

Gene Kushman found out that the slightly built Ernie Schlausky was really quite a gentleman. He wasn't at all like the neighbors said, a wacko motorcycle rider, always taking chances. Ernie would always broadslide whenever he saw the opportunity, even if it was on a city street. But once he talked Gene into taking a ride with him, he rode as though he were in a funeral procession. It was nice to have her back there, her arms around his waist. Sometimes she'd lay her head on his shoulder and quiet little Ernie felt warm inside. He wouldn't dare take any chances with Gene riding along. He'd take her everywhere, up to the garages at Gasoline Alley in Patterson, to the races, and sometimes just on long rides in the country. All the while he'd talk about the day he would be a famous race car driver. But first he had to be a successful motorcycle rider like his idol, Crocky Rawding.

Most of the time Gus and Ernie would sneak in the Midget races they attended, but every Wednesday and Sunday they had to pay forty cents to get into Nutley. It was OK they agreed, Nutley was worth paying for. The track was open only two seasons, 1938-39 and Ernie didn't miss one race either year.

* * *

After his successful debut at Nutley, Tony was ready to start running the circuit; the AAA circuit, the one the pros raced on. They were real racers, towing up and down the East coast on warm summer days. Jobs? Nobody had a job, driving race cars for a living wasn't like punching a time clock. Everybody had a good time. Not like real work at all. And none of them would admit that their chosen profession demanded more hours and more concentration and paid less than most eight-to-five jobs did. Among themselves, though, especially when the going got rough, they'd say, "If I put this much effort into regular work, I'd be a millionaire." What regular work offered the variety, the excitement of racing?

The tracks themselves even had an aroma you remembered -- like the smell of castor oil; an odor you couldn't find anywhere else. You could actually feel the action at a race track. When you were at a dirt track watching the cars warm up, you'd have to duck and turn your head sideways so the flying clods wouldn't hit you. But mostly, you just turned a little bit and it didn't hurt anything if a few clods blounced off your back. You could reach down and grab a handful of the moist clay and make a little ball out of it, toss it back and forth. And you knew that once you got your race car out there in the muck, you could powerslide through the corners so hard that everybody would think that bombs were going off under your tires. You'd leave behind a roostertail of dirt that made 'em all duck for shelter. Guys on regular jobs couldn't get that excited about their work. Why some tracks were so good that you'd race on them for free. Getting paid for racing a Midget was really neat.

For a young man yearning to go racing, the summer of 1938 offered all he could hope for. Tony read down the AAA schedule:

DAY	PLACE	PURSE
SUN	Nutley	$1,000
MON	Cedarhurst	750
MON	Bridgeport	550
TUES	Philadelphia	800
TUES	Bronx	700
WED	Nutley	1,000
THUS	New Haven	675
FRI	Philadelphia	800
FRI	Bronx	700
SAT	W. Philadelphia	600

Tony remembered that he had told Teddy Duncan he could drive the Midget a little if he came over East. Duncan knew Duke would probably be too busy to run all the time and he was looking forward to making his mark, along with the rest of the Chicago Gang, on the Easterners. Tony, however, was having second thoughts. He knew that only the bravest and the best could stand up to Nutley -- and he did -- on his very first try. He knew he'd get better. Just like indoors, he'd drive around 'em, or under 'em. He'd race with everybody. He had to WIN some races. First, though, he had to make the car reliable. He needed some help.

Crocky Rawding, the successful flat-track motorcycle racer, had taken an interest in the Nutley Midget races, probably because some of the cars, like Tony's, used motorcycle engines. Duke and Tony met Rawding after their first Nutley attempt. Could he look the car over and maybe offer some assistance? He'd had experience with bike engines.

When you had a problem at the race track, it was easy to locate the armchair mechanics who passed out advice and comments. Some wanted to say, "Yeah, I told 'em what was wrong with that box they're trying to race," but others would sacrifice their spare parts and help a fellow get back on the track. Then they'd go out and race you down to the wire. Crocky Rawding was not an armchair mechanic nor much of a spectator, and found that Tony's chain problem was just what he needed to get himself out of the grandstrands. Besides, he'd watched Tony and he knew talent, or maybe bravery, when he saw it.

"C'mon over to my place," he told Tony. "Got some tools

there. We'll make this little shaker run like a watch."

The week after Tony made his Nutley debut, he and Crocky worked on the car. They made a new chain sprocket and finished up in time to go back to the banked board speedway. If a car could survive Nutley, it'd survive anywhere. Tony told Duke the car was just fine now and he should drive it.

"Don't you want to run it?" Duke asked.

"Sure," Tony said, "but you'll really give 'er a test. I'll know it's OK if you say so."

On the way to the track the talk was the same. They wondered who won up at Hohokus that afternoon. The Nutley promoter, Jack Kochman, was staging a Big Car race there and Nalon complained that he didn't have a good ride so he didn't go. Who'd win the last indoor race back home? They'd read that McQuinn was in first place; he'd probably be the champ. He'd probably rather be here, over East, but he was doing OK in Chicago. He'd do OK wherever he ran. He was tough. How'd he like Nutley?

After warm-ups were over, Duke said the car felt pretty good, but he wasn't pushing as fast as he might. He'd try pretty hard in qualifying. Especially when Duke and Tony remembered Russo's greeting.

"That thing ready?" he asked.

"Sure." Tony said.

"Which one of youse is going to drive it?"

"Duke," Tony replied.

"Didn't ya like the place, Benski?" Paul asked.

"Sure, I love it. I just figured we'd win one right away. I might have to run a couple more times, but Duke can handle it."

"I ain't too worried," Russo smiled. "Last time I saw that thing it was tryin' to polish the fence off."

"Get outa here," Tony laughed. "Go tell that Offy of yours it's gonna have some competition tonight."

Announcer Nat Kleinfield told the crowd that Bobby Sall, before seven thousand fans, had won the Big Car feature at Hohokus and a couple of the boys were on their way from Hohokus to Nutley. He reminded them that the next Big Car race there would be held on May 30. They could take in two races in one day. Jack Kochman was staging some fine racing this summer.

Russo was first out on the track for qualifying. He'd said that he didn't want to give anyone a chance to drop oil on the boards before he made his run.

His Caruso Offy set a new record of 8.77 seconds. The fans gave him an extra ovation. He waved back at them. Then he waved down the pits to Duke and Tony.

THE BERGEN HERALD

NATIONAL AUTO RACING NEWS

SUPER SPEED

AMERICAN SPEEDWAYS' PICTURE NEWSPAPER

RACING EDITION

VOL. XVII, NO. 18 Entered as Second Class Matter Post Office, East Paterson, N. J. EAST PATERSON, N. J. APR. 7, 1938 Published Every Thursday I.A. 8-1346 PRICE TEN CENTS

PAUL RUSSO CAPTURES MAIN EVENT AT NUTLEY BOWL

(Story Page 2)

PAUL RUSSO, of Chicago, winner of the first race held on the board track at Nutley, N. J. Photo shows winner immediately after getting checkered flag.

BILL HEISERMAN, casting a critical eye over the gang as they start work on the guard rail at the Coney Island Velodrome. This plant is one of the Bill Heiserman Promotions.

CONEY ISLAND VELODROME—View showing how track will look to drivers coming down the back stretch on the Coney Island Velodrome, which will have its inaugural meet on Sunday, April 24, under the promotion of Bill Heiserman.

Paul Russo was a regular headliner at Nutley.

Red Redmond thrilled the Nutley fans weekly. [Harms Coll.]

"Cocky little bastard, ain't he?" Tony asserted.

Russo was right. When Duke went out the track had oil on it and he could do no better than 9.55 for eleventh quick time.

Russo got a second in his heat race; Nalon a third in his. Russo won the first semi and Duke the second, but the chain flew off as he crossed the finish line. They were parked for another night. In the feature Russo led for 29 laps and was virtually shoved out of the way by Red Redmond who went on to win. Paul finished second and commented to the Georgia driver after the event that he had pulled a pretty dumb stunt. Tricks like that, Russo said, got guys killed. Paul didn't like the idea of being put out of business by somebody else's mistake.

The following Wednesday night, Tony's car wasn't ready to run, but he went to Nutley anyhow. He'd help on Russo's pit crew. Again, Paul broke the track record with an 8.61 clocking. Everything was looking good for Russo in the feature until Frankie Bailey spun in front of him. Paul was forced to the rear of the pack. As Tony watched from the infield, the little Italian picked off car after car and was leading after twenty-five laps. He had passed Red Redmond, took over number one position and held it to the end.

"Boy, you were terrific," Tony said after the race.

"Did you learn anything?" Paul asked him.

"I just hope I can do *that* someday," Tony said as he nodded toward the track.

Announcer Kleinfield could see a definite battle emerging: Russo and Redmond. Who'd be King of the Nutley boards? C'mon back on Sunday night and watch another great battle. Tony wanted to be in that battle, too. But he was having trouble getting the car fixed. He needed a new shaft. You couldn't hurry a slow mechanic, though. But once the new piece was made, Tony

Pals, Paul Russo left, and Emil Andres.

reasoned, he'd be ready for the races. And now he had watched enough at Nutley to go out and run with the best of 'em. He'd memorized the groove that was fastest.

Russo won the next race, too; then Eddie Staneck found his stride and became a hot competitor and won the following event. It was near the end of May now and Tony wondered how Duke was doing at the Speedway. By the time Duke returned, he wanted to be doing well at the races. The Duke must be proud of him. It would have been nice, Tony thought, to have his name listed as "Winner" in the *National Auto Racing News*. Then Duke would be reading it back in Indianapolis.

The underground racing news wire informed the East Coast racers that Nalon had secured a ride in Henry Kohlert's Miller -- but he wasn't running very fast in practice. Probably not make the program. Emil Andres was running the Elgin Piston Pin sponsored car and although he wasn't considered one of the hot dogs, he'd be in the show. Harry McQuinn, who'd been running almost 120 miles an hour would probably be a contender along with Jimmy Snyder for the best performance by a Chicago driver. Duke had to make the show. He knew how important it was to be considered a Speedway driver. He mentally wished the Duke well. But for now, he'd have to concentrate on himself and make that Nutley feature.

Tony knew that if he could run around Nutley in less than nine seconds, he'd be in good shape. Usually only three or four guys ran less than nine seconds, though. You were a hot dog if you ran in the eights. Eddie Staneck had quick time with an 8.64 and Russo was second with an 8.70. Redmond's expected charge netted him an 8.93 for the next fastest time, but he wasn't alone with that clocking. Cecil Zent went out and tied Red's qualifying speed and so did a newcomer -- Tony Bettenhausen!

"It looks like you've got your head on straight tonight," Russo told him. "Now just keep it that way."

They were both in second heat race and Russo jumped to an early and comfortable lead. Behind him was Tommy Hinnershitz, a Pennsylvania Dutchman who claimed that he was, "Just a farmer having a good time." Tony followed Hinnershitz for the ten lap distance and finished in third place. Passing at Nutley took stuff, he thought. Still, third place in the qualifying heat wasn't good enough for the feature. He could run the semi. During the race little Eddie Staneck attempted to pass. Tony held firm and Staneck actually rubbed wheels with the newcomer. Staneck outpowered him and drove up next to Russo where he again had a wheel-rubbing incident.

After the fifteen lap event was over, Russo asked Tony, "Didja see how that Staneck put a wheel into me?"

"How could I miss it?" Tony said. "I was right behind you. He did the same thing to me."

"Welcome to the club," Russo said.

At last, Tony felt like a racer.

In the feature Russo and Staneck rubbed wheels again and Paul had to pull in with a flat tire. Memories were easy to build at Nutley.

The grapevine had brought news that on Memorial Day, Duke Nalon was to be an Indianapolis 500 starter. He was the slowest car to qualify out of the 33 allowed in the field. Emil had qualified 28th, Snyder 15th and Harry McQuinn was right next to him in 14th position. Tony would listen to the periodic race reports that were broadcast. He had read that Wilbur Shaw predicted an average speed of 115 miles per hour would be good enough to win and Shaw said that he'd drive to win.

One of the first reports broadcast had Jimmy Snyder leading the race. McQuinn was also running in the top ten and the announcer said Chicago driver Emil Andres had hit the wall in the northeast turn after his engine had frozen up. Andres' car had rolled several times and his condition was not known at the time. It was also reported that a spectator may have been injured as a result of the Andres crash.

Tony and Crocky Rawding had been listening together. Tony showed Rawding the copy of the *National Auto Racing News* that had him and Emil on the cover along with Chuck Andres.

The evening news reported a spectator had been killed by a wheel that had broken off the race car driven by Emil Andres. The man's name was Everett Spence. Driver Andres was in satisfactory condition. Floyd Roberts was considered an upset winner, as he averaged 117 miles per hour to win the event. Moments after Roberts crossed the finish line, rain began to fall. Tony was glad that Duke was able to finish eleventh, but he felt sorry for Emil. Killed a spectator, too.

Tony expected Duke back any day now and hoped they would be able to go out and run the circuit together. Russo had won another feature at Nutley the night before the 500 and went to Philadelphia the day after the race. He crashed at the Yellow Jacket Speedway and although he wasn't injured seriously, he had to go to Nutley all alone. It was different feeling. He didn't do well at all. It helps to have your friends around, he thought.

Russo wasn't gone long, only a week, and when he came back to Nutley he had quick time again. Tony's car wasn't running as well as it should and Russo asked him if he had been tinkering with it.

"Just a bit," Tony said, "I know I can make it faster."

"If somebody would take away your tools, you might just learn how to drive that thing," Russo told him. "First yo' gotta finish in order to win. You keep monkeying around with it and you're never gonna get past qualifications."

Tony the tinker. The engineer. Knew there was a better way. Give your machine the advantage, then drive around 'em. Tony had continuing car troubles. No, it wasn't his tinkering, he thought. Some things just had to be changed -- the engine maybe. He and Crocky had been talking, switch to the popular J.A.P. cycle engine. Besides, Rawding confided, he knew a lot more about the "Jap" than he did a Harley. They switched engines in mid-June and drove up to Bridgeport.

Tony didn't make the feature, but was happy when he came in after warm-ups. He had been among the fastest on the small dirt track. The dirt was nice and tacky and you could really broadslide through the corners.

"She'll go now," Tony told the motorcycle racer.

"You just keep your eye on the race track. It'll probably get hard and slick as pavement after a little while," Crocky told him. "You gotta know how to read a race track. Especially a dirt one. They'll fool you if you're not careful."

"Don't worry about a thing," Tony said. "We've got enough horsepower here to make up for any kind of track."

The track did get hard and Tony just spun the rear wheels as he tried to get traction. He had too much power.

"You were right," he told Crocky after his unsuccessful qualifying attempt. "But back on the boards we'll show 'em how it's done."

During the weeks Tony was having trouble with his car, he'd

Henry Banks in a 1935 photo in his Sprint car at Milwaukee. [Henry Banks Coll.]

traveled to Nutley each Wednesday and Sunday night to watch and learn. Sometimes announcer Kleinfield would interview a driver who'd run on the huge board speedways built before the war or during the Twenties. Most of them were over a mile in length, with banking like at Nutley and speeds then were tremendous. Newspaper writers treated the drivers like true athletes, superior to most mortals. Automobile racing was really something in the Twenties, they would say.

Yet in 1938, the Nutley race track had become the talk of the auto racing world. Drivers from all over the country came to at least take a look. One of the country's most successful Midget racers, Ronney Householder, towed his beautiful little white car from California to see the place. Householder was THE number one hot dog at the famed Gilmore Stadium in Los Angeles. Householder had class. He was always up front at Gilmore, the finest Midget racing facility in the United States.

"Nope," he said. "Think I'll pass it up. Doesn't look like my kind of race track," Householder said after one quick look at Nutley from the infield. Was he scared or just too sane to run at Nutley? Householder's reputation had spread East through the racing papers. The racing papers, (Tony had discovered another one, *Illustrated Speedway News*) detailed each event at Nutley and headlined the track in each issue. Writers around the country would ask their local stars what they thought of the place. Most had never seen the "boards" as the track came to be known but

This 1936 photo shows a 23 year old Henry Banks, already a four year racing veteran.

Henry Banks on the boards at Nutley in the Caruso Offy, 1938. Note the steep banking. [*Henry Banks Coll.*]

the continuing publicity was good for not only promoter Kochman, but the competitors as well. If you ran fast at Nutley you got good ink . . . important when you're trying to talk a promoter out of a "deal" or an owner out of a ride. And so they came from every part of the U.S. to challenge Nutley, Russo, Staneck and Redmond.

One driver who obtained some advance publicity was Henry Banks, from Royal Oak, Michigan, already a 500 veteran with an impressive record. The papers called him "A mild-mannered throttle stomper" as he showed at Nutley on a Sunday evening, July 3rd with a Jap-powered car that caught Tony's attention. They struck up a conversation and liked each other right away. Tony told him all he could about running Nutley and wished him well. Henry proved his mettle with a fourth place finish in the feature while Russo set a new track record of 8.37 seconds. Tony said his own car would be ready for the following Wednesday.

Tony pitted next to the Michigan driver for the Wednesday race and knew that Nutley had another challenger when Banks set second fast time in only his second race. Tony himself was sixth fastest of the evening and more than pleased with his performance. The car felt strong. He'd make the feature for sure.

He and Henry were in the same qualifying heat race, the one for the cars that qualified in the even number positions. They were running side-by-side down the backstretch when their front ends became entangled. It could have been serious, but luckily they both half-spun, right toward the infield. Tony could have shut it off and coasted in, but stood on the gas and shot all the way across onto the front stretch. Henry was right behind him, then he passed Tony fair and square. Banks finished second, Bettenhausen fourth. Back in the pits they laughed about the incident. Banks went on to register his first Nutley win and Tony rated a solid fifth.

The fifth place finish gave Tony a boost. He had expected it sooner. He wanted to be successful at Nutley. He wanted to be successful everywhere, but lacked the finesse and experience to succeed on the circuit's flat tracks. His performances throughout the summer of '38 were unpolished on the other tracks. He was often relegated to the consolation races while his friends were running up front. Henry would often tell him to take it easy and just follow some of the other drivers and learn. You had to be smooth, gentle with the gas pedal. But Tony knew better: Only one position for the gas pedal -- wide open.

Tony had good teachers for his first year in competition. He idolized Nalon and would always do his best to follow the Duke's orders. He could laugh with Russo, and just be at ease with Henry. To someone in central casting, Henry was the least likely of the foursome to be cast as a race car driver. He had left a job with General Motors that promised a bright future as an engineer. He loved automobile racing. Off the track he was the opposite of Tony. He could have been an accountant. A pharmaceutical salesman. A plodder. Maybe a lot like Clarence. But Clarence would NEVER think of driving a race car. Henry? Henry was a hot dog. In the pits and on the track his personality must have changed like day and night, Tony thought. Boy did he ever stand on the gas.

Russo could have been the little round Italian who owned the shoe store down on the corner. You could just hear him, "Listen lady, that's the last shoe I'm showin' you -- your feet stink."

Nalon was always ready with a toothy smile. He'd look fresh at the bottom of the ninth in the World Series with the bases loaded if he were the pitcher. The natural hero.

They were all big brothers to Tony. Little Tunni, probably a polite delivery boy who said, "Thank you, Ma'am," when he received a tip and flashed a smile. If the bank ever had to foreclose on Mama's mortgage, it would be Tony who would talk them out of it.

As the season wore on, Tony improved. He made it to the top four or five in qualifying at Nutley and up to a third place finish in the feature by mid-July. Then Teddy Duncan came to town and

Tony is congratulated on his fine drive to second place on July 27, 1938. [McCumsey Coll.]

talked Tony into letting him run the car at Cedarhurst. It was a long race, a hundred lapper, and Duncan had been running as high as third at the halfway mark. Then he spun. Tony and Henry were watching from the infield (Henry had gone out with mechanical troubles) and they ran to Duncan's aid.

"Just lost it," Teddy said from the cockpit.

"C'mon, turn it around and we'll push you off again," Tony said. "There's still forty laps to go."

"Never mind," Duncan replied. "I'm too tired. Forget it."

They pushed him into the pits and on the way Tony commented to Henry, "That's it. Too tired. From now on I'll drive this thing myself."

The following Wednesday Tony got a second at Nutley and Henry was right behind him. The next week it was another second and he won the semi. He was qualifying in the mid-eight second bracket now. Eddie Staneck, Russo and Ernie Gessell were swapping feature victories back and forth every week. Henry won another feature and Redmond two more. Tony was usually close behind. Both Staneck and Russo were extremely popular among the fans and always received the largest round of applause. Some fans were so appreciative of the driving performances that they brought gifts which were at first presented privately after the races. Announcer Kleinfield heard of the gift bearing and announced that fans could now make their presentations just before the running of the feature event, after the cars had been lined up.

On August 17th Kleinfield called Red Redmond to the starting line to accept a wooden crate that had been donated.

"And for our Georgia-born racer, Red Redmond," Kleinfield said, "we have some genuine Georgia peaches."

Redmond dutifully opened the box and took a bite of peach. He waved to the fans and said thank you.

"Will Paul Russo and Henry Banks please come up," Nat said. "We've got a couple of boxes here -- don't know what's in them."

Russo was ready to start the race on the pole -- number one position. He needed the win. Staneck was one up on him. Banks was set, too, he was starting right next to Paul.

Russo waddled up to the announcer, gave his wife Leona a short wave and accepted the unopened box. Banks did the same.

Russo shook the box, turned around and walked back down the race track. Even the straight-a-ways were banked. He didn't utter a word into the microphone and Banks gave him a glance like, "What the Hell you doing -- you're supposed to say thank you."

Banks shook his box also and followed Russo in duck-like fashion. When Paul stepped off the boards he side-armed the box into the infield and said to Henry, "Some sumbitch given me peanuts." He grabbed Henry's present, shook it and pitched it also. Then he said, "I ain't racin'. Them things are bad luck."

"Sick bastards," Paul continued. "Don't care if I am startin' on the pole, I ain't gonna run."

"I'm with you," Henry said.

And they both walked back toward their cars while the announcer stood silently on the track. A minute or two had passed and everyone noticed that nothing was going on. Were the presentations over? If so, you always heard a Midget roar to life. Kleinfield was always talking, right up to the time you couldn't hear him anymore for the drone of the engines. Men in the pits who saw Russo fling the boxes understood. The word spread fast. Somebody gave him some fuckin' peanuts. Assholes. Bloodthirsty bastards. We oughta find the sick son-of-a-bitch and bolt him in one of these things -- and wire the throttle open.

Russo got up next to his car, looked at it, turned around and walked back toward the pits.

"I ain't gonna touch that thing," he said.

By this time their crews had surrounded the two lead Midgets and were wondering what to say or do. Everybody looked at each other, and finally someone started pushing Ruso's car off the track, and Banks' followed it. Kochman told Kleinfield to call two more cars to the field: Everybody would advance two positions. Russo didn't want to talk to anybody and Henry was his usual quiet self. Mike Joseph and Jimmy McCarron were called to start the feature and Paul commented that it was bad luck to run out there tonight. Joseph spun and flipped in the feature race but he wasn't seriously injured. McCarron registered his best performance ever and took a second - behind Eddie Staneck.

The peanut jinx worked on Paul's mind and although he traveled to Cedarhurst the next night, he decided not to drive. He relinquished the Caruso Offy to Honey Purick, who barrell-rolled it down the backstretch and wound up with a factured skull, broken jaw and two broken ribs.

The Nutley story spread and spectators were turned away at the gate for the next several weeks. The grandstands were full. Russo and Staneck continued their battle for supremacy of the Boards and Tony continued to learn. Paul would tell him that he looked like he was "driving over your head", sometimes, but Tony would just laugh and say, "You're always talking about my head Russo -- you're going to have to start worrying about my foot pretty soon -- the one that works the gas pedal."

"You still got a hard head, Bettenhausen," Russo said. "Why don't you tell me about what happened at Cedarhurst. I heard you got upside down there last month. Is that right? I didn't see your car bent up."

"It was just a little flip," Tony said. "Didn't hurt a thing."

It was just a little flip. During warm-ups Tony hooked a rut and did a quick snap-roll and the car landed back on its wheels with the engine still running. He drove it back to the pits and parked it for the night. Nothing much was hurt.

"Well, it couldn't have hurt your head," Russo cracked. "How many times is that now you been upside down?"

"Don't worry about it," Tony ribbed back. "I ain't worried about getting upside down long as I can keep countin' the times."

The July 26 incident at Cedarhurst was the second time in Tony Bettenhausen's short career that he had been upside down. That's twice more than some guys could talk about.

* * *

Another solid member of the Chicago Gang joined the Nutley contingent in mid-summer, Cletus "Cowboy" O'Rourke, the racing Irishman who had a reputation for breaking as many hearts as he won trophies. And he won his share of trophies. He was a lot like Russo, but Russo's wife Leona accompanied him to nearly every race and Paul never had to look elsewhere for female companionship. Leona was a real looker and Paul was proud of her. Smart, too.

Tony and the Cowboy could really raise Hell together. The Cowboy was just as wild off the track as he was on. Tony didn't care. Tony didn't care about anything except becoming a champion race car driver. Booze, broads, race cars, good times. Tinley Park was never like over East. There was always something good going on. Like the night someone robbed Nutley.

It was on August 28th, right after the big 60 lapper that Staneck won with regulars Russo and Banks behind. Everyone had stayed around the pits for awhile after the feature, maybe even a little longer because there were more spectators milling around. It was a record crowd that they let in, over 9,000. Even the fire department was there because of the overflow. Boy, that Kochman is makin' dough tonight, the racers said.

Nutley's cashier, Archie Phillips, had asked for a police escort because of the additional cash he had to carry from the track. He even had two guards ride with him. The police escorted him to the Passaic city line and waved as he drove into Clifton. Right along Main Avenue, the trio was forced to curbside by four gunmen in another car. The savvy bandits first asked Phillips for the ignition key, then the money. They escaped with no trouble.

The racers thought it was funny. They had all received their money already, just like they did every night. You had to wait in line at the pit shack for it, but you were always paid right after the race in cash. They liked that. Cash, right now. They could trust Kochman and most other promoters on the AAA circuit, but watch out if you go to run an "outlaw" track. First, you're not supposed to run anything that isn't AAA sanctioned. Liable to get fined. Second, it's a good bet that the promoter will abscound with your funds. Happens all the time. Then somebody commented that it was probably four broke race drivers who staged the hold up. Everyone laughed.

Then the serious happened. Spins and crashes had been a common occurrence at Nutley all season long, but no one had been fatally injured. Not til Charlie Heliker made them vomit in the grandstands.

Charlie was another quiet, unassuming type of guy who had been racing for two years. He hadn't ever shown to have great potential, but he was likeable enough and made the shows now and then. Already thirty-four, he knew he wasn't really getting anywhere and told some of his friends that he'd probably give it up pretty soon unless he landed a top notch ride.

The accident happened in the second semi event, the race in which only the winner transferred to the feature event. Charlie was back in fourth spot racing with Lou Volk. Volk tried to pass on the outside and Charlie spun toward the infield -- then he spun again! This time back onto the track toward the guard rail and Volk. He slammed into Volk and the impact tossed Heliker out of his car. He was lying on the track. His race car continued up the track, into the guard rail and did a back flip. It landed right on top of Charlie -- and burst into flames. He didn't have a chance. Russo and Staneck went out and ran one-two again with Henry third. Tony wondered (as did everyone else) why Charlie spun and headed back toward the race track. Strange place this Nutley. Tony didn't like it as much as he had before. Who'd want to come back? Poor Charlie.

With only a few races left on the schedule Bettenhausen and Nalon headed back for the Midwest. The summer was nearly gone. There didn't seem to be much left for them over East. Especially after 'ol Charlie got it. Russo stayed and kept on winning. Everyone thought that West Coast newcomer Duane Carter would be another Nutley statistic after he slid down the backstretch upside down during the last meet that Tony attended. Carter was hurt alright, but he said he'd be back.

Of the 44 race meets that were held at Nutley in 1937, Russo won 15 of them and Henry managed 3. Staneck was the big winner with 16.

* * *

3

Jesus Paul, Don't Hit Me

After Tony had proven that both he and his little Dreyer Midget were capable of being competitive, he had received a few offers to sell the car. One came from a garage owner name A.C. "Pop" Leibensberger who said he'd wait until the end of the season to take delivery. The money was right and Tony agreed to sell. He was to deliver the car to Pop's mechanic, a fellow named Freddy Nickel who lived in Covington, Kentucky. Nickel was going to install an outboard engine in it and the car would ultimately become a part of Pop's racing team, a quartet of immaculate maroon and white racers that were feared wherever they ran.

After dropping the car off in Covington, Duke and Tony drove toward Chicago and re-ran the summer's races to each other. Tony said he knew he could win some races. Duke told him not to be so worried about winning right away, being the oldest driver around was more important than being the one they remembered. As usual, Tony told him that he worried too much.

Although he didn't admit it, Tony was glad to see the farmhouse. As he pulled the new Ford truck up the little incline next to the two-story structure, he gave the horn a couple of short taps and told Duke that Mom and Clarence would be surprised. He hadn't called in a couple of weeks and they didn't know when he'd be back. She'd whip up some food for them. But he was a little surprised when Mom didn't come running out the back door to greet him. She probably didn't hear the horn, he mused.

The two travelers walked through the back porch into the kitchen and saw Tony's mother standing over her stove. It was the middle of the day and she had a robe on. Sick? She had a towel wrapped completely around her head and face. She didn't hear them come in. She looked strange. Tony peeked over and saw a simmering pan of milk on the stove. She was breathing deeply, inhaling its fumes.

"Mom?" he said hesitantly, so as not to startle her and upset the hot liquid.

She pulled the towel from around her eyes and exclaimed, "Oh, my Tony. How are you? How are you? I'm so glad you're here."

"What in the world are you doing?" he asked.

Duke stood by and didn't say a word.

"Tony," she said, "I've tried everything. The healer said if I'd breathe these fumes, I'd drive out whatever's inside me making me sick."

Tony looked closely at her. She was pale. Lost weight. Not the strong farm woman he had left a few months ago. Something inside her? He didn't know what to think.

"A healer told you to breathe milk . . . boiling milk"?

"Yes, I don't know what else to do. It'll be OK. You and Duke . . . Hi, Duke. I didn't even tell you hello, did I?" She said. "You and Duke sit down for awhile and then I'll make you something to eat. Go on into the living room now. I won't be but a minute."

She turned and continued breathing the heat that was rising from the pan. Duke and Tony looked at each other, shook their heads and walked into the living room. The old couch looked inviting after spending the last couple days driving the truck.

"What do you think's wrong with her?" Tony asked.

"I don't know," Duke said. "But I don't like that stuff about something being 'inside her.' "

Then the sounds coming from the kitchen were alarming. A wretching, gagging. She was throwing up? Both men ran to her. She clutched her throat and had her tongue out. She pointed up.

"On the shelf," she managed.

Tony didn't know what to grab. All dishes. There was one bottle. Rubbing alcohol? She grabbed it from him and took a healthy swallow that she gargled and spat in the sink. She coughed hard, tongue still out. Tony turned her toward him and looked in her mouth. He reached inside with two fingers as though grasping for something. Duke stood by wide-eyed. Tony's hand started backwards and he was pulling it out. A long white noodle. Bigger than a noodle. A worm! A tapeworm!

Duke stood next to her, held her shoulders and was amazed at Tony's composure. He didn't shake. He didn't swear. He kept threading the living thing from inside her until it was all out. It must have been two feet long, and as soon as its tail passed over her lip, he threw it toward the sink.

Two days later she coughed up another one. Then she gained weight and went back to work. For a long time she kept both slippery looking noodles in a Mason jar and paid homage to the faith healer. She even told Tony that he should visit a fortune teller because there were some people on this earth who knew what was going to happen. After the tapeworm incident, he didn't doubt her word.

Tony had a few bucks in his pocket from the sale of his Midget and wasn't worried about the coming winter. Clarence had asked him if he was going to get a job and settle down a little bit now that he'd had his fun with the race car. Tony just laughed and evaded the question. What'd he need a job for? He knew that lots of the racers didn't work. Especially if they'd had a good summer. Besides, he had been talking with Emil and one of his pals named Jimmy Snyder and they'd said there were plans to build a board track inside the Chicago Armory for winter-time races. Tony figured he could race all winter. He could do well on a board track. He thought of Nutley.

Clarence had particularly liked Jimmy Snyder. Probably because the young racer was also a milkman. A good job, Clarence had said. Tony used to be sort of a milkman he'd told Snyder. Now though, Snyder and Emil were going to become partners in a bar and Clarence didn't think too much of the idea. He didn't have much time for bars. Tony told of Willie Belmont's place over East. Said that Emil and Jimmy's place could be a place in Chicago for the racers.

The talk of the racing gang in Chicago centered around the new Armory track. Wealthy Chicago publisher Thorne Donnelley was putting up the money and he had obtained the services of one Claude J. Girard, who was being heralded as a world famous bicycle track builder. Some of the gang scoffed at the idea of running on a bicycle type track, but they were quickly corrected by those who'd seen Nutley. Nutley had gained such widespread fame its first season that most forgot that it was originally built for the bicycle races..not Midgets.

Since Tony had been fortunate enough to receive a few lines of credit for his driving ability in the *National Auto Racing News*, the fellas back home were duly impressed. The last time they'd seen him, running indoors just a few months previous, he was a hazard like most newcomers. But those good finishes at Nutley, and even the good qualification runs he'd made were enough to cement his name as at least a potential winner. Anyone who could stand on the gas at Nutley had to have something going for him.

Thus it was without too much trouble that Tony talked himself into a ride for the indoor races. That was a step up itself: Somebody else, a car owner, had faith in him. There was a big difference between buying your own equipment and driving for the other guy. The real pros didn't own their cars, not unless they really wanted to. They showed up with their helmet bag while everybody else did the work -- or so the owners said so, anyway.

Donnelley announced that there would be a practice session for the drivers a week before the race. Tony had a Harley-powered job for the practice event and turned laps in the nine second bracket, the only driver to do so. He was then asked to test an Offenhauser powered Midget. An Offy. He'd arrived. You *had* to be good to get an Offy. He should have declined the offer. Going into the third turn he lost control and stuffed his new mount into the fence. Tony had a twisted ankle and the car had a twisted frame: It was not likely that it could be fixed in time for the race. The owner of the Harley didn't want Tony back in his car for the race itself. ("If it wasn't good enough for you during practice, then I guess it ain't good enough for you to race.")

Tony managed to get another car for the first Chicago board race but it wasn't competitive. He missed the show while a standing room only crowd of over 3,000 watched. Russo was back in town and he, Nalon and Harry McQuinn were the only drivers to lap the track in under ten seconds. Russo won the event and said it was real nice that the hometown folks were thoughtful enough to build a track especially for him. The mechanized rodeo spirit prevailed as Bernie Schecter went out of control into the infield, hit Pop Dreyer and mechanic George Gillet after being slowed by a couple of hay bales. Neither victim was badly injured.

Although the swelled crowd would have given any promoter visions of dollar signs, Donnelley decided that the first Chicago board racc would be the last: Cost of erecting the 636 individual sections on a weekly basis was prohibitive. The Armory also held weekly polo matches so the boards had to go.

Although the board track was being removed forever, the fact didn't affect the usual indoor season schedule. Weekly races would be held beginning the first weekend in January. Tony was ready for the 1939 season, but Duke wasn't. His lower back had been giving him problems, a result of the Nashville crash in '37, Tony could have sat out most of the indoor season as well. He was first plagued by mechanical difficultis in the rides he obtained, and later relegated to class "B" equipment.

Clarence had accompanied his little brother to the Chicago Armory numerous times in the first two months of '39 and since he witnessed no injuries and realized that Tony genuinely loved the sport, hc took more of an interest in it himself and started meeting more of Tony's new friends. He was becoming a racc fan. He had to admit that the unexpected was always happening. Plus, old

Twenty Grand Steinbock had obtained the announcing job and made even the smallest incident seem like a monumental affair.

By late March, Nalon was running indoors again, although still complaining of a minor back irritation. Duke had always been a front-runner in the indoor races and he didn't want to pass up the chances for winter-time winnings. Tony was still flogging around near the back of most races and wasn't in the top twenty in point standings. Although the indoor shows were considered fun, and hardly anyone ever got hurt, they could be dangerous under the right circumstances. One night during March, a driver named Orly Schlichter flipped during the semi-feature and was knocked unconscious, with unknown injuries. As attendants were carrying his body out of the arena to a waiting ambulance, newcomer Ed Teach crashed through the gate and knocked poor Orly some ten feet in the air and flattened one of the stretcher bearers. Orly finally woke up in Chicago Memorial with only a broken collarbone. Tommy Hammond, helping with the stretcher, needed four stitches in his forehead. Moments after Orly and Tommy were taken away, three cars tangled on the front stretch and one of them ran over starter Bill Vandewater while another ran into the judges table and knocked old Twenty Grand for a loop. Vandewater kept his wits about him and from a prone position grabbed for the red flag to stop the race. Twenty Grand couldn't pass up the opportunity to blare the calamities. After the race was over, drivers Warren Erwin and Earl Simmons exchanged blows. It wasn't Nutley, but indoors was always exciting.

A week after the racers themselves had nearly eliminated both the flagman and the announcer at the Armory, Nalon found his stride and won the feature. Spring was just around the corner, but the Armory was still drawing good crowds and the season would run for several more weeks. Over East, Nutley promoter Jack Kochman was anxious to take advantage of his standing room only crowds and opened the track in mid-March. Russo quit his truck driving job in Chicago and Henry Banks left the warmth of Florida for the Nutley bowl. Duke and Tony decided to stay in Chicago. Nutley might have paid OK, they decided, but things were getting worse there. Henry Guerand had just performed the most spectacular and gruesome auto racing accident of all time. While attempting to pass three cars that were side by side on the narrow track, he slammed into the outside guard rail and was half thrown from his mount. His head slid between the steel cables that surrounded the bowl and was sheared off by a supporting beam. With helmet intact, it rolled down to the infield while his arm dangled from a cable. The car continued with Henry's lifeless

A couple of dozen crew members check over Vern Orenduff after he slammed into Nutley's first turn guard rail and flipped twice. He was knocked unconscious. [*Crocky Wright Coll.*]

body in the cockpit and slammed into a car driven by one-legged driver Bill Schindler. It finally came to a stop after hitting the hay bales at the bottom of the track. Schindler received only minor cuts but Russo said, "I was right behind him and I pernt-near threw up."

Guerand was twenty-six years old and was one of the two drivers who plunged into a crowd of spectators the previous July at Hohokus Speedway injuring eighteen, one fatally.

While Guerand had met his death in the afternoon, Tony would once again come close to his own that evening. He was leading a heat race at the Armory when he entered the third turn too fast and flipped with no assistance from another car. He snap-rolled and was pitched out of the vehicle. It looked as though he'd broken his neck. They carried him away, unconscious, while the Duke looked on. Outside the arena he regained consciousness and said as though someone had pulled a joke on him, "What happened?" I was leadin' it."

"You got upside down again Tony," the Duke said. "How many times does that make now?"

Tony got up and shook himself off. He said to Duke, "It doesn't really matter, does it? Long as I can keep countin' the times, I ain't really too worried about it."

Then he marched back onto the track and gave the fans a wave. Duke went out and won the feature. The following week Tony was back in action and Duke won his second feature in a row. Nalon ran his string to three in a row and shared the headlines with Tony 'Flip' Bettenhausen.

"It looks like you've got a new nickname," Duke told him.

"We'll get it handled here pretty soon," Tony replied. "Besides, a little ink in the racin' papers can't hurt."

"It's a helluva way to get it," Duke remarked.

For the second time in as many weeks, Tony had flipped his Midget. The second occurrence wasn't nearly as lethal appearing as the first because he stayed inside the cockpit. After the car completed its full sideways revolution and landed on all four wheels, he motioned toward the pits for a push, which some dazed mechanics provided, and he was on his way again. Tony Bettenhausen was not winning Midget races, but the racing crowd was getting used to hearing his name. He just might turn into a race car driver, they said; if he lives long enough.

While the leaves were beginning to sprout in the Spring of 1939, Tony was continuing his weekly challenge at the Chicago Armory. He'd seen Duke win three races in a row. But Tony couldn't make the feature event. Duke would tell him, as he had over East, to "slow down and you'll go faster." Tony wasn't smooth yet and his wide-open driving style wasn't suited to the tricky indoor dirt surface. Duke would remind him that if he expected to make any money during the outdoor season he'd have to start learning how to read the dirt surfaces. Tony would always say he could make the car handle better. Tony didn't have any doubts about his driving ability, he was sure he'd start running right up front soon. He told Duke he could figure out which part of the race track to run on, he just needed a little more experience. And sometimes running indoors, just like with the car he bought from Wally Zale, Tony would look like a seasoned veteran. For a while he drove a car called "Mary Jane" named after the owner's wife. But he was never content with the way it was handling.

One night after Tony won a heat race, Nalon came over and said, "Now why are you fooling with that thing? Leave it alone or you'll jack yourself right out of the place . . . again."

"We're gonna win this one," Tony replied. "Just as soon as I make a couple of little changes here, it'll be just right."

And more times than not, Tony would make the wrong judgment for the indoor track. He should have left well enough alone. But he couldn't. He probably would have changed the car that Nalon was winning races in. Tony could always find something wrong with a Midget. He wanted perfection.

Clarence went along for the last Armory race in '39 and was happy to see Jimmy Snyder win the feature. Duke looked like he had the win, but hit a hole and the popular little milkman scooted past. Now they could start talking about the Midwest outdoor season and the Speedway. Everybody always talked about the Indianapolis Motor Speedway and someday racing there. Snyder was looking forward to his fifth race, Duke had lined up a ride with a man named Murrell Belanger and two other regular members of the Chicago Gang, Emil Andres and Harry McQuinn, were set for the annual big payday at the Speedway. Midget auto racing had soared from obscurity in 1933 to unforseen heights in the late Thirties, but no single Midget race could match the prestige of driving in the Indianapolis 500. No other race in the world could compare to Indy. It was possible, and even probable, that a consistent Midget racer like Nalon or Russo could pocket as much money as the winner of the 500 did, but to do so you'd have to race your tail off all summer long. And that meant running 60 or 70 races. It was easy enough to own your own Midget and feed yourself with its winnings, but a Speedway car was a different story. They didn't run them enough to justify the cost, so you had to find a Speedway ride. And everybody was looking for a Speedway ride.

Murrell Belanger was a Speedway car owner, a guy who could get you there. Even before he had purchased his first Midget, Tony had already asked Belanger for a ride in his Speedway car. It was back in '36, Tony had gone to Belanger's Chrysler-Plymouth agency in Crown Point, Indiana, just a few minutes drive from Tinley Park, when he was looking for a set of mirrors for his '36 Ford. He saw Belanger's race car sitting in the service area and asked the young car dealer if he could take a look at it. Sure enough, Belanger told him. Tony looked likeable enough. Seemed really interested.

"You know," Tony said, "You oughta let me drive this thing for you. I'd be good."

"What?" Belanger snapped. "Why you're still wet behind the ears. I'll bet you've never driven *any* kind of race car. You know what this thing is? It's a Speedway car. Ain't a toy, you know."

Tony was serious. Belanger was too. He was used to hearing people say, "Boy, I wonder what it'd be like to take a spin in this thing," but they didn't usually brush by you and tell you how good they'd be.

"Someday mister," Tony continued, "You're gonna ask me to drive for you. I'm going to be a Speedway driver. And then maybe I'll turn ya down," Tony grinned.

"You go home and put the mirrors on your hot rod, sonny, and leave the racing to the racers."

When Duke told Tony that he had secured a ride with Murrell Belanger for Indianapolis, Tony was happy. He hadn't talked to

Belanger since that first meeting, but he remembered him well. Tony wondered if Belanger knew that the kid who bought a set of mirrors from him was now on his way to becoming a bonafide race car driver.

"Sure," Duke said. "I'll bet he knows you. Murrell always comes to the indoor races."

Murrell Belanger had been around race cars since the Twenties. He almost made it all the way through high school, but left in the last part of his senior year to go motorcycle racing. Then one of his best pals was killed during a motordome act, and Murrell's mom said that his cycle had to go. That was OK, for he had wanted to buy a race car anyhow. He had a good job working for the Buick dealer and raced with the Central Illinois Racing Association for four years before he tore down forty feet of board fence at the North Shore Polo Grounds. After nearly being killed by the oncoming traffic outside, Belanger decided that he was more suited to the automobile business. He picked up a little money from the sale of his race car and along with a couple of friends and his brother-in-law, decided to try for an agency of their own.

The Chrysler people weren't particularly interested in this varied and undercapitalized group, but Murrell's determination impressed the regional manager. He had initially told the ex-driver no, in no uncertain terms, but found Belanger waiting for him every day for two weeks outside the office after work.

"Alright," the man said. "One thing's for sure -- you're persistent."

Initially, the foursome had Auburn, Cord, Packard, Chrysler and International Trucks to offer. The partnership didn't work out and finally a man from Chrysler appeared and told Murrell he'd have to make up his mind on what kind of vehicle he was gong to sell. Couldn't handle them all. Belanger chose Chrysler and his persistency was felt by those who walked into his showroom. Soon the factory was offering him a second dealership in Gary, Indiana where he also prospered. It was there that he couldn't suppress his longstanding desire to go to the Speedway, this time as a car owner.

Belanger had worked day and night to become a success and never passed an opportunity to make friends with potential customers. He was trying to sell cars to the State of Indiana and met many officials. One was Lillian Holley, who became the Sheriff of Crown Point after a berserk farmer murdered her husband. According to Indiana custom, she had been appointed to fulfill her husband's term. No one took her very seriously, especially when she suited up with her fringed buckskin shirt and vest, plaid and white kerchief under her chin. But Murrell liked her alright. She always appreciated his sending over a man to help start her Ford on cold winter mornings. Although she looked tough enough to forge a bit of snow, and any unsavory aspects of her job (she carried a pearl handled six-shooter at all times) Belanger usually obliged her requests.

Mrs. Holley's jail gained national fame when it was faced with the responsibility of keeping the nation's number one bank robber, John Dillinger. The lady Sheriff had asked if one of Belanger's men would come to the jailhouse with some welding equipment and help reinforce the cell that Dillinger claimed couldn't hold him. Murrell himself decided to perform the task for Lillian and recalls that Dillinger said, "I'll kill you for this someday."

Belanger's welding job was never put to the test. Dillinger managed to carve a pistol from a chunk of wood and after coloring it with shoe polish, made one of the most celebrated escapes of the century. He later died from FBI gunshot wounds and Belanger went on to sell the state 35 Plymouths. Then Murrell bought a Speedway car and took Jimmy Snyder to Indianapolis with him. Now he had Duke and struck up more than a nodding acquaintance with Nalon's companion, Tony.

Two days after the indoor races were over, Duke and Tony went to St. Louis for the first Midwestern outdoor race at Walsh Stadium. Duke won the feature and Tony trailed in fourth, right behind Jimmy Snyder. Tony had talked his way into a first class ride, an Offy-powered Midget owned by a man named Buzzard. And just like over East, the Midwest offered a seven night per week schedule of Midget racing. The only thing that was missing was the thrill of Nutley, and if the reports were true, Nutley just might be gone soon and Chicago would have its own board track.

After Guerand had his head chopped off, city officials began proceedings to close the place down. And they succeeded for a few weeks. No sooner had word of trouble been spread than Chicago promoters began advertising the "World Championship of Midget Auto Racing" would be held on a quarter-mile board track to be built in Soldier's Field. Duke and Tony had pointed out these facts to Belanger and tried to convince him that he should add a Midget to his stable of one. Belanger declined and told Duke just to come back from his planned East coast trip in one piece. It was May now and he should be concentrating on running the Speedway, Murrell told him.

Duke made a quick trip to Langhorne, Pennsylvania and won

the scheduled Big Car race there. Boy, that Duke was really great, Tony thought. When he got back, Tony went to Indianapolis with him. You really had to be somebody to get into Gasoline Alley, the garages where they worked on all the Speedway cars. Just as Emil had done at Riverview, Duke got Tony a pass.

Tony wanted to stay and really get to know the place and the people, but he also wanted to race. After his fourth place finish in front of seven thousand fans at St. Louis, he had to go back. Duke stayed with Belanger as they tried to work up to speed. Tony went to St. Louis and earned himself another line in the *National Auto Racing News* that called him an "impressive newcomer" with his fifth place finish. Now Tony was a second year driver. He'd met, and been accepted by the racers, the pros, the best in the business. No other profession appealed to him. Besides, he had it pretty easy. Most worked for a long time to get enough money just to buy a Midget. Not Tony. Mom was always around to help him through the tight spots. And with a few more of those top five finishes at places like Walsh Stadium where they were paying a thousand dollars prize money, he'd soon be on his own one hundred percent. He'd often times tell Duke, "I just want to win some races. Be a champion. Run at the Speedway, too."

Duke and Belanger were having mechanical problems at Speedway in '39. They didn't try to qualify the car. But Tony's buddy, Jimmy Snyder, was in his prime. He had set the fastest time of all during qualifications and was starting the race in the pole position. Maybe he'd win it. Even Clarence was rooting for him. Jimmy was a family man, had two kids. He wasn't like some of the others Clarence had met. He didn't leave the family at home for long periods just to go racing. Clarence was happy for the little milkman when he finished the 1939 "500" in second position, behind Wilbur Shaw. To many of the Midget racers, the 500 was just another race on the schedule. Many of them didn't really like the idea of taking off the month of May to work with the Speedway cars. The 500 was certainly important, they'd agree, but there was plenty of prize money to be earned outside of Indianapolis, too. So just as soon as Captain Eddie Rickenbacker passed out the cash (and said a few words in memorium for Floyd Roberts, the 1938 winner who was killed in the '39 race), the drivers were back on their Gypsy trail. Talk throughout the Midget racing fraternity centered upon the upcoming "World Series" that was going to be held in mid-June at Soldier's Field. Everybody would be there for that one. And it would be classy field, too. No outboards or motorcycle engines allowed. Just the Offy's and Millers. You had to be approved by the AAA.

The Duke went back over East and won the Big Car race at Williams Grove; Tony said that he wanted to drive the Big Cars soon. Duke told him to just keep plugging along in a Midget for awhile. The Big Cars could really bite you. Tony went to Riverview and missed the program. The first dozen cars qualified within a quarter of a second of one another. One little slip and you may as well put it on the trailer for the night: There was no margin for error. Then he and car owner Buzzard went back to St. Louis and suffered mechanical problems. It was a long tow for nothing. They decided to park the car and work on it until the board track was ready at Soldier's Field. The total purse there was going to be over $10,000 for five days of racing. You could afford not to race for awhile with that kind of money being offered.

The ads for the Soldier's Field race didn't say so, but the AAA Contest Board had decided to make the event an invitational. They didn't figure they needed a couple hundred Midgets to put on a program. They wanted only the cream of the crop. Just the names. Why make everybody go through hours and hours of qualifying and force the strong to survive once again? And they didn't particularly want a no-name winding up with all the marbles either. That wouldn't add much class to the event. When the final entry list was chosen, two names stood out. First, wild-man Wally Zale, one of the most consistent Midwest winners was denied entry. It had been said that Zale was just as mean off the track with officials as he was on. Then, Tony Bettenhausen was included in the all-star line up. He had yet to win a feature race and had driven in less races than any other driver at the meet. But his performances at Nutley and the single indoor board show that was held in Chicago made him a board track veteran. Some of the other drivers, stars throughout the Midget racing world, had never competed on a board track.

The trouble over at Nutley had continued and town officials managed to have five events cancelled. Another board facility had opened at Coney Island, and it was every bit as fast as the New Jersey velodrome. But no one had ever constructed a quarter-mile board track. The five meet Chicago series had received more advance publicity in the racing papers than even the "500" itself.

Russo and Nalon came back home to the series and were followed by a rare assemblage of talent who evacuated their favorite circuits for the show. Russo dominated from the start and turned the fastest qualifying lap at twelve seconds. More than 25,000 fans arrived and were treated to Twenty Grand Steinbock's public address act. He had plenty to talk about. The Shriners paraded before the event; the National Guard performed;

officials, drivers and crews were dressed in their racing best for the occasion and the entry blank stipulated that all cars "must be painted and chromed." Some new sod had even been laid on the football field that spanned the white board track. There could be no doubt about it, Midget automobile racing had come of age in the Midwest.

Russo's chances for victory in the first race were quenched by a worn tire and Sam Hanks, driving for the first time ever on the boards, came home first. Ronney Householder, the man who took a look at Nutley and decided to pass, finished second while Russo and Nalon followed. Tony had experienced handling problems from the beginning. He didn't make the top ten. For the next two days Tony didn't fare much better and managed only a fifth in a 25-lap consolation race. He made more changes to the chassis. Tried different tires. He'd ask Emil, Snyder, Duke and Russo for help. They were running up front -- where he wanted to be. In the next 12 lap heat race Tony finished second to "Bullet Joe" Garson. He was ready. On Saturday he said he could "blow 'em off the track."

Tony had said earlier that he wanted fast time today. Start on the pole and they'll never know which way he went. He told Buzzard to make sure he was clocking him, because he wanted to make sure he knew which groove to follow. The Soldier's Field track offered more running room than Nutley did, and more speed, too. Although the banks in the turns weren't quite as steep, they were still a full twelve feet high and more sweeping than Nutley. Maybe you could go better if you went higher, Tony thought. It was the worst error in judgment he could have made. As he came down the front straight at over 90 mph, he didn't dip down into the first turn, but stayed high. The car simply had too much momentum to follow Tony's chosen course. It hit the outer retaining wall and climbed skyward. Its occupant was dropped like a limp noodle. Dazed, and with his cheek pressed hard against the wood surface, Tony allowed his eyelids to roll back. He couldn't get up. There was a car coming at him. It was Paul. He prayed, "Jesus, Russo don't hit me!" Russo had nowhere to go. Tony was in the middle of the track, laying prone. If he spun, he'd probably back over the body. Couldn't turn left, already committed to the high side. Paul turned right, into the guard rail and his outer wheels pawed at the steel in an attempt to bring the rest of the car up there with them. He should have been sideways, ready to barrell-roll down the track. Instead, the car came back down to the wood and continued on its way down the backstretch. From the grandstands it appeared as though Russo simply drove up the rail with the outside tires while the inside ones narrowly missed Tony's head. Sort of like, "Bettenhausen, you screwed up good this time . . now don't move and I'll just drive around you."

Other than having the wind knocked out of him, Tony didn't suffer but a few bruises. He walked up to Russo after they let him out of the ambulance and said, "You know, I saw you coming and said to myself, 'Jesus, Paul, don't hit me.' "

"Yeah, Benski?" Russo replied. "Well, I was saying, 'God, Tony, please don't move.' "

Later in the day Ted Tetterton spun in front of Russo and he drove into the guard rail to avoid t-boning him. The report in the *National Auto Racing News* said:

> If there had been an award for sportsmanship it surely would have gone to Russo for his action in sacrificing himself to save another.

The second incident left Paul with a well-bent car and enough cuts and bruises to put him out of contention. Ronney Householder was ultimately crowned series champion. Tony had another story to tell about another time that he got upside down.

Clarence heard about the Soldier's Field accident and suggested that Tony consider giving up the sport before something really serious happened to him. On the following Thursday night, Clarence was certain he didn't want to ever see another Midget automobile race and now he had proof that "even the greatest drivers can get killed". Clarence's favorite, little Jimmy Snyder, had been fatally injured at the Cahokia, Illinois track after a quick flip. The Cahokia track wasn't paying enough purse to even make Snyder's trip there worthwhile, but the promoter was a former driver who asked Jimmy and several other friends to come down and help build his gate attendance. They passed the hat for Jimmy Snyder and presented his widow with a thousand dollars. Clarence didn't want anything to do with the sport anymore. Tony said that he wasn't going to worry about getting killed and left Tinley Park to join Duke, Russo and Henry Banks over East.

Tony managed to obtain a ride for some of the races at Yellow Jacket in Philly and a few races in the Bronx, but since he hadn't scored any feature victories yet, he was still considered just another young driver on his way up and had to settle for mediocre equipment. His 1939 performances on the Eastern circuit weren't as memorable, or as impressive as they were the prior year. He didn't go back to Nutley either. The place had been closed down for a few weeks following the investigation into Henry Guerand's fatal accident, and Duke suggested that they confine their activities to the many flat tracks that were open. By August Tony was on his way back home with Duke. They went to Milwaukee where Duke ran a Big Car race in front of 23,000 fans. All the Indy 500 stars were there. But it really wasn't a big deal, Duke and Tony agreed. They had just seen 55,000 people at a Midget show at the Roosevelt Raceway in Long Island.

Midgets were definitely the thing. Some of the Big Car drivers still didn't like them though. Too many guys getting killed, they said. In every part of the country, Midgets were attracting sell-out crowds on a regular schedule. The *National Auto Racing News* and the *Illustrated Speedway News* were reporting on over 60 races each week. Everyone had heard about the fabulous Gilmore Stadium in Los Angeles where 18,000 fans turned out regularly to witness what was called the best dirt track racing in the country. Tony wanted to go. He loved the dirt and had to see what this Gilmore place was all about. Besides, he had never been to California and the trip sounded exciting. Duke warned him that neither of them had a ride at Gilmore and it might be a little tough for Tony to obtain one. Again, Tony told Nalon not to worry so much. They'd do OK, he said.

The Gilmore facility turned out to be everything Tony had imagined. It had a horseshoe-shaped wooden grandstand that seated 18,000 and its infield was touted to be one of the best drained football fields in the country. It was located only minutes from downtown Los Angeles, at the corner of Beverly Boulevard and Fairfax, along side of the famed Farmer's Market, now the site of CBS Television Center.

Oil baron Earl Gilmore had taken more than a casual liking to the Midget racing sport when it began back in '33, and by 1934 he had invested $150,000 in his new Midget racing plant. The track itself, layered with moist clay and granite from the Hollywood hills, was a quarter-mile around and featured extra smooth and wide banked turns. Nalon was ready for Gilmore, but Tony wasn't. They started only 12 cars in the feature events there and the regular local competitors delighted themselves when they welcomed out-of-town challengers to try their hand and the fast oval. Most first-timers werc relegated to the consolation events, if they got to run at all. Gilmore didn't have car shortages, and just making the program was an accomplishment.

Nalon lived up to his reputation as a versatile competitor and finished second in the feature event. Tony had to watch from the pits on their first outing, but made the "B" race the second week and finished in sixth position, four spots behind another young man who raced under the name Reynold Coleman. Reynold Coleman was really Reynold McDonald, a youngster who didn't want

Bettenhausen and Emil Andres in the early days.

his well-to-do parents to know of his racing aspirations. Over the next four decades, Reynold McDonald would continue his interest in Midget auto racing, but a near-fatal crash would convince him to follow his leadership abilities and he would eventually rise to the presidency of one of the nation's largest steel companies.

Duke Nalon had already spent half a dozen years in a steel mill and knew that he didn't want any part of another one. And even though Tony Bettenhausen had already earned the name "Flip" he couldn't be convinced that his life should take any other course than the one he was following: The fastest route around a race track was Tony's goal, it didn't matter that you always wound up right back at the starting line.

Back home, the Armory was getting ready to begin its sixth season of indoor Midget racing. As usual, the mood was festive for the opening event in late October and Tony was set for another winter. This year he could also travel to Milwaukee on Friday nights and pick up some extra cash at the races there. By the end of the first week in November, however, Tony would lose another good friend. This time it was one of his peers: Chuck Andres, Emil's little brother, the guy he started racing indoors with just two years ago. Chuck had moved to Texas where he progressed rapidly into a feature winning driver. There was no one to blame for the accident, Chuck merely touched wheels with another driver and he was catapulted into the now familiar gyrations that Tony had not only seen, but lived through himself. The reports said that he was wearing a safety belt, and he died of a broken neck. They took up a collection at the Armory for Chuck's widow and three children as soon as the news spread, and when the body was shipped back to Tinley Park, Tony and Duke along with Cowboy O'Rourke and Frank Brisko and Emil served as pallbearers. Emil and Tony drove down to Houston to help clear out Chuck's belongings. They appeard at the Houston Speed Bowl and helped the announcer pay tribute to Emil's lost brother. Tony talked a fellow named Chenshaw into a ride and finished third in the feature shortly after the eulogy was given. It was now an accepted fact that drivers were going to be killed or maimed on a regular basis on the Midget racing circuits. Tony reasoned, as did most other drivers, that yes, they too could possibly get hurt, but it probably wouldn't happen today. Today it would probably be someone else. And that someone else was doing exactly what he wanted to be doing for a living. Getting killed in a race car was a lot better than getting yourself wrapped up in a punch press at some factory. When it's your turn to go, you're gonna go, no matter what. Just hurry up and get all the livin' in that you can, because you might not be around to get it done tomorrow. For now anyway, in January of 1940, Tony wanted to get back to the Armory and continue with the indoor races. He *was* getting better. Had a good car to drive, too, the Capper & Capper number eight, the Chicago haberdashers who loved Midget auto racing.

Tony had been making the features and running in the top ten consistently. Everying was going his way. He had traded the old truck in on a new Mercury, the make just introduced by Ford. It was a classy looking Coupe, had chrome trim around the windows, whitewalls and dual spotlights that he bought from Murrell Belanger. Tony didn't have any trouble impressing the girls with his new car. But then he never did. Except Val. She always thought Tony was showing off and didn't pay as much attention to him as he would have liked.

Tony wondered sometimes whatever happened to her. He hadn't seen or heard from Val in almost a year and a half. She'd gone back home to her parents and wasn't around Tinley Park much, even though she had some girlfriends there. He didn't blame her for not staying in Tinley, though. There wasn't much there. People were too conservative in Tinley. Sometimes Tony wondered what the folks back home would think of Nutley, or Gilmore and Los Angeles. Or even Milwaukee. He'd bet that most of them hadn't seen any farther than Chicago in their whole lives.

One night in late January, during a driving ice and rainstorm, Tony saw Val standing in the Tinley Park drugstore. He drove

A pre-war Tony Bettenhausen.

around the block but decided not to go in. He flashed his spotlight into the store, like the cops did after the place was closed for the night. Val looked out, saw who it was, and kept on talking to her girlfriend. She wanted to go see him, but stayed inside. If that Tony Bettenhausen wants to see me, she reasoned, he can damn well get out of that fancy car of his and walk in here. Shining his spotlight on me. Next he'll probably start honking his damn horn. Tony flagged down an old friend, Bud Berg, and told him to go outside and tell Val that he wanted to see her. Bud played messenger, but Val feigned indifference. Tony kept driving around the block and shining his spotlight. She finally went out to her Ford and heard Tony holler, "You can't drive home in this blizzard! Not by yourself. I'll follow you, OK?"

Val didn't say anything. How come, she thought, was Mr. Bettenhausen all of a sudden interested in her well-being. She could drive home just fine, thank you. But inside she was warm and happy. It felt good to know that her Tony was right behind her. Taking care of her. Making sure nothing happened. She did so love him. She had tears in her eyes now as she thought of her Tony. He must care. He had to, to drive fifteen miles out of his way to see her home. She pulled into her driveway and ran into the house. Tony parked right behind and walked up to the door, too. He expected Val's mom to invite him in. Probably offer him some hot chocolate. Boy, it was cold outside.

"Oh no you don't, Tony Bettenhausen. You're not coming in this house," Nan Rice told him.

She remembered Tony sliding around corners in his old Ford and then sauntering up to the doorstep and trying to look like a choir boy. She knew this Bettenhausen character. He wasn't fooling anyone. And she wasn't going to give him another chance to see her daughter either. The poor girl was lucky to be rid of him, she thought. Lucky she wasn't in a family way, too.

"I just," Tony stuttered, "I just wanted to see Val, Mrs. Rice," he managed.

"Well, I don't think Val's going to see you," she said firmly and closed the door.

But Tony saw Val smiling in the living room. He knew she wanted to see him. He could call her now. He felt better. That Val was sharp, Tony thought. She looked good. Even all wet. Tony always got excited when he thought of Val. Later Tony called and asked Val if she'd like to go to a Midget race, at the Armory with him. She'd be delighted, she said. Now that was more like it. Tony Bettenhausen was asking her this time, not telling her, like he used to do.

* * *

"Oh, shoot. Is *this* what I came for?" Val's eyes were watering from that horrible castor oil they were burning in the Midgets. And God, they were loud. Couldn't hear yourself think. She liked it better when none of them were on the track. And the smell. It was terrible. *This* is what Tony Bettenhause likes to do? He's gotta be crazy, she thought.

Charlotte Nalon agreed that the conditions indoors weren't really the best, but some of the races were pretty exciting. She said she liked outdoor racing much better, but Duke always won so much indoors that it made it worthwhile. Charlotte explained the race procedures to Val. Val had never been to a Midget race before, but said Tony took her to the 500 at Indianapolis two years ago and they didn't even really get to see the cars much.

Right before qualifying, Duke was walking across the track on his way to the restroom. A fella in a uniform, not a driver, maybe an usher, Duke thought, ran up to him and held out his closed hand. He wanted to give Duke something.

"Here, Duke," the man said.

Nalon thought maybe it was going to be a note from Charlotte.

Duke stopped in the middle of the north turn and turned his palm toward the man to accept the note. The messenger dropped a handful of peanuts in Nalon's palm. Duke looked at them, sighed as if to say, "That's a lousy joke," and dumped the merchandise on the race track. He didn't say anything about the incident to anyone. Duke wasn't overly superstitious, but he was a little upset. He thought that people ought to have better things to do than try to play stupid jokes on race drivers.

"I was driving on a doughnut," Duke recalled later. "My lower back was still giving me some problems from the old Nashville crash and the rubber ring I put on the seat seemed to relieve the tension.

"I went into that third turn hell bent for election. Wanted to set fast time, 'cause I knew it would put me on the pole for the feature. But I hooked a rut and knew it was going to be a wild ride. The car started doing sideways flips."

Charlotte screamed from the grandstand and Val did a little, too. It was all over so fast. And it began so quickly. One second Duke was coming into the turn, sliding sideways and looking like he had complete control, and the next instant he looked like a rag doll being tossed every which way. The car landed on all four wheels and Duke raised and twisted his head. He put his arms out to the side and started lifting himself from the cockpit of the number three Midget. The grandstands cheered. Nalon was a hero, and he had just cheated death. They didn't want to lose the Iron Duke. He was too good to get killed, many thought. He didn't make a mistake coming into the turn. It was just a bad break. Could have happened to anybody. Nalon's shoes crunched a couple of peanuts under them as he walked away from the bent racer.

I don't think that I'm going to like this indoor racing business much," Val said.

Charlotte agreed that the only time you can ever relax, around any kind of racing, is when there's nobody on the race track. Duke and Tony wouldn't let them relax tonight. Duke secured a ride in the Tomshe Offy after being checked over at the ambulance. Tony qualified fourth fastest, won his heat race, and had third money sewn up in the feature until the last three laps when Duke passed him. During the feature Val found herself rooting for her Tony and hoping Duke wouldn't pass him. Or crash into him. She forgot all about the castor oil fumes. Tony was good. He looked like he knew exactly where to put the car to stay ahead. But that Duke was good, too. One minute he was almost dead and now he was driving as though nothing had happened. She wondered if that sort of thing happened all the time and was just a part of the game. What a game, she thought. But if it's what her Tony wanted to do, then she'd like it as well. Or at least she wouldn't tell him that he shouldn't do it. She could see him joking with the other men in the pits. He was at home here. And she wanted to be at home with him. She'd still do anything to make him happy.

After the races they all went up to the Costello Brothers

"Midget Inn" on 81st Street. The place had become so much of a regular hangout that the enterprising brothers bought ads in the *National Auto Racing News* to "Meet Duke Nalon" after the indoor races. Val liked the people there. It was a party atmosphere. Tony liked having her back, too. Since Nalon had gotten married, he wasn't as interested as Tony was in picking up girls after the races. Sometimes, Duke was even a little cranky. He continued to complain about his back and with some coaxing, finally consented to having an operation performed in February. He had to give up the possiblity of winning the indoor championship, but the racing papers were still telling of the seven-night per week Midget racing circuits that would be coming up in the Spring. Duke also had a fine ride lined up for Indianapolis and he planned to continue racing on the half-mile tracks all season long in the Big Cars circuit. Now they were starting to call the cars that ran on the half-miles, Sprint Cars. Tony had expressed his own interest in driving the Sprint Cars and again wanted to go with Duke to the races.

"If you don't get your back fixed," Tony told him, "Then I can't go to the Sprint races. I gotta have my teacher around."

Tony always made the Duke feel like the old pro. Every time Tony would pass someone on the track, or do well qualifying, he would say: "Whatja think of that. Blew their doors off, huh?"

Nalon would smile and agree that indeed, Tony had done a good job. Then he'd go out and drive around Bettenhausen without ever infringing upon the part of the track that Tony was on. With some of the other guys he'd root his way through just like everyone else did, but Tony made him sound so good and so smooth that Duke wouldn't dare break the image. And he had to admit that it was becoming increasingly difficult to drive around Tony. Especially when he had a good car. Duke believed that Tony would be winning Midget races pretty soon. He wasn't quite ready for the Sprint cars yet, but the Midwestern Midget racers would soon have another front runner to contend with.

The outdoor season was just getting started. Duke was down in Indianapolis sorting out his 1940 Speedway ride when Tony and Emil drove over to Urbana for the opening Midget race. The story in the May 16 *National Auto Racing News* said:

> Urbana, Ill. -- Tony Bettenhausen, blond Chicago ace, cleaned up the inaugural cord of Midget races last Sunday afternoon at the new Urbana Speedway before a capacity crowd of wild-eyed fans. He turned in a time trial of 17.90 for the fifth-mile track, took the first heat, was second in the handicap event, and finished a clean cut winner in the feature.

Emil finished second behind Tony and he shared the victory celebration. The young man who had knocked on the old pro's door asking for help had just beaten his first teacher. Tony Bettenhausen had reached a milestone: He had won a Midget race driving another man's car. That was professionalism. He had been trusted with a very expensive piece of machinery and drove it with enough confidence and skill to out-duel the veteran who had taken him to see his very first Midget race. Now Tony talked about wanting to be a champion. Maybe even get a Speedway car next year. Drive some Sprinters, too.

After his initial victory, Tony didn't want to miss a chance at another race. He started following the circuit: St. Louis, Milwaukee, Cahokia, Crown Point and sometimes an out of the way track over in Iowa. In mid-July, he was in Dubuque, with a race car and Val. Since January, he'd been seeing more and more of her and once he even hinted that maybe they ought to get re-married. They had raced at Riverview on Friday night, went home and changed clothes and drove for the Iowa race. Along the way they stopped on a hilltop and Val joked that she was going to push Tony off it if they didn't get married soon. Tony drove into the city and found the courthouse.

"See, I'm trying," he said, "But the place is closed."

"Very funny, Tony Bettenhausen. It just happens to be 5:00 in the morning. Did you expect that they were waiting for you?"

Nonetheless, Tony and Val managed to once again take their "till death do us part" vows and on July 15, 1940 they were man and wife.

4

The Blond Blizzard

There was no formal honeymoon. From July 16 through August 23, Tony took his new bride to no less than 18 races and finished no worse than fifth in any event he entered. Soon he was saying that married life agreed with him. They moved to Chicago's South side, at 113th and Vernon and Tony continued his busy racing schedule for the rest of the season. In the latter part of the year he said he was going back to work at the Ford plant, and he could still race indoors.

In October of '40, talk in the racing world turned toward politics and government, subjects most participants said they weren't interested in whatsoever. The front page of the *National Auto Racing News* carried a picture of a new thing called a "Conscription Registration Form" that all men in the U.S. between the ages of 21-35 had to fill out. It meant simply that Uncle Sam had your name and there was a good chance that he might call upon you for service in the armed forces. The words Registration Card and Selective Service Board became a part of every man's vocabulary in 1940. Most termed it a threat to their freedom.

By the end of the 1940 racing season, Tony Bettenhausen was being referred to as a classy driver, could run with the best of them. He had paid his dues and was an accepted member of the feared Chicago Gang of racers. After he ran side-by-side with the ruthless Wally Zale at Chicago's Raceway Park in the last event of the season, even his fellow drivers took note of him. They'd said before that "Bettenhausen has the stuff to make it, if he doesn't kill himself first." Zale had won some 60 feature events in 1940 to make him the country's most succesful driver, so running second to him was certainly no disgrace.

It had been nearly a year now since newspapers nationwide had run banner headlines announcing that a part of the world was at

Tony's ride throughout the summer of 1940.

war. German troops had invaded Poland. Dictator Adolph Hitler was making territorial demands in Europe and there were attempts by the French and British to appease him, which had initially been successful in 1938. Hitler's bark had been heard worldwide and President Roosevelt had told Americans, "The epidemic of world lawlessness is spreading," and urged neutrality. Most racers could have cared less. They weren't involved in politics. They didn't see an immediate threat to their way of living. Who cares what some crazy German is doing over there? They knew that the Midwest, at least, was going to be blessed with prosperity in 1941 as steel mills throughout the region were working at capacity. But the munitions project just south of Chicago was also employing several thousand and the aviation program at Rantoul would have some 15,000 servicemen training. The threat of another World War involving America wasn't out of the question.

Tony was beginning to settle into a lifestyle now, one he could anticipate. He'd work at the Ford plant throughout the winter months while running indoors on the weekends and then go back to the outdoor circuit for the summer. He talked about moving up another notch in racing. He'd run some Sprint car races along with Duke in the summer of '41 and by the next year he'd be ready to get a shot at Indianapolis. Everybody wanted a chance to drive in the famous "500."

The indoor season had a new home at the Chicago Amphitheatre for the 1940-41 season and Tony was there for the first race. He ran fourth in the feature. The next week his picture was on page two of the *National Auto Racing News* with a headline that said: "Bettenhausen-O'Rouke Injured". The story said in part:

> Bettenhausen's accident occurred in the second heat race when his No. 20 Knight flipped suddenly after striking a hay bale coming into the front stretch. The car lunged directly in front of the judges stand on it's side. O'Rourke, driving the fast Muntz No. 2, was so close behind that his car's left front wheel became fastened inside of Bettenhausen's right rear, carrying the Cowboy over the top of Bettenhausen, who was pinned underneath. Bettenhausen after being taken to the first aid hospital and trying to hide his agony to assure his wife that all was okay, remarked, 'Well, it looks like I have the honor of being the first test case for the Prudence Insurance Company.'

Cowboy O'Rourke was uninjured in the first accident, but he too stuck a hay bale during the feature and slammed upside down into the retaining wall. Tony suffered a broken arm and strained muscles in his neck and the Cowboy had a broken nose, torn back ligaments and some internal injury. Again, Tony tried to shrug off the incident to no more than 'a little bad luck", and said his right arm would be back in good shape in no time. Meanwhile, the foreman at the Ford plant had become not only a pal of Tony's, but a fan as well. He told Tony that he really should be laid off, after all you needed two good arms to work in a factory, but found him a job of opening and closing one of the warehouse doors.

Since the indoor schedule had been considerably shortened for the '41 season, Tony and Val were able to spend more time with one another and wait for Spring. Tony didn't complain about the factory work like he had during their first marriage, but he was anxious to start driving again. Val was concerned that he might be called into the Army because of the new Selective Service Draft Act. A call had been put out to all able-bodied men of the country to enlist in the Army or Navy and the subsequent enrollment was the greatest in the history of the country. In February, Val was pregnant and her fears became worse. She couldn't stand the idea of her Tony leaving, especially with a baby on the way. She wasn't well and the doctor told her she was having problems with her gall bladder. She needed Tony more than ever now.

By Easter, Tony's arm had healed well enough to race and he proved that the four-month layoff hadn't affected his style when he finished fourth in the feature during a special race held at the Ampitheatre. As usual, Val worried about him and was still

A handsome young Tony Bettenhausen at Dayton in 1941. [Craig Racing Photos]

In 1941 Tony graduated to the larger Sprint cars. He's shown here in the Iddings number 5. [Craig]

battling her own problems. She'd had another gall bladder attack and was in general having a tough time with her pregnancy.

In May, Tony broadened his career and obtained his first Midwest Sprint car ride in the Iddings #5 at the high-banked half mile track in Dayton, Ohio. He had no trouble in adapting to the larger, more powerful Sprint cars and was victorious in his first race, a ten-lap heat. In the feature he finished second to Harry Robtoy and said he could have won it, had it not been for problems he encountered in lapping slower cars. After the first Dayton race, he started driving Wally Zale's No. 1 Midget and won the next two out of three races he ran at Cahokia and Chicago. Zale had broken his shoulder and was out of contention for the time being. Then it was back to the Ohio banked track and this time Duke Nalon was there with Tony. Nalon had missed the

Duke Nalon and his Sprint car during the 1941 season. [Alvarez-Craig Racing Photos]

Left; Bettenhausen, 5 and Elbert "Grandpappy" Booker during a 1941 Jungle Park race. [Craig Racing Photos]

Tony's first Championship car ride at Milwaukee on August 24, 1941. The car is very similar in appearance to a Sprint car, slightly larger. [Armin Krueger]

first show and commented, "You really like these things, huh?" after Tony had set fast time of the day. Tony kidded that he was going to give the Duke a hard time all season long running the Midwest Sprints and lived up to his promise by finishing second in the feature, a spot ahead of his respected teacher.

Now Tony was hungry. He wouldn't settle for an occasional Midget ride on the weekend or the day before a Sprint race, but wanted to run both as much as he could. He and Duke towed to Milwaukee for the opening Sprint race on the mile track inside State Fair Park on June 8 and the Duke was telling him to back off a little bit. There were plenty of races to run. But Tony would have none of the Duke's advice. From June 1 through the 8th, Tony ran half a dozen races, won two of them, ran a second, a third, a fourth and a sixth. The day of the Milwaukee race, which Duke won in the afternoon, Tony drove 90 mph all the way back to Chicago with Duke next to him in time for the feature at Riverview. The risky schedule could take its toll, however. Pete Romcevich nearly had his arm cut off when a tailpipe was jammed into the cockpit with him; Cowboy O'Rourke was in the hospital again, this time with a broken neck; Teddy Duncan had been badly burned; Zale had a broken shoulder and another character named JimMcClory had suffered the same fate that Cowboy had.

Tony averaged no less than one feature victory per week for the rest of the year. The next time he went back to Dayton, he won his first Sprint car race after a strong go with Harry Robtoy. The Duke wasn't there, though. He was busy winning a Championship event at Langhorne, Pennsylvania, and when he came back, he told Tony that maybe Tony Bettenhausen had a chance of winning the Midwest Sprint car title. Not too bad for his first year in the bigger cars. Then Duke allowed that Tony would, of course, have to beat him, because he too planned on running the rest of the races. In July, Duke made headlines when he was pictured riding on the tail of his Midget at Motor City Speedway in Detroit after being scalded by a broken water hose. He was driving again three days later with his legs bandaged and the racing writers called him, "The Iron Man from the Gary Steel Mills." Late in the season Tony took his first ride in a Championship car, the ones that meet the specifications to run at Indianapolis. It was at Milwaukee again, and the papers said he did "a grand job" in his first appearance. He finished sixth despite two lengthy pit stops, one for a tire change and the other to fix a stuck throttle.

Paul Russo showed for the Champ car race and had his usual wise-guy comments ready for Tony.

"Think you're ready for these things, huh, Benski?"

Tony was on his way to second place in the 1941 AAA Mid-Western Championship when this shot was taken with his contemporaries at Winchester, Indiana. Top row standing left to right: Tony Willman, Everett Saylor, Tony and Elbert "Pappy" Booker. Front row: Duke Nalon, George Connor and Emil Andres. [Bettenhausen Coll.]

Tony finished right behind Paul in two of the three days' races and later asked the black-haired little Italian why he didn't move back to Chicago and race. Russo had gone to Michigan and was winning his own share of races on the Michigan-Ohio circuit.

"We never heard of any of those guys you been beatin' lately," Bettenhausen told him. "Is that a Class B circuit you're runnin' up there?"

"Look who's talking. The guy who don't even know which way to drive on the highway. Now he's leading the Sprint car standings and getting a big head."

Russo wasn't serious. He was proud of Tony, as was Duke. Tony had been running in the top three in every Sprint race he entered and was leading Duke in the point standings. It was Duke, however, who was breaking track records throughout the summer on some of the most feared tracks in the country. It had been said that if you could go fast on the high banks at Winchester and Jungle Park, two Indiana tracks, you'd be a racer. Duke set a new half-mile record at both tracks in '41, and Tony finished second in both races. Tony himself set a track record at Hammond, Indiana

Tony and Joe Lencki with their pheasant and duck catch. [*Bettenhausen Coll.*]

in October and was called, "One of the most sensational pilots of the season," by the racing papers. At season's end he had finished second to Nalon in the final Sprint car standings.

The same day that Tony won every event he entered at Hammond, another close friend of his, Tony Willman, was killed at Thompson, Connecticut. They said he had been pitched out of his Midget and tossed over 75 feet. While laying prone on the track he was run over and died instantly.

After the last Sprint race, Tony and Joe Lencki took a short vacation to South Dakota to do some pheasant hunting. Lencki was well-known throughout auto racing as an innovator. He had constructed his own six-cylinder engine for competition at Indianapolis and was respected for the feat. Bettenhausen was becoming so popular among the racing fans that photographers took advantage of any publicity photo featuring the seemingly fearless young driver. He and Lencki were pictured on the front page of the racing news with their pheasant catch. Tony Bettenhausen was rapidly becoming a full-fledged star.

With the Midwest racing schedule winding down, Tony had more time once again to devote to Val at home. She needed it. There had been three gall bladder attacks, the baby was due in November and she was sure Tony would have to join the Army. Japan had demanded that the United States and Britian stop giving aid to China. The Japanese had aligned with Hitler and the Italian Mussolini in an effort to extend their conquests in Indo-China. The newspapers kept U.S. citizens informed of the aggression that had been taking place over the past three years and while most wanted peace, the threat of the U.S. in a second World

War was closer than ever before. In September of 1941, the Americans were having an undeclared naval war with Germany after a Nazi submarine had fired torpedoes at an American destroyer on its way to Iceland. President Roosevelt hadn't given Val much mental satisfaction while campaigning for an unprecedented third term when he said, "I shall say it again and again and again; your boys are not going to be sent into any foreign wars." He didn't say, however, that he would not consider fighting back after an attack.

On November 18, 1941, Valerie Bettenhausen managed to bear a son, Gary, for her Tony. She just made it, and it wasn't until ten days later that she was strong enough to go home. The next day she was rushed back to the hospital for further treatment and on December 5 they operated. While recuperating, she heard the news that the Japanese had attacked Pearl Harbor and the Americans had suffered some 4,500 casualties. The sneak attack fueled her fears that Tony would have to leave. She was only 20 years old, sick and now saddled with a baby boy. In the next week her condition improved, but the world situation didn't. Roosevelt had asked Congress to recognize that a state of war existed between the U.S. and Japan and Congress declared official entry into the fight on December 8. Three days later, Germany and Italy declared war on the United States.

Initially, automobile racing activity was not curtailed although some promoters voluntarily announced that race tracks would be closed "for the duration." Captain Rickenbacker, fully recovered from a near fatal airplane crash the previous year, said the Indianapolis Motor Speedway would not hold another 500 until the war ended and the facility would be made available to the government in any way possible to assist the total effort. During January and February of 1942, indoor races were held as scheduled and Tony raced as usual. Then in late February, Rickenbacker announced that the AAA would postpone all its racing activities for the duration. The American Automobile Association was the internationally recognized governing body of automobile racing and Rick's statement said the nation's best interests would be served by the cancellation of all auto races. Uncle Sam, on the other hand, said that state fairs could still be held and many drivers anticipated racing as usual at the fair dates and on so-called outlaw tracks.

Each week the racing paper would tell of another driver who had joined the war effort. But Tony didn't have to go. Along with his friend Joe Lencki, he went to work in the Maywood Buick plant and was assembling airplane engines. Val was relieved, and

Joe Lencki, far left, Tony and some of the gang at the Buick plant were featured in the racing news. [Bettenhausen Coll.]

for the first few months of the war there weren't any real changes in their lifestyle. Since the promoters had decided to stage races without AAA sanction, the winter schedule hadn't been affected. And when 26,000 fans showed at the opening Reading, Pennsylvania race, Midwesterners looked forward to their own season.

Val was back on her feet in a matter of weeks and she too was featured in the *National Auto Racing News* along with four other driver's wives at a local party. She had become popular with the other wives and enjoyed the weekly gatherings they'd have after the races. Sometimes they'd go up to Buster Novak's bar on Cicero Avenue. Novak was Wally Zale's brother-in-law and much like Willie Belmont over East, he was also considered a part of the racing crowd and he didn't mind the extra rowdiness the group sometimes displayed while they were re-running a race. One Saturday night in late April the gang was sitting around talking about the war and the effect it was having on their sport. Wally's brother, Johnny, had already joined the Navy and Mary Zale said she hoped that Wally didn't have to go.

He didn't get a chance. At exactly 1:55 AM the railroad crossing signal was flashing on U.S. 6, just a block away. Wally and fellow driver Bob Perrone tried to beat the long train that was approaching. Wally beat the first train to the crossing but was unaware that there was also a northbound freight on the second set of tracks. He hit the freight with such force that two cars were de-railed. Then, the first train slammed into them, killing both men instantly. The group at the bar heard the accident but were not notified of the deaths until 6:00 AM.

Twenty Grand Steinbock delivered a poetic eulogy to the pair at the next Ampitheatre race and writers from all parts of the country

AMERICAN SPEEDWAYS' PICTURE NEWSPAPER

VOL. XXI No. 22 Entered as Second Class Matter Post Office, East Paterson, N. J. EAST PATERSON, N. J., MAY 28, 1942 Published Every Thursday Tel. LAmbert 8-1346 PRICE TEN CENTS

BETTENHAUSEN WINS OVER STAR FIELD AT DAYTON

(Story Page 2)

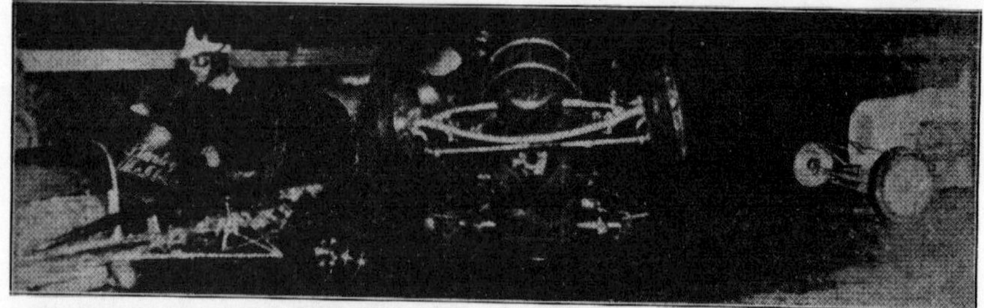

Photo by [illegible]

UNION THRILLER—Vernon Land in car balancing on its hind wheels after striking Walt Gregory, who had just crashed into Joe Garson who spun (out of foto). The rest of the field managed to miss the pile-up, in the consolation race at Union, N. J.

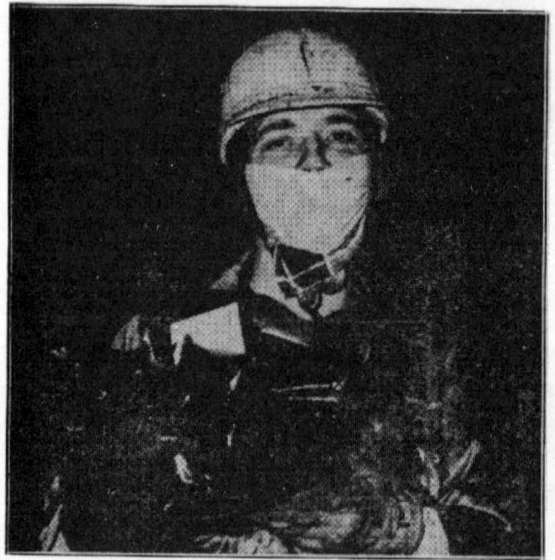

—O'Connell Photo

DOUBLE CROSSED—In Texas racing circles Junior Thomas is known for his rapid fire vocabulary. About the only time he is quiet is while he is prepared for a race. Waiting until he had tied his lips shut with a handkerchief, officials presented him with a birthday cake from an admirer. Junior is shown here in a bad way. He can't talk or eat. The scene: Houston Bowl.

—J. S. Sams Photo

MEET MR. AND MRS. HART—Driver Harry Hart being presented trophy by his charming bride of four weeks in honor of winning the trophy dash at Olympic Stadium in Kansas City. A few minutes later Harry was involved in an a bad spill in a special match race with Vito Calia, but luckily suffered only slight injury.

The front page of a May 1942 racing news told of Tony's accomplishments.

Tony teamed with owner Rudy Nichels in 1942 and dominated the Chicago area with this pretty black number 1.

expressed their sympathy in the racing papers. Zale had been known as "The Human Cyclone" and while not the most gregarious driver around, his consistent winning performances made him somewhat of a Midget racing legend in his own time. Over the past two years Tony had become extremely close to the man who had sold him his first race car. He accepted Wally's death with the attitude of, "I guess when it's your time to go, it doesn't make much difference what you're doing." Mary Zale told Tony that he could still run Wally's Midget when he had the opportunity and Tony said he'd continue to give her a portion of the prize money.

Now, in the first few months of 1942, Tony Bettenhausen was becoming one of the sport's most publicized stars and he didn't have to look for a ride. The main medium for becoming well-known in auto racing was still the *National Auto Racing News* and *Illustrated Speedway News*. Week after week Tony was receiving banner headlines for his stunning accomplishments. In May the paper said, "Blond Blizzard Sweeps Raceway; 3rd Opening Win." Tony had won his first three outdoor races of the season, all track openers. The same week he was featured working on an airplane engine at the Buick plant. The following week the headline read, "Bettenhausen Wins Over Star Field at Dayton." Throughout May, June and July, Tony absolutely dominated the competition at Raceway Park, Riverview and Milwaukee. On July 25, the largest crowd in the history of Raceway Park staged a "Tony Bettenhausen Night" and the report read:

> It was a night when the citizens of Tinley Park and the brush and shrubbery communities came to do homage to their idol, Tony Bettenhausen, also the gang from Buick was there.

Twenty Grand Steinbock made Tony come to the microphone to accept the many gifts bestowed upon him and he nervously stammered that he was deeply touched and he would try his best to please the folks by winning the feature. He not only won, but set three track records during the night against the largest field ever assembled at the facility. The next week he was trying to avoid a car in front of him and drove into Pete Neilson's path. Tony flipped and was shaken badly enough to sit out the rest of the evening. He said he'd be back for the next race at Riverview, the last scheduled for the duration of the war. Again, he was the winner. It was the last race Tony Bettenhausen would run for the remainder of the war. The government called a ban to all auto racing contests effective July 31, 1942.

As expected, the war effort would have its effect on all members of the racing fraternity. Nalon had already sailed into Cassablanca in June where he became the Rolls-Royce engine representative. Later he would go to Calcutta and then China. Henry Banks went to work for Intercontinental Air-Craft; Emil went into the Air Force; Russo stayed out of action by working in a Detroit machine shop and Tony stayed at the Buick plant.

For the remainder of the summer and into fall and winter, the racing papers continued on a weekly schedule reporting news of the boys overseas, "Remember When" columns, and news of the growing model Midget sport. Finally, a paper shortage, and the lack of races to report forced the termination of the weekly racing news. For Tony and Val the next three years would be remembered as one of the only quiet times in their lives. No longer did Tony rush to get everything done as he had in the past. Before the war it seemed like there were never enough hours in a day. Now, there were too many. Tony accepted his work at the Buick plant simply as something that had to be done. He'd often say he couldn't put up with factory work for the rest of his life. He sure wanted the war to end.

* * *

Little Ernie Schlausky hadn't been as fortunate as Tony Bettenhausen in avoiding war duty. On his birthday in 1942 he received his draft notice. He didn't like the idea that his racing career would have to be stopped, for he had set a goal for himself to be an Indianapolis 500 driver by 1948. Soon after he and Gus Gerhardt had started attending the races at Nutley, they built a flat-track motorcycle racer and Ernie was the rider. He wasn't a star, but considering their low-budget equipment he held his own against the more powerful (and expensive) machines. Gus, however, had lost interest in racing in 1939 and Ernie was on his own. He was still convinced he had the talent to be a professional. He'd always tell his girl, Gene, that someday he was going to win the Indianapolis 500. Now he had to say good-bye to her. He didn't know how long the war would last, but it was agreed that they would be married when he came home. Ernie knew that she was the girl for him.

They shipped Ernie to Hawaii and later to Saipan where he became one of the most respected members of the 762nd Tank Batallion. He had suggested that the unit obtain some motorcycles and he could be a dispatcher, take messages back to headquarters from the front lines. Ernie wanted to keep riding motorcycles, and he wasn't much interested in shooting guns. He'd rather take his chances on two wheels. But he came close to winding up like Henry Guerand did, over at Nutley, decapitated.

It was said that the Japanese would tie piano wire across the road at neck height to deter motorcycle messengers. Ernie had heard the stories and rigged up a branch that jutted out from the front of his motorcycle. He hoped it would catch the piano wire first and warn him in time to lay the motorcycle on its side, at speed. It worked. One late afternoon he was on his way back from the front when the branch suddenly shot upward. Ernie ducked and deliberately laid his mount over, an act which sent him sprawling on the dirt. He got up and couldn't see the wire until he was only inches away from it.

A few months later he was almost killed again. The guard had hollered, "Halt! Who goes there?"

Ernie didn't hear the man. His mind was in another universe. He had just received a letter from his beloved Gene: She was now married. Ernie couldn't understand, he had always written her letters, told her what he was doing and hoping for the day he could come home.

The guard cocked his rifle, ker-lick!

Ernie stopped in his tracks. He'd heard the bolt-action. Gene Kushman was gone forever. He'd still be a race car driver.

* * *

Val had become pregnant for the second time and even though he loved her, Tony was getting bored with going home to what seemed like the same old drudgery night after night. May as well stop and have a few beers with the gang. The drinking didn't help the situation on the home front. Jesus, Val thought, she worried about him when he was driving a race car, but at least she knew what her competition was. She didn't want him away, but sometimes it was just as bad when he was around. Awfully testy. She wished he had something to occupy his time, something that would make him give her the old compliments and hugs she loved so much. Damn war. It was miserable outside, too. Nothing worse than a dreary Chicago winter. But she'd make the best of things, she vowed. It'll get better when the war's over. This was her second time around with Mr. Tony Bettenhausen and you certainly knew what you were getting yourself into, Valerie, she told herself. She wondered if son Gary would turn out to have hers or Tony's traits. Well, at least he didn't have two different colored eyes, she smiled. Then she thought, oh Hell, what's the poor guy to do? He's right. He can't stand to be confined in that damn factory without letting off a little steam. And as much as anyone she ever knew, Melvin Eugene Bettenhausen worked up steam to let off. Having a couple of beers with the fellas couldn't be as bad as it sometimes seemed. Still, he didn't have to get drunk, did he? Maybe it'll be different when the new baby arrives.

The leaves came back to the trees and Val could see people on the streets again. She didn't feel so alone anymore. Soon after summer had arrived she presented Tony with their second son, Merle, named after Murrell Belanger who had by now become a personal friend of theirs. She liked Murrell, he was a little gruff on the outside, but she guessed he had to be, being in business for himself and everything.

Tony didn't have to worry about his own physical well-being for the duration, but he sometimes wondered about his sanity. Christ, this damn war could go on forever, he thought. He was convinced, more than ever before, that there was no other life for him than driving a race car. Boy, he was really beginning to show 'em how it ought to be done just before they shut things down. Tony thought he was pretty damn good behind the wheel, and he didn't mind telling you so. If they thought I was beatin' 'em before this fiasco started, just wait til it's all over.

Once a month now Tony was getting the old fire fueled even more. The *National Auto Racing News* had started publishing again on a monthly schedule with a new name: *National Speed Sport News*. Speed Sport. The sport of speed. Tony looked

As soon as the war was over Tony resumed his Midget racing activity in the Nichels number 1.

forward to each issue and remembering the races that used to be. Many times he'd found a picture of himself, usually getting upside down at the indoor races. And it was always funny. He could remember each time as though it had just happened. You forgot about the pain. And sometimes there wasn't any pain. And then he started thinking, that's all in the past. Probably won't get upside down much anymore. Smoother now. Besides, getting upside down was no big deal as long as you could keep countin' the times it happened.

* * *

The war seemed to drag on and on. Would it ever be over? Now Val was pregnant for the third time and it seemed like the same old thing. The whole country wasn't in a happy daily routine, and neither was the Tony Bettenhausen family. Finally things were starting to get a little brighter. The news from overseas had been prediciting a victory just about any day now.

The headline they were waiting for took up the entire front page of the August edition of *National Speed Sport News:*

RACE BAN LIFTED
MANY SPEEDWAYS READY

As Val had expected, Tony quit the Buick plant the day the war was officially over. Although he was already the father of two with another due next month, Tony wasn't about to consider a regular job. Old cement head. There was plenty of future in driving race cars. Besides, people had lots of money now, they hadn't been spending it on entertainment the last three years. The

The Tony Bettenhausen family just after the war. [Bettenhausen Coll.]

grandstands would be packed and that meant fat purses. And Tony Bettenhausen meant to relieve them of some of those hard-earned dollars with a driving performance or two that they'd remember.

Tony was right. Fans flocked to the late summer auto races like never before. The opening event over at Williams Grove in Pennsylvania drew 34,000; 15,000 went to Freeport up in Long Island; 11,000 went to Akron. And every seat in the house was filled at Blue Island's Raceway Park, one of Tony's favorite tracks. The promoters wanted to play the new boom for all they could, and after the standing room only crowd watched Tony Bettenhausen win the opening event, it was announced that races would not only be held every Sunday, but Wednesday nights as well. Throughout the next 18 race meets, Tony would win no less than a dozen of them. He teamed with Rudy Nichels from Hammond, Indiana and their black Number 1 Midget proved worthy of its number. During the first week in September of 1945, Tony became a father for the third time, as Val presented him a little girl. They named her Susan.

A successful day at the races could net you at least double what the normal working man took home for a week's toil. There were still no guarantees, however. You still had to roll your car out on the track and try to qualify just like everyone else. It didn't matter that you had racked up a couple dozen previous wins. Every race the meter was set back at zero. And lots of other guys wanted to be full-time racers, too. Now that there was more money around, it meant better (and faster) equipment for everyone. But Tony was up to the test. He had first class equipment and a cocksure attitude that he was able to back up.

In October there was a 100-mile Midget race in Toledo that was advertised as the biggest race of the new season. Stars from all around the country were there. It rained on qualifying day and for some odd reason all those who didn't qualify on Saturday were allowed a chance to make the field the morning of the Sunday race, but were forced to the rear of the pack, even if their times were faster than those of the first day. Tony had second fast time overall, but had to start 20th in the 33-car field.

"It don't bother me a bit," he told racing writer Len Milde. "We'll blow by 'em on the first couple of laps."

In his high, wide and breath-taking style, Tony passed car after car and by the fourth lap had command of the entire field. He didn't settle for a comfortable first, but lapped the field. Duane Carter, whom he'd met back at Nutley, finished a distant second. The ensuing headlines that Tony received from the Toledo win re-established his image as one of the nation's foremost dirt track Midget and Sprint drivers. He had been a quick-study. In reality, Tony hadn't driven for a number of years on the small unknown outlaw tracks of the country in order to hone his skills. His rise had been sure and steady.

Now he looked forward to the re-opening of the Indianapolis Motor Speedway and his debut there. Val could remember the night they sat outside the famed race track only a few years earlier listening to Tony tell her that someday he would race there. Would it come true?

The Speedway had set vacant throughout the war years and the entire 500 acre complex resembled a jungle that had a narrow brick road running around its perimeter. Captain Eddie Rickenbacker said he wasn't very interested in trying to renovate the facility as a race track and there was a good possibility it would be sold, probably as a housing development. Three-time "500" winner Wilbur Shaw took more than a passing interest in the plant and propositioned Rickenbacker to try and sell the track to someone who would carry on its tradition. Rick consented and Shaw began sending out proposals to various automotive oriented companies. He had several nibbles, but all wanted to utilize the race and its accompanying publicity to promote their own product line. Shaw finally convinced Terre Haute businessman Anton (Tony) Hulman to buy and perpetuate the Speedway tradition for a reported $750,000. Hulman had not previously shown an interest in auto racing, but likened the Speedway to Louisville's Kentucky Derby and said he believed the "500" should always be a part of Indiana. The deal was consumated and racing had a new hero in Tony Hulman. There would be a 1946 Indianapolis 500 . . . and

Entrance to the Speedway.

Three-time "500" winner Wilbur Shaw, right, convinced Anton [Tony] Hulman to purchase the Speedway and maintain it.

Melvin Eugene Tony Bettenhausen would be in the starting line-up, or he'd know the reason why.

Word spread among the Chicago Gang that Tony had secured a ride for the 500. He was to be officially entered in the Marchese Brothers car from Milwaukee. The Marcheses were old time racers themselves, and felt good about giving Tony his first real break. Good buddy Cowboy O'Rourke said they should celebrate the occasion and he threw a going away party at his "Last Lap Lounge" located in the fifty hundred block on Diversey. Indianapolis here we come.

Tony had time to stop at the Midget race in Crown Point on his way to Indianapolis on Sunday, May 5. While running in the second heat race, Pete Nielsen, a fine Midget driver and respected auto body builder (he had built the body for the Marchese car), flipped in front of Tony. He stopped and ran to Pete's aid, but

Nielsen was able to extricate himself from the car and started on a run toward the pits, grasping his chest along the way. He stopped, fell to the ground. Nielsen was dead of internal injuries. Another one. Tony went out and won the feature event. On to Indianapolis.

It was a great sense of accomplishment for Tony to be among the other drivers at the Speedway. He'd arrived. Now all he had to do was figure out how to drive at speed around the place, qualify the car and become a bonafide Indianapolis 500 race car driver. On his first lap around the old plant he found out that there was absolutely no similarity to any other race track he'd ever run. It was shaped like a rectangle with four very distinct corners. Two very long straights and two shorter straights in between the turns. They called them the short chutes. It didn't take long for a black groove to appear showing the line everyone took through the corners. They'd dip down low in the first turn, drift up toward the wall and head into the second turn. Same thing through three and four.

Within a few days Tony had worked up to speed they knew would qualify him for the race. Although nervous for his qualifying run, he handled the four trips around the rectangular track with no problem, but told the mechanics that the engine definitely had a bad vibration in it. They tore it apart and found the crankshaft cracked. Then they couldn't locate a replacement. Tony had qualified for his first "500" but it looked like he wasn't going to be in the starting field. Had to find another ride. The Marchese car would never make it.

Joe Lencki, Tony's fellow factory worker and the man he enjoyed pheasant hunting with, offered Tony his machine. Lencki had been working on the car throughout the war years; however, he wasn't as concerned with working on the old Speedway chassis as he was in developing his new fuel and carburetion system. His new blend, he believed, would produce considerably more power than conventional systems without much sacrifice in total consumption. That Lencki was a thinker, they said.

Bettenhausen had precious little time to waste. He'd have to work up to speed right away, and then qualify the car. The race was getting nearer. But after a couple laps everyone could see that he was in trouble. Tony would start into the first turn and he just couldn't make the car go where he wanted it to. Seemed like he was going to spin out at any minute. He'd have to slow down right in the middle of the corner when he wanted to be pushing on the gas pedal some more.

He thought it was all his fault, he never had any experience on a

Tony's first car at Indy, the Marchese Spl. [*IMS*]

place like this; he had to ask Duke what to do. Duke said he'd walk down in the first turn and watch. Lencki was getting a little excited, too. There wasn't anything wrong with the car, he reasoned. What's wrong with that Bettenhausen? Duke watched and later met Tony back in Gasoline Alley.

"That thing's doing all sort of gyrations out there," Duke told Tony. "It isn't your fault. It just isn't handling at all."

The pair wandered from one garage to another as they talked. Sometimes it was just idle conversation about the cars. Then Tony would ask a mechanic or another driver what he thought he could do to solve the car's handling problems. After a while, Tony leaned over to Duke and said, "You notice him?" pointing to a short, horn-rimmed little character carrying a clipboard. The black-haired man had turned sideways when Tony pointed toward him.

"Yes," Duke said. "I noticed he's been following us a bit. Maybe he's just a newspaper reported and wants to get a line on the one and only Tony "Flipper" Bettenhausen at the Speedway." Duke laughed at his own joke.

"Well, he's really starting to bother me. He oughta say something rather that just weasling around."

The pair walked to Paul Russo's garage where the mechanics were checking over the complicated looking car. It had two Midget engines in it. One in the front and another out back. What a nightmare, Duke thought. Tony liked it. And Russo was going fast in the new car.

Once again Tony glanced over his shoulder and there was Mr. Clipboard. And again, the beady little character turned and started looking at his notes so as to feign indifference to Tony's watching him. Tony brushed by Duke, walked up to this latest irritation and without so much as a greeting, grabbed the small man by the front of his shirt and slammed him up against one of the wooden garage doors.

"Alright you little bastard," he glared. "Now you have been following us for half an hour and writing things down. Just what in the hell are you doin'?"

Eyeglasses askew and standing on tippy toes, the note-taker held up a hand in a whoa-fashion and blurted, "Lencki . . . Lencki told me to follow you and find out how come you wasn't going fast!"

"Don't hurt him, Tony," the Duke said from behind. "It won't help you go any faster. I don't think anyone can go any faster in that thing that you are."

"Umm, I don't think so either, Mr. Bettenhausen," the petrified spy chimed in. "Matter . . . matter of fact, I think I'm going to go back and tell that to Mr. Lencki right now if you don't mind."

Tony released his grip and sort of flicked the little character away while he turned to Duke and laughed.

Afterwards, everyone agreed that Tony would probably do better in someone else's machine and he finally got a ride in the Bristow-McManus entry after waiting out a couple of day's rain.

Tony couldn't help but like the aura that surrounded the Speedway. It was the only race in the country where they took a full month to prepare. It was more like a convention of auto racing greats than a single race. He had known for some time that once you earned your way into a Speedway ride you were considered a real pro. This was the major league. Or it was supposed to be, anyhow. Still, one could walk though the heralded Gasoline Alley and see that it was full of shoestring operations. Most of the cars entered for the '46 event had been pulled out of mothballs and hurriedly prepared. But Tony loved all the activity. He liked to see the mechanics building, changing things. Here you had enough time to make a change, go out and try it and if it didn't work, make another change. He was used to unloading his Midget, taking two quick qualifying laps and then getting ready for the evening's races. At Indy you fine-tuned the chassis day after day and your time was based on four consecutive laps, ten miles.

You had lots of time to think while coming down the straights here. Initially, Tony wanted to, "back 'er in" dirt-track style the

When it was discovered the Marchese car couldn't run in the 500, Tony finally made the show in this old, but sleek Miller. [*IMS*]

same way he was used to driving all the small Midget tracks. But he soon found out that following the black groove laid down by the veterans before him was indeed the fastest way around. Tony's car wasn't built for dirt-track driving style either. It was a front-wheel drive Miller, originally built way back in 1924 and modified over the years to stay competitive. Tony had never driven a front-wheel drive vehicle before, but he liked it when he decided to let the front tires pull him through the corners rather than slide as he'd been used to.

Once Tony regained his confidence, he started to like the big track. He knew his car wasn't capable of going as fast as the ones some of the established Speedway stars like Rex Mays or Ted Horn had, but in practice he worked up to a speed he was sure would make the race. Even the way they talked about how fast you were going here was different. At all the Midget and Sprint car tracks, the announcer told the fans how many seconds the driver turned. At the Speedway, your miles per hour was the thing.

Emil, Duke and Henry Banks all congratulated Tony on his qualifying run. He'd gone faster than any of them. However, none were really considered potentials to win the race. They didn't have the equipment. But Russo did. His wierd little twin-engined car was really running. He qualified right up front. Would start in the first row. Tony told him, "What'd you expect? If you can't get 'er handled with two motors, Paul, you may as well hang it up." Russo allowed as to how he'd wave to Tony as he lapped him. Then on the serious side, he said, "Listen, Benski, this ain't indoors, you know. You just keep that thing between the fences. It ain't no world-beater. Run 'er all day long and you'll make some money."

After Tony had finally qualified for his first Indianapolis 500 Mile Race, he had a new sense of confidence about him. He'd already gained a good deal of self-satisfaction through his spreading reputation as a top dirt driver of Midgets and Sprints, but all the short track victories in the world didn't equal one first place finish at Indy. And while a goodly number of the competitors in the 1946 running of the Memorial Day Classic, as it was termed, would go back to the Midget and Sprint car wars throughout the rest of the summer, it seemed like the real hot dogs at the Speedway didn't even run the smaller cars. You never heard of Mauri Rose or Cliff Bergere or Rex Mays running a Midget race. They were in the exclusive club: Indy 500 drivers. None of them got there because they were nice guys, liked by everyone. You had to earn your way to the Speedway. And no matter how great you were on your own home turf, or even as a traveling man who'd raced in every part of the country, what you did at Indy was what counted. And you have just one time a year to prove how good you are.

Indianapolis was such an exclusive men's club that they didn't allow women in Gasoline Alley or the pits. They're no place for a woman. Just get in the way. So it was with great trepidation that Val allowed Tony to hide her in the back seat of their Mercury with a tarp covering her while Tony drove past the gate guards. He was going to work on the car some, and he wanted Val around. Oh well, she mused, it sure was better than waiting for him to come home from the aviation plant. She was proud of him. He said he'd race here and sure enough he was right. Lord, hope he doesn't get hurt or worse.

There was a full two hours of ceremony preceding the race that was to begin at 10:00 sharp. The track was turned into a city of its own on race day, and most everyone in the garage area had agreed long ago that all these people weren't your real racing fans. You wouldn't see these same folks at a Wednesday night Midget race. Some said they weren't even Indianapolis 500 fans. They just wanted to be there, so they could say they were. Going to the 500 was a day for a picnic. You could sit right there at the start-finish line and you couldn't tell what was happening all around the whole track. You could look up to your left and see the cars coming out of the fourth turn, way up there, over half a mile away. Then you could watch them drive down the front staight-a-way. And zoom. They were gone into the first turn and you didn't know what they were doing from there. You'd wait a while till they drove down the backstretch and pretty soon here they'd come again. Big deal.

It was hard to understand why the infield was full, too. Those people had a hard time even catching a glimpse of a race car, much less seeing some good side-by-side racing. But there was a big crowd down in the first turn. They figured that's where everybody had to turn left after picking up all that speed and if anything was going to happen, it'd probably be there. Up in the fourth turn you could pay and park your car pretty close to the track, too. That's where all the action would be, in the corners.

Action or not, they had packed the place. It didn't even matter that you couldn't see the cars go all the way around the track at Indy. There was nothing else like the Speedway. These are the best drivers and the most sophisticated cars in the entire world. Nothing else could even come close.

Tony would start the event back in the ninth row. There were eleventh rows in all, with three cars in each. A three abreast start. That was totally different, too. At most every other race in the country, it was a foregone conclusion that you started side by side, with two cars per row. And there was never an odd number of cars in the field. How come 33? It didn't really matter, that's just the way it was. Another of the things that added to the mystique of the Speedway. Sometimes, there would be a three-abreast field of 33 cars on one of the Midget tracks for a big special race and the design of the field was supposed to be somewhat of a salute to Indianapolis. And sometimes it got a little hairy. It was one thing to worry about what the guy next to you was going to do, but now you had to think about two guys. And it was a long ways from the starting line where they'd wave the green flag to that first turn. Everybody would be going like hell. From way back there in the ninth row you could sure see a lot of race cars up ahead of you. Boy, if one guy makes a mistake there could be a helluva mess. Maybe that's why the front straight-a-way grandstands were full.

Henry Ford II led the pack of 33 cars around the course with the official pace car, a beautiful cream colored 1946 Lincoln Continental convertible. It was a slick looking job, just had a half-dollar size push button where the door handle normally went. The car was to be presented to the winner of the "500". Would be an awful nice car to own, but it was a little hard to think about winning it when you were driving a mediocre car like Tony was. Besides, he was just a rookie, his first year. Just run all day, they'd told him, and you'll make some money.

Track owner Tony Hulman had allowed Wilbur Shaw to become the Speedway's official spokesman and the former driver wore his title of President well. Matter of fact, Wilbur looked downright business-like with his pencil-thin moustache and suit and tie. At 9:50 AM a microphone was handed to Shaw as he stood in the passenger seat of the pace car and he commanded the eleven rows behind him:

"Gentlemen, Start Your Engines!"

Cheers, hoops, yeah's and handwaving signaled the crowd's full acceptance of Wilbur's words and as the cars roared to life, the official starting bomb went off. In the middle of the track there was deafening noise from the unmuffled racers. A crew member was supposed to hold his hand high when the engine in his car started. But unless you saw a little puff from the tailpipe, it was really hard to tell just whose car had started. Was it yours or the ones in front or back, or next to you? The driver was supposed to tell you, but he could be so nervous he wouldn't know either. There was uncontrollable engine revving going on, driver's shaking their heads "OK" and crew members scurrying back toward the pits with cases of tools and litle battery carts they'd used to start the cars. Henry Ford would lead the field through one lap, pull in and the green would be thrown. You didn't get out of line, you didn't inch back or ahead, you were supposed to stay right where you started until the green was thrown.

The start was smooth and Tony just followed everyone else through the first couple of laps. Mauri Rose was the early race leader and looked like the class of the field. Russo was in the top four for awhile. There were 200 laps to go and it wasn't where you started that counted.

Henry Banks caused the first yellow to be displayed when he spun on the fourteenth lap, but he kept on going. Then just a couple of laps later Tony came around and was heading into the third turn when he saw Russo's car slammed up against the wall. He looked at Paul as he went by and although Russo wasn't slumped over in the seat, he didn't look too good either. He was sort of wiggling trying to get loose. But there wasn't any fire. He looked like he'd be OK.

Tony was driving as cautious a race as he knew how. He wanted to pass and get up there toward the front right away, but he could see there were guys dropping out, and every once in a while he'd go around someone himself. Slowly, he worked his way into the top ten by the 40th lap. Then he saw Duke pull in a couple of laps later. On the 45th lap he heard a slight change in the pitch of the engine and knew something was going to happen. Like right away. You can feel it. Or you're supposed to be able to he always believed. You're a part of the car and you should know even if the thing has an itch somewhere. It'll let you know, it changes just a little right before it gets ready to die. Or turn sideways. Something inside you tells you that something is out of synch. It's an "Oh, no" feeling.

The message had no sooner been transmitted to Tony when, Bang! Shudder . . . shudder . . . shudder . . .

Tony's reflexes pushed in the clutch, but it was too late. And it wouldn't have done any good anyhow. A connecting rod had snapped inside the engine and it's like a knife in the heart. There was no saving it. He would officially be credited with finishing the race in 20th position, good for $925. He was happy and upset all at the same time. He knew he could blow by these guys with the right equipment. But at least he was a bonafide Indianapolis 500 veteran now. You're only a rookie one time. From then on you don't make any mistakes. A rookie's liable to do anything, but once you've been in the race they look at you differently. You know what it's all about.

Twentieth finishing position wasn't too great, he thought. But it was better than what Russo was going through. He was in Methodist Hospital nursing a broken leg. The only member of the Chicago Gang who really did anything was Emil. He finished up in fourth spot and collected over $5,000. Emil would like that. He was a money racer if there ever was one. Harry McQuinn, one of the roughest Chicago Midget racers ever to come down the pike wound up in 13th. And they all got to rib fellow Chicago driver Danny Kladis who was driving for the Granatelli Brothers. He had the distinction of being in, to their knowledge, the only car in the history of the race that was forced to leave with absolutely nothing wrong with the vehicle. As it was being refueled, an anxious mechanic filled the tank to the brim and therefore left no space for air. It vapor locked. Kladis was forced to stop on the backstretch. A truck towed him back toward the pits, immediate cause for disqualification.

* * *

Ernie Schlausky had come back from the war with mixed emotions. He had wanted to become an Indianapolis 500 driver by 1948, but he had just lost four years of precious racing experience. He wasn't sure he could make it in two years. Nevertheless, he had

Ernie Schlausky in a 1941 pose.

Ernie Schlausky became Ernie Warren to drive race cars. He's shown here in a 1941 photo, leather-helmeted and ready. [*Crocky Wright Coll.*]

to make a trip to see his first ''500'' in 1946 to make up his mind for sure. It was even better than he pictured. He'd never been to another race track that even resembled the Speedway. It was huge. Why you could put the entire Nutley Velodrome in one end of the pits and not even notice it was there, he thought. He still wanted to be a Speedway driver.

On the way home from the race he made plans to buy a Midget. Plus, he could do some motorcycle racing too and run a Sprint car sometimes. Ernie Schlausky would be a full-time race car driver. But Schlausky was too long a name, he believed, for people to write in the programs and to remember. He'd be Ernie "Crocky" Warren. He still remembered Crocky Rawding, the great motorcycle racer who was his idol and he wanted to be like him.

5

The Kaiser-Frazer

Following his debut at Indianapolis, Tony talked about wanting to run in more of the championship events and keeping up his busy Midget racing schedule, too. His first race out on the Midget circuit was at the beautiful Walsh Stadium in St. Louis. He was in the familiar Nichels #1 on his qualifying attempt when he hooked just a little rut in the normally smooth dirt surface. By now the feeling was familiar, the sudden thrust of the car becoming airborne and snapping sideways. Sometimes your hands would fly off the wheel because they'd been criss-crossed so hard by the impact of hitting a wall that it was impossible to hang on. Then you looked like a rag doll inside the car being flopped side to side. Other times you knew you had a grip on the wheel and you could get your head down. The veterans would say, "Head for the basement when you know you're going to take a flier." Tony managed to hold on and the pretty black machine started snapping, rolling violently. It didn't care that you were a bonafide Indianapolis 500 driver. You might have believed it could hear you when you'd say, "C'mon, baby, hold together for just a couple more laps now, and we'll win us another one." Lots of the cars had names on them and were continually referred to as a sweet running little thing when it had done well for you, or a shitbox when you couldn't make it go where you wanted. Right now this shitbox could snuff out the father of three children and never mutter a word of compassion. The packed grandstand let out an, "Ohhhhhh" in unison as they automatically rose and leaned forward to witness one man's fate. They had paid one dollar for the right to judge a performance. They'd cheer for you if you risked your neck a little more than the others and passed everyone on the outside. They'd boo you if they believed you gave one of your fellow drivers a raw deal. And they'd mourn for you if you killed yourself right in front of their very eyes. But if you were going to kill yourself, don't be too messy about it. Don't be like Henry Guerand over there at Nutley the time he got up into the fence and cut his arm and head off. They didn't really mind seeing a wildly flipping Midget tossing its occupant every which way, but they didn't want to get sick over the matter, either. It'd be best if it was a horrendous crash, and the driver jumped out of the broken machine and waved up at everybody who'd paid their dollar. Then he was supposed to go back out in another car and win the race. They wanted to see the man beat the machine. That's what it was supposed to be like.

The engine had quit in the midst of the warm June air and the car slammed to the ground on top of Tony with a force that made everyone grit their teeth and grimace another "Ohhhhhh." They waited and looked. C'mon, Bettenhausen, scramble out of that sonofabitch. Tell us you're alright. Please. Jesus, don't be dead. You're too good to be dead. You get upside down all the time. Wonder how many times he's been upside down?

No matter how bad the accident, there's always someone in the pits who'll run up to the car without hesitation. It doesn't matter that the occupant may have just been deformed, decapitated or is bloody beyond recognition. Sometimes the drivers themselves would talk, and even joke about it. Mostly they agreed that it was reactions that made then run toward the car. Maybe there was something they could do in a hurry. Like get a buddy out before the damn thing catches on fire. But how about when you *know* the guy's dead inside it, somebody would ask. Aw, you're never positive. Guy might just be knocked out. How about if his head was missing? That's dumb talk. You gotta be an idiot to ask questions like that. You just don't talk about shit like that. It sounds like a question some damn newspaper reporter would ask.

Tony Bettenhausen's crash took place on June 11, 1946. Three days later he was back in the same car on the quarter-mile track at the Milwaukee State Fairgrounds. You couldn't tell that he had two different colored eyes now. You couldn't see the whites of his eyes because he had broken all the blood vessels and the whites had turned blood red. He said it didn't affect his vision, though, and he won the Milwaukee race. They had cheered for Tony at St. Louis when he gave them a limp wave after being dragged out of the black #1. He continued his summer pace of running at Blue Island, Milwaukee, St. Louis each week; he even managed to sneak in a side trip once in awhile to some non-regular stop. In July he won three races in a row and was winning almost every other Midget race he entered. He and Nichels had a combination.

Californian Johnnie Parsons and Tony became fast friends. Parsons was one of the first to wear a driver's uniform. [*Byers*]

You knew they'd be in the top three if they finished. Tony loved every minute of it.

In August Duke talked to Tony and told him to come on out to Gilmore. The Los Angeles track was still considered the best Midget track in the country, and if you won at Gilmore, you'd beaten the best.

Tony went to Los Angeles again and got a ride in Ted Halibrand's clean little Offenhauser. It was a capable car and Tony liked Halibrand right off. Tony said he wanted to make a few adjustments of his own on the car and Halibrand noted he didn't mind at all. It didn't matter that the car had been doing just fine without Tony's tinkering. If he was going to drive it, he'd have to make it just a little better. First, they went to the Los Angeles Coliseum where Tony was introduced to the 25,000 fans in attendance as one of the best Midget racers in the Midwest. Indy 500 racer, too. He missed the show. Flat. Maybe those guys in the Midwest ain't too tough, they said in the grandstands.

Two nights later they went to Gilmore. Tony made the feature and ran sixth. Duke had made a few suggestions and as usual, Tony took them seriously. Duke hadn't ever been wrong before, and he just won the feature here last week. Then Duke repeated his performance and upheld the honor of the Chicago Gang. Tony finished right behind Coast star Johnnie Parsons. He'd been drawn instantly to Parsons' easy-going attitude and rapid fire conversation. Maybe he liked the way Parsons was a little cocky, too. After the race Johnnie came up and said, "Didja see me wave

Tony in action on the mile track at the Indiana State Fairgrounds. [*Krueger*]

at you as I went by, Bettenhausen?" Handsome John. After the races they went out and drank together. That Parsons sure did attract the ladies, Tony thought.

Once back in the Midwest Tony had no trouble picking up where he left off. He landed a Championship car ride for the races at the Indianapolis Fairgrounds and on the Milwaukee mile, but wasn't a contender in either one.

The next Championship event on the schedule was at Goshen, New York, the site of the famed Hambletonian horse race. A man named Norm Olson had a car that was considered a conglomeration at best. The chassis was the one that Kelly Petillo had won the 1935 Indy 500 in; the engine came from the 1938 winning car. But Tony liked it. He told Emil he was going to go out and, "lead this race until she breaks."

By the second lap he had lived up to his prediction. And despite continual "E-Z" signals from Olson, Tony didn't let up once he had a comfortable lead. He lapped the entire field and was greeted by the reigning Miss America, Marilyn Bufered, in victory lane. Racing reporter Chris Economaki later wrote, "The state troopers had to circle to protect them from the pressing mob." A new face had won in Championship automobile racing, and it was a smiling one. The writers and photographers loved him. He answered their every question with interest and stood around signing autographs for two hours after the event. Then he went back home and won the last race of the year at Blue Island.

Postwar America was not only looking kindly on the auto

The 1946 National Championship

Before winning his first Championship race... [Craig Racing Photos]

Afterwards, Tony was greeted by the reigning Miss America.

racing sport, but business in general was prospering as never before. The automobile industry, although saddled with early 1940 designs that saw only slight facelifting for 1946, was turning out cars in record numbers. Tony was an automobile fan. Always had been. He especially liked Fords but took a keen interest in cars that were even slightly unusual. Americans had seen hundreds of car companies vie for a piece of the market throughout the first two decades of the century. By 1920 there were a little over 100 companies left and by 1940 eleven existed. Now, the factories couldn't keep up with the demand.

Tony had read of the plans that two men proposed, Henry Kaiser and Joe Frazer, to build a new brand of automobile bearing their respective names. Since America was close to a trasnsportation breakdown after the war had ended, Tony's interest in the new vehicle paralleled that of millions of others. It was estimated that Americans owned some 22 million vehicles in 1946, and half of them were ten years old. If ever the time was right for the introduction of a new car, it was certainly now. It would be considered a major calamity if the U.S. had only 18 million cars in driveable order. There wasn't much margin.

Tony asked Murrell Belanger what he thought of the idea of the new Kaiser-Frazer entering the market. He trusted Murrell's judgement in business and since Belanger had been telling Tony that he ought to put some of his time and effort into a business, Tony knew that Murrell would be interested.

"Why do you ask," Murrell said. "You thinking of going into the car selling business?"

"Maybe," Tony replied.

"You always told me that you were going to race until you were 65," Belanger kidded.

"Well," Belanger continued, "if Henry Kaiser has anything to say about it, it'll probably be a pretty good car. No matter what it is, if you had a thousand of them, you could sell 'em tomorrow."

Kaiser's name was well-known to Americans as the spearhead behind the great Hoover Dam and throughout the war years his ship building accomplishments were considered superhuman. He installed floodlights to work crews around the clock and was applauded by President Roosevelt as being one of the nation's key industrialists for the total effort. During the war he set up an experimental laboratory where a staff was designing a post-war automobile. Henry Kaiser saw himself as the new Henry Ford. He was a shoemaker's son who had already helped change the roads and major bridges of America, and now he wanted a car that would bear his name.

While Tony didn't have day one's experience in the business world, he had in innate capacity for recognizing things that were mechanically sound. And if they weren't, they could always stand a little of the Bettenhausen tinkering. He'd make the sumbitch perfect, or he'd know the reason why. From what he'd read about the new car, he didn't see any reason why it wouldn't be successful. But he was also interested in the radical new design that Preston Tucker was supposedly coming out with. In fact, Tucker was more his kind of guy. His heart had some roots in automobile racing and maybe his car would have also. Tucker was a long time associate of the great Harry Miller, the man who built the famed Offenhauser engine and some of the world's most successful racing cars. Tucker and Miller had laid down the basic plans for a new automobile in the late Thirties. It was to be of a rear-engine design. Miller had already built four radical rear-engine cars for the Gulf Oil corporation that were a good twenty years ahead of their time. George Barringer had driven one in Tony's first Indianapolis appearance this past May under the sponsorship of Tucker. It was called the Tucker Torpedo, the same name that was to be given to his new passenger car.

But Tony had his doubts about Tucker's new car as did everyone else who was following its debut. First, Harry Miller had died of cancer in 1943 so he couldn't be a part of the engineering team. Secondly, Tucker had always displayed a bit of questionable hustler-air about himself and reports in the *Chicago Tribune* didn't help his image. One, in fact, probably caused irreparable damage. Auto editor Frank Sturdy fueled the belief that the new Tucker didn't have a reverse gear after he heard Tucker's Chairman of the Board comment that the first prototype, "goes chug . . chug . . chug. . and I don't know if it can back up."

Tony had talked to Murrell about the new Tucker after it had been tested in the summer at the Speedway. It must have been sound, Tony thought. It had blown a tire while running close to 100 mph and flipped three times. But the driver walked away and the car also drove away under its own power. Nevertheless, Belanger advised that Tucker was in a heap of financial troubles with the government through his stock-selling antics and it probably wouldn't be long before they lowered the boom on him completely. Then one of the day's most respected radio announcers, Drew Pearson, said the same basic things that Belanger had and Tony decided to let Murrell put him in touch with the Kaiser-Frazer people.

In the winter Tony could have held down a full-time job as his racing activity was confined to running at the International

The Bettenhausen-Schuldt Kaiser-Frazer dealership. [*Bettenhausen Coll.*]

Ampitheatre on Sunday nights. He was looking forward to running at the Speedway again in May, but the idea of becoming a car dealer was appealing. Along with his brother-in-law Albert Schuldt, he formed a partnership and they planned to start selling the new Kaiser-Frazers as soon as they could get them. Since Tony's name was virtually a household word around Blue Island, near Raceway Park, they decided that would be a perfect location. Tony was impressed with the K-F organization and he told Emil that it'd be a good company to work for. Joe Frazer was an old-line automobile man who knew what he wanted in the way of sales and service, and the men he sent out to do his field work quickly gained the confidence of his dealer network. In reality, Henry Kaiser was using Frazer's years of automotive knowledge and contacts, but no matter what his motives, the dealers would be well cared for. Tony told Emil about the factory service rep's job that was open and helped his old tutor obtain the position.

Val's Dad was pulled into Tony's organization without much coaxing. He'd tired long ago of owing his soul to the Rock Island and welcomed the change. He'd learned to like Tony as did Val's Mother, now that she could see he was a devoted family man. His choice of professions, driving race cars, wasn't exactly her idea of a stable existence, but the gregarious Tony was able to charm her the same way he had done to so many others. And he *was* able to be easy going, at least around her. But Val said he was certainly stern with the kids. When Daddy was around you minded your P's and Q's.

The Bettenhausen-Schuldt Kaiser-Frazer dealership opened in an old Nash showroom up on Western Avenue along automobile row. Althought the new brands weren't priced as cheaply as the makers had originally hoped for, the press had given them good reviews which resulted in a steady stream of buyers. "Uncle Tom" McCahill, the respected car critic of *Mechanix Illustrated* said:

> Get a good grip on your hats, competitors, because the Frazer is one of the finest riding automobiles I have ever been in regardless of price, and from the standpoint of roadability, I don't know of a car that can touch it.

The Kaiser car was originally designed to be a front wheel drive (which Tony also liked, especially after his experience with one at Indianapolis) but gear problems were encountered, making it too noisy for passenger car use. The idea was scrapped and the Kaiser became rear drive also. Al and Tony wound up selling conventional cars.

Al Schuldt had respected Tony's ability with the mechanical end of things and his own background included that of an appliance and car salesman. He had suggested to Tony that they form a partnership for an auto agency. Al figured he'd run the showroom while Tony took care of the service, but it didn't really work out that way. Many of Tony's fans wanted to buy a car from him and weren't interested in talking to another salesman. Tony popped in and out of the place on an unscheduled basis, and poor Al wound up with a hectic existence. Despite the inevitable bickering that was caused by Tony's infrequent appearances, the business survived. It didn't take a P.T. Barnum to sell cars in the post-war years.

There wasn't an end to the 1946 season as far as Midget racers were concerned. Now they were running the small cars in parts of the country that had never seen them before the war. On both coasts, in the Midwest, and even down South, you could run seven nights per week if you wanted. No one thought it would ever end. The purses were fat and the cars were no longer the old ones pulled from unused garages during the war years. There was a man in California named Frank Kurtis who set up an assembly line to mass produce the small racers. The wheels of American were not only turning, they were churning up dirt that had lain dormant for years. And the public loved it.

After taking up his usual residence at the Chicago Ampitheatre in the winter, Tony became a three-in-a-row winner, got upside down in February and talked of the upcoming "500". He was firmly entrenched as not only a respected member of the Chicago Gang, but Tony's name wasn't left out of any race track or bar room conversations that spoke of the nation's winning race car drivers. He hadn't won the Speedway yet, but it was expected he would. You never won at the Speedway, or in the Speedway. You won the Speedway. It was like a ticket guaranteeing you passage through the Pearly Gates. That was it, you couldn't go *no* higher than winning the Speedway. What did you do after you won it? Umm, probably go back and win it again just to show 'em the first time wasn't a mistake. And then? May as well try for three.

While Tony was wrapped up in his auto racing world, partner Al Schuldt knew there was a different side to him that the fans in the granstands never got a chance to see. Or maybe they did, he would muse. He wondered what they would think if they saw him come storming into the new car showroom shoutin' orders and makin' everybody feel like they were a bunch of dumb shits. He hadn't even been around to know what was going on and he'd come in like the Genral. He always wanted to do more. Sell more cars. Promote a little bit. Make a little off a lot of cars rather than a lot off a few. Al and Tony didn't exactly see eye to eye on just how a car business should be run.

"You know what's wrong with you people around here?" Tony chided them one day. "You been in Tinley Park too long. There's a helluva lot goin' on in the world out there. Why I been higher in the air than you guys have been away from this place."

Confident Tony could sell cars. And the Bettenhausen tinkering could find and fix most mechanical problems while the mechanics were still thinking about them. Al Schuldt was relegated to the back seat, if any seat at all, when Mr. Bettenhausen decided to honor the dealership with his presence. But, Al had to admit, the place was making a few bucks so he endured. Tony liked him alright, he just wished he wouldn't be so goddamned conservative. Jesus, he must have Tinley Park-itis; like the rest of Tony's family, he believed, like his brothers Clarence and Herb, still out there on the farm. Herb had taken the place over from Mom and was still just pluggin' along. Then, Tony thought, at least he does have the biggest barn in all of Cook County.

It used to amuse Tony that once in awhile someone would mistake Herb for Tony on those rare occasions that Herb could be coaxed into going to a race track. He'd never forget the night when after a little bumping duel with Jimmy Knight, some lady came up to Herb and called him a "dirty driving bastard" and broke her clipboard over Herb's head. Tony wouldn't let him live that one down.

Throughout the winter of 1947, Tony was able to devote more time to the Kaiser dealership, but running the business wasn't foremost in his mind. He had to have a good car for the next

"500." He was able to make a deal with Lou Moore, one of the country's most respected car owners. Moore's cars were first class. He didn't spare anything to win. Now he had two new vehicles under construction that would be ready for the 1947 "500," The Blue Crown Spark Plug Specials were built specifically for the Speedway. He didn't care much about the other tracks on the Championship circuit; Indy was the big apple. Tony would be a teammate to Mauri Rose, Moore's number one driver and winner of the 1941 race. In his sophomore year at the Speedway, Tony Bettenhausen couldn't have asked for a better opportunity.

But he wanted more. Why couldn't he have a car of his own to run? It was OK to drive for Moore at Indianapolis, but Tony believed he should own an Indy car and maybe put someone else in it for the race. He could always use it for a back-up machine. Besides, not everyone wanted to run the rest of the Champ circuit and he didn't want to get stuck looking for a ride.

Murrell Belanger had just the ticket. He owned an old dirt car that had a broken engine. It was just sitting. Tony talked him into bringing it down to the dealership. "When I get done with it you won't be able to tell it from new," Bettenhausen told him. Murrell bought the idea, and for the next few months Tony spent so much time working on the car that Val referred to the car agency as the Kaiser Motel.

As Speedway time drew nearer, the talk around the racing crowd was that there'd be a driver boycott this year. A group of drivers formed their own association and called it ASPAR, (American Society of Professional Auto Racing). They didn't think the Speedway was paying out nearly enough in prize money. Their goal was to receive 40 percent of the total gate. The entry blank had promised participants of the 1947 event a guarantee of $75,000 but many of the sport's top names believed a substantial increase was in order. It had been said that Ralph Ammon up at the Milwaukee track was going to institute a 40 per cent policy, so if Milwaukee did, why shouldn't the Speedway? Emil Andres was a staunch supporter of the move among the Midwestern racers and he was soon joined by Duke and Tony. They reasoned, as did many others, that if such a prominent driver such as Ralph Hepburn, who was President of the group, was for the boycott, they'd have plenty of horsepower in obtaining their demands. Hepburn convinced owners not to send in their entry blanks and many drivers agreed they wouldn't break their own picket line. Even if a car owner entered a car, they wouldn't drive.

Lou Moore said he had a responsibility to his sponsor, the Blue Crown Spark Plug people, and he was going to have a car in the

1947 "500" come hell or high water. He told Tony to forget about the boycott or else he'd get someone else to drive the car. Mauri Rose didn't join the action and was at the Speedway the day it opened. He was an engineer for Blue Crown. Duke had a ride in the highly touted German Mercedes car and everyone believed the car was capable of winning the event, but it's owner, Don Lee, told Nalon the same thing: Either you get over here and drive this thing or we're going to put someone else in it. He, too, declined.

Speedway President Wilbur Shaw held a meeting with the ASPAR members in the infield and stated his side of the story. He said that track owner Tony Hulman would add to the purse if it were economically feasible. Wilbur was subjected to charges of being a turncoat. He wouldn't talk like that if he were still driving, they said. It was a poor circumstance. The ASPAR members had already missed the deadline for entering their cars, but the Speedway needed the additonal entries. The first weekend of qualifying made it clear there were not going to be enough cars and drivers available to make a 33 car starting field. By the time ASPAR and the Speedway reached an agreement, Bill Holland had been named as Tony's replacement. Tony landed a ride driving for wealthy sportsman Joel Thorne, himself a driver but unable to participate in the '47 race due to injuries received in a motorcycle accident only a few months earlier. Tony's own car, still registered to Murrell Belanger, was given to driver Mel Hansen.

Bettenhausen had only a few practice laps in the Thorne car when he attempted to qualify it on the last day. Going into the first turn he began what was later termed a "deadly slide." He recovered with no more than worn tires, went out a second time only to burn a piston on his first lap. He didn't like doing it, but Tony had to inform Hansen, who was waiting in the qualifying line, that he would not be allowed to run the car. Bettenhausen himself hopped in the machine and again qualified for the ninth row. And due to the boycott staged by ASPAR, the field wound up three cars short.

In the race itself Tony didn't fare much better than the year previous. A timing gear broke on him and he was credited with 18th position. Holland and Rose, however, were the stars of the show. Rookie Holland led much of the race and was seemingly assured of winning. His crew flashed him the "E-Z" sign on the 183rd lap, only 17 laps from the finish. Teammate Rose was in second spot by a comfortable margin over third. The Lou Moore team was headed for a 1-2 finish. And Tony believed he could have easily been where Holland was. Holland knew he had a

Tony's 1947 "500" ride. [*IMS*]

comfortable lead, but he wasn't sure of just how far. Then the crew gave Rose and "OK" sign as well. Rose drove around a willing Holland who would later comment, "I thought I had a two lap lead on him." Rose's pass came just seven laps from the finish and when he took the lead the crew gave them both the "OK" sign once more. As the checkered flag fell, they *both* raised their hands in victory. Holland could not believe he wasn't the winner. Had his crew allowed him to let Rose pass by? Did Lou Moore intentionally slow him down so that the veteran could take the win? Moore denied such allegations and tried to temper the action as much as he could. The incident was talked about for months after the race. Tony told Nalon that if he'd been in the car there was no way he would have let Rose by. But it didn't really matter now, Tony Bettenhausen and his 18th place finish went home with $1,500. Holland took $30,000 out of the total Speedway pot of $135,000. In reality the Speedway paid out some $98,000 and the remainder came from accessory and lap prize money. ASPAR didn't get their 40 per cent and Tony Bettenhausen wasn't considered a potential to win the race.

Tony went back to running the Midwestern Midget circuit and managed to win one out of every three races he entered for the rest of the season. As he had done the year prior, he went to Walsh Stadium the week following the Speedway . . . and flipped again during qualifying. The *National Speed Sport News* story said:

> When removing Tony from under the car, his first words were, 'I'm OK . . . how's the car? Can I still drive it?'

In July the paper said of Tony's performance at Milwaukee:

> Tony Bettenhausen lived up to his name "Flip" and did that in the Tuffanelli Offy . . . his life was probably saved by his crash helmet which was split right down the center.

* * *

Despite his disappointment of not driving for Lou Moore at Indianapolis, Tony was again enjoying a fine summer of racing. He liked the respect he had earned as one of the country's top Midget racers and never found himself in the midst of the many arguments that would crop up in the pits after a particularly rough race. It seemed like every once in a while, two drivers were ready to go to blows over a wheel banging incident. Tony would root his way through to the front in classic Midget racing tradition, but he was skillful enough not to get anyone but himself upside down in the process. Plus, he was becoming a master of the psyche school of competition. Sometimes he'd help out a fellow driver who would ask him to test an ill-handling car. Always throwing caution out of the cockpit, Tony would do his level best to drive the car just a bit faster than its regular driver. Then in typical fashion he'd come in and say, "Nothing wrong with that thing. You just gotta stand on it a little harder." And if he really felt that a chassis adjustment was in order, he'd casually suggest what should be done. He loved to tell a driver starting ahead of him that he was going to "blow by you" on such and such a lap. And because he'd grin as he was saying it, and would risk life and limb to live up to his prediction, he gained a Babe Ruth kind of respect. Drivers often waved or gave each other "the finger" as they passed one another even if it meant taking your hand off the wheel at a crucial moment. There was a camaraderie out there on the track and in the pits that the people in the grandstands were never privy to. Sometimes Tony would walk up to a fellow driver, elbow him in the ribs and say, "Where do you want me to go around you, on the inside or outside?"

It was a good time at the races. Like a reunion of the family several nights of the week. You came to know what to expect of your fellow competitors and among them, Tony Bettenhausen was right at home. Nothing about the whole business was boring. It was a new challenge every time you unloaded. You were all-consumed with making the car work for the particular race track you were on. Tony liked the feeling that he was earning everything that came his way. Nothing was given to you in this business, especially a good performance, and he didn't have much respect for anyone who wasn't willing to work for what they wanted. Overall, his attitude was easy-come, easy-go. "Money? Money's for spending," he'd tell Duke. Tony didn't have much time for free-loaders either.

One night in mid-July, on the way home from Walsh Stadium, along with Nalon and announcer Twenty Grand Steinbock, Tony pulled into a gas station some 200 miles from Chicago and said, "Now look at old Twenty Grand. There he goes again. Heading for the restroom. How come every time we get gas anywhere he does a disappearing act? He never lets loose with a nickel."

"I know," Duke replied. "But he's OK. He's just a little more thrifty, you might say, than we are."

"Well, let's see how the thrifty sonofabitch likes takin' the train. That's a train depot over there, isn't it?" Tony asked.

"Yep," Duke noted. "The Green Diamond train comes through here."

And without a word of goodbye to Twenty Grand, Tony dropped the Kaiser in low gear and roared off.

"I don't believe you did that," Duke said.

"Neither do I, but if feels good," laughed Tony.

Nalon recalls that neither his name nor Bettenhausen's was mentioned over P.A. systems much for the remainder of the summer while Twenty Grand was on the job.

Although the Midget races were drawing standing room only crowds several nights per week and were paying sizeable purses, the real money was still to be had at the few Championship car races. The Champ cars were the major league. When you were an established Championship Trail star, there was no comparison to being a Midget standout. Every part of the country had its own Midget stars, and while Tony was one of them in the Midwest, his accomplishments couldn't match Bill Schindler on the East coast who had racked up over 40 feature wins by August. And there wasn't really a national Midget champion because there wasn't just one circuit they all raced on. The term National Champion was reserved for the man who garnered the most points in the AAA Championship division. He was the unrivaled National Driving Champion. In addition to winning at Indy, Tony had his eyes set on the AAA National Championship.

At Goshen, New York, for the second year in a row, he proved himself an able competitor against the nation's best. He staged a race-long duel with two-time National Champion Ted Horn and ran in front of him all the way. Race reporter Chris Economaki called Tony a "master of the triangular shaped speedway." At one point in the race Horn had cut Tony's lead by five seconds. Duke

Tony and car owner Murrell Belanger with the Championship machine Tony ran in the summer of 1947. [*Bettenhausen Coll.*]

had dropped out of the race and was in Tony's pit. The racing paper report said:

> Nalon held up a blackboard which read: "HORNS TIRED -- R U?" Bettenhausen nodded in the negative and stepped it up to the finish coming home a good quarter of a minute ahead of Horn.

Duke then signalled Tony to keep on going after the checkered flag, which Tony did without question. Four laps. Duke told him later that he just wanted to make absolutely certain who the winner was. Tony grinned and said thanks.

While Tony somewhat flaunted his devil-may-care attitude to Nalon, he appreciated the concern. It was different with the others. Nowadays Tony would run against Russo at least once a week on the Midget circuit and they carried on a continual needling contest. Russo had maintained his status as a top-notch Midget driver over the years, but realized Tony was now capable of running with, or ahead of him on virtually any track they raced. Tony's friendship with Emil was closer now than ever. For the 1947 season they were running the Championship cars as teammates. Murrell Belanger had purchased a car from Emil and kept him on as driver. They made a formidable team. Emil was a past-master of the Champ cars and skillfully taught Tony some of the finer points of driving that would refine his style. Like the Duke, he too was always trying to temper the anxious Bettenhausen. Mechanics Frenchy Sirois and Buss Brownell called the drivers a couple of squareheads and the foursome usually made up one of the more jovial teams at a race track. It was Bettenhausen, they agreed, who always treated the problems with an attitude of, "This ain't work . . . it's fun."

The one Bettenhausen close companion who treated the sport more like a job was Henry Banks. Methodical old Henry. He'd check every detail and seemed to have a high respect for a machine he knew was capable of taking life's breath out of him. Henry planned on being around awhile and he'd already proven that his plodding along the same route had kept him from incurring injury while making him a threat to win most any race he entered. If something spectacular were to take plae, it was not expected that Henry would initiate it. Probably Tony. Emil, Duke, Russo, and Henry all treated him like the little brother who was going to get himself into trouble. Since they knew him before the war, they felt like they'd grown up with him. Take care of him a little. Tony didn't get the same response from buddies Johnnie Parsons and Johnny McDowell. They wanted to stand on the gas, too. Get there in a hurry. Duke and Tony's friendship was often written about in the nation's two racing papers. After Tony had won another feature at Blue Island, *National Speed Sport News* said:

> To elaborate further on the feature race, Nalon *had* his buddy Bettenhausen twice during the race when he held the lead momentarily.

When Tony beat Duke, there was a mutual respect that lasted without the wisecracks. Duke was always concerned about Tony's safety. He'd continually tell him not to take so many chances. He didn't have to *always* run up high. Be a little smoother, he'd say. Tony would tell him it looked better to be up there next to the guard rail. Felt good, too. There's nothing like giving 'er a big pitch and slidin' for all you're worth. The week before Bettenhausen and Nalon ran 1-2 at Blue Island, the paper had said Bettenhausen hit the outside guard rail no less than 11 times during the 25 lap feature. Duke told him that if he kept up that kind of activity, he'd be in for some serious sheet time in the near future. And as usual, Tony just laughed and told the Duke that he worried too much.

Tony always bragged with Henry too, but it was good natured. On his own Midget tour in the summer of 1947, Henry stopped by the farm, stayed overnight and was told by Tony: "Listen, I know where there's this keen little track where you haven't run before. Not too far from here. Let's go."

The track was a high-banked quarter mile, with no guard rail. It was located in Mazon, Illinois.

Henry Banks set a record that stood for over 20 years at Mazon, IL with this clean Midget. Tony's #1 car can be seen in the background. [*Henry Banks Coll.*]

Tony said, "Watch this, we'll set quick time for 'em." Then he went out and performed his prediction.

Henry countered, "That wasn't all that great. We'll really cut you a good one."

Banks went out and set a track record that would hold for the next 22 years. He won the race with Tony right behind.

Tony added more belief to the notion he was National Championship material after he beat Ted Horn again in the 100-mile race at Springfield in September of 1947. Now more than ever, it appeared as though a new American racing hero was budding. Tony Bettenhausen had paid his dues on every kind of track in the U.S. from the high-banked boards of Nutley to the bricks of Indianapolis. He didn't win on just one type of track in one kind of car, he drove Midgets, Sprints and now the Championship cars, all with equal prowess.

* * *

Ernie Schlausky had become Ernie "Crocky" Warren shortly after the war ended and had begun pursuing his Midget and Motorcycle racing career. He was plagued with mediocre equipment and was considered an "also-ran" in the Midget races. However, in the more evenly matched motorcycle races he usually ran right up front. One day he and three Italian friends were on their way to an unsanctioned motorcycle race, one where they could be fined if their own association (American Motorcycle

Ernie Schlausky became Crocky Wright while racing motorcycles.

Crocky and the checkered helmet he'd wear for many years.

Crocky Wright in 1946. He's in a "B" class Midget, a car that wouldn't be competitive on a professional circuit. [Crocky Wright Coll.]

Association) found out they were running. Each decided to take on a new name for the day. The Italians unwittingly adopted other Italian names and Crocky Warren saw a truck that said "Wright Truck Lines." Ernie Schlausky thus became Crocky Wright. The plan didn't work and all four were fined. But Crocky liked the name and continued to use it.

Although his racing career wasn't skyrocketing as he had hoped, he met a beautiful New York model named Josephine Protko, who became Jo Paris when she worked for all the big department stores. She loved going to the races with dapper looking Crocky and he finally felt a true replacement for his first lost love Gene Kushman. She wanted to marry him.

Crocky gave serious consideration to his stature in life. He was obsessed with the idea of winning the Indianapolis 500, but wasn't inching toward the goal. He wasn't winning Midget races, much less being offered a ride at Indianapolis. Maybe he'd become a journalist. He had liked writing for the Army newspaper and everyone always complimented him on his sports stories. Maybe he could go to college. Uncle Sam would pay the bill. But the officials he talked to said he'd have to go back and finish high school. They couldn't let him in a New Jersey school without a diploma. He took an equivalency test and was accepted at the Ohio State University.

On the drive to Columbus, Ohio the thought of racing at Indianapolis wore on his mind. He pulled into the campus, made one lap around and headed back to New Jersey without so much as stopping at the school. He was going to be an Indianapolis 500 race car driver. He reasoned that he just needed a few breaks.

Soon Jo Paris was telling him that she often dreamed of him being hurt in a race car. Wouldn't he please stop? She didn't want him to be hurt, or killed. Crocky couldn't concentrate with her around. She didn't understand just how *important* it was to be an Indy 500 driver. She said it was either her or the race cars. He told her good-bye.

* * *

Although several issues of both racing newspapers had proclaimed "Stock Car Racing Becoming Popular' in late 1947, the Midget racers were expecting another banner year. The AAA, the organization that held sanction over the Indianapolis 500 and the rest of the Championship circuit as well as many major Sprint car races, decided to enter the Midwest Midget racing field in full force. A seven night per week schedule was announced at tracks in

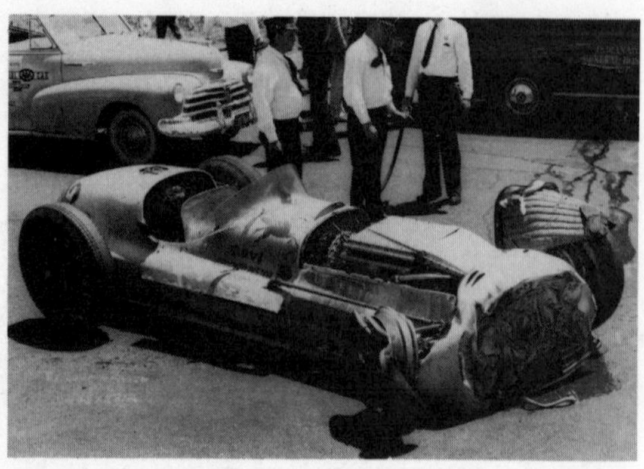

Ralph Hepburn's Novi after his 1948 crash.

Illinois, Wisconsin, Missouri and Michigan. The winter crowd at the Amphitheater was down a bit from previous years but no one seemed worried that there were too many Midget races being presented. Tony planned another full season campaign in the small cars in addition to running Murrell Belanger's Championship car not only at Indianapolis but the rest of the circuit as well.

The Kaiser-Frazer dealership was holding its own and allowed Tony to concentrate on his racing activity. Tony's ride as Belanger's number one driver for the 500 couldn't be considered as good as the chance he had with Lou Moore, but the car was considered better than average. Moore decided to give Bill Holland a ride for the 1948 race, especially in view of the fact that there was a strong possibility he should have won the '47 event. The Blue Crown cars were still considered the class of the field and the only cars around that anyone figured could beat them were the Novis. The Novis were over-powered brutes, they claimed. Had a personality of their own. Everyone agreed that if you could ever harness one, you might be long-gone from the rest of the field, but you just might become a Speedway statistic in the process.

Veteran motorcycle and race car driver Ralph Hepburn spun one of the Novi team cars on the second day of qualifying for the '48 500, and after heading toward the infield grass, he gave the low-slung machine a little more throttle. The front wheel drive machine pawed at the pavement and shot toward the outer wall. It took them 15 minutes to remove Hepburn's dead body from the wreckage. Just a few days earlier another Speedway veteran, Cliff Bergere, had spun the car and quit the team, declaring it unsafe. Indianapolis newspapers had a field day surveying the so-called "jinx car."

Duke Nalon and the Novi. [*IMS*]

Duke and Tony talked about the vehicle. It was true that Hepburn had set a Speedway qualifying record with it in 1946, but there must have been something wierd about the Novi. Good drivers like Bergere and Hepburn just didn't spin out for no good reason. Duke was offered the ride in the twin to the Hepburn car and after a few laps he said ok, he'd drive it. Then he too, spun. Tony told him maybe it wasn't such a good idea if he drove the Novi. Duke laughed and said, "Now look who's worried. I know what's wrong with the thing. The brake and clutch pedals are too close together and you get fouled up."

Duke had the team make some changes in the pedals and qualified faster than anyone else in the 33 car starting field. He wouldn't start on the pole because he wasn't ready the first day of qualifications. And Tony didn't get in the field til the last day, so he was starting back in the eighth row, 22nd spot. But his speed was good, so he was certain he'd be up front before too many laps had passed. Tony was happy to be in the race no matter where he started. He and Belanger had suffered mechanical problems all month long. He was better off than Henry Banks, who had missed making the field completely. Undaunted, Henry unloaded his Midget and went across the street to the 16th Street Midget race track and ran until the wee hours of the morning the night before the 500. They always held two Midget races the night before the big race and performed before a full house. The joke around the pits at Indy was always, "Well, it looks like I'm gonna get bumped out of the line-up here, so may as well go across the street and start lookin' for a ride."

At the end of the first 25 laps of the 1948 race, Tony had worked his way up to eighth position. Then he was seventh and looked like he had a firm hold on fifth for most of the event. The two Blue

Crowns with Rose and Holland were again the stars of the day until Duke proved to them he had the Novi under full control. The trio ran within striking distance of each other, but this year it was Nalon who was in the lead. On the 166th lap, Tony pulled into the pits with a broken clutch. He went toward the Duke's pit to see what they were telling him on his pit board. Duke wasn't scheduled for another stop and looked like he had the race in the bag. He's nearly a lap ahead of Rose. Then with only 16 laps remaining, he comes in. Needs fuel. What the hell happened? They were supposed to have filled the thing completely. He's re-fueled and Rose passes by. But there's still time to get back out and catch him. Nalon and the Novi have a faster combination. Then Holland passes, too. And the Novi dies. It won't re-start. Up goes the hood, then Ted Horn passes by. The engine starts but it's too late. Duke has time enough to go back out and pass Horn for third, but the deficit was too much to make up. Once again, Mauri Rose wins; Bill Holland second. And because of pit work, Duke Nalon misses the best chance he ever had for an Indy 500 victory.

Afterwards, Duke tells Tony that maybe they both ought to drive Novis next year. If they're around that long.

For the 1948 "500" Belanger had entered and run two cars. Tony's teammate was fellow Midget driver Duane Carter. Carter was as good a Midget driver as they came, and he, too, had fulfilled a long-time ambition of becoming a Speedway driver. In the race he was also victimized by mechanical failure. The rear axle broke, a wheel came off, and he was sent spinning into the outer retaining wall. You didn't mind so much when you made a mistake that caused a crash, but it was frustrating beyond hope, unexplainable, when some part decided to give up the ship. After the race it was again agreed that Tony would stay on and run Murrell's car on the rest of the Champ circuit. Tony would cut back a little on his Midget racing schedule, but was anxious to run the practically new Midget he had bought from Emil.

Andres had purchased the car only a few months earlier, but decided he didn't want to run Midgets much anymore and Tony was a willing buyer. Now he could try all the little tricks he had in the back of his mind that the other car owners were reluctant to experiment with. Yes sir, a little of the old Bettenhausen wrenching and he'd have this new Kurtis-Kraft whipped into shape in no time. They'd all be running for second.

Since Tony was track champion at Blue Island and up at Milwaukee again, he had earned the right to carry a number 1. The car appeared as the Bettenhausen-Schuldt Kaiser Frazier Special. But the number wasn't indicitive of the car's finishing position.

Tony, Al Schuldt and the Midget Tony bought from Emil Andres. [Bettenhausen Coll.]

Tony would have just as soon forgotten the summer of '48 as far as his Midget racing record was concerned. He was his own toughest competition. He couldn't buy a win. He registered a few 3rds, 4th, and 5th place finishes and some in the double-digit column as well.

"You are spending a fortune on that thing," Emil told him. "Why don't you just run it the way it is? Nothing wrong with it. You'll win if you leave it alone."

While some thought Bettenhausen's driving ability might be slipping, he proved just the opposite in the few Champ car races he ran. The week after the Speedway had run, he went to Milwaukee and qualified second fastest. Then a couple of weeks later he won at the same track. But it was the last Champ race of the year there in August that he really remembered. Going down the long backstretch, Russo, who was running far behind, crashed and was tossed out of his car. He lay prone on the track with a full field bearing down on him. Ted Lake, one of the AAA officials, jumped off his observer's stand and started waving the yellow flag while running toward the prostrate body. Everyone credited Lake with saving Russo's life. Paul was another one of the drivers who didn't believe in wearing seat belts. While they were taking him to the hospital, Tony was busy hopping from his own broken car to drive relief for Myron Fohr. Between the two they won the race.

The grandstand audience loved the performance. This was definitely Tony Bettenhausen country. The following week he

Twenty Grand Steinbock, behind microphone, presents Tony and Myron Fohr their win at Milwaukee. (Krueger)

went back to the beer producing city and won his first Midget race of the season. It was September now and not many weeks of racing left. But he had just proven that he could win with his own car. It didn't matter that it happened on the Milwaukee quarter, a track he knew as well as the deep creases in his hands. Now he could go to the biggest Midget race of the year, on the DuQuoin, Illinois, mile with some confidence. Most of the Midget racers were used to running on the quarters, the little tracks. He'd have a decided advantage. A win at DuQuoin would be good for his ego.

"He's on fire! they screamed from the pits. Tony was half in and half out of the car, heading down the straight-a-way. Smoke was streaming from the cockpit. You could see the smoke, but not the fire. Burning alcohol didn't give off a bright flame like gasoline did. Sometimes it was deceiving, you'd think a man was on fire and it was only steam from the radiator. But you never took a chance. Hit him with the fire extinguisher.

Tony didn't give them a chance. While still at speed he jumped from the burning vehicle and rolled on the Illinois soil. The driverless car continued into the pit opening and toward a large lagoon in the center of the track. Tony ran toward it as did several other men and all began pushing it into the lake. His legs were hot, but he didn't realize that his high felt boots were on fire until someone yelled, "You're on fire!" Then it all caught up with him. He dropped to the ground and began feverishly patting the boots. A blanket was thrown over his legs and the flames snuffed. The ambulance was on its way. Pain like he'd never felt before. Getting upside down is one thing, he thought, but fire's another.

Val wasn't in her grandstand seat as Tony started out in his qualifying run. She didn't see what happened. But she heard the crowd groan. As she came running back from a concession stand under the grandstand she heard the name "Bettenhausen" come from a spectator. There was a crowd gathering on the track. By the time she got there they were loading him in the ambulance.

"I'm okay . . . I'm okay," were Tony's first words.

She could see that he was at least conscious and talking. What's wrong? Burns! Oh my God.

After an overnight stay in the hospital, where they treated him for second and third degree burns on his legs, Tony insisted he be taken home. Val went out and bought sheets and along with mechanic Jimmy Siddle's help, turned their Kaiser Vagabond into a temporary ambulance. On the long drive home he couldn't get comfortable. He held his legs outside so the air would cool them. There was no talk about the next race, or any other race. She took him straight to the hospital. He never once mentioned the word "retirement," but he didn't get in another race for the remainder of 1948. Everyone came to see him, it seemed. Tony particularly liked the two Californians, Johnnie Parsons and Johnny McDowell, who visited. They had both moved to the Midwest for the summer season and had become part of the clique at the races. They were both winners. They called him hotfoot.

It was later discovered that a clamp around the fuel line had come loose and the underpan filled with fuel. Tony deemed himself lucky and had no one to blame for the loose clamp. He was the mechanic. Next year would be better, he thought.

* * *

Tony was shocked by the news: Ted Horn fatally injured at DuQuoin. Jesus, Horn was good. The absolute best. If he can get killed in a race car, then maybe anybody can.

Horn's accident also was due to mechanical failure. The left front spindle, the piece that connects the wheel to the axle had broken. Horn, too, was pitched out of the car and never regained consciousness. The race was only a token appearance for him. He had already clinched the AAA National Driving Championship for the third consecutive year and he didn't have to run. Tony was glad he hadn't been there to see it.

Tony busied himself in the winter of 1948-49 converting his Kaiser to V-8 engine power. The 1949 restyled Kaisers had arrived, but much to Bettenhausen's disliking, they had retained the old six-cylinder engine. Even though the company was able to claim more horsepower per cubic inch than any manufacturer other than Hudson, the switch to the V-8 engine had begun. And while Kaiser-Frazer continued to lead the industry, in the choice of interior and exterior color combinations, they couldn't call one of their models a "Rocket" like Oldsmobile did. Tony never did like the Kaiser engine. Said it reminded him of something that ought to be in a tractor. He ordered a new Cadillac V-8 engine and made himself a personalized vehicle. At the same time he started shopping for a good car to drive at the Speedway. He hadn't gone back to the Amphitheatre races in the winter as he usually did. And he didn't have any plans to compete in the opening races over East, either. Business wasn't too good at the dealership and he thought it might use a little more attention. Maybe he could get a ride in the second Novi car. He'd be Duke's teammate.

But it wasn't to be. Although Tony Bettenhausen was known and respected throughout the racing game, his reputation had come from his dirt-track performances. The second Novi car was given to Rex Mays. Even Tony admitted that Rex was probably the best choice. He had already proven himself a worthy Speedway competitor, he'd qualified for the pole before and finished second twice. Next to Ted Horn, Mays was probably the best known and respected driver in America. Tony kept looking. There wasn't any room on the Blue Crown team. He didn't want to take a ride in just any old shitbox, but it looked like he'd have to settle for something less than he hoped for.

When the line-up for the 1949 Indianapolis 500 was finally settled upon, Tony Bettenhausen's name was down at the bottom:

Alternate Starter

He'd been bumped. The procedure was simple. The first 33 cars to accept their qualifying attempts made up the field. Then the bumping started. The slowest man in the field was "on the bubble." The next driver who went out and bettered the 33rd man's time bumped that car rom the line-up. The displaced driver could go scramble for another ride, and usually the last day of qualifying from 4 to 6 o'clock saw a game of muscial chairs being played by owners and drivers trying to guess which way to go. What will the bubble speed be? Who should I put in the car?

While Tony was trying to accept his fate, Duke and Rex Mays were basking in their glory. They were starting 1-2, with Duke on the pole. It could be a Novi clean sweep. Duke deserved it, he should have won last year, they said.

Duke Nalon's Novi against the wall amidst a wall of flame. [*IMS*]

On the 24th lap of the race everyone pointed to a long, black column of smoke that was rising from the north turn. Nalon! The record-breaking leader. He was the class of the field just a moment ago and now he was feeling the same sensations about his face and hands that vibrated through Tony's legs at Duquoin. Dazed and burning, he made his way out of the car and toward the approaching ambulance. Even the Iron Duke hadn't tamed the Novi. A broken left rear axle had sent him crashing into the outer retaining wall. A few laps later Mays' machine broke. And Bill Holland won in a Blue Crown. Tony had offered to drive relief for Myron Fohr and showed up at his pit dressed for action. His services weren't needed.

The Duke wasn't disfigured by his second degree burns, but his cheeks were definitely a lighter color than the rest of his face. "There wasn't a thing I could do," he told Tony from his Methodist Hospital bed. "One second it was fine, and then bingo! The left rear dropped and she was sideways. I knew it was going to be a bad one."

It wasn't a particularly good "500" for any of Tony's close friends, save for Parsons. He "lucked into" second place finish in Tony's words. Russo was eighth, Emil was ninth and McDowell was 18th, and Henry Banks, like Tony, was bumped from the field.

At the Midget races following the 500 they asked, "Where's Bettenhausen?" He didn't go to Walsh Stadium, nor Raceway Park where he was usually assured of a healthy paycheck or even up to Milwaukee. Word was that Tony Bettenhausen had retired from Midget racing. Those DuQuoin burns had something to do with it, they said. Besides, he wants to race Champ cars. Most of the big timers in Champ cars don't run Midgets, anyhow, it was agreed.

Tony never mentioned the fact he was in fact taking a brief retirement from Midget racing. The racing writers themselves drew their own conclusions. More than one said he was conspicious in his absence. After a time, the Bettenhausen-Schuldt Midget began appearing with Gus Klingbeil as its driver. Gus was capable and ran right up front.

Tony was not the only one taking a retirement from Midget racing, many fans were as well. Now, in the late summer of 1949, the *National Speed Sport News* (NSSN) was devoting a full page of editorial matter to "Stock Car and Hot Rod Activities." An editorial by Pop Green said in part:

> Too much of any one thing makes anyone sick. Some years ago the Midgets came on to the stage and for a time, put new life into the sport and completely revived it. At first there were many different types of cars and the show was colorful. Now the field has narrowed down to virtually only two types of cars, Offenhausers and Fords, and one type of chassis . . . . it is certain that a complete radical change in racing is badly needed . . .

The stock cars and the hot rods have been invading Midget territory slowly but ever so surely. The Midget racers called them jalopies, but they did provide numberable crashes each evening and at least they all looked different. The Midgets ran more and more "parades" on the paved tracks and with the exception of color and number, they all looked like they were carbon copies of one another. Midget builder Frank Kurtis never anticipated he would turn out so many of the small cars that his own particular brand virtually dominated the entire sport. The Midgets still held full schedules in the Midwest, and on both coasts, but down South the stock car was taking hold. An "All Colored Boys" race was advertised in South Carolina and the ads said, "There will not be any drivers except the coloreds, but space will be reserved for all white spectators wishing to see this race." Stock cars. The Midget and Sprint car racers called them taxicabs. Fender benders. But like it or not, Midget auto racing was on a rapid decline.

The fans, however, still had a predilection for Championship car racing. They were always advertised as being the most sophisticated racing machinery in the world. And they were the only cars that featured true Indianapolis 500 stars as drivers. But even the Indy drivers would take an occasional ride in a stock car if the money was there. During the annual Milwaukee State Fair, Russo, Tony and Rex Mays ran stock cars before some 23,000 fans. Russo won it in a '49 Cad while Tony's new Olds lasted only 37 laps. It was good money, they agreed, and you couldn't get hurt with all that sheet metal around you.

But it was the Championship races that Tony was looking forward to. He had obtained a new ride in one of the most impressive cars ever to appear on the Championship Trail. Offenhauser engine builders Louis Meyer and Dale Drake had come up with the idea of installing a supercharged Midget engine in a lightweight Championship car. The red car carried the number 99 and looked more like a cross between a Midget and a Sprint car than it did a full size Indy racer. Ace mechanic George Salih was to campaign the vehicle during the 1949 season and he recommended Bettenhausen as its driver because, "this thing needs to be wound up in the corners . . . we need somebody who'll stand on it for all she's worth."

Some of the other Championship owners noted that it didn't really seem right that Meyer & Drake were competing against them. After all, they had unlimited capacity for replacing engine parts, and everyone who was competitive used an Offy. What were they trying to do? But since Tony didn't outclass everyone right off, the complaints amounted to no more than pit chatter.

Tony had waited until mid-July to take up his Midget schedule again, but only ran about 15 races and most of those were in one of the Bardahl Oil sponsored cars. He always ran in the top five and his own car was now being driven by one Clyde Young. Not surprisingly, Young fared better in the machine than Tony did because he wasn't continually experimenting with it. For the annual early September 100-mile Midget race on the DuQuoin mile, Tony obtained a ride in the Acme number 34 and led the first 85 laps. Late in the race an oil leak developed which blew a hot mist back on Tony's still tender left leg. Rather than pull in, he draped the leg outside the cockpit and continued to lead. He was finally forced to the pits as the oil pressure dropped and was quoted as saying, "Fill 'er up and we'll go back out." He had a two lap lead over the field. A broken spring was located, however, and his day was over. The entire car reeked with the oil fumes and heat. One writer called Bettenhausen either awfully tough, or awfully crazy. Who'd want to drive in that condition?

Just three days before the September 6 Midget race, Tony had proven the Meyer-Drake combination to be a winning one. He had won the 100-mile Championship race. The other owners started talking about the car again. A few days later, on the morning of the Detroit 100-miler, Murrell Belanger consumated a deal to purchase the little 99 and Tony was once again driving for his old

The Acme number 34 which developed an oil leak while Tony was leading at DuQuoin. Undaunted, Bettenhausen draped his leg out of the cockpit. [Gullick Photo Coll.]

boss. Meyer & Drake had practically given the car to Belanger. They not only sold it to him for $7,500, but promised to help him maintain it and agreed that George Salih would continue to help the team. Meyer and Drake were off the hook with the other owners, mechanic Salih still had a new toy to play with and Belanger had Bettenhausen back. They said they were going to re-write the record books. Just as soon as they worked the bugs out of the little supercharged engine, they added.

Five days after their DuQuoin win, Tony added another Championship victory in the 100-mile race at Detroit. He was interviewed after the race by Duke, who had also acted as honorary marshall. Nalon's bout with the Novi had relegated him to spectator status for the 1949 season. The new Belanger 99 team went to three more races in the next three months but encountered mechanical difficulties in every event. Tony wished he hadn't gone to the last race at Del Mar, California. It was there that he saw the great Rex Mays tossed out of his car and run over by two other drivers. Last year it was Horn, this year Mays. Two of the all-time greats. Tony had respected and idolized Mays.

There weren't many drivers who Tony said were absolutely great, but Mays was one of them. The racing community was sickened over the handsome Mays' death. Some guys had just been around so long, and always looked so good driving a race car that you thought they'd already passed up all their chances to be killed. They'd be around forever. Tony went home to Tinley Park and contemplated his future. He'd never said anything to Val about retiring, but she knew he must have talked about it to someone. Sometimes she'd see Dr. Carmichael in the Tinley Post Office and he'd kid her that Tony owed him $50,000. That's how much the bet was for, he'd claim. What bet? Tony bet him $50,000 that he'd never sit in another race car after he was burned at DuQuoin. Val wondered sometimes. But she knew better than to ask him to quit. He was in this business when she married him and she wouldn't badger him to get out. Poor Rex Mays.

The year 1949 had also not been kind to Tony and Al's Kaiser-Frazer dealership, or any other K-F dealership for that matter. The organization had fallen from eighth place in the industry in 1948 with 180,000 car sales to sixteenth place with 58,000 sales in '49. Henry Kaiser and Joe Frazer had disagreed once again on the total outlook of the company. Frazer was still the automobile man, Kaiser the industrialist who refused to listen to Joe's prediction that the organization must retrench. He said they'd do well to sell 70,000 cars in 1949 and had to cut back everything accordingly. Kaiser wasn't one to retreat and claimed he could sell 200,000 cars. The 1949 annual report said it was a bad year because:

1. Insufficient financing
2. K-F had a lack of new models
3. There was a return of the competitive market in the automobile industry.

Frazer was right, but his position in the company had to be relinquished because the Kaiser team had infiltrated management at every level. Frazer was a broken man. Tony Bettenhausen and Al Schuldt became, with several hundred other dealers, victims of the manufacturer's decisions. It didn't appear as though Kaiser-Frazer would be able to complete their entry into the automobile manufacturing business on a long-term basis.

While Tony was trying to make a decision on the dealership (the factory said better things were coming, like a new car, V-8 engine, etc.), he was also wrestling with his thoughts about racing. It was hard to accept Mays' death. But he wanted to win the Speedway. Knew he could do it, if he just had the right car. The little Belanger 99, with its supercharged engine wasn't his idea of a Speedway winner. Now in fact, Belanger and George Salih were talking

Johnnie Parsons and actress Barbara Stanwyck at Indy in 1950. Clark Gable blended into the Speedway activity in 1950.

about putting a conventional Offy in the car. But everyone said it wouldn't fit. Too big. Tony called Lou Moore, the man with Blue Crowns. He knew that Moore and Mauri Rose had just fallen out of love with one another and Rose's ride was vacant. Rose's car had already won the 500 twice, maybe it could carry Tony to a win, too.

The 1950 month of May at the Indianapolis Motor Speedway was like another happy reunion for Tony. He hadn't been in any kind of a race car since Mays was killed at Del Mar and the Illinois winter had passed slowly. Now the Duke was back after having served his time as honorary marshal, starter and general celebrity at the races while waiting for his burns to heal. Russo was there with a new creation that was immediately dubbed "Basement Bessie" by the race crowd. Paul and Ray Nichels had constructed their own Championship car in Paul's basement over the winter. Henry had a good ride and so did pals Johnnie Parsons and Johnny McDowell. Parsons had become a star in his own right after the 1949 season. He had won enough races and earned enough points to be crowned AAA National Driving Champion. At the Speedway in 1950 he was continually smirking. Actress Barbara Stanwyck was always seen talking to the handsome Californian and the new driving champ delighted in the extra attention. Stanwyck, Clark Gable and their MGM crew were shooting the movie "To Please A Lady". Gable was the hero of the racing epic and of course, Barbara was the lady. Gable had

Tony's Blue Crown entry for 1950. [*Bettenhausen Coll.*]

been accepted as one of the boys among the racers and Miss Stanwyck also mingled freely without giving off too many Hollywood airs. Many of the drivers were called upon for not only track scenes, but a few, and Parsons headed the list, actually got screen parts.

Tony was feeling extra sure of himself after qualifying one of the Blue Crowns. Racing writer Russ Catlin reported Bettenhausen said: "Isn't it nice to be able to stand around and watch these guys beat their brains out?" Bettenhausen had been a notorious last-day qualifier in years previous.

While Tony would start the 500 in the third row, Duke and the powerful Novi wouldn't be in the race at all. Duke broke a supercharger part on the last day of qualifications and soberly commented, "It just wasn't meant to be."

Early in the event Tony was a contender. Parsons was leading and Mauri Rose, who had secured another ride with no trouble, was second. Russo was close behind in third and Tony was fourth. Tony went around Russo and car owner Lou Moore signaled Tony to "Get Rose." It didn't happen. Tony pulled in with mechanical trouble on the 38th lap and told Moore that maybe the car was out of the race, but Tony Bettenhausen wasn't. He stormed off looking for a relief ride. Less than a half hour later he took over Joie Chitwood's ride. Chitwood, billed as a Cherokee Indian (from Reading, Pennsylvania), had a hand problem and could use the help. Bettenhausen was back in the race pretending it was a

The respected Blue Crown team in the pits at Indy, 1950. [*Krueger*]

20-lap feature at Nutley. He had no idea of his position, but wouldn't be satisfied until the crew gave him the number 1 signal. It didn't matter that the leaders might have had a couple miles advantage, he'd make it up.

Tony had taken over the Chitwood car just past the 200 mile mark and was credited with ninth position at 250 miles. His crew flashed him #2 on the pit board at 300 miles to which Tony responded with a joyous waving of his fist. Only one car ahead and 200 miles to go! It'd be a cinch. The Tinley Park Express can be the winner of the Indianapolis 500 Mile Sweepstakes.

At 345 miles the Indiana sky unzipped itself and covered the track with rain. Johnnie Parsons is the winner of the 1950 Indy 500. And a recheck of the scoring tape showed that Tony Bettenhausen never was in second place. The scoring procedure is infallible for checking position after the race, but two plastic scoring cards had stuck together and a scorer had erroneously reported Bettenhausen in second. He and Chitwood were credited with fifth. But it was a good ride anyhow, Tony's spirits were up again. He'd run the whole Champ trail again. He'd even run some Midget races.

* * *

6

The Little Jewel

"It's not worth it anymore," Emil said. "The equipment, the help, the money. Nothin's right. I ain't gonna run anymore. That's it. My driving days are over."

Emil Andres was depressed. He hadn't made the Speedway this year and Tony had just lapped him at Milwaukee. Emil didn't consider that Tony had lapped everyone at Milwaukee (Russo finished 35 seconds behind him) to score a wire-to-wire victory in the June Championship race. Emil had his fill. His ego didn't need to be boistered by all the back-patters you find when you got out and set fast time or when you roll into victory lane. Even the money didn't seem important now. Emil Andres was retiring, and he meant it. He would not drive again.

Tony had sold his midget, "Smartest thing you ever did," Emil told him and in his occasional rides he was back up front again. Now, however, the rides had to be occasional, for Midget auto racing in the summer of 1950 was all but dead. More tracks each week announced that the Midgets would be replaced with Stock cars, Jalopies, Hot Rods. The front page of the *National Speed Sport News* sometimes resembled an overall view of a junkyard, crashed stock cars. But the Championship races weren't suffering, 29,000 watched Tony win the Milwaukee race.

Ironically, the Belanger car that Tony won the Milwaukee event in was not the new number 99, but the old #34 that Emil had sold to Murrell a couple seasons prior. Emil made the deal on the morning of a race in Detroit to sell the car to Belanger. The price was finally agreed upon, but no money exchanged hands. Emil went out and won the race and Belanger said he was mighty proud that *his* new car was already paying for itself. Emil took exception and said, "Sorry, it's still my car and prize money til you pay for it." After that, Emil and Belanger fully understood that each was a businessman in his own right.

Although Tony had won with the #34 car, Belanger mechanics Luigi Lesovsky, Tiny Worley and George Salih were all working on the 99. Meyer and Drake had agreed to fabricate some special engine mounts to install the larger Offenhauser engine in the small car, but everyone warned that the combination might not work. Belanger and Bettenhausen weren't currently the best of pals anyhow; Belanger believed that Tony should have been his driver in the 500 and said he'd get someone else to run the 99. Tony didn't quibble, although he liked the little car, and secured a ride in the Shaheen Offy for the August Springfield race. Again, he looked like he would be the winner in the competitive field (some 38 cars took qualifying runs) as he set fast time of the day and led the first 25 laps only to have a tire let go. Russo and "Basement Bessie" won the race. The next day Tony won the rugged 100-mile Midget race at Milwaukee. On the first lap of the race, handsome Al Duris, who was starting way back in 23rd place, flipped to his death in an end for end crash that saw him wind up in the Honey Creek Parkway river.

A week later Chuck Stevenson set a new track record with the Belanger 99 at Milwaukee. By the 20th mile of the 200 mile event Tony was running right behind the Belanger car and soon thereafter Stevenson broke a wheel, giving Bettenhausen the lead. Tony had to make a lengthy pit stop which put him far back and the report in *Speed Age* magazine said:

> Bettenhausen began driving like a madman to make up ground. With his foot down all the way around, he laid his yellow machine against the outer walls of the turns in broadslides that had the fans goggle-eyed......Tony went through traffic like a tornado.

On the 128th lap he broke a throttle shaft to end his day. For all his effort and daring, Tony won the grand sum of $340 which included lap prize money. The Duke was back in action along with Henry Banks (who was having his best year ever) and Russo was proving to be very competitive on the Champ Trail. Russo and Nalon finished fifth and sixth respectively. Now this foursome were all journeymen drivers, running a relaxed schedule of maybe one race per week. Not at all like the old Midget racing days. The Champ cars were supposed to pay big money, and you didn't have to look for a Midget or Sprint show to fill in the gaps. All you had to do was run up front in the Champ shows. Three-hundred and forty dollars for making the fans goggle-eyed. The pay didn't seem commensurate with the performance.

Bettenhausen and Belanger talked things over and agreed they could probably do each other some good again. Tony would drive

Tony and Murrell Belanger with Murrell's "Little Jewel." [*Bettenhausen Coll.*]

Tony took time out in August of 1950 to run a 100 lap Midget race in Milwaukee...and won. [*Krueger*]

Tony and the 99 car on the way to a victory lane in 1950. [Chernokal]

the 99 at Syracuse. In front of 70,000 fans he "performed his seemingly exclusive duty of breaking the track record," said *Speed Age*. He and Russo put on a wheel to wheel duel for the first 24 laps until 99's rear end locked momentarily coming down the main straight. Bettenhausen did a double-spin with cars sashaying on either side. There was no accident and Tony was relegated to 12th finishing position.

The next day there was a race scheduled at Detroit and after grumblings about "Who in the Hell schedules these back-to-back races?" Tony again set another track record and led the race for the 49th thru 88th lap. Patient Henry Banks, who had been riding along in sixth position for the first 40 laps, had inched his way forward and took the lead when Tony went out on the 89th lap. Bettenhausen told Belanger he might win them some races if the little shitbox ever decided to finish. Bettenhausen was one of the major record setters of the season, but he wasn't in the top ten point standings. Russo and Henry were second and third after the Detroit race and the AAA National Driving Championship title was second in importance only to a win at the Speedway.

Three weeks later at Springfield on October 1st, Tony led 99 laps, was passed momentarily by Neal Carter on the last lap, but regained the lead coming down for the checkered flag. Once again he had set fast time of the day and as he drove into victory lane Belanger proudly asked him, "How do you like this little jewel now? She's a honey of a car ain't she?"

To which Tony replied, "If you think this little son-of-a-bitch is getting the job done by itself, turn 'er loose."

Bettenhausen didn't believe he was informed accurately of his position at Springfield by Belanger. He thought he had a comfortable lead and when Carter went around him he wasn't sure if he was in first or second for a moment, but decided to take no chances and gave the car a wild ride to re-pass Carter for the win. Carter had in fact driven a spectacular race and surprised Tony when he pulled up alongside him. It had seemed like only a few minutes earlier that the Belanger crew had given him a pit board telling him he had a 20 second lead on the field. After taking the checkered flag side by side, Tony and Carter saluted each other much to the delight of the packed grandstands.

Bettenhausen and Belanger were the talk of the Championship Trail. Tony now held more one lap and 100 mile records than any other driver on the circuit. The racing writers were running out of adjectives to describe Tony's 1950 performances. At mid-way in the season he wasn't in the top ten in point standings, but now had a clear cut shot at winning the driving championship. There were still four races left on the schedule:

Sacramento
Phoenix
Bay Meadows
Darlington

The Phoenix race was being promoted by J. C. Agajanian, a Stetson wearing Armenian who had been voted the single most popular individual in all of automobile racing by a poll taken by *Speed Age* magazine. Aggie was known throughout the sport as a rich pig farmer who didn't flaunt his wealth. He'd been in racing since the Thirties. His first aspirations were as a driver, but his father informed him that there'd be no place in the Agajanian household for him if he took up the profession. Still enamored with the sport, he became a car owner and later a race organizer when he realized that he and many of his peers were being victimized by shady race promoters who often absconded with the day's purse. The racers themselves came to trust him around the Los Angeles area and he was instrumental in setting up organizations and staging events on a professional level. He had met Tony at the Speedway in '48 and had gained his friendship immediately. Aggie wasn't a car owner who sat in the grandstands. He didn't work on the vehicles he owned; but his white hat and flashy mode of dress were a fixture in the pits, not only at Indianapolis but every race on the Champ Trail. Aggie was ok, they said. He supported the whole circuit. He wasn't like some owners who came just to Indy for all the glory. You'd see him at the Midget and Sprint races too. Most drivers wished they were as recognizable to the public as J. C. Agajanian.

Aggie and Belanger had also become friends and carried on a friendly rivalry. Agajanian had painted a pig on the cowl of his familiar number 98 car and Belanger responded by having an ear of corn drawn on the tail of 99.

"You know we're going to be running ahead of you," Belanger joked. "Just thought we'd put that ear of corn there so your pig knows which car to follow."

At Sacramento Tony once again set fastest time of the day and started in pole position. Aggie's car, with Walt Faulkner aboard, was discovered to have a broken tie-rod just as the race was getting underway. Chief Mechanic Clay Smith decided to change the part and let Faulkner start, although he was some nine laps behind before the replacement was made. On his first lap in the race, Faulkner hit a deep hole and slid in front of Bettenhausen, who was attempting to pass the late comer. Tony missed the car with

Sacramento, 1950 as described in text. [*Bettenhausen Coll.*]

his front wheels, but his left rear climbed over Walt's right rear tire, throwing the 99 out of control into the wooden rail fencing. The car blasted through the white posts, knocked down three small trees and caromed into four spectators standing in a forbidden part of the grounds.

One elderly man was killed almost instantly, another suffered a broken leg and the other two received only minor injuries. Tony was not hurt in the accident.

"How in the Hell could those people have been standing there in the first place?" Tony asked after the wreck. "Jesus Christ, what happened to Faulkner, he just jumped out in front of me?"

Published photos later showed that Faulkner's car had in fact literally bounced out in front of Bettenhausen, but no matter what the reason, Tony was sick over the incident. Now he knew how Emil felt after he, too, had taken a life at the Speedway a few years back. There was no party after the Sacramento race.

A month later the Championship Trail led to Phoenix for another 100 miler. Although Tony started second he was clearly the class of the field once again and led until the race was stopped on the 14th lap. Russo had blown a tire and wound up with a fractured shoulder. His chances for the AAA title were gone. With a victory however, Tony would be the new point leader. Henry was in second place. Bettenhausen led the rest of the day, til the 80th lap when he, too, blew a tire.

Two weeks later they gave a race to Bettenhausen that they shouldn't have. At Bay Meadows, California, there was a 150 miler scheduled and once more Tony was fast qualifier of the day. He led for 149 laps and coasted across the finish line out of fuel. The referee had lost count of the laps and gave Tony the checkered flag. Sam Hanks was close behind in Russo's car. A re-check of the scoring tapes showed Tony had not completed 150 miles, but it was ruled that since the officials had determined at the time that the 99 was the winner, the decision stood. The race went into the record books as a 149 miler.

Walt Faulkner and Henry Banks were running 1-2 for the AAA title and Tony was third going into the last show at Darlington on December 10. Henry wound up winning the title by virtue of his third place finish while Tony was forced out with a broken fuel line while running second. Bank's day was diminished when Walt Brown crashed into the pitwall and hit Henry's long-time helper Julius Schaff. Julius lived to once again help the mild-mannered Banks, and everyone agreed it had been a memorable season.

Now 34 years old, Tony set aside any thought he entertained about retiring. It had been written in the race papers that he had retired after the DuQuoin burns and came back only to drive the famed Lou Moore car at the Speedway. If he ever did retire, Tony had said, he'd still run the Speedway. Retiring meant not driving Midgets or Sprints or the rest of the Champ Trail. Besides, Midgets were just run for fun now anyhow. And Tony didn't drive Sprint cars anymore much to Val's satisfaction. He hadn't been in one since the war ended. There was just something different about those Sprint cars, everyone said. They were over-powered man eaters. Too small for all the horsepower. Seemed like somebody was getting killed in one every week of the summer.

* * *

Another blistery Chicago winter had come and with it the opening of the Amphitheatre. A steady member of the Chicago Gang, little Harry Turner asked Bettenhausen if he'd like to run his car indoors. Turner was a good Midget chauffeur himself, but liked building and tinkering with the cars as much as he did driving. Turner was another one who didn't care if the sun ever came up again. A little music, few beers, some good broads, a buck or two in your pocket and where in the hell's the next race? Harry Turner had spent many a year tucked away working on a race car til the early morning hours and didn't care much about anything else. He didn't hae any aspirations of wearing a suit and tie to work someday. Let's go run indoors and blow their doors off.

A mid-January 1951 shot showing Tony trying to get past Myron Fohr. Myron didn't move and Tony finished behind him. [*Krueger*]

Tony proved that he hadn't forgotten anything about indoor Midget racing by winning the opening 1951 race after a rollicking good time with Cowboy O'Rourke. O'Rourke would nudge him and you could see Bettenhausen laughing behind his bandana. Tony finally gained half a lap lead and held it. Leroy Warriner provided the evening's thrills when he spun, ran over four hay bales, and pinned started Bill Vandewater to the judges table. Van finished out the show but later went to the hospital for x-rays..it was just like old times. After qualifying on a smooth track for the second race, Tony commented that they oughta "dig the place up a little bit and make it rough" so he could drive around it. The third and final indoor show saw Tony get upside down again in spectacular fashion. On the 57th lap he tangled with Ralph Pratt and came to rest upside down with his head in Pratt's cockpit. Laughing at his own predicament he said, "Turn this sumbitch over and get me going again." They re-started the pair and both wound their way back through the field to finish 5th and 6th with Pratt ahead. There was still nothing like running indoors they said. Too bad it didn't last all winter. Now there was nothing to do until Speedway time again.

* * *

Considering the success that Tony, owner Belanger, and mechanic George Salih had during the 1950 season, most Indy 500 followers were surprised when they read that Lee Wallard and not Tony Bettenhausen would be driving the now famous number 99 car for the 1951 Indianapolis 500. Bettenhausen had an agreement

The 99 car in its garage at Indy.

with Lou Moore again for the 1951 race in one of the now dated cars that once dominated when they were known as "Blue Crowns". The Blue Crown spark plug sponsorship was gone and the cars appeared as the Mobilgas Specials. Bettenhausen and Duane Carter would be teammates for the 35th running of the Indianapolis Classic.

While Tony was re-acquainting himself with the characteristics of the front-drive Mobilgas car, Lee Wallard was having his first impression of the little 99. It was reported that after only a few warm-up laps he emerged from the dark blue machine and said to Belanger, "Wot A Car!" The ever-proud Belanger commissioned a sign painter to install the description on a banner that would hang the full-width of 99's garage all month long. Wallard proved the car's versatility on Indianapolis' hard surface by qualifying at just a tick over 135 mph, which was considered a great run. Bettenhausen managed only 131 in his cumbersome old machine and was nearly bumped from the starting field. The once proud old Blue Crowns were now considered squatty fat girls in the field of slender racers.

There was one car, however, that basically resembled Tony's in appearance and seemingly upheld the design. Duke Nalon's Novi. Now they were referring to Nalon as the comeback man. He'd

Tony's 1951 Indy 500 car. [IMS]

battled the Novi and had survived the burns. He was back to prove that both he and the machine were still capable. The Floyd Clymer Indianapolis 500 Yearbook said later of Nalon's qualifying attempt:

> Nalon was a man with a heavy burden of deed upon his shoulders as he pulled away from the line to shoot for the record (Walt) Faulkner had taken but a year ago.

Between quips, of "He's all washed up," and "He'll do it, the guy is a miracle maker," that ran along pit row, the Iron Duke squelched the nay sayers with an all-time new track record. Amidst the cheers, Duke thanked the Lord for allowing him to stay on the track to complete his mission. The scene along pit row after Duke pulled in was described as being "near pandemonium." Thus it was with more than the usual amount of interest that the pit-siders watched Walt Faulkner on his qualifying attempt a week later. Nalon was with J. C. Agajanian, Faulkner's car owner, as Walt reclaimed the record at 137 plus. While Aggie jubilantly waved his Stetson, Nalon hoisted him upon his shoulders and ran with the Armenian toward the starting line to greet the new hero. Nalon hadn't lost any of his class either.

Because Tony had qualified early in the month, he had earned an up front starting position for the race. At the end of the first lap he was listed as being in fifth position and could easily see the leader slowly pulling away from the field. It was car number 99. Tony Bettenhausen's regular ride was out there leading the single most prestigious auto racing event ever staged and the car's normal driver was flogging around as an also ran somewhere in

Above: Henry Banks, left, and Johnnie Parsons along Indy's pit wall in 1951 checking times.

Left: Duke Nalon hoists owner J. C. Agajanian for a triumphant ride while Speedway President Wilbur Shaw offers congratulations. Incident detailed in text. [IMS]

Below: The start of the 1951 "500" shows the 99 car in the middle of the front row. [IMS]

the top ten. By the time Tony's car decided to give up, just past the 425 mile mark, Murrell Belanger had displayed a pit board to Lee Wallard that said "EZY LEAD 2" which told him that he could relax a bit as he had a two lap lead over the field. Tony was credited with a ninth place finish. Duke dropped out a couple of laps after Bettenhausen did for a tenth spot, and Lee Wallard found out what it was like to visit victory circle at the Indianapolis 500. Wot A Car, said Belanger.

After the 500 had been run, Wallard knew that Tony would again be the regular driver for the rest of the Championship Trail. The weekend following the big race there was a Lee Wallard Day being staged at the Reading, Pennsylvania, half mile. After the "Welcome Home" celebration in which Wallard took part with the local mayor, the new Indy winner was interviewed by Chris Economaki along with Johnnie Parsons. Wallard said he had prayed to the good Lord that he would win the 500 and thanked everyone in attendance for their kindness. Less than two hours later he was in the Reading Hospital suffering from first and second degree burns about his arms and legs. His car had caught fire just as he crossed the finish line to take fourth place in the feature event. The *National Speed Sport News* published some gruesome photographs showing the burning Wallard sprawling on the ground trying to remove his flaming uniform. The hostile Sprint cars had again proven that they have less respect for their masters than any other form of racing vehicle ever bred.

* * *

There were 14 more Championship races left on the schedule after Indianapolis had been run, and Belanger pledged his support to each. Although he was approached by more than one firm wishing to sponsor his 99, he refused them all with the admonition of, "Ain't nobody around who's going to tell me how to run this little jewel." Other than a Mobilgas flying horse on it's hood, the "Baby Belanger" No. 99 would carry only a couple of accessory company decals and the words Belanger Motors Special in gold leaf lettering on its dark blue body. Murrell Belanger and his normal crew that included George Salih, Frenchy Sirois, Tiny Worley, Louis Meyer, Jr. and Melvin Euguene "Tony" Bettenhausen would begin their assault on the 1951 AAA National Championship at Milwaukee. (The hundred lap race on the Milwaukee dirt mile usually had the largest field of cars, other than Indianapolis, of any race on the schedule, and just making the program was considered an accomplishment.) Tony was

Tony gets a grease rag doused with water after his 1951 Langhorne win. [*Imlay*]

judged nearly a home-town favorite at Milwaukee for his previous outstanding performaces only only in a Championship machine, but the Midgets as well. Now that he had reached the big-time, many fans didn't expect him to risk injury in the Midgets as he used to, but Tony still had an affection for the small cars even though Belanger would have much preferred that he confine his activities to the Championship machinery and maybe an occasional Stock car ride. Tony said that the Midgets, "keep you sharp" and managed to run two races before the Milwaukee event was held. He told Belanger that he was ready this year. He'd just set fast time at Walsh Stadium in St. Louis and he was going to blow by all of 'em at Milwaukee. Belanger reminded him that the St. Louis Midget races had previously been unkind to Tony Bettenhausen, and had to jog his memory about the horrendous flips he had taken there. "Don't worry about a thing boss," Bettenhausen told him. "Milwaukee is going to be just the first one in a string they'll remember for a long time."

And it was. Never before in the history of Championship automobile racing did a driver dominate the entire circuit the way Tony Bettenhausen did in the year 1951. It was considered a quirk when they didn't win. Tony won and set a new record at Milwaukee. Then they went to the treacherous Langhorne, Pennsylvania track and won again. They finished second at Darlington and then made a rare appearance on a half-mile track at Willams Grove, Pennsylvania, where they finished second again. Tony saw another acquaintance go as Walt Brown died from injuries he received in a pre-qualifying crash.

It was considered a devastating weekend as Cecil Green and Bill Mackey both plunged to their deaths in almost the same spots on

Tony, outside, passes buddy Paul Russo at DuQuoin for the lead. Again, Bettenhausen won. [*Krueger*]

the Winchester, Indiana, high-banked Sprint car track. Both died in qualifying attempts and Tony's Indianapolis teammate, Duane Carter, solemnly watched both accidents and then went out and set an all-time new track record. The Sprint cars bite again.

Tony went back to Milwaukee for a 100 lap Midget race and won. Then he came home first in the Champ race at Springfield, to take over the AAA point standings lead. After each race he'd call Lee Wallard in the hospital and tell him the results. Wallard had held the point lead by virture of his Indianapolis win and knew it was only a matter of time before he would be surpassed. He wouldn't be driving any kind of car during the summer of 1951 and it built his spirits to talk to Tony. The next time Wallard heard from Bettenhausen, Tony reported that the team had suffered its first mechanical problems of the season at Milwaukee with a balky carburetor. Then it was on to DuQuoin for a pair of races on September first and third. Bettenhausen won them both. Next stop was Syracuse and another victory after Tony led lap 1 thru 67 when the race was halted for a multi-car crash. The following day at Detroit he led the first 97 laps of the scheduled 100 miler and ran out of fuel, but still finished fourth after a hasty pit stop. Russo won the race and commented, "Hey Benski, you only gotta lead the last lap you know. But you'd rather lap the field, right? See you at the gas station. Meanwhile, I hope you won't mind if I stop off here at victory lane and pick up some cash."

Russo had been running strong all season, but was plagued by one misfortune after another and he delighted in needling little Tunni. Pal Henry Banks had been plodding along all year, too, and was well up in the point standings, but couldn't be expected to successfully defend his 1950 AAA crown unless something drastic

VOL. IX—No. 37 RIDGEWOOD, N. J., SEPTEMBER 12, 1951 Entered as Second-Class Matter at the Post Office at Ridgewood, New Jersey (ISSUED WEEKLY)

Bettenhausen, Russo Win 3A Big Car Titular Events

(Stories on Page Three)

Hinnershitz Sets Grove Mark

(Story on Page Two)

STAFF PHOTOGRAPHER HARRY LUTHER snapped these on-the-spot pictures of the four-car crash at Syracuse, N. Y., on Saturday afternoon, September 8th. Upper left photo shows Jack McGrath immediately after hitting Bill Schindler in No. 10. Schindler precipitated the accident when he hit the wall after his steering failed. Upper right shows Schindler still in the car waiting for assistance. Middle left photo shows the damage done to the two machines. Middle right and lower two photos show the wrecks of Buzz Barton's No. 79 and Chuck Stevenson's No. 8. Schindler suffered the most injury, requiring ten stitches in his forehead. Cars involved were the Chapman No. 10, Hinkle No. 9, Richter No. 79 and Marchese No. 8. (Story on Page Three)

Bettenhausen and Russo shared headlines in September of 1951.

happened to Tony. The Duke wasn't around much now that he had taken a job with Ford's aircraft engine division and moved to Ft. Worth where he was an area field service supervisor. Tony missed running with Duke, he loved for Nalon to be proud of him.

Tony's talk during the late summer of 1951 included the fact he was going to be a father again soon as Val was expecting her fourth child. Overall, he was in a happy state of mind. However, he wasn't pleased with the way the Kaiser-Frazer dealership had been going the past few months as the auto industry in general was down some 27 percent from 1950 due to the Korean war conflict. But he had the AAA Championship in sight and a good finish at Denver could wrap it up for him.

The Championship cars had not appeared in Denver for some 26 years and owner-promoter J. C. Agajanian believed he could draw a crowd on the Centennial horse racing facility for the drivers advertised as "Indianapolis 500 Stars." The large crowd was treated to an extra bit of the Bettenhausen humor and confidence late in the race. Tony's car was experiencing minor mis-firing that caused a slight pop-pop sound on the straight-a-ways. An experienced mechanic could lend an ear and say, "That thing's shootin' ducks." While Tony was sure his crew was aware of his situation, he didn't want to miss a chance to needle Belanger about the performance of "the little jewel" as it was so often referred to. Coming down the front chute, Bettenhausen propped his left knee up under the steering wheel and took both hands off the wheel and pointed an imaginary shotgun skyward just as a flock of ducks flew over the track. The crowd clapped as Tony lowered his often-battered hands gently back on to the wheel and commanded the car through the first turn. He ultimately beat Henry to the finish line to score his seventh major victory of the season. Tony Bettenhausen was the undisputed 1951 AAA National Driving Champion and a guy he used to bang wheels with over on the boards at Nutley was right behind him. If it hadn't been for a slick spot that Paul Russo was forced into on the 90th lap, they would have finished 1-2-3. Now they were three old Midgeteers at the top of their chosen professions. The people in the grandstands surrounding the one mile facility had never seen anything like the high-banks of Nutley and they couldn't really appreciate the celebration the trio had after the race. Some asked of Bettenhausen "What are you going to do now?" after his victorious ride and the answer was an easy one: Get ready for San Jose, Phoenix and Bay Meadows.

Thoughts of San Jose and the old man who died under his wheels were hard to keep out of Tony's mind, but his basic

VOL. IX—No. 39 RIDGEWOOD, N. J., SEPTEMBER 26, 1951 Entered as Second-Class Matter at the Post Office at Ridgewood, New Jersey (ISSUED WEEKLY)

Bettenhausen Clinches Championship at Denver

(Story on Page Three)

Hinnershitz Grove Benefit Star

(Story on Page Two)

Milwaukee Trophy and Winner

WEE WALT FAULKNER, still grimy from his 200-mile victory ride at Milwaukee on August 25th, poses with car owner Jay Agajanian and Mrs. Faulkner. The trophy, nearly as tall as its winner, was donated by race promoter Tom Marchese, and Charles Kotovic of the East Side Chevrolet agency in Milwaukee, both great friends of racing. NSSN Staff Photo by Army Krueger.

Sports for Mrs. America 1952

Mrs. Peggy Duncan of New York City shown beside her first prize Austin A40 "Sports" convertible at the Convention Hall in Asbury Park, New Jersey, immediately after she was acclaimed winner over 32 other married beauties. For those interested in statistics:

	Mrs. America	Austin "Sports"
Height	5'7½"	4'9"
Weight	124 lbs.	2250lbs.
Waist	24"	None
Hips	36"	5'1"
Bust	36"	Twin Carburetors
Power	Unlimited	46 h.p.

BOB KING, winner of the 200-lap Mutual Racing Ass'n Roadster race at Funk's Speedway, Winchester, Ind., being interviewed by famous announcer Harold "Dutch" Hurst, after King's hard fought victory. The MRA heads the list of Roadster Organizations in the mid-west, running three and four times a week. Muncie Press Photo.

Here's a popular combination for competition in the 200-lap Grand National Circuit race for late model cars at Occoneechee Speedway, Hillsboro-Durham, N. C., Oct. 7th. Frank Mundy, Atlanta, right, and his car owner, Perry Smith of Columbia, S. C. talk over the chances of their 1951 Studebaker which held the second fastest time in time trials at Darlington and the fastest time at Detroit recently. Some 40 to 50 top drivers will compete in the Occoneechee race with time trials starting at 1 o'clock and the race at 1:30 p.m.

The newspaper proclaiming Tony National Champion after his Denver win.

fatalistic attitude kept him standing on the gas as hard as he had the year previous. After setting fast time of the day he again dominated the event and was followed across the line by Russo and Henry. These were the salad days now, racing and winning. Making money. Your pals were up front, too, on the same circuit that they all used to talk about. Tony was beating the rest of the Championship drivers now as easily as he used to dominate the Midget competition. Blowin' their doors off, he'd say. Belanger, Salih and Tiny Worley still had a hard time, however, keeping the Bettenhausen tinkering to a minimum. He still wanted to change things. Experiment some more. Make it a little better. A little faster. Really blow by all of 'em.

Everyone shook their head at Phoenix and wondered how it could be possible the Bettenhausen and 99 could outclass the rest of the field so easily. He wasn't again merely leading the race, he had lapped everyone but the second place driver, Johnnie Parsons. And he had a three-quarter lap lead on Parsons. Tony finally encountered mechanical problems on the 93rd lap of the 100-lap event and had to drop out. Parsons won the race and Henry was in second place.

Parsons won the last race of the year at Bay Meadows as well, but Bettenhausen's performance was at least as memorable as Johnnie's win. Tony led the 150 lap affair from the 32nd to the 129th lap when a worn tire forced him into the pits. He re-entered the race a lap down and made up half a lap by the time the checkered flag fell. He had worked his way back through the field and passed Henry for second spot on the 142nd lap. Henry shook his head and wondered just what it was that Tony was trying to prove. It was November ll, the year had ended. There would be no changing of the record books, Tony was the the champion and Henry had plodded along nicely to finish second. But there was Bettenhausen, driving hell-bent-for-election to try and catch Handsome John. That guy could kill himself out there, some said, driving the way he does. What the hell's the rush now? You're supposed to sit back and enjoy the fruits of the AAA title. Tony had no such notion. He never could idle around, take it easy. Just put the pedal to the metal. The fans at Bay Meadows received a first hand illustration of why Tony Bettenhausen had won the driving title. And even more importantly, he gave them a dust-blown description of his attitude and life-style. Wide-open Bettenhausen. Talking about it was for other folks. Get it done now. Who knows, maybe you won't be around for tomorrow. Absolutely no one back in Tinley Park would ever understand how a son of the Illinois soil could live such a rough-shod existence.

Tony's 1951 Championship winning machine, the Belanger 99. The car won at Indianapolis but Lee Wallard was driving it. [*Bettenhausen Coll.*]

They'd cringe if they ever saw what Christian Bettenhausen's last-born did to the dirt of the world.

* * *

At the end of 1951, Tony Bettenhausen had fulfilled one of his great ambiltions in grand style. He had unmercifully waxed the competition. Except at Indianapolis. He didn't much like to think about that. Lee Wallard had been the one to achive racing immortality at the Speedway. Wallard and car 99. Nobody ever though of Wallard and car 99. Everybody in racing called them "The Big B," Bettenhausen-Belanger and 99. But sure enough, Tony thought, Wallard and 99 had won the Speedway. All the god-damn Championship victories in the world didn't even come close to one first place finish at Indy. It was like some little kid walking up to you and saying, "Hey mister, you ever won the 500?" And you'd have to reply No. Then the kid would probably say, "Aw you ain't a *real* race car driver. Real race car drivers have won the 500, haven't they?" Now in the winter of 1951 there wasn't much time to think about last year. Probably 1952 would be good Tony thought. There was a new car agency, a Chrysler agency for Al Schuldt and Tony along with brother Herb. Al and Tony had decided to rid themselves of the Kaiser-Frazer store even though the 1951 Kaisers were among the most striking new cars on the market. They weren't selling, and the factory was losing money. Emil was still working as a service rep for the brand, but he had a salaried job. K-F continued to keep the old six cylinder and now performance was beginning to sell. They needed a V-8. Tony had driven a few Stock car races this past season, one in an Olds and another in a Chrysler and both of them would have no trouble showing their tail pipes to a Kaiser. The Kaiser factory had gone so far as to purchase a few Olds engines and install them in their own 1951 cars and the results had been great. Too great, in fact. Initially, the Kaisers had believed a deal could be made with General Motors to buy Oldsmobile V-8 engines and install them as standard equipment in the Kaisers and few Frazers they were building. They could simply change the valve covers and put their own name, or any name they wanted on them. In their stock form they were stamped "Rocket 88". But when GM found out just how well the sleek new Kaisers performed with the Olds engine, they upped the price so the engine was too expensive for K-F to handle.

There had even been a new addition to the Kaiser line, the "Henry J" that noted writer Uncle Tom McCahill of *Mechanix Illustrated* described by saying, "At a quick glance the car resembles a Cadillac that started smoking too young...Like a lot of girls, the chassis looks familiar but you can't quite place the face." Henry J. Kaiser had envisioned a car for the multitudes just as Henry Ford had done half a century earlier. But sales were soft. The 1951 buying public wasn't interested in economy and austerity. Bettenhausen and Schuldt weren't either. Together with Herb, who owned a nice little piece of property the new dealership could be built on, they would sell Chryslers. Murrell Belanger had certainly done well enough with the brand. Tony Bettenhausen would have the great new "Firedome V-8" to sell and a pair of Tinley Park partners. What a combination. Fire and ice.

* * *

By 1951 Ernie Schlausky had sucessfully changed his public name to Crocky Wright through his motorcycle and Midget racing activities. While he displayed a great deal of talent and bravery on motorcycles, his lack of interest in things mechanical hurt his car racing career. When the races were available, he ran Midgets seven nights per week but didn't earn enough money to maintain first class equipment. He went through a scattering of jobs and would quit each May so he could attend the Indianapolis 500.

With the rise in interest in stock car and jalopy racing, Crocky's Midget racing activity was almost non-existent now. He was accepting the fact that he probably wouldn't ever win the Indianapolis 500, but he was still so addicted to the sport that he refused to follow another profession. In 1951 another one of his idols, Putt Mosman, offered him a job traveling with the "Putt Mossman International Daredevils." Putt was one of the nation's champion horseshoe pitchers who later combined his talent with stunt motorcycle riding. He entertained fairground audiences standing atop his motorcycle and pitching horeseshoes. Soon he had a traveling troupe and brave little Crocky Wright became a star of the show by crashing a motorcycle through a burning wall.

Every once in a while Crocky would think about his first lady love, Gene Kushman, tender face and long brown hair that would cascade over her shoulders like a pretty waterfall. His second girl, Jo Paris, had married the first man she met after Crocky told her that he couldn't give up his driving career for a woman. Still, Crocky didn't fit the mold of the devil-may-care vagabond who would drive from one county fair to the next leaving a string of broken hearts in his path. As you watched him shatter flaming boards at high-speed, you wouldn't guess that under the checkered helmet was a shy young man whose vocabulary didn't include four-letter words. After each performance you'd find him puffing his pipe and answering any questions the awed spectators might pose. Sometimes the conversations would lead to the discussion of a racing performance one of the customers had seen. Crocky was always interested in how the stars of the day were doing and he'd usually comment, "Yeah, that guy's terrific. I just love the way he slides around corners, throwing up a roostertail." He would never say anything derogatory about a competitor, even if he didn't respect the man's driving tactics. Crocky was too gentle to verbally abuse another man. Even after winning several motorcycle races at a particular track he could never say, "I'm going to blow by all of 'em today." Rather, he'd bow his head in victory lane a little and say, "Gee, it's really great to be here. Terrific."

Crocky Wright liked being around the races too much to quit entirely. He wasn't sure exactly where his career would lead him, but it didn't seem to matter. He was happy being with those who entertained others and he couldn't leave.

* * *

7

Retirement

As 1952 approached, Tony had more to consider than ever before. A week and a half after the October San Jose race Val had made him a father once gain and the new child was to carry his father's name: Tony, Jr. Their little bungalow on 67th Court in Tinley was already cramped enough so that Gary and Merle had been given permanent quarters on the porch. It was cold out there, they said.

Late in the year friend Karl Kiekhaefer, the Wisconsin manufacturer of Mercury outboard motorboat engines, called and asked Tony if he'd like to try his hand at road racing. There was a five day race utilizing passenger cars from Tuxtla Gutierrez to Ciudad Juarez known as the Mexican Road Race, a grueling 1,933 mile event that would pay the winner over $23,000. The race was run in eight separate legs, or stages, and at the end of the first day Tony and his mechanic Ed Metzler were in 66th position. Tony gave the following report in the *National Speed Sport News*:

> We were the seventh car to get going, but by the end of the first day we were in 66th position. About 100 miles out we discovered we had lost our brakes. It was a funny feeling reaching for that pedal and find it laying on the floor. The next day, after Eddy worked all night, we were moving pretty well until we popped a wheel. Despite the fact that we were almost last, we got one of the biggest ovations I've ever heard as we pulled into Mexico City that night. The Mexicans are real race fans. Maybe it's because they don't have to pay.
>
> On the third day we got a little lucky and had moved up to 48th place by the time we had reached Durango. We learned that our time was 47 seconds off the pace set by Ascari (the eventual winner). The next morning we cut their lead to about 40 seconds through the mountains, but their cars weighed between 2,000-2,200 pounds and ours was 3,800-4,000.
>
> About this time Eddy and I decided we had to do something to catch these guys so we really set sail and the next day we were

Tony's Stock car for the Mexican Road race. [Bettenhausen Coll.]

> fastest by four minutes. I know we must have been hitting 140 because we had a plane going along with us and we kept passing it while it was doing 130.
>
> Toward the end we devised a plan so the plane could really help us. We had the pilot fly a little ways ahead over the road. If the plane went straight ahead we knew the road was straight, but when they banked one way or the other we knew a turn was coming. Using this system we finished seven minutes ahead of the Ferraris on that leg.
>
> The final day people were lined up by the thousands from eight miles out all the way to Juarez. They'd stand right in the road until we were near and then a path just wide enough for the car would open up, filling up right again behind us. This was quite a thrill at 130 mph.

Although he didn't win, Tony was one of the main heroes of the event through his showing a bulky Chrysler against the sleek Ferraris. When he arrived home, some 250 friends gave him a party at Chicago's fashionable LaSalle Hotel where he was not only presented a plaque from fellow Kaiser-Frazer dealers but he was the recipient of the prestigious Champion Sportsmen of the Month Award from Champion Spark Plug Company. Other great sports stars, such as golfer Ben Hogan and ball player Connie Mack, had recently received the award as well. Tony said, "I never thought I was this popular. I've been trying for a long time and I promise you I'll be back next year."

Val was put on stage, too, and she noted that she was just very proud to be Mrs. Tony Bettenhausen. It had only been a couple of months earlier that Val had mustered enough courage to ask Tony about something she'd wanted for a long time. She didn't know how he'd react but she had to try. She remembers the conversation exactly. It was just after Tony had sat down for a bowl of Val's meaty chili.

"Tony?" she said warmly.

"Yeah, hon?"

"Is there something you'd do for me?"

"I guess so, I've never denied you anything yet, have I? What do you want?"

"Will you buy me your mother's farm?"

"You *gotta* be kidding," he said as he dropped the spoon into the chili and turned around. "Hell, I would have bought the damn place three years ago if I thought you'd live out there."

"But I gotta have my own car, too," Val replied.

"You got it," he smiled and went back to the chili. The very next day Val talked to Tony's mom, who was equally surprised.

"You? You girl?" she asked with a deep gutteral accent. "Why I thought you were a city girl. I thought you wanted it easy. Okay, I'll sell. But I have to have cash, you know."

And cash it was. Tony withdrew every bit of savings he had, took a loan and went to take the money to Mom. She instructed him to divide it up and distribute it evenly to all his brothers and sisters. He did, and Mevlin Eugene, the boy who always said he wouldn't give a plug nickel for living on a farm, made arrangements to completely renovate the home before moving his family in. It ought to have a basement. No problem, he said. We'll just put 'er up on some jacks and dig out underneath it. Tony the caterpillar driver. By the time the house was completely off the ground there were 13 jacks under it and Tony said something else would have to be used to help prop it up. That 13 was a damn unlucky number. Tony took his superstitions seriously, so no one argued with him. The kids knew that if a black cat ran out in front of the car, Daddy would pull over to the side of the road and wait until another car had "broken the path" before he'd proceed. You didn't question Daddy, you just did what he said.

Gary and Merle were kept busy for days helping to pull out all the old lath and plaster. Then they were told to remove all the little nails from the thin lath and wood strips and pile them neatly. How come, they'd say to each other. He ain't never gonna use it.

The house renovation turned out to be a family affair with Tony, "The General" leading. He'd make up lists for everyone and there was never any question that the jobs would be done. Gary and Merle couldn't even think about playing. Daddy was strict. But he was also pretty smart, they agreed. After the Bettenhausen family had moved to its new farm on January 25,

Tony gives Merle the checkered flag at the family's new farmhouse. [Bettenhausen Coll.]

1952 everyone said it sure was a lot keener than the old bungalow. Plenty of room for Gary and Merle and their cousin Harlan Bettenhausen and friend Roger Klickner to play. Harlan was Herb's son and they called themselves the four Musketeers. Definitely buddies to the end, pledging loyalty to one another, exploring everywhere. And when they grew up they'd be like Tony and race. So they'd stage serious bicycle races which had to be official. There was always a specific number of laps and boundaries you had to stay inside of. Gary always won, but the others didn't mind because, after all, he was the oldest. And when something went wrong they shared equally in the blame.

Once they found a miniature barn, a model someone had patterned after the one on the Bettenhausen farm. They took it and were going to show if off to their friends, but somewhere along the way they got tired of carrying it and threw it in a ditch. When Daddy found out they all had to write, "I will not steal," a thousand times. They wondered: Did Daddy know he was talking to the famous four Musketeers? None were brave enough to ask.

When the Bettenhausens moved into their newly refurbished farmhouse, Tony had reached an enviable position. He could easily be considered Mr. Automobile Racing in the United States, through not only his accomplishments during the 1951 season, but by the accompanying publicity as well. He endorsed many products (even a milk ad) and his photo appeared in newspapers throughout the country. His family unit seemed stable and now that he was becoming involved in the new Chrysler dealership, his business future looked secure. There was no talk in the winter of

'52 about retiring from racing. Tony didn't consider himself in his prime, he just knew he was capable of blowin' their doors off at any race track he went to. Except the Speedway. He still hadn't won the Speedway. That bugged him. Next year would be different, though. He would drive little 99 and do just like Lee Wallard the year before.

He made a quick trip to the West Coast during the winter to run a Midget race at Bay Meadows and "had 'er won till the damn thing started poppin." He came home and continued to work on the basement which he was turning into a racing oriented family room. He had envisioned the basement months before, and while the house was up on jacks his mother had warned him that the place could surely fall over. Val recalls him laughing from his seat atop a Caterpillar and saying, "Ma goddammit, if the good Lord wants this house blown halfway out into the field, then that's the way it's gonna be. Now quit worrying about me."

Tony's attitude was on one hand always superstitious, but on the other he believed you made your own luck.

His outlook was well stated on the front page of the May 29th edition of *The Indianapolis Times*. It devoted nearly the entire page to him and his picture was reproduced in full color all the way across the top. Tony bylined the story himself: "I'm called Tough Luck Tony, But This May Be My Year." He said in part: "Less than a week ago it looked like I wouldn't get into this year's race. That was when I cracked up against the wall in Murrell Belanger's No. 99."

There would be no Tony Bettenhausen and the familiar number 99 in the 1952 "500." Bettenhausen had sufficiently damaged the car during a qualifying attempt so that it couldn't be fixed in time to race. But he was still optimistic. His article continued: "Within a few hours I had a new assignment to drive. In the Blue Crown Special owned by Lou Moore, the car I drove in last year's race.

"That was a 'good break' for I qualified the Blue Crown at 135.382 mph and now I'm in the race.

"I'm starting this year's race in the hopes that this might be my big year. Like every driver I want to win the "500" more than I've ever wanted anything.

"And I will win it one day."

Tony's *Times* story appeared on the day of the 1952 "500." Less than two weeks later, the *National Speed Sport News* headlined:

Tony Quits Except For 500 Miler

In between May 29 and June 8, Bettenhausen had run the 1952 "500" and never was considered a contender for a top ten spot, much less a winner. He completed 93 laps and was credited with finishing in 23rd position. Nevertheless, a week after the race his spirits were high. He'd get back in form during the traditional Championship race held at Milwaukee a week after the Speedway. Early in June, Henry Banks had just spent a couple of days with Tony on the farm and they were driving together. Val was ahead of them along with daughter Susie.

A sharp looking '48 Ford Coupe that was lowered in the rear caught Tony's attention as it cruised by on the left. It emitted a low exhaust rumble that was a popular hotrod sound of the day. Probably had "Smitty" mufflers on it, Tony thought. He always appreciated a good looking car. And he really preferred one that sounded a little snappy, too.

As the coupe began around Val and Susie, it hesitated and slowed, just matching Val's pace. The boys in the car could only see Val, a good lookin' redhead. Susie was on the floorboard looking for one of her lost jacks. Tony heard the distinct rumble of a man letting off the gas pedal when the coupe slowed and he half cocked his head into a position as if to say, "What the hell's going on up there?"

The boy on the rider's side rolled down his window and shouted something to Val. Tony could see her look at the youth, and then he caught her eyes glancing in the rearview mirror. Her Tony was back there. She felt protected.

"What did that punk say to her?" Tony said aloud to Henry. Complacent old Henry had simply been sitting there, hands folded and looking at the familiar scenery. Bettenhausen swapped lanes and gave the horn a short tap, as if he had been following the coupe for a long time and wanted to pass. The youngster on the right leaned far out of the window and shouted something at the two men as he gave them the finger as if to say, "Buzz off, we're gonna talk to this chick here."

Henry looked over at Tony and then glanced at the speedometer, 60 miles per hour. He didn't have any comment to make. Tony honked again, this time a meaningful blast. Once more the youth leaned out the window and flashed the universal sign of contempt, middle finger held high.

"Goddamn punks," Tony said. "If one of my boys ever did that I'd kick his ass."

Henry still didn't have anything to say. He was too busy watching the whole thing.

"I'll give 'em a little driving lesson," Tony said. "Watch this."

Banks looked over at him and his fears came true. Bettenhausen was going to shove them out of the way. Christ Tony, he thought, we're going 60 miles per hour and you gotta start playing around. If you just leave them alone they'll probably get bored and go away. Nevertheless, Henry knew that a bit of action was about to occur, so he subconsciously straightened up in the seat and braced his legs up on the floorboard.

Tony gently pushed the accelerator, as if he were barefoot on a wet sponge wanting to feel the coolness through his toes. The passenger in the coupe stared momentarily at the oncoming vehicle and quickly jerked back inside to nudge his buddy.

Both cars sped up just a bit, enough to pass Val and Susie. Tony inched closer and closer to the coupe until he was actually pushing it. Henry heard a little click, like a ball point pen being retracted when their car met the one ahead. Bettenhausen was grinning now.

"What the hell are you doing?" Henry finally broke his silence.

Tony offered no reply. He felt like a kid who had just amazed his parents with some new magical trick. He kept pushing the coupe until it was moved over into the right hand lane. He grinned again as he watched the Ford accelerate away. Val and Sue drove alongside and he offered them a short salute. Then he dropped in behind her again and laughed out loud.

Christ, Henry thought, what if we had locked bumpers with those kids.

The Sunday following the incident with the teenage boys, Tony announced his retirement. It came on the day he was to have raced at Milwaukee, as he'd done for so many years. Both he and Henry attempted to qualify for the race, but their runs were too slow. Missed the show. They had both drawn late qualifying numbers and the track was fairly well worn out by the time they made their attempts, but there was another problem that was bothering them.

Their friend Johnny McDowell had been killed on his own qualifying run. McDowell was thrown out of his car to his death when a wheel failed. Grief stricken, Tony made a slow, deliberate retirement announcement after the race.

At last, Tony Bettenhausen was retiring from racing. Or so some thought. He was visibly bothered by McDowell's death and talked about it to Val and the kids on the way home from Milwaukee. Would it actually be true that Tony wouldn't be off somewhere every weekend, running a Midget or one of those god-awful Sprint cars? Valerie Bettenhausen could think back over many, many years of waiting and wondering, is he alright? There was always that slight twinge she'd feel every time she answered the telephone when he was gone. Could this be the time that there'd be bad news? He was quoted in the racing papers:

"I've got a nice family, a nice home and good business prospects. The best time to quit this game is when you're on top. I'll say though, that everyting I have I owe to racing.

"I'll keep trying at Indianapolis because nobody passes up that kind of money. If you win, it's worth about $70,000."

McDowell had two kids, a boy ten and girl age eight. Tony talked about him all the way home and grieved for a long time. Johnny was a great Midget chauffeur, having proven his worth at the 1937 Pacific Coast champ and he was second behind the great Rex Mays in the West Coast big car title chase. Tony reasoned that he was almost too good to get killed. He'd been racing for so long. If it was going to happen it would have happened by now. But a wheel failed. You can't do anything when the shitbox falls apart on you, Tony had said.

Val felt some relief after Tony's retirement, but she didn't really believe him. They went to a few races during the summer and his helmet and driving suit were still in the trunk. He held true to his word and didn't get in another race car for the rest of the calendar year of 1952. Tony was thinking about some of the other greats who had died someplace other than Indianapolis. He remembered that the front end had come apart on Ted Horn's car. And there probably wasn't anybody any better than Horn. Or Rex Mays. Now they were both gone.

But Tony knew that he himself would go back to Indianapolis, that Tony Bettenhausen's name ought to be included when they talk about Indy 500 winners and be emblazoned on that Borg-Warner trophy. That's about as close to immortality as you can get. But even Indy 500 winners can get killed. Sure, if it's your time to go, the drivers agreed, anybody can get snuffed. But they'd sure remember you a lot better if you'd won the Speedway. Thus a few of the old veterans confined their racing activity to just the Indianapolis 500. They took two trains of thought: 1) They didn't have anything to prove to themselves on the other tracks that were mostly low-paying and pretty risky anyway, and, 2) they knew that winning the Speedway is the only thing that counts, nothing else can come even close. It's the reason you spent all those years bustin' your ass in the Midgets and Sprint cars, just to get to the Speedway. Tony said he'd run only the Speedway. He didn't hear himself talking when he used to say that running Midgets keeps you sharp. And in the meantime, it wasn't important to go to every track and blow their doors off. He'd already done it. He thought he was good enough to suit up once a

Tony being congratulated by J. C. Agajanian and crew after qualifying for the 1953 "500." Regular driver Troy Ruttman shown far left, arm in sling. Note the pig on the cowling. [*Krueger*]

year. Be as competitive as the rest of the yokels who ran their fannies off.

One of those who thought like Tony was a 50-year-old named Chet Miller, a throwback to another era in racing. He'd run in the Halycon days of the Twenties, on the big board speedways and he was at Indianapolis when they had two-men cars. Old Chet, some said, would keep on running at Indy until he collected Social Security. Hell, he's been running so long that there ain't nothin' that's gonna kill him. If he ain't bought the farm by now, he never will. Guys who wanted to keep racing past age 40 used Miller for an example. He didn't just come to Indy and stroke along, he was a Novi driver. And if he could still have balls enough to try and tame the often-erratic and overpowered Novi, running just once a year couldn't be all bad. If you ever got the Novi percolatin', everybody said it would run off and hide from the rest of the field. Duke Nalon had just very nearly won the race in one, but it bit him when he was leading. And it was a Novi that Ralph Hepburn died in just five years ago.

In the 1953 "500," Chet Miller and Duke were entered as teammates in the twin Novi cars. For the first time since Milwaukee, Tony would get back in a race car. But it wasn't in his familiar 99. He had made a deal with old friend J. C. Agajanian to drive Aggie's 98, the car that Troy Ruttman had driven to victory

Bill Vukovich, Sr.

in the 1952 race. Ruttman was walking around Indy with his right arm in a sling, the victim of a Sprint car crash in Des Moines. Sprint cars, Novi and injuries. All could usually be mentioned in the same sentence.

Although Tony was driving the car that had won the previous year's race, it hadn't been the class of the field. Last year Bill Vukovich literally dominated the event and looked like a sure winner until eight laps from the finish when a piece of steering mechanism let go. He wasn't injured in the ensuing crash and vowed that he'd come back to win. He was the odds on favorite for 1953, but since Agajanian's famed number 98 was a first class piece, Tony had a good chance himself. He sure wanted to beat that Vukovich.

Bettenhausen had become friendly with California Bill Vukovich now, and it was good to see him again. Vuky's early day Midget racing career had nearly paralled Tony's and they had many stories to trade each May. Vukovich was a quiet and reserved man, almost to the point of being withdrawn. Short, black-haired, sharp featured, he could scare a little girl into tears if he took a mind to. Vuky didn't have much time for talking to the press, fans or even too many other drivers, but he felt comfortable around Tony and in his company was usually good-humored. He liked to rib Bettenhausen about how he was going to beat him.

Once again Tony enjoyed the Speedway scene in May of 1953. It was great to be back among all your buddies again, using the same language you'd been used to for so many years: "You don't really think you're goin' anyplace in that shitbox, do you?" one would say to another. "Hello, featherfoot, you look like my grandmother out there." And there was always the serious as well. One driver going down in the corner to watch a friend. Or just to watch. And then stopping by someone's garage and making a sincere suggestion. Tell a buddy, or a rookie, or someone you don't even know too well what his problems looked like from the infield. You wanted to win the race, beat the best in the business. But you also want to help anyone who's having problems because you know that if you don't have them yourself this year, you're liable to the next. It happens to everybody, even the good guys. And you know how hard every other driver here worked just to get a chance.

While Tony was as respected a man who ever donned a crash helmet for a dirt track race, he hadn't yet obtained the title of Speedway master. He was sometimes accused of driving the place as though it were dirt. He'd sort of back in. He wasn't known as the smoothest driver ever to race on the old two and one-half mile rectangle. But nobody could ever really say anything to him about it, because he had beaten about every man in the place on some other kind of track. Except Duke. Tony always took the Duke's advice. If Nalon said that Bettenhausen was going into the first turn a little high, Tony would lower his approach. Sometimes he listened to Emil, too.

As always, this year again, the talk centered around the speed it would take to win the pole, and just make the race. Some said that the magical 140 mile per hour mark might be reached but no one had come close to matching Chet Miller's track record of 139.5 mph. Old Chet himself went out on May 15, the day before qualifications and cut a lap of 137. On his next time around he lost control of the unmistakable sounding Novi in the first turn and slammed head on into the retaining wall. The car bounced away, slid 300 feet and hit again. He was dead of a basal skull fracture and brain hemorrhage when they removed him from the car. The accident was a virtual re-enactment of Ralph Hepburn's five years prior. And Duke Nalon was supposed to try and qualify the other Novi the next day.

"This is a Godsend for me," Nalon commented as he watched the rains wipe out Saturday qualifications. Duke knew that nothing had broken in the car, Miller just dipped down too low, skidded in the grass and lost control. Observers said Chet momentarily looked as though he might regain control, but there was too much momentum built up and he didn't stand a chance. Around Gasoline Alley, the Novi was again referred to as a "Killer Car."

Nalon ultimately qualified the second Novi, but made a total of

Henry Banks

eight pit stops in the race and finally spun in order to miss Gene Hartley. He received the "Sportsman of the Year Trophy." Tony qualified up front but was victimized by the searing heat that caused many drivers to drop out. It was the hottest day in the history of the 37 year old event and driver Carl Scarborough died in the infield hospital from heat prostration. Bill Vukovich, "The Mad Russian," led 195 of the 200 lap contest and joked after the race about the heat. "Every time I went by a car it had a different driver in it."

After the race, Vukovich was ribbing Tony about being a pansy. "You probably could have run second if you'd stayed out there all day. Not too tough, huh?" Tony was used to Vuky's wisecracks. So were his sons, Gary and Merle. Last year when he visited them, Vukovich had said, "My kid's so tough he can chew nails!" Merle recalls that in the summer of '53 when Vukovich brought his family to the farm Merle greeted Bill, Jr. with a handful of nails and said, "Here, Billy, let's see you eat these." They didn't become good buddies, especially after Gary and Merle took Billy out and ran him through one of their serious bicycle races. "We waxed him good," they said.

Vukovich was taking a busman's holiday on his way to the Milwaukee race as he had already said he wouldn't run the remainer of the Championship Trail. He and Tony both were supposedly going to be Indianapolis 500 drivers only. At Milwaukee their ranks were joined by Henry Banks. Going down the backstretch, Henry felt the desire to race in his foot but not his heart. He didn't really bend 'er in to the corners the way he knew he could. He didn't want to. He could have come in and made an excuse or two about the chassis not working very well, dry track, etc. Henry knew all that. He also knew he didn't have to prove anything to anyone. But the fun wasn't there anymore. It had just sort of drifted away. The importance of doing well was gone. The addiction he had known for so very many years to stand on the gas had subsided. He came in from hot laps and told an official, "That's it. I quit. I ain't gonna run," he said with his usual wry smile.

"Why you gotta run," the official said. "You already warmed up. You gotta run."

"I don't *gotta* do nuthin'," Henry mocked back. And without a further word he turned and walked away. "Hey Nazaruk," he said. "You want to run my car?"

Sure," the upcoming star commented. "But what about you?"

Henry didn't elaborate and Mike Nazaruk didn't ask many questions. He had a ride. And he *wanted* to race. Henry said he'd probably confine his activities to the Speedway now like Tony and Duke. Paul Russo was still running, however. And running hard. He came from 14th to 4th at the Milwaukee race and never talked about giving up the dirt tracks. He still had the bug.

Tony did too. He was a little irritable around the house after Milwaukee and Val figured it was only a matter of time before he'd climb back into a race car at a track other than Indianapolis. In the meantime, he was going to work every day at the new Chrysler agency. He and brother Herb, along with Al Schuldt, had set up a three-way partnership to run not only the car dealership but shared in a John Deere tractor agency across the street. There wasn't anything formal drawn up among the trio. Al and Tony were supposed to run the car dealership for the most part, and Herb would take care of the farmers. Herb owned the new building that housed the auto agency and Tony often complained that he let everyone know just who owned the joint.

Once, salesman-bookkeeper Dick Brosius and Tony spent half the day arranging seven cars in the tiny showroom. They were first driven in and then jockeyed into position by means of a floor jack. Pick up the front end and move it a few inches. Then do the same to the back. It was sort of a pain in the ass Tony agreed, but the end result would be worth the effort. It'd look like a big-time agency. People really had a choice, right inside. Herb came in and said there was too much weight on the floor. "Too much weight on the floor?" Tony asked unbelievingly. Brosius and Tony moved three of the cars back outside.

Dick Brosius didn't really mind. He liked working for Tony. He had been a racing fan since '46 and traveled all over the Midwest helping Midget star Mel Hansen. In pit talk he was a stooge, willing to do just damn near anything to be around the races. Dick Brosius had the bug, too. He didn't like his regular job, in the legal claims department for the Sante Fe Railroad. He worked there for 12 years and used to leave work undone on Friday afternoons in order to meet Hansen so they could go to the races. He liked the congenial atmosphere at the Midget races. Everybody said what was on their mind. If somebody was an asshole, you said so. It wasn't like that at all working for the Sante Fe. Why, even in the mornings, riding up the elevator, when one of the top brass got in everybody shut up. Afraid of their own shadows, it seemed. Boy, he thought, if these guys ever went to the races they'd get introduced to a whole different kind of life. A place where the people are people, not a bunch of sheep. Although he had a dozen years in with the Sante Fe, he felt like Clyde Rice, Val's dad, that he owed his soul to the company store. Clyde had welcomed the opportunity to go to work with Tony, mostly keeping books. Brosius himself enjoyed hanging around the dealership. One day he quit the railroad and didn't have anything specific in mind. He was killing time, chewing the fat with Tony when Bettenhausen suggested, "Why don't you come to work here? Sell cars and help out. We'll all make it just fine." Dick accepted without hesitation. It wasn't a job in racing, but he'd be working with Tony and that was good enough for him.

Herb, Tony and Al built a cohesive little crew in the dealership. Brosius, Tony and Al were the salesmen, Charlie Harmill took care of the parts department and old Adolph and Jimmy Styx were the main mechanics. Bud Petersen was a combination man who did body and paint work along with a mechanical job or two. From the day they opened their doors they made money. And had a good many petty arguments. There was a vein of jealousy that prevailed. Hard working Al Schuldt was supposed to get off work every night at six, but more times than not he stayed until nine. Tony was always in and out of the place, wheeling and dealing, talking to prospective customers and letting people know that yes, of course, you could buy a car directly from Tony Bettenhausen, the race car driver. It seemed to irritate a bit that some people refused to buy a car unless Tony sold it to them. There were money squabbles, too. They were all to draw $450 each per month and divide up the year end profits. But it was mentioned that Al seemed to be working a little more than the others. And he did, without complaint. His wife, Bertha, (Tony's sister) reminded him once in awhile, but she was always assured of driving a new demonstrator. That ought to appease her. Val didn't

Speed Queen boats featured Tony in some of their publicity photos. [Bettenhausen Coll.]

get one and neither did Herb's wife.

Bettenhausen, always scheming with a way to make the place better, came up with the idea that he could become a Mercury outboard engine dealer. He was good friends with manufacturer Karl Kiekafer. Nowadays Karl bought all his company cars from Tony and he obligingly made him an engine dealer. Along with constant Tinley Park buddies Curly McBride and Jack Ryan, they also obtained a deal to sell Speed Queen fiberglass boats which were made in nearby Orland Park. The boat deal caused more friction in the dealership. Al and Herb didn't share in the profits and felt Tony was taking advantage. Tony never mentioned that they probably wouldn't be selling half the cars they were if it weren't for his name and popularity. He took the petty bitchiness in stride and thought they were doing pretty well for a small town car dealer. He always personally took care of the complaints.

Every once in awhile, someone would come in and tell Bettenhausen that the new Chrysler he had just purchased wasn't running right. Tony would check it out and delighted in taking the owner along with Dick Brosius on a demonstration ride. He'd smile and wink as Dick got in the back seat and braced himself. They would head out of the agency up to the right, along Highway 42-A. The dealership was on 175th Street and they'd go a few miles up toward 126th, through the long sweeping curve Tony liked so much. He'd turn around and cruise about 75 mph and say, "She seems pretty good to me. Let's see if she can do better." After pushing the accelerator all the way to the floor, he would comment, "Yeah, that's more like it, 105." They would run through the long sweeper curve with Tony asking questions to the

The Bettenhausen-Schuldt dealership in Tinley Park. [Bettenhausen Coll.]

occupant like, "You think she runs okay now?" And more times than not the wide-eyed passenger would say, "Yeah! It's just fine. Think we oughta, uh, slow down a bit?"

"Mister," Bettenhausen would sometimes comment, "I think you might be driving this thing with a bent knee. Either that or you got shit in your blood," he'd say with a grin.

Bettenhausen could tell someone they didn't know what they were talking about and have them like it.

Tony never forgot about McDowell's death completely, but it filtered into the back of his mind as did Rex Mays' and Ted Horn's. You never thought about some guys who got it. You figured all along that they were good candidates. Squirrels. Shouldn't be runnin' in the first place. You believed that you could handle the situation, you'd probably never kill yourself. You just hoped that some asshole never spun in front of you, or stuck a wheel into you. And you always hoped that nothing really important would fall off the car. Or break. Like that spindle on Horn's car. And sometimes, just driving down the highway, you could easily imagine what it would be like to be back in a race car. You didn't want to drive on straight stretches of road, they were boring. When you saw a curve you really didn't want to stay on your own side of the road. You wanted to dip down close to the opposite shoulder and really make some time through that baby. Kinda punch the gas pedal just as you were in the middle of the curve and let the car have its head up to the other side. And you could never figure out how all these assholes killed themselves on the highway. Christ, driving a passenger car on the road was just about as simple as going to the bathroom. You couldn't understand why people had such trouble driving on ice and snow. You could see them up ahead, the car would start to slide a little, and ON would go the brake lights. All they really had to do was turn the steering wheel into the direction of the slide and keep right on going. You could feel that the car wasn't going to spin. So what if you were going sideways up the road for a ways? It'd straighten itself out with a little help from the gas pedal. Matter of fact, driving on snow was more interesting than just a plain old blacktop dry road. You could slide around the corners a little, and grin because you knew exactly, precisely, spot-on-the-button, where the car was going to go. How in the hell could all those people wind up in the ditch? You could tell that most of them were scared shitless from the way they were choking the steering wheel. They'd chigger the wheel back and forth every time the car made a little twitch. You knew it was easier to drive on the snow with one hand than it was with two. You could spin the wheel all the way from one end to the other with one finger and feel you were accomplishing something in the meantime. You just had to have a feel for it. Sometimes you'd come up to a left hand curve in the road and you cold imagine it was dirt, and right-about-here, you'd be bending the wheel to the left a little and you could feel the back end coming around behind you . . . it was back there just over your right shoulder, and if you glanced back you could see it about 4 o'clock. And just as it was starting to come around you'd blip the gas pedal a bit and snap the steering wheel back to the right. You'd be going around a left hand curve, just like turn 1 or 2 at any race track, and you wanted to be standing on the gas, throwin' a roostertail of dirt over the fence.

But normal people didn't have any idea of the feeling you could get running on the dirt. They could all have that very same feeling if they'd just do the same thing in the snow, but they were afraid to turn the steering wheel to the right, when the curve went left. They didn't know how to enter the corner. Enter the corner. The most important part of getting into the corner. You had to know how to get into the corner, so you could get off the corner. At the races everybody would say, "How's she gettin' off the corner?" If you don't get in right, you can't get off right. Tony sure did miss gettin' in and gettin' off.

* * *

8

Just Like Old Times, Huh Mom?

"Hey Boss," he said to Murrell Belanger, "let's go to DuQuoin."

Tony Bettenhausen had come out of retirement. On September 7, 1953 he led the first 70 laps of the Championship race driving his old 99. Now it was painted differently and said MIRACLE POWER on the hood. Belanger had taken a sponsorship. Ten-year-old son Merle was standing in the infield with his Mom and said proudly, "Just like old times, huh, Mom?" Val frowned, a little scared and said, "Shhhhh, Honey." On the 71st lap Tony went out of the race. The grease plug had come out of the rear end. Somebody didn't tighten it. Another case where something fell off the damn car.

The big "B" was back in business and the following week the team went to Syracuse. Tony won the race on his birthday, but a celebration wasn't in order. Drivers Chuck Stevenson and Jimmy Bryan tangled, hurtling Stevenson's car into the crowd. One dead and twelve injured.

In October the Chrysler Corporation decided to utilize Bettenhausen for an attempt on the 24-hour continous run record. Driving a new Chrysler at the Speedway along with assistance from factory men, Tony broke the existing marks and set a new average speed record of 89 mph and covered a distrance of 2,157 miles. His run attracted much publicity, but the end result still wasn't an Indianapolis 500 victory.

Following the Chrysler test, it was on to Phoenix. Tony set fast time of the day and won the season ending race. Now it was only five months until Speedway time again. The thoughts of McDowell, Horn, Mays and all the others that he'd known over the past 15 years faded into the back of his mind like a lost love. If you allowed yourself to dwell on them you could become melancholy. The only way to combat the feeling is to go out and concentrate on new things. The next race. You'd force yourself to remember all the good things about the particular track when you were happy. Then there's always the chance that the next circumstance will be better. If you started thinking about the possibility of getting hurt, you'd be like Henry. The thrill wasn't worth the risk.

Tony had dominated three out of the four races he entered in 1953, and the old feeling was back. McDowell just had some bad luck, he thought. A wheel broke. That probably wouldn't happen to Tony Bettenhausen. C'mon, let's get ready for the new season.

* * *

Before Tony settled down for the winter, he and Val made a trip to Mexico City for the Pan-American Road Race. Belanger had entered an Indy-type car outfitted with a Chrysler engine for Tony to drive, a far cry from the stock bodied Chrysler Tony had driven previously. The Chrysler offered a roof for protection along the grueling 1,912 mile course while the Indy machine represented an all-out competition vehicle. A simple roll-over that may have resulted in no more than a few dents in the top of the Chrysler could easily prove fatal in the Belanger entry. But Tony didn't have to worry about the treacherous roads, because by the end of the second day he was so sick from the food that he was forced to withdraw. Pal Duane Carter took over his car; he suffered mechanical problems the next day.

Nineteen hundred and fifty-four appeared as though it would be another good year in the Bettenhausen house. The economic picture was bright, cars were selling well and Tony thought he could even make time for a side deal or two. Val had a vacuum cleaner that needed repair and after taking it to a downtown Chicago dealer, Tony arrived back home with a contract authorizing him as an official Cadillac Vacuum Cleaner Distributor.

"What in the world are we going to do with 40 Cadillac vacuum cleaners?" Val asked.

"Sell'em," was Tony's matter-of-fact reply.

Bettenhausen had been hooked into believing that the loud little machines would make him a tidy side income. They sold them from the farm, the dealership, out of the trunk of Dick Brosius' car . . . anywhere they could. No one was overjoyed about Cadillac Vacuum Cleaners.

Although she never said so, Val had hoped Tony would retire from racing altogether. She had a vague dream of him working for

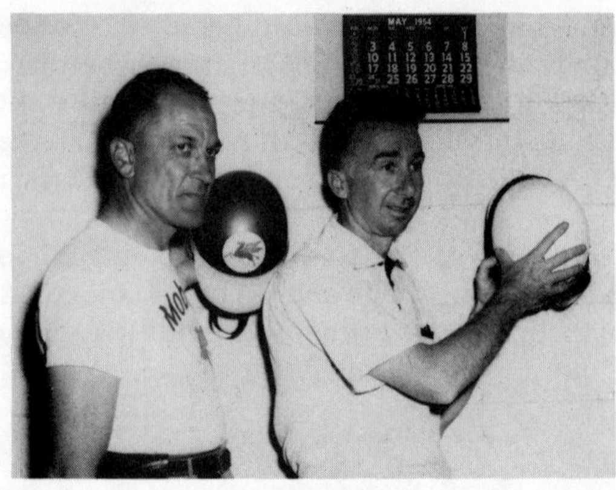

George Connor, left, and Henry Banks pose for a publicity photo showing them "hanging up their helmets," in 1954.

an accessory company. Maybe he could be a tire representative, or sell spark plugs, she mused. It wasn't quite so bad when he said he was only going to run at Indianapolis, but now with a full schedule all the old fears were back. Neveretheless, she told herself, "Valerie, you knew he was a race car driver when you married him and that's what you accepted. So keep your mouth shut and don't badger him." Around the house she knew that he was, overall, a pretty content man. Not at all like during the war years when he didn't have anything to keep him occupied. He never had lost his habit of giving orders, however, and sometimes the kids referred to him as The General. They never said it to his face, though. He'd always leave lists of things that were to be done, especially if he were going out of town for a few days. You came home from school and did your chores. You didn't have a chance for excuses, either. One late evening during the winter Tony and Henry came home after having a few beers and Tony hollered up the stairs, "Gary . . . Merle . . . did you kids feed your pony?"

"No, Daddy," was the reply.

"Well, you're going to right now, aren't you?"

"Yes, Daddy."

Henry was stopping over during a Ford training session he was taking. Henry had an eye toward the future but he said he'd run at the Speedway in May. Duke and Russo would be also. The gathering of the clan was always something to look forward to.

A few days after arriving at Indianapolis in '54, Henry and fellow driver George Connor posed for a photo showing them hanging up their helmets. Henry had decided he probably wasn't going to win as much as he might lose by continuing his racing career. He'd be content to sit on the pit wall, meander through Gasoline Alley and talk with friends. And reminisce. Remember

Nutley? Boy that was some joint. There aren't many of us around now who ran there.

Russo and Nalon remembered it. Now they were getting older and still trying for the big golden apple. A Speedway win. If the truth were ever known, it took more balls to run around Nutley in eight seconds than it ever did to run the Speedway. If they could race at Nutley, and Langhorne, and seemingly a zillion other circles all over the U. S. and win, then by God they oughta be able to win at the Speedway. Or so they believed. The Duke was entered once again in the Novi and Russo had drummed up a ride in a nice Kurtis roadster.

The term "roadster" was used frequently now. Car evolution at Indianapolis was taking place and the traditional "upright" like Belanger's 99 was rapidly becoming obsolete. For the Speedway the roadsters were wider and lower, most with engines offset to the left hand side to aid handling the continual left hand turns. You didn't race roadsters on dirt, but then who cared? The Speedway wasn't dirt, although Tony always wished it were. Tony himself was driving for car owner Mel Wiggers in another Kurtis roadster. Frank Kurtis, the man who churned out hundreds of Midgets that all looked alike, was doing a good business at Indianapolis. He was a constant innovator and had the same addiction to the sport that most drivers have.

And some fans. And all the mechanics. Plus each of the officials. And the car owners. And some sponsors. And a guy like Dick Brosius. Absolutely nothing else in the world becamse as important or all consuming as racing. For many, they didn't just become narrow-minded about the sport, they were one-track. You could walk through the pits and hear a story about a man who had 12 years tenure built up in his job. Retirement plan and benefits had been paid into. The boss tells him he has to work late on Friday and the man says, "Sorry, I gotta be at the races." The boss says you can get fired. The man says okay. The man gets fired. You can believe the story because you've lived through a similar incident yourself. You'd sacrifice absolutely anything to be around the races.

Car builder Frank Kurtis knew about the addiction. Although his factory turned out production line Midgets and had built more Indy 500 cars than any other company in history, Kurtis-Kraft didn't turn much of a profit. But Frank Kurtis probably would have paid the Indianapolis Motor Speedway to let him build a car for the race if he had to. Starter Bill Vandewater, who had been knocked silly more than once by an errant indoor Midget, would have paid to do his thing at the Speedway, too. And old Twenty

Since 1949, Larry Bisceglia, "Mr. First In Line," has been camping out in front of the Speedway each May.

Grand Steinbock reveled in the fact that patrons of the most famous race track in the world would listen to his continuing monologue. If you arrived in Indianapolis a couple of weeks before the race you'd find Larry Bisceglia sitting at the main gate in his 1933 Desoto with a sign proclaiming himself "Mr. First In Line." This was the fifth consecutive year he had the distinction of being the first man inside this speed capitol. Larry had spent his lifetime re-grooving tires by hand, but one look at him and you'd swear he was a railroad engineer. He had the right cap, Levi's rolled up with big cuffs. Car owner J. C. Agajanian could have easily been hob-nobbing with Hollywood movie stars and not worrying about getting grease on his tailor-made slacks. But he'd had the racing bug since the Thirties. He loved to around guys like Tony.

You could go down in turn one and find a photographer who hasn't missed a race in 20 years. He schedules his vacation around the month of May and has shoeboxes full of negatives that represent thousands of hours of work. He gives away his photos just to be friends with those who are closer to the sport than he is. When he dies, his wife will probably throw away the seemingly worthless film. All around the track you'll find guards who have manned their posts for years, each with a favorite story.

The Speedway is the Harvard of all racing institutions. It not only becomes a bustling city throughout the month of May, but it has its own levels of intertwined society. Here millionaire car owners mingle freely with high school dropout mechanics, members of the press, braggart drivers, nervous writers, pushy photographers, would-be stars and has-beens.

Oftentimes, however, you'd hear a disgruntled member of the racing fraternity saying to his peers: "Why I've put my whole life into this damn business. I've worked day and night, towed thousands of miles, given it everything I've got. And what have I ever gotten back? Not a damn thing. That story they just did on Charlie over there, why they should have done one on me a long time ago. You know, there's no retirement plan in this business. No guarantees. It doesn't even take care of its own. They gotta pass the hat when someone gets screwed up. Sometimes I think it's really dumb to devote your whole goddamn life to this shit. I don't know, I guess I've done it because I've liked it, but after thinkin' about all the guys I've known who've been killed . . . and . . . just everything . . . I wonder if it's worth it."

Sometimes the addicition goes away in a hurry. You don't care if you ever hear the drone of an Offenhauser. That driver who just got killed was one of your friends. Or that decision made by the officials was really lousy. So once in a while you'd find an addict who says he's leaving the sport. But you can usually lay odds that the self-imposed treatment isn't permanent. He'll be back.

Just like Tony. That line of bullshit he gave at Milwaukee, about the fact there was too much money at Indy to pass it up wouldn't hold water with anyone who's ever known a race car driver. They'd run for peanuts, popsicles or pennies so long as the peanuts weren't presented in the pits. And at the Speedway, they'd run for nothing. Tony Bettenhausen, along with the other 32 starters in the 1954 race just . . wanted . . to . . win . . the . . Speedway! He wouldn't rest until he did. And he wouldn't quit until he did, either.

Tony's mathematical chances for winning the 1954 "500" weren't good. He'd be starting the race from the seventh row. There were 11 rows of three in all. It was usually proven that if you're any further back than the fourth row you weren't running for the win. The pre-race favorite, Bill Vukovich, was also starting in the seventh row and the pair continued their needling of one another.

"Just follow me Bettenhausen, if you can, and I'll show you where the front of the pack is," Vuky said.

"You take the easy way on the inside," Tony said, "and I'll go by 'em on the outside. We'll see who gets there first."

Tony had no trouble in keeping up the needle with Vukovich, but he knew that it wouldn't really have much effect. Ever since he first set foot in the place, Vukovich performed like a verteran. Tony knew he was a smooth, hard charger. Deep down, Tony envied Vukovich's Speedway record. He knew that the quiet man was a terrific Midget driver, but he'd never followed the rest of the Championship Trail the way Tony did. Tony had commented that he'd like to get Vukovich, "out on the dirt and show him a thing or two." Nevertheless, the two men respected one another and Tony was one of the few that Vuky continued to feel comfortable with. Vuky liked to let his driving performance do his talking and still didn't have time for the reporters always asking questions. The antithesis of Tony Bettenhausen.

Two of Tony's other close buddies were also in the '54 race, Johnnie Parsons and Paul Russo. But Duke Nalon and the famed Novi were on the sidelines. Duke had missed the program. Gone too slow. It was said that he missed the signals from his pit crew on his fourth qualifying lap to pull in because he wasn't going fast enough, and everyone was surprised when he headed for the checkered flag under full power. He could have backed off and had another attempt. The foiled run was blamed on lack of communication. Some said, however, that just maybe Duke was driving her about as fast as he wanted to go. The ranks of the old Chicago Gang in the Indianapolis 500 were dwindling. Russo just barely made the race and was starting in the 11th and last row.

The 1954 "500" for Tony was nondescript. He went a little over halfway, had a bearing go out and was credited with 29th place. He watched a comely Marie Wilson, TV star of My Friend Irma, kiss Bill Vukovich in victory lane. Bettenhausen said he'd be back. Vukovich did too. He wanted to be the first man in history to win three 500's in a row.

* * *

The day after the race, Tony made an arrangement to test drive the infamous Novi. The same car Duke had missed the show in. A Novi had claimed Ralph Hepburn, it had burned the Duke when he was leading the "500," and another had bludgeoned wily old Chet Miller to death. Duke had gone 136 mph in his this year, far off the fastest time set by Jack McGrath of 141. McGrath was the only car in the field to top the 140 mark. After a briefing from Duke, Tony became a bonafide Novi driver and wished he'd had the car for the race. He turned in a lap at 141.4. He came in and everyone was all smiles. Anyone who ever appreciated the sound of an engine beamed when they heard the Novi. They described it like "a screaming banshee." The eight-cylinder Novi engine virtually wailed in comparison to the low drone of the rest of the cars, which were all powered by the familiar four-cyclinder Offenhauser. Bettenhausen made it scream for mercy. But he was careful because he knew how it could bite back.

The Chrysler Tony drove in a 24 hour factory test. Referred to in text.

Once again Tony made the annual trek to Milwaukee for the Championship race held the week after the Speedway. Evolution was taking place there, too, as the nation's most famed dirt mile track had been paved. Mechanical problems kept him out of the race that day.

Ten days later, on June 16, he was one of the guests and participants at the Chrysler Corporation's new proving grounds. The brochure read:

> On Wednesday, June 16, 1954 six hundred prominent newspaper, magazine, radio and television representatives from across the country gathered together on a green and sprawling 4000 acre tract of land near the town of Chelsea, Michigan. Here at a ceremony filled with color pageantry and fast paced events, they witnessed the dedication of the newest, largest and most extensive automotive center in the world.

Tony arrived two days early and the morning before the ceremonies, began another 24 hour speed and endurance run around the 4.7 mile oval track that featured 36-degree banking with parabolic curves built so perfectly that it was possible to drive through them with hands off the wheel. The banking at Indianapolis is only 9 degrees. Tony hadn't seen anything like it since the old days at Nutley where the boards shot up at a 45 degree angle. Along with some factory co-drivers assisting, Bettenhausen was credited with a new world's record of 2,836 miles in 24 hours at an average speed of 118 mph. He was driving a new 1954 Chrysler and was congratulated by President L. L. "Tex" Colbert as being the world's fastest car dealer. Colbert liked racing and his own son Nick would become a successful drag racer a decade later.

It was a gala affair and Chrysler spared no expense to entertain.

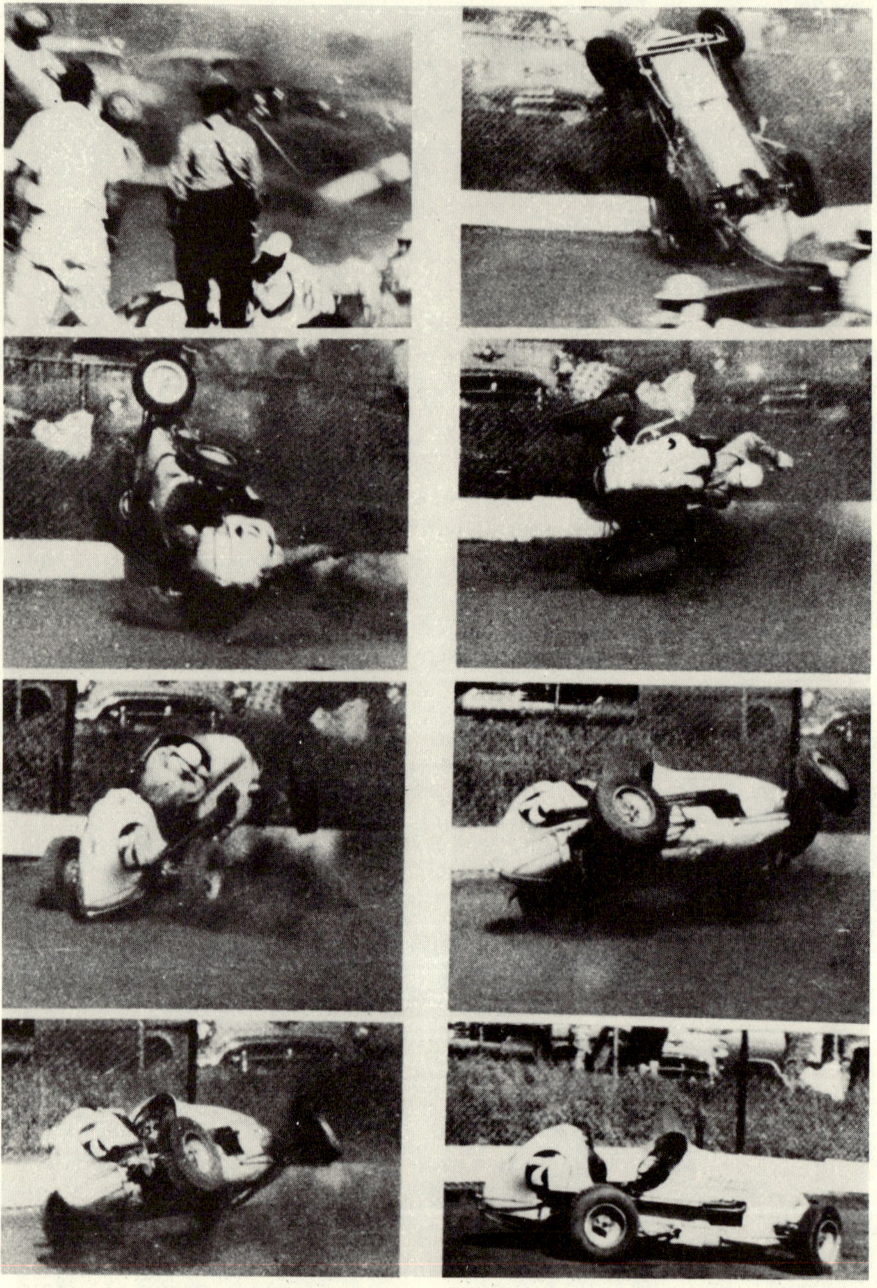

The Midget Tony crashed at Reading in June of 1954, referred to in text. [Chernokal]

Tony's 24 hour run was timed to end soon after the guests arrived. He made the Chrysler officials proud as he displayed his public speaking talent and extolled the virtues of the new car. He said he was sure he could win almost any stock car race with the new Chrysler, and proved it by coming in first at Milwaukee three weeks later in a 150 mile event. He almost didn't make it to the race though, as he very nearly killed himself at Reading, Pennsylvania, on June 27, just 11 days after the Chrysler test.

Reading promoter Sam Nunis decided to stage the first annual 100 Lap National Midget Championship and was bringing in the best in the business in an attempt to pack the grandstands. He called Emil Andres and asked him to drive the pace car, and then made a deal with Duke and Tony to compete. Duke hadn't been on a dirt track in three years and after missing the show at Indianapolis only two months earlier, reports of his total retirement were circulating. Announcer Chris Economaki had a great day telling the fans about these Chicago Gang members -- Andres, Nalon and Bettenhausen.

Duke proved that he hadn't forgotten anything about driving on the old Reading half mile dirt and was the fastest qualifier of the day, an honor that would allow him to start last in the inverted field. Tony qualified midway in the line up and before the first lap of the race was completed, everyone was again able to ask him: "Hey Bettenhausen, how many times you been upside down?"

The report in *Speed Sport News* said:

> As they roared into the start, Jimmy Bryan slammed into the outer guardrail with Bettenhausen also ploughing into the fence. Jimmy was unhurt and his car was ironed out for the restart. Bettenhausen flipped spectacularly without bodily injury but his car was out of action from then on.

Tony's son Gary had accompanied him on the trip and took off on a dead run while his father was gyrating through the air. He was the first to reach the twisted Midget and screamed, "You okay? You okay?"

"Yeah," was Tony's reply. "But I knew this damn car number wouldn't be any good. And that Bryan sure screwed up."

Tony had been scheduled to drive car number 76. Prior to the race he said, "Seven and six make 13 . . that's unlucky." So he put tape across the number 6 and drove the car as 7.

Two nights prior to the Reading race, entrepreneur Andy Granatelli brought Duke and Tony to Chicago's Soldier's Field for another 100 lap Midget race. He had publicized their appearance widely throughout the Chicago area. Midget racing had nearly been given the death knell for the past several years and there was no more seven-night-a-week racing. Now a few dedicated clubs throughout the country staged races wherever they could convince a promoter that the small cars still had crowd appeal. With the decline in popularity the format of the races had changed. Rather than short races on a weekly basis, smart promoters scheduled long races with well established stars. The races themselves were given prestigious titles such as Midwest National Championship, when in reality the event amounted to no more than a 100 lap program.

Andy Granatelli was a showman. Along with his brothers Joe and Vince, they had become Chicago's most successful racing promoters. Utilizing profits from their Grancor Automotive garage, they had seen the trend moving away from Midget racing to stock cars and jalopies. They formed the Chicago Auto Racing Association and were filling the grandstands in a way reminiscent of the 1946-48 era. But Andy was himself a racer and almost made the starting line up at Indianapolis one year. He had driven some Midgets, too, and had a soft spot for them. But he didn't allow his emotions to overcome his pocketbook. He figured that having Nalon and Bettenhausen at Soldier's Field would surely attract many fans of the two Midwestern greats.

Some 5,253 fans showed and had to watch Duke flog around in the consolation event while Tony missed the show entirely. It wasn't exactly like the old days when a Nalon-Bettenhausen 1-2 finish at a Midget race could almost be anticipated. The diehard Midget fans enjoyed the program and the Granatellis made a few bucks. But they liked it a lot better when they attracted 18,586 two weeks later for a stock car race.

After a couple more mediocre performances, some said that Tony Bettenhausen was in the autumn of his career. Was it really necessary to go back to the Midget races and try to prove something? Maybe he should just stick to Indianapolis like some of the other veterans were doing. Running Midgets was still a balls-to-the-wall propostion and there were lots of young bucks out there just itching for a shot at recognition. Bettenhausen and Nalon were considered elder statesmen of the Midget fraternity, but they didn't have any intention of finishing out their careers in the small cars as some drivers did. Sometimes you'd hear a driver say, "Running Midgets is just plain fun. It's close and competitive. I don't have any desire to get back in the Indy cars, too much politics. I'll keep runnin' the Midgets because I like to."

In reality, some of the oldtimers couldn't get a ride in an Indy car any longer, and they'd been racing so long they didn't know how to give it up. They remembered the days when they ran right up front in the Midgets and loved the praise so much they had to strive for it again. This kind of behavior was out of character for Duke Nalon. He displayed an enviable gracious attitude in victory and usually thanked the Lord that he was still fit after defeat. He had built up a fan following nationwide who'd rather not see him risk his neck in the Midgets. But Tony was as hardheaded as ever. Old cement head knew he could still blow 'em off the track and wasn't about to admit defeat. He could come up with an excuse for any poor performance.

Late summer found him teamed once again with scruffy little Harry Turner. Turner himself had a tough attitude and they made a perfect pair. If they didn't win they could come up with a good reason why they failed. And wait till next time. They'd show you how it ought to be done.

The biggest Midget race of the season was held in mid-August, again at Soldier's Field. It was to be a 250 lap affair and was paying enough money that even retired Midget owners were taking their cars out of mothballs. Some 14,000 arrived to watch the season ending spectacle. Tony made headlines again:

BETTENHAUSEN SERIOUSLY HURT AT CHICAGO

The *National Speed Sport News* report said:

> Tony was leading the event by a half lap when the engine of his Harry Turner Offy No. 3 blew up in the south turn. The car turned over on its side and struck the outside cement wall with terrific force with Bettenhausen himself caught between the wall and the car.

A second story reported:

> Melvin "Tony" Bettenhausen is now described as in "good condition" here at Walther Memorial Hospital by his attending physician, Dr. B. L. Coniglio. He has been removed from the critical list. One indication of his improvement, according to Dr. Coniglio, is the fact that 'he regained complete consciousness Saturday and immediately began complaining when we refused to let him leave to make the big races at Springfield and Milwaukee. He apparently doesn't know yet how badly he was hurt.' It has now been established that Tony suffered a severe fractured skull, a broken right shoulder and some six deep lacerations about his face and head. His first skin grafting operation took four hours Thursday morning and a couple more are still believed necessary. Although many believed that his crash Wednesday night was due to a blown engine, Bettenhausen revealed that this was not the cause shortly after he regained his full senses. He reported that he had run out of brake fluid and had no stopping power. While he is now considered on the road to recovery, Tony still has quite a distance to go before

Chicago's Soldier's Field, site of Tony's 1954 Midget crash. [*Byers*]

> he is considered a well man. Dr. Conigilo indicates that the famed "Tinley Park Express" will be hospitalized at least a month and cannot be permitted to have visitors.

Ran out of brake fluid. What Tony failed to mention to the press was that it was his own fault. He and Turner had been working on the Midget and Bettenhausen left off a brake line clip that allowed a hole to be worn in the brake line itself through constant vibration. Mechanical failure again. And upside down one more time. Tony's kids witnessed the accident, but once again Val didn't. She was out of her seat at the time, under the grandstands, and came running back only when she heard the ominous groan of the crowd. She had to get to her Tony. Duke and Lee Wallard spotted her and hoisted her over the wall. Duke had missed the show and was giving Tony signals before the accident. He began thinking that maybe it was about time to give it up for good.

But there was one more big Midget race left on the Mid-western schedule. A 200 lapper at the new Terre Haute half mile that had opened last year. Duke was offered a ride with veteran Midget mechanic Johnny Pawl. While Tony was recuperating, Duke made his bon voyage performance to automobile racing a memorable one. First he set fast time of the day and staged a race long duel with none other than chunky little Paul Russo. Russo finally faded back to sixth on the 188th lap and Duke went on to win. This is as good a place as any, he thought, to retire. But not Russo, he still had the bug. Then the Duke reconsidered. He had a ride for the Championship race at Phoenix and maybe he'd just give it another try. After all, the race papers had just said he'd made a successful comeback. He missed the show at Phoenix and watched Tony make his own comeback. The recuperated Bettenhausen himself harbored thoughts of retirement, but didn't say anything to Val about them. Tony qualified poorly, but passed eight cars on the first lap and looked like he was back in form again. Then he rode up over Jimmy Reece's wheel and the ensuing crash sent Reece to the hospital with broken ribs, punctured lung and shoulder fracture. He was in serious condition. Tony continued in the event, but went out with mechanical trouble. The following week they went to Las Vegas for another Champ car race and Duke missed the show again. Tony was involved in a second lap crash that left him uninjured. Val was glad the season was over. Then Tony reminded her the Mexican road race was being held next week. Bettenhausen didn't figure in the final standings at all, and complained that his Chrysler just couldn't keep up with the big Lincolns. The Indy drivers didn't fare too well; his pal Bill Vukovich wound up with a broken vertebra in his neck when he slid down a 40 foot bank. They hoped 1955 would be better.

* * *

"Oh, for Christ sake Tony," Val said. "A Sprint car? Why in the world do you want to go run a Sprint car?"

She was disgusted. But still she didn't harp. Tony had just informed her that he was going to drive a Sprint car in 1955.

"You haven't been in a Sprint car since before the war," she reminded him.

That was okay, Tony said. He could still run with 'em.

The Sprint car. The most feared, fire-breathing, God-awful creation ever designed for a race track would be on Tony's agenda for the new season. The Sprint car was a cross between a Midget and a Championship car. It is sized just between the two. But it didn't act like either. One the dirt half miles where they were most popular, you could always see the driver in kitchen chair like position, strong arming the wheel from lock to lock in an attempt to harness the overpowered animal. Sprint cars were for guys who wanted to prove to the world that their balls were made out of stainless steel. They were the up and comers. Prove yourself in a Sprinter and some sharp Indy car owner is going to offer you a ride. You should be able to drive one on dirt, and on the "hills." The same hills that Tony and Duke ran 1-2 against each other for the Midwestern title before the war. The hills were those steeply banked tracks at Dayton, Salem, and Winchester. Winchester was the place where two men got killed in one day, just qualifying.

Tony's 1955 "500" ride.

It had been 13 years since Tony had climbed into a Sprinter but he made his debut at Dayton (in a car owned by Mary Hulman, daughter of the man who owned the Indianapolis Motor Speedway) and finished a creditable fifth. He ran three more Sprint shows to "get ready for the Speedway." He finished fourth at Salem after a crash in the first turn made the place look like an exploding junkyard. Val was nervous. And the kids weren't too happy with him, either.

Mr. First In Line, Larry Bisceglia arrived at the Indianapolis Motor Speedway on April 18th to insure the longevity of his title for 1955. After practice and qualifying were over he was happy to see that his Month-of-May friend, Tony Bettenhausen, would be starting the event in the first row. "Yahoo!" exclaimed Bettenhausen. "We got a good chance at winning this thing from here."

Luck and fate coupled to put Tony in the first row, because he wasn't the fastest qualifier; he was just close. There was a rule at Indianapolis that roughly stated: "The fastest qualifier on the *first* day of qualifications will sit in the pole position and all other first day qualifiers earn up front starting spots. Consequently, only those who qualified on the first day were eligible for the pole, even if someone else went faster during one of the three other qualifying days."

High gusting winds kept qualification attempts to a minimum on the first Saturday. Finally at 5:30, a half hour before qualifications ended, Jerry Hoyt went out and turned in a 140 average. Tony followed some four minutes later with a 139 plus. Hoyt was on the pole and Tony was in the middle. He was the only Chicago Gang member in the event also. Russo missed the show,

Paul Russo was entertained by Dean Martin and Jerry Lewis at the '54 "500."

Duke retired. Old buddy Henry Banks came back and took a few laps in a turbine-powered racer, but he too said he was all done. Tony and Russo worked out a plan whereby Russo would drive relief. Hot weather conditions the past couple of years had demanded more relief drivers than at any other time in history. The years had not mellowed either the confident Bettenhausen nor the wisecracking Russo. Now they were two scarred old war horses who had seen each other in action. They shared an unspoken mutual respect. There was a time when the curly-haired Italian was the cream of the field. Those inspiring nights on the Nutley Velodrome where your very life was put to a test nearly every lap had left them both with a confidence that they had met the roughest and survived. Tony couldn't ask anyone else to drive relief for him. No one else quite measured up to what they'd been through together. It didn't matter that Russo had missed the show. Bettenhausen knew just what the little character was made of.

Once again Bill Vukovich grabbed the lead in the race but staged a memorable duel with Jack McGrath. Tony was a top five runner in the early stages but he, like everyone else, was bothered by the gusting winds on the backstretch. A long, white fleecy cloud of smoke appeared along the back straight shortly after Vukovich had completed 56 laps. Announcer Tom Carnegie said, "There appears to be an accident of a serious nature." The description was appropriate. Bill Vukovich had died in an attempt to win his third consecutive Indianapolis 500. The headlines screamed "Vukovich Burns to Death" but a later report showed that he died of a basal fracture. In all probability, the wind was to blame. Rodger Ward's car was virtually picked up by a gust and spun. Two other drivers took evasive action and Vuky hit Al Keller and

Bill Vukovich's car upside down.

Below: Paul Russo takes over for Tony during the 1955 race.

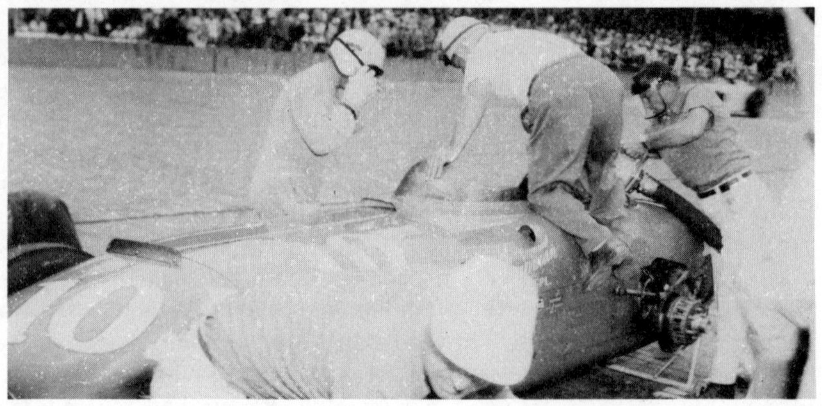

was catapulted over the guard rail into three parked cars. He brushed a telephone pole and came to rest upside down, burning.

Henry Banks broke the news to Esther Vukovich of her husband's death. Many spectators left. The carnival atmosphere of parading bands, Dinah Shore waving to the crowd, balloons floating skyward, that had all taken place just prior to the race, wasn't even a memory. The winner was dead. The favorite. He was leading the race just moments ago. How could they possibly keep the race going? It seemed like it was time to fold the tent and go home. What kind of fun could possibly come out of this day now?

"Watch that damn wind on the backstretch, Paul," Tony said when he turned the car over to Russo. "I swear it moved me over six feet."

Russo watched and drove as cautiously as he knew how. He was also driving with the knowledge of Vuky's death. Every lap he'd drive right over the black tire tracks leading into the wall. With about 70 laps remaining in the 200-lap affair, he handed the car back to Tony. Bettenhausen was assured of a third place, but a long pit stop by the second place car gave him the runner-up position. He had no chance of beating winner Bob Sweikert who had a lap lead. Second place was all right, they agreed. But they'd rather not run at all if Vukovich could be brought back. Esther Vukovich would go back to Northern California and try to rear her son and daughter alone. She didn't care if she ever heard the word Speedway again. She didn't care what anybody else said about "The Mad Russian." Sometimes they called him taciturn. All she knew was that she never did like these damn race cars in the first place.

* * *

Vukovich was mourned for a time, but once again, there was another race to be run. The traditional trip to the Milwaukee mile took place a week after the Speedway had been run. Bettenhausen climbed back into a race car and went home from Milwaukee with a grand total of $25. The retirement speech he had once given was long forgotten, and Bill Vukovich would fade into a memory as well.

It was easy to think of the good times you had with friends who were now gone. Their names constantly came up at parties. You'd remember a particular incident and get a fleeting glimpse of a friend who wasn't around any longer. You didn't want to remember how he was killed. You wanted to think of the happy times that you had shared.

Often, it was party time after the races. Sometimes you'd just break out the beer and stand around your race car for hours and re-run the day. Then you'd reminisce. Sometimes there was a party. Maybe one of the racing crowd lived close to the track and everyone was invited over. Val and Tony planned a gathering for all their friends after this year's Milwaukee race. Tinley Park was on the way back to Indianapolis and over 200 showed up to see where the Tinley Park Express called home.

The week following the party at the Tinley Park farm, the racing fraternity was awakened with some startling news. In Paris the French cabinet decided that automobile racing would be banned. Reason: 79 spectators had been killed when an errant car rocketed into the stands and disintegrated. Over 90 others were hospitalized. Board members of the AAA in America were considering their withdrawal from the sport. By August, their decision had been made and the announcement took up the entire front page of the *National Speed Sport News.*

AAA QUITS RACING

The AAA had been the nation's premier auto race sanctioning body for 54 years. It's president, Andrew J. Sordini, pinpointed the LeMans, France accident and the possibility that "it could happen here" as the major consideration for his organization disassociating themselves from the sport. He said, "The AAA feels it should no longer be identified with this activity." Hours after the official announcement was made, Tony Hulman, owner and President of the Speedway, set up a meeting to take the first steps toward forming a new organization to replace the AAA and continue sanctioning of the nation's premier races. AAA would remain in effect for the rest of the calendar year 1955. Word came through from Indianapolis in the autumn of '55 that a new, non-profit organization had been formed to replace all of the AAA functions. It would be called the United States Auto Club (USAC), rapidly dubbed "yew-sack" by the racers. Driver Duane Carter was appointed Director of Racing. Duane Carter had beaten the boards at Nutley, too.

* * *

Tony wasn't making his friends nor family happy with his participation in Sprint cars. Famed Sprint car driver Bobby Grim was once quoted as saying, "Sprint cars are for a young man in a hurry to get there . . . and an old man with no place to go." Bettenhausen was trying to prove he still had what it took. For the most part, the Sprint cars were all evenly matched and it took some genuine talent and skill to be a front-runner in one. Running a car at the Speedway where you could pick your nose going down the straightaways was one thing, but you didn't dare blink in a Sprinter. No sooner did you exit one corner than you had to get ready to set up for the next one. You had to get into the corner right, or you couldn't get off. And usually there was some guy on either side of you trying to get in the same place. But a lot of times someone would try to get in underneath you, on the inside, force you up high so you'd lose your line. Then there were the times that

Illinois Governor Adali Stevenson visits with Tony, Gary and Merle after a 1955 race. [*Bill Hill Coll.*]

the man going underneath would try too hard, he'd slide up into your car. Maybe he'd just spin you out. But maybe your wheels would ride over his and that was enough to get you upside down in a hurry. You had to trust the sumbitch running next to you in a Sprint car. And if your name was Tony Bettenhausen and you were a National Champion you were really fair game. It'd be awful nice for some youngster to call you to a showdown and let everybody see how he can out brave you. Tony Bettenhausen had a lot of notches on his belt and there would always be someone ready to challenge the old fighter. Nobody understood why in the Hell he had to get back in Sprint cars. But then no one understood why he never slowed his pace when he had a lap lead on the field of any race, either. Tony didn't want to just beat 'em, he wanted to disgrace 'em. Besides, it felt absoultely *great* running out front. one of your buddies, or the car owner would be standing in the infield giving you hand signals like he was describing the length of a fish. It was good to see that big, wide span between his hands.

Much to his family's satisfaction, Tony ran only one more Sprint race after the Speedway in 1955. He stayed busy throughout the summer with his stock car (Val liked it, it had a roof over his head), an occasional ride in Harry Turner's Midget and he ran some of the Championship Trail races. He won a couple of Stock car races, did fairly well int he Championship shows, and came on strong near the end of the season in the Midgets. He also sandwiched in a 12-hour run on the Bonneville, Utah Salt Flats in an Osca sports car to set 15 world's records.

At the end of the year he dug out the ledger book he and Val had started the year before. They began on the last page and worked their way forward, entered all their expenses and income in a methodical manner until late that night. "Just keep pourin' the coffee," Tony told her. "Who knows, someday you may have to do this yourself."

Such talk always scared Val. It still seemed as though there weren't enough hours for Tony. When he was racing Midgets six and seven nights a week and there was always someone getting killed, Val was nervous. Then back in '51 when he was winning all the Championship races by such a wide margin, he made her cringe, too. Couldn't he let up a little? Not even in his everyday existence. He was always volatile, impatient. It was easy to remember when he was pulling out of the Pole Drive-In in Indianapolis and he got impatient with all the cross traffic coming from the Speedway. There was honking and even a little shoving. Tony got out of the car and wound up in a fight with a fan from Colorado. He came back to the motel with two black eyes. They had to go out and buy him the biggest pair of sunglasses in Indy so he could go to the Speedway the next day without answering too many questions. And then just a few months later on the way home from Milwaukee with Dick Brosius, he got into it with some character in a coffee shop. He never scrapped with anyone at the races, but on the outside he never did back away from a quick one. Val knew he'd never really change. Something big inside him became satisfied after running a good race. Maybe if he ever won the "500" he'd quit, she thought sometimes. She hoped so, for until then he'd sure keep on scaring her.

What Tony didn't ever tell her was that he also scared himself, along with every other guy who was ever ready to bolt himself into a race car. At virtually any track. The fear or anxiety was especially bad at the Speedway. None of them would ever admit it. On the way to the race track it would start: you'd get a few butterflies. Sometimes they were bad. It depended on how much you wanted to remember about that particular track. If you'd seem somebody get zapped there, and you happen to think about it, you could get a really sick feeling in your gut. But you always played the Academy Award winning part. You'd keep up the chatter, keep up the psyching-out of your buddies. You'd talk about your car, changes the mechanics had made. You'd talk about broads, tires, officials. Anything. Just before the start of the "500" it was horrendous. Quiet drivers became talkative. Friendly ones became passive. Nobody looked scared. If anyone ever did walk up to you and ask if you ever got nervous, you'd reply indignantly, "Hell, no. About what?" And you knew you were lying through your teeth. Sometimes it even happened at the indoor races. To be afraid of dying you didn't have to be starting in the great Indianapolis 500. And every once in awhile you'd think, "Jeez, today just might be my day."

But there was always one thing that kept everybody coming back. You might be nervous on the way to the race, and at the track, and a little more so as you buckled into the car, but once the engine fired off, your head was clear. You'd say to yourself, "Okay, here we go. Hope this thing holds together. Let's see how we can do." And you immediately addressed yourself to your car. It felt great to be out there on the track trying to prove to yourself and everyone else how good you were. You didn't spend two seconds being afraid. Then a refreshing calmness came over you. Sometimes the race would be stopped for one reason or another and you'd grab a quick catnap before the re-start.

From the grandstands the spectators would never guess that the men walking toward their cars could sometimes have heartbeats that sounded like a jazz drummer. The announcer could interview a driver the moment before he stepped into the cockpit and even a lie detector wouldn't reveal his nervousness. The race car driver who tells you he doesn't get scared or anxious is a liar. But you'll probably never find the one who'll admit it either. It's a closed club.

Tony knew and understood the fear so well he now used it. So he never gave up the friendly needling. When he walked up to someone and jokingly said, "Watch out for me now, I'm gonna have my wheels in there right close to you," he was not only trying to bring a little comic relief to the time, he was doing his level best to instill a little fear of God. And maybe, when a competitor saw Bettenhausen coming up he'd think just an extra split second, and maybe not challenge the old codger. Bettenhausen wanted 'em to believe that he was the single, bravest chauffeur ever to come down the pike. Not braver than anyone else, but he did have probably more determination to win. He never went sliding into a corner figuring maybe he'd get upside down. He'd figure he was savvy enough to drive through the corner faster than anyone else. Yet they all should have seen him at home. He could be a real baby. He liked and needed attention. Sometimes he'd run Val ragged:

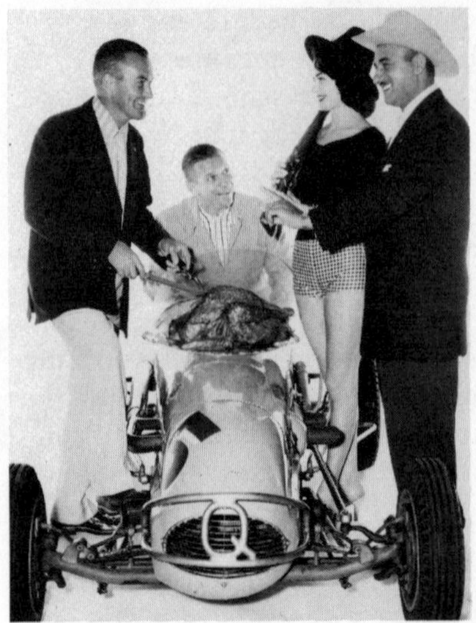

Promoter J. C. Agajanian always staged a few memorable publicity photos for his races. Here he utilizes Tony, Johnnie Parsons, Bob Hope and a pretty model.

"Val . . will you get me a Kleenex . . Val . . will you bring me a cup of coffee . . Val . . I could use an aspirin, hon."

He'd kick off his shoes and lie on the couch. He'd remind one of the kids that he wanted to get up at a certain time and when awakened he'd half laugh, half wimper, "Lemme alone . . let me sleep . . go away . . go away."

Then when he'd get up late he'd complain, "Why in the hell didn't you wake me?"

Daddy may have been awfully tough on the outside, they thought, but he was an old marshmallow inside.

* * *

During November of 1955, Tony took off the entire month to run some California Midget races. Most likely, his West Coast trips coincided with a call from J. C. Agajanian, who'd say, "Hey, I need a star. You want to run?" Aggie always made sure he had at least a couple of Indianapolis 500 drivers in his races and Tony was a popular draw. Bettenhausen and Johnnie Parsons were often the featured drivers for Agajanian's shows and he promoted them heavily. They could usually count on a photo session with either a buxom blond, a Hollywood starlet, or sometimes a genuine star like Bob Hope. Usually Tony took Val along and they were guests of the Agajanians. Over the years they'd become close friends and even though some of the Armenian's advertising had to suggest somewhat of a huckster come-one, come-all attitude, most everyone respected his honest policies.

Once he advertised that Indianapolis 500 winner Johnnie Parsons would participate in the next Midget race. Parsons called from the snowy East and said, "I'm socked in, can't get a plane out." Agajanian immediately purchased radio time that announced his advance publicity promises would have to be altered. Parsons can't make it, so don't come expecting to see him. Then at all the ticket windows he posted announcements telling of Parsons' delay: Most racers agreed they'd run an extra mile for Aggie, the sport could use more promoters like him.

* * *

Although Tony made it a point to try and return to the Chrysler dealership after his weekend sojurns to the races, it was usually Tuesday before he got back to work. He'd frequently leave on Friday morning in order to make it to a race as well. But Bettenhausen's absence still wasn't the main point for dissention in the dealership. Moreover, Tony was a liberal trying to deal with a pair of Tinley Park conservatives. Although both the Chrysler agency and John Deere store were making money, the partners got on each other's nerves with more frequency. They would split everything, right down to the last nuts and bolts in the parts bins, three-ways and close their doors. Tony wound up with some farm equipment and announced to Val, "Well, since we got the stuff we may as well start using it."

* * *

9

I Don't Think I Ever Want To Quit

After the three-way Bettenhausen-Schuldt partnership was disbanded as informally as it was formed, Herb opened a Dodge franchise and Al Schuldt moved across the street and retained the Chrysler dealership, along with Dick Brosius as his first salesman. Tony took home his newly acquired equipment and informed sons Gary and Merle that they wouldn't be looking for things to do after school now. Their summers would be busy as well. Beginning with 1956 Bettenhausen and sons would once again make the land pay. Tony still knew, however, that there were more exciting things to do on dirt than mosey along sitting atop a tractor. He'd run the Speedway again, and then pick and choose some of the fun races throughout the rest of the year. When asked directly he answered yes, he just might run some more Sprint car shows, too.

Tony was now 39 years old and by the beginning of the 1956 season he had accounted for more post-war Championship victories (19) than any other active driver. His performances, however, weren't as consistent as in the old days. Val and the kids, as well as the race fans, had seen his sometimes erratic driving and quietly wished that he would accept the success he'd already had. But Murrell Belanger had a nice roadster ready for the 1956 "500," and it carried his traditional number 99. Bettenhausen and even his old pal Paul Russo would be considered potential winners soon after practice began for 1956 "500."

Russo was 43 years old and a grandfather. He was entered in the event as a Novi driver, and his wife thought much like Val: Maybe if he wins the 500 he'll give it up. Early in May, Russo set an unofficial all-time record of 146 mph to top Tony's previous high of 144.

The last two members of the Chicago Gang were upholding the old spirit whenever the name was mentioned. Russo and the Novi clearly became the class of the field soon after the race was

Tony's 1956 roadster for the "500." [*Bettenhausen Coll.*]

underway and the press box comment was, "Well, there goes the race with the Novi..if something doesn't happen." Tony was in a top five spot early in the going, a desirable place considering normal attrition of the field. Russo's early pace was nearly ten miles per hour faster than anyone had predicted, especially the tire engineers. Going into the first turn on the 22nd lap, Paul blew a tire and crashed into the outside wall. A sheet of flame leapt skyward, reminiscent of Duke Nalon's crash in the Novi. The car bounced off, spun and again hit the concrete. There was another flash of fire as the car came to rest in the center of the track. The plucky little Italian popped himself out, ran to the infield, uninjured. He later said over the track public address system:

"Thank God I'm still here. All I could think of was Nalon when I saw that first burst of fire. I know that this medallion my priest gave me helped carry me throught."

The legend of the Novi and its devastating capabilities had once again been reinforced. Some said that maybe if a Novi ever won the 500 they'd retire it too; it had casued the end for so many. Not for Russo, he said he'd be back.

Bettenhausen, meanwhile, was having fire problems of his own, but not serious enough for him to get out of the car. He came in for a pit stop and began shouting to the Belanger crew. There was a fire under the seat and in the noise and confusion he had a difficult time talking to his servicemen. Finally a CO-2 bottle aimed under Tony and the small blaze was extinguished. It had been a long pit stop and while he was waiting, Tony pointed at one pitsider eating a hotdog, motioning him toward the car. Only so many men were allowed over the wall into the pits and the

Below: Tony had a minor fire during the 1956 race, not serious.
Right: Paul Russo ready for action.

bystander didn't know what to do. Bettenhausen kept pointing at his hotdog and finally the man got the message and passed it to the hungry driver. Tony wolfed down his snack while the crew changed tires and added fuel. As usual, he believed he could go back out and make up for lost time.

In an attempt to regain ground, he set a fast pace, as Russo had, and suffered the same consequence. A tire let go in almost the same spot and he headed full steam into the first turn wall. The Floyd Clymer 500 Yearbook said of the accident:

> "Again, the good luck held as Bettenhausen suffered only a broken shoulder in an accident that could have been fatal."

Both Russo's and Bettenhausen's crashes were recorded in full

Tony and his clan during the mid-Fifties. [*Bettenhausen Coll.*]

sequence by track photographers and reprinted side by side in the 1956 edition of the 500 Yearbook. The crash took a bit of wind out of Russo's sails and he said he'd continue in his new job with Ford Aircraft division and not run the rest of the Championship Trail. Bettenhausen said his shoulder would be fine in no time at all and he'd be back in shape before the summer was over. The Tinley Park Express still didn't see any reason for altering his schedule. You should keep runnin' to keep sharp.

Oftentimes after a driver is injured there is speculation that, "He won't be the same when he comes back, if he does." Deep down, after an accident, the drivers themselves may question their own self worth. Was there something they could have done differently. How would someone else react? To a man, they agreed that sometimes they would have to try a little harder. It is almost expected that you put in some memorable performances the first few times back in a car after your crash. Everyone is watching you with critical eyes. You could be tabbed as a squirrel or washed up.

Tony spent a restless summer waiting for his shoulder to heal and, much to Val's chagrin, said he would enter the Sprint car race at Williams Grove, Pennsylvania in mid-August. His comeback race was sucessful as he finished second and drove like a man half his age all day long. But it was rare that he found a combination the rest of the year. He ran another 15 races and had some mechanical problems, some qualifying problems. He bounced off a few fences, finally won a Midget race and then another Championship race at Syracuse. The injury was healed, but it wasn't the Tony Bettenhausen of yesterday out there. You could hear the terms "washed up" and "over the hill" once in awhile.

Everyone knew that his star could still shine brightly, but nowadays there were more clouds out front than there used to be. Tony, however, didn't think anything was different. He could come up with an excuse for every sub-performance that he, himself, believed. He wasn't about to make any drastic changes. He'd keep expanding the farm and go right on racing. One day in early 1957 he announced to the family that this was the year he was probably going to win the "500" for sure. He had just made a deal to drive the most powerful car ever to turn a wheel at Indianapolis, the Novi. He'd be teammates with Paul Russo.

The Novi had been named in honor of the town where car owner Lew Welch lived. Legend had it that originally the town had no name, just a number on the railroad stop: No. V1.

The cars Tony and Russo were driving weren't the same ones that had been run in the early Fifties. The original front wheel drive cars had been replaced with conventional rear-drive Kurtis chassis last year. But it didn't matter at all. They still sounded the same, they contained the same screaming engine that let off a higher, and different pitch than all the rest of the cars. Even the first time visitor at Indianapolis would say, "What's that?" as he heard a Novi coming down the straightaway. Bettenhausen and Russo received standing cheers when their cars were rolled out for practice.

"You think they're rootin' for us, or the cars?" the stubby little Russo asked Tony.

"Probably a little of both," Bettenhausen replied. Then he continued, "No I don't think so. You probably got all of your Wop relatives up there cheering for you," Tony nudged.

On the serious side, Russo said, "You know it's about time one of us wins this goddamn thing. I knew I could have done it last year if the rubber would have held up."

"Yeah, you gotta finish to win," Bettenhausen said in a reflective tone.

"I'd probably quit, if I ever won it." Russo noted.

"I don't think I ever want to quit," Tony said. "I love it too much. Hell, I still like runnin' the Midgets even. I'll probably be racin' when I'm on Social Security," he continued.

"Yeah, me too." Russo sighed.

Nearly two decades had passed since these two had thrilled the overflowing grandstands around the Nutley Velodrome. Back then, when they'd finally stop needling one another, their dreams were of "runnin' the Speedway." Be a star there. Then blast down the highway to some obscure little Midget race and blow 'em all off. After the Midget race you'd go eat breakfast at some greasy spoon cafe and you'd know that you were on your way to the next race. You weren't like all the other people in the restaurant. You were doing what you wanted. You could bet your bottom dollar that they were all leading dull, common lives. Get up in the morning, clock in, put in your eight hours and go home to the same old bullshit. Those people didn't know anything about livin' at all.

They also didn't know about dying either the way Paul Russo and Tony Bettenhausen did. They hadn't seen old Henry Guerand cut his head off over at Nutley. They didn't know what it was like to see Bill Vukovich over the wall on fire, when just a few minutes before you were jabbing him in the ribs. Russo and Bettenhausen were two war torn veterans reflecting on their years. They figured if they quit, they'd be just about like everybody else. And they'd known for a long time that they were different molds from everyone sitting up there in the grandstands. Now they kidded each other about a Novi 1-2 finish. Who'd be #1 and who'd be #2? They never did settle the question. Bettenhausen finally nudged Paul in the shoulder and said, "I'm gonna go get some laps in."

It was back to work as usual. You'd spend your month of May taking a few laps and then trying to communicate with your Chief Mechanic. You'd try to tell him exactly what the car was doing in the corners. The back end is a little loose, you'd say. Let's give 'er a little adjustment. Communication with the Chief during May was at least as important as talking to the man upstairs on any other day. Sometimes you'd make a suggestion and the mechanic would agree. If you didn't respect your mechanic, you were on the wrong team. You'd think that maybe something was going to fall off the car if you thought he was lazy. Or maybe you didn't think he was really too savvy about setting up a chassis. At the Speedway you fine-tuned the chassis. You gave the adjusting bolts just a little tweak to try and gain a mile an hour. Sometimes just a half mile an hour. The mechanic could say, "I've been watching down in the corner . . here, let me do this." And his mechanical change would make the car feel better. You loved him. He was a genius. Up in the grandstands the people knew only that the mechanics "toiled over the cars like they were babies." It was hard for them to understand that two identical cars, same engines and chassis, could react so differently on the track. It was probably the difference in drivers, they thought. What they didn't know was that a couple of turns of an adjusting bolt here and there could make a champ look like a chump. And vice-versa. If the car wasn't "working," no one could drive it fast.

Russo and Bettenhausen lived up to the crowd's expectations. Paul set the fastest qualifying speed of the month and Tony's run was termed "heroic" as he went out during an extremely windy period. Many other drivers refused to attempt a qualification run because of the wind. Tony nearly crashed once during his run but shrugged off the incident and said he was glad he was in the show. It was what you did in the race that really counted.

On race day the fans weren't treated to the traditional, "Gentlemen, Start Your Engines!" command as a new procedure was instituted whereby the cars pulled on to the track, single file from the pits. The new method didn't work and two cars crashed. Up in the grandstands, Crocky Wright was happy to see Paul Russo leading the race. Early in the event Tony was running as high as third and the Novi fans were hoping for that 1-2 finish. But it wasn't to be, as Tony suffered throttle linkage problems and finished 15th while Russo managed a fourth. The race was won by veteran Sam Hanks, who announced his retirement from the sport in victory lane. He was driving a car built by Tony's former chief mechanic, George Salih. It worked fine.

* * *

Crocky Wright knew better than most that a car had to "work" before it could be competitive. He never had given up Midget racing himself. Each year since 1946 he'd make a pilgrimage to Indianapolis in May for the 500 and take in several Midget races in the area. Crocky didn't come to the Midwest to race, although he wished he could, but his car racing performances had always been mediocre. He had a hard time making second class equipment work well enough to run up front. He continued to live in New Jersey and raced when he could pick up a ride in the local shows. When he came to the Midwest each year he renewed acquaintances with many of the traveling pros he'd met over the years.

There was always reminiscing, maybe the best part of going. Somebody would do something, spin, get upside down, pass a lot of cars, and it would remind you of another time and another place. Out of all his experiences, not only as a driver but as a spectator, the board track at Nutley continued as Crocky's all time favorite. Nothing had ever replaced those memories of that old bicycle velodrome, and nothing ever would.

Tony and the Novi at Monza. [*Bettenhausen Coll.*]

Crocky had seen Tony and Paul Russo along with Henry Banks and The Duke run Nutley and watched with envy as their respective careers took them to the pinnacle of the sport. His own career as a bachelor race car driver hadn't ended in 1957 and way back there in the caverns of his mind he saw himself driving around the Indianapolis Motor Speedway. Leading.

* * *

"You-a-Bettenhausen?" the skinny Italian asked.

"Yep, that's me," Tony replied.

"You-a-crazy," the man said as he tapped his finger on his temple.

The scene was Monza, Italy and Tony had just made a run in the Novi at better than 177 miles an hour to set the fastest qualifying time. The Italians had invited a contingent of Indy 500 drivers for a well-publicized "Race of Two Worlds." The European equipment was no match for the high horsepower American machinery and Tony was the class of the field. The only tracks he had ever seen where the turns looked similar to Monza were back at Nutley and the Chrysler proving ground. The Monza track was 2.6 miles around with 38 degree banks. They were ominous looking compared to the turns at the Speedway where the nearly flat corners were banked only eight degrees.

Although he didn't win the event, the Europeans remembered Bettenhausen. After Tony made a lengthy pit stop, Chris

The Jones & Maley number 33 in which Tony led the "500".

Economaki reported: "He returned and immediately blew off the leaders in an effort to 1) regain lost ground, and 2) set up a lap record."

Tony finally retired with a broken suspension part. The foreigners had now seen why they called him the "Tinley Park Express."

* * *

For the remainder of the 1957 season Tony drove Harry Turner's Midget (he won one race) and ran another half a dozen Championship races but didn't fare any better than a middle-of-the-pack performance. His career was definitely in a valley but his determination was as strong as ever. He'd been around long enough to know that a driver can have an off season. Sometimes the combinations were hard to come up with. In this business the best driver in the world can't do much when the car isn't working, he mused. Meanwhile, he and his sons were working the dirt. Gary and Merle weren't taking part in many after-school activities. There were chores at home.

* * *

"Stay tuned now for the greatest spectacle in racing," Sid Collins had said in May of 1958. In the three-story control tower located midway in the pits, along the front straight-away, the race announcer had once again let his radio audience know that they were listening to another Indianapolis 500, "the greatest spectacle in racing." It was a phrase that Sid had coined and he used it a couple of dozen times each broadcast when he broke away for a commercial. Although he had a little aristocratic air about him and was continually straightening his tie, or pulling his shirt cuff out to just the right length for the jacket, Sid Collins knew all about every driver in the race. There was no chance you'd ever see him at a dusty little Midget race somewhere, for he wasn't addicted to the sport the way old Twenty Grand Steinbock was. Nevertheless, he was a fixture at Indy. He'd been given a crack at the radio announcer's job and helped make the Speedway Radio Network. When Sid Collins came through Gasoline Alley on practice days you talked to him. You knew the folks back home would be listening to his every word, and to millions, Sid Collins *was* the Indianapolis 500. You'd believe him if he told you there was a giant oak tree beginning to sprout in the middle of the first turn. Knowledgable spectators even brought a radio to the race so they could hear him as well as track announcer, Tom Carnegie.

"Our leader at this point is veteran Tony Bettenhausen, the Tinley Park Express, driving the Jones and Maley number 33," Collins said.

In the grandstands Valerie Bettenhausen had started to cry. A landmark had been reached. She had sat next to a young man in his Ford coupe and waited all night just to get inside this place over 20 years ago. She remembered, "Someday I'm gonna race here." Now Melvin Eugene Bettenhausen was finally leading the Indianapolis 500. Gradually she recalled the talk had changed to, "Someday I'm going to win that Indianapolis 500." In reality, he'd never come close to winning. He hadn't even led the race before. Val thought, "God, Tony, please don't get hurt. Win the damn thing. Then quit."

Val had every right to be scared. She'd just witnessed the worst wreck in the history of the 500. Before one lap had been completed, 11 men were involved in a crash in the northeast turn that saw cars spinning, flipping, heading toward the infield in clouds of smoke with screeching tires. Driver Ed Elisian had spun and claimed the life of driver Pat O'Connor. The P.A. system announced that it was "remarkable" that Tony and three other drivers had made it through without contact with another car.

Tony was in the top two positions for half the race but long pit stops forced him to a final fourth place finish. The wire services carried photos of the first lap accident world-wide and a cigar-smoking cowboy named Jimmy Bryan claimed a victory kiss from actress Shirley MacLaine. But 80 million radio listeners had

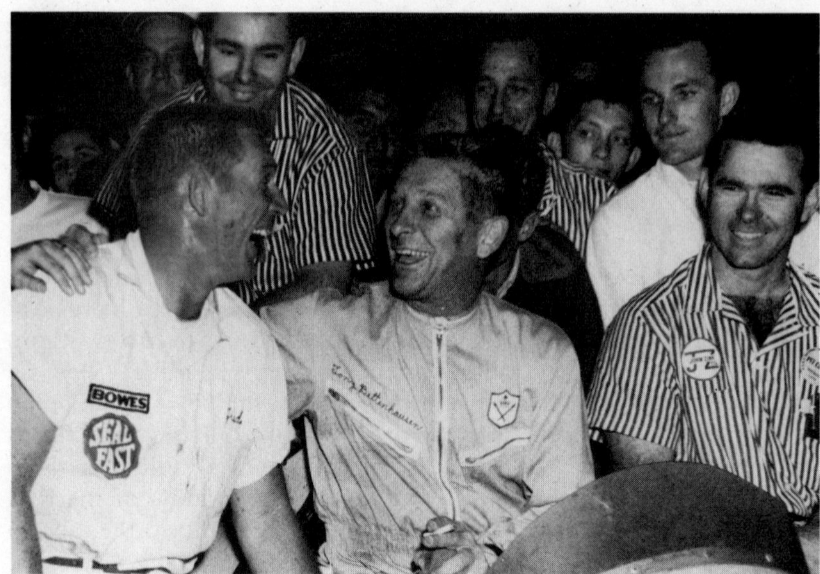

A happy Tony Bettenhausen and crew celebrate in Phoenix after Tony clinched his second National Driving Championship [1958]. [Bettenhausen Coll.]

known that Tony Bettenhausen was a contender this year. The performance helped Tony's ego. He said he'd run the rest of the circuit. Although he didn't win even one of the next 11 Championship races, he performed steadily and consistently to earn enough points to once again be crowned the 1958 National Driving Champion. The season wasn't at all like his sterling performances back in '51 when he had virtually dominated every race, but he proved to himself and the race fans that he was still a competitive driver. He figured he'd go on racing forever. Two National Driving Championships now, may as well try for a third. National Driving champs ought to claim a victory at Indianapolis, too, he believed. Next year.

* * *

1959

"Tony Bettenhausen is upside down in the south turn," Tom Carnegie said over the public address system. "We don't have a report on what happened yet, or the condition of the driver. We should know momentarily."

The murmur among the crowd at Indianapolis always turns to an eerie silence when it has been announced that something out of the ordinary has taken place. Then the speculation starts. Fans rise

The car Tony crashed in 1959. Note the roll-bar is packed full of mud. [Lower photo: Krueger]

and look toward the scene. They already know they can't see anything that has happened probably over a half mile away, but they look anyway. They want every detail. They want to be able to say, "I was there."

It was the morning of the first day of qualifications and the grandstands looked nearly as full as on race day. For a dollar you could have any seat in the house. It was first come, first served. Today was Pole Day. The fastest driver would start in the number one position. It was second in importance only to winning the race itself. Before qualifications the track was always opened up for a few last practice laps. Then you got in the qualifying line and waited your turn.

Tony was practicing when he lost control and slammed into the outer retaining wall between the first and second turns. He caromed across the track and came to rest upside down in the infield. Although the roll-bar was packed full of mud showing that it had dug in its full depth, Bettenhausen was slammed down in the cockpit far enough to avoid serious injury. He had a cut on his nose and a bruised leg. After treatment, Henry Banks picked him up at the track hospital in a golf cart and Bettenhausen commented, "You know, there's an opening in the inside fence out there and I'm sure that a big gust of wind came through and got me out of control and upside down."

Henry chuckled, raised one eyebrow and said, "Hey there, Tony. Rembember me? Henry? Henry Banks? I've been around this joint a few times myself, pal. Now there wasn't any gust of wind big enough to come through that little old hole in the wall to get you upside down. Man, you're something else. A hole in the wall . . and a gust of wind. I think you just lost it, right?"

Tony didn't reply, but managed a little chuckle himself.

Henry Banks had returned to the Speedway each year since his retirment to renew acquaintances and generally be a part of the scene. Auto racing had always been his baby. Now, in May of 1959 it was once again his livelihood. He had quit his job with the Ford Motor Company's aircraft division to accept the post of Director of Competition with USAC, the club that had been formed in 1956 to replace the AAA. It all happened rather quickly for Henry, not at all like his methodical way of doing things.

He received a call from a USAC Board member asking him if he'd consider the position. Sure, Henry said, he'd catch the next plane out and talk it over. When he arrived in Indianapolis, he was greeted by a headline that said:

Carter Fired, Banks Hired

His racing friend of nearly twenty years, Duane Carter, had been fired after a USAC Board meeting and the former driver was as surprised as Banks. Carter had been running USAC since its inception and had received a few warnings that he shouldn't consider his position as one of ruler. There was a Board to answer to, it was noted, and it was felt that Banks' background in business might suit him for the job a little better.

Carter said that USAC was looking for a "yes" man and Duane wasn't about to answer to anyone. He figured that if they gave him the job as boss, then they oughta let him call the shots. He wasn't too happy about the idea of being replaced.

Henry Banks walked into the USAC office and said, "Well, Duane, it looks like I've got a lot to learn."

"You sure do," Carter replied. And with that statement he turned around and walked out. Henry would have to plod his own way through.

* * *

Tony Bettenhausen and Howard Linne [holding Val] made a formidable team. This is a 1960 photo taken after a win at Milwaukee. [Krueger]

Henry took Tony back to the garage area and Bettenhausen began searching for another ride. Now Henry was an executive and Tony was still a full time race car driver. Tony found another ride, qualified and ran consistently enough in the 1959 race to place fourth. Throughout the rest of the season he defended his National Driving Championship admirably and wound up second in points. He made time for a few Midget races and teamed with Howard Linne, a hulk of a man, a friendly bear who had been addicted to Midget auto racing nearly as long as Tony had. If you had a ride in a Howard Linne Midget, you were in the best equipment available. He had only one piece of advice for any of his drivers: "Just stand on the gas."

Linne and Bettenhausen won some Midget races together and they spoke each other's language. If there was something new that Tony wanted to try, Howard would buy it. Plus, Howard knew all about the Illinois soil; he was a farm implement dealer.

Toward the season's end Tony teamed with another man, who also could always buy the best, Lindsey Hopkins. Lindsey had been a car owner since before the war and Tony had known him as the man who supplied Henry Banks with good equipment. Lindsey was a true Southern Gentleman. Quiet and shunning publicity, he had become a refreshing part of the racing crowd through his reserve and good nature.

"Suh," he'd quip. "Money? Money can't buy you friends, can't buy you happiness . . . . confederate money that is."

Lindsey was probably the wealthiest of all the car owners. Many thought he owned Coca-Cola, or at least controlled it. Fact was, he had a seat on the Board of Directors and a few knew that he had vast real estate holdings in Miami Beach. But at the races no one cared. He was one of the gang. Sometimes you could even talk him into doing a magic trick. Hopkins was respected by the rest of the car owners because he never made any demands on the officials, didn't boast, and left all the decisions about running his racing team up to the chief mechanic, Jack Beckley. Beckley was another addict. He too had worked his way up from Midgets, to become an Indy mechanic. Getting to the Speedway for a mechanic was every bit as important as obtaining a starting position in the line-up for a driver. On the side of every Speedway car three names were always mentioned: Owner, Driver, Chief Mechanic.

By the end of 1959 Tony had celebrated his 43rd birthday and taken on another new responsibility: He had joined the Champion Spark Plug company's Highway Safety Program. Tony's job, along with several other Indy 500 drivers, was to give talks on highway safety to high school classes. He was well received whenever he spoke and soon built up a file of congratulatory letters from high school principals. Tony found it easy to identify with the students, as two of his sons were high schoolers now, and he had drilled them constantly about safe driving. He had recently purchased each one a new 1959 Chevrolet and he didn't want to hear any reports about them becoming hotrodders. Just get your butts home after school and get to work, he had told them more than once.

* * *

Life on the Bettenhausen farm at the beginning of the Sixties was good. Money was never a problem and Tony looked forward to another year of racing on the summer weekends, expanding the farm, but most of all running at Indianapolis. He knew he could still go to an occasional Midget race and be a winner. Do the same in a stock car event and there was no doubt in his, or his competitors minds that he would be a winner in the Indy type cars. Tony was the last member of the old Chicago Gang to continue to run the rest of the Indy car circuit, the Championship Trail, as it was still called.

Henry Banks had hired Paul Russo in the Ford Aircraft Division and Russo returned to racing only once a year now, at Indianapolis, and found it increasingly difficult to get a ride. The Duke showed up every May along with Emil and countless other others who still had gasoline in their veins. Dapper Johnnie Parsons had recently joined the ranks of ex-drivers. He'd said, "Damn, I gotta quit. This is the hardest thing I've ever had to do. But I know inside that I just don't want to stand on the button enough through the corners. And that's not fair to the car owners.'' But handsome John would come back to the Speedway also. He had to come for the atmosphere. The friends. You just didn't walk away from 20 years involvement. Now he could needle Tony and his other pals, sit back on top of the pit wall and laugh about it. Besides, John liked the admiration he received every May. Parsons had been receiving admiring glances from pretty ladies all his life. You'd always find a few unattached ladies sitting behind the pits in that long section known as the Tower Terrace. Like all other spectators of that section, they couldn't see a race car on the track for over five seconds, but they knew all the action going on in the pits. Sometimes they'd wander up to the wire fence separating the pits from the bleachers and talk to a mechanic, driver or owner. Soon, a girl might be tabbed a fence-hanger. Her anatomy would be discussed by the pit population. Oftentimes she was a waitress, barhop or the like from an Indianapolis spot the drivers might frequent. The invitation was always the same: ''C'mon out to the race track tomorrow and we'll, uh, talk some.'' Girls reacted to you differently when you were in your race driving uniform. It was better than a sailor's suit. You had to be brave to drive a race car. Lots of balls. And it was a rare man who didn't bask in the admiration of some admiring female. But you had to be careful; there were always wives around and you didn't want to hear, ''I heard you were talking to some little fence-hanger today. Who was she?''

* * *

By the time Tony arrived in Indianapolis in 1960 his spirits were high. The month previous he had waged a race long duel with Rodger Ward in the season opener at Trenton, New Jersey and finished second. He had even gone so far as to let son Gary become a part of his pit crew at Indianapolis. Gary and Merle had always avoided conversations with their dad about their aspirations to become professional drivers because they knew he wouldn't approve. Tony knew, however, that Gary was mechanically minded and could see some of his own traits in the boy. Gary didn't think much of most school classes and showed only an interest in art and drafting classes. Gary figured he'd be a race car driver someday soon and wasn't even vaguely interest in going to college, much less finishing high school. He'd just as soon spend his time working out behind the house in the garage. There

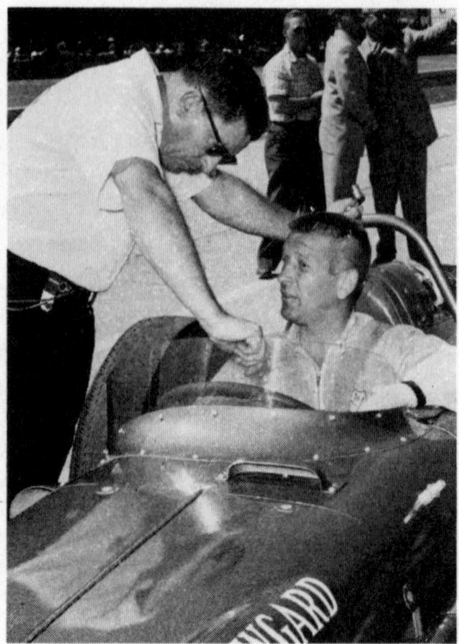

Left: Gary helped on his dad's pit crew in 1960. Right: Chief Mechanic Jack Beckley, left, listens to Tony at Indy in 1960. [*Krueger*]

was always something around the farm that needed fixing and by the time he was 18, Gary had a working knowledge of all the mechanics tools you used. He liked tools, you could do things with them. Merle wasn't jealous that Gary was the one who went to Indy to work in the pits. Merle didn't like taking things apart as much as Gary did. For him, school was okay, he didn't have too hard a time with his classes and always turned his work in on time. Like Gary, he sure wanted to see his dad win the 500. Then Merle figured, Gary would win at Indy and later on he would, too. Bettenhausens, they thought, were a part of 1) racing in general, and 2) the Indianapolis Motor Speedway.

Tony was a top five runner at Indy in 1960, no more and no less. The car Lindsey Hopkins had provided for him was good, but it didn't outclass the field. With the right luck, Tony might have won the race. But it turned out to be just another year where the Bettenhausen luck at the Speedway wasn't enviable. After running as high as second, Tony's car started smoking. He ultimately wound up with a fire in the engine compartment and came driving into the pits sitting atop the roll bar, steering with one hand. He was surrounded as soon as he stopped by men with fire extinguishers and was able to exit the car uninjured. Lindsey Hopkins and Jack Beckley told him he had done a fine job of saving the car. But, they added, it wasn't necessary for him to risk

Gary and Tony in a 1960 photo, loading Dow Weed Killer. The Dow Company utilized some farm photos for publicity. [*Bettenhausen Coll.*]
Below: Lindsey Hopkins and Tony with their 1960 "500" entry.

being burned just to bring it in. Race cars can be replaced, they said.

Throughout the rest of the summer Tony went back to all the old tracks he had known for so many years now: Milwaukee, DuQuoin, Syracuse, Sacramento, Phoenix, Springfield, Indianapolis Fairgrounds. He always ran in the top five and his fans and family seemed to expect that Tony Bettenhausen would be racing forever. Henry Banks had asked him, "Tony, how long you going to keep up in this business? You think it might be about time to hang it up?"

And the answer was always the same.

"Nope, probably keep on drivin' race cars till I collect Social Security." Tony did, however, make a decision about one race car driving career. He said to his son Gary, "Pal, your racin' days are

Ladies weren't allowed in the pits at Indy, so Tony had to talk to Val over a fence in 1960.

over. Don't get any ideas now about you bein' a race car driver. You're going to be a poppa, and that's it."

Gary had managed to get one Pat McBurnay pregnant and when Tony learned of the situation, he promptly aided in having the couple married. Gary moved off the farm and lived above Bettenhausen's Hardware Store in town. Gary Bettenhausen didn't really care what the old man said; he'd be a race car driver anyway. It was just going to take a little time to figure out how to get a ride, that's all.

* * *

"I've got some red roses for a blue lady," Tony sang as he and Val drove toward downtown Phoenix.

"Y'know hon," he said, "We don't have to work as hard as we do. Someday you and me ought to move out here while the snowballs are hittin' everybody else in the butt back home."

The 1960 season was over and Tony had taken Val on an extended holiday first to Phoenix, then a lazy two week stay in Hawaii, and back to Phoenix. There wasn't any rush to get back to Tinley Park. It was nice to see Tony in such a relaxed mood, she thought. He wasn't rushing around trying to get everything done before leaving for a race. And she had to agree that winter in Phoenix was awfully nice. She liked the farm, but it wouldn't be too long before Merle and Susie were out of high school. Then maybe they could move to Phoenix, bring little Tony and let him go to school here. It was a nice thought. Tony would probably have to have a big garage out back of the house. Just to tinker. He'd always have to have his hands in the engine compartment of something. She looked at him and thought, Mr. Tony Bettenhausen is going to be a grandfather pretty soon. Imagine that. He's 44 years old. A grandfather. She smiled to herself when she thought about him. Back in the old days, he'd skid around a corner and give her a wave, "Hi ya babe." A grandfather. A racing grandfather. Oh well, he certainly did know what he was doing when it came to driving a race car. Just second nature. She couldn't ask him to quit.

* * *

10

Hello, Val?

"Shit, Tony, I'm havin' a helluva time. I don't know, maybe I'm over the goddamn hill. But I want to keep on runnin'. You know what it's like. Can't get it out of my system. But I just want to run the Speedway."

Pudgy Paul Russo was talking. To the Bettenhausen kids he was "Uncle Paul" sometimes when he came to visit, but in reality the little Italian had been a grandfather himself for a good many years now. He was confiding in his best racing pal. Russo had missed the show at Indianapolis in 1960. The Novi he was practicing in blew a supercharger and the shrapnel cut a brake hose. Paul had to drive figure-eights in the infield to get it stopped. Then he couldn't drum up another ride. Everybody was friendly, but the old excuses were becoming familiar now.

"Like to give you a ride, Paul, but I've got this young kid here I wanna give a break. You understand."

"Yeah," Russo replied to more than one owner.

It was late in the year. Tony knew what Russo was going through. He'd had some over-the-hill feelings himself, but never admitted them. All the while he knew he was just having a bad season. He knew he'd come out of it. And so would Paul, he reasoned. Man, if they'd ever seen him blast around the boards over at Nutley, they'd be beating a path to his door just to give him a ride.

"Listen," Tony said. "C'mon up to the farm and spend the winter with me. We got lots of work here and we'll drum you up something for the Speedway. It'll do you good to live some farm life for awhile."

Russo had left his job with Ford and spent the winter of 1960-61 helping Tony install some new grain dryers and an elevator. Many nights they'd go into town and have a beer at Funk's Tavern, shoot the breeze with the boys. Talk about the old days.

Left: Murrell Belanger, right, talks with Tony and Paul Russo [left] about a new tractor. Right: Paul Russo

Remember Yellow Jacket Speedway? Remember Ascot? Tony could look back and think about the times when he really should have won the Speedway, so could Paul.

First, he was supposed to be in Bill Holland's car. Holland was leading the race, far and away, when he let Mauri Rose pass by. If I'd been in the car, Tony thought, there would be no way I would have lost.

Then he decided to let Lee Wallard drive the little 99 in the 1951 show. And sure enough, Wallard won the thing hands down. Nobody every thought about anyone but Tony Bettenhausen in the 99. What a screw-up, he mused.

That was all past history, now, Tony could tell himself. The year 1961 could be the one. He had a good car, professional crew, he felt fine, reflexes and ability just as good as ever. It was going to be the 50th anniversary of the Indianapolis Motor Speedway. It'd be a gala year.

For the first time in his life, Tony became the early favorite at Indianapolis. He received banner headlines all week in the *Indianapolis Star*:

May 7: Bettenhusen Turns Three Hot Ones, 145 MPH
May 8: Bettenhausen Hikes Hot Lap to 147
May 11: Bettenhausen Tops 149

Tony at home, reading to an amused Val. [*Bettenhausen Coll.*]

After running 149.25 mph, Tony came in and grabbed a cane from oldtimer Henry Hartz. He danced a little jig in the pits and said, "See there, it takes an old man to do it. We'll get 150 for sure.

Tony wanted to be the first man in history to turn 150 miles per hour around the Speedway, not only for the record itself, but the speed would surely put him on the pole for the race. He was clearly the odds-on favorite. This year he had found the combination. The car was right, the engine was right. Tony's driving pattern around the famed old two and one half mile plant was smooth. He had finally adapted to traditional Speedway driving style. No one could accuse him of trying to "back in" the way you did on dirt. Old Cement Head had come to terms with the Indianapolis Motor Speedway. And it was about time. He had driven more miles around the place than any other active race car driver. On Friday morning he turned some additional 149 laps and called Val.

"You and the kids going to be down here tonight?"

"Yes hon, just like usual. Soon as they get out of school we'll leave."

"Did you get the brake shoes for me from Bill Harris?"

"No, they haven't come yet."

"Dammit, call him up. I want to start plowin' first thing Monday morning and need them."

Above: Gasoline Alley, the garage area of the Indianapolis Motor Speedway, in the early 1960's.
Right: Tony confers with mechanic Jack Beckley after nearly running 150 mph. at Indy.

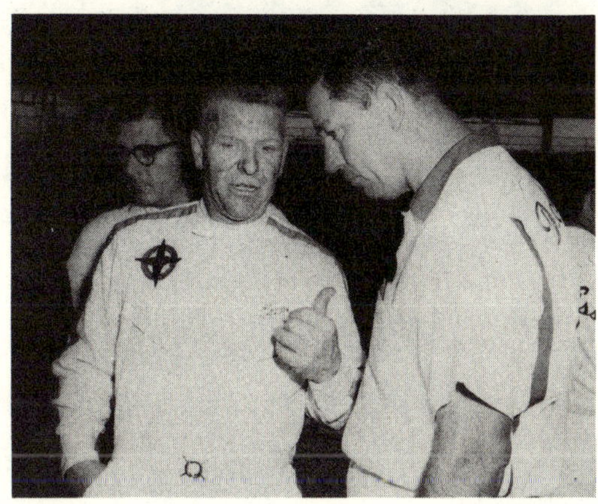

"Okay, I'll call right away. Are you going to run some more today?"

"Nope, don't think so. Man, oh, man, what a sweet runnin' machine. We'll be number one tomorrow."

"Then you're not going to run anymore today?"

"Naw, don't have to. Best car I've ever had. Sweet running thing."

"Okay, we'll see you tonight."

"Drive careful. See you later."

Tony had called shortly after lunch. Val was in a relaxed mood, the car was packed and she was just waiting for the kids to come home from school She was sitting at the kitchen table doing her nails, gently whistling the tune, "I want some red roses for a blue lady," when the phone rang.

Upside Down 28 Times... 29th Is Fatal

Bettenhausen Drove Like There Was No Tomorrow

(This story is reprinted in the Tinley Park Times by courtesy of the Indianapolis Star)

By BOB COLLINS

Tony Bettenhausen drove a race car like there was no tomorrow. And Saturday his world ended — upside down on a retaining wall at the Indianapolis Motor Speedway.

He was going like Tony Bettenhausen, fast and reckless and seeking whatever it was he searched for in his wild rides around the track.

AND THEN his time came. And a man, aged 44, who seemed to have an unswerving belief in his own immortality, was locked in a battle with run-away machinery that even he, with his incredible toughness, finally could not survive.

So they said, in newspaper parlance, write a "background" story on Tony Bettenhausen. But Tony always was in the foreground, wrapping his glamorous career in headlines, from the first race—a midget — in 1938 when his car flipped all the way over and landed on its wheels until Wednesday when he practiced at over 149 m.p.h.

THERE HAVE BEEN all kinds of race drivers, but there never was one like Tony. He had his own groove, his own theories on how to get there fastest.

He was upside down 28 times in a race car and survived, building a legend of indestructibility that was as much a part of racing as the names of the tracks where he ran his one-man thrill circuses. Tony would crank one up too fast and something would happen and guys would laugh and say "Tony got on his head again." And pretty soon he would be back, all patched up and wisecracking about it.

AND pretty soon you almost had yourself believing he always would climb out of them.

But yesterday was No. 29. And Tony didn't get out. And there was nothing but shock and sadness and the kind of silent tribute that is paid the great ones at the Speedway.

It all started for Melvin Eugene Bettenhausen in the Chicago Armory in 1938. His first race, his first flip. But Bettenhausen, then 22, soon became so proficent in the midgets, driving his own way, in his own groove, that he was winning with almost monotonous regularity.

And later came the dirt track cars and the stocks and the Speedway. Anything that would race.

ON THE DIRT he was fantastic. He won more 100-mile championship races -- 21 -- than any man who ever raced. He was the national champion in 1951 and 1958. He was all-time championship point leader with 11,535, way ahead of the nearest active driver.

But he never won the 500-Mile Race. And, oh, how he wanted to win this one. This was to be his 14th try.

He logged 1,904 laps in competition at the Speedway. And he always was charging, always pushing for the lead.

BUT HIS record is a long tale of mechanical woe . . . broken rod . . . broken clutch shaft . . . broken axle . . . spun out.

With the aid of Paul Russo, whose car he was testing yesterday, he got a second in 1955. But he couldn't go the full 200 laps until 1958 when he finished fourth.

But he never quit trying, never quit believing that the big prize one day would be his.

And this time the cocky, nervous little man had a hot car. He was going over 149 mph in practice. Guys were saying he was practically a cinch to go 150. And Tony's legions of loyal fans were crossing their fingers and saying, "Maybe old Tony is going to win one after all these years."

SO SATURDAY Tony Bettenhausen, gentleman farmer, father of four, was doing what he did best. He was doing something that was more important to him than anything else; something that had brought him international fame and a considerable amount of money.

He was driving a race car -- fast.

And Saturday it ended, as race drivers, with their fatalistic inclinations accept and as Tony must have known it eventually would, upside down on a retaining wall.

TONY BETTENHAUSEN AT THE START OF HIS RACING CAREER IN 1938.

Tinley Park Times

Published every Thursday by Semmler Press, Inc., at Tinley Park, Cook County, Illinois. Entered as second class matter at the Post Office at Tinley Park under the act of March 3, 1879. Subscription $3.50 Year. K. S. Johnson, Publisher; Glenn F. Lagoo, Managing Editor; Anne M. Rodgers, Associate Editor; Lester Rabenau, Advertising. Phone KEllogg 2-4738.

Volume 33, Number 22, Thursday, May 18, 1961 2 Sections TINLEY PARK, COOK COUNTY, ILLINOIS 10c PER COPY

'RIDE FOR PAL' KILLS TONY

FLAMES ENGULF BETTENHAUSEN'S CAR, SECONDS AFTER CRASH.

ROOKIE DANNY JONES AIDS AS FOAM IS LAID.

1957 WINNER SAM HANKS HELPS GUARD FIGHT FIRE Hanks, Speedway Racing Director, was burned on the hands.

(Photos through permission of Indianapolis Star)

Crash Due To Mechanical Failure

The death of Tony Bettenhausen, internationally famed, all - time racing favorite from Tinley Park, came in a violent crash on the main straightaway of the Indianapolis Speedway Saturday, May 13 during the pre-qualification runs.

The 44-year old "Flying Farmer" from Tinley who was national driving champion in 1951 and 1958 was battered to death instantly between the outside retaining wall and the roll bar of the No. 24 Stearly Motor Freight Special.

Tony was test-hopping the car for his close friend, Paul Russo, 47 year old racing veteran from Fortville, Ind.

Bettenhausen was killed when the car hit the retaining wall at a speed of approximately 140 mph, rolled 325 feet along the three foot high barrier, gathering up wire fence like a snowball and stopped, upside-down and caught fire.

Although the fire broke out immediately, Bettenhausen's coveralls were hardly singed due to speedy action by the track safety crew.

MECHANICAL TROUBLE

The U. S. Auto Club investigation board blamed the crash on mechanical trouble. "The anchor bolt fell off the front radius rod support allowing the front axle to twist and misalign the front wheels when the brakes were applied, which forced the car into the outer wall on the front straightaway."

Bettenhausen had averaged 145 mph on one lap, then had slowed down as if he was preparing to come in at the end of the lap previous to the crash.

But, then he raised one finger into the air to signal "just one more lap".

In the test run Tony had been using an onboard weight-jacker on the car, trying to correct handling problems for his long-time racing pal, Russo.

Since Bettenhausen had driven the No. 5 Autolite Special through the first 149 mph lap in Speedway history, prior to the qualification runs, he was almost assured of the pole position on the start.

PROMISED TO GO SLOW

His car owner, Lindsey Hopkins of Atlanta, Ga. and Miami, had consented reluctantly to allow Tony to test-hop the red and gold Stearly car for Russo. "He was a friend of Russo," said the broken-hearted Hopkins. "He asked us to let him test hop it. He promised not to run fast."

Saturday, Russo had received permission from Hopkins to drive Tony's car, the No. 5 Autolite Special in an attempt to qualify it for the race as a special tribute to Bettenhausen. He will have to average better than 143.062 mph, to put the car on the starting grid Memorial Day. He has already made several practice runs at over 144 mph.

TONY BETTENHAUSEN

Hundreds Pay Tribute To Bettenhausen

Tony Bettenhausen was laid to rest in the Tinley Park Memorial cemetery, located near his farm home on 171st st., on Tuesday, May 16. Tony died Friday, May 12 in a racing car at Indianapolis Speedway, which he was testing for his friend, Paul Russo, another veteran driver, prior to the qualifving trials.

The funeral cortege stretched for 2 - 1/2 miles . . .the exact distance of one lap at the Indianapolis track.

The funeral services held at the West End Funeral Home in Chicago Heights Tuesday afternoon were attended by some 400 persons. The Rev. Kenneth Crandall, pastor of the Tinley Park Methodist church, officiated. Masonic rites were conducted at the chapel Monday night under the auspices of Calumet lodge No. 716, A.F. & A.M. Tony was also a member of the Consistory and Medina Temple, United States Auto club, and Helms Foundation Hall of Fame.

The pallbearers were Emil Andres, a former race driver; and Paul Schuldt, a brother-in-law, both of Tinley Park; and five well-known figures of the auto racing world, Jack Beckley, "Tiny" Worley, Merle Belanger, Paul McBride, and J. C. Agajanian.

The flower arrangements filled five station wagons.

Many residents of the area came in a steady stream to the cemetery during the afternoon and evening on Tuesday to pay tribute to Tony and to view the magnificient floral pieces, some of which were in the form of racing cars and checkered flags.

Leading the funeral procession was a motor cycle escort from Chicago Heights, a state police car, and the Tinley Park police car, driven by Chief Harold Moore.

There were about 200 cars in the funeral procession, many of these from out of state.

Christened Melvin Eugene Bettenhausen -- Tony, as he has been called since boyhood -- was born on the farm on 171st st. that is now his home.

Besides his wife, the former Valerie Rice, he is survived by three sons and a daughter Gary, 19, Merle, 17, Tony Lee, 9, and Suzanne, 17. Merle and Suzanne are students at Carl Sandburg High school, and Tony Lee attends the Kirby McIntosh school.

Also surviving is his mother, Mrs. Amelia Bettenhausen, four sisters, Mrs. Lillian Brandau, Mrs. Florence Breitbarth, Mrs. Laura Younker, Mrs. Bertha Schuldt, and two brothers, Clarence A. and Herbert C.

"Hello, Val?" the voice said.

"Yes, uh, Murrell?" She was expecting a call from Murrell Belanger. Tony had some pit passes for him and he was supposed to come by and pick them up.

"No, hon," the voice said. "This is Jack."

"Jack . . ?"

"Beckley, honey. Jack Beckley."

"Well, what . . ?" She knew. Right away she knew. The fact raced across her mind. Tony's mechanic calling from the Speedway. Oh, no.

"I think you better get down here right away," Beckley said.

"Well, my God, what happened . . what's wrong?"

"Tony got in some shitbox . . and . . and he got into the wall!" Beckley blurted.

"Well how bad is it, what happened, where . . ?"

"I'm afraid it's all the way."

"Oh, no . . no . . no . . no ...."

Valerie dropped the telephone, slammed through the screen door and ran toward the road screaming hysterically, "Oh my Tony, my Tony, my Tony . . . "

The Tinley Park Express had come to its last stop. Tony Bettenhausen was dead of neck and skull injuries. The *Tinley Park Times* would headline:

RIDE FOR PAL KILLS TONY

After his call to Val, Tony had a cup of coffee in the cafeteria with Paul Russo. Paul had obtained a ride in the Stearly Motor Freight Special. He was having trouble getting up to a speed they hoped would make the race.

"You're not doing so good in that box, are you?" Tony asked.

"Not really," Paul replied. "I wish you'd take a few laps in 'er. We don't really have a Chief Mechanic, you know. The owner's the mechanic. I can't seem to get it working."

"Okay," Tony agreed. "Let's go. I can figure out what its doing."

Tony approached his car owner, Lindsey Hopkins and Beckley. He asked them if it'd be okay if he took Paul's car out for a few quick test laps.

"I'd really rather you didn't," Lindsey told him.

Beckley agreed that car hopping wasn't the greatest idea in the world. But both Lindsey and Beckley knew how much Tony liked to take a few laps in someone's car, go faster than they did, and then make a suggestion on how to make it handle better.

Tony's fatal accident.

"Listen, maybe you don't have to Tony," Russo said. "We're getting closer to really making it work okay. I don't think I'll have that much trouble getting in the show. Besides, look at those tires. They don't have any laps left in them."

"They got plenty of laps left," Bettenhausen said. "Go get a tire engineer."

One of the Firestone men checked the tread left on the tires and gave his full approval. At least 25 good hot laps left, he said.

Tony took several laps in the car at respectable speeds, then slowed down as though he were going to come in. He held up a finger as if to say, "One more lap," as he tinkered with the car's on-board chassis adjustments. Everyone was watching him come down the front straightaway. He reached the point just past the start-finish line where everybody gently taps the brake pedal to slow for the first turn.

Tony touched the brake and there was one of those immediate, "Uh, oh" feelings. The car turned right, into the knee high retaining wall. The front axle buckled under and the machine began a series of quick snap rolls along the top of the wall, gathering wire-fencing in snowball fashion around it. It knocked down six steel support beams that held up the fencing, and came to rest upside down on top of the wall. It was the 29th time Tony Bettenhausen had been upside down in his career.

It was the time he couldn't count.

* * *

USAC officials began searching for the cause of Tony's death. It was evident to all who saw the accident that something broke, or a part had fallen off the car. Cars just didn't turn right, into the retaining wall for no good reason.

The accident was attributed to human error: someone forgot to tighten an anchor bolt that holds the front axle in place. The bolt and nut were found on the race track. It had only been a few hours previous that the car had been undergoing many chassis adjustments. It was normal procedure to loosen the bolt that ultimately fell out.

Under most circumstances the car's chief mechanic would come under harsh scruntity. In the case of the Stearly car, however, the car owner served as his own mechanic, aided by several assistants. Blame could not be placed, other than to say someone was most assuredly not qualified to be trusted with normal, every day chassis adjustment. Henry Banks immediately had a rule passed that every car at Indianapolis must have a qualified chief mechanic.

But it was too late. Word spread throughout Gasoline Alley that someone forgot to tighten a radius rod bolt. Unforgivable. Every swear word in the book was used to describe the culprit. Tony Bettenhausen had died by the hand of another man. He couldn't have accepted that. But he had known full well for a long time that the possibility existed.

His dream of the Bettenhausen name winning the Indianapolis 500 wouldn't die with him. He had sired three sons who would all inherit the same singular goal. Nothing else in the world would become so all consuming as first, getting a ride at the Speedway and then, winning. Melvin Eugene Bettenhausen could never shake the addiction he had for winning automobile races. It had become so much a part of him that he passed it on to the next generation: a lethal hope that brings highs and lows that most men could never identify with. The Bettenhausen name would not be gone long from the race tracks of America.

* * *

The 1960's were a time of reformation for the Bettenhausens. Although Tony was gone, his personality would have a life-long effect on all family members. In later years the sons and daughter of Tony Bettenhausen would come to realize just how versatile a man he was. At the races he was both "Tough Tony" and a man with a ready smile. He had always liked the idea of psyching out the competition and making them believe that he had a God-given edge in a race car.

At home he was the Chairman of the Board. The General. He was The Tinley Park Express and he wanted to make sure that everyone stayed right on schedule. There was never a challenge that couldn't be overcome. In those times of financial hardship he'd wink at Val and say, "Old money all gone? That's ok...go get new money." When times were good he always believed, "money's for spending."

He had bought both Gary and Merle brand new 1959 Chevrolets and had told everyone Susie was going to have a new Corvette. Susie was definitely Daddy's little girl. He didn't have to look very hard to see much of himself transferred to her. He didn't want her to get too friendly with boys too soon. He was probably afraid she'd meet a charmer like Tony Bettenhausen and get herself in a family way. While he thought he was guarding her from the town's male population by restricting her to double dates with brother Merle, just the opposite was happening. Often times she would accompany Merle to a high school function and afterwards she would be the only female among her brother and his friends. Susan Bettenhausen became very comfortable around men in general. Tony's censure of his daughter's dating activities would later be an asset to her as she would find herself in competition with men in her work. She would never feel subservient with the opposite sex.

He was never terse with his little girl nor did he ask Merle to do things twice. Merle had always been the cherubic member of the family. He didn't argue. He looked like the chubby little kid who would wind up selling insurance. Tony didn't think he needed much encouragement, or direction. He'd bark at Merle one time and it was "Yes sir!" But he thought Gary needed some management. At times, Tony's first-born wouldn't listen to reason. Tony Bettenhausen's reason, anyway. You didn't argue with The General, even if you knew he was dead wrong. Physical violence between the two occurred on more than one occasion.

Gary would get so mad he'd say to himself, "I wish you were dead you son-of-a-bitch."

Merle felt a loss, but not one that totally devasted him when he heard the news of Tony's death. The middle Bettenhausen son had always been obedient but suffered from a lack of encouragement and support from his strict father.

Susan was shattered at the news. A part of her, irreplaceable, was gone forever. When she had announced to her father she wanted to go to college and asked permission rather than receiving a new Corvette, Tony put his arm around her and said, "Sure," in his own special warm tone of voice. Susie loved that look in his eyes when she knew that he was really concentrating on her. Tony thought it was nice that his little girl would want to give up a car and go for an education. But he thought she should have a car too. He bought her a Corvair Monza, bright red, and would have been proud of his petite blond had he ever seen her changing the seemingly endless string of fan belts that broke on it.

Namesake Tony, Jr. was just a tyke when the Indianapolis Motor Speedway claimed his father. He wouldn't have any vivid recollections of a harsh or gentle man. He knew he loved Daddy and realized that Daddy could get hurt driving race cars. When he was eight years old he began praying for him in Church. The prayers lasted a year and went unanswered. Tony, Jr. would have to meet his own father through friends and books.

Tony, Jr. didn't know his father was a serious man who seemingly utilized every hour of the day for something productive. He didn't know that one day might find him plowing a field while the next might find him dressed in suit and tie, freely mingling among corporate presidents, making them laugh. He wouldn't recall that his father could go down to Funk's tavern and come home staggering drunk and argue with Gary. Nor would he know that Tony Bettenhausen had an innate business sense. In later years Tony Bettenhausen, Jr. would see among his brothers and sister all the assets and liabilities his father possessed, and would finally learn that neither all the good, nor all the bad had been passed on to a single one. Rather, it took a wide combination of personalities to equal the rare individual they called The Tinley Park Express.

* * *

11

And Your Winner Is

"Let's all wait until he gets his helmet off folks . . there, now he can hear you. Let's all give a great big hand to our winner Gary Betten . . . hous . . . en!"

Gary Bettenhausen had just won his first USAC Midget race. The date was April 28, 1967 and the track was located at Lubbock, Texas. The car number: 99. The next night on the same race track he took a second and a few weeks later he won another Midget race at Muncie, Indiana. Tony Bettenhausen's eldest son had served ample notice that not only some desire, but talent as well had been passed on from father to son.

Nearly six years had passed since Emil Andres, Jack Beckley, Tiny Wearly, Murrell Belanger, Al Schuldt, Curly McBride and J. C. Agajanian had carried Tony to his final resting place. The funeral cortege stretched two and one half miles and was attended by over 400 persons. The town of Tinley Park was virtually shut down for the day. As the cars passed by the two-story Bettenhausen farmhouse, the passengers saw a "B" in script stylized along the chimney that stretched astride the house from the first floor past the roof. Much of Tony's farm equipment sat along the road, waiting for its master. There were shoes to fill.

But The General was gone. Valerie Bettenhausen had found herself lying in the dirt road in front of the house, knees and elbows bloodied from a fall. She was sobbing uncontrollably when two passers-by stopped. They helped her back into the house which was soon overrun with photographers, flashbulbs, reporters, movie cameras. All she knew was that Jack Beckley had said "all the way." Val Bettenhausen would try to keep the farm going without her Tony. It turned out to be more than one person without motivation could handle.

Gary had the additional responsibilities of being a father as of August 6, 1961 when Pat bore him a son: Gary, Jr. Merle

The Bettenhausen homestead in Tinley Park. [*Chini*]

graduated from high school only weeks after his father's death and much of the responsibility of running the farm would fall in his hands. Soon Susie would go off to the University of Denver to study Food and Restaurant Management and youngest son Tony was toddling along as a nine year old grade schooler. At the time of Tony's death, the family was farming nearly 500 acres and it took a strong chain to work the land. Now the master link was gone and there was no replacement. Tony used to walk around the farm with a notebook and leave lists of things to do when he was away. It was said he ran the place like it were a corporation. Gary was usually the brunt of his brief tirades, but underneath they knew he was soft as Jello. One night after a particularly hard day when he'd been terse with everyone, he broke down and cried, and said, "Don't you understand that I'm doing this all for you?"

Once he caught Merle smoking and immediately put a "For Sale" sign on Merle's Chevrolet. Susie wasn't allowed to date until she was a Senior in high school. It was okay to double along with Gary or Merle, but there was no chance that some young Tinley Park buck was going to get his hands on Susie Bettenhausen. Susie was in gym class in May of '61 anticipating the qualifying weekend when she was paged over the P.A. system. She thought she was being excused to leave early, and everyone wished her luck. As she ran down the hall and turned a corner, she saw Milford "Sleepy" Bettenhausen, a town cop of no relation. She stopped cold and said, "Oh no, how bad is it?" They took her to the principal's office and brought Merle in, too. She said, "Daddy's dead, Merle."

Gone now were the days when Susie and Val would bring hot

Valerie Bettenhausen, 1965. Merle Bettenhausen, 1961 graduation photo.

dinners to their men harvesting in the fields. There weren't any more nights when Tony would gather them all in the den and tell them an old racing story and refer to his clan as "The Tinley Park Express & Company."

In 1963, at 22 years of age, Gary had announced that he would indeed become a professional race car driver. Val replied, "You're going to have a roof over your head if you get in anything young man." Her comment did not refer to his residence, but to the type of racing vehicle she would even think of condoning. If you have a roof over your head it is generally understood that you are driving a Stock car: A modified, stock-bodied automobile with its interior gutted and replaced by a maze of tubing that formed an entire roll cage assembly. It is a rare case when a Stock car driver is injured.

Gary went to work for Beckstein Construction, the same man who had sold Val and Tony their first little bungalow. He convinced three friends to help him buy a stock car and obtained some sponsorship money from Esserman Dodge. Chicagoland residents had long been familiar with the Esserman radio commercials that always ended with a voice singing, "Es-Sir-Man Dodge" and followed by horn blasts that mimicked each syllable.

In March of 1965 Merle decided to join the Army. He knew that he would soon receive 1-A status, be drafted and have no choice to his assignment. Gary was a father, which provided adequate deferment. Susie was in school and Val decided to take a trip to Phoenix to visit old friends. While waiting for the McDaniels (who were running a little late for dinner,) she struck up a conversation with the bartender, an amiable sort of man named Webb Stephan. For the first time since Tony's death she found a sparkle back in her eye and a feeling of sensuality running throughout. Later, when Val returned to Tinley Park, Webb went out and bought an entire box of Christmas cards, threw them all away save one and sent it to her. Soon a couple of letters per day started passing back and forth between Tinley Park and Phoenix.

There wasn't much left for her on the farm. She had auctioned off the equipment and leased much of the land. She would marry Webb Stephan in August of 1965 and move to Phoenix with Tony, Jr.

While Val was moving to Phoenix, Gary was becoming totally immersed in his race car driving career. He wasn't about to leave Tinley Park, although there had been times in the past few years when he had jokingly said he might do better if he joined the French Foreign Legion. He'd made his share of problems with the girls he knew.

It all began on the night of his eighteenth birthday with Pat McBurnay. Pat was the first girl Gary had dated and he'd been seeing her for two years when he wanted to celebrate at a drive-in movie. Pat resisted, she was afraid of getting pregnant. Gary assured her that he knew what he was doing. He'd pull out. A couple of months later, Pat learned she was pregnant, ran away from home and wound up with relatives. Soon she was Mrs. Gary Bettenhausen. After a short stay in the small apartment above Bettenhausen's Hardware, her folks put a down payment on a house for the pair and Gary managed to make the payments.

One night Gary awoke at about 3 a.m. and felt that Pat was gone. He went to the garage and saw that his car was missing as well. His pride and joy, a cherry red 1959 Chevy with a four-speed and six carburetors that he affectionately referred to as the Tinley Park Terror wasn't there. He was furious. Pat came home and said she had simply gone out for a drive. A couple of Gary's friends later asked who the guy was, the other night, driving his car. Gary was livid, no one drove his car. He moved back to the farm, later tried a one-night reconcillation with Pat, but was informed that he was to sleep on the couch. He moved out again for good.

Soon he was seeing a curvaceous young lady named Joyce Hughes and he thought she was dating other fellows as well. Shortly after they broke up, Joyce informed Gary she was pregnant. Too bad, Gary said, it wasn't his problem. Joyce would bring forth a paternity suit.

Next, Gary began seeing a pretty, busty girl named Wavelyn Kent. He'd met her at the Tinley Park Bowling Alley, always a good place to pick up on the locals. Wave's parents had once bought a Kaiser-Frazer from Tony and the Bettenhausen name was familiar to them. Wave's grandparents owned Jardine's Restaurant, a popular spot the Bettenhausens frequented after the races. Wave's folks asked Gary to come live with them when Gary explained he wasn't getting along very well with his mother, after his scenario with Pat and Joyce. Gary wasn't divorced from Pat yet, she was reluctant to let go. Soon, however, Pat discovered that she herself was pregnant by one of Gary's best friends: Pat Militelo and decided to give Gary the divorce. Then Wave became pregnant. Gary was going through a divorce, a paternity suit and his girl-friend was pregnant. He was working in a Marathon gas station making $65 per week and paying out $50 in child support. He had to sell his prized Chevrolet (as well as Wave's roller skates) for survival. A professional auto racing career looked like it was a long way off.

Ever mechanical, Gary located a 1955 Chrysler in a junkyard that was missing its engine and transmission. He towed it to the farm and soon it was his everyday vehicle, but not without problems. Each night during the winter he had to carry the battery up a flight of stairs in his and Wave's new one-bedroom apartment in nearby Oak Forest. Wave's father had advanced Gary money for his divorce and told the young couple to get themselves a place to live.

Wave's pregnancy didn't last as long as it was supposed to. On January 22, 1964, after only six months and 10 days from conception, she gave birth to twin boys. They were named Cary and Todd and spent their first 45 days of life in an incubator. It would later be learned that a lack of oxygen had caused an eye disorder.

The boys were nearly blind and later years would see them holding books less than six inches away in order to decipher words. It was a sure bet that they would never announce Cary and Todd Bettenhausen in the starting line-up at the Indianapolis 500.

Throughout his bumblebee activities in bed, Gary had also managed to complete his first season (1963) as a USAC Stock car driver. He had previously run some go-karts to launch his career as the small racers at least afforded some wheel-to-wheel competition.

Through the help of his friends at Beckstein Construction, Gary ran 14 USAC Stock car races in 1963 and came home with one, glorious shining moment. He finished second to A. J. Foyt in a 100 miler on the Indianapolis Fairgrounds mile track. Foyt was one of the current young stars of USAC. He had already won the Indianapolis 500 that everyone thought was clearly earmarked for Tony Bettenhausen in 1961 and was versatile in Midgets and Sprint cars as well.

The Stock cars were often referred to as "taxicabs" by those who regularly drove Indy cars, Sprints and Midgets, but they were still race cars. Once in a while Gary would overhear someone saying something about, "He's got a long ways to go if he wants to fill his old man's shoes," but most everyone was helpful. It was common knowledge that Bettenhausens and racing went together like a horse and carriage.

The last race of the year Gary ran in 1963 was held on the half mile at Illiana, a town not far from Tinley Park that bordered Indiana. The proceeds were scheduled to be donated to the Tony Bettenhausen Memorial Hospital Fund, a charitable plan that had been fostered by Tony's good friend Dick Brosious. After Tony's death Brosious came up with the idea to build a memorial to the man so many had admired. Brosious envisioned a 100 bed hospital to be erected in Tony's memory. Emil Andres served as vice-president of the fund and friend Glen Pyles was the treasurer. For a couple of years they had regular meetings and beat the drums for their cause. They garnered over $25,000 in cash and had pledges for several times that amount. But Brosious' dream became a political football and finally the Chicago Hospital Planning Council suggested that the funds be turned over to exisiting hospitals. The money was donated to the South Suburban Hospital in Hazelcrest and a small plaque on a wall states that the Emergency Facility has been named in honor of the late Tony Bettenhausen.

Although Gary managed only one top ten finish during his rookie season, he was in the right type of racing vehicle for the times. Stock cars were not only safe, they were popular. Detroit was heavily involved in racing programs and the backing was felt all the way down to the dealer level. Esserman Dodge was satisfied with the exposure they were receiving from sponsoring Gary's car. At the first of the year Benson Ford himself had said, "The race track and road rally are the test ground for this new era. Here are being created improved engines, drive trains, suspension systems, all the components that will add up to a vastly improved breed of automobiles."

In addition, Gary was able to display his youthful determination to a number of professionals he might not have met had he been attempting to race Midgets, or any other vehicle for that matter. At Indianapolis Raceway Park, for example, he finished 14th, one spot behind a successful sports car driver named Roger Penske. Penske had recently been named "Sportsman Of The Year" at the Philadelphia Motorboat and Sportsmen show.

If you were an oval track driver and had any aspirations of running Midgets, Sprints and Championship machinery, you didn't have much respect for the gentlemen sports car drivers. They were most often referred to as tea-cuppers and squat-to-pee racers. Little did the eldest Bettenhausen son know how profound an effect sports car driver Roger Penske would have on his life.

The first Bettenhausen son was totally dedicated to the sport. On his wedding night to Wave, he stayed out all night preparing a car so he would drag race at Chicago's Amphitheatre the next day. Sometimes he would stay in the shop for two weeks at a stretch, Wave would bring him clean clothes and they would slip off to a nearby car and make love in the back seat. Wavelyn Kent had just completed a year of college before meeting Gary Bettenhausen and she wasn't too sure that she liked, or understood her new husband's obsession with this auto racing business. She didn't know anything about the car races, but reasoned that she'd get along better if she didn't nag. She had to admit that Gary was indeed a hard worker, sometimes too hard.

During the winter of 1964 Gary went to work at the Ford plant on Chicago's southwest side. The assembly line foreman soon saw that his new employee was a quick study, he learned all the jobs on the line and was known as a utility man. When someone was sick or didn't show up, Gary was given the job. He worked ten hour shifts and would come home with numb and bleeding fingers. When Wave would complain that he was pushing himself too hard, he'd tell her to keep quiet, there was a lot to do. You had to be fast to be good on an assembly line. What all do you have to do, she would ask.

Gary explained that a frame would come down the line and the first thing you did was stick a big rubber grommet in the center, up front, for the radiator to sit on. Then you go to the right front wheel and open a little bolt that bled the brake. Then you tightened a nut down on the right front steering arm, put a cotter key through it and bent it over. Then you go back to the exhaust pipe, grab an asbestos gasket out of your apron, slip it over the pipe, put the pipe in place and start three bolts. All the while the car is moving past you. Then over to the right rear wheel and bleed its brake. You had a minute and three seconds to perform all these operations before the next chassis had come down the line. Gary said he'd rather go racing, but as long as he was working on the assembly line he was going to do as good a job as he knew how.

* * *

While Gary was serving his apprenticeship in stock cars, the profile of the starting field at the Indianapolis 500 had changed drastically since his father had run there last in 1961. Ever since the first "500" was run in 1911, most every car in the race was front-engined, just like passenger cars. The year Tony was killed, an Australian named Jack Brabham arrived at Indy with a tiny, rear-engined vehicle that most thought wouldn't go fast enough to make the starting field, much less be competitive. Brabham not only qualified the car, but ran all day and finished a creditable ninth. The rear-engine revolution at Indianapolis had begun. Initially, European car builders dominated the scene but gradually, American ingenuity took hold and the men who had once built the tried and proven "Indianapolis Roadster" were now building smaller, torpedo like machines with the engines in the rear.

The new rear-engine cars were flimsy in comparison to the stout, wide old roadsters. The new breed had little struts holding the wheels on, whereas the roadsters utilized hefty straight axles that looked like they'd survive a crash. When one of the rear engine cars hit a wall, tires would fly in every direction and it appeared as though the car itself would disintegrate. The roadsters would merely receive bent frames and bodywork.

Ironically, the fact the rear-engine cars would disintegrate made them much safer vehicles: When driving a roadster, the driver would absorb much of the shock from a crash because nothing gave-way. The progress was not accepted easily by the Speedway's old guard. The new machines didn't look anything like a roadster and many didn't believe that they should even qualify for the term Championship race car. They looked funny. They were called "Funny Cars" for many years to come. Some drivers had a difficult time adapting to the different characteristics of the rear engine machinery and their seemingly endless maze of suspension adjustments. But most had to admit they could go faster in a rear-engine car if and when they could make the thing handle properly. When they crashed they were afraid of fire.

The cockpit of the rear engine machinery was fabricated much in the same fashion as the fuselage of an airplane. The driver slid down into his tubular capsule and was surrounded on both sides

Parnelli Jones' number 98 roadster is shown in comparison to Jimmy Clark's Lotus, both cars raced in 1963. By the time Gary arrived at Indianapolis, the Clark style car had obsoleted the roadster.

by fuel tanks. If you hit the wall hard enough, or another car, it was quite possible that you'd rupture a fuel tank and spew gasoline on the track, the engine and yourself.

The morning of the 1964 Indianapolis 500 saw Henry Banks walk up to rookie Dave MacDonald and say, "Dave, glad to see you're in the race. I was watching you during practice, and it looks like that thing is a little bit squirrelly. Take a hint from an old-timer who's been there. Just run all day and make some money. Don't go out and hot-dog it and get yourself in trouble."

No one ever saw Dave MacDonald again. He spun coming out of the fourth turn and was hit by the man everyone called "The Clown Prince of Auto Racing," Eddie Sachs. As Sachs hit MacDonald, both cars burst into flames that shot a trail of black smoke a quarter of a mile in the air. Neither survived, and it was called the most horrendous accident that had ever occurred at the old speed plant. Gruesome photos of the wreck appeared in many major daily newspapers around the country and television views as well were witness to the burning. Some sponsors considered quitting the sport amid the ghastly scene. Ford Motor Company was deeply involved in the 500, as it had developed the first engine ever to challenge the supremacy of the Offenhauser. Of their involvement in auto racing and the Indy 500 specifically, Ford's general manager Lee Iacocca said, "We will continue our public competition program as long as it contributes to our object of building better production vehicles. We feel the lessons learned and experience gained in these events would help build better cars."

* * *

Detroit's involvement in automobile racing might have been a boom to a Tony Bettenhausen, but it became evident early in his career that Gary did not share the same gregarious attitude his father had. Gary was all business, didn't feel comfortable talking to people. He was right at home either under the hood, under the car or behind its steering wheel. He was on a mission: He wanted to become a professional race car driver and someday run at the Indianapolis Motor Speedway. He didn't particularly have time for comparisons of his driving to his father's and he felt that all the talk in the world wouldn't get him any closer to his goal. He just wanted to go out and turn left. The car was the important thing. It was the only thing.

* * *

Merle Bettenhausen had driven in one race before he entered the Army in 1965, a jalopy event at Sante Fe Park Speedway. His job in the service saw him shuffling a lot of paperwork and he got along nicely with everyone. He was even promoted a rank before being discharged in 1967. While stationed in Oklahoma, he drove in a few Modified races and wrote a letter to Chris Economaki telling him of his activities. Chris Economaki was still *the* man most famous for writing about American oval track auto racing through his *National Speed Sport News.* Economaki had become the Hedda Hopper-Walter Winchell of the sport through his weekly column titled, "The Editor's Notebook." In addition, he was ABC's man in the pits when a race was televised on Wide

Merle in a 1964 photo, driving a jalopy style stock car. [Bettenhausen Coll.]

World of Sports. Economaki duly mentioned that yet another second generation driver was on his way up with a sentence about Merle and told he was joining not only his brother Gary but Johnny Parsons, Jr. and Billy Vukovich, Jr. as well. The beat would continue.

* * *

Susan Bettenhausen graduated from the University of Denver in 1966 at age 20. She worked continually as either a waitress or hostess throughout college, and managed to gain nearly a year's extra credits by going to summer school. She could have graduated at age 19, but thought, "Who's going to hire a 19 year old?" and decided to spend the customary four years obtaining her degree. She had previously reasoned she would enter the food and restaurant management field as she thought it was there that a female had an equal opportunity with a man.

Upon graduation she was hired by Northwest Airlines and given the title of Supervisor of Administrative Food Services. It was a heady beginning for a recent college graduate, but the airline realized that she wouldn't be drafted into the Viet Nam war effort and convinced her to move to Minneapolis, Minnesota with a starting salary of $550 per month. She would soon prove her perfectionist attitude and not her inherent good looks and desirable figure was her most important asset.

* * *

Susan took time out from her studies at the University of Denver to act as a trophy queen for the local Midget races one evening. She's shown here with John Hollingsworth. [Byers)

Valerie had relocated in Sun City, Arizona where her new husband Webb Stephan managed the lounge at Del Webb's King's Inn. Her youngest offspring Tony went to work shagging golf balls in the summertime and was soon being given free lessons by the club pros. He showed a good deal of early promise, as he was only a junior high school student when he first picked up a golf club. Both Val and Webb would encourage his new activity.

* * *

When Gary Bettenhausen had removed his helmet on April 28, 1967 at Lubbock, Texas and heard the crowd's roar for his first-ever Midget race victory, another career had begun as well. The records show that brother Merle finished 11th in the same race. It was Merle's first Midget ride, he'd only been out of the Army a few months.

Gary had completed four years of stock car racing (1963-66) while Merle had been behind the wheel of a racing vehicle only a few times. Gary had run in no less than 37 automobile races during the 1966 season, his year of change. He was now working for Esserman Dodge as mechanic, body and paint man. Service Manager George Hopkins owned a Midget and gave Gary his initial rides. Gary also obtained a ride in an Indianapolis 500 style car, but not one that was considered to be a front runner.

Although Gary had been hired by an owner name Dave McManus to drive his Indy car, there was no chance that the eldest

Bettenhausen son would be allowed to take a rookie test at the Speedway. USAC officials gave him a Championship driver's license, but Gary knew better than to ask permission to come to the Speedway. First he'd have to prove himself out on the Championship Trail. They went to many of the same old tracks Tony had run on like Trenton, and Langhorne, but Gary encountered either mechanical or personal problems. He finally made a race at Phoenix, but was an early retirement with an oil leak which put him out of the race.

His career was progressing, however. He had shown himself well in the Hopkins Midget and in October of 1966 a respected Midget owner named Bob Nowicke called him and asked if he'd like to drive his car. Gary was ecstatic. Getting a ride with Bob Nowicke was big-time. He had first class equipment. Nowicke also had a second Midget in pieces that Gary offered to put together for Merle. The year 1966 saw Gary Bettenhausen drive Stock cars, Midgets and even Championship cars. The ony thing he didn't run was a Sprint car. He had previously told wife Wave, "Listen, I'll never drive those things. They're dangerous as hell. You don't have to worry about me."

During Gary's early career, Wave went to as many races as possible, often times towing a race car while Gary slept in the back seat, drained from the exhaustion of preparing the vehicle. At first she wondered what was so all-fired important about these different kinds of races. She didn't know the difference between Midgets, Sprints, Indy cars. But it was all Gary talked about and he was racing with increasing frequency.

In June she read that two USAC Sprint car drivers had died at Reading, Pennsylvania: Red Riegel and Jud Larson, both veterans who knew what they were doing. It was another of those devastating weekends as two Midget drivers were killed also: Midget driver Dave Whitehorse (who's name wasn't familiar) and Jimmy Davies was killed at nearby Sante Fe Park. Davies was a three-time USAC Midget champion. Wave was definitely worried. Then two weeks after the Riegel-Larson accident, a pair of Northern California Sprint drivers were killed. Ron Lux, a USAC Sprint driver followed two weeks later in a Tulsa USAC race and just a few days before Gary was supposed to run at the annual "Turkey Night Grand Prix" that J. C. Agajanian was promoting at Ascot Park in Los Angeles, Don Branson and Dick Atkins were killed in the season ending USAC Sprint car race. They burned to death.

"Jesus," she would later say, "walking a tight rope is safer than driving one of those damn Sprint cars."

Gary showed that he had come of age as a Midget car driver in the Turkey Night race as he started on the front row and led for a time before going out with mechanical trouble. Young Billy Vukovich finished the prestigious event in second place but wasn't friendly toward Gary. There was some animosity between the two second-generation drivers, and it would soon be carried to the race track. Both were fighting for recognition and a chance in a Speedway car. Although there was a common bond, both their fathers had died in Speedway cars (Vuky's father was killed in a car owned by Lindsey Hopkins, the man Tony was to drive for in 1961) they hadn't ever become friends. Their sibling rivalry had been carried over to young adulthood. Vukovich didn't respect Gary's driving and was insolent toward him. Billy had been running Midgets in Northern California and was currently King of the Hill. Bettenhausen, he figured, was an upstart in the open-cockpit machinery. Gary's experience came from stock cars. Vuky referred to them as taxi-cabs. He believed that real men drove Midgets and Sprinters. If you're going to be a race car driver, he believed, then you have to drive real race cars. Real race cars didn't have doors.

Gary wanted to do well in the 1966 Turkey Night Grand Prix. His father had won the event in 1959. All in all, however, Gary would remember the year 1966 fondly as he convinced himself that he could most assuredly be a winning race car driver. And that's all that was really important in his life. Drive race cars and then win the Indy 500; Gary didn't know or care anything about the war going on in Viet Nam, or who was Secretary of State or anything else. His world was confined to the schedule of the United States Auto Club and the more he could participate in its activities, the better he would like it.

As the year 1967 dawned, 25 year old Gary started seriously entertaining thoughts about getting a ride at the Speedway. He hadn't as yet served a full apprenticeship, but his desire to be a Speedway driver was insatiable even after his insignificant performance in a Championship car the season previous, he decided he was ready. Consequently, when the announcer in Lubbock, Texas announced to the crowd that Gary Bettenhausen was the winner of the Midget feature, his hopes were at an all-time high. Regulars along the USAC Midget circuit said it was a miracle that he was even alive, much less winning. Only two and a half weeks before the race in Lubbock, Gary had nearly broken his neck in his first Midget crash.

Another driver had spun in front of Bettenhausen at Phoenix, and Gary had no place to go. The other car suffered a rear-end malfunction and spun in the middle of the front straightaway. Bettenhausen hit him and flipped violently all the way down the main stretch and into the first turn. They wanted to take him to the hospital, but he convinced the medics that he was ok. Besides, he had been promised a Championship ride the next day on the Phoenix mile track and he didn't want to miss it for anything. Soon, however, the pain in his neck was unbearable. A late trip to have x-rays revealed he had broken several vertrabrae. It was no big deal, he said, he'd be ready for the race at Lubbock. All he had to do was get the car straightened out. Brother Merle had been the first one to reach the scene of the accident and Gary responded by saying, "I'm ok...I'm ok...how's the car? That asshole. Did you see him? Spun right in front of me?"

Merle towed the car back to Chicago and called on old family friend Harry Turner, who had a greasy little race car shop within earshot of Chicago's Loop. Gary had a neck brace on when he arrived, but still worked on the car day and night. They didn't have time to start the Midget before leaving for Lubbock and Merle had to drive nearly the entire distance by himself, while Gary slept. Upon arriving at the race track Merle got lucky and located a Midget without a driver. In reality, it was an old, uncompetitive machine, but to Merle it was the best thing he'd ever seen. A race car owner had said, "Yes, you can drive it." That's all he was waiting to hear. Gary went about the business of firing up his car and getting the engine warm. It sounded terrible. He had just completed two weeks of day and night labor only to find out that the engine had suffered some internal damage from the Phoenix crash. It sounded, Gary thought, like it had a bent valve. All the way from Phoenix to Chicago, Chicago to Lubbock, and now he discovers the engine needs work. Rather than swearing and getting mad, or looking for another ride, Gary reached in his tool box and found a long, tubular piece of steel called a socket-extension. He pulled a spark plug from the ailing motor, fished around until he felt the bent valve and proceeded to beat on the extension with a hammer. Bettenhausen engineering was once again being practiced at a Midget auto racing track.

Gary won the feature event and the next night finished second. Merle ran 11th and 12th, respectively, in the two nights of racing and was smiling all the way home. They had to get to Indy practice for the 1967 "500" was going to start in just a couple of days.

Gary believed he was ready for Indy. His prior performance in a Midget, coupled with his famous name would at least get him a chance to take the mandatory rookie test. He'd worry about obtaining a car for qualifying and the race later. The rookie test

Gary, left, and Merle with their Bob Nowicke owned Midgets. [*Bettenhausen Coll.*]

was the important part. There was always a considerable amount of car hopping going on during qualifying at Indy and chances were that Gary would have been able to pick up a ride.

Val, however, had other ideas. She came to the Speedway and had a talk with Chief steward Harlan Fengler. Fengler was a former driver from the 1920's era who had seen it all. He had a reputation for running track activities his way. Val said Gary needed more time, he was too green yet. Please, she asked, don't let him on the track. Deny him the rookie test.

"Whaddya mean I can't run," Gary sobbed. He was crying in the USAC office. "I just won a Midget race...been running stock cars for years and...."

USAC officials informed Gary that he didn't have the necessary experience. You couldn't just go out and run for a few years and expect to be an Indianapolis 500 driver. If you really want to run here, they told him, get back out there on the circuit and get some more miles. There'll be another Indy 500.

Gary's tears didn't last long. He went to Muncie, Indiana on May 26 and registered another first place finish against USAC's best Midget drivers. Then he went home and started putting together a second Midget for Merle to drive.

For the remainder of the year Gary ran every possible Midget race and the record shows that he wasn't able to live up to his word with his wife: He drove a Sprint car in November of 1967. The season ending Midget races were still traditionally held in California and it was seemingly etched in stone that no Midget

J. C. Agajanian and Henry Banks flank Gary after his first trophy win in a Sprint car. He won a trophy-dash at Ascot in November of 1967.

driver worth his crash helmet would ever miss a chance to run in the famed Turkey Night Grand Prix. Consequently, Gary headed to Los Angeles a couple of weeks early and was offered a ride in the Knox & Hill Sprint car at Ascot. Gary's USAC Sprint debut was impressive as he was among the four fastest qualifiers of the night and came home victorious in the night's three-lap trophy dash. Even A. J. Foyt, who had just won the 1967 "500," told him he looked pretty good. He had beaten Foyt in the trophy dash and finished the feature race two spots behind the three-time Indy 500 winner. Foyt won the Sprint car race.

Gary knew the Sprint cars were awesome in comparison to a Midget. Nowadays they mostly all had snarling Chevrolet V-8 engines that provided far too much horsepower for the average race car driver to handle. Gary knew how many men had been killed in the machines that often displayed malevolent behavior. The family didn't like it when Tony had announced he was going to return to Sprint car racing. But all that horsepower under your right foot felt good. Gary could handle a Sprint car, he knew he could.

With a blissful feeling inside after his initial Sprint car race, Gary felt like he was where he ought to be, close to winning, all the time. He knew he was racing with the nation's best, not just some local racing organization that ran one or two nearby tracks. He was traveling with the United States Auto Club and running third in point standings after only his second year in Midgets. He was

Right: Car owner Bob Nowicke watches Gary after his Manzanita win.

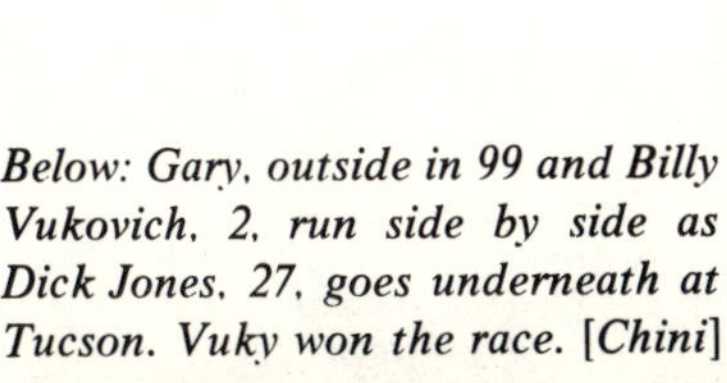

Below: Gary, outside in 99 and Billy Vukovich, 2, run side by side as Dick Jones, 27, goes underneath at Tucson. Vuky won the race. [*Chini*]

ready for the Turkey Night Grand Prix, the world's most famous Midget race. But first, there were four quick dates to run.

He went to El Cajon and ran fifth. Then it was on to Tucson and Phoenix where there'd be at least fifty Midgets each night trying to make the 18 car starting field. At Tucson he and Billy Vukovich banged wheels with one another as the oldtimers shook their heads and said, "Those kids are gonna kill themselves if they don't cut that crap out."

Vukovich won the Tucson race with Gary right on his bumper. The next night at Phoenix was November 18th, Gary's 26th birthday and he celebrated it with a win. Auto racing writer Ronnie Allyn reported in the *National Speed Sport News*":

> Second Generation Stars...Vukovich, Bettenhausen Win in Arizona Midgets
>
> Bettenhausen and Vukovich, both sons of late Indianapolis greats were dueling wheel to wheel for the lead going down the backstretch of the half-mile oval on the final lap when Bettenhausen's car touched wheels with Vukovich's, sending it

After a win at Phoenix, Gary and promoter Agajanian shared victory circle. [*Chini*]

> bouncing into the crash wall in a wild spin. Third place driver Sonny Ates rammed Vukovich and then the wall with his car bursting into flames.
>
> Although neither driver was injured some hot words were spoken between Vukovich and Bettenhausen following the race.

The six-foot, lanky Vukovich had learned that he couldn't intimidate Gary Bettenhausen. Gary had privately said, "I'll make that sumbitch like me...ain't nobody going to dislike Gary Bettenhausen for very long you know. But they're gonna have to respect me out there on the race track 'cause I ain't gonna give an inch."

From Phoenix it was on to the Turkey Night Grand Prix. As usual, promoter J. C. Agajanian was blessed with enough cars to make up three Midget races. Even A. J. Foyt and two-time USAC National Champion Mario Andretti were entered. Aggie still knew how to attract the big names. Once again, racing writer Ronnie Allyn was able to report:

> Gary Bettenhausen scored a surprise win in Thursday night's 27th running of the annual Thanksgiving Day Night 150 lap USAC Midget Grand Prix at Ascot Park before 5,500 fans.
>
> The 26 year old Tinley Park, IL pilot became the first son of a former winner to take the southern California Midget racing classic. His famed father, Tony, won the 1959 event.

Gary had not only won the race, he lapped the entire field. He ignored motions from his pit to slow down. He didn't know how.

Gary in his Turkey Night winning Midget, 1967. [*Chini*]

He had a rhythm going and couldn't quit. Mario Andretti finished fourth; A. J. Foyt was hit in the face with a rock and suffered a badly bruised eye and nose. Gary had dirt in his teeth at the checkered flag, but it tasted sweet. They'd have a tough time turning him down at Indianapolis now.

Chris Economaki would later comment that the driving tactics of Gary Bettenhausen and Billy Vukovich toward one another should be tempered before the results became serious. Neither Bettenhausen nor Vukovich walked up to one another and offered their hand in truce. They just sort of started smiling at one another when the new year began.

* * *

Although the appearance of the vehicles at the Indianapolis Motor Speedway had changed drastically since Tony Bettenhausen was killed, much of the Gasoline Alley population had stayed the same. There were welcome additions in the way of foreign race car drivers and designers, bringing an international flavor to the event. When Gary arrived in May of 1968 he was witness to one of the most controversial technological advances ever made at the Speedway. If Andy Granatelli had his way, all the cars would be silent. No more roar. No more vroom. No more wacka-wacka. Just a whoosh.

Granatelli had progressed from Chicago street urchin, to auto

Andy Granatelli being interviewed by Economaki. [Torres]

mechanic, to race car driver, to racing promoter and finally what some termed, "automotive snake-oil salesman." Granatelli had successfully packaged a very thick petroleum product called STP and sold hundreds of millions of dollars worth. He utilized Indy 500 racing as a rolling billboard for STP and pasted STP stickers on everything from bumpers to breasts. Andy Granatelli was another who had a dream of winning the Indianapolis 500 and while he didn't get the chance to accomplish it as a driver, he wanted more than anything to do it as a car owner.

The year previous he had set the Indy establishment on its proverbial ear by bringing a turbine-powered car to the race. Parnelli Jones silently whooshed to nation-wide headlines and came within three laps of going to victory circle. The turbine broke a gear on the 197th lap of the 200 lap contest. Most every car owner at Indy cried "foul" when the turbine outclassed them and USAC responded by restriciting Granatelli's new machines to a smaller engine size. Andy and his turbine had become so controversial and famous that the Tonight Show's Johnny Carson had even come to Indy in the off season and run the original car at over 140 mph. Granatelli garnered more publicity for the Indianapolis 500 than it had ever had before. He also made sure that an STP decal was always located somewhere near the camera's eye. For 1968 he brought three new wedge shaped turbine cars to the "500." It turned out to be a fortunate circumstance for Gary Bettenhausen.

* * *

Before Gary came to Indy in 1968, he had run Joe Hunt's Dirt car on some of the paved tracks. He's shown here at Phoenix outside of Arnie Knepper who's driving a conventional rear engine car. [*Chini*]

"Look at that," a mechanic said. "Who in the Hell does that Bettenhausen kid think he is. There's no way he's going to make the show in that old box."

Gary Bettenhausen had arrived at Indianapolis in 1968 with a car that looked like the one his father had driven back in 1950. Amidst the new, low-slung, rear-engine machinery, Gary's Championship Dirt car looked like a Model "T." Bettenhausen had received permission to take his rookie test and had teamed with car owner Joe Hunt. Hunt had installed a turbocharged Offenhauser in his Dirt car and Gary managed to run 149 mph, the same speed his father had run seven years previously. Hunt's car, however, was designed to run on the one-mile dirt tracks and wouldn't stand a chance of making the starting field. Officials suggested that Gary try to obtain another ride as soon as possible.

Billy Vukovich was also in his rookie year at Indy in 1968. He had convinced J. C. Agajanian to bring him to the Speedway. Aggie had two cars and soon Bettenhausen was in Vukovich's back-up machine breezing through his test. Gary and Billy were learning to like each other, Vukovich was duly impressed when Gary drove the back-up car faster than Vuky was going in the team's number one entry. Aggie worried about both young drivers.

Gary ultimately landed a ride in Fred Gerhardt's Thermo-King entry when regular driver Art Pollard went to drive a Granatelli turbine. One of Granatelli's turbine drivers, Mike Spence, was killed during practice when he hit the wall and received massive head injuries. Fred Gerhardt had tried both Bettenhausen and Bob Hurt in his machine before making a decision on who the new

Rookie Billy Vukovich in Aggie's 1968 Indy car. [*Mahoney*]

driver would be. Hurt got into another machine and wound up as a paraplegic when he too hit the wall. He would spent the next 15 years undergoing experimental operations all over the world in an attempt to live up to his vow: "Someday, I'll walk through this place."

Both Bettenhausen and Vukovich qualified for their first Indianapolis 500's. Val had mixed emotions about the situation: She could remember sitting outside the track in the front seat of a Ford Coupe and hearing her man say, "Someday I'm going to race here." This plot of ground in Indiana that had caused her more pain than glory would still be on her mind. She was both proud, and scared. One more time now, all she could do would be hope for the best. Old friend J. C. Agajanian had acutally helped the sons of his old time friends make the race that had taken their lives. How would he feel if they lived the cliche of following in their father's footsteps? Andy Granatelli could remember the day when he really had an eye for Valerie Bettenhausen, but now he would look at her differently. He knew, as she did, that in late May, some engines would roar to life when the man said, "Gentlemen, Start Your Engines," and they all realized that there was a magnetism about the place that would bring them back again and again. You could look at one of Indy's participants and if you knew their history you'd probably be able to find some compassion inside you for something that happened, somewhere along the auto racing trail that involved them. They all have an unspoken camarederie for one another. Gary Bettenhausen and Billy Vukovich making the 1968 starting field could only lead to more memories.

* * *

Above: Gary qualified this car for his first 500, 1968. Indy cars were changing drastically in the early 1960's.

Right: Henry Banks congratulates Robert Wagner and Paul Newman on their entry into USAC during the film "Winning." [*IMS*]

Gary ran an uneventful race in his first year at the Speedway: He went out after 43 laps with oil cooler problems. Vukovich ran all day and was given "Rookie of the Year" awards. Once again, a turbine appeared to be a sure winner, but leader Joe Leonard had victory whisked from his grasp with only eight laps to go when a fuel pump broke. USAC would effectively ban the turbines for the following year and Granatelli would sue, causing the most expensive lawsuit in the history of the club. More focus by the media was now being placed on the Speedway than at any other time in history. Even Hollywood had taken an interest and made a movie there titled, "Winning," starring Paul Newman, JoAnn Woodward and Robert Wagner. As the cars became more sophisticated, commercial interest would grow in Indy 500 racing.

Granatelli's example of utilizing racing as an advertising medium would be exemplified by car owners and drivers seeking sponsorship. Talk around the Speedway had it that auto racing was becoming big-time. Soon, some said, the American public would know that Indy 500 drivers were more than greasy-fingernailed jalopy drivers seeking thrills.

* * *

12

Tony Would Have Been Proud

Gary Bettenhausen had proven his versatility after the running of the 1968 "500." He had been competitive in Stock cars; had won Midget races; knew he could drive a Sprint car with the best of them, and was now a bona fide Indianapolis 500 driver. Car owner Fred Gerhardt was so impressed with Gary's performance that he offered him a permanent ride in his Championship car. In all probability, Gary could have made an above average living if he confined his driving activities to only the Championship cars, as there were 12-15 races per year and each offered substantial prize money. While Gerhardt's operation was considered competitive, it wasn't blessed with an over-supply of money. The team wasn't in the same class as the top half-dozen or so who always had the latest, and fastest equipment readily available. Still, Gary wouldn't have to put his neck on the chopping block just to make the races. Least of all, he didn't have to drive Sprints and Midgets to put food on the table. But he wanted to. There was something about driving a Sprint car that made his motor run full speed. He loved driving Midgets and there were still several one-mile dirt tracks that took a special car called a Championship Dirt machine. He wanted to run them all.

A month before the Speedway had opened in 1968, Gary received an opportunity to drive a Sprint car at Reading, Pennsylvania. He finished second in the race and everyone said it was an outstanding performance for a rookie. Then car owner Willie Davis offered him a ride in another Sprint car. Davis had a car, a few tires and wheels and three hundred dollars in his pocket when he left Los Angeles in April. He was ready for an assault on the Midwest Sprint circuit. If the money ran out, he said, he'd load up and go home. Gary had actually driven Davis' car once in 1966, but stuffed it into the fence and was told, "Go on home and learn how to drive a race car. Maybe I'll talk to you again someday."

Left: Willie Davis [Chini]

Below: Billy Vukovich, 98 and Gary run side by side at Milwaukee in 1968. [Mahoney]

Willie Davis was one of the original Southern California hot-rodders who had gained a reputation for fielding quality equipment. His involvement in the sport dated from mid-Forties and he thought he was a pretty good judge of talent. Gary ran second in the Davis machine (at New Bremen, Ohio) the week following the Reading race, and the portly Davis was all smiles. He had enough money to get ready for the next show at Dayton, Ohio, held only a couple of days after Indy. He'd found himself a young hot-shoe who was ready to stand on the gas for all he was worth.

The USAC Sprint car circuit had been dominated throughout early 1968 by a driver named Larry Dickson. By the time the Sprint cars visited the famed high-banked track at Dayton, Dickson had racked up five consecutive wins. Dickson knew Bettenhausen was good on the dirt tracks, but everyone still agreed that the true test of a Sprint car driver came on the paved highbanks. The tracks at Winchester and Salem, Indiana along

Larry Dickson, 1968 [*Mahoney*]

with Dayton half-mile hadn't changed significantly since Tony and Duke Nalon ran them in the Forties. It was one thing to hop in a little Midget and do your stuff on the quarter-mile tracks, it was said, but only those with brass balls would try the "Hills" as they were still referred to.

Dickson pushed his winning streak to six in a row after the Dayton race and Gary Bettenhausen held his breath for a seventh place finish. Just making the show was an accomplishment, however, and Gary admitted he had a bit to learn about the Hills. Only five days after his inauguration to the highbanks, Gary came within a whisker of death in a Midget. During the running of the three-lap trophy dash at Hales Corners, Wisconsin, he tangled with Mel Kenyon and went for one of those breath-taking spills that could have once again broken his neck. He wound up with broken blood vessels in his eyes, a common injury to the open-cockpit drivers. He was able to joke about the incident and said he'd be ready for the Championship race in a few days at Mosport, Ontario. He looked terrible but his determination wasn't affected.

Following the Mosport event, he and Willie Davis scored their first-ever USAC Sprint car win and received headlines in *National Speed Sport News* that said;

"Bettenhausen Unseats Dickson"

Left: Gary in the Davis Sprinter at Clovis, Ca. in 1968. [*Chini*]

Opposite: No less than eight USAC Midgets can be seen in this first turn photo taken at El Cajon, Ca. Gary is in car 99, learning his trade. [*Chini*]

Larry Dickson had set an all-time USAC record and won seven consecutive Sprint races when Gary logged his first win at Terre Haute, Indiana, on the dirt half mile. Gary not only won the race, but was the fastest qualifier among 38 cars. Sprint car rookies usually had a difficult time just making the starting field and weren't expected to be competent in the machines until at least their second or third year. Larry Dickson was a veteran who didn't like the idea of some upstart with a famous name cutting in on his territory. He figured he'd have to give this kid a few driving lessons.

But Gary didn't need any. He had found his element. He was running some kind of open-cockpit car almost on a daily basis now. Two days after his win at Terre Haute in June, he drove a Midget for Harry Turner at Davenport, Iowa and won. The next night he finished second in Illinois and then made a quick trip to Pennsylvania where he won another Sprint car race. Two days later he registered his best Championship finish to date by taking a third on the tricky Langhorne oval. The following weekend he came home first at New Bremen, Ohio in another Sprint race.

He would continue his fearless schedule throughout the remainder of the summer and well into fall and winter. Often times he would sleep in his driving uniform and not be aware of the day of the week.

By fall, the headline that both Merle and Gary had been waiting for appeared in *Speed Sport News*:

"Tony Would Have Been Proud"

Merle was in his second season as a Midget driver and had been

slowly progressing toward the front of the pack. He didn't display the same all-or-nothing gut determination for blasting around a race track that Gary had, but looked consistent and smooth. His apprenticeship had paid off in September when he outclassed 67 of USAC's best Midgets and won his first race on the fast five-eights mile track at Indianapolis Raceway Park. The same night Gary won a Sprint race at Reading. They were in the big-time. Sometimes you'd see a license plate that said, "USAC-The Major League of Auto Racing." The names Gary and Merle Bettenhausen were now know to every open-cockpit fan in America.

Throughout the 1968 season Gary ran in 27 Sprint car races and won an amazing seven of them to finish second in points behind champion Larry Dickson. He basked in the admiration he received from being a winning Sprint car driver. It was common practice among Sprint car drivers, owners, fans to boast of the difficulty of mastering the perilous machines. When they'd hear someone espousing the virtues of a particular non-Sprint car driver, they were apt to say, "Bring him to Winchester...let's see how he does on the hills." Or "Bring him to Terre Haute and let's see how he does running through the ruts." Gary Bettenhausen hadn't mastered Winchester, but said he'd be back full time next year. Merle didn't have enough miles under his belt, to try his hand at Sprint racing yet. He wanted to go slowly up the ladder, take it a step at a time.

* * *

By 1968 the United States Auto Club had become the most

prestigious and respected auto racing organization in the world. Through Henry Banks' cautious leadership, all four divisions of race cars were enjoying full schedules. USAC sanctioned Indy cars, Sprints, Midgets and Stock cars. The most famous Stock car drivers of the country were concentrating on the southern NASCAR circuit, but most agreed that the South was Stock car country and they could keep it. Auto racing in general was enjoying increased popularity and once in a while you could see a race on TV. As the last year of the decade approached, Henry Banks was looking forward to continued prosperity. He had brought the club from a near zero bank account to its present status of number one in the industry. When he took over leadership from former race driver Duane Carter, the USAC offices consisted of three rooms atop a dress store. Now, USAC had its own two story building located only two blocks from the entrance to the Indianapolis Motor Speedway.

Thus it was with an open mind that he greeted a young man named Carl Hungness who had asked for an appointment. Henry was always willing to at least listen to someone with an idea:

"Hi, Mr. Banks. Carl Hungness is my name. I've, uh, written you two letters and haven't received a reply to either one of them. So I thought I'd come see you."

"Oh yes," Henry replied. "I've got them right here. Well, we've been awfully busy with this Granatelli lawsuit you know. Let's see now, what is it you want to do...change our newsletter to a regular newspaper?"

"Right."

"Where you from?"

"Denver."

"Did you come back here for the races?"

"No sir. I came back here to see you."

"You mean you drove all the way from Denver just to see me...because I haven't answered your letters?"

"I figured it was the best way to get an answer. Besides, it's real easy to say 'No' on the phone."

"Are you driving that old car out there? What is it?"

"It's a 1928 Graham-Paige, sir."

"A Graham-Paige? I remember those things. Had a six-cylinder in it, right."

"That one's got a new Mustang engine in it."

"Well," Henry laughed. "If you drove that old clunker all the way from Denver just to see me, and see if you could start a weekly newspaper I have some bad news for you. I can't make that kind of decision. I'm just the Director of Competition around this place. I get all the flack if something goes wrong, but they don't really let me have a free-hand in running the place. We have a board of directors, as you probably know and they get to make all the decisions. I just have to live with them."

"Will you get me an appointment to see the board?"

"Well," Henry scratched his chin and looked toward the ceiling. "You might be in luck yet. They're having an Executive Committee meeting tomorrow, downtown. I'll get you on the agenda. But don't get your hopes up. We've had this little weekly newsletter since 1956 and it has been serving us just fine. Besides, there's lots of racing papers that cover USAC. I'm sure you've seen *National Speed Sport News* . . . old Economaki has been around as long as I have. I don't think we need a newspaper."

"That's ok, just let me talk to the board. If they say no, I'll go back home."

J. C. Agajanian had previously befriended Hungness in Denver and had given him the same basic advice.

"Listen Carl," the Stetson-shod promoter said, "I've known those people back in Indianapolis for many, many years. They're a conservative bunch. You don't look like you have a lot of money and I wouldn't go wasting any of it on a proposal for a weekly newspaper. They've already got a newsletter. Take my advice and forget it."

Utilizing a sales pitch and presentation that convinced the USAC board that they didn't have a tool to fight back toward some of the allegations that were often made toward them, and the fact a prestigious organization should have a newspaper, the board bought Hungness' plan. He offerd to work for $100 per week, plus a percentage of any advertising he sold. He convinced them that the paper would not only make money, it would serve to bring USAC news to race fans nationwide. Worldwide. USAC was in the newspaper business. In January of 1969 the first issue of the new *USAC NEWS* was published and it was an immediate success. No one in professional auto racing had ever heard of its editor Carl Hungness, but they agreed that a newspaper printed on white paper rather than newsprint certainly was pretty. Besides, the old newsletter gave them only the barest essentials in results and photos. Henry Banks was proud of the new publication. Chris Economaki was slightly jilted. He commented that he though USAC was in the business of sanctioning automobile races, not publishing racing news.

* * *

"Hi, I'm Merle Bettenhausen," the chubby young man had

MERLE

Above: Winter of 1968-69, Merle at Western Springs Speedway in Auckland.
Right: Friend Willie Kay and Merle celebrate with Champagne in Auckland.
Below: Merle and Bob Tattersall in a publicity photo at the Sydney Showgrounds. [*Merle Bettenhausen Coll.*]

Bob Tattersall, foreground and Merle were treated like royalty during their Australian, New Zealand tour in the winter of 1969. [Merle Bettenhausen Coll.]

said. "I guess you're the editor and founder of our new newspaper. Nice job. I just wanted to stop in and introduce myself."

"Yeah, fine...I'm Carl Hungness. Nice of you to come by. You're doin' good in Midgets."

"Thanks. Wanna go to lunch?"

"Sure. Love it. What'll it take to ever get your brother Gary to say 'Hello'?"

"Oh, Gary?" Merle mused. "Well, he's kind of got to get to know you. Why, have you tried talking to him?"

"Yeah, he don't say much. Sort of curt, know what I mean?"

"That's just his way. Hang around a while, he'll soften up."

Merle Bettenhausen would take the time to meet someone new in the sport. His attitude was that a stranger might be a friend he hadn't met yet. Gary Bettenhausen would initiate a conversation with someone only if there were a direct relationship with one of his goals. And even then he was hesitant, insecure. At the races he was thinking about tire combinations, gear ratios, how to drive the race. He'd rather take a look under the hood of the car than make small talk with the army of photographers and writers who were always hanging around. Merle figured that the car had a mechanic (usually its owner) and he'd do better if he relaxed and talked to reporters. Besides, Merle thought, the engine either runs or it doesn't and there wasn't a lot he could do to help it.

Merle's value as a public relations man was proven early on in his career when he went to Australia and New Zealand to race

Midgets. During the winter of 1968-69 he substituted for Gary in the races "down under." The promoters had requested that the elder Bettenhausen make the trek, but Gary's busy schedule kept him home. He convinced them, "My brother Merle has been racing too, you know. Take him. He'll do a terrific job." The promoters were at first hesitant because Merle's name hadn't as yet appeared in the win column but they hoped the crowd would come see a Bettenhausen race.

Merle traveled with a New Zealander his own age named Willie Kay, who was also hooked on racing. Merle not only ran against the locals and won, but was put up against veteran Bob Tattersall in several match races. He performed extremely well and the experience paid off when he got back to the states for the early 1969 races. The Aussies invited him back for the following season. He not only won races, but made friends everywhere he went. After talking with Merle, Willie Kay wanted to come to the United States.

* * *

"Look at that young man broadsliding through the corners! He's running *dangerously* close to the guard rail! He' powersliding and throwing up a rooster-tail just like his Daddy used to do!"

The voice came booming over the public address system and was nearly drowned out by the roar of the engines. Chris Economaki was standing up, microphone touching his lips and blood vessels straining in his neck. He was describing Gary Bettenhausen's driving performance to some 31,000 people inside the Houston Astrodome. Economaki had long ago out-classed old Twenty Grand Steinbock, the golden voice of the speedways from yesteryear. When you heard Chris Economaki announcing a race, you knew absolutely, positively, beyond-the-shadow-of-a-reasonable-doubt that he was describing the greatest spectacle you had ever seen to date.

"Just like his Daddy used to do," Economaki had blared. He was right, but most occupants in the capacity crowd had never seen Tony Bettenhausen run a Midget, or anything else. Economaki didn't care. By the time he was done with them they'd believe that Gary Bettenhausen was the world's greatest Midget driver. Economaki had spent enough years blasting up and down the nation's highways to famed and obscure race tracks to know what the grandstand population wanted to hear. If he could have been as excited about selling toilet paper, the world would have looked white from afar.

But on this night in March of 1969, Economaki was rightfully

Above: It isn't the Astrodome, just an indoor race at Ft. Wayne where the Bettenhausens were regular competitors.
Right: Gary following his Astrodome win in 1969. [Chini]
Below: Gary on his way toward winning the Astro Grand Prix inside the Houston Astrodome. [Messer]

Left: Tony, Jr. [Chini]
Below: Merle at the Astrodome in 1969.

frenzied. Not since the days immediately following World War II, had the Midgets played to 31,000 spectators. It was a Midget racing weekend that would go down in racing annals as a classic. All the big-guns of the Indy 500 were racing including A. J. Foyt, Mario Andretti, the Unser brothers, Lloyd Ruby, Johnny Rutherford, etc. During the first night's race, Gary Bettenhausen was out-shining them all. He won the race by a full lap over A. J. Foyt, while Billy Vukovich finished third. The second night Gary was also leading the race when he was parked trying to avoid a crash. Gary was featured on the cover of *Speed Sport News* the following week along with little brother Tony, who was attempting to "open his first bottle of champagne."

The race inside the Astrodome had received several months of prior publicity and the promoters went to tremendous expense to construct a quarter mile dirt track inside the dome stadium. The city of Houston was inundated with publicity about the upcoming indoor race and it paid off. Houston residents had long been proud of their native son A. J. Foyt and his exploits in the world of auto racing, but most had never had a chance to see him race. There were few, if any USAC races held near Houston. Foyt gave them their money's worth as he came from 24th position to second in the first night's action.

One of the constant followers of the daily publicity was Tony Bettenhausen, Jr. He had recently moved with Val and step-dad Webb to Houston where Webb was offered a job with Indy car owner Gordon Van Liew. Van Liew was the proprietor of the Vita-Fresh Orange Juice Company and needed a dispatcher. Tony had allowed his interest in golf to wane, although he was shooting near par. He had talked about quitting school and "going racing." Webb, Val and Van Liew all took a deep interest in him and tried any ploy they could to make him finish his basic education. Van Liew went so far as to offer him a Stock car if he'd just stay in school and graduate. Further, Van Liew told him that he'd pick up the tab for college if he wanted to go. They all thought he seemed like such a nice young man. He didn't appear to have the temperament to be a race car driver. He had talent in other areas. Webb tried to encourage his golfing. But when the news of the Midgets coming to the Astrodome hit town, they could see he was enamored.

Excitement filled the air as four tiers of grandstands around the perimeter of the stadium cheered the small cars on. It was next to impossible to hear Chris Economaki describing the races as they were being held, but every once in a while you knew that someone was in the announcer's booth going wild. The alcohol-burning engines generated a noise inside that had never been heard before. The place was nothing like a serene golf-course where you could detect a cough in the gallery, and the loudest rumble was a "whack" as club struck ball. The thoroughly-proper and well dressed golf course gallery would clap ever so gently when a fine shot had been made. They wouldn't understand a Midget race fan shouting, "Pass on the outside! Get underneath him! Give him a god-damn slide job! Stand on that son-of-a-bitch!"

Golf didn't have a chance. As Valerie-Rice-Bettenhausen-Stephan watched her first-born lap the entire field she could only smile and holler, "Go Gary!" It was usual practice to paint the driver's name on the side of the car along with the mechanic and car owner's. Old line Midget owner Howard Linne aptly described the attitude within the sport when he had a sign painter inscribe under the word Driver: "One Who Stands On The Gas." Valerie Stephan would soon see the name Tony Bettenhausen painted on the side of a race car. Again.

* * *

Throughout the 1969 season Gary competed in no less than fifty-seven automobile races. He learned how to drive the "Hills" in a Sprint car and won a race at the ominous Winchester Speedway. He dueled with Larry Dickson on a weekly basis and racing writers were referring to the USAC Sprint car circuit as "The Larry & Gary Show." Gary won eight races and was declared Sprint Car Champion. Dickson finished second in points as the pair see-sawed back and forth in what was termed some of

Gary and Willie at New Bremen, OH in early 1969. [*Mahoney*]

the best Sprint car racing ever seen. Both drivers were taking Russian-roulette style chances to gain an edge on the other. This was no boyish rivarly, but a full-bore race to the finish where the stakes were life, limb and very few dollars for the victor. Sometimes it was a game of Chicken to see who would back off first in a turn. Dickson wasn't sure how far he could trust Bettenhausen when running next to him. Would he back off and give you racing room? Or would he let his car drift out toward yours, put a wheel underneath you that might send you sailing clear into next week? There was a laser-beam look when the two met each other's eyes at the race track and King-of-the-Hill Dickson wouldn't relinquish his status without a fight. Many predicted a double-death on the Sprint car circuit if the pair didn't stop running so close to one another.

It wasn't a Sprint car that nearly claimed Gary Bettenhausen once more, however. He got upside down in a rear-engine Championship car and lived to tell about it. It was unheard of to flip a modern-day Indy car and talk about it. They were too low to the ground to get upside down, unless you ran over someone's wheel. And if you were dumb enough, it was said, to do that, then you probably shouldn't have been given a license to drive one in the first place.

Just a week after the 1969 "500" was held, Gary went to the traditional Milwaukee Champ car race and was involved in a 13 car pile-up triggered by Art Pollard. Bettenhausen ran over a wheel on Wally Dallenbach's car and skyrocketed upside down toward the infield. Billy Vukovich was one of the first on the scene and saw a small fire behind the cockpit, in the engine. He grabbed a fire extinguisher from a nearby fireman and doused the area. The he bent down and jammed the extinguisher in the cockpit and

[Mahoney]

Above: Billy Vukovich
Left: Gary and his winning trophy after coming home in a 1969 Winchester Sprint car race.

turned it on once more. "C'mon you guys," he hollered. "We gotta get this thing turned back over."

Several drivers and safety crew members righted the overturned vehicle and saw that Gary was ok, but coughing.

"I damn near choked on that fire-extinguisher stuff," he said. "Who's the guy who blasted that extinguisher in there?" he asked.

"Don't know," Vukovich quipped. He saw that his friend was physically ok and walked with him to the ambulance. Had Vukovich known that Bettenhausen was alright in the overturned car, he would have most likely sprayed the cockpit anyway. There's always a chance of fire, he would say, and besides, it probably would have been funny. It would have been like spraying a pal with a garden hose.

Vukovich took every opportunity available for a practical joke. A couple of weeks after the Milwaukee race he walked into the USAC NEWS office and spotted driver Cy Fairchild reading a newspaper.

Hiya Cyrus," Vuky said.

"Umm, hello Billy," Fairchild noted. Fairchild was engrossed in the paper.

"Tell me," Vuky said, "are you really a big rough and tough Sprint car driver? Do you spit on the sidewalk and snarl at little girls?"

Vukovich had recently given up driving Sprint cars and

concentrated on Championship cars and an occasional Midget race. He said there wasn't any future in running Sprints. A guy could get hurt in those things he claimed, and in his normal, animated, wise-cracking tone of voice, took every opportunity to needle anyone who boasted about the difficulty of driving a Sprint car.

Vukovich sat next to Fairchild and continued the chiding: "C'mon, tell me what it's like to be a hero Sprint car driver. Do all the girls like it?"

As he was talking, Billy reached in his pocket, took out a book of matches and lit the bottom of the paper Fairchild was reading.

"Listen Fairchild," he continued. "Talking to you is boring. One thing's for sure though," he chuckled. "I really think you're gonna be the hottest driver on the circuit soon. See you later."

Within seconds Fairchild's newspaper was ablaze and he jumped up and said, "You bastard," as he looked around for the arsonist. Vukovich was gone and all you could hear going down the hallway was, "He-yah...ha-ha-ha."

Vukovich, like many others, made Indianapolis his summertime headquarters. He had purchased a trailer and lived just across the street from the Speedway. Many of the Championship teams were given free garage space in Gasoline Alley for the summer. Often times the summer days could be boring after experiencing hectic night and day activity throughout the month of May. During May, the town's population seemed to triple. You'd spend days at the Speedway and evenings were a time for socializing at the nearby motels. There you'd meet car owners, sponsors, women and seemingly every would-be Indy 500 driver in the country.

Merle Bettenhausen was standing in the Holiday Inn Northwest, a popular hang-out located only a couple of miles west of the track.

"Hi Merle," the gruff voice said. "What's happenin'?"

It was pudgy Paul Russo, making the nightly rounds. Russo had finally retired from driving in the mid-Sixties and landed a job with the Perfect Circle Piston Ring Comany as a racing representative. Essentially, Russo passed out free piston rings.

"Not much Paul," Merle replied. "Just taking in the sights and the sounds."

"How'd you like to take in a little of that," Russo noted as he spied a mini-skirted blonde walking by.

"Hey sweetie," Russo said. "You wanna get laid real good? This guy here can handle it....I guarantee it," he said as he motioned toward Merle.

"Aw Paul," Merle said. "Ease up. She's probably a nice gal."

Driver Bob Tattersall, center, could always be counted on for some risque humor.

Russo was drunk. It seemed like he got drunk a lot during May and there was always a little trepidation in his voice as he approached Gary or Merle. Deep down inside he felt guilty for allowing Tony to take a ride in his car back in '61.

The blonde gave Russo a cold stare and glanced at Merle as if to say, "I can only judge you by the company you keep," and walked on.

She headed toward the bar where Midget driver Bob Tattersall was sucking on a can of beer. She had her back to the old Midget driver and he eyed her up and down and made pantomine motions with his hands as if to outline an hour glass. He definitely approved of the rear view. Tattersall was an aging driver who was known for his happy-go-lucky attitude. He was a hold-over from the bygone days and still sported a crew cut that was speckled salt and pepper gray and black.

"Say Miss," he said.

The blonde turned around looked at him askance and timidly said, "Yes?"

"Nobody' here's giving you a hard time, are they?" Tat said in his best fatherly tone of voice.

"Well a little," the young lady said. "Maybe you have to expect some...." and her voice trailed off.

"Well tell me," Tat continued. "Have you ever been to Australia?"

"Why..why no," she said puzzled.

"I have," Tat laughed. "You wanna fuck?"

Tattersall roared back on his barstool, took a swig of beer and roared again.

The girl turned and walked away. Disgusted. Tattersall

The brothers Bettenhausen: Merle in car 69 about to be passed by eventual winner Gary in Harry Turner's number 82 Midget at New Bremen, OH in July of 1969. [Crucean]

continued laughing at his own joke and broke out in one of his usual nee'r-do-well Sailor style rhymes:

"Once I knew a Lady,
Margie was her name....
She got chocolate hair
And big boobs....Yahoo!
But best of all
She liked to do,
The things that I do too....
The things that I do too..."

Tattersall looked around and saw that no one was paying much attention to either him or his verse. At the Holiday Inn he was just another boisterous drinker. At the Midget races he was a man to be reckoned with, but he liked the spotlight as often as possible. Merle looked over and laughed and Tat gave him a shrug as if to say, "It ain't no big deal. There'll be another one come walking in pretty soon."

Merle was continuing his Midget racing apprenticeship throughout 1969 and becoming a respected member of the traveling circuit. He had teamed with the father and son combination of Bob and Danny Lockard, long time Midget owners from Joliet, Illinois. He usually traveled with Danny and split motel expenses in the cheapest place they could find. The Lockards owned a junkyard in Joliet and worked on their car in a dirt-floor garage. They were known as innovators in Midget racing and fielded competitive equipment. Although Merle was considered to be a conservative driver, he drove hard enough to keep the Lockard's happy and rarely spun or crashed the car.

On July 4, 1969 however, Merle was involved in a spectacular Midget crash in the Lockard car. He was racing at Springfield, Illinois on the quck, high-banked quarter-mile dirt track that even his talented father didn't care for. Tony had commented more than once, "I don't like that joint," in reference to the little Springfield track.

Merle was racing side-by-side with Tattersall, who was the current point leader in Midgets. Merle had been running the top half-dozen cars all year and was always in contention. The pair had started in the back of a preliminary race and were working their way toward the front of the pack when they touched wheels coming off the second turn. Both flipped violently and Merle's car came down atop the wooden guard rail. Tattersal barrell-rolled at least three times. Fortunately, only the cars were damaged.

Later in the year Merle tried running a few Sprint car races but didn't find the combination and missed more shows than he made. He was becoming proficient in Midgets, but he was no Gary Bettenhausen in a Sprint car yet. Most members of the Midget racing clan said Merle would do even better in Midgets if he'd just get a little tougher. For the most part Merle was a gentleman driver. It wasn't often you'd see him attempt to nudge someone out of the way. He'd try his level best to beat a fellow driver, fair-and-square into a corner. Gary's attitude was, "Watch out assholes, I'm comin' through."

* * *

While it was true that Merle was racing proof that nice guys finished second, Henry Banks was learning that the old adage would even apply to the executive side of auto racing. The USAC Board of Directors had been increasingly criticized for fickle decisions and Banks had no power to enact some of his own plans. In early 1969 he had recommended that a new position of Executive Director of USAC become available, and along with the title was to go some real executive power. The board thought it was a dandy idea, but it backfired in Henry's face. In August they announced that one William J. Smyth would be the new Executive Director and would be vested with, "the total management of the corporation and in this capacity he will have sole responsibility." President Charlie Brockman added to the statement, "of course the Board is not abdicating and will continue to establish policy."

It wasn't exactly "Good-bye Henry," but it was close. He was shuffled upstairs of the USAC office and allowed to keep his title, for a time, of Director of Competition. His long-time secretary Jo Huffaker cried at the news and said, "It isn't fair Henry. You've brought this club from nothing to something. Who does the board think they are?"

Smyth had been nominated for the new post by J. C. Agajanian who said: "Automobile racing has graduated to a multi-millon dollar sport in the Unted States, and for USAC to continue in a dominant position we had no choice but to find an executive director with executive and administrative abilities."

Smyth's biography showed that he had been a zone supervisor for the old AAA racing organization, had been associated with Chilton publications for a dozen years and was currently associated with Texas oil magnate John W. Mecom and Mecom's son. Mecom, Jr. owned the car that won the 1966 "500" and maintained an interest in auto racing.

Henry quietly trudged upstairs and didn't make any regretable statements to the press. He did, privately, agree with *Indianapolis Star* Sports Editor Bob Collins who said, "The best thing that could happen to the USAC Board would be to cut it in half....and cut it in half again."

Often times when a driver or mechanic was frustrated with a USAC decision they'd say: BeTARS which meant Big Time Auto Racing Sucks.

* * *

Late in 1969 Gary debuted a brand new Midget he and Harry Turner had been working on for many months. It was one of the most unique machines ever to appear in the 40 year history of Midget racing. Gary had awaken Wave one early Sunday morning and said: "I got it. I dreamed about it last night. It's all here in my head."

"What? What is?" Wave said sleepily.

"A brand new design for a Midget. I gotta have some drafting and drawing tools. Will you go get me some?"

"Gary," Wave said calmly. "It is *Sunday* morning in Tinley Park, Illinois. Just where in the Hell do you expect me to find *drafting equipment* now?"

"It doesn't make any difference. Just don't come back without it. This design is really gonna blow their door's off. It'll work."

"Ok, ok," Wave sighed. "I hope you'll let me get dressed first. I'll see what I can do. And Midgets don't have doors, so how can you build a car that's going to 'Blow their doors off,' " she smiled.

After a several hour search, Wave located the necessary instruments, went home and presented them to her man.

"Good...good...now leave me alone...don't bother me til I'm done."

Through the day and all night Gary drew, erased, designed and smiled. He was building an edge. He'd have a better Midget than anything he'd ever seen. He believed he had to have that competitive edge. He couldn't be satisfied with just a first class machine like everyone else had and utilize the talent that he had worked so hard for. He wanted the car to do the work and he'd simply steer it around the track. Out in front.

"Bettenhausen, you're crazy. This thing will never fly. It ain't gonna work. It looks flimsy. You'll waste a lot of money."

It was old Harry Turner talking. Gary had rolled up his drawing and marched into Turner's shop as the great emancipator.

"This looks like something your old man would dream up," Turner continued. "He was a great one for engineering too you know. Why I remember the time....."

"I don't care about any of that old yesterday crap, "Gary said, smiling. "This thing is simple. See, all we do is bend up a piece of aluminum in a "U" shape and bolt everything to it. We don't even need a frame anymore. If you crash it, you just bend up another piece of aluminum. Why didn't somebody think of this years ago? It'll be lighter, the chassis will respond to weight-jacking better and it won't have all that frame garbage to worry about."

Turner wasn't going to win the argument. He never did win an argument with Tony and he didn't have any reason to believe he'd win one with his son. Besides, it was Bettenhausen's money and he could throw it away any way he wanted Turner surmised.

The new machine didn't outwardly look any different than the conventional cars of the day and after a good deal of trial and error, blown engines and Gary Bettenhausen's blind determination, the machine worked. It worked well and Gary himself did all the testing and racing. He'd make the thing win races or spend a fortune figuring out why it wouldn't.

* * *

While Gary was playing with his new Midget in-between his busy racing schedule, Merle was continuing his 1969 Midget racing campaign. At season's end Gary was crowned USAC National Sprint Car Champion and at the Victory Banquet commented that he'd be back next year for another try at the title. Gary couldn't complain about his Sprint car driving record, but hoped for better

Merle drives the Lockard Midget under Bob Lithgow at Davenport. [*Chini*]

performance in the Indy cars and a higher finish at the Speedway in 1970. All in all however, he was happy with his Indy car ride. He got along very well with the car's chief mechanic, Phil Casey. Casey had a reputation around Gasoline Alley for being the first one to arrive in the morning and the last one to leave at night. Gary said he was a racer. Gary also spent a good deal of time with his Sprint car owner Willie Davis andd was continually trying to talk Willie into experimenting with new ideas. Willie was a racer too, Gary would say.

Although Merle wasn't making much of a living driving Midgets, he was steadily progressing in proficiency and notoriety. Fans and writers alike found that Merle always had time for them and he was looked upon as being the nice guy in the Bettenhausen family. Merle said he simply wanted to do better in 1970 than he had done in 1969. Merle didn't think he was perfect, but some believed Gary was.

Beth Turner, tall thin red-headed wife of car owner-builder Harry Turner, had recently taken to calling Gary "Little Jesus." For the most part, Beth didn't have much use for race car drivers. She'd watch them come to the track, helmet in hand, jump in one of Harry's cars, crash it and say, "Well, see you next week." She had one of the most descriptive vocabularies ever heard on the Midget circuit. Often times she could make a Marine Drill Sergeant blush. Sometimes you'd think, "Easy lady, I got a picture of my mother in my wallet." It wasn't uncommon to hear her say about a particular driver: "That asshole's no race car driver. Hell, he can't even drive nails." But Beth liked Gary. He could do no wrong. Gary strood on the gas and knew what made the car work. He could also appreciate the amount of hours it took to build, or fix a race car. In Beth's book, Gary was "Little Jesus."

Gary's perfectionist spirit filtered down to his Sprint car owner, Willie Davis. Gary was continually convincing Willie that a new gizmo ought to be bolted on the Sprint car, something that would make it better, give them an edge. They'd go to the races and Bettenhausen would constantly want to tinker with the machine.

"Little Jesus," Willie would say. "Peter Perfect. Well Gary, what's the latest hot-tip going to be today?"

The new monickers didn't get printed in the auto racing newspapers, nor did the track announcers refer to Gary by his unique nicknames, but his close pals could always be counted on to call him something other than Gary. Early in 1970 Gary bought a new dog. It was a cute little Schnauzer he and Wave name Lady. Vukovich saw the animal, laughed and said, "What's that?"

"It's my new dog, asshole. What do you think it is?" Bettenhausen replied.

"He don't look big enough to qualify for being a dog," Vuky said.

"It ain't a he, it's a she. And she's big enough to do anything I want her to."

"What kind is it? Vukovich asked.

"It's a Schnauzer."

"He-yah, ha-ha-ha! A Schnauzer? A German? Just like You? Boy, I'll bet she's really dumb," Vukovich cackled. "A Schnauzer for a Bettenhausen. A Schnauzer-Hausen, right Peter?" Billy continued.

"Just never-you-mind," Bettenhausen retorted. "She'll be a great little dog. Leaver her alone."

He-yah, ha-ha-ha! A genuine Schnauzer-Hausen. You gonna modify it? Knowing you Bettenhausen, you'll probably put a roll-bar on the poor thing so she won't get hurt when she falls down. A Schnauzer-Hausen. Peter Perfect and his Schnauzer. Bettenhausen, I want you to know that you are definitely fucked-up. You heard it here first. He-yah, ha-ha-ha!"

All Gary could do was smile. Vukovich was performing again. No one else in the country could walk up to Gary Bettenhausen and give him as hard a time as Vuky could. Vukovich was entertainment. Gary sure liked him.

* * *

13

To The Top

1970-71

The years 1970 and 1971 were a basic continuation of the successful 1969 season for Gary. He was still battling with Larry Dickson in every Sprint car race and few other drivers received much publicity in "The Larry & Gary Show." Often times the USAC Sprint car circuit was referred to as the "Thunder & Lightning" cars division. Between the two of them, Dickson and Bettenhausen usually caused some sparks to fly and once in a great while tempers would as well. Consequently, it was a thoroughly surprised Dickson who commented to Bettenhausen: "What are you trying to pull? Is this some gimmick?"

Bettenhausen had approached his arch rival at the hotdog stand during the April (1970) Reading Sprint car race and said: "Hey, I need a team-mate to drive my other Indy car. You interested?"

Dickson wasn't quite sure how to reply to the offer. He wasn't convinced Gary was serious. But on second thought, Dickson mused, he just might be.

"Yeah, sure," Larry said. "I'd like to run the second car. I don't have to stop driving Sprints though, do I?" Dickson laughed.

"No," Bettenhausen smiled back. "We've got some good cars. We'll do ok."

Dickson was elated. Later in the evening he went out and passed both Gary and Merle and won the feature event. Merle was driving a new Sprint car for his Midget owners, Bob and Danny Lockard. He started out the season in great shape, and finished the Reading race in fourth place. Unfortunately, it was to be his best Sprint performance all year, although he attempted another 16 races. Merle and the Lockard car just weren't a combination.

At the Speedway in 1970 Gary tested not only his own car but

The Larry & Gary Show

The "Larry and Gary Show" spanned several years which saw a controversial change in Sprint cars from roll bars to roll cages. The defending champion Dickson [1] was unable to hold off Gary B. [2] in 1969 [above] and 1971 [below] as Gary went on to win the titles.

Dickson's as well. Gary made the 33 car starting line-up with no problems, but Dickson's mount broke in qualifying. Bettenhausen wasn't sure what Dickson thought about him as a Sprint car driver, but Gary respected Larry's ability. Besides, Bettenhausen wanted to make a friend out of him. They both continued their 1-2 finishes back out on the Sprint car circuit, and in 1970 Dickson wrested the title back from Gary.

* * *

Gary's Sprint car had been called the "City of Syracuse" special for the season and the sponsorship money eased the burden on Willie Davis. Two Syracuse businessmen, Pat Santello and Bernie Gerthoeffer had started attending automobile races on the

Above: Bernie Gerthoeffer, left and Pat Santello pose at Reading with their favorite driver. [Bettenhausen Coll.]

Right: Long-time racing team manager John Laux found sponsors for Willie and Gary.

Below right: A May 1970 photo shows the different attitude of the Sprint car on pavement. Photo taken at Indianapolis Raceway Park, a five-eights paved oval.

Below left: During 1970 Gary's Sprint car carried a number 1 and had a roll cage installed. This shot taken on the Terre Haute half mile dirt track. Note left front wheel. [Chini]

weekends and made a trip to see the Daytona 500 stock car race. While in a local bar, they struck up a conversation with one John Laux, a successful manager for an Indy car team. Pat and Bernie allowed as to how they thought they might buy a race car next year. John querred them and asked if either was a driver. No, was the answer. A mechanic, John asked. No again. Did they have some product they wanted to push, put a name on the side of the car? Once more, the pair replied no. They just wanted to own a race car.

Laux sugested that they sponsor a car. That way, he told them, you simply put out a few dollars and let the car owner worry about getting the thing to the races and taking care of it. Then, he added, they could show up at the track and enjoy the car's performance.

Pat and Bernie were interested. All they really wanted to do, they agreed, was go to the races and be a part of the scene. Have a good time.

Laux said, "I've got just the team for you. Gary Bettenhausen and Willie Davis. I'm sure you can get them pretty cheap. Matter of fact, I've got Gary's phone number right here. Let's go call him now."

Thus, from a bar in Daytona Beach, Florida, John Laux sold all parties concerned on getting married. Pat and Bernie were from Syracuse, so they thought it'd be nice if they called "their" car the City of Syracuse Special. The arrangement worked for everyone.

* * *

"Hey Webb, can I, uh, borrow a few bucks 'til next week?"

"Sure Merle. Will twenty do? Got a hot date over there? She's sorta pretty."

Professional race car driver Merle Bettenhausen was hitting on his step-dad for a small loan. The scene was the Holiday Inn across the street from the Speedway during May of 1970. Merle was on a blind date with a tall, willowy, blue-eyed brunette that he wanted to treat differently from most of the females you met at the race tracks. Leslie Saure looked a lot better to Merle than anything he had previously known.

It wasn't Merle's style to pick-up on the available females at the race tracks. Usually, the racers referred to them as fence hangers. It was said that a good fence hanger could graduate to the status of star-fucker if she played her cards right. Leslie Saure didn't fit into either category. On their first date Merle saw some blending taking place. She was a lot better, Merle thought, than that cowgirl back in Phoenix who was so impressed with him when he won a Midget

1970 Remembrances

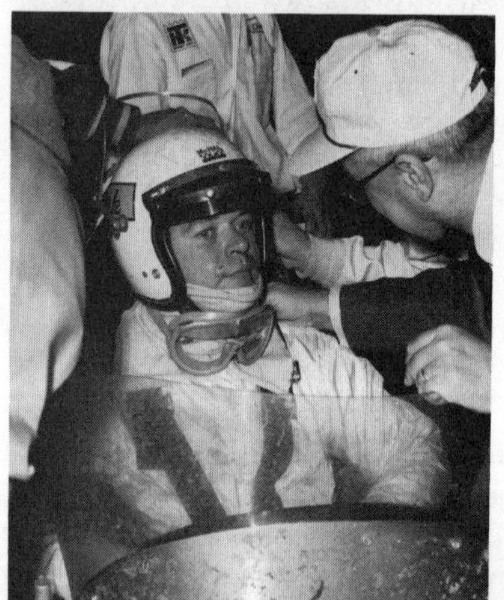

Above: Merle started off 1970 with a win on the tough dirt half mile at Phoenix. He was joined in victory lane by car owner Danny Lockard, left, Dick and June McClung and sister Susie [far right.]
Left: USAC Midget supervisor Bob Stroud congratulates Merle on his feature win.
Below: Merle Bettenhausen inside the Houston Astrodome, 1970.
[Chini Photos]

Merle Bettenhausen and car builder Harry Turner in the lounge on the ship that took Merle to Australia. [*Chini*]

race. The cowgirl had found Merle after the race and hung around until he finally got together with her. It turned out to be one of those quick-hits that was as easily forgotten as a bad qualifying lap. Leslie wasn't impressed that Merle was a race car driver. In fact she wasn't impressed when Merle walked up to her door. She saw him through the window, took one look at the way he was dressed and figured, "this guy has no taste at all. Mother, tell him I'm not home."

"I'll do nothing of the sort," Leslie's mom told her. "Now you get down here and act like a lady."

Merle Bettenhausen had found himself a lady. Within a year he would be married.

* * *

In late 1970 Gary proved that his Midget design was not only workable, it appeared to be superior to anything else that was running. In November he had gone west once more for the annual Turkey Night Grand Prix, this time he was entered in his own car. While 66 other Midgets arrived for the annual event, Gary outclassed them all. He became a two-time winner of the race and in the process lapped the entire field. By now, his helpers knew there was no use in giving him pit signals to slow down, he wouldn't pay any attention to them.

Merle ran in the same race and finished tenth. Then he prepared to say good-by to girlfriend Leslie and spend the winter racing Midgets in Australia. Merle Bettenhausen may not have been winning races with the same fequency as his elder brother, but his

Gary's Unique Midget . . .

Top: When it first appeared, Gary's new Midget didn't have a roll-cage assembly. He's shown here running next to Billy Vukovich at San Jose. Middle: Astrodome, 1970: While it doesn't look much different than a standard Midget, this car's side panels make up its frame. Bottom: On the San Jose high-banks. [Chini Photos]

Brought Cash , Trophies, Glory

A confident Gary Bettenhausen bet Phoenix Midget promoter Keith Hall that he'd break the track record in qualifying with his new Midget. Above, Hall pays off. Gary won the three lap trophy dash on Turkey Night in 1970 and posed with Aggie and didn't find one of Aggie's usual models in victory lane. [Chini Photo] Then he went on to win the feature event [and became a two time winner] so Aggie gave him a hug. [Earl's Racing Photos]

Merle made the trip to Australia again in the winter of 1970-71 and found the going easier than his first trip. Above, he shows off while winning a heat race driving with his left arm only. [*Merle Bettenhausen Coll.*]

gregarious attitude had reached far. The Australians had discovered Midget racing nearly forty years ago and annually welcomed one or two Americans to compete in their summer series. Merle and Bob Tattersall were the chosen stars for the early 1971 campaign.

Occassional reports sent back from Australia would appear in the *National Speed Sport News* and in early 1971 stateside fans were informed that Merle had won 14 races out of 26 starts. He was crowned The New Zealand Speedcar (Midget) Champion.

Tony Bettenhausen had stayed in high school and graduated in 1970. As promised, Gordon Van Liew bought him a Stock car and the youngest Bettenhausen son started his career in 1969 at the local Meyers Speedway. By 1970 he was brancing out to some of the surrounding tracks in Shreveport, Baton Rouge and a track or two in Alabama. He was working for Van Liew as an all-around utility man on the Vita-Fresh trucks. Tony was in Stock car country and had his eye set on running the entire NASCAR circuit someday soon. He didn't see any reason to move to the Midwest and start running Midgets and Sprint cars as his brothers were doing. Val was glad that her youngest decided to stay in the Stock cars. At least, she surmised, it's awfully difficult to get hurt in a Stock car.

By 1971 the Midgets and Sprint cars were becoming safer as well. USAC had instituted a rule, as did many other racing organizations, that an entire roll-cage assembly of tubing must be installed above the driver's head. Ever since the turn of the century, open-cockpit cars were just that: Open-cockpit. In the early days they weren't even equipped with a roll-bar. Finally, after the second World War, small, seemingly insignificant roll-bars were installed behind the driver's head. Still, if you got yourself upside down in a Midget or a Sprint car it was usually fate that told you whether or not you came out of the ordeal dead or alive. The old-timers complained the new roll-cage rule was pure heresy. It would ruin open-cockpit racing. Drivers, they said, have been running these things for years like they should be. As men. Brave men who aren't afraid. The whole idea, they claimed, behind Midget and Sprint car racing was that it was traditional. You ran a Midget or a Sprinter the same way today as you did thirty years ago. For the most part they were right. The Midgets and Sprints showed very little evolutionary design change over the past thirty-five years. Unfortunately, it was just as probable that a driver would wind up with a broken neck in 1970 as it was in 1940. The roll-cage rule was passed and drivers became more brave overnight.

* * *

During 1971 Gary was again USAC's most active race car driver as he ran in nearly 60 races. For the fourth consecutive year he and Larry Dickson fought for the USAC Sprint car title. With only two dates left on the schedule and the title up for grabs by either driver, Bettenhausen displayed what was termed one of the finest, driving performances ever seen in the history of Sprint car racing.

The schedule called for a pair of races to be held on the old Winchester half mile, both events being 50 laps. Gary finally blew an engine in Willie Davis' car in the first race. Davis had compiled an amazing consistency record with Gary at the wheel. Their car simply didn't break. Gary obtained a ride in an unfamiliar machine for the second 50 lapper and was forced to start last in the 20 car field. It was always said to be not only difficult but dangerous as well to pass at Winchester and if you didn't start in the top six cars, your chances of winning were considered slim at best. Gary passed cars on the high side, on the low side, on the front straight and on the back straight until he was in third place on the last lap. On the last corner of the last lap he made an all-or-nothing dive and went under the checkered flag in first place. This was the same Winchester cathedral of speed where two men were killed in one afternoon of qualifying twenty years ago. Winchester, the most feared and famous of the Sprint car Hills. Driving around the flat Indianapolis Motor Speedway was

1970 Remembrances

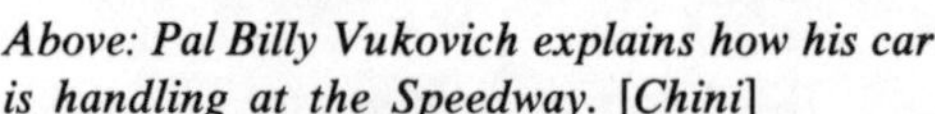

Above: Pal Billy Vukovich explains how his car is handling at the Speedway. [Chini]
Right: Gary Bettenhausen in short pants, a real first. Here, he's hoisting fellow driver Bruce Walkup for an easy shot in a benefit basketball game. [Mahoney]
Below: Gary and Mario just before the start of the 1970 "500." [Chini]

Above: At the time, they were USAC's three winningest Sprint car drivers: Gary, A. J. Foyt, center and Larry Dickson posing at Terre Haute in 1970. [Mahoney]

Left: The twins and wife Wave join Gary in victory circle at Michigan 1970. [Chini]

Below: Some days are better than others. Gordon Johncock is a bit miffed at a non-committal Gary Bettenhausen. [Bettenhausen Coll.]

1971

Gary and Larry Dickson before the start of the Winchester feature Gary won from last place. [*Mahoney*]

Gary just after winning a 50 lap race at Winchester from last place. [*Mahoney*]

Gary displays classic dirt track style on the high-banked half mile Sprint track named Eldora. June 1971 photo. [*Mahoney*]

Some Sprint car owners remind drivers how they want them to perform.

kid's-stuff in comparison to passing somebody at Winchester. With the win, Gary all-but clinched the 1971 USAC Sprint car crown. He took a fifth in the next race to formally take the title back from Larry Dickson and with it went a feeling of satisfaction that you couldn't buy at any store in the world.

Earlier in the season Gary had taped a photograph of Larry Dickson to the dashboard of his Sprint car. Usually, over 40 cars would vie for starting positions in the 20 car Sprint races, but to Bettenhausen's way of thinking there was only one man he wanted to beat. Once, the pair finished sixth and seventh respectively after dueling the entire race. Gary came in smiling and Willie said, "You're happy? You weren't even close to the front?"

"Yeah," Gary allowed. "But me n' Dickson had a helluva race. The guy's an animal. If you beat him, you know you've done something. I'd race him side-by-side all day long."

At the annual USAC banquet, Gary graciously accepted the award for winning the 1971 Sprint car championship. While at the podium he virtually bequeathed the upcoming 1972 Sprint title to fellow Sprint driver Sammy Sessions. Gary said he wouldn't be able to run in all the Sprint car races because he had just signed a contract with Championship car owner Roger Penske. Penske had requested Gary not run in any races the day before a Championship race.

Bettenhausen had reached star status. Roger Penske was considered one of the best, if not the absolute best, Championship car owners in USAC. Penske's equipment was Class A, top-of-the-line, best money could buy. At the Indianapolis Motor Speedway, some of the lesser teams jokingly referred to Penske as God.

Penske had retired from driving sports cars himself at age 27, back in 1964. He disappeared from the auto racing scene for a time, but was soon back as a sports car owner. He rapidly built a reputation for fielding first-class equipment. At one point near the end of his short but successful driving career it was rumored he would be an Indianapolis 500 driver. But while racing, he had also become obsessed with the desire to be very, very successful in business. He found he was unable to obtain the business backing he wanted if he continued driving, although respected automotive journals had him picked for international stardom as a driver. He parlayed a downtown Philadelphia Chevrolet dealership into wide and varied enterprises that were centered around the automotive world. He treated automobile racing like a business and was determined to make a profit from his business efforts. To make a profit from automobile racing, it was evident that you must obtain sponsors to pay for your equipment: Penske set out to obtain the best sponsors and keep them happy on a long-term basis.

Thus, when he arrived at Indianapolis as a car owner he wanted to command respect from not only fellow owners, but potential sponsors who would be in the neighborhood. He took a look at his assigned garage in Gasoline Alley and transformed the old wooden-door stall into an antiseptically clean racing laboratory. Walls were paintd and the floor was tiled in his team colors. Soon, other owners, some who had been at the Speedway for years, began to copy his act. The racing press referred to Penske as The Captain. His number one driver, Mark Donohue, was called Captain Nice and the pair were considered to be a winning team in any type of auto race they entered. Donohue was an engineering graduate of Brown University and one of the nation's most successful sports car drivers when he came to Indianapolis in 1969 with Penske. It didn't take the team long to learn the ins and outs of Championship auto racing and in the early Seventies you expected a Roger Penske car to be an Indy 500 winner. Gary Bettenhausen would be a part of the creme de la creme for the 1972 season. He would receive a monthly retainer of $1,500 to drive for Penske, and Roger's only request was that he refrain from driving in Midget or Sprint car races the day before a Championship Indy car race. Consequently, Gary was beaming at the USAC banquet when he said he wouldn't be able to compete in all of the 1972 Sprint car races. He added, however, that there was no way he was giving up his involvement in Midgets and Sprints and that he'd run them whenever he could. Gary believed that 1972 would be the best year yet for the Bettenhausen family.

* * *

1972

Phoenix, Arizona: March 17, Night

"See I told you," Gary said to a nearby mechanic. "Merle's got the talent, all he needed was the right car."

Merle had just won a Midget race at the Manzanita Speedway, considered one of the fastest and most feared half-mile dirt tracks in the country. He had driven the Midget that Gary designed and Harry Turner built.

"A lot of people have said that Gary was the reason that this car went so fast. Gary wanted to prove that the car was the answer and that anyone could drive it to a win," Merle commented after the race.

The week previous, Gary had driven the car to another victory inside the Houston Astrodome before 21,000 fans, and detractors of the car's design were heard to say, "It isn't the car. Gary could win in anything."

The day following Merle's Manzanita win there was a Championship race scheduled on the mile paved track at Phoenix, and Gary was honoring his committment to Roger Penske by not running the night before. The publicity generated by Merle's win was good for his morale and he anxiously looked forward to the remainder of the year. Merle wanted to become a driver at the Indianapolis Motor Speedway, just as most of his peers on the Midget circuit did. It was getting increasingly difficult, they all agreed, to talk an owner at the "500" into hiring you. The cars were becoming more expensive and it was a rare owner who would take a chance on an unproven rookie. Still, they all believed, if you did well in Midgets and Sprints your phone might ring. Maybe a Champsionship car owner would read about how good you were and give you a try.

* * *

Roger Penske had never seen a Sprint car race, so he was duly impressed when ABC's Wide World of Sports asked him to serve as a color commentator for their scheduled broadcast of the April 30th Sprint race to be held on the famed Terre Haute "Action Track." Gary would be a competitor and would do his best to impress his new boss. Penske was already happy with Bettenhausen's performance, they had just scored their first Championship victory a week before the Terre Haute race when Gary came home first in the 200 miler at Trenton, New Jersey.

"Holy mackerel," Penske noted. "Those things can be devastating."

Roger had just watched Gary perform a horrendous flip in the first turn at Terre Haute. Gary ran over Carl Williams' wheel and headed skyward. He landed upside down in the first turn atop the guard rail. Bettenhausen was uninjured, save for a good shaking up, but Penske had received a first-class inauguration to the world of USAC Sprint cars. He talked to many of the drivers and found they all mostly hoped for a chance in a Speedway car someday. After the event Penske said he'd see about making one of his own cars available if he could talk Goodyear into supplying engines and tires. He had been properly impressed with the competitiveness of Sprint car racing. There was no comparison of Sprints to sports cars on gently winding road courses or even to Indy cars for that matter. Sprint car drivers definitely had balls. He didn't think that he liked the idea of his Indy car driver taking part in Sprint races, however. It was a good thing they had roll-cages on them, he mused.

* * *

"I don't know Gary, do you really think he's ready?"

"Sure he's ready. You should have seen him at Manzanita."

"Well, maybe so, but I'm not real sure. Merle's been driving for a while that's true. But he hasn't done that great in Sprints and hasn't won that many Midget races. A Speedway car is a lot different you know."

"I know. I'll help him. I'll give you five thousand dollars if you get Merle through his rookie test at the Speedway and give him a chance to qualify."

"It's not the money that's important, I'm just not sure he's ready yet."

"He'll do fine. He's an old-smoothie. He'll adapt to a Speedway car right away."

Gary Bettenhausen was talking to car-owner-builder Grant King. No one had yet offered to give Merle a chance at Indianapolis and Gary believed it would be a cheap investment to put up five thousand dollars so Merle could join the ranks of Indy 500 drivers. Grant King was an Oriental car builder who had always dreamed of building Speedway cars. He started his building career in the Pacific Northwest and finally got up the courage and cash to come to Indy. He built everything in his own shop and was known as a workaholic. His Indy cars were considered mid-field equipment at best because he didn't have the

Above: Car owner/builder Grant King put Merle in this 1972 entry. [*IMS*]

Right: A pensive Grant King watches Merle in practice.

dollars to compete with the big teams, yet you always expected Grant King cars to make the race.

It was agreed that King would bring Merle to Indy in 1972 and do his best to put him in the field. It was a major step up in Merle's career. Once you made the show at Indy you were a bona fide "500" driver, not just another Midget or Sprint car driver praying that someday you'd get a chance. You could call up an Indy car owner and he'd know who you were. You were only a rookie at Indy the first year, then you were a veteran.

When the Speedway opened in 1972 Gary became one of the early favorites and for the first time in his career he was headlined as an Indy driver:

"Bettenhausen's 190 Run Stamps Him Pole Favorite"

He had adapted quickly to the Penske operation. He even looked different at the Speedway. With his old ride he could be seen hovering over the car, helping mechanic Phil Casey upon occasion. With Penske, Gary wore one of the expensive racing

Gary and mechanic Phil Casey, left, fire up an Indy car while Merle and Johnny Parsons, Jr. [*in uniform*] *look on.* [*Chini*]

parkas around Gasoline Alley and wasn't expected, or for that matter allowed, to get too close to the mechanical side of things. On the Penske team there were drivers, mechanics, public relations men...everything was in order. There was a small corporation doing business back in Gasoline Alley.

"Boy, this thing is so shiny and clean that it's gotta be good for another five miles an hour at least," Gary noted about his Penske-Sunoco special.

Gary told Roger he was going to take Merle's car for a test drive. See how it was set up. Roger reluctantly said, "ok," but would rather he wouldn't. Penske didn't disrespect Grant King's cars, but he'd feel better if Gary didn't do any car-hopping.

"It's easy Merle, Gary said, "Drivin' these rear-engine cars is easy. Now what's wrong...where are you having a problem? Are you looking at the gauges in the middle of the corner."

Big brother was giving little brother some advice.

"I'm a little too busy to be looking at the gauges in the middle of the corner, Gary," Merle said disdainfully.

Gary had run Merle's car and declared it ok. He thought Merle should have been running faster. As it was, Merle went through the phases of his rookie test without problems, but wasn't quite running a speed that would qualify him for the 33 car line-up. Merle was nervous. Grant King couldn't spend all his time with

Merle and Gary talk over Merle's Indy debut. [IMS-Scott]

him as he had entered another car and considered Merle the number two driver on the team. Merle wasn't familiar with the characteristics of the high-horsepower, rear-engine machinery and he had never driven anything with a 'wing' on it.

Aviation theory had invaded Indianapolis 500 cars since the rear-engine machines appeared, and all cars were equipped with upside-down airplane style wings both fore and aft to create the reverse effect they did on a plane. Moreover, curvature of a wing on an airplane created lift as the vehicle went through the air: On an Indy 500 car, an upside down wing created downforce, thereby holding the car on the track in a more stable fashion. The theory worked beautifully, but wing angles were continually being changed on Indy cars through adjusting bolts, and a few degrees up or down could radically affect a car's handling characteristics. Gary could rattle off wing settings from years of prior experience, but a rookie had to get a feel for things. About the best a rookie could hope for was a car and mechanic that was basically good. You had to worry about driving the thing at speeds near 180 mph average to make the program. You ran about half that fast in Midgets and Sprints. The Speedway was a two and a half mile rectangular track: Midgets and Sprints ran on quarter and half-mile tracks. Was he looking at the gauges in the middle of the corner? Merle had a few choice thoughts he wanted to lay on Gary, but maintained his composure. He knew Gary was trying to help, but he wasn't a very patient teacher.

The mechanics on Merle's car made a major wing adjustment, Merle went out and SPLAT! hit the fourth turn wall. One side of

A smug Billy Vukovich about to accept a dollar payoff on a bet that Gary lost. [*Chini*]

the race car was wiped out. His chances for qualifying looked like they were gone.

Grant King and crew loaded up the car and took it to King's shop, located just a few miles west of the track. They worked around the clock and straightened the crumpled hulk. They got back to the track just in time to push into the qualifying line on the last day, but time ran out. Merle Bettenhausen was left in line when the final gun went off. He wasn't sure, but fairly confident he could have mustered up the extra couple of miles per hour he needed to make the show. Grant King had lived up to his part of the bargain. He spent well over $5,000 preparing and fixing Merle's car. On race day Merle occupied a spot in Penske's pit. Gary was doing what a Bettenhausen had always wanted to do, leading the Indianapolis 500. Penske gave Merle a headset so he could communicate with his brother on the car's two-way radio.

''Terrific,'' Gary shouted into helmet microphone. ''Everything is working great!''

Up in the grandstands Val, Webb, Tony and Susie, along with Susie's husband Lowell were in awe of the sight. Over 350,000 spectators were watching Gary Bettenhausen and his beautiful blue Sunoco number 7 lead the Indianapolis 500 lap after lap. Millions more on ABC Wide World of Sports saw throughout the

Gary being towed to the pits after leading the "500." [*Mahoney*]

race that it was Gary Bettenhausen, eldest son of the famed Tony Bettenhausen, the rest of the field was chasing. In the announcer's booth Jim McKay was telling the viewers that this, the world's largest single-day sporting event, looked like it belonged to Gary Bettenhausen. On the radio Sid Collins was broadcasting world-wide to over 100 million listeners once again and told of how he used to watch Tony Bettenhausen, the Tinley Park Express, drive around this same race track. It was a 200-lap contest and Gary was being paid one hundred and fifty dollars for every lap he would lead. The total purse was over one million dollars and the winner would take home nearly a quarter of that amount. Gary was making money:

20 laps Gary Bettenhausen 3rd
40 laps Gary Bettenhausen 1st
60 laps Gary Bettenhausen 1st
80 laps Gary Bettenhausen 1st
100 laps Gary Bettenhausen 1st
120 laps Gary Bettenhausen 1st
140 laps Gary Bettenhausen 1st
160 laps Gary Bettenhausen 1st
175 laps Gary Bettenhausen 1st

"Ohhh.....this son-of-a-bitch! Damnit! She's poppin!"

Gary was on the backstretch, swearing. Merle had no trouble hearing his voice over the two-way radio. His day in the sun at the Indianapolis 500 was coming to an end with 17 laps to go. Racing immortality was just a few miles around the bend, but once more a Bettenhausen would not visit victory lane and drink the milk that

Left: Car owner Roger Penske taking lap times. [IMS - Duffy Photos] Below: Team-mate Mark Donohue with Gary Bettenhausen.

was given to the winner. Gary Bettenhausen completed 183 laps of the 1972 Indianapolis "500" and broke all exisiting records along the way. His family cried in the grandstands. Team-mate Mark Donohue inherited the lead and went on to collect over $200,000. Mark Donohue had never sat in a Midget nor driven on a dirt track. He had no heritage that dated back a quarter of a century in automobile racing. Yet his likeness would be etched on the Borg-Warner trophy as the winner of the one and only Indianapolis 500. As the winner at Indianapolis you would receive countless offers to endorse a wide variety of products. Little did it matter that Gary Bettenhausen had just won the Indy car race at Trenton, New Jersey a few weeks previously nor did it matter that he was a two-time USAC National Sprint Car Champion. He could walk into a bar in Denver, Colorado and say, "I just won the Championship car race at Trenton,'' and the occupants would reply, ''Umm..oh yeah..yeah. Trenton..do they hold car races there?''

Yet a man could walk into any establishment in the entire world and say, ''I just won the Indianapolis 500,'' and somebody would offer to buy him a drink. As far as the world was concerned, there was really only one automobile race; the Indianapolis 500. Most of the people who attended the Indy 500 didn't even know there was such a thing called the ''Championship Trail,'' where these same cars and drivers competed on a dozen or more different weekends throughout the year.

As one spectator was leaving the track after Donohue's victory, he said in a Kentucky hills accent: ''It's too bad about that Bettenhauser. He done had 'er won today. Why I saw him drive right past that Donohue character. But the best jockey in the world kaint win if his horse dies.''

One of Roger Penske's horses had died. Gary's car suffered an electrical malfunction.

* * *

14

He's Conscious, But His Arm Is Bad

After the "500" was run, Gary and Merle both resumed their Midget and Sprint racing schedules. Gary went to the traditional Milwaukee Champ car race the week following the Speedway and registered a creditable third. Grant King said he'd take Merle to a few more Championship races, he felt badly that Merle didn't make the Speedway and wanted to give him some more experience in an Indy car. But, he said, Milwaukee was too flat and it was easy to get in trouble there. He didn't take Merle to the Milwaukee race, but said they could run the next 500 miler at Pocono. Grant believed, as many others did, that the bigger tracks were easier to drive than the one mile tracks like Milwaukee and Phoenix. Merle got in a few practice laps at Pocono, but the show was cancelled due to a flood in the area. The next race was to be held on the high-banked two-mile track at Cambridge Junction, Michigan. Grant said Merle could run the car there. Merle loved the idea.

The Michigan track is located in the scenic Irish Hills in lower Michigan. The area is a popular tourist spot and has several attractions located only minutes from the race track. The race track itself is a wide, steeply banked two mile oval where the fastest speeds of the year are annually logged by the Indy cars. Drivers would back off their throttle pedals only momentarily going through the corners. The 18 degree banking through the turns was much easier to negotiate than Indianapolis' nearly flat corners.

Bobby Unser set a new track record at Michigan when he went 199 mph in 36.04 seconds. Gary qualified a tick of the watch behind at 36.67 seconds for third place on the starting grid and Merle was in 19th starting position with a qualifying time approximately three seconds behind the front runners. Merle was justifiably happy with his performance, considering it was his first-ever Championship race and seven other drivers qualified

The fiery crash that cost Merle Bettenhausen his right arm. [M. Bettenhausen Coll.]

behind him. The experience of running the 200 mile race will be great Merle thought, and besides, he could certainly use the money. He and wife Leslie had left their house trailer in Indianapolis with only $20 to their name the day before the race. Merle's application for a MASTERCHARGE had been accepted and he received his credit card the morning they were leaving.

"Well," he quipped to Leslie, "we can at least charge our own motel room now."

Since Merle was starting the race in 19th position, it meant that nine rows of cars were ahead of him. He immediately noticed a tremendous amount of turbulence buffeting his head around in the cockpit as the field came down for the start. He wondered if the windshield was too low, was this what you expect when you start in the back of the pack?

On the third lap of the race as he was coming out of the second turn, head still being buffeted side to side, he lost control. Had something broken, did he just lose it? He didn't know....it all happened too fast. The car turned right spun and slammed into the outer guard rail, shearing its left side wheels off and bursting into flames. The cockpit was on fire, and the car was still spinning. Merle unsnapped his safety belts and began to raise himself up from the blazing pod when the vehicle hit the wall again. It came down across the flat backstretch on fire. Merle couldn't push himself up out of the car. "Why can't I get out?" he thought. "Why doesn't my right side raise up?" He looked to his right, and there was no arm. "Oh my God! Oh my God!" he cried, "Help me.....please!"

Firemen were on the scene immediately, dousing the wreckage, but no one made an immediate move toward the cockpit. "Help me please!" came another cry, and fireman Jerry Murray heard the plea. He dove in amidst the inferno and extricated Merle from the wreck. The driver was alive and conscious, bleeding profusely from the right shoulder where his arm had been ripped off.

He was taken to the track hospital within minutes. Wave, Leslie, Susie and Lowell all rushed toward the emergency building while the race was stopped. Gary had gone by and thought he saw Merle trying to push himself up out of the spinning car. He pulled in and ran to the hospital.

When Leslie arrived she saw Grant King walk from the building, head down. "Oh my God," she thought. "Merle's dead."

The family waited for endless minutes outside the building. No one was allowed immediate admittance. Finally, driver Johnny Rutherford's wife, Betty, (who had been an RN before marriage) came out and said; "He's conscious, but his arm is bad."

Leslie had visions of broken bones protruding from the skin. Well, she thought. At least he's alive. Maybe has a broken arm.

Track physicians called the hospital at Ann Arbor and told them to get ready for an emergency patient. Merle Bettenhausen and his severed arm would be on the way within minutes. The arm was placed between Merle's burned legs.

Upon arrival at the Ann Arbor facility, Merle started apologizing to Leslie for putting her through such an ordeal. She told him to be quiet, not to worry. Everything would be ok. It was hard for Leslie to look at him. He was burned about the face, his eyes were working, but they were surrounded by mass of raw flesh. Throughout the ordeal Merle remained conscious and courteous. Dr. Henry V. Larabee accompanied the 29 year old race driver on the ambulance trip to University Hospital and later recalled that his patient never forgot to say, "Please," and "Thank you."

Merle had reached the hospital less than an hour after his crash thanks to a state police escort. Dr. Larabee explained to Leslie and the rest of the family that they would do all they could, but the chances of re-attaching Merle's arm were slim. Soon, Dr. Robert W. Bailey, Professor of Orthopedic Surgery at the University of Michigan Hospital, arrived and took charge. He surveyed the situation and explained that there had never been a successful implant between the shoulder and the elbow, that is, successful to the point of restoring hand operation. The arm had been crushed, then pulled apart. It was agreed that a functional prostesis would be better than a useless extremity.

Merle replied, "Whatever you say, Doc."

The family had gathered in Dr. Bailey's office. It was decided that he should be the one to call Val.

"Oh my God," was her first reaction.

"Well," Dr. Bailey continued, "we're pretty certain we can bring him out of this alive."

Alive? Everyone looked at each other. No mention had ever been made that Merle might die.

"Gimme that phone," Gary demanded. "Listen Ma, this asshole don't know what he's talking about. Merle isn't going to die."

The rest of the family tried to calm Gary down. Give him back the phone they admonished. Gary handed the phone back and said the man was crazy. There was no way that Merle was going to die. He couldn't die.

And he didn't. Leslie stayed with him every night for the next two months and for the first six weeks they didn't go a single night without a visitor. Soon Merle was joking that he was a member of the "Crispy Critter" club and he was telling visitors that Gary was out looking for a power-steering unit that he could adapt to a Midget. Merle said he'd be back racing next season. One arm style.

* * *

After he had undergone surgery for skin grafts and the wound was closed where his arm had been severed, Merle was fitted with an artificial arm. Upon his return to Indianapolis he stopped by a local racer hangout called the Beverage Inn and showed everyone how proficient he had become with the hook that had replaced his right hand. Merle could pick up an inch-long cigarette ash with the new appendage while everyone else would crush it while attempting to lift the ash with their fingers.

In mid-August, just three and a half weeks after Merle's crash, Gary himself slammed into the retaining wall at Toledo during a Sprint car race and broke his left arm. Val's phone rang again. For a time he was listed in serious condition in the intensive care ward as having a mild concussion. A pin was inserted in his upper left arm. He was released and spent the remainder of the summer recovering....without pay. Roger Penske had exercised a clause in Gary's contract that allowed Penske to terminate the contract if Bettenhausen was hurt in someone else's race car. Gary had been driving his usual ride, the Willie Davis Sprint car.

Bettenhausen figured he was a free agent. Penske had cancelled his contract, which to Gary's way of thinking left him free to seek another ride. During his convalescence, Teddy Mayer of Team McLaren called Gary and asked him to drive for the famed team.

Then he talked with George Bignotti, chief mechanic of the Patrick Racing Team, and found he could strike a deal with them for the 1973 season. Bignotti had been chief mechanic on more Indy 500 winning cars than any man in history. Gary was elated. He'd felt like a puppet driving for Penske, as he couldn't make any of the important decisions concerning the race car. Besides, Gary knew, the Penske car in 1972 didn't have an enviable finishing record. Gary dropped out of more races than he completed.

Gary wasn't able to sign with either Bignotti or Team McLaren. He believed that politics within the sport kept him tied to Penske. Gary recuperated sufficiently enough by November of 1972 to once again make the annual trek to the West Coast and run a couple of Midget and Sprint races. Shortly thereafter he negotiated a new contract with Penske that would give him his monthly retainer plus a straight 40 percent of his winnings. The year previous, Penske had given him a sliding scale percentage that only went to the traditional 40 percent after Bettenhausen had compiled a determined amount of winnings. Gary asked for and received the straight 40 percent. He hoped the Penske cars would do better in the reliability department for 1973.

1973

Since Gary had been spending an increasing amount of time in Indianapolis, he had asked Leona Russo, Paul's wife, to try and find him a home. Leona was in real estate and located a 46 acre plot in the nearby town of Monrovia. The beautiful, rolling land was heavily wooded and had a four acre lake on it as well as two houses. Gary and Wave, along with the twins left Tinley Park and relocated. The lake was stocked with catfish, bluegills and bass. Gary, Vuky and other pals envisioned good summertime fishing.

Vukovich was always looking for something to do on summer days and could usually be found inside the Speedway on the golf course. He had been pestering Bettenhausen to take up the game but Gary said he didn't see much future in chasing a little white ball around. He finally relented and found that he actually enjoyed it.

"See there, Schmuck," Vukovich would say. "I told you it's a good game. Did you ever think about how much money the guys on the pro golf tour make? And they never had to eat dirt."

Schmuck. It was another one of Vukovich's nicknames. He'd heard the term being bandied about somewhere and didn't know what it meant. Schnauzer-Hausen. Schmuck. They were all the same. Vukovich was always tagging people with a nickname. But this one stuck. Soon, other drivers were referring to Gary as "The Schmucker" and he didn't mind. It had come from Vukovich and was intended as a term of endearment.

No one had ever told Billy that the literal Yiddish translation of Schmuck is....prick. It was difficult, if not impossible to find either a Jewish race fan or driver. They didn't serve matzo balls or gefilte fish at the Speedway. Consequently, the word Schmuck was just something that sounded keen. Soon, Gary became "The old Schmucker." None of the racing journals, however, ever headlined: "The Schmucker Wins at Winchester."

* * *

"Gee, this is terrific," the old man in the grandstands said. He was watching an early 1973 USAC Midget auto race. He'd probably seen more Midget races since 1934 than any other person in attendance. The voice came from Crocky Wright, the Midget race fan who had started going to the races back in the days when Tony and Duke Nalon were running at Nutley. Now, in January of 1973 Crocky was watching Johnny Parsons, Jr. win an indoor Midget feature at Fort Wayne, Indiana. Crocky had never allowed his interest in Midgets to lapse even for a moment. He finally gave up driving the small cars when he was well past forty, and then dusted off his typewriter and began writing about them for some of the Eastern auto racing newspapers. He moved to Indianapolis when the Eastern club he had followed all these years decided to put not only roll cages, but wings on Midgets as well. Crocky accepted the roll cages, believed they made the Midgets safer. But he said the wings were "ridiculous." He could fondly recall what a Midget looked like in the Thirties, Forties, Fifties and Sixties. When they put wings on Midgets, he'd said, there was nothing left for him on the East Coast. He'd move to Indianapolis and continue going to the Midget and Sprint car races just as he always had. But he'd never go to a Midget race if they were running wings.

The young driver he was watching, Johnny Parsons, Jr., was the son of Tony's old friend of the same name. The man who had won the 1950 Indianapolis 500 and who was considered to be one of the most handsome race car drivers. His son spelled his first name Johnny rather than Johnnie, but there the difference stopped. John Jr. was blessed with his father's good looks. He had been campaigning with USAC since 1968, but had yet to earn a ride in an Indianapolis 500 car. Parsons, Jr. had, however, earned

Johnny Parsons, Jr.

a reputation for knowing that the gas pedal on a race car has only one position...wide open. His youthful enthusiasm caused him to crash a lot and Indy car owners had shied away from him.

Vukovich loved to needle him.

"Hey Parsons," Vuky would say. "Did you get upside down this weekend?"

"No," Parsons replied.

"Did you hit the fence?"

"No," was the reply again.

"What's wrong, were you sick?" Vukovich laughed.

Johnny Parsons, Jr. was envious of Gary and Billy Vukovich. They had all known each other since childhood and he was the one left without an Indy car ride. By 1973 he figured he had paid his dues and should have been given a chance in an Indy car long ago. He was getting tired of running just Sprints and Midgets.

For now though, Crocky Wright thought his performance was just fine. There was nothing Crocky liked better than seeing a good Midget race. It was frosting on the cake that he had seen Johnnie Parsons, Sr. win the 1950 "500." Many times Crocky had said, "I don't think I'll go to any more races. It's sort of ruined my whole life. It's all I've ever done. I don't know....maybe...."

* * *

While Gary could count on not only having one of Roger Penske's machines for the 1973 Indianapolis "500," but a chance in Penske's stock car as well, he was still enamored with dirt track racing. His Sprint car sponsors, Pat and Bernie had purchased another car for him to drive, one of the special machines called a Championship Dirt car that ran only on the mile dirt tracks. There were only a few mile dirt tracks left on the schedule, a hold-over from the old days. Yet the Champ Dirt races continued to draw large fields of cars, and crowds were good. The Champ Dirt cars looked just like a Sprint car to a bystander, but they were a bit longer, heavier and were allowed a little larger engine. Their design hadn't changed drastically since the days when Tony was running the old 99.

Gary believed he had a better idea for a Championship Dirt car. He wanted Willie Davis to completely revamp the front end of their car so it had suspension similar to an Indy car.

"This independent suspension stuff has been tried before," he told Gary. "I think we're going to waste a lot of time trying to make it work."

"It'll work just fine," Gary replied. "It's about time there was some progress made. We'll blow their doors off."

Throughout April of 1973 Willie put in long hours to build the new front end. Gary wanted the car itself to look different as well, and contacted master body builder Don Brown to fabricate new aluminum panels that would make the car unique from the rest of the field. Brown had been nicknamed, "The Prince of Darkness" for his preference in working after the sun went down.

The 300 pound, cigar smoking Davis had also picked up a new nickname. Driver George Snider saw him cleaning out one of the large refueling tanks at Indy and all that was visible was Willie's hind-section as he was stretched inside through an opening cavity.

"Hey look," Snider said. "A Cork. Willie would definitely make a good Cork for that tank."

Again, the name stuck. Thus, The Schmucker, The Prince and The Cork all toiled in the wee hours over Gary's latest pet project.

"What's wrong?" Willie asked Gary. "Why are you shaking your head like that?"

"That music," Gary noted. "It's about to drive me crazy. How do you put up with it?"

Willie laughed. "Ha," long pause. "Ha," long pause again. "Ha," third long pause. You could hear Willie's laugh from a block away. Three long Ha's with a long pause between each.

"What's wrong, Schmuck, don't you like my Nighttime Engineering Music? You oughta listen to it once in a while. What do you play when you're doing all this Kitchen-Table Engineering?" Willie asked sarcastically.

"Oldies," Bettenhausen replied. "Good-shit. Not that long-haired crap," he smiled.

Tchaikovsky's Nutcracker was blaring through the garage. Often Willie would break momentarily from a part he was working on, close his eyes and let his head roll from side to side in tune with the music. Bettenhausen would look over, shake his head as if to say, "God, how can anybody like that stuff?"

The car was finally finished the night of April 23 and Gary had obtained permission to test it at DuQuoin, Illinois on the mile track. It was virtually unheard of to ever test a Dirt car. You simply showed up at the race and took your best shot. You either made or missed the show.

"Everybody be back here early," Bettenhausen said. "DuQuoin's a long ways and we'll have to hustle."

A young mechanic named Billy Brown, a 24 year old California surfer type, was designated to drive the borrowed truck. Willie and writer Carl Hungness were to ride with Brown while Gary and constant helper Larry Journay would follow. Hungness overslept and missed the trip.

Bill Brown was driving a truck known as cab-over. You climbed up, into it and sat next to the engine. It didn't have a long hood out front. Willie had climbed into the sleeper shortly after the team stopped for coffee. Along Interstate 70, just past the Indiana-Illinois border, Billy Brown rammed headlong into the back of a semi-truck that had just pulled out of a rest area. It was surmised that he had fallen asleep.

"Oh no," Gary said. "I think Willie's dead too."

The front of the cab had been smashed all the way back to the sleeper. Willie had been knocked unconscious, but after a time said, "What happened?" They had to cut him out of the wreckage.

* * *

"Sorry, I gotta go to work," Gary said to the battery of photographers in the Speedway pits who were snapping pictures. Once again, Gary was one of the favorites at Indy and drew a lot publicity. As he was walking toward his car a cute young brunette came up to him and said, "How's Merle?"

"Fine," Bettenhausen replied as he looked her up and down. "He's back in the garages somewhere. He's doing just fine."

A female was in the pits at the Indianapolis Motor Speedway. The pits and Gasoline Alley had been strictly off-limits to women since 1911, but the recent Women's Lib movement had torn down the gate.

"Tits in the pits," said more than one driver and mechanic.

The beautiful 1973 Cadillac pace car pulls into the pits as the field comes down for the green flag. [*Laycock*]

They weren't allowed to wear shorts or sleeveless tops. The sports car oriented people in attendance had long been used to females in the pits, but oldtimers at Indy felt as though one of their last bastions had been invaded.

Merle had been spending time at Indy in 1973 saying hello to all the well-wishers. He told them that he expected to be back in a race car in a month or so.

"Boy, Merle, what'd you do with your bandage?" Johnny Parsons, Jr. asked.

Merle had been wearing a bandage across his skin-grafted nose.

"Took it off. Feels a lot more comfortable. Feels neat."

"You look like an animal," Parsons said. "I'm glad I'm not eating dinner."

Parsons had finally talked his way into a Speedway ride. Another second generation driver was at Indy. Parsons' ride wasn't competitive and he wasn't expected to make the show. Still, he was there. It was a lot better than walking around and praying.

It was the first day of qualifying at Indianapolis and more than 250,000 people were in attendance. Seemingly, everyone who was anyone in the sport over the last thirty years came to Indy qualifying. The morning had started off badly when driver Art Pollard hit the wall in the first turn. The accident looked bad, it wasn't expected Pollard would survive.

Gary qualified easily in the top half-dozen starters and just before his official photo was to be taken the announcer notified the throng that Pollard had died. Merle didn't hear the announcement and Gary looked across at him and said, "Pollard's dead." It had been twelve years to the day and nearly the hour that Tony was fatally injured on the same race track. Merle quickly changed the subject and said, "Everything, OK. How'd it feel?"

Roger Penske looked over at the burned Bettenhausen and winked.

The photo was taken and everyone but the car's crew stayed in the pits. You wanted to know what the competition was doing. You chatted with all the oldtimers. In the pits you could still find remnants of the old Chicago Gang: Duke Nalon, Paul Russo, Emil Andres, Harry McQuinn among other old racers. Johnnie Parsons, Sr. sat with his pals and nervously watched his son.

Johnny Rutherford was on the track and had just completed the fastest run of the day. He had won pole position. Gary ran to the pit wall and gave Rutherford a hand clasped cheer as he went by.

Al Unser walked up to Bettenhausen and said with a smile, "Hey, don't you have a car just like his?"

"Yeah," Gary grinned. "But not the same foot."

Penske and Bettenhausen spent time trying to help driver Al Loquasto. Loquasto had purchased a year old Penske machine and Roger wanted to see the car in the race. Gary looked the car over from end to end, nervously walking up one side and down the other. All the while he held his hands together, pushing his cuticles back. Whenever Bettenhausen would stop, either in the garage area or pits, he'd put his hands together and work on his cuticles.

"Hell, he's ok." Penske said. "I put the wings up and moved the bars forward. We'll put thirty gallons of fuel in it and zap him in the show tomorrow. He'll make it just fine."

Tech talk. Moving wings, adjusting stabilizer bars. It was the usual language of the pits. Chris Economaki, ABC Wide World of Sports' man on the scene, was standing nearby. Economaki always had a nose for news.

"Where are you looking at the gauges," Gary asked the skinny Loquasto.

Loquasto looked up, shrugged and shook his head no. He didn't say he wasn't looking at the gauges. He didn't have to.

"Tires look great." Penske noted.

Gary explains to Loquasto that he should adjust the right front wing up a little if the car is handling in a certain fashion.

Loquasto replies that he didn't know where the wing setting was

Above left: Gary and Roger Penske wait for the track to dry out, Indy 1973.
Right: A bit of frisbee playing helps the time go by.
Below left: Gary's rear-view mirror doubles as a hat rack.
Right: Gary and Merle during the National Anthem. [*Chini Photos*]

right now. He just hoped everything was ok, that he'd make the show.

Gary turned around, rolled his eyes upward at Penske and smiled. Penske grinned back as if to say, "Don't worry. Don't worry. Not everyone is a perfectionist."

Loquasto hit the fourth turn wall on the last day of qualifying and wiped out the right side of his car. He wasn't injured but there was no chance he'd be in the 1973 Indianapolis 500 either.

The race itself turned out to be a bad memory. It started on Sunday and ended on Wednesday after only 332 miles had been run. Rain, fire and crashes were the talk of the year. Driver Swede Savage died of track injuries and a pit man was killed by a safety truck traveling in the wrong direction. Rich kid Salt Walther got upside down and cameras zoomed in on his feet, sticking out from the front of the car. Miraculously, he lived and raced again. Gordon Johncock was finally declared the winner. Billy Vukovich was flagged in second place when the final day's rain came and Gary ended where he started, in fifth position.

* * *

"There, how's that Merle? Think you can drive like that?"

Gary had concocted a swivel device he bolted on the steering wheel that accepted a pin that would replace Merle's hook.

"Yeah, feels ok," Merle said. "Let's go Midget racing."

Gary had acquired a large building on Indianapolis' west side, he was turning it into a race car shop. There, he'd said, he would build race cars and maintain his own. He believed he'd make money. He wanted the place to be as clean as a Penske operation. It never was.

The first project of the season was readying Gary's Midget for Merle. A power steering system had been installed and with the new steering wheel device, Merle was ready to become the one-armed driver of the USAC Midget circuit. His face looked like hell.

"Your winner is Merle Bettenhausen!" the announcer proclaimed. The scene was a bullring of a race track in a town called Lost Creek, Kentucky. Merle won a preliminary event in his first race back. He was on the USAC Midget Trail once again and determined to prove that he could drive a race car, for all intents and purposes, with one arm. His car carried "Steed" Oil and Marathon sponsorships. The Marathon credit card came in handy

The pin and swivel that attaches Merle's arm to his Midget wheel. Below: Merle's good friend Ted Siemsen squeezes his cheeks after Merle won a heat race at Lost Creek, KY. Long time Bettenhausen friend John Stagnero is on the left. [*Chini Photos*]

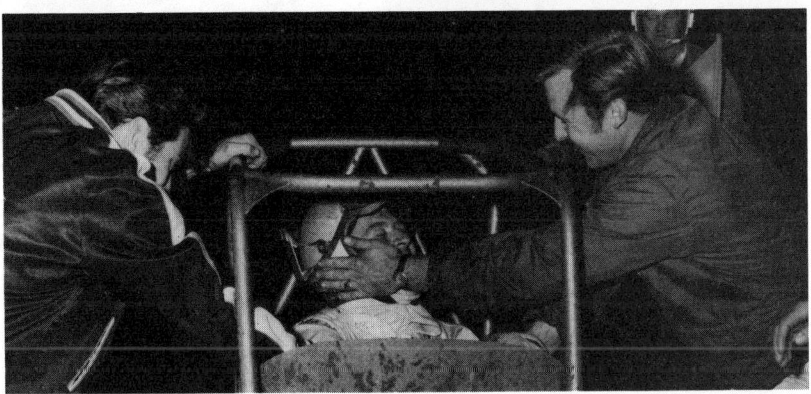

when he and Leslie took a seven thousand mile trip to run the USAC tour that took them to the Pacific Northwest. While the other Midget racers were complaining about high prices due to the shortage of '73, Merle was able to concentrate on his driving. The driving went alternately good and bad. Usually, he wasn't among the top ten finishers, but every once in a while his star shined. At the end of August he won a feature event down in Johnson City, Tennessee. Merle was once again caught up in the aura that surrounds the races. When someone would ask him if he expected to run at the Speedway again and he always replied, "Sure." But deep down inside he knew he was a one-arm race car driver who wouldn't have had a prayer in a Speedway car.

* * *

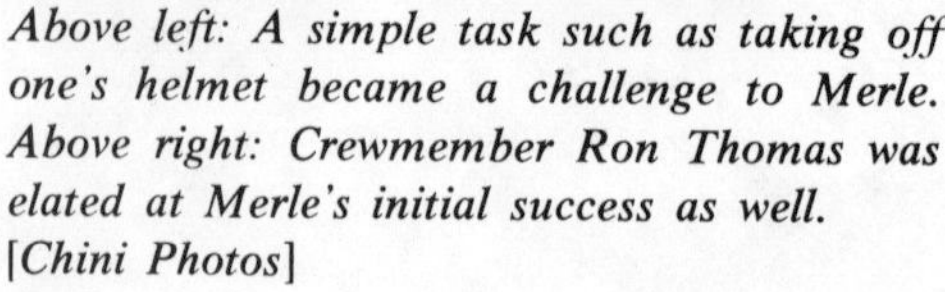

Above left: A simple task such as taking off one's helmet became a challenge to Merle. Above right: Crewmember Ron Thomas was elated at Merle's initial success as well. [Chini Photos]

Right: Merle signals Gary that he has two laps to go at Terre Haute. [Mahoney]

The car Gary designed, repainted for Merle with Steed and Marathon sponsorship. [Chini]

Right: Clockwise: Pancho Carter, Billy Vukovich, Gary and mechanic Danny Jones watch Merle qualify on the Phoenix mile track. [Chini]

Below: In a rare temper outburst, Gary shakes his fist at Sprint driver Rich Leavell after a track incident with him. [Mahoney]

Gary continued running Sprints and Midgets whenever possible throughout 1973 in addition to his Indy car activity in the Penske machine. He won what was termed the world's fastest automobile race at College Station, Texas in October on a track that was a duplicate of the one at Michigan where Merle lost his arm. Overall however, Gary encountered more mechanical difficulty in the Penske machine than he expected and wound up sixth in year end point standings. He hoped next year would be better.

* * *

Tony Bettenhausen, Jr. visited Gary's Indianapolis race car shop in mid-summer of '73. He was campaigning his Vita-Fresh Stock car and had decided to come to the Midwest to run some of the USAC races. In July he accompanied Willie Davis to one of

Left: Tony shares a joke with another second generation driver, Pancho Carter, son of Duane Carter. [Chini]
Above: Tony brought his Stock car to the Midwest in 1973 and ran a few races. [Chini]
Below: He also took a practice spin in Gary's Sprint car at Salem. [Mahoney]

the Sprint car Hills at Salem, Indiana, and practiced in Gary's car. He said, "My mother would shoot me if she knew I was in this thing." Tony could appreciate what it took to drive a Sprint car and thought it best if he continued his Stock car driving career.

* * *

The 1973 season ended on a sad note when word came down from Chicago that builder Harry Turner had been struck by a Midget while he was standing on a race track at Kankakee, Illinois. It was reported that Turner may have been attempting to cross the track; someone shouted at him and diverted his attention. An oncoming car smashed into him and threw him upward into the roll cage. Harry Turner would spend the rest of his life in a wheelchair. He'd spent half his life racing the small cars and the remainder of it building them. He said he'd continue building.

* * *

15

A Farewell to Arms

1974

With the winter of 1974, once again came the traditional indoor Midget races inside the Fort Wayne, Indiana Coliseum. The hockey-rink sized track provided the same type of close competition and car-bumping that used to go on back in Tony's days at the old Chicago Amphitheatre and Armory. Usually, over 50 Midgets turned out for the January races and only ten made the feature line-up.

Merle displayed his smoothness to the packed house by not only making the feature event, but finishing third in the 75 lap race. Gary had built another new Midget and drove it to fifth position. The star of the day was an itinerant race car driver named Dennis (Super Duke) Cook. Cook qualified poorly and had to run some consolation events in order to work his way into the feature event. He won three separate races and finally finished right behind Gary in the feature.

Many of the racers in attendance had attended Duke's Christmas party only a couple of weeks prior. Cook was one of the regulars on the USAC Midget and Sprint circuits and it had been said for years that if he could drive as well as he could talk, he'd have won the Indy 500 half a dozen times by now. Usually, where you found Vukovich and Bettenhausen throughout the summer months, you'd find Duke Cook. The racers had come to accept him as being a "pretty nice guy, way deep down." Outwardly, Duke was one of auto racing's most obnoxious individuals.

At his party he spied a well-endowed unescorted female. Duke walked, up, looked her straight in the eye, then down at her breasts and said: "Nice tits."

"Well!" the girl replied. "Is that your very best opening line?"

"Uh, hadn't thought about it. I just think you got nice tits. Don't you know how to take a compliment?"

Duke Cook

"If that's a compliment, you better look up the meaning of the word," she said and stormed off.

Duke turned around and said to nobody in particular, "What's she all pissed off about? She oughta be glad she ain't flat-chested."

Conversely, Duke was the first man on the scene to raise funds for an injured driver. Sometimes he'd organize an auction to assist someone in the sport who had suffered an ill twist of fate. And surprisingly, Cook found his share of females who were rather attracted to his gutter-level manner of speech.

* * *

A couple of weeks after the Fort Wayne race both Gary and Tony were racing in a NASCAR event in Riverside, California. Gary had been given a ride in Roger Penske's Stock car, and he was proud that little brother Tony was running with the pros. Tony planned on running the entire NASCAR circuit in hopes of becoming "Rookie of the Year."

While two of the Bettenhausen brothers were on the West Coast, leadership of USAC back in Indianapolis was changing. Executive Director Bill Smyth had tendered his resignation and it was accepted by the board of directors. Rumor had it for many months that Smyth would be asked to resign at the annual board meetings after his four and a half year tenure. Gary was still on the board.

Upstairs, Henry Banks quietly chuckled to himself. Henry had been given the title of Director of USAC Properties, a position

Streakers were a part of the Indy 500 scene a few years ago. [*Mahoney*]

Left: Racing photographer Jim Chini allows Gary to borrow his camera for a better view of Indy's sights. [*Whitlow*]

that had nothing to do with racing. It was Henry's job to license firms to use the USAC emblem and conduct certified tests for various automotive oriented companies. Henry had been shuffled out of the way and told to promote USAC Certification wherever he could. Sometimes a Detroit manufacturer would want to conduct a test and it was Henry's job to convince them that a USAC Certification would add credence to results they could advertise. Once in a while you'd see an ad on TV stating in part: This Test Conducted By The United States Auto Club. While Henry made his own little division profitable single-handedly, the general public never did become very familiar with either the USAC emblem or the name of the club. Most thought it was one of those clubs you join which offers road assistance. Henry Banks was far removed from automobile racing activities yet his heart was still in it. Each May you'd find him in the pits at Indianapolis, reminiscing. His old car owner, Lindsey Hopkins, continued to be an entrant at the Speedway and the pair continued their life-long friendship.

Gary's luck at Indianapolis in 1974 wasn't enviable. He went out after only two laps with engine failure. Streakers livened up the usual month of May activity and it wasn't uncommon to see a naked person in the grandstands or running down the track. Girl watching in the grandstands immediately behind the pits had long been a past-time of pit occupants and this year's viewing was the best ever.

"Let me see that camera," Bettenhausen said to photographer Jim Chini.

Gary had spied a halter-topped brunette in the grandstands who had a habit of leaning over to the seating section in front. Her white top bulged when she sat upright and flopped just right so that huge mounds of flesh would seemingly come pouring out of it when she leaned over. Chini had a camera with a telephoto lense on it and you could occasionally find a driver making friends with a photographer who at other times may have been considered to be somewhat of a pain. At Indianapolis a driver's time was never his own. There were photographers in the pits, in the garages, cafeteria, in the parking lot. You didn't want to stand around talking to some fence hanger for very long otherwise your activity would forever be recorded on film.

"Bettenhausen, what are you doing?" Billy Vukovich asked.

"Taking pictures of the crowd," Gary smiled without taking the camera from his face.

Vukovich looked toward the direction of Bettenhausen's camera, spied the white-topped brunette and said, "Schmuck, you are a pervert. Looking at some chick's tits through a camera. I'll bet you're a god-damn peeping Tom, too."

"Shut-up," Gary laughed. "I think she's getting ready to bend over again."

"One thing's for sure," Vuky continued. "Your old lady ain't here today. Does she know she's married to a pervert? You going to go home and tell her how hard you worked at the track today? You really had to spend a lot of time getting the car straightened out, right Schmuck?"

"There!" Gary exclaimed. "That is be-you-ti-ful!"

Johnny Parsons came walking by the group and looked up. Parsons had another Speedway ride and this year it looked like he would make the show.

"Something good up there?" he asked.

"Good...bad...what's the difference?" Vukovich said.

The handsome Parsons looked at Vukovich, smiled and walked on. He knew he had no trouble attracting females and didn't have a reply for Vukovich.

Bettenhausen handed the camera back to photographer Chini and said to Vuky, "Did you run this morning?"

He was bored with watching the girl in the white top. Now it was time for tech talk with Vukovich. They walked through the pits and headed toward the cafeteria where they spotted driver Pancho Carter and a man in a gray suit. The balding man had a double chin, but a ready smile. He was familiar to the drivers, went to many Sprint races with Pancho. His name was Larry Conrad, Secretary of State of Indiana. A race fan politician.

Bettenhausen was still in his uniform and so was Vukovich. Carter was in street clothes. After ordering an iced tea, Gary pulled a chair out from the table and sat down. A. J. Foyt had just got up from the table next to Bettenhausen's, looked over at Billy and Gary and said, "Sheet...look at that...hero race car drivers," and laughed to himself. "I'll bet you guys even wear them uniforms to bed," Foyt laughed again and kept on walking.

"How's it going?" Vukovich asked Bettenhausen.

"Shit, don't ask," Gary replied. "It's like I gotta send everybody in that garage to school. It's a screwed up operation."

Larry Conrad looked toward Gary and said, "Hey Gary, you knew that George Washington, our first president, was a General in the Army before he was president, don't you?"

Bettenhausen thought for a moment, eyes glanced left and right. Scared. George Washington, President. History. Bettenhausen didn't like history and didn't answer immediately. Conrad wasn't looking for an answer. He continued.

"Well, you see General George was getting ready to fight the British and he had fifty men with him, and it was late at night and he didn't have anywhere to sleep. So he said, 'Men, we have to find a place to sleep so we can fight in the morning. There's a house, let's see.' "

Conrad continued, "So General George walked up to the door and a lady came out. He said, 'How do you do, ma'am. General George Washington here, getting ready to fight the British in the morning and need a place for my men to stay.' "

The lady replied, "Oh yes General. Well how many men do you have?"

"Fifty plus myself, ma'am."

"Oh my, General. I might be able to handle one, but that's all."

"That's ok," George said. "Lieutenant Cox, fall out. Stay here tonight and meet us down by the bridge tomorrow morning, 5 a.m. sharp."

"Yes, sir," was the call from the back of the troops.

"Well," Conrad continued. "George walked up the road aways and saw a big mansion. What he didn't know was, the place was a house of ill-repute. The madam was inside looking out the window and she was smiling when she saw all these men walking toward her door. So once again, George knocked on the door and said,"

" 'How do you do, ma'am. General George Washington here. Getting ready to fight the British in the morning and need a place for my men to stay.' "

" 'Why that's wonderful,' the madam said. 'how many men do you have?' "

Gary and Larry Dickson had become pals by 1974. [*Mahoney*]

“ ‘Let’s see,’ George said, ‘Without Cox we have 49 plus myself.’ ”

“ ‘You gotta be shittin’ me,’ the madam said and slammed the door in his face.’ ”

Everybody at the table rocked back in laughter. Without Cox Bettenhausen said.

* * *

Although Gary won a couple of Sprint car races before the Speedway was run in 1974, his activity in Midgets and Sprints had slowed down considerably from prior years. He was concentrating more on running Bettenhausen Racing Enterprises and building race cars at his new shop. He had hired Merle for a hundred dollars per week to act as general manager and the plans were to make a profit from building and selling Sprints and Midgets. While Merle was able to organize inventory and take care of the general office work such as paying salaries and ordering supplies, the feeling was that it was Gary’s personal hobby shop. He had convinced Willie Davis to bring his equipment and merge with the new enterprise, Willie reluctanly agreed.

Gary was continually doing favors for fellow racers and had a notion that he would build and drive his own Sprint, Midget and Championship Dirt car to success and thereby insure customer orders. Early on, Merle saw that procedures weren’t being conducted on a businesslike basis and tried without success to operate with some specific goals and objectives in mind.

Gary would usually show up dressed in grey work pants with a matching shirt. A bystander looked at him and said, "Hey GB, you look like a Maytag repairman!"

"A what?" Bettenhausen replied caustically.

"A Maytag repairman, you know, like the guy you see on TV in the ads."

"I can fix anything," Bettenhausen retorted and walked off.

Often times he'd see an employee making a part, fixing something and he'd walk up and say, "That isn't how you do that. Here give me that. Jesus, there's a right way and a wrong way to do everything. I want the shit that comes out of this shop to be absolutely perfect, understand?"

Employees would refer to the demanding Bettenhausen as "der Fuhrer" and give each other Hitler-style salutes when explaining how Gary would want something done. He was impatient both in and out of the shop.

One day while waiting for a long line of traffic to pass, Gary looked around and said to his lunch-time passengers: "What are all these assholes doing on *my* road...where'd they all come from?"

Sometimes the one-armed Merle would ask for assistance in performing a small task. He asked, "Hey Gary, help me put up this bulletin," to which the elder brother replied: "You can handle it yourself...figure it out."

The tough Schmuck. If he thought that it would have really helped Merle, Gary would have cut off one of his own arms to lend assistance. Inside he believed that if you demanded perfection from someone it would help them. Outwardly he was the leather-skinned "Fuhrer," and once you got past the outer layer he was jelly inside. When he heard about a fellow driver getting injured, he could be found at home, alone, crying. He'd light up his pipe and reflect on the good times he had with the man. A pipe? Gary Schmucker Bettenhausen the pipe puffer? Everyone at the races was used to seeing him hot-lapping a Midget or a Sprint with a cigarette held between his teeth, just like Tony used to do. No one in the outside world could ever imagine a pensive Schmucker with a pipe in his mouth.

* * *

Merle continued his campaign along the USAC Midget circuit from January through June of 1974, and his consistency put him second in overall point standings. Many were saying that he was a better driver with one arm than he was with two. He had tried a couple of Sprint car races without success in May but wasn't discouraged. On May 20th he became a father when Leslie presented him with an eight pound eleven ounce baby girl they named Tracy.

He claimed that having the additional responsibility of a child didn't affect his thinking during the summer of '74, but he admits to having a nagging feeling about getting hurt once again in a race car. He'd experienced the usual butterflies that take place on the way to the track and nervous anticipation just before the start of any race, but these feelings were different: He thought something bad might happen to him.

He was justifiably upset when another driver spun him out of the feature race at Chesteron, Illinois the night of June 28th.

"Jesus Christ," he shouted. "Why in the hell don't you stick to your typewriter. You motioned me around one direction and then you went the same way! You can't do that!"

He was venting his anger at his good friend Carl Hungness. Hungness had been racing a Midget directly in front of the second Bettenhausen son when he motioned him by on the right during a restart. The restart of the race, following a long caution flag, took several laps and Hungness moved high on the track when he had already motioned to Merle that he would move low. A minor bumping incident ensued, leaving the man who was fighting for the point championship parked sideways on the track. Spectators could see the angry Bettenhausen shaking his one good fist at Hungness. Before the race he had commented, "All right Carl, keep your nose clean...and don't spin me out of the feature. You spent two years building that thing and don't bend it either."

It was the last time that Merle Bettenhausen would ever drive a race car. The man who turned out to be his biographer had spun him out of his last race.

Merle had every intention of participating in the next Midget race to be held, but received news that brother Gary had crashed at Syracuse, New York. Gary was practicing for the one mile dirt race to be held on the famed old track when his car dug into the first turn and flipped wildly. He was listed as being in good condition in a Syracuse hospital with two broken collar bones, broken ribs, broken thumb, a fractured eye socket, and a broken nose. The night before the Syracuse crash, Gary had received the broken nose in a Sprint car race at Reading, Pennsylvania, but still made the long drive to run in the heavily publicized Championship Dirt race. It was the same track where Tony had won his first Championship event, and the July 4th event promised such stars as Mario Andretti and Al Unser as participants. Gary hadn't planned on running the Syracuse race, but was informed by Roger Penske that he wouldn't be driving his stock car as planned the July 4th weekend at Daytona. Effectively, Bettenhausen had been replaced in the stock car by NASCAR standout Bobby Allison. Gary thought he had a contract to run Penske's AMC Matador, but was somehow ousted in favor of Allison.

Gary called Willie Davis and asked him if he could put in an around-the-clock effort to put the Dirt car together. Willie was in the midst of changing the front end back over to a standard set up rather than the independent suspension design Gary had conned him into earlier in the year.

"I'll do my best," Willie told him.

Prior to qualifications on any track the cars are allowed to "hot lap" in groups. Gary wanted to test the new front end, make sure the car was working well before qualifying. It was the first time in years that the Dirt cars had run on the old one mile track, and he had every intention of winning the race.

On his very first hot lap Gary drove into the first turn and didn't lift at all from the throttle. The dirt surface was moist. Drivers said it was "heavy" under such circumstances early in the day and it was normally possible to easily broadslide all the way from the entrance of the corner, through its radius, to its exit on the backstretch. That's what the fans came to see, a Dirt car going around a turn in a sideways position. Everybody expected it, especially early in the day when the track was in good condition and hadn't turned hard and slick yet.

Bettenhausen's car dug in with its right rear wheel and Gary thought it was going to go for a long slide when it suddenly hit a rut and took off skyward as though shot from a cannon. The force threw his arms off the wheel stretched them upward, outside the roll cage. The car cleared the fence, punched a hole in a vacant concession stand roof and tumbled back down on the track, tail first as though ready for an upward launch.

Merle told Leslie he wasn't going to race in Wisconsin: He wanted to think. He brooded about the house all day and Leslie kept her distance. Something very wrong was happening, she knew. Merle wouldn't pass up one of his favorite tracks unless something was eating at him. Merle was second in USAC Midget point standings and the possibility of winning the championship existed: Leslie tried to console him when he said, "I'm going to Syracuse."

"But it's ten o'clock at night, Merle. Wait til morning. The hospital said he was in good condition. You don't have to leave right now, do you?"

Gary's violent Syracuse flip which partially paralyzed his left arm. [*Irvins*]

"Yes," was the simple reply.

Merle drove all night and through the next morning before reaching the Syracuse hospital. Upon entering the hospital room his elder brother looked up and said, "I just feel sorry for mom. Poor MOM! he cried." Now she has to go through this again."

Merle looked at his bandaged brother and cried, "You don't ever have to worry about ME, because I'll never get in another race car again."

"Please Merle," Gary choked. "Please, don't ever change your mind."

The next day the *New York Daily News* devoted the entire centerspread to Gary's accident with a headline of: "A Race Against Death." Because he wasn't killed the paper said you could call him "Mr. Lucky."

When Gary's twins Cary and Todd got close enough to recognize the figure who was coming down the causeway at the airport, they looked closer, screamed and ran away. His left arm in a sling and face heavily bandaged, Gary told Wave that he'd be ok in a few weeks. He wondered how bad the car was.

It had been discovered that in addition to the injuries already mentioned, Gary's left arm was partially paralyzed and he would have to undergo an operation and extensive therapy. Gary said the arm would be fine in no time at all and soon he was back at his race car shop learning the ways of a one-armed man. He said he wanted to get in shape for the annual Turkey Night Grand Prix at the end of the year.

For the remainder of the summer Gary Bettenhausen was a spectator at the races and a self-employed one as well. Roger Penske dropped Bettenhausen from the payroll.

Gary diligently went to therapy several times per week but saw little immediate improvement in his left arm. When he walked it dangled. He could give it a swinging motion and raise it up to table height. His wrist was curved inward, and he worked continually to try to restore it to a normal position. When the other racers saw him they said privately, Bettenhausen's got a gimp arm. He's all through. Even their macabre sense of humor was displayed: "Hey Schmuck," photographer Jim Chini said, "I hear somebody's going to do a book on your family. What are they going to call it, 'A Farewell To Arms?' "

Bettenhausen understood the vein in which the statement was made, laughed and replied, "No, can't do that. Tony's still got two good arms." Then he added, "Keep it up Chini, we'll see who laughs last. The 'ol Schmuck ain't done yet."

* * *

Gary attempted to run the 1974 Turkey Night race at Ascot Park in Los Angeles in November, but finished a poor 20th. The West Coast crowd had read of his plight and everyone made it a point to take a look. Gary walked around with his arms crossed, trying to look as normal as possible. Sometimes he'd lift the dangling appendage to pocket height, hook his thumb in his left pocket and try to look cool, just standing around. There was no way he was going to drive a race car like that, they said. Hell, it was mentioned, even Merle had a hook to help him out. How's he going to grab hold of the steering wheel if he can't even pick his arm up?

Two months after his Ascot encounter the first issue of the 1975 *National Speed Sport News* headlined on the front page:

"BETTENHAUSEN 'ONE ARMS'
WAY TO FORT WAYNE FLAG"

Inside the headline read:

ONE-ARM GARY B. IS COMEBACK KID
IN FORT WAYNE GO

VOL. XLIII No. 1 RIDGEWOOD, N.J., JANUARY 8, 1975

Bettenhausen 'One Arms' Way to Fort Wayne Flag

(Story on Page Three

Jax Drivers Brawl, Police Called

(Story on Page Two)

TOP READING MEN — Reading Stock Car Assn. promoter Lindy Vicari is shown with the top men in points as the group celebrated at the annual awards banquet Saturday night. L. to r. Gerry Chamberlain, fifth; Kenny Brightbill, first; Vicari; Johnny Botz, third; and Jim Keppley, fourth. Missing was runnerup Dick Tobias. (Ty Berger photo)

MIXING IT UP — Gary Irvin (42), Bob Wente (25), Steve Cannon (67) and Gary Byers tangle on the tight tenth of a mile track at the Allen County Memorial Coliseum in Fort Wayne, Ind., during Sunday's USAC indoor midget races, as a crowd of more than 4,000 race-hungry fans looked on. (Bud Miller photo)

WHAT IT's All About — Bobby Albert (right), champion of the Super Midget Racing Club, accepts his titular hardware from Paul Kuhl, promoter of the Flemington, N.J. Fair Speedway. The SMRC fete was held in Flemington. (Dave Innes photo).

THE MYSTERIOUS CHARLIE BROWN is revealed as a dachshund. NASCAR ace Darrell Waltrip and his perky wife Stevie snapped with "Charlie" in Pensacola last month. A story circulated on the NASCAR circuit that Charlie had a radio in his collar and as he roamed the pits, he was gaining intelligence from other crews. It was a season-long standing joke on the Grand National Circuit as some believed and some didn't. (Don Barnes photo).

SENTIMENTAL PRESENTATION — Veteran midget pilot Ed (Dutch) Schaefer with Christine Sanders, daughter of fellow driver Sonny Sanders, chosen to present the Tony Bonadies Memorial Award to Schaefer. Bonadies, a former compatriot of Schaefer, died in a crash several years ago. The trophy is for achievement, fair play and dedication to midget racing. (Ace Lane photo).

Above: Although barely visible in this photo. Gary in car 93, is driving one-armed. [Mahoney]
Left: Cockpit of Gary's Midget in 1975: Sign on the dash says "Super Schmuck" and tape on the wheel aids his right hand. [Mahoney]
Below: Tony and Merle were on hand to congratulate Gary in his comeback. [Mahoney]

Auto racing writer Bill Hill said of Gary's performance:

> It's a known fact that you can't keep a Bettenhausen down very long, and Sunday afternoon that was proven once again when Gary Bettenhausen won the 75 lap U. S. Auto Club indoor Midget feature.......
>
> Driving with his right arm only, Gary capped an almost unbelievable day by pulling into victory lane amid a standing ovation from 4,289 race hungry fans. Waiting there to meet him were brothers Merle and Tony, Jr. and Chief Mechanic Howard Lehmann.

What Hill failed to mention was that during the course of the race, Gary's left arm fell from the steering wheel and could be seen dangling outside the cockpit. There was no time for rest along the straights at Fort Wayne, as it took less than nine seconds to make a lap around the small, indoor track. Gary wasn't interested in hearing anything about having a gimp arm. All he knew was that fifty Midgets took time trials for the Fort Wayne race and he had beaten them all. The 'ol Schmuck had returned. Two weeks later he repeated his winning performance in the next race at Fort Wayne and once again the pit population shook their heads in amazement. Gary said he'd be ready for the outdoor season as usual.

* * *

16

That's A Lot of Work

Gary returned to his Midget, Sprint and Championship car activity in 1975 and found his arm injury had affected not only his driving, but the rides he was able to obtain. Having been fired from the Penske operation, he was rehired by Fred Gerhardt, the man he drove for from 1968-71. His first race back in an Indy car netted him a 14th place finish in the California 500. Gerhardt's Thermo-King sponsored team was still competitive, but it wasn't in the same class as the Penske operation. Gary had no trouble in the California event (he also ran a 100 mile qualifying race) and said he could handle a Speedway car just fine. He noted that you only move the steering wheel a quarter of a turn or so in the Indy cars and the real test would come in the Midgets and Sprints, on dirt.

For the first time in his life, Gary Bettenhausen was fired out of a Sprint car ride. He teamed with a knowledgeable owner named Junior Knepper early in the season and failed to make the shows at both Reading, Pennsylvania, and Rossburg, Ohio, two tracks where he had previously excelled. The team then went to Winchester and Gary managed a fifth. Knepper said he'd get someone else to drive the car. It was a new experience for Gary, he was one of the three winningest Sprint car drivers in the history of USAC. He told Wave he wasn't going to give up, he'd win races. He confided that he was glad he had an Indy car ride though.

Two nights before the 1975 Indianapolis "500" a twin bill of Sprint car races was held on the mile track at the Indianapolis Fairgrounds. Gary's race car shop had recently completed building a new Sprint car for a driver named Bob Richards and Gary was driving the machine. Bettenhausen led the first 50 lapper briefly but later spun and wound up in a duel with old foe Larry Dickson for ninth position. Gary edged his way back up to fourth at race's end. After getting out of the car he walked up to Merle, made a gesture as though he were masturbating and said, "I just couldn't run up high." Fellow driver and good friend Steve Chassey unbuckled Gary's helmet for him, while mechanic Lou Ligino wiped the oil and sweat off the back of Gary's neck. All the while Gary was giving orders to the crew as to what to change on the car for the second 50 lapper. He finally looked around and saw that everyone was busy, sat down on a pile of tires and said, "Boy Merle, that's a damn lot of work with one arm." Merle just nodded his head as if to say, "Yeah, I know. I really know."

In the second race Gary was running third when he spun again. Brother Tony looked over at Merle and said, "Jeez, he *just* did that. And he did it at Terre Haute too and it cost him about three grand."

Merle noted, "He gets tired with one arm, but he's not going to ever tell you about it."

"He's really gonna skin his ass if he doesn't realize it pretty quick," Tony said.

After the race Gary was pissed. Merle asked him what happened and he said, "I got sideways and tried to straighten it out. The left front touched the fence and I didn't want to run into Sammy (Sessions) so I had no where to go. Screw it. Gimme a beer."

It was definitely a different Gary Bettenhausen driving a Sprint car on the Indianapolis Fairgrounds track. In a previous day, he would have driven the place like he owned it. If he had been up as far as third, or leading, it would have taken a mechanical malfunction or mistake on someone else's part to make him lose a position. The old Schmuck would have to learn a new driving technique.

Gary was justifiably miffed, it was the second race at the Fairgrounds mile within a week where he hadn't performed well. A week prior to the Sprint show Gary missed the show entirely in the scheduled Midget race. He came in after hot laps and told Merle, "It's just flat-out all the way around...not going anywhere. If I had a different engine I'd really blow their doors off."

Merle suggested that a gear change be made and Gary said no, that wouldn't help it. Then Gary turned to Steve Chassey and said, "you feel like racin' tonight?"

"Sure," Chassey noted.

"This thing's a slug," Gary said. "The chassis is working, but no horsepower. If I don't have a chance of winning, I don't feel like running around in the back and taking a chance on bustin' my ass. I can't afford to miss the Speedway....gotta make some money."

As soon as the subject of putting Chassey in the car was raised, so was it dropped. Again, Gary began walking around the car telling his crew what changes to make in the chassis. When it came time for him to qualify, he got back in the car and required help buckling his helmet. He could do battle, but it was a little tough getting the armor on. Gary had drawn a very late qualifying number, which meant that most every other car at the race had already made an attempt. Consequently, the track conditions had changed significantly from the time the first few cars went out. On a dirt track you always hoped for an early qualifying number so the track wouldn't be "worn out." It was usually extremely difficult to log a good qualifying time if you'd drawn a late number. Gary made his run and missed the show completely. He hadn't gone faster than the slowest car. He came rolling into his pit area and crew members shook their heads, turned thumbs down as if to say, "Nope, missed it."

Gary unbuckled himself and with his helmet still on picked up a hammer and walked toward the front of the car and smacked it on the nose a couple of times: "Rotten Pig!"

Billy Vukovich saw the brief tirade, walked up and said, "Oh wow! Tough Guy! Look at him in action. Shit Bettenhausen, you ain't tough...they don't know you...you're like putty inside."

Bettenhausen turned toward Vukovich, eyes smiling. He unbuckled his helmet, laughed, looked at the car, shrugged and said, "Shitbox."

"Let's go see who else is left to qualify," Vukovich said. "If everybody misses the show, you'll feel good Schmuck."

"Watch that guy!" Gary quipped as a car went by on the track. "I was behind him earlier...he's gonna wear that thing."

Gary Bettenhausen had missed the show, fair and square. He expected to be one of the last cars out and show everyone how it was done: set fast time of the evening. He'd done it before, there was no better feeling than going out on a dirt track when it was seemingly, "all gone" and finding a groove that would still carry you around faster than anyone else. But now, nine days before the running of the 1975 Indy "500" it wouldn't happen. Gary was a spectator. He and Vukovich went down into the first turn to watch the races.

* * *

At Indianapolis in 1975 Gary didn't enjoy the limelight, nor the prestigious equipment he had with the Penske team. Gary knew he would make the 33 car starting line-up but he couldn't expect to be a front-runner unless a miracle occurred. The Indianapolis 500

Chief mechanic Mark Stainbrook, left, waits for Gary to don his helmet in 1975. [Mahoney]

wasn't like running an everyday Midget or Sprint race where you could still take a mediocre car and put a superior driver in it and expect to win. At Indy, especially in the mid-Seventies, it was beginning to be said that you could take a superior car and a mediocre driver in it and garner a win.

On Thursday May 22, only three days before the "500," Gary almost wiped out his chances of running in the race. Traditionally, a few days before the race, the track is opened for a day called "carburation tests." Just past noon, Gary spun some 600 feet in the first turn when the car broke traction. Pancho Carter saw that he was ok and waved to him as he drove by. Gary came back in the pits and told his new chief mechanic Mark Stainbrook: "Mark, they tried to give us a used tire again. Take this thing back to Goodyear and tell 'em to stick it."

"Ok," Stainbrook said.

With the Thermo-King team, Gary didn't generate the same interest among the pit population as he had with the Penske car. He wasn't considered a front row contender, he'd be starting the event back in 19th position. Ironically, the driver who gave him a friendly wave, Pancho Carter, went back out late in the day and spun himself. Pancho's crew had to work straight through from Thursday until Sunday morning to straighten the wreck.

On race day Gary was progressing to the top ten and it appeared as though he would at least make some money for all his

Top: Tony stands at the pit wall and watches Gary slide along Indy's front straight. [*Wick*]
Center: Gary's right rear is missing and left front is off the ground as he heads toward the infield. [*IMS*]
Left: A visibly shaken Val in the garage after the 1975 race. [*Shuck*]

Gasoline Alley in the mid 1970's. [*Torres*]

frustration. Then as suddenly as it happened to hs father before him, something broke on the car just as he was entering the main straight-a-way. The right rear tire exploded along with the suspension pieces that hold it in place. The car veered into the wall and the left front tire came off the ground. All the way down the front stretch the car rocked back and forth, being guided by a one-armed driver. The right front and left rear tires were the only ones touching the race track. Skillfully, Gary guided the car down from its 180 plus mile per hour speed and off onto the grass in the first turn. Brother Tony stood at the pit wall in amazement as Gary went by on the verge of destruction. Val and the rest of the family saw the incident from the grandstands. For hours after the race, Valerie was visibly shaken: She knew full-well what the consequences could have been.

* * *

Tony Bettenhausen, Jr. had been assigned the job of being Gary's "board man" at Indy in 1975. It was the board man's job to stand out next to the race track, just behind the retaining wall with a blackboard and communicate with the driver. Tony had recently moved to Indianapolis when he found that his Stock car wasn't competitive on the NASCAR circuit down South. Tony had been running Stock cars on a regular basis for the past six seasons and hadn't ever shown an interest in running Midgets and Sprint cars. His car owner, Gordon Van Liew, had decided he

The Bettenhausens at Terre Haute, IN for the annual "Hut Hundred" in 1975 with Gary's Porsche-powered Midget. [*Crucean*]

didn't want to be directly involved in ownership any longer and gave the racing vehicle to the youngest Bettenhausen brother. He basically said, good luck, it's all yours.

Tony hoped his luck would be better on the Midwestern USAC Stock car circuit, but his car wasn't competitive there either. He ran nine races and logged a couple of seventh place finishes for his best performance. Tony was a welcome addition around the Bettenhausen Racing Enterprises shop as he usually had a smile on his face. He didn't have Gary's blind determination and understood Merle's concern for business matters. He, too, had visions of someday becoming a Speedway driver, but his Stock car career wasn't carrying him toward that direction. By the end of 1975 he would decide to sell the Stock car and go Midget racing in 1976.

* * *

After the "500" was run in May of 1975, Gary usually raced once per week until the end of the season. He had a couple of shining moments in Sprint cars: He won a race on the paved half-mile at Illiana and then teamed up once again with Willie Davis and came home first on a slick track at Terre Haute. Gary could handle the flat paved tracks and the dirt tracks that were sometimes referred to as hard-slick, but when conditions on the

Gary and A. J. Foyt discuss mutual problems. [*Chini*]

dirt made the track rutty and heavy, he was flogging around. He could remember the days at Terre Haute when he'd reach up in the middle of the corner, while his car was going sideways, and wipe his face shield. Sometimes he'd reach up and tighten his saftey belts. He was showing off. He knew he had the car dialed-in and it was his way of saying, "There assholes, take that. Drivin' through these ruts is nothin'."

This year though, he had different comments to make. After the traditional "Hut Hundred" Midget race held at Terre Haute in September, Gary commented to sister Susie, "This arm has sure taught me a lot about how not to wear myself out." He wouldn't tell everyone, however. Prior to the race A. J. Foyt had walked by the Bettenhausen pit and said, "What are you doin', GB?

"Getting ready to blow their doors off," Gary replied.

"Sheet," Foyt laughed. "I'm going to wave to you as I go by."

Then Foyt got serious and asked Gary about the tire he was running on the right rear. It wasn't often that the King himself, A. J. Foyt, could be talked into running a Midget race, and when he did he wanted to know that he had the right set-up. He trusted Gary's judgement. Foyt didn't win the Midget race and neither did Gary. Foyt, however, was running for fun, and it was speculated that race promoter Don Smith paid him handsomely to make an appearance. Bettenhausen was racing for career survival. He figured the top-notch Indy car owners would give him a chance again if he went out and tallied up some additional Midget and

Left: The Bettenhausen-Davis team re-united for a Terre Haute win in August of '75.
Middle: Ready for a Sprint car race, Illiana 1975.
Lower: Championship Dirt Car, DuQuoin 1975.
[Mahoney Photos]

Right: Concentrating at Winchester. Moments later he would crash.
Below: Gary flipped a Sprint car down the backstretch at Winchester but was uninjured.
[Mahoney Photos]

Sprint car victories. Nevertheless, he had to do it his own way. Gary didn't attempt to secure a first-class Midget ride, he brought his own new creation, a Porsche-powered Midget he was sure would outclass the field. He finished 11th in the race.

* * *

Throughout the 1975 season Gary proved he was capable of winning an occassional race. He wasn't the same old Bettenhausen on the rough and rutty dirt tracks but he had no problems with either the Indy cars and most Midget Sprint races. His arm still looked abnormal. The Indy car owners had seen it and made their judgement. They didn't ask if it was progressively getting better.

Probably no more than a third of the cars that made the starting field at Indianapolis could be considered potential winners under normal, competitive circumstances. The owners of those top 10-12 cars, for the most part, didn't have a great deal of knowledge, or interest, in Sprint or Midget racing and therefore couldn't appreciate the versatility and skill it took to win in one of the vehicles.

Bettenhausen's chances of landing a first-class, capable-of-winning vehicle at the Speedway were slim. Still, the top stars of the day were all Sprint and Midget graduates. Drivers such as Johnny Rutherford, A. J. Foyt, Gordon Johncock, Mario Andretti the Unser brothers had all excelled in Sprints and Midgets, but when most had reached star status at Indianapolis, such as Gary did with Penske, they more or less gave up their Midget and Sprint activity. When Gary was running for Penske, he felt he wanted to accomplish even more than he already had in the other divisions. He didn't see himself leaving his roots behind. Now, as 1976 approached, he had two choices: 1) He could continue with the Gerhardt team and be thankful he at least had a *good* Indy car or, 2) He could go out and try to obtain a sponsor for an exisiting top-notch team, approach the car owner and literally buy the ride. Gary Bettenhausen didn't know how to buy a ride. He didn't even know how to call up a car owner and ask for a ride. Gary had said his phone number was in the book and his racing record should speak for itself. In vernacular of the pits, he wasn't going to kiss anyone's ass.

1976

During the winter of 1975-76, a new Midget for Tony was constructed in Gary's shop. The youngest Bettenhausen son had sold his Stock car and was gearing up for his rookie season on the USAC Midget circuit.

Merle continued to manage the shop and run the racing tire distributorship the Bettenhausens had obtained. Each summer weekend at the Sprint car races, Merle could be found with the huge Bettenhausen Racing Enterprises trailer selling Goodyear racing tires. The Bettenhausen shop was a subdealer for the tires through Roger Penske, who bought directly from the manufacturer. If you wanted to sell Goodyear racing tires in the Eastern half of the United States, you bought them through Roger Penske.

Gary was claiming that his arm was progressively getting better and planned a continuation of his racing career with no additional outside interests.

Sister Susan was steadily climbing through the corporate ranks in the airline industry. She had gone to work for Frontier Airlines in 1970 and by 1972 was Director of Dining Services. By 1975 she had been given the additional responsibilities of cabin services and aircraft interior design and modifications. In the airline industry she was Sue Wilson and few knew that her father was a race car driving, farmer-businessman. Through the many suppliers she dealt with, Susan was gaining a reputation of driving a hard, but fair bargain. Her knowledge and corporate spirit belied her impish smile. In 1975 she became Ms. Sue Wilson when she divorced Lowell Wilson in an amiable separation. They would remain good friends in the coming years and Lowell would maintain the interest he had discovered in professional automobile racing. A psychologist, Lowell was surprised that he became so engulfed in the sport through his association with the Bettenhausens. He once commented, "It's an all consuming thing. I find myself trying to get my non-racing friends interested in it. Lowell saw that Gary had some insight to psychology when Bettenhausen commented to him "The Indy 500, it's like there's 33 penises starting out there and each one is trying to outdo the other.

* * *

Whereas the Midwest indoor Midget racing season used to take place in the Chicago Amphitheatre and Armory in Tony's day, the scene had merely moved to Indiana by the Sixties. A couple of events were held annually at the Fort Wayne, Indiana Coliseum, and in 1976 the Coliseum in Indianapolis also scheduled a pair of races. Not much had changed in thirty years, even some of the same faces were familiar from the old Chicago Gang days. Running indoors could still be equated to performing in a mechanized rodeo.

Gary held his spirits high and with his conviction that he could prove his mechanical brainstorms were viable. He put a few more trophies in his case after the 1976 indoor season was over by winning a pair of races and finishing second in another. He was crowned indoor Midget champion. He had proven his Porsche-powered car worked. You could put an entire indoor Midget race track in the space that two pits at the Indianapolis Motor Speedway occupied. A crowd of 7,500 indoor fans was considered excellent and just maybe you could gross six hundred and fifty dollars if you won the main event. There wasn't an Indy 500 car owner within rifle range of an indoor Midget race, but the challenge was the same as at any other race track. Trouble was, you impressed the Midget racing clan but they couldn't help you get a ride in a first-class Indy car. Gary continued to believe that an impressive record in Midgets and Sprints would once again put him among the Speedway's upper echelon.

Vukovich, right, about to lecture Bettenhausen. [*Wick*]

Consequently, Gary kept his name in the racing newspaper headlines in early 1976 by winning a pair of Sprint car races and finishing second in another before the Speedway opened in May. At Indianapolis he was back with the Gerhardt team and qualified for the race right next to Billy Vukovich. Although they were both in the third row of the field, both had qualified a full seven miles per hour slower than the drivers in the first two rows. Neither of their names were mentioned as probable winners of the event. Vukovich however, understood the value of running all day long and simply being consistent. He'd already logged a second place Indy finish with his attitude and loved those Indy 500 paydays. Thus once again, he was going to give Gary a hard time for running in a Sprint car race just two days before the 1976 "500." There was another twin bill of Sprint races scheduled at the Indiana State Fairgrounds. Vukovich the spectator was giving Gary Bettenhausen more sage advice. He found Gary in the pits, climbed atop the roll cage of Willie Davis' Sprint car with him and held court: "Bettenhausen, you're really dumb, you know that don't you? They're having a million dollar race on Sunday and here you are beating your brains out for...how much? A grand? Two grand? You really ain't too smart. I just wanted you to know that."

Gary needed the diversion to smile. Vuky was good entertainment. Bettenhausen's right hand was swollen and hurting from a horsefly bite he encountered that afternoon while mowing the lawn. The raspy-voiced Vukovich continued his lecture: "You'll never learn, Schmuck. You know that nothin's ever gonna change, leastwise you. Why, what's changed around here in the last fifty years?" "Look," he pointed toward the grandstands, "they still got the wives in the nickel bleachers. They oughta give 'em hundred dollar seats...if they had hundred dollar seats."

Billy continued to chide Gary about the unsavory aspects of Sprint car racing and said, "Now you tell me, how do these things look any differently than they did thirty years ago?" Vukovich points toward the clouds when he really wants you to understand a point, then looks you directly in the eye as if to say, 'There, beat that.'

Bettenhausen grins, mulls over what he was just heard, looks down at his car and says, "Whaddya mean? Why now we've got wider tires, bigger torsion bars and uh....," he realizes Vukovich has a point. Not much as changed in the last thirty years. To nail the lid on his speech, Vukovich asserts, "The only smart thing that the Sprint car drivers have ever done is put these things on," he says as he pounds on the roll-cage that is currently serving as his seat of judgement. Billy hops down and walks off without another word. It's seldom he says good bye. He just leaves. You're supposed to sit there and think about his last statement.

It isn't often that the Sprint cars run on a one mile track such as the one at the Indiana Fairgrounds and Gary notes to Willie that he hopes everybody keeps their head screwed on straight tonight.

Vukovich walks down pit row and overhears driver Bruce Walkup saying to fellow driver Tommy Astone, "Tommy, do you want to go to the big race track in the sky?"

Vukovich falls forward in a thunderous roar of laughter, looks at the pair and laughs again. Astone is Vuky's brother-in-law and a relative newcomer to Sprint racing. Vuky is one of his heroes. His hero is laughing at him.

"Do you want to go to the big race track in the sky?" Vukovich mimicks. He laughs again and Walkup is still waiting for an answer.

"No, I don't," Astone says like a little boy who's just been caught doing something wrong.

"Then just why in the hell are you running that God-awful tire on the back of your 'lil racer, Tommy?" Walkup asks in a fatherly tone of voice.

Vukovich is interested. He doesn't allow Astone to answer but demands an explanation from Walkup. What's wrong with the tire, he wants to know. Walkup tells him how the car will handle with the particular tire and Vukovich nods his head, and says,

"Wait here," to Astone. Vukovich marches back toward Bettenhausen's pit. Gary'll know. He'll know precisely what the tire will do. This time there are no jokes, no wisecracks. Vukovich is the interrogator and witness Bettenhausen is telling him everything he wants to know about the tire. Vuky got it. Again, no good-by, no thanks, no see ya later. He turns and walks back toward Astone. Mission completed. Astone listened to Vukovich's advice and qualified for the race in tenth position, not bad for a rookie. Vukovich has been in a few Sprint cars himself and he can soon forget the nicknames, arm waving and needling in general if he thinks there's even a remote possibility that someone might get themselves in trouble with a particular set-up. It's an unspoken creed. You race the guy next to you down to the wire, but you don't let him out on the track if you see something wrong with his car. He might bust his ass. Even worse, he might bust his ass right in front of you and you could wind up in the same situation.

The year previous at the Fairgrounds, Gary performed poorly and was upset about the outcome of the races. The Fairgrounds track is located only ten minutes from the Indianapolis Motor Speedway and annually draws a good crowd because of the throngs who are in town for the "500." Occasionally some of the Speedway car owners attend the Sprint races at the Fairgrounds just to see what the lower class is doing. The pits, like the track, are dirt and you find more Levis in sight than double-knits. Some of the Madison Avenue types attend the Sprint race and look curiously at the narrow, boat-tailed Sprint cars. Within the last year *Sports Illustrated* and *People Magazine* had done a feature stories on Sprint car drivers and referred to them as being a part of grass-roots America. Although the "500" track is just a few minutes down the street, it's years away in terms of wheel-to-wheel competition and balls-to-the-wall bravery. At the Speedway, an out of town sponsor, car owner or even writer might obtain a seat in one of the guest suites located just off the second turn and can sit back in a lawn chair, sip a cocktail and watch the cars zoom by. You're liable to step in a mud puddle at the fairgrounds and your ears will hurt from the exhaust pipe blast that is created when 24 Sprint cars thunder violently by.

Johnnie Parsons, Sr. is walking through the pits and is justifiably proud of his son's up front starting position. The greying but still handsome Parsons says, "He knows how to get around this place ok," and smiles.

After only five laps are completed in the race, two drivers flip violently and tear their machines to pieces. The race is stopped. Gary comes to a stop on the front straight and immediately tells

Pancho Carter

Willie to put a cold rag on the fuel pump. He doesn't want to have a hard time re-starting the car. Willie tells him that it was Sleepy Tripp and Jackie Howerton involved in the accident. They're both ok. Tripp has recently been a well publicized Midget driver and Gary comments, "Guess Sleepy's been reading his press releases too much."

The race is re-started and another ten laps goes by when Jack Hewitt starts flipping wildly in the third turn. He's flipping so rapidly you can't count the number of times he's gone over. It's at least seven or eight.

During this red flag period Gary gets out of the car as do many others. Merle walks up and can see that Gary is reaching for his goggles with his one good hand. The other arm dangles. Merle reaches out with his left arm, his only arm, and grabs one side of the goggles. Gary reaches up with his right arm and pulls on the other side. In unison they stretch the goggles away from the helmet and upward. If was a smooth operation.

"I'll bet that rung his bell," Gary notes about Hewitt.

On the restart Pancho Carter and Gary run 1-2. Gary passes him and holds the lead for eight laps and is re-passed by Carter. They finish in that order. Bettenhausen comes in and asks who finished third.

"Dickson," Willie replies.

Bettenhausen smiles to himself, nods his head up and down as if to say, "I beat him."

In the second fifty lapper Pancho Carter is long gone. He's going to win by half a mile. Then Johnny Parsons spins, Pancho has nowhere to go and hits him broadside. No injury, and the race

Larry Dickson, 1, and Gary entering the first turn at Indy Fairgrounds. [*Dick*]

keeps on going. Both Carter and Parsons are out of the running and Gary inherits the lead. Old arch rival Larry Dickson, is right on his bumper. With only three laps to go the two journeymen fight for supremacy on the fastest track on the circuit. They're running side by side under the lights and the legion of Sprint car fans who remember the old "Larry and Gary Shows" from 1969-72 are yelling themselves hoarse in the grandstands. On the 47th lap Bettenhausen spins in the first turn and is parked.

Dickson takes the checkered flag, comes around to the starting line, unbuckles himself and starts a walk toward the stage to receive his trophy. It seems as though the entire grandstand is booing him. They think he spun Gary Bettenhausen out. Gary is pitted next to the stage and complaining to Willie Davis that Dickson, "flat ran into me." He is shaking his fist and cursing. A crowd gathers around the irate Bettenhausen and is joining in the tirade. The boos go on for more than a minute. Announcer Bob Forbes looks at the crowd gathered next to the stage and wants them to shut-up. He finally speaks into the microphone, "Well Larry, what do you think? What happened down there?"

"We never touched," the black haired Dickson says. Last year his hair was all grey. "What am I supposed to do, give him the race and forget about it?"

Forbes places the winner's garland around Dickson's neck and Bettenhausen looks up at the stage. He's still cursing to no one in particular but has drawn a crowd of about 40 onlookers. Suddenly he jumps up from the beer cooler he has been sitting on and starts toward the stage.

"Bet he's gonna punch his lights out," someone in the crowd says.

Gary looks like a vigilante leader with the crowd behind him as

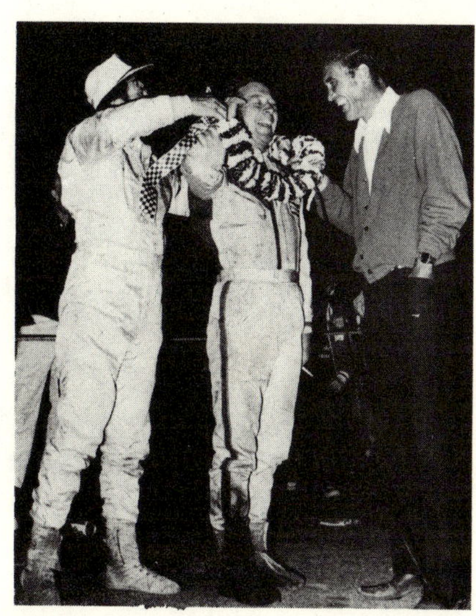

Winner Dickson gives the garland to his old arch rival.

he marches onward. He jumps up on the stage, eyes squinted and jaw set tight. Forbes eyes widen. Then Gary turns and flashes a full grin. The entire stadium cheers. He moves up next to Dickson and gives the fans a wave as Forbes carefully moves the microphone between the duo and says, "What...what do you think Gary?"

Gary smiles and says, "I think it's just like old times. The Larry and Gary Show. It was a helluva race."

Dickson removes the winner's garland from around his own neck and places it around Gary's and the crowd roars again. Gary fumbles with a can of beer and tires to lift off the ring. He's smiling wider than ever, but can't lift the ring with just one hand. A cigarette dangles in his left hand. Useless. Dickson glances at the beer and relieves Gary of the burden. Bettenhausen lifts off the garland and places it around Forbes' neck. Dickson opens the beer for him. It was a helluva race.

* * *

Gary's luck in the 1976 Indy 500 was similar to what he had experienced in his previous eight attempts at the track: A mechanical malfunction put him out of the race. He lasted only 53 laps. He had yet to finish an Indy 500. Pal Vukovich fared even worse and ran only three laps.

While Vukovich played golf and the Indy front runners waited out their time until the next Championship race, Gary trekked

Above: After winning the "Hut 100," an interview with Bob Forbes. [*Mahoney*] *Left: Once again photographers took a photo of Andres, Bettenhausen and Nalon at a Midget race track. This time however, it was Emil Andres, left along with Tony, Jr. and the old Iron Duke. Scene was Indianapolis Raceway Park the night before the 1976 "500."* [*Mahoney*]

back to the anachronistic Midget and Sprint car circuits. He had already broken the track record at New Bremen, Ohio, a month before Indy was run, then proved he was as capable as ever when he went to one of the Sprint car Hills at Dayton, Ohio, and set another track record. He won a total of four Sprint races during 1976 and registered his eighth career victory on the Terre Haute half-mile in a well publicized last lap pass he performed on "Little Joe" Saldana. He went back to Terre Haute a month later and won the prestigious "Hut Hundred" Midget race while driving for one of his father's old car owners, Howard Linne.

Little brother Tony wasn't adapting to his new Midget with the same success his brothers had before him. He went to a couple of dozen races throughout the year and made the field in about half the events. His best finishes were a pair of sixths. He had trouble

The Sprint car Gary designed and built. [*Tippy*]

making the car handle and it wasn't equipped with the latest, most competitive Midget engine. Tony also claimed a liking for the larger tracks such as he had run in Stock cars and didn't particularly care for the quarter and half-mile ovals the Midgets were running on. He said he'd stick with it though, and try a little harder in 1977.

* * *

1977

Bettenhausen Racing Enterprises had ultimately turned out to be one big hobby shop for Gary and his dreams. It didn't turn a profit and the building payments along with salaries were more than Gary could handle. The shop was sold. Merle wound up with a truck and trailer and would continue to service the Sprint car races with tires. Gary took a few pieces of equipment home to Monrovia and started building a brand new Sprint car that had more tricks on it than you find in your average magic show.

Gary had installed some side mounted oil tanks on the car and built accommodating bodywork around them. Sons Cary and Todd were excited about the project. He called a USAC official to come take a look at his work to see if it would pass inspection and the official said, "Yes, I don't see anything wrong with what you've done." When Bettenhausen unloaded the car for its maiden race at Salem in March of 1977, protests were lodged. They said the bodywork around the oil tanks acted as a wing, and

Car owner-builder Grant King and Gary at Indianapolis. [Hunter]

Opposite: Gary's 1977 Speedway ride was sponsored by Evel Knievel and J. C. Agajanian.

Sprint cars in USAC weren't allowed to have wings. Gary wasn't allowed to run the vehicle in its present form.

He had recently received additional bad news: His Indy car owner Fred Gerhardt, was pulling out of the sport. Gerhardt had been a supporter for three decades but business was bad and rising costs of fielding a Campionship car were prohibitive to him. Gary was left without an Indy car ride. He wasn't considered one of USAC's hottest properties. His telephone wasn't ringing. He finally teamed with old friend Joe Hunt for a pair of West Coast Championship races, but Hunt's equipment was mediocre at best and Gary finished the two races in 10th and 11th position.

He finally struck a deal with Grant King to drive at Trenton and then the Speedway in May. King had teamed with J. C. Agajanian and Aggie had convinced stuntman Evel Knievel to sponsor the car. Bettenhausen wasn't at the bottom of the barrel, but he was close. After Merle had crashed in Grant King's car at Michigan, Gary had privately called Grant everything from a dumb Chinaman to a lousy car-builder. Initially, Gary believed that something on the car broke, but King kept the wreckage at his shop for months just for inspection purposes to anyone who would claim that it was the car's fault. Grant King had never been known as an innovator, but he was considered the best copier in the business. He could look at the latest Speedway car, have a few photos to work from and turn out a duplicate in his own shop. He couldn't afford the testing programs and the expensive well-tuned engines the moneyed teams had, but King had pride in his own craftsmanship. He expected that Gary would bad mouth him and felt deeply hurt when Merle crashed. Grant never had a driver

seriously injured before Merle. Gary's tirades about Grant King's cars were brief in the aftermath of the accident and at the time Gary himself had one of the best rides in the business. Now, in the winter of 1977 a Grant King car for the Speedway was the best thing he could obtain.

At the Speedway in May Bettenhausen was frustrated. On his way back from the pits to Gasoline Alley he commented, "Well, we oughta get the trophy for laying down the most oil on the track around here."

Grant King's cars had always made the race, but often times King tried to do too much with the crew he had and disorganization resulted. Once back in the garage Gary said to Tony and Steve Chassey, "It's always a hassle around here the month of May. Even if everything in the engine is right, then something else is going to go wrong. I been thru this old shit for ten years now and it's not going to change.

"We gotta get organized around this god-damn place. We look like a Chinese fire drill."

Bettenhausen paced back and forth in the garage, pushing his cuticles back, thinking.

"Now I want everyone to have one job. Even if it's just one guy putting a cold rag on the fuel pump every time we come in it should look like an instant replay. Got that? Everybody do one thing, do it right. Jesus, what a mess."

A man in brown corduroy pants and a tan shirt walked in the garage with a paper sack, lunch size, and said, "I've got some real good heim joints here for sale. Only two bucks each."

Heim joints are critical components that attach suspension parts to the chassis. If one fails, disaster usually follows.

"Let me see them," Gary said.

"These things ain't no god-damn good," he said after quick glance. "Look, they got grease fittings in them and they're . . . . ."

Bettenhausen went on to explain to the man that there are many different grades of heim joints and the ones he was trying to sell oughta be used on tractors. They didn't belong on Speedway cars. He fairly well ran the man out of the garage and said, "Some dumb-shit will probably buy some of those things and wind up pasted against the wall. I don't think these guys around here know anything."

The Grant King crew worked hard enough to not only put Bettenhausen in the 1977 Indy 500, but team-mate Sheldon Kinser as well. Again, Gary didn't complete 500 miles. He was out with clutch failure after 138 laps of the 200 lap contest. Bettenhausen felt as though he was a major league pitcher who just a few seasons ago was in the limelight, throwing no hitters in the World Series. Now he'd just finished a race with Grant King, a tireless worker who could drum up no better than minor league dollars. Gary was still an Indy 500 driver, but he couldn't be one of consequence with a Grant King car. He hoped for better days.

While he was often lamenting the situation at Indianapolis throughout the month of May and saying that it's, "always the same old stuff around here, you gotta accept it," the Speedway once again became the site of one of the biggest surprises of his life.

There was a young lady waiting to see him, he had been told. She was right over there, leaning up against the fence that separated the pits from the spectators. Over the years dozens of young ladies had requested his presence, sometimes for an autograph or just a chat. Gary walked up her, blinked, and their eyes met.

"I knew," he would later say. "Right away I knew. I had a daughter."

Her name was Shawn and she turned out to be the product of Gary's involvement with Joyce Hughes, the girl who had sued him in a paternity suit. Gary was convinced that Joyce was sleeping with other men and he wasn't responsible for her pregnancy, but after taking one look he broke into a wide grin and said, "Hi, Umm, hi." The girl's grandmother had told her of her mother's involvement with Gary Bettenhausen the race car driver and soon father and daughter got to know one another. Wave accepted the situation and while Shawn had no plans to live with her father, she was understandably relieved to have met the man. She would learn

Merle in a usual pose, selling Sprint car tires at Winchester. [*Mahoney*]

that she had a half-brother also named Gary living in Illinois and would meet twins Cary and Todd. Wavelyn grinned, raised an eyebrow and said, "Is that all of them?" when she learned of Shawn's existence. Gary said, "I think so."

Every weekend throughout the summer of '77 Merle Bettenhausen could be seen at a Sprint car race selling tires out of the back of a trailer. Gary was usually in attendance as a driver, but managed to gross only $7,500 for risking his neck some 16 times during the year driving Sprints. Although he wasn't a contender to win in the Championship cars, the Grant King entry did earn him a gross of over $60,000 for eleven races. Normally, the driver received forty percent of the purse so financially, he was at least ahead of the average American. Gary competed in 26 Midget races and grossed just over $9,000; four Championship Dirt races brought in nearly $5,000 and a new style of race called a Mini-Indy vehicle contributed just under a thousand dollars for a pair of races. The Mini-Indy cars were called the wave of the future but initially, the veteran Sprint and Midget drivers called them pee-pee racers.

Gary's weekly summer sojurns back to the Sprint car tracks meant that he was still willing to risk not only his physical well being but reputation as well. Once in a while you'd hear a brash rookie claiming, "Hell, I' ain't gonna get hurt in one of these things. I got it handled."

The race hardened veterans would look over and sarcastically say, "Yeah, sure," either to themselves or sometimes out loud. They knew that if you kept driving a Sprint car, or any kind of race car long enough, you'd get bitten. Sometime. Gary survived another brush with disaster in September of 1977 when the high

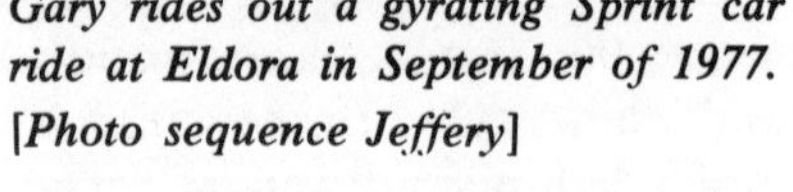

Gary rides out a gyrating Sprint car ride at Eldora in September of 1977. [Photo sequence Jeffery]

banked dirt half mile of the Eldora track treated him as though he were just another piece of clay, on its surface. Eldora had a way of taming even the bravest Sprint car driver.

Merle had managed to squeak out a living from the sport through tire sales but little brother Tony took home a grand total of $1,554 dollars after attending 22 Midget races that took him from Fort Wayne to Seattle. He made the starting line-up only nine times throughout the year and had two finishes in the top ten. Privately, Gary and Merle said they wished he'd give up the idea of being a race car driver. He wasn't doing himself any good. And he wasn't doing much for the Bettenhausen name either.

* * *

17

I Have To Get A Job

Although the racing press in general had been referring to automobile racing as "The Sport of The Seventies," the latter years of the decade seemed to obscure the Bettenhausen name. Gary never wavered in his belief that given the right equipment, he could easily drive to an Indianapolis 500 win. He understood only too well, however, that he was responsible for his own station in his chosen profession and wasn't one to complain. He was never a whiner. He held fast in his attitude that good fortune would come his way once more and in the interim he'd keep his name in front of the racing public through up front performances in Sprints and Midgets. He actually enjoyed driving a Championship car for Grant King because King would allow him to make any change, no matter how preposterous, that Gary's heart desired.

He took his own Sprint car to a couple of dozen races in 1978 and found himself taking less chances, driving more conservatively.

"Sometimes it's nice to go to a race and run only as hard as I want to," he explained, "I can remember back from 1969 through 72 when I used to do things because...well, I guess because it was expected of me. We were running balls-to-the wall every weekend, me 'n Dickson. It's a wonder we survived. Now if everything's right and I want to stand on the gas, I do. I don't have to please some car owner...and risk bustin' my ass every time I get in one of these things."

He liked the idea of running his own Sprint car and maybe proving that his engineering ideas were sound. He and the car performed well throughout 1978, but he didn't win any races in it. Sprint car regulars knew Bettenhausen was still a potential to take the checkered flag first and the thought throughout the pits was, "Gary can still get ' em hooked up, especially if he drives for someone else. He always seems to out engineer himself."

Once a year, 33 Midget drivers race in an event known as "The Hut 100" held on the Terre Haute half-mile. This shows the start of one such race. [*Coles*]

At the Championship events the King-Bettenhausen team were considered mid-field finishers and didn't draw much attention. They qualified in the last row at the Speedway and lasted 147 laps out of the 200 needed to finish. At the rest of the races along the Championship Trail Gary obtained a ride in one of the new Mini-Indy cars that were now becoming popular. The Mini-Indy cars were scaled down versions of their bigger brothers and fitted with Volkswagen engines. Short races were being held as preliminary events to the Championship races at many tracks throughout the country. Volkswagen of American was backing the series and dumping some $12,000 in prize money into each race. The cars were competitive and staged close wheel-to-wheel races. It was said that they'd probably replace the Midgets and Sprints as training ground for aspiring Indy car drivers.

Tony Bettenhausen was still attempting to earn his way toward a "Speedway ride" through the Midget ranks however. At the rate he was going, pitsiders said his chances were slim and none that he'd ever make an Indy 500 driver. He went to 18 Midget races in 1978 and made the feature event only half a dozen times. Other than a couple of top ten finishes running indoors, he was what is known in the trade as a back-marker. Gary let him take the Sprint car to a couple of races but his performance in the high-powered vehicles was just as poor.

During the winter of 1977-78 Merle came to the realization that the sport he had given an arm to wasn't supporting he and his family. "I have to get a job," he told Leslie. "A stock job."

When everything was going well, a traveling race car driver might hear from a mechanic, "Race car drivers? Hell, they don't

Above: Sprint cars on the high banks of Winchester: Sheldon Kinser, on the outside drives a roadster styled car while Gary run his own creation. It's a warm-up lap and the drivers appear as though they're trying to communicate.
Left: Same car on the Terre Haute dirt. [Mahoney Photos]

work. A few hours on the weekend, that's all. Most of 'em are too lazy to work, and too chicken to steal.''

Merle came to terms with a fellow driver named Eldon Rasmussen. Rasmussen was a Canadian with his eye on running the Speedway. He had moved his family to Indianapolis to follow his quest for glory and fabricated race car parts to put food on the table. But Eldon always had a deal going. His latest was to manufacture tiny vehicles called Rent-A-Racers that would look like minature Indy 500 cars. Tracks would be set up throughout the country and people would pay to drive the cars. Merle would run the shop for him.

Sister Susie was the only family member in the real world work force. She was steadily progressing through the corporate ranks at Frontier Airlines and in 1978 was promoted to Director of

Consumer Services. Her brothers had no idea what her responsibilities were, they were just happy to see her when she flew in for a race. Many other members of the racing clan liked to see her too. Privately many of them said she'd definitely be "good stuff." Susie would often socialize with the racers at the track but never dated any of them. She could trudge through a muddy infield with the best and watch a race with as discerning an eye as you'd find on the grounds. But on Monday morning she was a Frontier Airline executive, one of the best managed airlines in the industry. She had learned more about the value of a dollar bill than her brothers ever imagined. She knew about things like return on investment, long term capital gains, and could slit you wide open if you tried to lay some line of bullshit on her about the profitability of some whiz-bang idea you had.

She worried about Gary's involvement with his race car shop and could only shake her head when he told her how much money he was going to make in it. She wasn't surprised when he had to close its doors, but didn't chide him about his lack of business expertise. Gary would delight in telling her a risque joke and they could often be seen huddling together sharing only those things that you'd tell your own sister. She wished Gary would conduct his affairs on a more business-like basis but knew that any attempt to change him was futile. So she laughed with him, and let him confide in her. Sometimes, however, she wished that her family knew that she was winning her own version of the Indiana 500 right inside the Frontier corporate offices in Denver, Colorado. Since her divorce she was often lonely and couldn't count on her family for the understanding she needed. Gary and Merle were proud of her and Tony would always ask, "Can I tell my friends you're a vice-president yet? A vice-president sounds impressive, you know." She worried about Tony. She liked his gregarious manner and secretely hoped that maybe a car owner would offer him a job that sparked his interest. She hated to admit it, but one of her father's sons wasn't going anywhere on the race track. She hoped he wouldn't get hurt.

* * *

Gary notched another personal accomplishment during the 1978 season when he won the Championship Dirt car race named in honor of his father at Springfield, Illinois. "A dozen second place finishes doesn't match one win," he commented after the event. Some of those in attendance came up to him and told of the times they used to watch Tony blast around the place. A driver named

Left: Shirley McElreath Bettenhausen [*McQueeney*]
Right: Father and son: Jim McElreath and son James ponder their Speedway car. James was one of USAC's brightest young stars when he crashed to death on the famed Winchester half-mile. Jim has continued his own career and remains an active driver although he's over 50. [*Link*]

Jim McElreath finished behind Bettenhausen in the 100 mile event. McElreath had known Tony Bettenhausen and had raced against him before his death. He had also watched his own son James master the sport in a few short seasons. Then he saw him crash to his death in a Winchester Sprint car accident. It had been said that Jim McElreath would never again go to another automobile race track, but here he was, running right behind Gary. Before the end of the year 1978, he would have a new son-in-law named Tony Bettenhausen who would marry his daughter Shirley. At the wedding in McElreath's hometown of Arlington, Texas, Merle would tell him, "I know Tony isn't James, but give him a chance. Maybe he'll surprise us all."

* * *

A few months after Tony married Shirley McElreath he found himself running in the Championship race at College Station, Texas (April, 1979) on a track that was a duplicate of the one in Michigan where Merle lost his arm. The car owner was listed as Shirley McElreath, Jim's wife. The speeds didn't bother Tony as his stock car driving experience paid off and he collected ninth position money. Ironically, race winner A. J. Foyt said that a late

One of the closest finishes of a Champ car race occured in April, 1979 at Texas World Speedway when A.J. Foyt [14] beat Gary to the finish line by 0.03 seconds. [Whitt]

race yellow flag caused by Tony when his engine blew, may have helped him win the event. Foyt was able to make a precautionary pit stop for fuel. Gary wasn't happy about the situation because even though Foyt had more horsepower than the elder Bettenhausen, Gary had been running right behind him all day. Bettenhausen had the grandstands on their feet when he made a last-lap, last corner attempt to get around Foyt for the win but fell short by a few feet.

After the race was over Foyt said, "That Bettenhausen's a good race car driver...he was running good all afternoon."

Gary had shined throughout the day. He was driving what was considered an uncompetitive vehicle and very nearly pulled off a win in it. He had made a one race deal with car owner Sherman Armstrong to pilot the machine and would have to go back to the Grant King operation for the upcoming 1979 Indy 500.

Although Gary had turned in a tremendous performance for the College Station race and ran second to Foyt, Bettenhausen's high finish could be deceiving. The race was in fact a USAC Championship event but it lacked many of the top name drivers and car owners of the day such as Mario Andretti, the Unser brothers, Johnny Rutherford, Gordon Johncock, etc. Had the aforementioned drivers been in attendance Bettenhausen (and Foyt) would have found a completely different set of circumstances.

The reason for the lack of participants in the event was that there had been a major split amidst the ranks of the Championship teams. Late in the summer of 1978 a faction of car owners banded together and formed a new organization they called Championship Auto Racing Teams (CART). They had previously

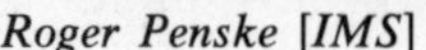

Roger Penske [*IMS*]

Pat Patrick [*IMS*]

lodged justifiable complaints with USAC stating they wanted more of a direct hand in the operation of Championship racing in general. The championship cars, they felt, were in need of larger purses, additional TV coverage and rule revisions concerning mechanical specifications. Initially, the owners had no intention of breaking away from USAC but their requests met with the same bureaucratic shuffle the club had been criticized for previously.

They ultimately withdrew from USAC in an unprecendented move and began signing their own races, on tracks previously sanctioned by USAC since 1956. The move caused a tidal wave of controversy throughout professional automobile racing and everyone from drivers to sponsors tc the television networks were affected. The words CART-USAC appeared on an almost weekly basis in the headlines of the *National Speed Sport News* and the country's other racing papers. The most bitter fight in the history of American automobile racing was taking place and sides were being chosen. The staid USAC Board of Directors was at last being challenged by a new generation of businessmen-racers who wanted more of a direct vote in guiding their own destiny. Gary Bettenhausen had been a USAC board member as driver representative for a number of years. His regular Championship car owner, Grant King was also a board member and they were being forced to choose sides just like everyone else.

The CART movement had been spearheaded by car owners Pat Patrick and Roger Penske and four other top flight teams. USAC believed it held the upper hand because it still held sanction rights to the Indianapolis 500. In April USAC sent a telegram to the CART owners who represented the cars of Al and Bobby Unser, Johnny Rutherford and Gordon Johncock, all previous Indianapolis 500 winners, denying them entry into the 1979 Indianapolis 500. Three other top name drivers would be affected as well. The news shocked the racing world. USAC claimed their entries were being returned to them because, "you are not in good standing with the United States Auto Club."

The CART owners brought suit in Federal court against USAC in early May just as the Speedway was opening and within days Judge James F. Noland ruled in their favor. The CART owners and drivers could run at Indianapolis but the fight for supremacy in Championship auto racing would continue.

Gary remained a staunch USAC supporter, but it didn't help his efforts at Indianapolis in 1979. For the first time in his career he failed to qualify for the race. His Grant King entry was too slow. He was at the bottom of his ladder. The race was won by Rick Mears in a Roger Penske car.

* * *

The King and Bettenhausen team attended four other Championship races in 1979 and both were resolute in their support of USAC. Gary said, "This club was good enough for my dad, it was good enough to make the Unsers, Rutherford, Mario and all those guys stars and I don't see any reason to change. I wish some of these guys who are bitchin' could attend our board meetings. The board works it's tail off for the club."

The USAC Championship schedule was being chipped away by men who flew around in Lear jets and who couldn't be bothered chaperoning three other divisions of race cars: Midgets, Sprints and Stock cars. The CART owners appreciated the care it required to run USAC as a whole, but they'd had enough vacillation from the USAC board. The Championship car owners weren't the only ones who weren't in concert with the board's decisions. There were rumblings in the Sprint car division as well.

You were still considered to be an outlaw driver if you didn't run your Midget or Sprint car in USAC sanctioned races. The terminology dated all the way back to AAA days when stiff fines were assesed for running in unsanctioned races. Throughout the Seventies, however, racing promoters in various parts of the

Gary takes a wild ride at Winchester in July, '79. [*Shuman*]

country began staging "open" races, open to anyone who wanted to race. There was no visible sanctioning body.

The open shows were of course labeled outlaw programs by not only USAC but the racing press in general. It had once been considered an honor and an achievement to run with USAC. Drivers and car owners from all parts of the country looked upon the club as the absolute leader in open cockpit style racing. Once a driver mastered his home tracks and was able to beat the competition he looked forward to proving his mettle with USAC, the club of the stars. USAC maintained a haughty attitude about its members and made it a policy never to recognize, in print, the existence of the many clubs across the nation that supplied the bulk of its membership. Once a driver made the transition from his local club to USAC his former club was never mentioned in USAC's newsletter or press releases. The general felling among many was that USAC was doing you a favor letting you run with them. The Bettenhausens were rare cases among USAC membership as they started their careers with the professional club. Most Midget and Sprint drivers spent a minimum of three seasons running with a local organization before trying to take on the USAC veterans.

It was becoming increasingly evident that many of the outlaw drivers were covering a wide geographical area and many names became familiar to the racing public. When a rich open show was publicized you expected a core of outlaws to attend and some of their races were not only receiving as much publicity as USAC's, the grandstands were full.

* * *

Merle's job with Eldon Rasmussen didn't work out and he found himself running Smiley's Car Wash on Indianapolis' west side. Gary was amazed at Merle's discipline.

"How can you do it, Merle? I couldn't get up every morning like you do and go to some job I hate. I'd tell 'em to stick it."

Merle was simply meeting his responsibilities. In addition to daughter Tracy, Leslie had given him a son they named Ryan in June of 1977 and the middle Bettenhausen son had mouths to feed. He didn't seek sympathy and realized the best helping hand he had was located at the end of his arm. He managed to give up smoking two packs of cigarettes per day and said he was going to lose weight too. He and Leslie looked forward to moving out of the cramped trailer, into an apartment...and maybe someday buy their own house. Merle would put in a full week at the car wash and spend the weekends selling Sprint car tires. There was never enough money but Leslie's constant sense of humor eased the burden.

* * *

Although the Indianapolis Motor Speedway holds one race per year, over 350,000 visitors annually pass through the turnstiles in the Hall of Fame Museum located in the infield. It is a multi-millon dollar white marbled facility that displays not only many famed race cars, but antique passenger vehicles. Ticket sales offices are located within, as well as a complete gift shop and the general executive offices for Speedway personnel and management.

It is 7 a.m. in the morning and there is one person stirring inside the Hall of Fame. He's a short, frail looking man with sad eyes. He smokes a pipe and likes to laugh, but when he does you notice that he bows his head ever so slightly. Some of his teeth are a little crooked and he thinks they ruin his smile. He's dressed in a matching outfit, dark blue shirt and pants. He's a custodian.

If you were able to peer through a window at this early hour, before the doors have opened, you might see him sitting in one of the old race cars. Tony Bettenhausen's little number 99 is on display, restored and race ready. But it's not the old man's

The sign on W. 16th Street directs visitors to the world's most famous racing facility. The Hall of Fame Museum is open year round and attracts hundreds of thousands of visitors. All of the Museum's cars are fully restored and in running condition. A few make appearances on the track each May. [IMS Photos]

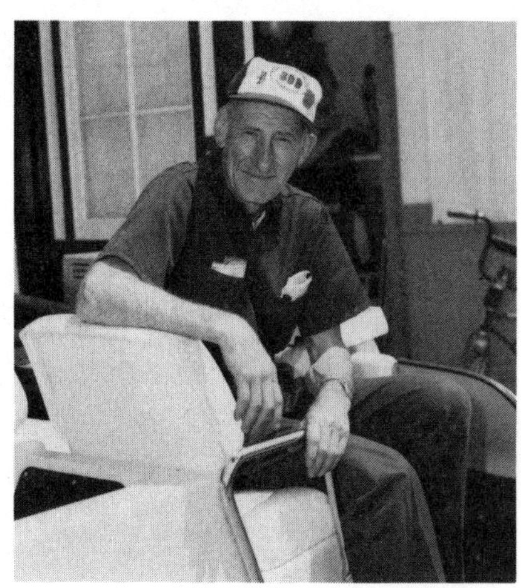

Crocky Wright, custodian at the Indianapolis Motor Speedway takes a break for a photo in Gasoline Alley. [*Mahoney*]

favorite. There are some others he likes better. He sits in them often and pretends. He can imagine himself driving around the one and only Indianapolis Motor Speedway, way out in front, leading the pack.

Crocky Wright sits in the cockpit of a vehicle the way a man is supposed to, he thinks. Bolt upright, hunched over the steering wheel just a little. He doesn't care for the new, low-slung rear-engine machinery where you get in and almost lay down. This is his kind of race car, ones that they ran just after the second World War. They look like big Midgets, the kind he used to watch run over at Nutley when he was a boy. And a thousand other race tracks since.

Little Ernie Schlausky, Crocky Wright, finally made it to the Indianapolis Motor Speedway.

During the summer of 1980 Crocky Wright would attempt to recapture some of the glory he experienced back in the days when he was a performer in a thrill show. Although he was now in his late fifties, Crocky still yearned for the cheers of the crowds. They used to cheer for him when he rode his motorcycle through a burning board wall. He believed he could still perform the stunt. Arrangements were made to stage the act at a local track, the Indianapolis Speedrome on a night when the Midgets were running. Crocky's friends treated the circumstances lightly, it was more or less a joke to them.

Crocky didn't have any knowledge of how to construct the wall, or even what type of materials to use. He claimed that in the old days he never paid any attention to such things. He just crashed through it, that's all.

Crocky Wright crashing through a wall of boards and flames at the Indianapolis Speedrome. [*Mahoney*]

Announcer Jep Cadou with Crocky. [*Mahoney*]

After a suitable wall was constructed and moved into position on part of the track's paved surface, workers doused the boards with buckets of gasoline. The boards should have been lightly painted with the volatile liquid so the surface entering and exiting was dry. Once aflame it was apparent that Crocky couldn't judge where the middle of the structure was located. No one thought to mark the pavement with lime, or flour. No one considered the consequences of having a slick surface under the wall.

Crocky said he thought he knew where to drive through the mini-inferno, and headed toward the blaze. The moment his front end made contact with the boards it was thrown sideways on the slick surface underneth, which was also burning. Crocky went through the flames and down, sprawling on the pavement. His only protective gear was a crash helmet and a leather jacket. Bruised, he pulled himself up and from his embarrasing position and waved while racing journalist Jep Cadou asked the crowd to "give him a hand." Race fans in Indianapolis, Indiana were applauding for Crocky Wright.

* * *

18

I Think Gary's Going To Win The 500!

As the decade of 1980 arrived the destiny of the racing Bettenhausen name was in doubt. For the first time in many years the winter indoor Midget races came and went without a Bettenhausen in the feature line-up. Tony attempted and missed the features at Fort Wayne and Gary didn't bother to go.

Gary had parted company, amicably, with Grant King and was left wondering what he would do for a Speedway ride in May. Tony at least had a car lined up to take his refresher test in at Indianapolis but it was agreed he'd need a tremendous amount of good fortune to actually make the race.

The racing paper headlines continued to reiterate the USAC-CART problems and winter time peace talks had failed. Speedway President John Cooper finally suggested a plan for the two warring groups to consider and "The Cooper Plan" was basically adopted in April of 1980. The new Championship Racing League outline was amenable to both CART and USAC. Everyone breathed a sigh of relief after the long fight.

The cost of an Indianapolis 500 car in 1980 hovered right at $90,000, less engine and support equipment. The newly developed Cosworth V-8 powerplant that the top teams were switching to cost $40,000. A serious team couldn't show up at Indy with one chassis and one engine. To be guaranteed of just making the race a $200,000 investment for Indy alone was judged on the cheap side. If you wanted to run up front and attend the rest of the races on the circuit a million dollar budget might squeak you through. Owners Pat Patrick and Roger Penske had budgets that neared the three million dollar mark for a single season. Nowadays, top teams had their own car designer, fully equipped shop facility, a budget for wind-tunnel testing, usually an 18 wheel tractor and trailer, outfitted with a mini-machine shop to haul a pair of cars and a complement of anywhere from six to 18 men to run the

A Speedway badge [1977]. Given to drivers, owners, mechanics, press, etc. to allow entry to the pits and other places not open to the public. [Hunter]

operation. The situation was light years away from the days when Murrell Belanger hired a couple of mechanics to work on his little 99.

There was no possibility that Gary Bettenhausen was going to put on a three-piece suit and make formal presentations to major companies in search of sponsorship. He couldn't call up an owner and tell him that he could bring his helmet bag and a six-figure check in order to get a ride. Nevertheless, some youngsters were able to ante up seemingly astronomical figures for a Speedway ride. Thus, the term "buying a ride" was being used more and more by those who didn't have a car lined up. It was generally agreed that for around $50,000 you could probably buy a ride at Indy but not in a machine that would run anywhere near the front.

Gary Bettenhausen was in serious trouble. Even though the CART teams had reconciled with USAC for the 1980 "500," Gary continued to back USAC. It wouldn't have made much difference who he supported, his telephone still wasn't ringing. Tony was receiving some support from old friend Gordon Van Liew and now even his little brother's ride was beginning to look good to Gary. His only chance was to show up at the Speedway every day and hope that someone would hire him.

A car owner named Sherman Armstrong, whom Gary had driven for in Texas, entered four machines at Indy. Most insiders chuckled when they walked past the Armstrong garages and referred to the beehive of activiity as a three-ring-circus. Armstrong himself was an act to watch. A short, banty-rooster type of man, he wore a Panama hat emblazoned with buttons, each with a different saying or company logo. One said, "I'm the

Sherman Armstrong, Midget, Sprint and Championship car owner. [*Whitlow*]

boss." Armstrong was a self-made man, said to be one of the nation's largest manufacturers of glass moulds for the production of bottles and jars. He was headquartered in Winchester, Indiana and had caught the racing bug a few seasons prior. His stable consisted of Midgets, Sprints, Dirt Cars and Indy cars. He'd even gone so far as to purchase the old Salem, Indiana Speedway. Sherman Armstrong considered himself a racer. He was sold on Gary as a driver but had no plans to run the fourth car. It was considered a back-up, and a poor one at that. It was fitted with a four-cylinder Offenhauser engine and didn't incorporate any of the latest developments. Gary swallowed every bit of his pride and told Armstrong that he'd not only work on the car, but drive it in the race for twenty-five percent rather than the usual forty.

Three days after the track opened Tony was warming up his Vita-Fresh Fruit Juice Special in preparation for his test when he spun. He slid some 240 feet up to the outside wall, crunched the rear of the vehicle, and then slid an additional 380 feet to the inside of the track. He was uninjured but it looked like it would a lot of midnight oil to repair the car.

* * *

Willie Davis hobbled up to the fence that separates the pits from the spectator seating area and nonchantly peered at the car Gary was driving. Every time Willie took a step he was reminded of a gopher hole he stepped in years ago at a Sprint car race.

"Willie!" Gary exclaimed.

"What are ya doin, Schmuck?" Davis offered.

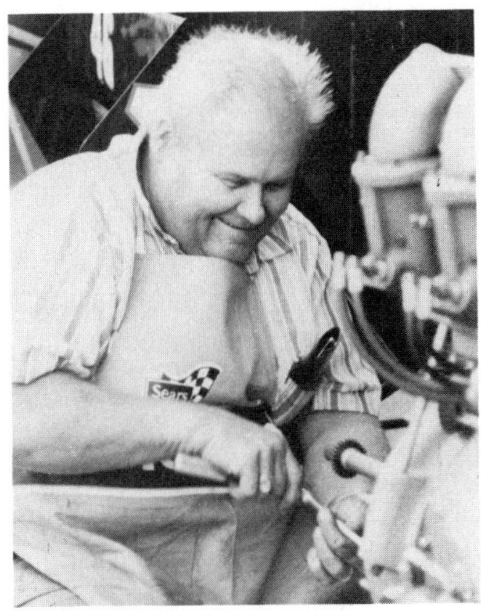

Once convinced to work with Bettenhausen again, Willie was in his element. He deserves much of the credit for Gary making the race in 1980. [*Kincaid*]

The once winning duo hadn't been on the best of terms since Gary closed up his race car shop. Bettenhausen had convinced Davis to bring all his own equipment to the new enterprise and work with him. The deal had gone basically sour and Willie was left without a job. He didn't return to his native California but stayed on in Indianapolis. His Sprint car was home in the garage, crashed. He hadn't bothered to fix it in the past couple of seasons. He was working for a local welding shop. A stock job. After work he decided to see what was going on at the Speedway. Just for the sake of old times.

"The throttle's stickin' on this damn thing," Bettenhausen continued. "You wanna give me a hand?"

Davis reached back, scratched the back of his neck and said, "Naw, I don't want to infringe on Leffler's operation."

He was referring to Paul Leffler, the mechanic who was supposed to be responsible for Armstrong's kaleidoscope of cars.

"C'mon," Gary said. "I'll get you in the pits."

Willie found the trouble right away, a bent cable was causing the problem. He knew a stuck throttle could end any driver's career.

Later that evening Gary called Willie and asked for his help at Indy. He said he needed him. Willie declined, said he had a stock job now. He finally relented and said he'd take off work an hour or two early.

"I'll make it right," Gary said. "I'll take care of you."

Willie remembered the headlines back in the days of the Larry

Tony, Jr. receiving some advice from big brother at Indy in 1980. [*Walker*]

and Gary Show. It was always "Gary Bettenhausen Drove The Willie Davis Sprint Car To Another Win Today...." Willie knew it was Gary's last shot. If he missed the race this year, he was all washed up. They'd called him "The Cork." Oh well, Willie mused, everybody in racing gets some kind of nickname. He supposed the Cork wasn't as bad as The Schmuck. Willie would give him a little help, but he wouldn't give up his vacation time to do it. He knew there was only a week left to get up to speed, the last weekend of qualifying was soon approaching.

* * *

Tony made it back on the track after the first weekend of qualifying was over and successfully completed what is known as a refresher test. He didn't have to take a full rookie test because of his previous experience in a Championship car last year. Tony had veteran chief mechanic Tommy Smith taking care of the car and a toothless old gent named Jess Alu as first assistant. Jess was a tireless worker who'd been coming to Indy since pre-War days and he could be trusted not to leave anything loose on the car.

"Ok," Smith noted to Tony, "get some laps in but don't push it. We're not in any hurry to get anything done. Just get the feel of the place. And for God's sakes don't go out there and hurt yourself.

Tony idled off down pit lane. Tommy turned around and said to Jess, "Jesus, I don't know. I think the kid is just so damned scared."

Tony made his debut at Indy in this car but was bumped from the starting line-up. [*IMS*]

Tony took a few warm-up laps and then moved out into the groove. He ran some laps at speed and came in.

"We're not doin' too good," Tony grinned. "But honest Tommy, she's flat out all the way around."

The best Tony had run was 168 mph. It would take at least a mid 180 mph run to make the starting field. Smith looked the car over and said, "You're right. She's flat out all the way around. The pop-off valve is broken. Let's take her back to the garage."

* * *

Gary was going from garage to garage himself, borrowing parts and seeking advice. His old Offenhauser didn't look like it was going to get up to speed either. He visted Herb Porter's garage, the man the racers referred to as "Horsepower Herb" and "Father Time." Porter maintained a garage in Gasoline Alley to build Speedway engines and was considered one of the professors of the business. He had known Tony throughout his entire career and liked Gary's appreciation of things mechanical.

"Let's take a look at what you have," he told the second generation driver.

The last Saturday of qualifications was rained out and the Speedway officials announced that an extension of the trials would be held if necessary. Everyone hoped they'd get their chance on Sunday.

Tony took a qualifying speed of 176 mph. which only the most optimistic believed would make the race. He was sure to be

Left: Willie Davis changes a left front tire while Gary waits. [Mahoney]
Below: Gary's official 1980 qualifying photo. He not only made the race in this car, but drove it to third place. [IMS]

bumped. While waiting in the qualifying line-up Sherman Armstrong informed Willie Davis that he'd give him a thousand dollars for his efforts and Willie noted, ''Fine.'' He just wanted to see Gary make the show.

Gary accepted a speed in the low 183 mile per hour range, a speed that was considered shaky at best. Greg Leffler, the chief mechanic's son, went just a tick of the watch faster for his four lap average and put Gary "on the bubble." He was the next car to be bumped out of the starting line-up. It was only four o'clock, two hours to go. It appeared as though there were at least three or four other cars in line capable of exceeding Gary's speed.

One of them was Howdy Holmes, a diminutive sports car driver who bore a distinct resemblance to the old TV puppet Howdy Doody. Holmes went out, warmed up, but didn't take the flag.

Wave gives her man a hug after his successful qualifying run. [*Miller*] *Below: Gary happily attended the "Last Row" party after qualifying for the 1980 race.* [*Mahoney*]

Bettenhausen sweated. Next out was Ron "The Shoe" Shuman, a rookie but a famed Sprint car driver who would throw caution to the wind. It started to sprinkle at 4:20 just as Shuman was warming up his engine and the yellow flag was thrown. The rain came, the field was full and Gary Bettenhausen would be a starter in the 64th running of the Indianapolis 500 Sweepstakes. He'd have to start in the last row of the 33 car field, but at least he was starting, he mused. Now he'd be a guest at the traditional "Last Row" party.

* * *

Race day dawned bright and clear and over 350,000 spectators jammed into the old speed plant. Festivities began promptly at 8 and 10:15 dapper looking Johnnie Parsons, Sr. was taking a lap around the two and one half mile oval in the car he had won with back in 1950. It was the 30th anniversary of his win and the senior Parsons was up to the task. "How do I look?" he asked while

Johnny & Johnnie Parsons. [Talley]

divulging a straight-toothed smile. "I'm really ready for today," he continued. "I think I could go 500 miles easy."

His son Johnny had convinced his father's original sponsor, Wynn's Friction Proofing, to return to the Speedway this year in honor of the event and the younger Parsons would carry the company name on his entry. It was a banner day for the Parsons family. Johnnie, Sr. stuffed a white handkerchief in his mouth and toured the track ever so slowly, jazzing the engine of his restored racer every few feet. He came back in and started toward the official pace car, which he was to drive throughout the day. The magnetism of the track had grown stronger for him over the years. He wished his son well, turned and said, "That's m' boy," before getting in the pace car.

Track owner Mrs. Mary Fendrich Hulman gave the traditional "Gentlemen, Start Your Engines," command and the sound of the engines was once again nearly drowned out by the cheers of the population. As the engines came to life thousands of colorful balloons were released from an infield tent in a continuing tradition. This year, three Pontiac Trans-Am pace cars led the field around on the warm-up, and then the parade lap. The drivers waved to the crowd as they allowed engine temperatures to rise. Then the eleven rows of three cars settled in behind the pace car driven by Parsons as the other two token vehicles pulled off the track.

The start of the Indianapolis 500 is often described as one of the most awesome spectacles in all of sports. Everyone talked about the first lap, the start. The veterans worried about the rookies who might get nervous, do something dumb and screw up the whole field. It was a rare occasion that a rookie qualified fast enough for an up front starting position though, so if you were in the first

Top: The area called the "Tower Terrace." Pits are on the left. You are looking down the main straight-a-way, toward the first turn. [*Whitlow*]

Center: Part of the throng exiting on Georgetown Road, if you were at street level, you'd see heat waves rising just above the crowd.

Above: The spectator area inside the first turn is affectionately known as the "Snake Pit." Here, the young and young at heart may be observed doing everything from bleeding to breeding. The area is getting smaller now, with the addition of more seats. For the most part the spectators are a well behaved lot.

couple of rows your chances of survival were better. Then too, it was generally accepted that if you didn't start in the first three or four rows your chances of winning the race were slim. Slow cars qualified in the back and they weren't going to pass anybody anyway. Usually.

The start went smoothly and Bobby Unser got the jump from the outside. Mario Andretti was squeezed back just far enough to drop in behind, but Johnny Rutherford was still accelerating. He overhauled Unser going into the first turn and in some 50 seconds traveled around the two and half mile distance to earn first place. There were only 199 laps to go.

More than a half a mile behind Rutherford, Gary was passing cars immediately. After three laps he had improved his position by 12 cars! A few laps later Gary had to dodge the debris left by an accident that caused no injuries, then once again took up his charge. Gary Bettenhausen had never finished an Indianapolis 500 Mile race so the odds weren't in his favor today. He figured he'd let them know he was on the race track before this old box he was in decided to pack it in for the day.

A couple of days before the race Gary and Willie locked themselves in the garage and completely revamped the car's fuel system. They checked everything from stem to stern, declared it ready and tried to drum up a pit crew. Willie's wife Mary handled the scoring and Gary's long-time friend Mike Garabedian made his annual trek from California to help out. Month of May mechanics Jack Ford and a hulk of a man known to the racing fraternity only as "Big Dave" helped on the car as well. Another Indy regular named Joe Dragus was to handle the refueling but it wasn't expected he'd have to work all day.

Gary continued to pick off cars and at 60 laps he was up to 10th position. At 70 laps he was 8th and his pit crew was ecstatic. At 76 laps he was sixth and becoming the darling of the crowd. His pit stops were as rapid as the leaders. By the 98th lap, just near the half-way point, Gary passed another car and took over fifth position. The race was being dotted with many yellow caution periods for various spins and accidents, none which resulted in serious injury.

By the 124th lap only six cars, including Gary were on the same lap. Everyone else had been passed by the leaders. The pit population, as well as the grandstands and even his own family, was astounded at Gary's performance in the underpowered Armstrong machine. Gary continued to run with the leaders and was staging a duel with Gordon Johncock. They swapped fourth and fifth position back and forth three times in four laps. While cars were ducking in and out of the pits, Gary beat Johncock to the finish line and was listed as being in second place just past the 150 lap mark. At the 160th lap, race leader Johnny Rutherford was two and a half seconds ahead of Bettenhausen. Family members could hardly believe what they were seeing.

The cars being driven by Tom Sneva, Johnny Rutherford and Rick Mears were clearly faster than Gary's mount, but he was maintaining a top four position throughout the ending laps of the race. Mears dropped off the pace and at 190 laps Rutherford had a 15 second lead over Tom Sneva. Gary was still dueling with Johncock, some 20 seconds behind.

"I think Gary's going to win the 500!" a writer in the press box shouted. "Look at this. The leaders have screwed up. Last year they could only go 25-26 laps without fuel, right?"

The man caught attention from a few around him. What was he talking about?

The writer did some quick calculations and figured that both Rutherford and Sneva would have to make one more pit stop before the end of the race. And Gary Bettenhausen had just refueled. He was the only one running who wouldn't have to stop. He could easily pick up 10-12 seconds while the leaders pitted, and by the time they got back on the track Bettenhausen would be long gone.

"Is that right?" one reporter asked another. "Do they have to make another stop?"

"I'm not sure, now," was the reply. "Maybe."

"Wouldn't that be something," another shouted. "Gary Bettenhausen winning the Indianapolis 500 front the last row. He missed the show last year. I thought he was all washed up."

The writer was wrong. Sneva and Rutherford didn't have to make another stop. The fuel allocation this year was allowing the cars to go just over 30 laps before making a pit stop.

Johnny Rutherford came across the finish line first, followed by Tom Sneva. Gary Bettenhausen and Gordon Johncock raced side-by-side to the cheers of the throng for third place. Bettenhausen won. There was pandemonium in his pit. Up in the Tower Merle cried. Valerie cried.

Gary pulled in after the race and without removing his helmet kissed Willie Davis. Willie rocked back and forth from the bear hug Gary was giving him and the crew danced as though they were barefoot on a hot griddle. Gary Bettenhausen had finally finished an Indianapolis 500. It took him 12 years to do it. It took his father before him 12 years to do it as well. Beer, wine, champagne and tears flowed back in Gasoline Alley after the race was over and more came from the Bettenhausen garage than any other.

"It's tough to keep a Bettenhausen down," red-headed Val laughed. "By God, you sure showed 'em today Gary!"

There probably wasn't another place in the whole world where the lady born as Valerie Rice had shed so many tears.

* * *

19

A Champion Again

A week following his $86,000 drive to third at Indianapolis, Gary raced a Championship Dirt car on the now familiar DuQuoin, Illinois mile. It was the same track where Tony had shined so brightly on numerous occasions. There was very little difference between the Dirt machine Gary was to drive there in 1980 and the one his father drove thirty years earlier. The cars now had roll cages surrounding the cockpit, but the configuration was the same and lap times weren't even significantly faster. The DuQuoin mile was the scene where Tony guided a burning Midget into the infield lake once. It was about to accept another Bettenhausen.

Gary's Dirt car was owned by two Illinois residents named Tim Delrose and Dale Holt. Timmy Delrose was often referred to by the racers as Mafia not only because of his Italian heritage, but his magazine distribution business was located in Joliet, Illinois, scene of more than one memorable murder that seemingly had underworld ties. Everyone at the races remembered that Midget standout Henry Pens had been bludgeoned to death and left in his car in front of his body shop. It was said that Henry had been messing around with somebody's wife. When you saw a handsome, but portly Timmy Delrose walking down the pits toward you, you'd kid him, "Oh, oh...straighten up, here comes the Mafia."

Dale Holt was a restauranteur whose interest in racing went back to his childhood days. As a boy he remembered seeing Tony Bettenhausen drive and even went for some rides with him in one of Tony's Chrysler passenger cars. He'd always been impressed with the Bettenhausen name and loved being around the races.

While the Delrose-Holt combination could be considered well-to-do, they weren't in the Indy car owner class. They could both be found at varied races throughout the country and derived

Above: Dale Holt, left and Tim Delrose [with Gary's 1982 Dirt car.] [Mahoney]
Left: Bettenhausen, 12, and Pancho Carter thrilled the fans at DuQuoin during the 1980 season. [Mahoney]
Below: Gary cooled off after the DuQuoin win. [Figler]

Bettenhausen ran the Armstrong at a few other races in 1980 but didn't match his Indy performance. He's shown above on the road course at Mid-Ohio. Note the addition of a wing on top of the nose. [*Mahoney*]

great satisfaction from the Midgets, Sprints and Champ Dirt cars. Since USAC had scheduled some seven Champ Dirt races this year, a record high for the antiquated looking machines, they were looking forward to the season.

"C'mon Bettenhausen...hold on...don't let that sumbitch around you!" A crew member was shouting his lungs out as Gary roared by on the 99th lap of the DuQuoin race.

For most of the race Gary had held a comfortable lead over Pancho Carter but blew a head gasket on the 98th lap. Pancho quickly closed the gap, but slid behind slightly when he hit oil dropped by Gary's car. As they rounded the fourth turn of the final lap Pancho made a heroic dive to get past Bettenhausen and finished nose to nose with him in what was called a photo-finish. Bettenhausen was ahead by a couple of feet. Chief mechanic Robert Galas looked around and said, "Any more like that and I'm liable to have heart failure."

Gary came in and drenched himself in the infield lake. The 100 miler had been held in 94 degree temperatures. The racing papers ran a photo of a soaking wet Gary Bettenhausen walking out of the water. His fortunes had changed.

Sherman Armstrong gave Bettenhausen the car he ran at Indy and told him he could take it to the rest of the races. on their next outing at Milwaukee Bettenhausen could manage no better than 12th in in the old machine, some seven laps behind the leaders. Tony attempted the Milwaukee mile also, but timed too slowly in his machine to make the show. The Bettenhausen brothers fared

Gary, on the inside, takes the lead from A. J. Foyt at the Hoosier Hundred. The Championship Dirt cars look almost identical to the Sprints. [*Mahoney*]

no better at the next event, the Pocono 500 in late June when Gary's clutch went out after one lap and Tony lasted four laps before a piston burned.

The Indianapolis Motor Speedway dropped a bombshell on USAC during the Pocono race when President John Cooper said, "There is growing evidence that USAC has become an organization governed by selected car owners. That, of course, would not meet our criteria of having an independent authority sanction the 500." It was reported that the Speedway was considering dropping USAC as the sanctioning body, a move that would for all intents and purposes, kill the club. Cooper wasn't happy with the make-up of the new Championship Racing League board of directors, even though everyone thought that he himself had been the architect of the plan. He pointed out that originally only three car owners were to be represented on what was to have been a seven man board. CART and USAC had come up with a six man board which included five car owners.

The Speedway wasn't very interested in seeing a board that was heavily weighed with a special interest faction of car owners. The Speedway, most surmised, wanted to avoid any conflict with the car owners in future years over issues such as purse, purse and purse. Roger Penske took issue with Cooper's view by saying, "USAC can put any three people they want on the CRL board. This year they happen to be car owners, so his point is not valid."

Nevertheless, USAC called an emergency meeting for oxygen. They voted to drop out of the Championship Racing League pact. USAC was back in the Speedway's good graces but the CART owners trudged right along and continued with the schedule they'd set last year. USAC and CART were divided again.

Along the Championship Dirt trail the Bettenhausen-DelRose-Holt team was grabbing headlines sometimes just above, and just below those of Pancho Carter. Carter and Bettenhausen

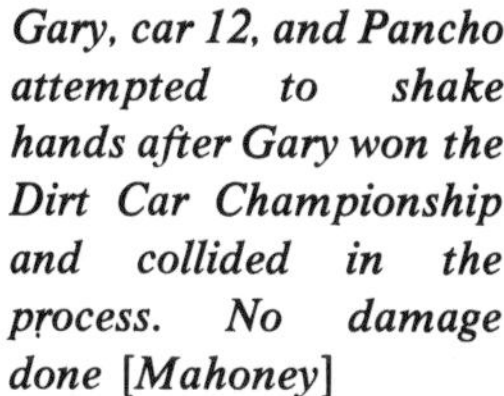
Gary, car 12, and Pancho attempted to shake hands after Gary won the Dirt Car Championship and collided in the process. No damage done [*Mahoney*]

were dominating the circuit and they staged a near re-run of their May DuQuoin race when the cars went back in August. Bettenhausen wore out a tire and the white cords were showing near race's end. Again, they finished side by side, less than a second apart with Bettenhausen ahead. Two weeks later Gary won the prestigious "Hoosier 100" on the Indiana State Fairgrounds and stood up in the cockpit immediately after taking the checkered flag. He explained; "I took the seat cushion out of the car before the race so I would sit lower in the cockpit. It was a bad mistake. I was sitting on a 280 degree oil tank. It wasn't so bad when we were racing, but on the yellows it was almost unbearable. I almost pulled in on that yellow at 45 laps it was hurting so bad."

The team went to Tulsa where Gary scored a pair of second place finishes and then to Terre Haute for the season ending race that would decide the Championship between Gary and Pancho. Carter's luck went sour when an inner tube broke and cost him a three lap pit stop. Gary went on to win the race, although Pancho rejoined the event and passed Gary just to show him he could do it. After the checkered flag was thrown, Pancho pulled up alongside Betenhausen and offered his outstretched hand in congratulations. Gary responded and did the same. The two cars touched wheels and Bettenhausen nearly flipped in the process. During the post-race celebration Tim Delrose slipped off the victory platform and fell on a trash receptacle, hurting some ribs. Gary credited Merle over the public address system for his tire strategy. "Without Merle's help," Gary offered, "I don't think I could have won this one today. He sure knows his stuff."

Gary Bettenhausen was duly crowned 1980 USAC Dirt Car Champion. There wasn't a CART owner in sight.

* * *

Merle had taken son Ryan to the Terre Haute race as he had on many previous occasions. Ryan stayed out of the way and often times sat atop Merle's trailer in his own little lawn chair watching the cars for extended lengths of time. He never seemed bored. Once in a while he'd watch a car go into the first turn, put his hands on an imaginary steering wheel and gently twist to the left, then all the way back to the right, just the way the racers were doing.

* * *

Gary ran third in the season ending CART race at Phoenix while driving for Armstrong, but Armstrong wasn't going to follow the CART races in 1981, so Gary had to start shopping for a ride at season's end. The Championship racing scene was still in limbo. He wondered who he'd drive for at the Speedway in 1981.

* * *

During the years Gary had his race car shop, the Bettenhausen brothers frequented a lounge on Indianapolis's west side for lunch and dinner named the "Pair of Jacks." It was jointly owned by Jack Rogers and Jack Unland. After the shop closed, Tony in particular continued his relationship with the owners. At the end of the 1980 season Tony met with Jack Rogers and a close friend of Rogers' named Wayne Hillis. Hillis and Rogers were drawn to the youngest Bettenhausen and wanted to help the advancement of his career. The two businessmen formed a corporation along with Tony and put out a call to other friends to build a racing team. They promised no return on investment and told everyone that the best that they could possibly hope for was to spend money and in return might receive a few passes to races. Moreover, Jack and Wayne were out beating the drums in an attempt to garner enough money to buy Tony a Speedway car that had a half-way even chance of making the race.

They were successful and the newly formed H & R Racing team purchased the car that Tom Sneva drove to second place in the 1980 race. Tony Bettenhausen had himself a fair chance at becoming a rookie in the 1981 Indianapolis 500 starting field. Along with the purchase of the car, Tony took along mechanic Paul Diatiovich who had served as an assistant on the Sneva team. Diatlovich hadn't been an Indy 500 chief, so the team was considered brand new.

* * *

Lindsey Hopkins

Gary's phone still wasn't ringing. While his name was well known among not only Indy 500 car owners, but fans as well, in the winter of 1980 he was the Bettenhausen without a ride. He didn't want to go through another scenario as he had last May with the Armstrong team, so for the first time in his life he called a car owner and asked him for a ride.

The man was an old family friend, Lindsey Hopkins. Rumor had it that Lindsey might not even come to the Speedway in '81. He wasn't feeling well these days, was past 70 and had a bad taste about the current USAC-CART situation. Lindsey had served for many years on the USAC board and said publicly that CART "was born out of avarice and greed."

Lindsey Hopkins was one of the last car owners not to side with CART. By 1981, the Indianapolis 500 was the only Championship Indy car race on the USAC schedule. The CART owners had the cars, the tracks, the television networks, the sponsors. They had everything but the Speedway, which they didn't need. They could race at the Speedway without sanctioning it. The United States Auto Club was a cancerous shell of its former self. Steps were taken to merge the Championship Dirt cars back into what was known as the National Driving Championship and names such as Gold Crown Series and Silver Crown Series were publicized, but race fans understood that Championship Indy car racing was being conducted by an organization called CART. CART began adding road courses to the schedule, lobbying for additional television coverage, searching for race sponsors and in general conducting business as businessmen, rather than sportsmen willing to spend significant dollars on a hobby. Lindsey Hopkins was still a sportsman. He'd been entering cars in the 500 longer than any other man on the scene. He'd seen his driver Tony Bettenhausen take a friend's car for test-hop and crash to his death. Lindsey had seen his familiar rabbit-in-a-hat logo on pre-War Midgets and enjoyed decades of friendship with those close to the sport.

It was often said that Lindsey Hopkins was a true Southern Gentlemen, his word was his bond. A handshake would do with Lindsey. He told Gary, ok, he'd come back for one more race at Indianapolis.

* * *

Gary's insecurities about himself and his dealings with the general public had vanished ever so slowly over the years as he was forced to make public acceptance speeches for his accomplishments. While he was driving for Roger Penske he found that being an off-track public relations man was as important as being an up-front race car driver. Thus the Help Them Walk Again Foundation chose him for their annual 500 Racers Roast for Charity during the 1981 month of May.

The affair was attended by several hundred people who enjoyed the old grace and charm of Indianapolis' Atkinson Hotel. Merle and Tony were scheduled to roast their brother along with a host of fellow drivers, some former car owners and a few members of the media. Bettenhausen went along good naturedly with the affair and took his place at the head table, elevated above the crowd. Part of the reason for Gary's good humor was that he had already qualified for the 500 in one of Lindsey's cars without encountering too many problems. He wasn't among the fastest of the month, but he felt comfortable. He thought he could run all day and be in the hunt near the end.

Susie had flown in for the affair to join the rest of the family. Most of the audience was made up of the general populous who weren't attuned to some of the private jokes understandable only by the racing crowd, and for the first part of the evening they quietly maintained.

The loquacious Duke Cook entertained. He told of the true story when Gary was racing at Pocono a few years back and also had his Midget in tow, to run when he wasn't busy with the Championship machinery. Cook said: "There was this Midget race scheduled at Flemington one night after practice at Pocono. So Bettenhausen says to his pal Vukovich, 'C'mon, let's go to Flemington...we'll blow their doors off.' It'll be P-One E-Z' Right Schmuck?" Cook joked.

"So they haul ass and they drive like a maniac...and they get the map out. Tell you what," Cook continued, "race drivers has got

A slightly inebriated Gary Bettenhausen addresses the crowd at a charity roast held in his honor. [*Talley*]

nerves of steel right? Gary's got a head of concrete to match. He lets Vukovich read the map."

"So here they go. Down the highway. Gary says, 'Do you see Flemington?' Billy says, 'Yeah I got it...I got it...right here it is...take 19 to 22, 37' and boy they get there about 5 o'clock. Hot laps about five-thirty."

"They pull into a gas station and ask the guy," 'Where's the race track?'

"The guy says," 'Race track?'

"Some old Dutch farmer," Cook continued. 'Ain't no race track here,' the farmer said.

"So Gary says, 'Don't give me no shit. They're racing tonight in Flemington. Right here's the entry blank.' "

Cook went on: "So the guy's looking and he says," 'Wait a minute...that's Flemington, New Jersey...you're in Flemington, Pennsylvania.' "

Gary bowed his head and laughed along with the crowd. Duke Cook had told a true story. Cook hadn't let him and Vuky live down the tale for years.

"I wish they'd quite feeding him drinks up there," Susie commented. "Gary's going to make a fool out of himself if he has to get up and talk if he keeps drinking that way."

She was right. Gary was drunk by the time he was called to the podium. The racers in attendance realized the fact, gave him a

Tony explains how his car is handling at Indy while Gary furrows his brow in concentration. [IMS-LINK]

Opposite: The Brothers Bettenhausen: Tony, Jr. became an official Indianapolis 500 driver in this car, 1981. [IMS]

round of applause and said, "That was very nice, Gary," before he had a chance to say a word.

Bettenhausen responded, "Shit...shit down and shut up."

"You sound great Bettenhausen."

"I want to tell you all that I hope you're...you're not in a hurry because this is going to take a while," Gary continued.

"I'm going to read my notes to you. The first page says...bunz, bert, mis-take, Schmuck......"

The crowd took Bettenhausen's situation good-naturedly. Susie buried her head in her hands and said, "Oh, Gary!"

"The second page says, Steve, see, mirror, eleven to four."

Bettenhausen rattled on for another five minutes while some of the prim and proper fund-raisers looked askance at him. Wave glanced around, shook her head in despair.

"Another month of May," she offered after Gary finally stepped down.

* * *

The 1981 Indianapolis 500 had both Gary and Tony as starters. As kids, Merle and Gary used to talk about racing there but now Merle was spending his days as a truck department service manager for the local Roberts Dairy, it was a step-up from the car wash. He obtained the job through the help of Russ Roberts, a race fan who also helped out on Tony's crew.

Tony and mechanic Paul Diatlovich made a good accounting of themselves at Indianapolis and put their car in the program without a major hitch. The back page of *National Speed Sport News* carried a photo of the brothers with a caption that read:

Tony's Boys - Not 100 feet from where there father met death just 20 years ago this month, the Bettenhausen brothers smile for the cameraman as Tony, Jr. qualifies for his first Indy 500. Gary and Merle are at left.

At the top of the page readers were informed that Al Unser's son had just won a race. He may have been competing against Michael Andretti, Roger Penske, Jr., Bobby Unser, Jr. The beat would continue. The old beat never really died out. Tony's closest pal of yesteryear, Duke Nalon, would be driving the official Buick pace car this year.

Val, Webb and Susie would be able to do their worrying from the comfort of Gordon Van Liew's suite located just off the second turn. Tony's car owners had found a sponsor for the race named Provimi Veal. Tony said it stood for, "Protein...vitamins and mineral." He wasn't very interested in sliding around the dirt at Terre Haute or holding his breath at Winchester, but he knew that he was now an Indianapolis 500 driver. He said he just wanted to do well in the race, keep his nose clean.

Gary had an eventful day fighting fire in his car, throttle linkage problems, long pit stops to try and sort out all the malfunctions. He was never considered winning material and officially completed only 69 laps.

Tony ran smoothly and was in the top ten on his way to the best pay day of his career when he noticed that the profile of his right front tire was distorted while driving down the backstretch. He was losing air. He slowed entering the third turn and bobbled ever so slightly in an attempt to continue his chosen line, and not affect anyone behind him. Second year driver Gordon Smiley attempted to duck under him and the pair brushed wheels. Smiley did a reverse spin, slid out and hit the wall with the left side of his car. He was through for the day. The yellow light flashed on immediately and Diatlovich radioed Tony, "The yellow is on again."

Quick-witted Tony shot back, "I know. I'm it. I'm coming in."

Gordon Smiley was vocal about the driving talents of one Tony Bettenhausen in an interview on the world-wide Speedway Radio Network. He said he didn't belong on the race track, was a hazard, etc. Smiley had, in fact, been running fast this year and looked like he was assured of a top five finish until the tangle occurred.

After the race was over, Gary was extremely proud of Tony's performance and took exception to Smiley's statements. He sent a friend down to Gordon's garage (he was driving for Pat Patrick and had him ask Smiley if he'd consider a retraction tomorrow night at the victory banquet. Smiley refused to talk about the incident.)

Gary stormed off on his own, but was followed by a small cadre of supporters. He attempted to reason with Smiley, but the two had verbally attacked one another previously. Smiley had chided Bettenhausen for his USAC support and Gary had countered with, "Gordon, you wouldn't have a ride in this place if it weren't for your checkbook. Or somebody's checkbook."

Gary was fuming. Odds makers would have bet that the elder Bettenhausen was going to take a poke at Gordon Smiley.

Back in his garage Tony was saying to his crew, "Dammit, I wish Gary would let me fight my own battles. It was just one of those things. It was racin'. Whatever Gordon said over the radio will probably hurt him more than it does me."

It was beginning to drizzle and Smiley popped his umbrella open. Gary looked at him, slammed the umbrella down around Gordon's head, turned and walked back to the garage. It was post-race celebration time and Gary Bettenhausen was going to tell the world what a good job his kid brother had done.

Patrick crew member John-John Anderson commented about the incident: "We keep tellin' Gordon to keep his mouth shut. He goes fast, but his mouth gets him in trouble. I told him last week, 'Listen Gordon, next time they put a microphone in your mouth, sneeze. Walk away. Tell 'em you got a cold and can't talk.'"

No one ever figured out why Anderson was called John-John

but he usually tried to make a humorous circumstance out of most any trying incident.

Car owner Pat Patrick said, "Smiley is an ass for talking that way on the radio."

Tony's car owners threw a party in his honor after the race and all family members attended. He'd been driving race cars for a good number of years, but it was though he had just been inducted into a secret society. Making the starting field and racing at the Indianapolis 500 was still one of the most important things that could happen in the life of a race car driver.

A few days after the race it was learned that Gordon Smiley was fired from the Patrick team. Tony would campaign with CART for the rest of the summer. Gary said he would probably have to go run some Sprint races. Maybe he'd call a car owner or two.

* * *

Tony gained wide recognition for a driving performance late in the summer during the running of the Michigan 500, on the track where Merle lost his arm. Many of the early leaders dropped out and Pancho Carter and Tony found themselves out in front of the pack with the race to themselves. Pancho's car was faster than Tony's 1977 mount, but the youngest Bettenhausen was dialed-in on this day and enjoyed the run. He knew that his machine wasn't capable of overtaking Carter's under normal racing circumstances but kept up with the leader and delighted the overflowing crowd. After the race was over track owner Roger Penske commented that Tony had indeed done an admirable job.

Members of the press were introduced to the namesake's humor when he referred to Pancho: "I was like a dog chasing a car. I don't know what I'd done with him if I'd caught him."

Gary managed a ride for the CART event, but had to compromise himself to do it. He talked with car owner Jack Rhoades, an Indiana based aircraft dealer. Rhoades allowed as to how he didn't have a sponsor for the race and didn't know if he could afford to go.

Gary said, "Well if things really get rough for you, and we don't make any money up there I'll drive it for twenty percent. But don't tell anyone. I'll do it to help you out."

Gary finished a creditable sixth in the balky machine and was running at the end. Rhoades sent him twenty percent. The team had earned $13,000. Gary didn't complain but Wave told him he was a "dumb shit" for letting people take advantage of him. For the first time in her life she read the riot act to Rhoades' mechanic over the phone as well. She'd always made it a practice to stay out of Gary's business affairs but this time she believed someone had pushed just a little too far. There were 37 cars in the race and she figured the Rhoades team had certainly been the recipient of a good driving performance by one Gary Bettenhausen. Sending him twenty percent was an insult. Wave herself never complained about money and had obtained a job a few years back at nearby Hall Elementary School in the office. She was, she had to admit, getting just a little fed up with the current state of affairs in Championship automobile racing.

"Do you know how many of those clowns up there, or even at the Speedway, bought a ride?" she asked. "I think I'm getting ashamed of some of these car owners. I feel like frizzing my hair up, walking around in a t-shirt with big boobs that says, 'Money Talks and Talent Walks.' "

"Take it easy," Gary says. "Just shut-up and be the quiet little housewife and let me worry about the racin' end of things."

"You're worried about it and letting people screw you," she retorts. "You always say 'Everything comes back in the end.' Well, in The End is where you're getting it."

"Calm down," Gary continues. "We've never bad-mouthed anybody and we ain't gonna start."

"Maybe you ought to," Wave claims. "Sprint car champion, Dirt car champion, the guy who's won the fastest Indy car race ever run. Midget winner, car builder. You've done it all. What do they want? I'll tell you what they want. Money. You got more talent in your little finger, than most of those assholes have in their whole bodies. It just makes me sick that you don't have a first-class ride."

Gary didn't reply. He was digesting what his wife of 18 years had just told him. He knew that he could always count on her to stay out of the way, not say something dumb, something that would embarrass him in front of other drivers, or an owner. Wave was always behind him. He trusted her, she didn't go out and run around on him. Wave knew that some race car drivers had "escapades" but she never wanted to hear about any of them.

Gary is sprawled out on the couch at home. Wave has just served dinner and she's cleaning off the table. It's late in the summer of 1981. The Bettenhausens are being interviewed.

"I'll tell you one thing." Wave says, "there's very few of the car owners out there today who aren't looking for money from a driver."

"Lindsey isn't." Gary interjects.

"Lindsey's one in a million," Wave asserts.

The interviewer asks: "How do you feel about Tony running second up at Michigan?"

"He did a good job. He was dialed-in," notes Gary.

"How would you feel if he won next year's Indy 500? Would you be jealous?"

"No, I'd be happy for him."

"Aw, c'mon, wouldn't you feel a little jealous."

"No," Gary continues, "I don't think so. Tony isn't great in a Champ car yet, but he's learning. He'll get better. Besides, I've learned that it isn't just all your own talent that makes you win in one of those things. It's guys like Patrick and Penske and Jimmy McGee (a chief mechanic) and lots of money."

"What would you do if Roger Penske called you up, right now, and asked you to drive for him?"

"I'd be back on top of the world. I'd say, 'Yes Sir, Roger...and whatever you'd like me to do Roger.' "

"Would you keep driving Sprint cars?"

"I'm sure that I'd never look at another Sprint car or Dirt car again."

"Well, why didn't you give them up the first time you drove for him, back in the early Seventies?"

"It was different then," Bettenhausen continued. "I just had some goals that I wanted to accomplish. I don't think I'd have been happy if I had given them up back then. It was a whole different deal then, you know. I felt like I was a puppet driving for Penske. At first, I couldn't even come in and change a spring without first asking Mark Donohue. But things did get a little better after a while. I didn't really feel like I was my own man when I drove for him then. Now, it'd be different. He's different now too, you know. Do you realize that when I drove for Roger Penske that I finished four races in two years? It seems like everybody forgets that. He didn't exactly have the greatest finishing record, and engines. Do you remember? Traco was doing our engines, and they were like a bunch of hand-grenades."

"What would you do if the best Midget owner in the world called you up, right now and asked you to drive his Midget?"

Gary rocked back, laughed and said, "Well...uh, I think I'm gonna be sick next week...try somebody else."

Then Bettenhausen stares off into the distance. He glances down at the carpet and offers: "You know, it is really kind of horseshit way of makin' a living. If I had it to do all over again, knowing what I know now...I'm not so sure I'd do it."

"Would you encourage your boys to drive?"

"You mean if they had good eyesight? No. No I wouldn't."

"Would you help your nephew, Ryan?"

"Only after he's decided on his own that's what he wants to do."

"How would you feel if you'd just won the Indy 500. Or let's say you win it next year."

"I'd feel like someone just took a big load off my shoulders."

"Do you think your dad's proud of you?"

"I guarantee you my dad's proud of me. That's one thing I don't have to worry about."

"How do you think he'd look at Merle?"

"He'd be damn proud of Merle. That damn Merle has got more discipline in him than any of us. He used to be the laziest good-for-nothing you ever met. Then he cut his arm off and he had to do something. I dunno. Maybe it was get discipline. Merle wanted to quit smoking and zap (Gary snaps his fingers) he did it. Hell, I can't do it. Merle gets up every morning, drives down the same road and goes to a job. He's quit eatin' meat, lost weight. Merle's got his shit together."

"And Tony?"

"Well, Tony was pretty young when Daddy got killed. But he'd be proud of him too. I don't know if he'd want him driving race cars...but then again, if he were alive I wouldn't be driving race cars. He told me when I got Pat pregnant, 'Pal, your racin' days are over.' And they hadn't even started yet. That's just the kind of guy he was. He said something and you'd better jump. Or else."

"Or else what?"

"He used to get physical with me. I mean, he'd whale on me. We'd be down on the kitchen floor, wrestling around. Sometimes I used to say to myself, 'I wish you were dead you old bastard,' about him. He was tough on me. But I know it was good for me. I'll bet my own kids have said the same thing about me...that sometimes they wish I were dead. You don't really mean it like that."

"Do you feel like you're driving with one arm?"

"I know I'm driving with one arm. I've probably got sixty percent of what the normal, average guy has got."

"It doesn't seem to bother you in a Speedway car?"

"It doesn't. Not at all. Not one tenth of one percent. Just at places like Winchester, or muddy rough dirt tracks. Places where I'd be wipin' my face shield and I gotta be steering. But it didn't bother me last Sunday at Eldora and that's a rough joint to drive."

"Would you quit if you won the Indy 500?"

"If I won the Indy 500 for the next three years in a row,"

(laughter) "then I guess you could say I'd consider slowing down some."

Bettenhausen pauses and adds, "And then of course I'd just run the Speedway," (more laughter.)

"Do you have any other interests at all, other than racing?"

"Not really. My interests in life are my little forty six acres here and racing."

Wavelyn finally chimes in, "I think that's sad Gary. I've always told you I think that's sad."

Gary turns his head sideways, looks out the window and says, "Sure it is," (sigh)...but that's the way it goes."

"What are you going to do if you ever quit racing?"

"I'm not exactly sure right at this point. But something. I always come up with something. Always come through in the worst of storms."

"Have you ever considered retiring?"

"When I was in the hospital after the Syracuse wreck. Everything hurt so much. But then it got better and I thought, 'Well, maybe it wasn't so bad after all.' "

"What are you going to do for the 1982 '500'?"

"Lindsey Hopkins has given me two of his Speedway cars. The ones I had this year. I'm going to bring them home, rebuild them. Do a little re-design."

"Do you honestly think you can win with them?"

"Yeah, sure. Think about it. This year, with very little preparation they were pretty fast. If I have good pit stops, a little luck, I could win the race with one of Lindsey's cars."

"Would you rather drive for Penske?"

"That's a dumb question."

"Why do you keep driving Sprint cars now?"

"Gotta keep my name out in front of the car owners. I can't just sit here on my thumbs."

"Do you still enjoy it?"

"Not as much as I used to. But everybody gets like that. You do so much of it and you get a little burned out. Then you just want to go to the fun races."

After a while, Gary invites the interviewer down to see his shop, located out behind his house. His Sprint car is sitting in one corner and his boys start pointing out some of the innovations that have proven workable on the vehicle. They show you the wood stove their father built and say, "It'll run you out of the place." The shop is immaculate. Upstairs, Gary finds a couple of bolts lying on the floor, picks them up and inserts them into little bins, neatly stacked. He looks around, smiles and says, "Yup."

"Yup, what?" the interviewer asks.

"Yup, this is just the way my old man would have had this place. Everything in its place, and a place for everyting. It could have been his shop too. We're going to get Lindsey's cars in here pretty soon and start working on them."

"Do you like the idea of being your own mechanic?"

"Well, I'll hire some help for the Speedway," he says. "But yeah. I like the idea that if I win or lose, it's my fault. Know what I mean?"

"Yes."

"You know," Bettenhausen continues, "everybody thought I was all washed up after my Syracuse wreck, including you, you sumbitch," he says to the interviewer. "Do you think I've won enough races, on enough kind of tracks to prove that ain't so?"

"Yeah, I guess you're right," the interviewer says sheepishly.

Bettenhausen was right. Talk among the racing crowd had him over the hill. Washed up. No one expected him to come back and become a champion again.

"Now," Gary says, "little by little, every year, I can tell some difference. My arm gets stronger and stronger. It's a helluva lot better now than it was in 1975. I tell everybody they're getting older. And I'm getting better," he laughs.

* * *

The man who provided the Provimi Veal sponsorship money for Tony at Indianapolis in 1981 was sold not only on Championship auto racing, but Tony Bettenhausen as well. In the jargon of the pits, Tony's H & R racing team had found an angel. Aat Groenevelt, an immigrant from Holland, had come to the United States in 1958. For the 1982 running of the Indianapolis 500 he would be able to ride in his Citation jet to see his car run in the race. He had provided the backing necessary to buy Tony a new car and enough support equipment to make him feel more than comfortable as a professional automobile racer. Tony's personality, his approach to business through the H & R corporate strategy and Tony's partners in the corporation were all to Aat's liking. He wanted to become involved in auto racing. He'd been bitten by the bug that few often shake. Tony not only had the latest in on-track equipment, but also an 18 wheeler semi tractor and trailer with Provimi Veal Racing Team painted on the side became part of the stable.

The closely-knit team worked out of a small garage facility located less than a mile from the gates to the Speedway. Tony looked forward to the 1982 Indianapolis 500 with much more confidence than he had the year prior. He knew he was capable of making the race, and his second place finish at Michigan last year let him know what it was like to run with the leaders. Given the right equipment and circumstance he knew that a Tony Bettenhausen could win the Indianapolis 500. He now carried himself with a sense of belonging and maturity. Last year he'd made more money than any other year in his life. It would come in handy now too, as he and wife Shirley were parents to a little girl, Bryn.

Shirley Bettenhausen had always felt comfortable at the races. It was the only life she'd ever known. It seemed as though her brother James (no one ever called him Jim, a name reserved for her father) had a pre-destined course in life. James would be a professional race car driver. When asked about her brother's death in a Sprint car at Winchester Shirley commented, "Well at least he was doing what he liked to do best."

Racing people often said that about someone who had been killed in the sport. When asked, how would she feel, God forbid, about the sport if it ever took away her Tony she replied again, "Well, at least I'd know that he was doing what he liked best."

Shirley McElreath Bettenhausen is totally dedicated to her daughter and her husband. Brother James was a standout in Sprint cars and in the few Midget races he drove, but now her man is an Indianapolis 500 race car driver, just like her dad. Dad is over 50 now and he's still driving race cars.

The previous May Tony and Shirley were walking through Gasoline Alley toward the race track with Merle and Leslie. The cars were on the course, mechanics ready. Nearly 400,000 people were inside the track waiting for the race to start in a few moments when rookie Tony turned to Merle and said nervously: "Boy Merle, I can't believe I've waited my whole life to feel like I feel now."

* * *

Susan Bettenhausen Wilson was performing those painful seemingly endless sit-ups she had perfected in her local health club when a black-haired, mustachioed man walked by. He took a quick glance and simply said, "Faster." Brash character, she thought. Did he know just *whom* he was telling "Faster." If he knew anything at all about the little blond working up a sweat he would have known that she was performing the exercise as it should be done. Exactly. The right speed, the right stretch. Susan

Left: Susan Bettenhausen Anselmi with her brother, Tony.
Right: Donald Davidson, a walking computer of Indy 500 statistics. He's committed to memory the record of every car and driver who have run at Indy in the past 66 races. You can hear him annually on the world-wide radio broadcast.

Wilson had earned her title of perfectionist. She just happened to be a Virgo to prove it, in case anyone ever asked. She could have thought, "Just who in the hell does he think he is, anyway?"

He turned out to be a no-nonsense executive named Bob Anselmi who was a perfect match for Ms. Susan Wilson. Later in the summer of 1982 they would be married at Denver's fashionable Cherry Hills Country Club. But first she would take her man to see the Indianapolis 500 mile automobile race. She had some roots that went very deep there she explained.

* * *

Gary Bettenhausen had worked throughout the severe Indiana winter behind his house preparing Lindsey Hopkins' now dated Speedway cars. Often times when he needed a part fabricated he'd go see his old friend "The Prince of Darkness," Don Brown. Brown would toy with him and say, "Listen Gary, I know how we can build an intake manifold that will over-ride the pop-off valve. You'll blow their doors off at the Speedway if you can handle the horsepower."

The pop-off valve is a simple device installed by the USAC technical committee on each car to limit the amount of turbocharger pressure that can enter an engine. Over-riding it can give a definite advantage, but cheating on an Indy car is a rare and risky circumstance.

"No, no, no," Bettenhausen advised. "I've never cheated yet and I don't intend to start."

Brown knew that Gary would rather miss the show than cheat but continued with his charade: "Aw, c'mon, we could make Patrick and Penske and Foyt and all those hot-dogs over there crazy. You could just tell them that you've re-engineered the car! Maybe you'll sell 'em one if they're nice to you."

"No, no," Gary said. "Come on, we've got work to do. Don't you ever work in the daytime?"

"I like to work when the moon's out," Brown noted eerily. "Strange things happen at night...woooooo."

Gary did re-engineer much of the bodywork on the cars but when he got on the track in May of '82 it looked like his winter's work had been in vain. There was a tremendous jump in speeds from the year previous and the odds-makers wouldn't have given him a 50-50 chance of making the program. Although the country was in the midst of an economic recession, there was a record number of entries for the 66th running of the 500 and brand new cars were the order of the day. Speeds of over 200 mph. were reached soon after the track opened for practice.

As usual, track regulars were discussing the latest pit gossip, new drivers, sponsors. Statistically, the most knowledgeable human being in the world on the facts and figures of the Indianapolis 500 is a 39 year old Englishman named Donald Davidson. As a teenager he obtained every book he could locate on the race and surprised himself when he found that he had total recall of statistics. He moved to the United States in 1964 and got a job as statistician with USAC. Each May he was a part of the world-wide radio broadcast of the 500, being called upon for his expert commentary and often humorous anecdotes. He was talking to another writer at the track: "How about that Smiley?" he said. "I think someone rattled his cage."

"I haven't talked to him this year," the writer offered. "Don't really care if I do either. That character's mouth makes him his own worst enemy. Why do you say someone rattled his cage?"

"He's a changed man. Did you hear him on the radio last night?"

"No, what'd he say?"

"It was a brand new Gordon Smiley. He didn't act like he was a twenty year veteran of the place. Matter of fact he was quite self-effacing. He was saying, 'Well, I'm still new around here you know,' and things like that. It wasn't the Gordon Smiley we came to know, and not love."

"The Gordon Smiley? Gordon "The Lip' Smiley?"

Gordon Smiley met his death on a warm-up lap at the Speedway when he went out to qualify. The photo is gruesome: the accident described as the worst ever seen in nearly three quarters of a century at the Speedway. Smiley was a good driver but veterans said he was simply trying too hard. [Mahoney]

"Yeah. You should have heard him. I don't know if it's an act or what, but he talked like his head was used for something else besides putting a helmet on.

I dunno. Any guy that roams around with a license plate on his car that says 'Flash G' has still got an ego problem."

Two days later the writer saw Donald Davidson standing at the track, walked up to him and said, "Well, unfortunately that takes care of Gordon Smiley. It looked like a dozen sticks of dynamite went off when his car hit the wall."

"I know," Davidson offered. "That was the worst I've ever seen. Nothing like it. He never knew what hit him."

"It's too late now," the other said, "but maybe he had changed. I'll give him the benefit of the doubt."

It was Saturday May 15th, just past noon when Gordon Smiley

went out to make his four-lap qualification attempt. He had arrived at Indianapolis with a new car and team, organized by his friend Dave Anderson. Anderson believed in Smiley's ability as a driver and as previously stated, he could indeed run fast. The general consensus of the pits was that Gordon was running too fast. He'd looked scary in the corners during practice, he didn't have the car dialed-in. Going into the third turn on a practice lap he lost control and the car made a sharp right turn into the concrete wall. Upon impact it exploded into three sections, his body remaining in the cockpit.

Writer Tom Callahan penned an article for the May 31 edition of *Time* magazine that was run next to grisly color photos of the accident. Callahan had spoken with Merle years ago and filed away a Bettenhausen quote for nine years that he would use at an appropriate time. Merle had just decided to return to racing, one-armed. Callahan's story said in part:

> That these men know something the rest of us don't is undeniable. Merle Bettenhausen, a man with shiny pink skin and a hook for a right arm, said one time in Indy's Gasoline Alley: 'I know why you feel sorry for me, but you don't know why I feel sorry for you.' The name Bettenhausen is engraved at Indianapolis everywhere but on the trophy. The father, Tony, died in a practice run in 1961. Two of his sons, Gary and Tony, Jr. both drive at Indy. Merle would too, but his arm happens to have been sliced off ten years ago in the Michigan 200. 'We are discovers,' Merle said. 'You may be alive, and you may have two arms. But you have never felt it.'

Callahan earlier in his story alluded to a line written by sportswriter Jim Murray and termed it, "Like the last note of taps. 'Gentlemen, start your coffins.' "

Later in the summer, after Indy had been run, Merle and Leslie were sitting at home on a Sunday afternoon when a program about racing came on. They both watched the show with one eye, carrying on an unrelated conversation all the while. The show featured numerous crashes and Leslie commented, "I can't believe I was married to a race car driver," and as the last word came from her mouth Merle said, "I can't believe I *was* a race car driver," then they both laughed.

"It all seems so illogical," Merle says. "Everything I do in my life is logical. I am a logical thinking person. Driving a race car is not a logical thing to do."

Logical or not, his two brothers were working hard to make the 1982 "500." Early in the month Tony experienced a mechanical failure that sent him spinning into the backstretch wall. Parts would have to be air-freighted from England in time to repair the car.

Tony's new car for the 1982 "500." [*IMS*]

Gary had to wait until the second (and final) weekend of qualifying to make his attempt. His first lap average is only 191 mph. and his crew waved him in. He has two attempts left. Back in the garage he and the crew make more changes to the car.

Tony went out and turned a speed of 195, considered safe to make the race. He came in and said over the public address system: "Thank you very much. This one belongs to the crew. And I'll tell you what. We've had a tough go the last three months and they haven't stopped working yet. They get ninety-nine percent of the credit."

Tony continued on to thank his sponsors, car owners and crew again. He ended with, "I think we might just happen to have a spare engine that would fit into Gary's car, if he needs it."

Gary needed more than an engine. It was now the last day of qualifying and he was stuck at 189 mph. He didn't know what else to change on the car. It appeared as though it would go no faster, safely.

Close to 4 o'clock on Sunday afternoon, Gary rolled his car into the qualifying line and readied for an attempt. The field of 33 cars was already full, he'd have to go faster than the slowest man. To have some margin so he himself wouldn't be "on the bubble" he'd have to go quite a bit faster. Crew chief Chuck Buckman and first helper Ronnie Breen had taken advice from the car's designer David Bruns and cocked the right rear tire in a few degress. Gary said, "Let's try somethng radical and move the rear wing way up, perhaps that will help."

The changes worked. He picked up over six miles per hour to

Lindsey Hopkins shared Gary's delight in qualifying for the 500. [*Talley*]

average over 195 mph. and bumped rookie Chip Mead from the starting line-up. Gary came in and gave the longest speech of any driver in the field. "I'm so happy right now I could cry," he noted in the middle of his detailed explanation. Gary too thanked everyone but his wife for the effort.

The moment Gary crossed the line on his fourth and final qualifying lap and it was announced he'd made the field, a couple of dozen cars in Monrovia High School parking ot began honking their horns and cheering in jubliation. It was Cary and Todd's graduation day and they, along with their eager classmates waited in anticipation of Gary's run. Cary and Todd said it seemed like the whole school wanted their dad to make the race.

Billy Vukovich came by the Lindsey Hopkins garage after qualifying was over and as he entered he said, as though he were on the public address system: "And if it's Smuckers, it's gotta be good sports fans!"

Gary looked up and smiled.

"Isn't that what they say about the jelly?" Vukovich continued. "You think they'll ever say, 'And if it's a Bettenhauser it's gotta be good?' Naw, that don't sound right," Vukovich answered his own question.

They were standing in the same garage where their fathers before them had been. All that was left of the men who had

After a winter's work with help from his sons and a neighbor, Gary and his Indy crew found just enough speed in the waning hours of qualifying to put his machine in the 1982 race. Merle and Tony pose with their brother. [IMS]

Left: Billy Vukovich toying with his pal, Gary.

brought them into the world were framed photographs on the wall.

"Are we playing golf tomorrow?" Vuky continued.

"Yeah...yeah, I guess," Gary answered while he looked at the car.

"C'mon smile, Bettenhausen, you just made money," Billy said.

"Money." Gary laughed, "The old ka-vitcher, always thinking about money. What are you going to do with all the money you got?" Bettenhausen asked.

"He yah-ha-ha!" Vukovich roared. "All the money I got? Well one thing's for sure. I ain't gonna buy one of these shit-boxes," the lanky driver says as he kicks one of the car's tires. He turns and walks out of the garage. No good-bye.

He gets to the doorway and adds, "And if I did own one I

wouldn't put you in it...He yah-ha-ha!"

Bettenhausen laughs, the crew laughs and Lindsey shakes his head and smiles.

Merle and Leslie came by the garage and offered congratulations. Val and Webb were again splitting their time between Tony's and Gary's garages. Val hides her nervousness about the upcoming race well. She sits on a lawn chair and directly in her line of sight is a photo of Tony, taken about 1959. Lindsey's next to her and they chat. If you were a knowledgeable passery-by, you'd say they earned their wrinkles.

Merle and Leslie bid adieu to everyone to go home to suburbia, a few miles west of the track. Merle Bettenhausen lives a different life nowadays. He's moved up another notch in the work force. He's earning a middle-class wage as a supervisor for the Indiana Farm Bureau Co-op. He runs the vehicle department. It's not a job that taxes his mind, and he knows it isn't his last job, so he endures and makes friends along the way. He's not quite sure what he'll ultimately do, but he knows his capabilities far surpass his present position. He reminds himself of the fact frequently. If he told you to grab a beer out of the referigerator you'd see a small newspaper clipping taped to the door that says:

> "Mobilize the powers of your mind. Develope your faith, think positively every day all the way. If your goal is specifically conceived and firmly fixed in your conscious, powerful influences out of the life force within you and around you will come to your aid. Don't reject but drawn upon the tremendous power with the mind."

Later in the summer Leslie will be able to answer the phone and say "Oh Merle's gone racing today. No, not a car race, he's entered in a marathon." Merle discovers jogging and finds yet another satisfaction he didn't experience while driving race cars.

After qualifying for the "500" there is always a week's wait for the race. Three days before the actual event the track holds what is known as Carburetion Day, the name stemming from the days when the cars actually used carburetors. The cars are allowed on the track one final time so crews may check to see if everyting is set for a 500 mile run. Normally, no more than a third of the field runs the entire distance. For the past several years the track has been open to the public on Carburetion Day. The place represents a convention of those interested in the sport from today and yesteryear. The Speedway also has an Oldtimer's Club, membership requirements being that you were first involved with the track twenty years ago. Most of the Oldtimers are out on Carburetion Day.

Speedway sightseers: From left, Timmy Delrose, part owner of the Champ Dirt car drove to the championship; the "Iron Duke" Nalon, and Cowboy O'Rourke, both long-time Bettenhausen pals. [*Flynn*]

Tony's pals from the Forties, Fifties and Sixties are members of the oldtimer's club now and frequent the track each May. Carburetion Day is one of the last times they'll see one another for another year. It is a trying circumstance to find anyone on race day.

You can sit in the pits and see a balding old man walk by. He's medium of build and wears thick glasses now. His name is Emil Andres and he can remember the day that a youngster knocked on his door and said, "Hi, Mr. Andres. My name's Tony Bettenhausen and I'm going to be a race car driver." No one recognizes Emil Andres other than his peers.

A still handsome Duke Nalon will appear, neatly outfitted and displaying the same winning smile that used to make the girls giggle. Duke will tell you of his son's progress as a Sprint car driver. Look closely and you'll see that the skin on his face is in two shades. He can tell you long stories about a car they called the Novi. People still walk up to "The Iron Duke" and ask for his autograph. They remember when he and Emil were members of the feared Chicago Gang.

Their little buddy, rotund Paul Russo can't come to the Speedway any more. Paul died in his sleep a few years back. He was around a race track to the end though. Russo was in Florida ready to watch the Daytona when his time came.

Henry Banks takes a break from his job as Director of USAC Properties and comes across the street to mingle with old friends. Henry is 67 years old now and ready to celebrate 47 years of marriage to his wife Rosie. Henry is afraid to retire, says he's worked all his life and he's not sure he'd know what to do with

Emil Andres, Henry Banks and Crocky Wright at Emil's annual Oldtimer's Banquet. [*Crucean*]

himself. He laments the situation that USAC is in, even though he's had no connection with the auto racing end of the club in a decade now. He can't understand why they need some 19 employees to do less of a job than he did with half a dozen. Thirteen years ago his club held over 70 Midget races, close to 40 Sprint races, almost 20 Championship races and a couple of dozen Stock Car races. In 1982 the Championship division has one race, Indianapolis. There are less than 20 Midget races and it's been so long that a USAC Stock car race has received any publicity many race fans wonder if the club still sanctions Stock cars. The Sprint cars have a couple of dozen races now, but many are held on obscure little quarter-mile dirt tracks that are known only to local fans. He thinks the USAC Board of Directors made one of the biggest mistakes in the history of the club when they replaced him with Billy Smyth.

Henry tries to joke about the situation and says he could write a book called "The Rise and Fall of USAC." Today a man named Dick King is at the USAC helm and some say he's the captain of rudderless ship. Gone now are the days of the Larry and Gary Sprint car shows. Gypsy Midget racers still tow the nation's interstates and put on good shows, but no one has ever heard of the clubs that have sliced up the USAC pie.

Auto racing has been oxygen to Henry Banks, but now he sees the patient lapsing into what may very well be a permanent coma. Like his peers, he relives some of the old days. He'll jump on an airplane and attend the "Gilmore Roars Again" party that is held annually on the West Coast. In the winter he'll drive up to Chicago and attend Emil Andres' Oldtimers Banquet. They'll talk

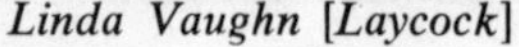

Linda Vaughn [Laycock]

Larry Bisceglia [Rowe]

about Blue Island and Riverview and Nutley: Nutley. Henry can think. Boy, that was a one of a kind place. Emil's party isn't held too far from Tinley Park and they'll talk about "old Tony."

This year they'll miss old Gays Biro, dead at 73. Gays was one of Tony's peers back in the halycon days of Midget racing and was a feared competitor. He and Tony raced each other many times. Gays Biro died Friday November 10, 1982, on the race track at Williams Grove, Pennsylvania. He had attended the annual Old Timers gathering there and had taken a Midget for a couple of hot laps around the track. A radius rod broke and Biro died in the crash. It was a radius rod bolt that had fallen out of Tony Bettenhausen's car twenty years earlier.

* * *

Johnnie Parsons, Sr. will go bouncing by on Carburetion Day and when he stops to talk to you, he'll use the language of the day. Handsome John will never be an Oldtimer, it's not his style. You ask him how it's going and he'll tell you that everything's coming up roses. Just great. Johnnie Parsons, Sr. never really made a nickel in or out of auto racing, but he's happy to be here anyway. He can't imagine being anywhere else the month of May.

Buxom Linda Vaughn walks through the pits and up to a small gathering of men.

"Hi, y'all," she drawls in a Georgian accent. She joins the conversation and isn't bothered as the men gaze now and then at her huge, well-rounded breasts. She's been Miss Hurst Golden Shifter for twenty years and has learned the art of public relations through thousands of race track appearances. None of the cars use

Left: The 500's Chief Steward, Tom Binford. [*Mahoney*] *Right: Paul Page, the Voice of the 500 to millions of radio listeners world-wide.* [*Wendt*]

Hurst shifting devices, yet they still send Linda to the Speedway every year just for the publicity she'll garner.

Another old man in an engineer's cap is wandering through the pits. Sometimes a mechanic will speak to him, ask him how he's been. He's Larry Bisceglia, Indy's Mr. First in Line for 34 years now. If you'd arrived at the Speedway in late April you would have seen his van parked outside the gate, waiting. The truck is a collage of racing decals and serves as Larry's home on the road. Last year he said he probably wouldn't be back in '82 but just laughs and says, "Well, here I am again."

Just behind the start-finish line, the line that still exposes a couple of rows of brick, there's a man in a short sleeved shirt, wearing a tie and Hush Puppy shoes. A pipe is held in the side of his mouth. He looks like a college dean for an Ivy League school. Maybe he's just removed his sport coat because it's so hot out. He's the man who runs the race, his title is Chief Steward. Although he can only see less than a quarter mile of the race track in both directions, he's responsible for everything that happens around its two and one half mile perimeter. Last year he had to bear the brunt of a decision to take away the win from Bobby Unser when it was shown that Unser passed on the track illegally. On the night of the race he was fairly well humiliated on national television when Ted Coppel of ABC's "Nightline" was unrelenting in his line of questioning. It made no difference to

Coppell that he was talking to Tom Binford, Chairman of the Board of the Indiana National Bank and one of Indiana's most respected citizens. To Coppell, he was just another race car official at the Indianapolis 500. It was one of the first times in history the track received any publicity for an event other than a death. Tom Binford had been involved in the sport since the Fifties and knew that the incident was unfortunate but had to be dealt with. Binford was unflappable, he'd been dealing with unfortunate auto racing incidents since Ted Coppell was a kid.

Binford can look over and see the Borg-Warner trophy sitting on a table not far from his position. The seventy available spaces reserved for the winner's likeness are almost all full now. Only a few more races and there will be no place left. What will happen when the trophy's full? Binford smiles and says he doesn't know. Never been asked that question before.

Paul Page, the new "Voice of the 500" over the world-wide radio broadcast walks by. He stops and talks to Tom Binford momentarily, makes a note and continues on. He'll have a briefcase full of notes for the race on Sunday, in preparation for everything from rain to death and all circumstances in between.

Track Superintendent Charlie Thompson pushes a button on his two way radio and says, "Yeah that's ok. Just make sure they're in place for Sunday morning." Charlie Thompson has over 6,000 track employees to worry about for the race on Sunday but still makes time to wander through the pits on his daily rounds.

A few feet from the entrance to the pits two young men are sitting in a golf cart. One of them has a Goodyear apron on, the other a brightly patterned shirt, his hair is frizzed. The lanky fella with the Goodyear apron could have become a successful commercial artist, he'd been blessed with talent. His name is Bobby Grim and he's a tire buster for Goodyear. He's worked for the giant corporation of over a decade, doing the same job. He goes to all the Championship races. He's been going to races all his life. His father, of the same name, was once a famed Sprint car driver who finally made it to Indy late in his career. Bobby Grim, Jr. has a Midget of his own, home in the garage, but doesn't harbor any thoughts about becoming a Speedway driver. He watches as one of the Whittington brothers' cars is pushed toward the track, turns to his pal Al Freedman and says, "Now there's a perfect example of no talent what so ever. Mega bucks is the only, *the only*," he emphasizes, "thing in the world that got them here."

Freedman lays back, props a foot up on the end of the cart and says, "Yeah, money still talks and bullshit walks."

Left: Charlie Thompson, track superintendent at Indy has to worry about 6,000 employees on race day. [IMS]
Right: Chris Economaki, whether it happens in the pits or Paris, he has a line on it if it's auto racing news.

Everyone at the Speedway who knows him calls Al Freedman, Einstein. He's been around for twenty years and nowadays can always be found outside the Goodyear garage dispensing humorous witticisms about the current crop of drivers. Einstein used to be a crew member back, "in the days when it was fun." But he still comes to the Speedway every year to soak up the atmosphere, be among his friends. Grim looks at the Whittington car and shakes his head.

Chris Economaki is walking by and noted Grim's gesture. Economaki is outfitted withphones and an ABC Sports cameraman in tow. Economaki gives the pair a short wave and continues towards the pits. No one knows exactly how long Chris Economaki has been coming to Indianapolis, but it seems like forever. Next week his column in his *National Speed Sport News* will be datelined: Indianapoplis. The following week he may be in South Africa, then Monaco and then Daytona the week after. In mid-summer you might find him covering and announcing the Knoxville Nationals, famed Sprint car races held next door to an Iowa cornfield. Economaki will once again work the pits for ABC. He'd much rather be up in the announcer's booth, but ABC producers know that no one else can approach the racers the way

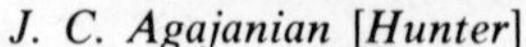
J. C. Agajanian [*Hunter*]

Al Bloemker [*Crucean*]

Chris Economaki can. If possible, he'll be on the scene before the car stops spinning asking the driver, "Exactly what happened out there?"

Photographers roam and snap pictures. One of them sees a man sitting on the pit wall, smoking a cigarette. He carries neither a smile nor a frown. He straightens his fedora, looks left, then right. He's seen it all before, but he's still interested. He's been writing about the "500" since the early 1920's. His name is Al Bloemker and he's the only public relations man the Speedway has had since 1946. He's 74 years old now, but looks like he's in his fifties. If you ask him if he knew Tony Bettenhausen he'd laugh and say, "Old Tony? Sure. Why I remember the time when I had dinner with him up in Chicago. He was telling me what he was going to do *after* he won the 500. I think he was going to be driving one of the Blue Crowns. The race was months away, yet old Tony had 'er in the bag. Running the race was just secondary. Winning it was going to be a breeze. He was quite a character."

One of the only other men around the Indianapolis Motor Speedway to wear a hat with a brim all the way around is J. C. Agajanian. Aggie's expensive Stetson has been publicized more in the last forty years than the face that wears it. Aggie just comes back for the race these days, and now he rides around in a golf cart. The ravages of age are taking their toll on the friendly Armenian. Yet you can still hear some of the grandstand population shout, "Hey Aggie!" as he goes by. It has been many

Roy Grugel saw the 1921 race, he has been a Speedway guard for decades. The job attracts the same people back year after year, so longevity is not uncommon. [*Talley*]

years since Aggie has had an active part in Speedway racing, his once famed number 98 cars are being relegated to auto racing history books. Auto racing is still a part of his daily life, however, as he is the proprietor of Los Angeles' Ascot Speedway, one of the nation's busiest half-mile dirt tracks. Aggie's sons are involved in the operation and will carry on with their father's first love. Aggie's Beverly Hills home still sports beautiful hedgework, trimmed in the numerals 98. Midget and Sprint car racing are alive and well at his Ascot plant, but he doesn't stay away from Indy each May. It is still, as the sign on the museum in front says, The Capitol of Auto Racing. To those like J. C. Agajanian who have lost life-long friends maybe it's Valhalla.

Just to the north as you leave Gasoline Alley you see the cafeterias located under the grandstands. One's for drivers, crews, etc., the other for the general public.

A busty brunette wearing a red and white stripped top, designer jeans and high heels walks into the driver's cafeteria. She's stopped just inside the door by a craggy faced old man sitting in a chair. He's wearing a white cap and has a large silver badge on his yellow shirt.

"See your badge, Miss?" the old man says with a smile.

She aims a finger at the oversize badge on his shirt and says, "Badge?" as though she's supposed to have a badge like the old man's.

He grins, glances toward the gleaming piece of metal on his shirt and replies, "No, no...not like this. Pit badge. Do you have a pit badget?'' and holds up his thumb and forefinger showing a length of about an inch and a half.

"Pit badge?" She asks. "No, I don't have *any* kind of badge."

"Sorry, you'll have to go to the other side then. You have to have a pit badge, like that one, " he says as he points to one clipped on a customer's shirt.

''But I was supposed to meet somebody here,'' she protests.

''That's fine,'' the guard says with a grin again. ''You can wait right there outside the door. I'm sure he won't miss you,'' the old man continues. Then he nods his head as if to say, ''Run along now sweetie, you're not the first little girl I've talked to today.''

Nor is she the first girl old Roy Grugel has ever talked to at the Speedway. He can remember seeing more women's styles being displayed before his very eyes than most have seen in magazines. He's been coming to the Speedway as a fan and then a guard for over 60 years now, and he doesn't have any plans to quit.

"Been here a long time," he'll agree. "But a lot of us have," he says. He's right. It's not difficult to find guards who are in their second and third decade of service at Indy. You're not really considered a member of the club until you've been there at least ten years.

Gary and Vukovich walk in and Gary says, ''How ya doin?'' to Roy as he squeezes the old man's shoulder when he walks by. Roy sits down most of the time now, his legs aren't what they used to be, but his memory is as clear as his blue eyes.

Ask Roy Grugel if he knew Tony Bettenhausen and he literally beams when he says, ''Sure did. The whole family. Why they used to come in my station up north all the time. That old Tony was a character, you know. One time he came skiddin' in to the station and said, 'Quick, open the door.' He looked plenty serious, so I didn't start asking a bunch of questions. I just threw up the garage door fast as I could.

'Now close it,' Bettenhausen said.

So I closed it. I walked up next to the car and said, 'What's going on?'

Tony said, 'You'll see, just wait a minute.'

Well sir, we didn't have to wait a minute. I thought I'd heard sirens off somewhere and sure enough here they come. This police car went barreling by my place, must have been doing eighty. Tony was still in the car. He looked out over the back seat and watched them go by."

"Then he laughed," the old man continues and said "We beat 'em that time!"

"He was laughing and carring on, he thought that was just

Left: George the T-Shirt Man and lady. Right: T-shirts have a colorful language all their own.

great. Pretty soon I thought it was pretty good myself."

Miss Candy Stripe was still waiting outside the door, tapping a toe that looked like the farthest point down on a long, sleek appendage. She finally blinked momentarily, turned and walked away.

In walks George-The-T-Shirt Man with a little blond cupie doll holding his arm. George is about five-seven, 210 pounds at least. He's sort of a short Jackie Gleason with an Afro and a moustache.

"Hi ya podnuh," he says to Roy. "Getting along ok? Everything fine? You're looking good."

"Good, good," Roy replies.

George walks up to the cafeteria line and is immediately recognized by several of the restaurants occupants. George has arrived. The electricity has been turned on, power restored. For the next fifteen minutes he won't stop entertaining long enough to gulp down the iced tea he's about to order. Every once in a while one of the drivers or mechanics or owners he's talking to will notice that George's date has an absolutely beautiful face, magazine cover quality. Maybe she's 19.

No one knows George's last name, but now he's one of the crowd. He showed up a few years back to peddle t-shirts and his rapid fire speech, coupled with a Boston accent made more than one potential client back up. He kept hanging around, entertaining.

"Hey George," a voice from the crowd hollers. "How many *grand* did you pay for the Seville you're driving? Pretty snazzy."

Without a second's thought George shoots back, "How many grand? Why you're lookin' at the only *grand* thing around here," as he outstretches his arms. There's a small chorus of laughter and several heads glance his way.

George's infectious personality has opened all of Indy's doors for him. A. J. Foyt will walk up to him, poke him in the tummy, smile and say "How you doin', Porky?" He gets invited to the suites located just off the second turn where he can sip a scotch in comfort. If he's sitting alone in the Speedway Motel dining room, Roger Penske invites him to his table. George came to Indy to sell t-shirts but got caught up in the racing scene and became a fan. He's wearing a gold bracelet on each wrist, five gold rings on his fingers, a gold chain and another gold chain that holds a piece of gold sculptured in the shape of a t-shirt. He'll hand you a t-shirt shaped business card and is most likely to send you on your way with two shirts, one for you...and one for your lady.

He orders his tea and decides he doesn't like the look of the cafeteria's hot dogs, so says to the lady he's been introducing as "my daughter" or "my niece from the country," "C'mon sweetie, we'll go where they got some good food."

He struts out of the cafeteria, to the left where's there's a long one story cinder block building. He knocks on one of the many doors. It opens and a voice from behind the bar proclaims, "George! C'mon in."

He's just entered the Miller room. Miller Brewing Company rents one of the many hospitality suites for the month to entertain clients. Miller adds to the purse and also sponsors a pit stop contest held a few days before the race. They distribute over $40,000 to participating teams who race against the clock. A couple of years ago Johnny Rutherford won it in his Budweiser Special.

The man who greeted him behind the bar is Ron Burton, an artist Miller retains annually to produce point-of-purchase poster art that depicts an Indy 500 scene. Its a plum of a commission for Burton, one he's waited for. Ron Burton has dedicated his life to being *the* Indy 500 artist. The room is decorated with his work, ranging from realistic to impressionistic. He's just past 40 now and has been attempting to make a living drawing race cars for twenty years. A few years back he reached the zenith of his career when the Miller Company made a deal with the Speedway to install a Miller Wall of Fame inside the museum featuring only Ron Burton originals. Burton choked up at the opening and gave a tearful speech. He likened the occasion to winning the race.

It wasn't the only time he's cried around a race track. His father

Ron Burton, racing artist.

Everett was killed in a roadster race at Kokomo. He's said that, "once racin' gets in your blood, it's hard to get it out." His three brothers are also involved in the sport. He lives within earshot of the track and can be found having his daily lunch inside the Speedway Motel, surrounded by his paintings. He's proud they have replaced the Leroy Neiman work that was there previously.

As the day nears end and the spectators file out, a short stocky man climbs up and into a giant street sweeper. His well muscled arms and spring like movements belie his fifty plus years. His name is Hal Minyard, a famed Sprint car driver who was once the champion of the prestigious California Racing Association. Back in the days when an admission ticket to a ride at the Indianapolis Motor Speedway was earned through talent and accomplishment in a Sprint car, Hal Minyard earned a red-carpet welcome. Luck and circumstance prevented him from ever being a starter in the "500." He's raced not only against the Bettenhausen sons, but their father as well. Nowadays if you attend an obscure backwoods Sprint car track with a name like Putnamville or Bloomington or Paragon, Indiana, you're liable to see Hal Minyard buckling up as he has for over three decades. During the day, he drives at the Speedway.

Minyard isn't the type of man who would be bitter at his situation of not being able to claim he's an Indy 500 driver, past or present. He'd throw his head back laugh and say something like, "Hell, racing's fun....that's why I've done it all my life and it's why I continue to do it once in a while now."

* * *

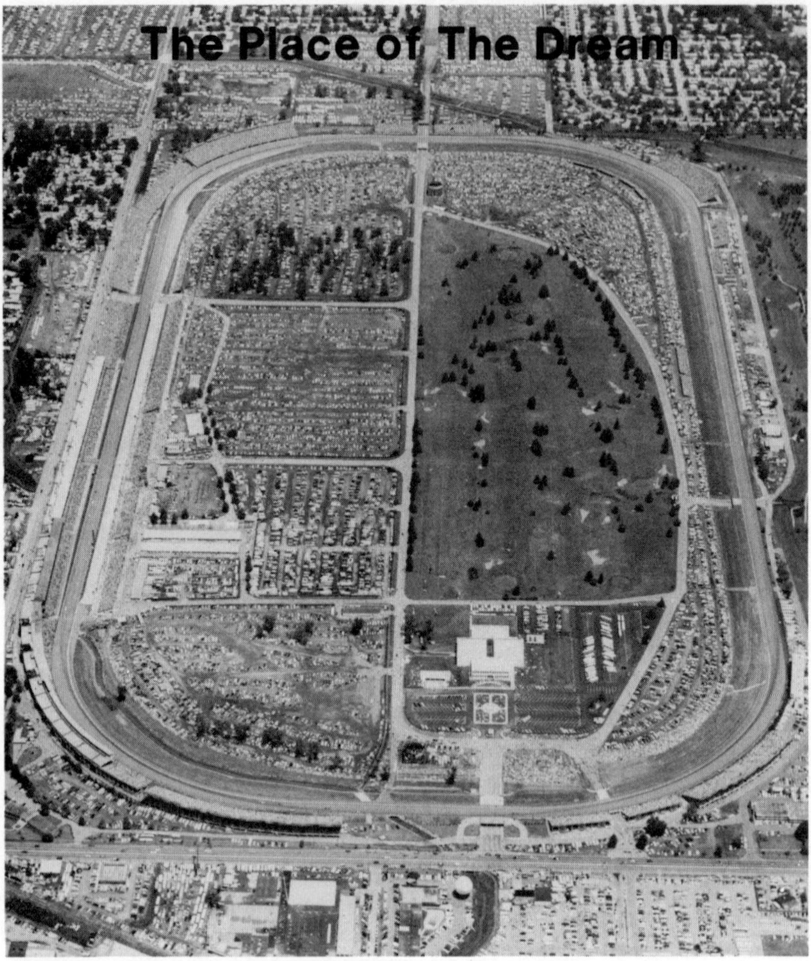

The Place of The Dream

The Indianapolis Motor Speedway covers 529 acres, distance around the track is two-and-one-half miles and is a city within itself the month of May. Front straight-a-way is on your left, the first turn, lower left. There's a full size golf course in the infield where the PGA used to hold tournaments. [IMS]

Left: Mrs. Hulman gives the traditional, "Gentlemen, Start Your Engines!" command. [IMS]

An hour before the running of the 1982 Indy 500, Henry Banks stops by Lindsey Hopkins' garage to wish Gary well. Henry can't visit every garage the way he used to, there are so many new faces who just look at him as though he's another old geezer at the race track. As he leaves, Tony comes in the door and Henry says, "Oh, there you are. Was just on my way to find you." Tony exchanges greetings and gives Henry a long handshake, and a short hug on the shoulder.

"Well," Henry sighs, "you have a good ride out there today."

He pauses momentarily, considers saying something else, changes his mind, looks back and once more says, "Have a good ride. I'll be seeing you."

He hopes.

* * *

Race morning 1982 dawned grey and overcast, the result of a torrential rain that hit the night before. Once again, widow of the track's late owner, Mrs. Tony Hulman gave the traditional starting command: "Gentlemen, Start Your Engines!" On the start of the race, just as the green flag was being unfurled, the often feared circumstances happened: A car in the front row got sideways and caused a multi-car accident. Second year driver Kevin Cogan, driving one of the flawless Roger Penske machines, broke traction and veered left. There were no injuries. Cogan would claim something broke while his detractors said he just flat lost it when the horsepower came in.

After nearly an hour's delay the race was re-started. Tony maintained position while Gary headed toward the back of the field, experiencing mechanical ills. On the 36th lap Tony was barrelling down the front straight-a-way when SNAP! Something broke. He was going over 190 mph. and like his father before him, didn't have time to utter more than "oh...." before the car turned into the outside retaining wall.

He was lucky. The car hit the wall nose first and spun completely around. No one was directly behind him at the time and he climbed out unscathed. Later he joked, "Well, the first part of the month the car did that on the backstretch so this time we did it where everyone could see it." Gary flogged around at the back of the field for most of the day and finally pulled in twenty-five laps from the end. The race was the closest and most exciting in the history of the track. Rick Mears and Gordon Johncock staged a race to the checkered flag for the last ten laps that had half the population hollering "Go, Rick!" while the

Indy crews can fuel a car and change tires in under 15 seconds when everything goes right. This is Johnny Rutherford's crew. [*Whitlow*]

Above: Gary and Tony at Milwaukee with their Provimi Veal sponsored cars. [*McQueeney*]

Left: Valerie at the Provimi-Bettenhausen 200 gave a hearty, "Gentlemen! Start Your ENGINES!" Then she backed away from the microphone, laughed and said, "How'd I do?" [*McQueeney*]

others shouted "Go Gordon!" There had never been a duel to the finish such as the one that was unfolding at the '82 event. The drivers trusted one another with their very lives as they ran side by side at full throttle. Johncock nosed out Mears by 0.16 of a second as the two cars came across the yard of bricks almost side by side. Johncock was driving for Pat Patrick and Mears was in Roger Penske's car.

Gary knew Lindsey wouldn't send his cars to the rest of the races along the CART circuit and began shopping for a ride after the Speedway. He hooked up with a man named Dick Hammond, an upstate New York beer distributor who fielded nice Championship cars he called Genesee Beer Wagons. Hammond's cars aren't in the Patrick and Penske class, but very few are. Hammond ran a solid racing operation and Gary could once again concentrate on driving only. Hammond's main crew includes Chief mechanic Galen Fox and Willie Davis. Willie had told everyone that he was going to move to Phoenix last year and get a job. A stock job. He'd been turning wrenches on race cars long enough. Old Sprint racing buddy Galen called him and said, "C'mon Willie...you don't want to move to Phoenix." So once again, GB and The Cork are a team.

Gary's Sprint car sits in the garage most of the time now. There was a race at Indianapolis Raceway Park, just a few miles from his house, so he ran mostly as a favor to the promoters. He finished an easy second. He'd consider running some of the Championship Dirt shows, but he could live without them too. He's a regular on the Indy car circuit once again and it feels good.

For the annual Tony Bettenhausen 200 held in early August each year, Tony's car owner provided a car for Gary to drive (Gary's Genesee car was broken) and also sponsored the race itself. It was re-named the Provimi-Bettenhausen 200 and became a Bettenhausen family affair. Valerie was brought in to perform the official starting command at the track that so honored her late husband that the race was named in his honor. She would send her own boys on their way with the same, "Gentlemen, Start Your Engines!" she'd heard so many times before. They both came home safely, mechanical problems put them out before the race's end. But Gary didn't make it all the way home safely.

On the way home with Wave driving, a couple in a pickup truck ran a stop sign and slammed into the side of the Bettenhausen station wagon. It's occupants, including Gary and the twins were knocked unconscious. The boys and Gary woke shortly after the crash and sustained cuts and bruises. Wave woke up a week later, her memory gone. She slowly regained it and was sent home from

Merle and Leslie and their handsome offspring. [*Mahoney*]

Above left to right: Cary, Gary and Todd Bettenhausen at the 1982 Hoosier Hundred.

Left: The namesake: Tony Bettenhausen, Jr. midgets and Sprint cars weren't his cup of tea, but he's been very successful in the Indy cars and has a promising career ahead.

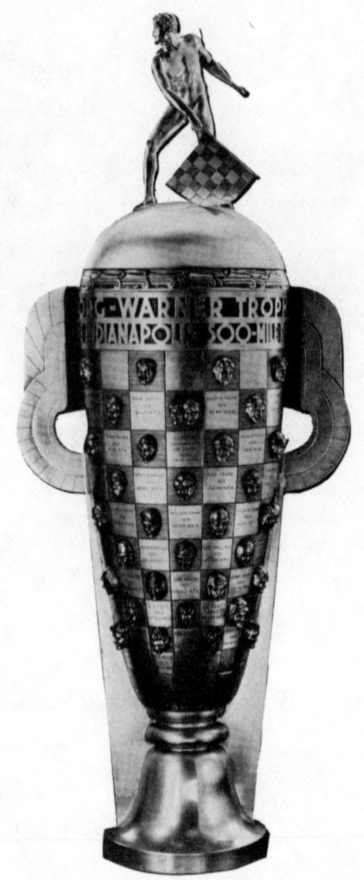

The Borg-Warner Trophy, 80 pounds of sterling silver, is the symbol of Indianapolis victory. The winner of the race has his likeness emblazoned on it - the dream of every "500" driver. It is on permanent display in the Indianapolis 500 Museum. [*IMS*]

the hospital. She continued to complain of body pain, re-entered the hospital and was discovered to have eight broken ribs.

Soon she would find herself bedridden most of the day, waiting for the ribs to heal. Her boys had gone off now to begin their engineering studies at Indiana State University at Terre Haute, Indiana, the town where their father has won more races on the "Action Track" than any other man in history. They want him to be proud of them. Todd even wrote a detailed article for *Open Wheel* magazine about his father's Sprint car. It was printed and he was paid for it. Gary liked that. He also likes the idea that Gary Bettenhausen has two boys in college. They didn't just slide in the door either, he'll tell you. They're National Honor Society members, which means they've graduated in the top two percent of graduating seniors, nation-wide. He's glad they're not home working on some old box, getting it ready for Kokomo, or Springfield or some other dusty little bullring where they pay five bucks to see you risk your neck. He's just past 40 now, and Gary Bettenhausen is coming to terms with himself. He knows it isn't too late. He knows he'd never pull a stunt like that Cogan did on the start of this year's 500. And he knows that everybody else at the Speedway knows it.

There's still a few spaces left on that Borg-Warner trophy and Gary wants to get his hands on one of them. Then just for good measure he'll let his little brother have one too.

The Tinley Park Express will continue down its narrow track.

* * *

Author's Notes

In 1972 Merle and Gary Bettenhausen agreed to allow me to begin work on a biography of their family. Unknown to them at the time, their mother had told one Joe Scalzo that he could do the same thing.

Joe Scalzo can probably be considered one of the finest racing journalists this country has ever known. He now possesses a command of the English language that is second to none.

After Merle phoned Scalzo and told him, "it looks like two guys have been hired to drive the same car," and relieved him of the assignment, he turned to me and said, "You better win the race with this book, buddy."

For the next ten years Merle's statement has stayed with me. The day after I received the green light to write the book, I left on a seven thousand mile interview trip to begin disecting the lives and careers of the Bettenhausens. It was only the first of many such journeys I would make.

A year after writing began, Gary saw me running the welding machine in his shop. He walked up and said, "Welding? Who taught you how to weld?"

"Don Brown and Grant King," I replied.

"I thought you were a writer," the eldest Bettenhausen son asserted. "How are you going to finish our book if you're building a race car? I hope you're faster at writing than you are at building."

I was engrossed and enamored with the racing scene. I wanted to be as close to it every day as possible. Building and driving my own race car, right in the Bettenhausen shop seemed to be the best way to accomplish all my goals at once. So I said, "Well, there's so much going on in your family right now I figured we better wait to finish the book. You've got a Penske ride, you're liable to win Indy, right? Besides, that's the best possible ending for the book isn't it?"

Winning the Speedway. Running the Speedway. It was *the* topic, *the* thing. I thought it was just around the corner for Gary Bettenhausen to win at Indy. Then we'd have a fitting ending for the book.

It soon became evident that a win at Indianapolis was more than 500 miles away. How then would I finish the book? Then I came to realize that even a win at Indy wasn't the end. The victory would have just become the deepest notch in a racing belt that sometimes chokes.

There is no end. A. J. Foyt talked about how badly he wanted his fourth Indy victory for ten full years before achieving it. Now, after twenty-five consecutive starts at Indianapolis, he's searching for the fifth win.

Mechanic George Bignotti is well into his Sixties, financially secure and working every day toward his seventh trip to Indy's victory lane. Every year he talks about retiring and every year the writers say, "Old George will never quit, they'll have to carry him out of the place."

It's not the win at Indy the racers want, it's the challenge. The way of life. It's the feeling that can't be conveyed until it's experienced. I can't tell you what a watermelon tastes like, you have to taste it yourself. Merle Bettenhausen used to be consumed by the aura surrounding the fervor for driving a race car. So was his father. So was Roger Penske when he was a driver. He too was ready to come to the Indianapolis Motor Speedway as a driver when he was under thirty years old but fate kept him away. Henry Banks had suspended him from USAC for running a non-sanctioned race. Today in late 1982, a Roger Penske makes winners in the Indy 500.

If he were to call up Gary Bettenhausen there's no doubt in the writer's mind that the Bettenhausen dream might finally be fulfilled. Will a Tony Bettenhausen, Jr. ever win at Indy? He's becoming capable and given the right set of circumstances and equipment it is entirely possible he could become a winning race car driver.

When a Bettenhausen has his likeness engraved on the Borg-Warner trophy, will the anticipation be as great as the realization? Probably not. It will probably be just like life in general. There will be another race, another mountain.

For decades, the sport of auto racing has fought for recognition in the media. Today there are more televised events than ever before but the general public doesn't equate their own interest with the risk factor involved. While racing is safer than it has been before, it is still a deadly game. "The price you pay for an error is too severe," says Merle Bettenhausen. He was a fiery flash across news pages one day for making a bobble that you can equate to a second baseman tripping over the bag. One man picks himself up and knocks the dust from his knees while the other dreams about the appendage that isn't there. One player belongs to a team that sends him a regular paycheck while the other sacrifices everything including pride sometimes just for the chance to participate.

What makes the breed of man they call a race car driver tick? I hope that by reading the foregoing you've come to at least the shores of their mind. But if you aren't willing to strap on the helmet I'm afraid you'll never know what they do.

Some respect them and others pity them. Don't pity them, they've seen the consequences. They all think they'll beat the odds. For some, driving in the race is living and everything else is just waiting. They're more alive inside the car than out of it. I hope next time you see one of them race you'll know more than when you read the first page of this book. If so, I will have won my own race.

* * *

RACING RECORDS

The following statistics have been mostly compiled by historian Bob Mount of Lebanon, Indiana. Additional work was done by Statistician Donald Davidson of the United States Auto Club, the author and racing journalist John Mahoney.

The records do not represent every race the Bettenhausens have entered since 1939, but we believe well over ninety percent of the events are represented. Some early day statistics are not as complete as we'd like, but our exhaustive research over a ten year period has failed to turn up a more complete listing than what is represented.

Racing Record of Tony Bettenhausen, 1939

Jan. 15	Chicago, Ill. (40 lap midget)	Mary Jane #6	——
Jan. 22	Chicago, Ill. (40 lap midget)	Mary Jane #6	crash-heat
Feb. 14	Chicago, Ill. (40 lap midget)	Mary Jane #6	crashed
Apl. 30	Chicago, ILL. (40 lap midget)	Buzzard Offy	——
May 9	St. Louis, Mo. (35 lap midget)	Buzzard Offy	4th
May 16	St. Louis, Mo. (35 lap midget)	Buzzard Offy	5th
May 23	St. Louis, Mo. (35 lap midget)	Buzzard Offy	——
June 14	St. Louis, Mo. (35 lap midget)	Buzzard Offy	5th
June 20	Chicago, Ill. (40 lap midget)	Buzzard Offy	5th
June 23	Chicago, Ill. (50 lap midget)	Buzzard Offy	——
June 24	Chicago, Ill. (50 lap midget)	Buzzard Offy	——
July 3	Philadelphia, PA (75 lap midget)	?	——
July 11	Bronx, NY (35 lap midget)	?	——
July 17	Philadelphia, PA (50 lap midget)	?	——
July 25	Washington, DC (25 lap midget)	?	——
Aug. 2	Philadelphia, PA (25 lap midget)	?	——
Sept. 28	Los Angeles, CA (? lap midget)	?	6th-consi
Oct. 29	Chicago, IL (40 lap midget)	Mack #8	——
Nov. 3	Chicago, IL (40 lap midget)	Mack #8	6th
Nov. 5	Chicago, IL (40 lap midget)	Mack #8	——
Nov. 9	Houston, TX (30 lap midget)	Crenshaw Spl.	3rd
July 17	Philadelphia, PA (50 lap midget)	?	——
Oct. 29	Chicago, Ill. (40 lap midget)	Mack #8	——
Nov. 3	Chicago, Ill. (40 lap midget)	Mack #8	6th
Nov. 5	Chicago, Ill. (40 lap midget)	Mack #8	——
Nov. 12	Chicago, Ill. (40 lap midget)	Mack #8	5th
Nov. 19	Chicago, Ill. (40 lap midget)	Mack #8	——
Nov. 25	Chicago, Ill. (40 lap midget)	Mack #8	——
Dec. 3	Chicago, Ill. (40 lap midget)	Mack #8	——
Dec. 10	Chicago, Ill. (40 lap midget)	Mack #8	——
Dec. 17	Chicago, Ill. (40 lap midget)	Dauplin 38	5th

1940

Jan. 14	Chicago, Ill. (40 lap midget)	Capper #8	6th
Jan. 21	Chicago, Ill. (40 lap midget)	Capper #8	6th
Jan. 28	Chicago, Ill. (40 lap midget)	Capper #8	4th
Feb. 4	Chicago, Ill. (40 lap midget)	Capper #8	6th
Feb. 11	Chicago, Ill. (40 lap midget)	Capper #8	gave car to Nalon
Feb. 25	Chicago, Ill. (40 lap midget)	Capper #8	6th
Mrh. 3	Chicago, Ill. (40 lap midget)	Capper #8	——
Mrh. 10	Chicago, Ill. (40 lap midget)	Capper #8	4th
Mrh. 17	Chicago, Ill. (40 lap midget)	Capper #8	——
Mrh. 24	Chicago, Ill. (40 lap midget)	O'Day	6th

Mrh. 31	Chicago, Ill. (40 lap midget)	O'Day	5th
May 12	Urbana, Ill. (20 lap midget)	Hansen Offy	1st
May 14	St. Louis, Mo. (35 lap midget)	Hansen Offy	——
May 19	Urbana, Ill. (20 lap midget)	Hansen Offy	——
May 28	St. Louis, Mo. (35 lap midget)	Hansen Offy	1st
June 2	Urbana, Ill. (20 lap midget)	Hansen Offy	2nd
June 13	Cahokia, Ill. (25 lap midget)	Hansen Offy	2nd
June 14	Milwaukee, Wis. (35 lap midget)	Willison #21	5th
June 17	Cahokia, Ill. (25 lap midget)	Willison #21	gearbox-out
June 18	St. Louis, Mo. (35 lap midget)	Willison #21	5th
June 19	New Berlin, Ind. (25 lap midget)	Willison #21	2nd
July 2	Urbana, Ill. (20 lap midget)	Willison #21	3rd
July 3	Cahokia, Ill. (25 lap midget)	Willison #21	3rd
July 4	St. Louis, Mo. (25 lap midget)	Willison #21	——
July 5	Milwaukee, Wis. (35 lap midget)	Willison #21	——
July 7	Kansas City, Mo. (35 lap midget)	Willison #21	crashed
July 16	St. Louis, Mo. (35 lap midget)	Willison #21	2nd
July 18	Cahokia, Ill. (25 lap midget)	Willison #21	out-practice
July 19	Milwaukee, Wis. (40 lap midget)	Willison #21	4th
July 23	St. Louis, Mo. (35 lap midget)	Willison #21	4th
July 25	Cahokia, Ill. (25 lap midget)	Willison #21	——
July 27	Milwaukee, Wis. (40 lap midget)	Willison #21	3rd
Aug. 1	Cahokia, Ill. (25 lap midget)	Willison #21	4th
Aug. 2	Milwaukee, Wis. (40 lap midget)	Willison #21	5th
Aug. 3	Chicago, Ill. (30 lap midget)	Willison #21	3rd
Aug. 6	St. Louis, Mo. (45 lap midget)	Willison #21	5th
Aug. 8	Cahokia, Ill. (25 lap midget)	Willison #21	3rd
Aug. 9	Milwaukee, Wis. (100 lap midget)	Willison #21	5th
Aug. 11	Crown Point, Ind. (15 lap midget)	Willison #21	3rd
Aug. 11	Chicago, Ill. (30 lap midget)	Willison #21	4th
Aug. 16	Cahokia, Ill. (25 lap midget)	Willison #21	——
Aug. 21	Urbana, Ill. (20 lap midget)	Willison #21	2nd
Aug. 22	Milwaukee, Wis. (30 lap sprint)	?	ran in the semi
Aug. 23	St. Louis, Mo. (50 lap midget)	Willison #21	7th
Sept. 1	Mazon, Ill. (20 lap midget)	Willison #21	4th
Sept. 1	Chicago, Ill. (30 lap midget)	Willison #21	4th
Sept. 2	Chicago, Ill. (20 lap midget)	Willison #21	3rd
Sept. 4	Urbana, Ill. (20 lap midget)	Willison #21	2nd
Sept. 7	Chicago, Ill. (30 lap midget)	Willison #21	——
Sept. 11	Urbana, Ill. (20 lap midget)	Nichels #7	1st
Sept. 12	Farmer City, Ill. (20 lap midget)	Nichels #7	3rd
Sept. 14	Chicago, Ill. (30 lap midget)	Nichels #7	4th
Sept. 29	Chicago, Ill. (30 lap midget)	Nichels #7	2nd
Oct. 10	Chicago, Ill. (30 lap midget)	Nichels #7	2nd
Oct. 20	Chicago, Ill. (25 lap midget)	Nichels #7	2nd
Nov. 24	Chicago, Ill. (30 lap midget)	Nichels #7	5th
Dec. 8	Chicago, Ill. (100 lap midget)	Nichels #7	——

1941

Jan. 5	Chicago, Ill. (40 lap midget)	Knight #20	4th
Jan. 12	Chicago, Ill. (40 lap midget)	Knight #20	flipped-broke arm
Apl. 16	Chicago, Ill. (40 lap midget)	?	4th
May 10	Chicago, Ill. (30 lap midget)	?	——
May 11	Dayton, Ohio (25 lap sprint)	Iddings #5	2nd
May 15	Cahokia, Ill. (25 lap midget)	?	1st
May 17	Chicago, Ill. (30 lap midget)	Zale #1	2nd
May 26	Cahokia, Ill. (25 lap midget)	Zale #1	1st
June 1	Dayton, Ohio (25 lap sprint)	Iddings #5	2nd
June 4	Danville, Ill. (20 lap midget)	Zale #1	1st

June 5	Cahokia, Ill. (25 lap sprint)	Zale #1	6th
June 7	Chicago, Ill. (30 lap midget)	Zale #1	1st
June 8	Milwaukee, Wis. (25 lap sprint)	Iddings #5	4th
June 8	Chicago, Ill. (30 lap midget)	Zale #1	3rd
June 13	Monticello, Ill. (20 lap midget)	Zale #1	1st
June 15	Ft. Wayne, Ind. (25 lap sprint)	Iddings #5	3rd
June 18	Danville, Ill. (30 lap midget)	Zale #1	2nd
June 22	Dayton, Ohio (25 lap sprint)	Iddings #5	1st
June 23	St. Louis, Mo. (35 lap midget)	Zale #1	2nd
June 26	Farmer City, Ill. (20 lap midget)	Zale #1	1st
June 29	Winchester, Ind. (25 lap sprint)	Iddings #5	4th
July 1	St. Louis, Mo. (35 lap midget)	Zale #1	didn't make feature
July 4	Milwaukee, Wis. (100 lap midget)	Zale #1	mech.
July 20	Dayton, Ohio (25 lap sprint)	Iddings #5	1st
July 28	Danville, Ill. (25 lap midget)	Zale #1	5th
Aug. 1	Milwaukee, Wis. (100 lap midget)	Zale #1	— —
Aug. 3	Ft. Wayne, Ind. (25 lap sprint)	Iddings #5	3rd
Aug. 10	Winchester, Ind. (25 lap sprint)	Iddings #5	3rd
Aug. 13	Urbana, Ill. (20 lap midget)	Zale #1	1st
Aug. 22	Milwaukee, Wis. (25 lap sprint)	Iddings #5	5th
Aug. 23	Milwaukee, Wis. (30 lap sprint)	Iddings #5	6th
Aug. 24	Milwaukee, Wis. (100 mile champ)	Blue Crown Spark Plug #25	6th
Sept. 1	Syracuse, N.Y. (100 mile champ)	Blue Crown Spark Plug #25	2nd
Sept. 7	Dayton, Ohio (25 lap sprint)	Iddings #5	3rd
Sept. 14	Indianapolis, Ind. (25 lap sprint)	Iddings #5	— —
Sept. 15	Winchester, Ind. (25 lap sprint)	Iddings #5	3rd
Oct. 5	Rockville, Ind. (25 lap sprint)	Iddings #5	2nd
Oct. 12	Hammond, Ind. (25 lap sprint)	Iddings #5	1st
Oct. 19	Hammond, Ind. (20 lap midget)	Zale #1	2nd

1942

Jan. 11	Chicago, IL (100 lap midget)	Tomshe	6th
Feb. 8	Chicago, IL (40 lap midget)	Subjak	mech.
Feb. 15	Chicago, IL (100 lap midget)	Subjak	3rd
Apr. ?	Hammond, IN (? lap midget)	Muntz-Nichels	1st
Apr. ?	Rockville, IN (? lap sprint)	?	1st
Apr. 9	Chicago, IL (30 lap midget)	Subjak	6th
May 16	Chicago, IL (? lap midget)	?	1st
May 19	Chicago, IL (30 lap midget)	Subjak	7th
May 23	Chicago, IL (? lap midget)	Nichels #1	1st
May 24	Dayton, OH (15 lap sprint)	Iddings	1st
May ?	Grand Rapids, MI (20 lap sprint)	Zale	1st
June 6	Chicago, IL (100 lap midget)	Nichels #1	2nd
June 12	Milwaukee, WI (25 lap midget)	Oswald	1st
June 19	Milwaukee, WI (25 lap midget)	Oswald	DNF
June 26	Milwaukee, WI (25 lap midget)	Nichels #1	2nd
June 27	Chicago, IL (330 lap midget)	Ulmer	1st
June 28	Chicago, IL (30 lap midget)	Ulmer	DNF
July 3	Milwaukee, WI (100 lap midget)	Nichels #1	1st
July 4	Chicago, IL (30 lap midget)	Nichels #1	1st
July 7	Chicago, IL (100 lap midget)	Nichels #1	DNF
July 10	Milwaukee, WI (50 lap midget)	Nichels #1	2nd
July 11	Chicago, IL (30 lap midget)	Nichels #1	1st
July 14	Chicago, IL (100 lap midget)	Nichels #1	2nd
July 17	Milwaukee, WI (30 lap midget)	Nichels #1	1st
July 18	Chicago, IL (30 lap midget)	Nichels #1	1st
July 24	Milwaukee, WI (100 lap midget)	Nichels #1	1st
July 29	Chicago, IL (100 lap midget)	Nichels #1	1st

1945

Aug. 29	Chicago, IL (25 lap midget)	Nichels #1	1st
Sept. 1	Chicago, IL (25 lap midget)	Nichels #1	1st
Sept. 5	Chicago, IL (25 lap midget)	Nichels #1	1st
Sept. 17	Farmer City, IL (20 lap midget)	Nichels #1	——
Sept. 26	Chicago, IL (25 lap midget)	Nichels #1	1st
Oct. 21	Toledo, OH (100 lap midget)	Nichels #1	1st

1946

May 5	Crown Point, Ind. (25 lap midget)	Nichels #1	1st
Indianapolis Speedway:		Blue Crown Spark Plug #9	practiced
		Marchese #27	qualified, but withdrawn broken crank.
May 30		Bristow-McManus #42	20th-47 laps
June 11	St. Louis, Mo. (25 lap midget)	Nichels #1	flipped
June 14	Milwaukee, Wis. (30 lap midget)	Nichels #1	1st
June 29	Blue Is, Ill. (25 lap midget)	Nichels #1	withdrew-mech.
July 2	St. Louis, Mo. (25 lap midget)	Nichels #1	4th
July 5	Milwaukee, Wis. (25 lap midget)	Nichels #1	1st
July 6	Blue Is, Ill. (25 lap midget)	Nichels #1	4th
July 7	Blue Is, Ill. (25 lap midget)	Nichels #1	1st
July 11	St. Louis, Mo. (25 lap midget)	Nichels #1	3rd
July 12	Milwaukee, Wis. (50 lap midget)	Nichels #1	1st
July 13	Blue Is, Ill. (25 lap midget)	Nichels #1	1st
July 14	Blue Is, Ill. (25 lap midget)	Nichels #7	1st
July 18	Farmer City, Ill. (20 lap midget)	Nichels #1	2nd
July 18	St. Louis, Mo. (25 lap midget)	Nichels #1	3rd
July 19	Milwaukee, Wis. (25 lap midget)	Nichels #1	9th
July 20	Blue Is, Ill. (25 lap midget)	Nichels #1	4th
July 21	Blue Is, Ill. (25 lap midget)	Nichels #1	2nd
July 23	St. Louis, Mo. (25 lap midget)	Nichels #1	2nd
July 26	Milwaukee, Wis. (30 lap midget)	Nichels #1	1st
July 27	Blue Is, Ill. (25 lap midget)	Nichels #1	2nd
July 30	St. Louis, Mo. (25 lap midget)	Nichels #1	blew engine-practice
Aug. 2	Milwaukee, Wis. (30 lap midget)	Nichels #1	1st
Aug. 3	Blue Is, Ill (25 lap midget)	Nichels #1	2nd
Aug. 9	Milwaukee, Wis. (100 lap midget)	Nichels #1	1st
Aug. 11	Chicago, Ill. (25 lap midget)	Nichels #1	1st
Aug. 20	Los Angeles, Cal. (Col. 30 lap midget)	Halibrand	——
Aug. 22	Los Angeles, Cal. (Gil. 30 lap midget)	Halibrand	6th
Sept. 3	St. Louis, Mo. (50 lap midget)	Acme #5	hit wall
Sept. 5	S. Bend, Ind. (25 lap midget)	Oswald Elto	1st
Sept. 8	Chicago, Ill. (25 lap midget)	Acme #5	2nd
Sept. 13	Milwaukee, Wis. (50 lap midget)	Acme #5	3rd
Sept. 15	Indianapolis, Ind. (100 mile champ)	Corley #67	5th
Sept. 22	Milwaukee, Wis. (100 mile champ)	Corley #67	9th
Sept. 29	S. Bend, Ind. (25 lap midget)	Oswald Elto	1st
Oct. 6	Goshen, N.Y. (100 mile champ)	Norm Olson #7	1st
Oct. 13	Blue Is, Ill. (50 lap midget)	Acme #5	1st
Nov. 10	Chicago, Ill. (25 lap midget)	Nichels #1	4th
Dec. 14	Chicago, Ill. (25 lap midget)	Tomshe #1	1st

1947

Jan. 11	Chicago, Ill. (25 lap midget)	Nichels #2	1st
Jan. 25	Chicago, Ill. (25 lap midget)	Nichels #2	2nd

Feb. 8	Chicago, Ill. (25 lap midget)	Nichels #2	flipped 2nd heat
Apl. 27	Terre Haute, Ind. (25 lap midget)	Nichels#2	didn't finish
May 2	S. Bend, Ind. (25 lap midget)	Nichels #2	1st
Indianapolis Speedway:			
May 30		Thorne Eng. #21	spun S.W. turn
		Belanger #29	18th 79 laps-gear train
June 2	Chicago, Ill. (25 lap midget)	Nichels #2	5th
June 5	Detroit, Mich. (25 lap midget)	Nichels #2	4th
June 3	St. Louis, Mo. (25 lap midget)	Nichels #1	flipped qualifying
June 4	Kenosha, Wis. (25 lap midget)	Nichels #1	didn't finish
June 8	Milwaukee, Wis. (100 mile champ)	Belanger #16	43 laps mech.
June 11	St. Louis, Mo. (25 lap midget)	Nichels #1	2nd
June 11	Chicago, Ill. (20 lap midget)	Nichels #1	1st
June 20	Milwaukee, Wis. (30 lap midget)	Nichels #1	1st
June 22	Langhorne, Pa. (100 mile champ)	Wolfe #15	14th
June 24	St. Louis, Mo. (25 lap midget)	Nichels #1	3rd
June 25	Blue Island, Ill. (25 lap midget)	Nichels #1	1st
June 26	Sisters Lake, Mich. (25 lap midget)	Tuffy #23	didn't finish
June 27	Milwaukee, Wis. (25 lap midget)	Nichels #1	4th
June 28	Crown Point, Ind. (25 lap midget)	Nichels #1	2nd
June 29	Chicago, Ill. (25 lap midget)	Tuffy's #23	didn't finish
July 1	St. Louis, Mo. (25 lap midget)	Tuffy's #23	4th
July 3	Sisters Lake, Mich. (25 lap midget)	Tuffy's #23	7th
July 4	Blue Is, Ill. (25 lap midget)	Tuffy's #23	1st
July 8	St. Louis, Mo. (25 lap midget)	Tuffy's #23	5th
July 10	Sisters Lake, Mich. (25 lap midget)	Tuffy's #23	2nd
July 10	Blue Is, Ill. (25 lap midget)	Tuffy's #23	1st
July 11	Milwaukee, Wis. (25 lap midget)	Tuffy's #23	flipped qualifying
July 13	Bainbridge, O. (100 mile champ)	Wolfe #15	4th
July 16	St. Louis, Mo. (25 lap midget)	Tuffy's #23	5th
July 21	Chicago, Ill (50 lap midget)	Tuffy's #23	didn't finish
July 26	"Rendevous Bowl" (25 lap midget)	Tuffy's #23	1st
July 27	Milwaukee, Wis. (100 mile champ)	Olson #6	11th
July 27	Chicago, Ill. (25 lap midget)	Tuffy's #23	5th
July 31	Sisters Lake, Mich. (25 lap midget)	Tuffy's #23	3rd
Aug. 1	Milwaukee, Wis. (100 lap midget)	Tuffy's #1	4th
Aug. 2	Blue Is, Ill. (25 lap midget)	Tuffy's #1	2nd
Aug. 7	Sisters Lake, Mich. (25 lap midget)	Tuffy's #1	1st
Aug. 8	Milwaukee, Wis. (25 lap midget)	Tuffy's #1	1st
Aug. 9	Blue Is, Ill. (50 lap midget)	Tuffy's #1	2nd
Aug. 10	Chicago, Ill. (50 lap midget)	Tuffy's #1	2nd
Aug. 13	Blue Is, Ill. (25 lap midget)	Tuffy's #1	3rd
Aug. 14	Sisters Lake, Mich. (25 lap midget)	Tuffy's #1	3rd-beat Mays in a special match race
Aug. 17	Goshen, N.Y. (100 mile champ)	Belanger #16	1st
Aug. 18	Indianapolis, Ind. (25 lap midget)	Tuffy's #1	——
Aug. 20	Blue Is, Ill. (25 lap midget)	Tuffy's #1	12th
Aug. 21	Milwaukee, Wis. (20 lap sprint)	Belanger #16	6th
Aug. 22	Milwaukee, Wis. (20 lap sprint)	Belanger #16	4th
Aug. 23	Blue Is, Ill. (25 lap midget)	Tuffy's #1	1st
Aug. 24	Milwaukee, Wis. (100 mile champ)	Belanger #16	4th rel. by Mays
Aug. 27	Blue Is, Ill. (25 lap midget)	Tuffy's #1	1st
Aug. 28	Sisters Lake, Mich. (25 lap midget)	Tuffy's #1	2nd
Aug. 29	Milwaukee, Wis. (25 lap midget)	Tuffy's #1	2nd
Aug. 30	Blue Is. Ill. (25 lap midget)	Tuffy's #1	1st
Sept. 2	Mendota, Ill. (25 lap midget)	Tuffy's #1	1st
Sept. 5	Milwaukee, Wis. (25 lap midget)	Ullmer #26	4th
Sept. 6	Blue Is, Ill. (25 lap midget)	Tuffy's #1	5th
Sept. 11	Milwaukee, Wis. (50 lap midget)	Tuffy's #21	1st
Sept. 13	Blue Is, Ill. (25 lap midget)	Tuffy's #21	1st

Sept. 18	Sisters Lake, Mich. (25 lap midget)	Tuffy's #21	6th
Sept. 28	Springfield, Ill. (100 mile champ)	Belanger #16	1st
Oct. 5	Crown Point, Ind. (150 lap midget)	Tuffy's #1	10th
Nov. 2	Arlington, Tex. (100 mile champ)	Belanger #16	50 laps-mech.

1948

Feb. 8	Chicago, Ill. (30 lap midget)	Tuffy's #22	spun out 1st lap
Feb. 21	Chicago, Ill. (30 lap midget)	Tuffy's #22	3rd
Apl. 17	Wms. Grove, Pa. (30 lap sprint)		didn't finish
May 31	Indianapolis, Ind. (500 mile champ)	Belanger #6	14th-167 laps clutch

20 laps-8th 120 laps-7th
60 laps-7th 140 laps-5th
80 laps-5th 160 laps-5th
100 laps-5th

June 6	Milwaukee, Wis. (100 mile champ)	Belanger #16	16th
June 20	Langhorne, Pa. (100 mile champ)	Belanger #16	10th
July 17	Chicago, Ill. (50 lap midget)	Bettenhausen #16	didn't make feature
July 18	Milwaukee, Wis. (25 lap sprint)	Belanger #16	1st
July 21	Rockford, Ill. (30 lap midget)	Bettenhausen #1	9th
July 23	Milwaukee, Wis. (100 lap midget)	Bettenhausen #1	4th
July 24	Chicago, Ill. (60 lap midget)	Bettenhausen #1	didn't make feature
July 25	Indianapolis, Ind. (75 lap midget)	Bettenhausen #1	11th
July 26	Anderson, Ind. (30 lap midget)	Bettenhausen #1	didn't finish
July 27	St. Louis, Mo. (30 lap midget)	Bettenhausen #1	5th
July 31	Chicago, Ill. (40 lap midget)	Haddad #2	4th
Aug. 1	Indianapolis, Ind. (30 lap midget)	Haddad #2	5th
Aug. 3	St. Louis, Mo. (30 lap midget)	Bettenhausen #1	3rd
Aug. 8	Milwaukee, Wis. (100 mile midget)	Bettenhausen #1	12th
Aug. 10	Milwaukee, Wis. (20 lap sprint)	Belanger #16	10th
Aug. 11	Milwaukee, Wis. (30 lap sprint)	Belanger #16	hit wall qualifying
Aug. 15	Milwaukee, Wis. (100 mile champ)	Schoof #78	6th
Aug. 17	St. Louis, Mo. (30 lap midget)	Bettenhausen #1	3rd
Aug. 18	Rockford, Ill. (60 lap midget)	Bettenhausen #1	3rd
Aug. 21	Springfield, Ill. (100 mile champ)	Belanger #16	6th
Aug. 24	St. Louis, Mo. (50 lap midget)	Bettenhausen #1	4th
Aug. 25	Rockford, Ill. (30 lap midget)	Bettenhausen #1	4th
Aug. 28	Chicago, Ill. (40 lap midget)	Bettenhausen #1	7th
Aug. 29	Milwaukee, Wis. (200 mile champ) rel. Myron Fohr	Thorne Eng. #22 Marchese #32	20th-20 laps 1st
Sept. 4	DuQuoin, Ill. (100 mile champ)	Belanger #16	10th
Sept. 10	Milwaukee, Wis. (50 lap midget)	Bettenhausen #1	1st
Sept. 12	DuQuoin, Ill. (100 mile midget)	Bettenhausen #1	car caught fire qualifying and he was burned on legs.

1949

May 28	Indianapolis, Ind. (Speedway)	Flavell-Duffy #46	qualified and bumped
May 29	Indianapolis, Ind. (Speedway)	Alfa-Romeo #16	too slow
July 16	Arlington Downs, Tex. (50 lap sprint)	Meyer and Drake #99	4th
July 18	St. Louis, Mo. (50 lap midget)	Bardahl #37	4th
July 20	Fairbury, Ill. (35 lap midget)	Bardahl #37	3rd
July 22	Milwaukee, Wis. (50 lap midget)	Bardahl #37	4th
July 26	St. Louis, Mo. (50 lap midget)	Bardahl #37	4th
July 29	Milwaukee, Wis. (25 lap midget)	Bardahl #37	1st
July 31	Kokomo, Ind. (25 lap midget)	Bettenhausen #1	2nd
Aug. 7	Kokomo, Ind. (25 lap midget)	Bardahl #37	2nd

Aug. 5	Milwaukee, Wis. (100 lap midget)	Bardahl #37	8th
Aug. 14	St. Louis, Mo. (30 lap midget)	Bardahl #37	3rd
Aug. 14	Kokomo, Inc. (30 lap midget)	Bardahl #37	2nd
Aug. 15	St. Louis, Mo. (30 lap midget)	Bardahl #37	5th
Aug. 20	Springfield, Ill. (100 mile champ)	Meyer and Drake #99	out-mech. trouble
Aug. 21	Milwaukee, Wis. (100 lap midget)	Bardahl #37	28th
Aug. 26	Milwaukee, Wis. (100 lap stock)	Oldsmobile	24th
Aug. 28	Milwaukee, Wis. (200 mile champ)	Meyer and Drake #99	15th
Aug. 30	St. Louis, Mo. (75 lap midget)	Bardahl #37	5th
Sept. 3	DuQuoin, Ill. (100 mile champ)	Meyer and Drake #99	1st
Sept. 6	DuQuoin, Ill. (100 lap midget)	Acme #34	led laps 1-85 out with oil leak
Sept. 10	Syracuse, N.Y. (100 mile champ)	Speedway Cocktail #45	9th rel. by Otis Stine
Sept. 11	Detroit, Mich. (100 mile champ)	Belanger #99	1st
Sept. 25	Springfield, Ill. (100 mile champ)	Belanger #99	9th
Oct. 16	Langhorne, Pa. (100 mile champ)	Belanger #99	failed to qualify
Nov. 6	Del Mar, Cal. (100 mile champ)	Belanger #99	mech. trouble

1950

May 30	Indianapolis, Ind. (500 mile champ)	Blue Crown Spark Plug #14	31st-30 laps wheel bearing
	(rel. Joie Chitwood at 84 laps)	Wolfe #17	5th
June 4	Chicago, Ill. (40 lap midget)	Haddad #17	11th
June 11	Milwaukee, Wis. (100 mile champ)	Belanger #34	1st-led 1-100
June 16	Milwaukee, Wis. (75 lap midget)	Haddad #17	didn't make feature
June 25	Langhorne, Pa. (100 mile champ)	Belanger #34	14th
July 30th	Chicago, Ill. (100 lap midget)	Holton #73	14th
Aug. 4	Milwaukee, Wis. (100 lap midget)	Pat Clancy #22	1st
Aug. 6	Kokomo, Ind. (30 lap midget)	Pat Clancy #22	2nd
Aug. 13	Chicago, Ill. (40 lap midget)	Lund #93	1st
Aug. 19	Springfield, Ill. (100 mile champ)	Shaheen #39	12th-led 1-25
Aug. 20	Milwaukee, Wis. (100 mile midget)	Lund #93	1st
Aug. 27	Milwaukee, Wis. (200 mile champ)	Shaheen #39	18th
Sept. 9	Syracuse, NY (100 mile champ)	Belanger #99	12th-led 1-24
Sept. 10	Detroit, Mich. (100 mile champ)	Belanger #99	10th-led 49-88
Sept. 17th	Chicago, Ill. (100 lap midget)	Lund #93	2nd
Oct. 1	Springfield, Ill. (100 mile champ)	Belanger #99	1st-led 1-100
Oct. 15	Sacramento, Cal. (100 mile champ)	Belanger #99	17th-crashed
Nov. 12	Phoenix, Ariz. (100 mile champ)	Belanger #99	2nd-led 1-80
Nov. 26	Bay Meadows, Cal. (150 mile champ)	Belanger #99	1st-led 1-149
Dec. 10	Darlington, S.C. (200 mile champ)	Belanger #99	20th

1951

Jan. 13	Chicago, Ill. (25 lap midget)	Turner #82	1st
Jan. 21	Chicago, Ill. (25 lap midget)	Turner #82	failed to make feature
Jan. 27	Chicago, Ill. (100 lap midget)	Turner #82	6th-flipped, continued
May 30	Indianapolis, Ind. (500 mile champ)	Mobiloil #5	9th-178 laps spun NW turn
June 3	Chicago, Ill. (100 lap midget)	Lund #93	12th
June 6	St. Louis, Mo. (100 lap midget)	Bardahl #93	spun lap 75
June 10	Milwaukee, Wis. (100 lap champ)	Belanger #99	1st-led 81-100
June 16	Milwaukee, Wis. (100 lap midget)	Bardahl #93	13th
June 24	Langhorne, Pa. (100 mile champ)	Belanger #99	1st-led 85-100
July 4	Darlington, S.C. (250 mile champ)	Belanger #99	2nd

July 7	Chicago, Ill. (100 lap midget)	Bardahl #93	7th
July 15	Milwaukee, Wis. (150 mile stock)	Oldsmobile #99	2nd
July 29	Wms Grove, Pa. (50 lap champ)	Belanger #99	2nd
Aug. 9	Moline, Ill. (100 lap midget)	Bardahl #93	failed to make feature
Aug. 11	Milwaukee, Wis. (100 lap midget)	Bardahl #93	1st
Aug. 18	Springfield, Ill. (100 mile champ)	Belanger #99	1st-led 20-100
Aug. 19	Milwaukee, Wis. (100 mile midget)	Bardahl #93	24th
Aug. 23	Milwaukee, Wis. (100 mile stock)	Chrysler #99	11th
Aug. 24	Milwaukee, Wis. (100 mile stock)	Mercury #87	5th
Aug. 26	Milwaukee, Wis. (200 mile champ)	Belanger #99	10th
Aug. 31	Chicago, Ill. (100 lap midget)	Bardahl #93	15th
Sept. 1	DuQuoin, Ill. (100 mile champ)	Belanger #99	1st-led 8-100
Sept. 3	DuQuoin, Ill. (200 mile champ)	Belanger #99	1st-led 1-101
Sept. 6	Moline, Ill. (100 lap midget)	Bardahl #93	failed to make feature
Sept. 8	Syracuse, NY (100 mile champ)	Belanger #99	1st-led 1-67
Sept. 9	Detroit, Mich. (100 mile champ)	Belanger #99	4th-led 1-97
Sept. 23	Denver, Col. (100 mile champ)	Belanger #99	1st-led 1-100
Oct. 21	San Jose, Cal. (100 mile champ)	Belanger #99	1st-led 6-100
Nov. 4	Phoenix, Ariz. (100 mile champ)	Belanger #99	13th-led 3-89
Nov. 11	Bay Meadows, Cal. (150 mile champ)	Belanger #99	2nd-led 32-129
Nov. 20-25	Mexican Road Race (1933 miles)	Kiekhaefer Chrysler Saratoga	16th

1951 National Championship Standings

1. Tony Bettenhausen
2. Henry Banks
3. Walt Faulkner
4. Jack McGrath
5. Mike Nazaruk
6. Johnnie Parsons
7. Lee Wallard
8. Manny Ayulo
9. Andy Linden
10. Paul Russo

1952

Mrh. 2	Bay Meadows, Cal. (100 lap midget)	Fuel Injection	6th
May 24	Indianapolis Speedway (qualifying)	Belanger #99	hit wall-south chute
May 30	Indianapolis, Ind. (500 mile champ)	Blue Crown Spark Plug #27	24th-93 laps stalled
June 8	Milwaukee, Wis. (100 mile champ)	Belanger #99	failed to qualify

1953

May 30	Indianapolis, Ind. (500 mile champ)	Agajanian #98	9th-196 laps crashed turn 3 by Hartley

20 laps-7th 140 laps-8th (Stevenson)
60 laps-5th 180 laps-10th (Hartley)
120 laps-6th

Sept. 7	DuQuoin, Ill. (100 mile champ)	Miracle Power #99	18th rear-end 87 laps led laps 1-70
Sept. 12	Syracuse, NY (100 mile champ)	Miracle Power #99	1st
Sept. 26	Indianapolis, Ind. (100 mile champ)	Miracle Power #99	6th
Oct. 25	Sacramento, Cal. (100 mile champ)	didn't enter	
Nov. 11	Phoenix, Ariz. (100 mile champ)	Miracle Power #99	1st
Nov. 19-23	Mexican Road Race (1833 miles)	Kurtis Kraft (drove with Merle Belanger)	DNF

1953 National Championship Standings

1. Sam Hanks
2. Jack McGrath
3. Bill Vukovich
4. Manny Ayulo
5. Paul Russo
6. Art Crass
7. Don Freeland
8. Chuck Stevenson
9. Jimmy Bryan
10. Tony Bettenhausen

1954

May 30	Indianapolis, Ind. (500 mile champ)	Mel Wiggers #10	29th-105 laps bearing
June 6	Milwaukee, Wis. (100 mile champ)	Mel Wiggers #10	failed to qualify
June 25	Chicago, Ill. (100 lap midget)	Krech #76	failed to make feature
June 27	Reading, Pa. (100 lap midget)	Krech #76	flipped after hitting Bryan
July 11	Milwaukee, Wis. (150 mile stock)	Chrysler	1st
July 16	Kokomo, Ind. (100 lap midget)	C. Nalon #58	3rd
July 17	Indianapolis, Ind. (100 lap midget)	C. Nalon #58	failed to make feature
July 23	Chicago, Ill. (100 lap midget)	H. Turner #3	13th-spun out
Aug. 7	Detroit, Mich. (75 lap midget)	H. Turner #3	failed to make feature
Aug. 10	Jeffersonville, Ind. (100 lap midget)	H. Turner #3	3rd
Aug. 18	Chicago, Ill. (250 lap midget)	H. Turner #3	crashed 120th lap while leading. Skull fracture & shoulder injury.
Nov. 7	Phoenix, Ariz. (100 mile champ)	Blakely #41	16th-50 laps, brake line
Nov. 14	Las Vegas, Nev. (100 mile champ)	Blakely #41	17th-2 laps-crashed

Note: On May 31 he drove the Novi at the Speedway on a test and ran a lap at 141.4.

1955

Apl. 3	Dayton, Ohio (30 lap sprint)	HOW #2	5th
Apl. 10	Oklahoma City, Okl. (30 lap sprint)	HOW #2	——
Apl 17	Kansas City, Mo. (30 lap sprint)	HOW #2	spun on lap 10
May 1	Salem, Ind. (30 lap sprint)	HOW #2	4th
May 30	Indianapolis, Ind. (500 mile champ)	Chapman #10	2nd
	20 laps-4th	120 laps-6th (Russo)	
	40 laps-6th	140 laps-8th	
	60 laps-5th	160 laps-4th	
	80 laps-7th (Russo)	180 laps-3rd	
	100 laps-7th (Russo)	200 laps-2nd	
June 26	Dayton, Ohio (30 lap sprint)	LaVilla #1	8th
July 2	Knoxville, Tenn. (100 lap stock)	Chrysler #99	2nd
July 13	Illiana, Ind. (50 lap midget)	H. Turner #82	3rd
July 17	Milwaukee, Wis. (150 mile stock)	Chrysler #99	crashed qualifying
July 22	Galesburg, Mich. (50 lap midget)	H. Turner #82	3rd
July 30	Jeffersonville, Ind. (100 lap midget)	H. Turner #82	2nd
Aug. 20	Springfield, Ill. (100 mile champ)	Chapman #10	failed to qualify
Aug. 21	Milwaukee, Wis. (100 mile stock)	Chrysler #99	——
Aug. 25	Milwaukee, Wis. (250 mile stock)	Chrysler #99	1st
Aug. 28	Milwaukee, Wis. (250 mile champ)	Chapman #10	2nd
Sept. 3	DuQuoin, Ill. (100 mile stock)	Chrysler #99	——
Sept. 5	DuQuoin, Ill. (100 mile champ)	Chapman #10	failed to qualify
Sept. 11	Indianapolis, Ind. (150 lap midget)	H. Turner #82	failed to make feature
Sept. 17	Indianapolis, Ind. (100 mile champ)	Belanger #99	4th
Sept. 18	Milwaukee, Wis. (200 mile stock)	Chrysler #99	18th
Oct. 9	Terre Haute, Ind. (100 lap midget)	H. Turner #82	1st
Oct. 23	Fresno, Cal. (100 lap midget)	Quellia #5	——
Nov. 1	Los Angeles, Cal. (100 lap midget)	Quellia #5	1st
Nov. 6	Phoenix, Ariz. (100 mile champ)	Sweikert #55	8th
Nov. 13	San Diego, Cal. (100 lap midget)	Quellia #5	1st
Nov. 24	Los Angeles, Cal. (150 lap midget)	Quellia #5	failed to make feature

1955 National Championship Standings

1. Bob Sweikert	6. Jimmy Davies
2. Jimmy Bryan	7. Pat O'Connor
3. Johnny Thomson	8. Pat Flaherty
4. Tony Bettenhausen	9. George Amick
5. Andy Linden	10. Walt Faulkner

1956

Mar. 4	Clovis, CA (100 lap stock)	Parsons Dodge	5th
Apr. 8	Fresno, CA (100 lap midget)	?	flipped/warmups
Apr. 21	Gardena, CA (100 lap midget)	Ken Smith Spl.	12th
Apr. 22	Vallejo, CA (100 lap stock)	Parsons Dodge	21st
May 30	Indianapolis, IN (500 mile champ)	Belanger #99	22nd-crashed
Aug. 4	Knoxville, TN (100 lap stock)	Everett Chevrolet	9th
Aug. 12	Wms. Grove, Pa. (30 lap sprint)	Schmidt #44	2nd
Aug. 18	Springfield, Ill. (100 mile champ)	Schmidt #44	hit fence qualifying
	Rel. Rex Easton lap 30	Iddings #57	13th
Aug. 19	New Bremen, Ohio (30 lap sprint)	Schmidt #44	6th
Aug. 25	Milwaukee, Wis. (100 lap midget)	H. Turner #82	mech. led most of race
Aug. 26	Milwaukee, Wis. (250 mile champ)	Schmidt #44	failed to qualify
	Rel. Elmer George lap 155	HOW #21	20th-200 laps transmission
Sept. 1	Jeffersonville, Ind. (midget)	H. Turner #82	1st
Sept. 2	DuQuoin, Ill. (30 lap spring)	Schmidt #44	4th
Sept. 3	DuQuoin, Ill. (100 mile champ)	Schmidt #44	8th
Sept. 8	Syracuse, N.Y. (100 mile champ)	Schmidt #44	1st-led laps 19-100
Sept. 15	Indianapolis, Ind. (100 mile champ)	Schmidt #44	18th-5 laps hit fence turn one
Sept. 23	Salem, Ind. (100 lap sprint)	Schmidt #44	4th
Sept. 30	Dayton, OH (100 lap midget)	H. Turner #82	3rd
Oct. 7	Terre Haute, Ind. (100 lap midget)	H. Turner #82	1st
Oct. 13	San Bernadino, CA (100 lap midget)	Turner #82	11th
Oct. 21	Sacramento, CA (100 lap champ)	Dayton Steel #96	14th-61 laps spun turn one
Nov. 12	Phoenix, AZ (100 mile champ)	Dayton Steel #96	9th
Nov. 22	Gardena, CA (150 lap midget)	Turner #82	

1957

May 12	Indianapolis, Ind. (practice)	Jim Robbins #35	spun in turn one
May 30	Indianapolis, Ind. (500 mile champ)	Novi Air Cond. #27	15th-195 laps
	20 laps-5th 40 laps-8th 60 laps-9th		
June 8	Chicago, Ill. (100 lap midget)	H. Turner #82	3rd
June 29	Monza, Italy (500 mile champ)	Novi Air Cond. #27	12th-45 laps mech.
July 10	Blue Island, Ill. (100 lap midget)	H. Turner #82	2nd
July 27	Chicago, Ill. (100 lap midget)	H. Turner #82	5th
Aug. 21	Chicago, Ill. (100 lap midget)	H. Turner #82	——
Aug. 24	Milwaukee, Wis. (100 lap midget)	H. Turner #82	early leader-mech. tro.
Aug. 25	Milwaukee, Wis. (200 mile champ)	Morcroft #27	21st-72 laps-brakes
Sept. 2	DuQuoin, Ill. (100 mile champ)	Morcroft #27	15th-68 laps-hit fence turn four
Sept. 4	Illiana, Ind. (50 lap midget)	H. Turner #82	1st
Sept. 7	Syracuse, N.Y. (100 mile champ)	Federal Eng. #33	failed to qualify
Sept. 14	Indianapolis, Ind. (100 mile champ)	Federal Eng. #33	11th-96 laps
Sept. 29	Trenton, N.J. (100 mile champ)	Federal Eng. #4	7th-98 laps

Oct. 6	Terre Haute, Ind. (100 lap midget)	H. Turner #82	mech.-failed to start
Oct. 20	Sacramento, Cal. (100 mile champ)	Las Vegas Club #45	18th-0 laps hit fence turn one
Sept. 15	Blue Island, Ill. (100 lap midget)	H. Turner #82	3rd

1958

Jan. 19	Riverside, Cal. (100 lap midget)	London #5	7th
Mrh. 30	Trenton, N.J. (100 mile champ)	Hardwood Door #35	2nd-led laps 11-18, 39-54
May 31	Indianapolis, Ind. (500 mile champ)	Jones & Maley #33	4th-led laps: 19-20, 22-25, 35-49, 53-65, 105-107
	20 laps-1st	120 laps-5th	
	40 laps-3rd	140 laps-4th	
	60 laps-1st	160 laps-6th	
	80 laps-2nd	180 laps-5th	
	100 laps-2nd	200 laps-4th	
June 8	Milwaukee, Wis. (100 mile champ)	Hardwood Door #35	2nd-led laps 80-93
June 15	Langhorne, Pa. (100 mile champ)	Hardwood Door #35	5th
July 4	Atlanta, Ga. (100 mile champ)	Hardwood Door #35	18th-14 laps magneto
Aug. 16	Springfield, Ill. (100 mile champ)	Hardwood Door #35	12th-82 laps-mech.
Aug. 23	Milwaukee, Wis. (100 lap midget)	Hardwood Door #35	1st-led only last lap to beat Branson
Aug. 24	Milwaukee, Wis. (200 mile champ)	Hardwood Door #35	25th-36 laps magneto
Sept. 1	DuQuoin, Ill. (100 mile champ)	John Zink #5	2nd-led laps 57-96
Sept. 6	Syracuse, N.Y. (100 mile champ)	John Zink #5	3rd
Sept. 13	Indianapolis, Ind. (100 mile champ)	John Zink #5	5th-led laps 2-48
Sept. 28	Trenton, N.J. (100 mile champ)	John Zink #5	3rd
Oct. 26	Sacramento, Cal. (100 mile champ)	John Zink #5	5th
Nov. 11	Phoenix, Ariz. (100 mile champ)	John Zink #5	2nd
Dec. 28	Los Angeles, Cal. (100 lap midget)	London #5	7th

1958 National Championship Standings

1. Tony Bettenhausen
2. George Amick
3. Johnny Thomson
4. Jud Larson
5. Rodger Ward
6. Jimmy Bryan
7. Eddie Sachs
8. Johnny Boyd
9. Don Branson
10. A. J. Foyt

1959

Apl. 4	Daytona, Fla. (100 mile champ)	Racing Assc. #75	18th-6 laps-oil leak
Apl. 19	Trenton, N.J. (100 mile champ)	Central Exc. #81	1st-led laps 2-25, 27-34, 49-87
May 16	Indianapolis, Ind. (practice)	Ansted Rotary #1	flipped in south chute
May 30	Indianapolis, Ind. (500 mile champ)	Hoover Motor Exp. #1	4th
	20 laps-7th	120 laps-6th	200 laps-4th
	60 laps-6th	140 laps-6th	
	80 laps-5th	160 laps-4th	
	100 laps-7th	180 laps-4th	
June 7	Milwaukee, Wis. (100 mile champ)	Central Exc. #81	17th-75 laps-blew engine spun turn tour
June 14	Langhorne, Pa. (100 mile champ)	Dean Van Lines #83	17th-21 laps-mech.

July 19	Milwaukee, Wis. (150 mile stock)	Ford #99	1st
Aug. 22	Springfield, Ill. (100 mile champ)	John Zink #1	17th-10 laps-piston
Aug. 23	Milwaukee, Wis. (150 mile stock)	Ford #99	——
Aug. 29	Milwaukee, Wis. (100 lap midget)	Linne #96	64 laps-fuel line led laps 48-64
Aug. 30	Milwaukee, Wis. (200 mile champ)	John Zink #1	16th-159 laps-spun turn three-led laps 6-61, 73-159
Sept. 6	DuQuoin, Ill. (100 lap midget)	Linne #96	1st
Sept. 7	DuQuoin, Ill. (100 mile champ)	John Zink #1	3rd
Sept. 12	Syracuse, N.Y. (100 mile champ)	John Zink #1	6th-spun turn one after finishing
Sept. 19	Indianapolis, Ind. (100 mile champ)	Hopkins #16	15th-57 laps-spun turn 2 after clipping Hurtubise
Sept. 27	Trenton, N.J. (100 mile champ)	Simoniz #16	2nd
Oct. 11	Houston, Texas (50 lap sprint)	Sherk #5	5th
Oct. 18	Phoenix, Ariz. (100 mile champ)	Hopkins #16	1st-led laps 46-100
Oct. 25	Sacramento, Cal. (100 mile champ)	Hopkins #16	8th-72 laps-mech. led laps 1-16
Nov. 20	San Antonio, Tx. (50 lap midget)	Linne #96	1st
Nov. 22	Houston, Texas (100 lap midget)	Linne #96	5th
Nov. 26	Gardena, Cal. (100 lap midget)	Linne #96	1st
Aug. 1	Champaign, Ill. (40 lap midget)	Linne #96	7th

1960

Apl. 10	Trenton, N.J. (100 mile champ)	Dowgard #2	2nd
May 30	Indianapolis, Ind. (500 mile champ) 20 laps-5th 80 laps-5th 40 laps-3rd 100 laps-4th 60 laps-4th 120 laps-4th	Dowgard #2	23rd-125 laps-rod
June 5	Milwaukee, Wis. (100 mile champ)	Dowgard #2	4th
June 26	Milwaukee, Wis. (twin 50 sprints)	Competition Eng. #8	1st: 5th 2nd: failed to finish
July 24	Milwaukee, Wis. (200 mile stock)	Ford #99	1st
July 31	Dayton, Ohio (30 lap midget)	Linne #96	3rd
Aug. 20	Springfield, Ill. (100 mile champ)	Dowgard #2	15th-30 laps radius rod
Aug. 21	Milwaukee, Wis. (250 mile stock)	Ford #99	——
Aug. 22-23	Indianapolis, Ind. (tire test)	Braund Plywood #45	
Aug. 25	Milwaukee, Wis. (200 mile stock)	Ford #99	1st
Aug. 27	Milwaukee, Wis. (100 lap midget)	Linne #96	1st
Aug. 28	Milwaukee, Wis. (200 mile champ)	Dowgard #2	14th-182 laps-rear end led laps 60-182
Sept. 4	DuQuoin, Ill. (100 lap midget)	Linne #96	2nd
Sept. 5.	DuQuoin, Ill. (100 mile champ)	Dowgard #2	2nd
Sept. 10	Syracuse, N.Y. (100 mile champ)	Dowgard #2	2nd
Sept. 17	Indianapolis, Ind. (100 mile champ)	Dowgard #2	2nd
Sept. 25	Trenton, N.J. (100 mile champ)	Dowgard #2	6th
Oct. 30	Sacramento, Cal. (100 mile champ)	Dowgard #2	5th
Nov. 20	Phoenix, Ariz. (100 mile champ)	Dowgard #2	16th-4 laps-spun turn 1 hit by Branson & Hulse

1961

Apl. 9	Trenton, N.J. (100 mile champ)	Autolite #5	19th-31 laps-magneto
May	Indianapolis, Ind. (practice)	Autolite #5	
May 12	Indianapolis, Ind. (practice)	Stearly Motor Frt. #24	crashed-fatal

Racing Record of Gary Bettenhausen, 1963

Apl 28	Clermont, Ind. (300 mile stock)	Esserman Dodge #99	14th
June 2	Illiana, Ind. (50 mile stock)	Esserman Dodge #99	——
June 23	Illiana, Ind. (50 mile stock)	Esserman Dodge #99	22nd
July 7	Clermont, Ind. (150 mile stock)	Esserman Dodge #99	21st
July 14	Milwaukee, Wis. (200 mile stock)	Esserman Dodge #99	21st-flagged
July 28	Meadowdale, Ill. (200 mile stock)	Esserman Dodge #99	——
Aug. 11	Milwaukee, Wis. (150 mile stock)	Esserman Dodge #99	26th-eng.
Aug. 15	Milwaukee, Wis. (200 mile stock)	Esserman Dodge #99	20th-hit wall
Aug. 23	Springfield, Ill. (100 mile stock)	Esserman Dodge #99	11th
Sept. 1	DuQuoin, Ill. (100 mile stock)	Esserman Dodge #99	spun out
Sept. 4	Indianapolis, Ind. (100 mile stock)	Esserman Dodge #99	2nd-qual. 14th
Sept. 8	Langhorne, Pa. (250 mile stock)	Esserman Dodge #99	22nd-overheating
Sept. 15	Milwaukee, Wis. (250 mile stock)	Esserman Dodge #99	36th-cracked cyl.
Oct. 6	Illiana, Ind. (50 mile stock)	Esserman Dodge #99	crashed-hit wall

1964

Apl. 26	Langhorne, Pa. (150 mile stock)	Esserman Dodge #99	crashed over the fence in practice
May 3	Clermont, Ind. (300 mile stock)	Esserman Dodge #99	29th
July 12	Milwaukee, Wis. (200 mile stock)	Esserman Dodge #99	26th
Aug. 16	Milwaukee, Wis. (150 mile stock)	Esserman Dodge #99	17th
Aug. 20	Milwaukee, Wis. (200 mile stock)	Esserman Dodge #99	21st
Aug. 30	Springfield, Ill. (100 mile stock)	Esserman Dodge #99	——
Sept. 6	DuQuoin, Ill. (100 mile stock)	Esserman Dodge #99	crashed into Eddie Meyer on lap 56
Sept. 9	Indianapolis, Ind. (100 mile stock)	Esserman Dodge #99	——
Sept. 13	Langhorne, Pa. (250 mile stock)	Esserman Dodge #99	21st

1965

May 23	Illiana, Ind. (50 mile stock)	Esserman Dodge #99	——
May 30	Clermont, Ind. (100 mile stock)	Esserman Dodge #99	7th
June 13	Indianaola, Iowa (200 mile stock)	Esserman Dodge #99	7th
July 4	Illiana, Ind. (50 mile stock)	Esserman Dodge #99	5th
July 11	Milwaukee, Wis. (200 mile stock)	Esserman Dodge #99	11th

Aug. 15	Milwaukee, Wis. (150 mile stock)	Esserman Dodge #99	6th
Aug. 19	Milwaukee, Wis. (200 mile stock)	Esserman Dodge #99	18th
Aug. 20	Springfield, Ill. (100 mile stock)	Esserman Dodge #99	5th
Aug. 27	Ft. Wayne, IN (40 lap midget)	Hopkins #54	15th
Sept. 7	Indianapolis, IN (100 mile stock)	Esserman Dodge #99	25th
Sept. 19	Milwaukee, WI (250 mile stock)	Esserman Dodge #99	37th
Sept. 26	Clermont, IN (40 lap midget)	Hopkins #54	5th
Oct. 10	Wentzville, MO (200 mile stock)	Esserman Dodge #99	16th
Nov. 20	Phoenix, AZ (40 lap midget)	Hopkins #54	missed feature
Nov. 27	Gardena, CA (150 lap midget)	Hopkins #54	missed feature
Nov. 28	Hanford, CA (200 mile stock)	Esserman Dodge #99	81 laps-mech.

1966

Jan. 9	Ft. Wayne, Ind. (100 lap midget)	Hopkins #54	7th
Apl. 17	Langhorne, Pa. (150 mile stock)	Dodge #99	14th
Apl. 24	Trenton, N.J. (150 mile champ)	American Eagle #61	blew engine-practice
May 1	Clermont, Ind. (300 mile stock)	Dodge #99	8th
May 29	Kokomo, Ind. (100 lap midget)	Hopkins #54	18th
June 3	Grand Rapids, Mich. (50 mile stock)	Dodge #99	6th
June 5	Milwaukee, Wis. (100 mile champ)	McManus #61	failed to qualify
June 26	Atlanta, Ga. (300 mile champ)	McManus #61	crashed in practice
July 2	Indianapolis, Ind. (100 mile stock)	Dodge #99	5th
July 4	W. de Pere, Wis. (50 mile stock)	Dodge #99	2nd
July 10	Milwaukee, Wis. (200 mile stock)	Dodge #99	11th
July 15	Santa Fe, Ill. (100 lap midget)	Hopkins #54	spun, but cont.
July 16	Springfield, Ill. (50 lap midget)	Hopkins #54	17th
July 22	Grand Rapids, Mich. (50 mile stock)	Dodge #99	9th
July 24	Clermont, Ind. (150 mile champ)	American Eagle #61	failed to qualify
Aug. 7	Langhorne, Pa. (150 mile champ)	American Eagle #61	failed to qualify
Aug. 14	Milwaukee, Wis. (150 mile stock)	Dodge #99	21st-transmission
Aug. 18	Milwaukee, Wis. (200 mile stock)	Dodge #99	35th-engine
Aug. 19	Springfield, Ill. (100 mile stock)	Dodge #99	15th
Aug. 20	Springfield, Ill. (100 mile champ)	American Eagle #61	valve-practice
Aug. 26	Indianapolis, Ind. (100 mile stock)	Dodge #99	6th
Aug. 27	Milwaukee, Wis. (200 mile champ)	McManus #61	failed to qualify
Sept. 3	DuQuoin, Ill. (twin 50's midgets)	Hopkins #54	1st: 5th - 2nd: oil leak
Sept. 4	DuQuoin, Ill. (100 mile stock)	Dodge #99	7th
Sept. 10	Indianapolis, Ind. (100 mile champ)	American Eagle #61	failed to qualify
Sept. 11	Langhorne, Pa. (250 mile stock)	Dodge #99	6th
Sept. 15	Milwaukee, Wis. (250 mile stock)	Dodge #99	26th-blew engine
Sept. 25	Trenton, N.J. (200 mile champ)	American Eagle #61	failed to qualify
Oct. 9	Wentzville, Mo. (200 mile stock)	Dodge #99	13th
Oct. 16	Terre Haute, Ind. (100 lap midget)	Nowicke #2	5th
Oct. 20	Reno, Nev. (50 lap midget)	Nowicke #2	failed to make feature
Oct. 21	Livermore, Cal. (40 lap midget)	Nowicke #2	12th
Oct. 23	Sacramento, Cal. (100 mile champ)	American Eagle #61	failed to qualify
Nov. 13	Gardena, Cal. (50 lap midget)	Nowicke #2	15th

Nov. 19	Phoenix, Ariz. (40 lap midget)	Nowicke #2	7th
Nov. 20	Phoenix, Ariz. (200 mile champ)	Lynch #55	19th-32 laps-oil leak
Nov. 24	Gardena, Cal. (150 lap midget)	Nowicke #2	22nd

1967

Apl. 7	Tucson, Ariz. (40 lap midget)	Nowicke #99	spun lap 35
Apl. 8	Phoenix, Ariz. (40 lap midget)	Nowicke #99	flipped on mainst.
Apl. 28	Lubbock, Tex. (50 lap midget)	Nowicke #99	1st
Apl. 29	Lubbock, Tex. (50 lap midget)	Nowicke #99	2nd
Apl. 30	San Antonio, Tex. (50 lap midget)	Nowicke #99	3rd
May 26	Muncie, Ind. (100 lap midget)	Nowicke #99	1st
May 27	Clermont, Ind. (300 mile stock)	Ford #68	5th
May 29	Kokomo, Ind. (100 lap midget)	Nowicke #99	18th
June 2	Lake Geneva, Wis. (50 lap midget)	Nowicke #99	failed to finish
June 3	Sycamore, Ill. (40 lap midget)	Nowicke #99	14th
June 11	Granite City, Ill. (40 lap midget)	Nowicke #99	3rd
June 18	Louisville, Ky. (50 lap midget)	Nowicke #99	6th
June 22	Grand Rapids, Mich. (40 lap midget)	Nowicke #99	4th
June 23	Santa Fe, Ill. (50 lap midget)	Nowicke #99	5th
July 4	Daytona, Fla. (400 mile stock)	Ford #68	5 laps-flipped over fence
July 8	Springfield, Ill. (50 lap midget)	Nowicke #99	2nd
July 16	N. Bremen, Ohio (30 lap midget)	Nowicke #99	11th
July 20	Rockford, Ill. (50 lap midget)	Nowicke #99	11th
July 21	Santa Fe, Ill. (50 lap midget)	Nowicke #99	16th
July 22	Kokomo, Ind. (50 lap midget)	Nowicke #99	4th
July 29	Champaign, Ill. (40 lap midget)	Nowicke #99	1st
July 30	Granite City, Ill. (40 lap midget)	Nowicke #99	5th
Aug. 13	Milwaukee, Wis. (150 mile stock)	Ford #68	5th
Aug. 17	Milwaukee, Wis. (200 mile stock)	Ford #58	38th-23 laps blew engine
Aug. 18	Springfield, Ill. (50 lap midget)	Nowicke #99	17th-spun out
Aug. 23	Fairbury, Ill. (twin 50's midgets)	Nowicke #99	1st: 2nd - 2nd: 12th
Aug. 27	Wentzville, Mo. (200 mile stock)	Plymouth #68	15th-33 laps-crash
Sept. 2	DuQuoin, Ill. (twin 50's midgets)	Nowicke #99	1st: 6th - 2nd: 17th
Sept. 3	Florence, Ky. (20 lap midget)	Nowicke #99	3rd
Sept. 4	Columbus, Ohio (100 lap midget)	Nowicke #99	3rd
Sept. 9	Indianapolis, Ind. (100 mile champ)	American Eagle #61	failed to qualify
Sept. 10	Louisville, Ky. (30 lap midget)	Nowicke #99	7th
Sept. 24	Terre Haute, Ind. (50 lap midget)	Nowicke #99	2nd
Oct. 1	Sacramento, Cal. (100 mile champ)	Joe Hunt #47	12th
Oct. 8	Knoxville, Tenn. (50 lap midget)	Nowicke #99	2nd
Oct. 21	Fresno, Cal. (50 lap midget)	Nowicke #99	16th
Oct. 22	Hanford, Cal. (200 mile champ)	Joe Hunt #47	11th
Nov. 11	Gardena, Cal. (30 lap sprint)	Knox & Hill #30	3rd
Nov. 12	El Cajon, Cal. (50 lap midget)	Nowicke #99	5th
Nov. 17	Tucson, Ariz. (40 lap midget)	Nowicke #99	2nd
Nov. 18	Phoenix, Ariz. (40 lap midget)	Nowicke #99	1st
Nov. 19	Phoenix, Ariz. (200 mile champ)	Joe Hunt #4	19th-clutch
Nov. 23	Gardena, Cal. (150 lap midget)	Nowicke #99	1st

1968

Jan. 7	Ft. Wayne, Ind. (50 lap midget)	Nowicke #99	6th
Jan. 28	Irwindale, Cal. (40 lap midget)	Nowicke #99	4th
Feb. 4	El Cajon, Cal. (50 lap midget)	Nowicke #99	17th
Feb. 18	San Jose, Cal. (100 lap midget)	Nowicke #99	3rd
Mrh. 3	El Cajon, Cal. (50 lap midget)	Nowicke #99	5th
Mrh. 17	Hanford, Cal. (200 mile champ)	Joe Hunt #99	10th
Mrh. 31	Las Vegas, Nev. (150 mile champ)	Joe Hunt #99	10th

Apl. 5	Tucson, Ariz. (40 lap midget)	Nowicke #99	4th
Apl 7	Phoenix, Ariz. (150 mile champ)	Joe Hunt #99	13th
Apl. 20	Reading, Pa. (30 lap sprint)	Leader Card #2	2nd
Apl. 28	N. Bremen, Ohio (30 lap sprint)	Davis #24	2nd
May	Indianapolis, Ind.	Joe Hunt #99 Agajanian #97	practiced took drivers test
May 30	Indianapolis, Ind. (500 mile champ)	Thermo King #11	24th-43 laps: hit debris from Al Unser crash
		40 laps-10th	
June 2	Dayton, Ohio (30 lap sprint)	Davis #24	7th
June 5	Avilla, Ind. (50 lap midget)	Nowicke #99	7th
June 7	Hales Cor., Wis. (50 lap midget)	Nowicke #99	flipped-trophy dash
June 15	Mosport, Ont. (twin 100 mile champ)	Thermo King #11	1st: 9th 2nd: 13th-13 laps-oil leak
June 16	Terre Haute, Ind. (50 lap sprint)	Davis #24	1st
June 18	Davenport, Iowa (40 lap midget)	H. Turner #82	1st
June 19	Sycamore, Ill (40 lap midget)	H. Turner #82	2nd
June 21	Heidelberg, Pa. (30 lap sprint)	Davis #24	1st
June 23	Langhorne, Pa. (150 mile champ)	Thermo King #11	3rd
June 30	N. Bremen, Ohio (twin 30 sprints)	Davis #24	1st: crashed into Mosley 2nd: 7th
June 30	Kokomo, Ind. (50 lap midget)	H. Turner #82	5th
July 4	Salem, Ind. (30 lap sprint)	Davis #24	11th-blown engine
July 5	Kansas City, Mo. (30 lap sprint)	Davis #24	4th
July 7	Castle Rock, Col. (150 mile champ)	Thermo King #11	7th
July 13	Nazareth, Pa. (100 mile champ)	Thermo King #11	4th
July 14	Oswego, N.Y. (twin 50 sprints)	Davis #24	1st: 9th - 2nd: 6th
July 19	Santa Fe, Ill. (50 lap midget)	H. Turner #82	7th
July 20	Rossburg, Ohio (30 lap sprint)	Davis #24	1 lap-mech.
July 21	Clermont, Ind. (twin 100 mile champ)	Thermo King #11	1st: 21st-8 laps 2nd: 12th
July 26	Stafford Spg, Conn. (30 lap sprint)	Davis #24	1st
July 27	Reading, Pa. (twin 50 sprints)	Davis #24	1st: 4th - 2nd: 3rd
July 28	Langhorne, Pa. (twin 100 mile champ)	Thermo King #11	1st: 13th - 2nd: 12th -49 laps-steering
July 31	Knoxville, Iowa (40 lap midget)	Linne #99	16th
Aug. 4	Mt Treblant, Qub.(twin 100 mile champ)	Thermo King #11	1st: 14th-29 laps, sway bar 2nd: 13th-7 laps sway bar
Aug. 10	Clermont, Ind. (30 lap midget)	H. Turner #82	16th-blew engine
Aug. 11	Terre Haute, Ind. (50 lap sprint)	Davis #24	8th-led laps 1-20
Aug. 13	Davenport, Iowa (40 lap midget)	H. Turner #82	17th
Aug. 16	Springfield, Ill. (50 lap midget)	Nowicke #99	16th-crashed
Aug. 17	Springfield, Ill. (100 mile champ)	Thermo King #11	13th-71 laps, blew engine-led 1-7
Aug. 18	Milwaukee, Wis. (200 mile champ)	Thermo King #11	5th
Aug. 19	Granite City, Ill. (30 lap sprint)	Davis #24	3rd
Aug. 21	Fairbury, Ill. (twin 50 midgets)	H. Turner #82	1st: 5th - 2nd: 2nd
Aug. 22	Rockford, Ill. (50 lap midget)	Linne #99	blew engine practice
Aug. 24	Hamburg, N.Y. (30 lap sprint)	Davis #24	15th
Aug. 25	N. Bremen, Ohio (twin 50 sprints)	Davis #24	1st: 8th-led laps 1-21 2nd: 1st
Sept. 1	Dayton, Ohio (triple 33 lap sprints)	Davis #24	1st: 2nd - 3rd: 16th
Sept. 2	DuQuoin, Ill. (100 mile champ)	Thermo King #11	4th
Sept. 6	Knoxville, Iowa (30 lap sprint)	Davis #24	1st
Sept. 7	Indianapolis, Ind. (100 mile champ)	Thermo King #11	4th

Sept. 8	Terre Haute, Ind. (50 lap sprint)	Davis #24	1st
Sept. 13	Springfield, Ill. (50 lap midget)	Nowicke #99	mech.
Sept. 14	Valley Park, Mo. (40 lap midget)	Nowicke #99	4th
Sept. 15	Winchester, Ind. (100 lap sprint)	Davis #24	failed to make feature
Sept. 21	Reading, Pa. (30 lap sprint)	Davis #24	1st
Sept. 22	Trenton, N.J. (200 mile champ)	Thermo King #11	12th-158 laps turbo charger
Sept. 29	Sacramento, Cal. (100 mile champ)	Thermo King #11	2nd
Oct. 13	Cambridge Jct, Mich (250 mile champ)	Thermo King #11	21st-21 laps-clutch
Oct. 26	Gardena, Cal. (30 lap sprint)	Davis #24	2nd
Nov. 3	Hanford, Cal. (250 mile champ)	Thermo King #11	21st-41 laps-engine
Nov. 9	Gardena, Cal. (30 lap sprint)	Davis #24	13th
Nov. 10	Clovis, Cal. (30 lap sprint)	Davis #24	10th
Nov. 16	Phoenix, Ariz. (40 lap midget)	Nowicke #99	1st
Nov. 17	Phoenix, Ariz. (200 mile champ)	Thermo King #11	1st-led laps 184-200
Nov. 28	Gardena, Cal. (150 lap midget)	Nowicke #99	15th
Dec. 1	Riverside, Cal. (300 mile champ)	Thermo King #11	19th-51 laps oil pressure

1969

Jan. 5	Ft. Wayne, Ind. (50 lap midget)	Hopkins #54	3rd
Feb. 16	San Jose, Cal. (100 lap midget)	Stryker #99	3rd
Mrh. 8	Houston, Tex. (100 lap midget)	Nowicke #7	1st
Mrh. 9	Houston, Tex. (100 lap midget)	Nowicke #7	20th
Mrh. 28	Tucson, Ariz. (50 lap midget)	Nowicke #7	10th
Mrh. 29	Phoenix, Ariz. (40 lap midget)	Nowicke #7	4th
Mrh. 30	Phoenix, Ariz. (150 mile champ)	Thermo King #8	20th-24 laps gear shift
Apl. 6	Rossburg, Ohio (30 lap sprint)	City-Syracuse #2	2nd
Apl. 13	Hanford, Cal. (200 mile champ)	Thermo King #8	10th-126 laps, hit wall in turn 2
Apl. 20	Salem, Ind. (30 lap sprint)	City-Syracuse #2	6th
Apl. 26	Reading, Pa. (30 lap sprint)	City-Syracuse #2	crashed 2nd heat
Apl. 27	N. Bremen, Ohio (30 lap sprint)	City-Syracuse #2	2nd-led laps 13-21
May 4	Cincinnati, Ohio (30 lap sprint)	City-Syracuse #2	3rd
May 30	Indianapolis, Ind. (500 mile champ) 20 laps-4th	Thermo King #8	26th-35 laps-piston
June 1	Dayton, Ohio (30 lap sprint)	City-Syracuse #2	7th
June 8	Milwaukee, Wis. (150 mile champ)	Thermo King #8	21st-0 laps-rode over Dallenback in turn 2 and flipped
June 11	Avilla, Ind. (50 lap midget)	Nowicke #7	10th
June 14	Reading, Pa. (50 lap sprint)	City-Syracuse #2	1st
June 15	Langhorne, Pa. (150 mile champ)	Thermo King #8	7th
June 17	Davenport, Iowa (40 lap midget)	Sohm #9	failed to make feature
June 19	Knoxville, Iowa (40 lap midget)	Nowicke #6	13th
June 20	Springfield, Ill. (40 lap midget)	Sohm #90	failed to finish
June 21	Toledo, Ohio (30 lap sprint)	City-Syracuse #2	3rd
June 29	N. Bremen, Ohio (30 lap sprint)	City-Syracuse #2	1st
July 4	Charleston, W. Va. (30 lap sprint)	City-Syracuse #2	9th
July 6	Granite City, Ill. (30 lap midget)	Sohm #90	2nd
July 12	Nazereth, Pa. (100 mile champ)	Thermo King #8	2nd
July 13	N. Bremen, Ohio (30 lap midget)	H. Turner #82	1st
July 19	Trenton, N.J. (200 mile champ)	Thermo King #8	16th-74 laps-spun
July 24	Heidelberg, Pa. (30 lap sprint)	City-Syracuse #2	8th
July 26	Rossburg, Ohio (30 lap sprint)	City-Syracuse #2	7th
Aug. 2	Grand Rapids, Mich. (30 lap sprint)	City-Syracuse #2	2nd

Aug. 3	Pocono, Pa. (twin 30 sprints)	City-Syracuse #2	1st: 2nd - 2nd: 2nd
Aug. 10	Terre Haute, Ind. (50 lap sprint)	City-Syracuse #2	1st
Aug. 17	Milwaukee, Wis. (200 mile champ)	Thermo King #8	13th-178 laps-rear end
Aug. 18	Springfield, Ill. (100 mile champ)	Thermo King #8	6th
Aug. 22	Stafford Spg, Conn. (50 lap sprint)	City-Syracuse #2	10th
Aug. 23	Hamburg, N.Y. (30 lap sprint)	City-Syracuse #2	1st
Aug. 24	Dover, Del. (200 mile champ)	Thermo King #8	5th
Aug. 31	Cincinnati, Ohio (30 lap sprint)	City-Syracuse #2	1st
Sept. 1	DuQuoin, Ill. (100 mile champ)	Thermo King #8	10th
Sept. 6	Indianapolis, Ind. (100 mile champ)	Thermo King #8	2nd
Sept. 11	Jefferson City, Mo. (40 lap midget)	H. Turner #82	engine trouble
Sept. 12	Springfield, Ill. (50 lap midget)	H. Turner #82	failed to make feature
Sept. 14	Winchester, Ind. (50 lap sprint)	City-Syracuse #2	1st
Sept. 21	Trenton, N.J. (300 mile champ)	Thermo King #8	19th-58 laps-throttle shaft
Sept. 27	Stockton, Cal. (50 lap midget)	Bettenhausen #7	14th
Sept. 28	Sacramento, Cal. (100 mile champ)	Thermo King #8	2nd
Oct. 5	Salem, Ind. (30 lap sprint)	City-Syracuse #2	6th
Oct. 12	N. Bremen, Ohio (30 lap midget)	Bettenhausen #7	3rd
Oct. 19	Terre Haute, Ind. (30 lap sprint)	R. & Z. #12	1st
Oct. 26	Syracuse, N.Y. (twin 50 sprints)	City-Syracuse #2	1st: 1st - 2nd: 2nd
Nov. 14	Phoenix, Ariz. (40 lap midget)	Bettenhausen #7	13th
Nov. 15	Phoenix, Ariz. (200 mile champ)	Thermo King #8	10th-88 laps-piston
Nov. 27	Gardena, Cal. (100 lap midget)	Bettenhausen #7	20th
Dec. 7	Riverside, Cal. (300 mile champ)	Thermo King #8	valve in practice

National Sprint Standings

1. Gary Bettenhausen
2. Larry Dickson
3. Bill Puterbaugh
4. Sam Sessions
5. Greg Weld
6. Cy Fairchild
7. Todd Gibson
8. Bruce Walkup
9. Tom Bigelow
10. Larry Cannon

1970

Feb. 22	San Jose, Cal. (100 lap midget)	Bettenhausen #7	15th
Mrh. 6	Hollywood, Fla. (40 lap sprint)	City-Syracuse #1	4th
Mrh. 13	Hollywood, Fla. (40 lap sprint)	City-Syracuse #1	led laps 1-30-stalled to miss tow truck
Mrh. 14	Houston, Tex. (100 lap midget)	Bettenhausen #7	17th-hit fence
Mrh. 27	Phoenix, Ariz. (40 lap midget)	Bettenhausen #7	1st lap flipped over Vukovich
Mrh. 28	Phoenix, Ariz. (150 mile champ)	Thermo King #16	17th-41 laps hit wall to miss a pile up
Apl. 3	Vallejo, Cal. (100 lap midget)	Rossi #24	5th
Apl. 4	Sears Point, Cal. (150 mile champ)	Thermo King #16	21st-3 laps-throttle
Apl. 5	Rossburg, Ohio (40 lap sprint)	City-Syracuse #1	1st
Apl. 12	Dayton, Ohio (40 lap sprint)	City-Syracuse #1	3rd
Apl. 25	Reading, Pa. (40 lap sprint)	City-Syracuse #1	10th
Apr. 26	Trenton, N.J. (100 mile champ)	Thermo King #16	12th
May 2	Rossburg, Ohio (40 lap sprint)	City-Syracuse #1	4th
May 3	Cincinnati, Ohio (40 lap sprint)	City-Syracuse #1	18th-spun
May 10	Madison, Wis. (40 lap sprint)	City-Syracuse #1	5th
May 18	Clermont, Ind. (50 lap sprint)	City-Syracuse #1	1st
May 30	Indianapolis, Ind. (500 mile champ)	Thermo King #16	26th-55 laps-valve

May 31	N. Bremen, Ohio (40 lap sprint)	City-Syracuse #1	2nd
June 5	Odessa, Mo. (40 lap sprint)	City-Syracuse #1	1st
June 7	Milwaukee, Wis. (150 mile champ)	Thermo King #16	9th
June 13	Nazareth, Pa. (twin 45 sprints)	City-Syracuse #1	1st: 1st - 2nd: 15th
June 16	Langhorne, Pa. (150 mile champ)	Thermo King #16	5th
June 21	Terre Haute, Ind. (40 lap sprint)	City-Syracuse #1	5th
June 26	Grand Rapids, Mich. (40 lap sprint)	City-Syracuse #1	2nd
June 27	Toledo, Ohio (40 lap sprint)	City-Syracuse #1	1st
June 28	N. Bremen, Ohio (40 lap sprint)	City-Syracuse #1	7th
July 4	Cambridge Jct, Mich (200 mile champ)	Thermo King #16	1st-led laps 54, 76, 92-100
July 5	Salem, Ind. (40 lap sprint)	City-Syracuse #1	1st
July 11	Wms Grove, Pa. (40 lap sprint)	City-Syracuse #1	3rd
July 12	Heidelberg, Pa. (40 lap sprint)	City-Syracuse #1	2nd-led laps 3-38
July 16	Clermont, Ind. (50 lap midget)	H. Turner #82	18th
July 17	Madison, Wis. (30 lap midget)	H. Turner #82	1st
July 19	Minneapolis, Minn. (50 lap midget)	H. Turner #82	2nd
July 25	Rossburg, Ohio (40 lap sprint)	City-Syracuse #1	17th-hit fence
July 26	Clermont, Ind. (150 mile champ)	Thermo King #16	22nd-6 laps oil leak
Aug. 9	Terre Haute, Ind. (40 lap sprint)	LaFevre #32	18th
Aug. 15	Rossburg, Ohio (40 lap sprint)	City-Syracuse #1	4th
Aug. 16	N. Bremen, Ohio (40 lap sprint)	City-Syracuse #1	3rd
Aug. 21	Grand Rapids, Mich. (40 lap sprint)	City-Syracuse #1	4th
Aug. 22	Springfield, Ill. (100 mile champ)	Thermo King #16	20th-12 laps-hit wall in turn three
Aug. 23	Milwaukee, Wis. (200 mile champ)	Thermo King #16	17th-78 laps intake manifold
Aug. 29	Gardena, Cal. (30 lap midget)	Faas #37	2nd
Sept. 4	San Bernadino, Cal. (100 lap midget)	Faas #37	4th
Sept. 6	Ontario, Cal. (500 mile champ)	Thermo King #16	19th-93 laps-oil leak
Sept. 7	DuQuoin, Ill. (100 mile champ)	Thermo King #16	9th-56 laps-oil line
Sept. 11	Rossburg, Ohio (40 lap sprint)	City-Syracuse #1	3rd
Sept. 12	Indianapolis, Ind. (100 mile champ)	Thermo King #16	failed to qualify
Sept. 13	Terre Haute, Ind. (40 lap sprint)	City-Syracuse #1	3rd
Sept. 19	Sedalia, Mo. (100 mile champ)	Thermo King #16	16th-17 laps-fuel pump
Oct. 2	Wms Grove, Pa. (50 lap sprint)	City-Syracuse #1	3rd
Oct. 3	Trenton, N.J. (300 mile champ)	Thermo King #16	failed to qualify
Oct. 4	Sacramento, Cal. (100 mile champ)	Thermo King #59	9th
Oct. 25	Salem, Ind. (50 lap sprint)	City-Syracuse #1	1st
Nov. 21	Phoenix, Ariz. (150 mile champ)	Thermo King #16	19th-50 laps-water leak
Nov. 22	Phoenix, Ariz. (100 lap midget)	Caruthers #1	2nd
Nov. 26	Gardena, Cal. (100 lap midget)	Bettenhausen #7	1st

1971

Jan. 3	Ft. Wayne, Ind. (75 lap midget)	H. Turner #82	3rd
Feb. 28	Rafaela, Argt. (twin 75 mile champ)	Thermo King #16	1st: 11th - 2nd: 7th
Mrh. 17	Cincinnati, Ohio (40 lap sprint)	Thermo King #2	16th-blew engine
Mrh. 26	Phoenix, Ariz. (40 lap midget)	Bettenhausen #16	17th
Mrh. 27	Phoenix, Ariz. (150 mile champ)	Thermo King #16	20th-49 laps-pit fire
Mrh. 28	Reading, Pa. (40 lap sprint)	Thermo King #2 Chas. Chariot #37	crashed 1st heat 19th
Apl. 3	Corona, Cal. (50 lap midget)	Schweitzer #60	4th
Apl. 4	Rossburg, Ohio (40 lap sprint)	Thermo King #2	1st
Apl. 17	Gardena, Cal. (50 lap midget)	Schweitzer #60	14th
Apl. 18	N. Bremen, Ohio (40 lap sprint)	Thermo King #2	2nd
Apl. 24	Reading, Pa. (40 lap sprint)	Thermo King #2	4th
Apl. 25	Trenton, N.J. (200 mile champ)	Thermo King #16	16th-41 laps-clutch
May 1	Terre Haute, Ind. (40 lap sprint)	Thermo King #2	failed to make feature
May 2	Cincinnati, Ohio (40 lap sprint)	Werglund #46	9th

May 15	Clermont, Ind. (40 lap sprint)	Thermo King #2 Stapp #44	blew engine-practice 18th
May 30	Indianapolis, Ind. (500 mile champ)	Thermo King #16	10th-178 laps
May 31	Salem, Ind. (40 lap midget)	Bettenhausen #16	15th
June 2	Rockford, Ill. (50 lap midget)	Bettenhausen #16	2nd
June 5	Knoxville, Iowa (40 lap sprint)	Thermo King #2	7th
June 6	Milwaukee, Wis. (150 mile champ)	Thermo King #16	16th-80 laps throttle linkage
June 10	Cincinnati, Ohio (30 lap midget)	Bettenhausen #16	18th
June 11	Grand Rapids, Mich. (40 lap sprint)	Thermo King #2	15th
June 12	Rossburg, Ohio (40 lap sprint)	Thermo King #2	2nd
June 20	Nazareth, Pa. (100 mile dirt)	City-Syracuse #24	5th-led laps 33-41
June 26	Toledo, Ohio (40 lap sprint)	Thermo King #2	2nd
June 27	Winchester, Ind. (40 lap sprint)	Thermo King #2	7th
June 30	Wms Grove, Pa. (50 lap midget)	Bettenhausen #16	3rd
July 3	Pocono, Pa. (500 mile champ)	Thermo King #16	6th
July 4	Reading, Pa. (40 lap sprint)	Thermo King #2	2nd
July 11	Salem, Ind. (40 lap sprint)	Thermo King #2	1st
July 17	Selinsgrove, Pa. (40 lap sprint)	Thermo King #2	17th
July 18	Cambridge Jct, Mich (200 mile champ)	Thermo King #16	22nd-23 laps-ignition
July 24	Rossburg, Ohio (40 lap sprint)	Thermo King #2	4th
July 25	N. Bremen, Ohio (40 lap sprint)	Thermo King #2	1st
July 30	Peotone, Ill. (50 lap midget)	Bettenhausen #16	1st
July 31	Reading, Pa. (40 lap sprint)	Thermo King #2	4th
Aug. 1	Cincinnati, Ohio (40 lap sprint)	Thermo King #2	3rd
Aug. 8	Terre Haute, Ind. (40 lap sprint)	Thermo King #2	1st
Aug. 13	Hales Cor., Wis. (50 lap midget)	Haisman #47	2nd
Aug. 14	Toledo, Ohio (40 lap sprint)	Thermo King #2	8th
Aug. 15	Milwaukee, Wis. (200 mile champ)	Thermo King #16	3rd
Aug. 20	Springfield, Ill. (twin 50 midgets)	Bettenhausen #16	1st: 14th - 2nd: 25th
Aug. 22	Springfield, Ill. (100 mile dirt)	Thermo King #16	20th-25 laps-throttle
Sept. 5	Ontario, Cal. (500 mile champ)	Thermo King #16	3rd
Sept. 11	Indianapolis, Ind. (100 mile champ)	Thermo King #16	18th-66 laps-blew engine
Sept. 12	Winchester, Ind. (40 lap sprint)	Thermo King #2	3rd
Sept. 19&25	Pocono, Pa. (500 mile stock)	Dodge #6	15th-188 laps-lost lug nuts
Sept. 25	Wms Grove, Pa. (40 lap sprint)	Thermo King #2	2nd
Oct. 3	Trenton, N.J. (300 mile champ)	Thermo King #16	24th-77 laps-throttle linkage
Oct. 17	Winchester, Ind. (twin 50 sprints)	Thermo King #2 Leyba #1	1st: 19th-blew engine 2nd: 1st (from last)
Oct. 22	Phoenix, Ariz. (40 lap midget)	Caruthers #5	1st
Oct. 23	Phoenix, Ariz. (150 mile champ)	Thermo King #16	5th
Oct. 24	N. Bremen, Ohio (40 lap sprint)	Thermo King #2	5th
Oct. 30	Corona, Cal. (75 lap midget)	Caruthers #5	3rd
Oct. 31	N. Bremen, Ohio (40 lap sprint)	Thermo King #2	5th
Nov. 20	Phoenix, Ariz. (100 lap midget)	Caruthers #5	14th
Nov. 25	Gardena, Cal. (100 lap midget)	Bettenhausen #16	4th

National Sprints
Standings

1. Gary Bettenhausen
2. Larry Dickson
3. Rollie Beale
4. Sam Sessions
5. Lee Kunzman
6. Don Nordhorn
7. Dick Tobias
8. Darl Harrison
9. Karl Busson
10. Johnny Parsons

1972

Feb. 20	San Jose, Cal. (100 lap midget)	Caruthers #8	1st
Mrh. 11	Houston, Tex. (100 lap midget)	Bettenhausen #16	1st
Mrh. 18	Phoenix, Ariz. (150 mile champ)	Sunoco #7	4th
Mrh. 26	Grantsville, Pa. (40 lap sprint)	Thermo King #1	1st
Apl. 2	Rossburg, Ohio (40 lap sprint)	Thermo King #1	4th
Apl. 9	Winchester, Ind. (40 lap sprint)	Thermo King #1	15th
Apl. 23	Trenton, N.J. (200 mile champ)	Sunoco #7	1st
Apl. 30	Terre Haute, Ind. (40 lap sprint)	Thermo King #1	19th-flipped turn 1, lap 3
May 27	Indianapolis, Ind. (500 mile champ)	Sunoco #7	14th-182 laps, ignition led laps: 31-53, 57-161, 166-175
	20 laps-3rd	120 laps-1st	
	40 laps-1st	140 laps-1st	
	60 laps-1st	160 laps-1st	
	80 laps-1st	180 laps-3rd	
	100 laps-1st		
June 4	Milwaukee, Wis. (150 mile champ)	Sunoco #7	3rd
June 10	Rossburg, Ohio (40 lap sprint)	Thermo King #1	6th
June 11	Terre Haute, Ind. (40 lap sprint)	Thermo King #1	3rd
June 16	Grand Rapids, Mich. (40 lap sprint)	Thermo King #1	11th-led laps 12-17
June 17	Toledo, Ohio (40 lap sprint)	Thermo King #1	1st
July 1	Grantsville, Pa. (40 lap sprint)	Thermo King #1	18th
July 9	Milwaukee, Wis. (200 mile stock)	Dodge #10	9th
July 16	Cambridge Jct, Mich (200 mile champ)	Sunoco #7	24th-6 laps-withdrew entry
July 22	Philadelphia, Pa. (100 lap midget)	Linne #96	1st
July 29	Pocono, Pa. (500 mile champ)	Sunoco #7	19th-77 laps-ignition
July 30	Pocono, Pa. (500 mile stock)	Dodge #10	26th-48 laps lost oil pressure
Aug. 2	Independence, Iowa (40 lap midget)	H. Turner #82	1st
Aug. 3	E. Moline, Ill. (40 lap midget)	H. Turner #82	8th
Aug. 12	Toledo, Ohio (40 lap sprint)	Thermo King #1	14th-35 laps crashed in turn one
Nov. 3	Phoenix, Ariz. (40 lap midget)	Bettenhausen #16	9th
Nov. 11	Gardena, Cal. (40 lap sprint)	Thermo King #1	failed to make feature
Nov. 18	Gardena, Cal. (40 lap sprint)	Thermo King #1	15th-spun out
Nov. 23	Gardena, Cal. (100 lap midget)	Bettenhausen #16	19th

1973

Jan. 28	Ft. Wayne, Ind. (100 lap midget)	Bettenhausen #16	18th
Feb. 18	Roseville, Cal. (50 lap midget)	Caruthers #4	2nd
Feb. 25	San Jose, Cal. (100 lap midget)	Caruthers #4	1st
Mrh. 4	Gardena, Cal. (50 lap midget)	Caruthers #4	flipped in turn 3 in practice
Mrh. 17	Salem, Ind. (40 lap sprint)	Davis #24	12th-mech.
Mrh. 25	Reading, Pa. (40 lap sprint)	Davis #24	16th-led laps 24-27
Apl. 1	Rossburg, Ohio (40 lap sprint)	Davis #24	14th-mech.
Apl. 7	College Sta., Tex. (200 mile champ)	Sunoco D-X #5	2nd
Apl. 7	College Sta., Tex. (200 mile stock)	Dodge #4	35th-10 laps-handling
Apl. 8	Winchester, Ind. (40 lap sprint)	Davis #24	crashed turn 1 of 2nd heat
		Bill Easton #25	failed to make feature
Apl. 15	Trenton, N.J. (twin 150 mile champ)	Sunoco D-X #5	1st: 6th 2nd: 17th-44 laps-engine
May 30	Indianapolis, Ind. (500 mile champ)	Sunoco D-X #5	5th-130 laps
		100 laps-9th	
		120 laps-6th	
June 1	Hales Cor., Wis. (50 lap midget)	Caruthers #4	2nd
June 3	Knoxville, Iowa (40 lap sprint)	Davis #24	4th
June 10	Milwaukee, Wis. (150 mile champ)	Sunoco D-X #5	3rd
June 15	Grand Rapids, Mich. (40 lap sprint)	Davis #24	2nd

July 1	Pocono, Pa. (500 mile champ)	Sunoco D-X #5	27th-37 laps hit wall in turn 3
July 4	Cincinnati, Ohio (40 lap sprint)	Davis #24	failed to make feature
July 8	Salem Ind. (40 lap sprint)	Willard Coil #15	5th
July 15	Cambridge Jct, Mich (200 mile champ)	Sunoco D-X #5	24th-35 laps-stalled
July 15	Cambridge Jct, Mich (200 mile stock)	Matador #61	23rd-68 laps, oil leak
July 19	Engelwood, Col. (40 lap midget)	Linne #96	3rd
July 20	Lakewood, Col. (50 lap midget)	LInne #96	1st
July 22	N. Bremen, Ohio (40 lap sprint)	Davis #24	8th
July 27	Heidelberg, Pa. (40 lap sprint)	Davis #24	8th
July 29	Winchester, Ind. (twin 30 sprints)	Davis #24	1st: 10th - 2nd: 5th
Aug. 5	Terre Haute, Ind. (40 lap sprint)	Davis #24	9th
Aug. 12	Milwaukee, Wis. (200 mile champ)	Sunoco D-X #5	20th-77 laps-oil pressure
Aug. 19	Springfield, Ill. (100 mile dirt)	Penske #14	15th-70 laps-lost power
Aug. 26	Ontario, Cal. (100 mile champ)	Sunoco D-X #5	2nd
Sept. 2	Ontario, Cal. (500 mile champ)	Sunoco D-X #5	19th-79 laps-engine
Sept. 3	DuQuoin, Ill. (100 mile dirt)	Penske #14 Steed #16	mech. in practice 9th
Sept. 15	Indianapolis, Ind. (100 mile dirt)	Penske #14	brakes in practice
Sept. 16	Cambridge Jct., Mich. (twin 125 mile champs)	Sunoco #5	1st: 2nd led laps 36-61 2nd: 8th led laps 2-10
Sept. 23	Trenton, N.J. (200 mile champ)	Sunoco D-X #5	24th-27 laps spun in dogleg
Sept. 29	Cincinnati, Ohio (40 lap sprint)	Davis #24	4th
Sept. 30	Salem Ind. (40 lap sprint)	Davis #24	7th
Oct. 6	College Sta., Tex. (200 mile champ)	Sunoco D-X #5	1st
Oct. 14	Winchester, Ind. (twin 50 sprints)	Kemerly Gits #34	1st: 5th 2nd: 12th-hit fence lap 39
Oct. 21	Rossburg, Ohio (twin 50 sprints)	Davis #24	1st: 4th - 2nd: 4th
Nov. 3	Phoenix, Ariz. (150 mile champ)	Sunoco D-X #5	6th
Nov. 23	Gardena, Cal. (100 lap midget)	Linne #93	26th
Nov. 25	Phoenix, Ariz. (twin 50 midgets)	Linne #93	1st: 32nd - 2nd: 25th

1974

Jan. 6	Ft. Wayne, Ind. (75 lap midget)	Bettenhausen #93	5th
Jan. 26	Riverside, Cal. (500 mile stock)	Matador #16	7th
Feb. 18	Daytona, Fla. (500 mile stock)	Matador #16	12th
Mrh. 3	Ontario, Cal. (100 mile champ)	Penske Prod. #8	11th-28 laps-wing flap
Mrh. 10	Ontario, Cal. (500 mile champ)	Penske Prod. #8	20th-146 laps
Mrh. 17	Phoenix, Ariz. (150 mile champ)	Penske Prod. #8	14th-79 laps-gearbox
Mrh. 24	Atlanta, Ga. (500 mile champ)	Matador #16	9th
Mrh. 31	Rossburg, Ohio (40 lap sprint)	Davis #24	13th
Apl. 7	Trenton, N.J. (200 mile champ)	Penske Prod. #8	hit wall in practice
Apl. 14	Terre Haute, Ind. (40 lap sprint)	Davis #24	1st
Apl. 21	Winchester, Ind. (40 lap sprint)	Davis #24	20th-engine
Apl. 28	N. Bremen, Ohio (40 lap sprint)	Davis #24	1st
May 5	Talladega, Alb. (500 mile stock)	Matador #16	37th-105 laps-led laps: 19, 23, 38-42, 53-54, 63-76, 84-91, 98-100, 103
May 26	Indianapolis, Ind. (500 mile champ)	Score #8	32nd-2 laps-valve
June 2	Winchester, Ind. (40 lap sprint)	Davis #24	8th
June 9	Milwaukee, Wis. (150 mile champ)	Score #8	2nd
June 16	Cambridge Jct, Mich (400 mile stock)	Matador #16	4th
June 30	Pocono, Pa. (500 mile champ)	Score #8	31st-9 laps-piston
July 3	Reading, Pa. (40 lap sprint)	Davis #24	12th-hit in face by clod of dirt
July 4	Syracuse, N.Y. (100 mile dirt)	Thermo King #44	flipped in practice
Nov. 28	Gardena, Cal. (100 lap midget)	Linne #93	20th

1975

Jan. 5	Ft. Wayne, Ind. (75 lap midget)	Linne #93	1st
Jan. 19	Ft. Wayne, Ind. (100 lap midget)	Linne #93	1st
Jan. 25	Indianapolis, Ind. (100 lap midget)	Linne #93	7th
Feb. 8	Indianapolis, Ind. (100 lap midget)	Linne #93	failed to qualify
Feb. 14	Oklahoma City, Okl. (100 lap midget)	Linne #93	7th
Feb. 16	Oklahoma City, Okl. (100 lap midget)	Linne #93	9th
Feb. 23	San Jose, Cal. (100 lap midget)	Linne #93	13th
Mrh. 2	Ontario, Cal. (100 mile champ)	Thermo King #45	11th
Mrh. 9	Ontario, Cal. (500 mile champ)	Thermo King #45	14th
Mrh. 15	Phoenix, Ariz. (40 lap midget)	Weingarten #30	3rd
Mrh. 16	Phoenix, Ariz. (150 mile champ)	Thermo King #45	10th
Mrh. 23	Reading, Pa. (40 lap sprint)	Knepper #55	hit by rock
Mrh. 28	Chula Vista, Cal. (40 lap midget)	Weingarten #30	8th
Mrh. 29	San Bernadino, Cal. (100 lap midget)	Lloyd #25	17th
Apl. 5	Reading, Pa. (40 lap sprint)	Knepper #55	failed to make feature
Apl. 13	Rossburg, Ohio (40 lap sprint)	Knepper #55	failed to make feature
Apl. 20	Winchester, Ind. (40 lap sprint)	Knepper #55	5th
May 4	Terre Haute, Ind. (40 lap sprint)	Richards #15	15th
May 10	Clermont, Ind. (40 lap sprint)	Roesch #6	failed to make feature
May 16	Indianapolis, Ind. (50 lap midget)	Linne #93	failed to make feature
May 23	Indianapolis, Ind. (twin 50 sprint)	Richards #15	4th & 21st
May 25	Indianapolis, Ind. (500 mile champ)	Thermo King #45	15th-lost wheel
June 1	Terre Haute, Ind. (40 lap sprint)	Leyba #4	7th
June 7	Schererville, Ind. (40 lap sprint)	Leyba #4	1st
June 8	Milwaukee, Wis. (100 mile champ)	Thermo King #45	9th
June 29	Pocono, Pa. (500 mile champ)	Thermo King #45	5th
July 4	Syracuse, N.Y. (100 mile dirt)	City of Syracuse #97	6th
July 12	Rossburg, Ohio (40 lap sprint)	Leyba #4	2nd
July 19	Toledo, Ohio (40 lap sprint)	Leyba #4	19th-hit wall
Aug. 3	Terre Haute, Ind. (40 lap sprint)	City of Syracuse #24	1st
Aug. 9	Schererville, Ind. (40 lap sprint)	Leyba #4	3rd
Aug. 16	Springfield, Ill. (100 mile dirt)	City of Syracuse #97	15th
Aug. 17	New Bremen, Ohio (40 lap sprint)	Leyba #4	5th
Aug. 24	DuQuoin, Ill. (100 mile dirt)	City of Syracuse #97	18th
Aug. 31	St. Paul, Minn. (100 mile dirt)	City of Syracuse #97	mech.-practice
Sept. 6	Indianapolis, Ind. (100 mile dirt)	City of Syracuse #97	mech.-practice
Sept. 7	Terre Haute, Ind. (100 lap midget)	Linne #93	11th
Sept. 22	Terre Haute, Ind. (40 lap sprint)	Leyba #4	2nd
Sept. 29	Salem, Ind. (50 lap sprint)	Leyba #4	17th
Oct. 5	Rossburg, Ohio (twin 50 sprint)	Leyba #4	failed to make feature
Oct. 12	Winchester, Ind. (twin 50 sprint)	Leyba #4	13th & 18th
Nov. 2	Birmingham, Ala. (40 lap sprint)	English #45	3rd
Nov. 9	Phoenix, Ariz. (150 mile champ)	Thermo King #46	6th
Nov. 30	Irwindale, Cal. (100 lap midget)	Noffsinger #82	20th

1976

Jan. 4	Ft. Wayne, IN (75 lap midget)	Bettenhausen #93	failed to make feature
Jan. 18	Ft. Wayne, IN (100 lap midget)	Bettenhausen #93	1st
Feb. 7	Indianapolis, IN (100 lap midget)	Bettenhausen #93	1st
Feb. 14	Indianapolis, IN (100 lap midget)	Bettenhausen #93	2nd
Feb. 15	San Jose, CA (100 lap midget)	Lynch #27	6th

Mar. 13	Phoenix, AZ (30 lap midget)	Lynch #27	D. Carter in feature
Mar. 14	Phoenix, AZ (150 mile champ)	Thermo King #45	mech.-practice
Mar. 21	Madera, CA (100 lap midget)	Lynch #27	11th
Mar. 27	Gardena, CA (40 lap midget)	Linne #93	2nd
Mar. 28	Rossburg, OH (40 lap sprint)	Davis #24	10th
Apr. 4	Salem IN (40 lap sprint)	Davis #24	9th
Apr. 11	Rossburg, OH (40 lap sprint)	Davis #24	failed to make feature
Apr. 18	New Bremen, OH (40 lap sprint)	Davis #24	1st
May 1	Terre Haute, IN (40 lap sprint)	Davis #24	mech.-semi
May 9	Dayton, OH (40 lap sprint)	Leffler #8	20th-crash
May 15	Clermont, IN (40 lap sprint)	Leffler #8	2nd
May 23	Findlay, OH (40 lap sprint)	Leffler #8	1st
May 30	Indianapolis, IN (500 mile champ)	Thermo King #45	28th-mech.
June 4	Indianapolis, IN (twin 50 lap sprint)	Davis #24	2nd - 7th
June 6	Terre Haute, IN (40 lap sprint)	Leffler #8	failed to make feature
June 11	Schererville, IN (40 lap sprint)	Leffler #8	mech.-practice
June 13	Milwaukee, WI (150 mile champ)	Thermo King #45	mech.-practice
June 27	Pocono, PA (500 mile champ)	Thermo King #45	33rd-mech.
June 30	Clermont, IN (30 lap midget)	Bettenhausen #16	3rd
July 3	Findlay, OH (40 lap sprint)	Leffler #8	18th-mech.
July 10	Rossburg, OH (40 lap sprint)	Leffler #8	mech.-semi
July 11	New Bremen, OH (40 lap sprint)	Leffler #8	5th
July 14	Clermont, IN (30 lap midget)	Bettenhausen #16	7th
July 16	Schererville, IN (40 lap sprint)	Leffler #8	1st
July 17	Toledo, OH (40 lap sprint)	Leffler #8	11th
July 25	Winchester, IN (40 lap sprint)	Leffler #8	17th
July 28	Terre Haute, IN (30 lap midget)	Lithgow #28	qual. 11th-rain
July 31	Indianapolis, IN (tripple 33 lap sprint)	Leffler #8	22nd mech.-1st feature
Aug. 1	Terre Haute, IN (40 lap sprint)	Leffler #8	1st
Aug. 6	Schererville, IN (40 lap sprint)	Leffler #8	8th
Aug. 7	Rossburg, OH (40 lap sprint)	Leffler #8	crash-qual.
Aug. 18	Clermont, IN (40 lap midget)	Linne #99	mech.-1st heat
Aug. 21	Springfield, IL (100 mile dirt)	City of Syracuse #97	19th-mech.
Aug. 22	Dayton, OH (40 lap sprint)	Leffler #8	failed to make feature
Aug. 29	DuQuoin, IL (100 mile dirt)	City of Syracuse #97	mech.-practice
Sept. 3	Schererville, IN (40 lap sprint)	Leffler #8	5th
Sept. 5	Ontario, CA (500 mile champ)	Joe Hunt #99	27th-mech.
Sept. 6	Sandusky, OH (40 lap sprint)	Leffler #8	11th
Sept. 11	Indianapolis, IN (100 mile dirt)	City of Syracuse #97	failed to qualify
Sept. 12	Terre Haute, IN (100 lap midget)	Linne #99	1st
Sept. 19	Rossburg, OH (40 lap sprint)	Leffler #8	failed to qualify
Oct. 2	Syracuse, N.Y. (100 mile dirt)	City of Syracuse #97	2nd
Oct. 3	Salem, IN (50 lap sprint)	Leffler #8	15th
Oct. 17	Winchester, IN (twin 50 lap sprint)	Bowen #35	18th
Oct. 31	Terre Haute, IN (40 lap sprint)	Dorathy #21	R. Beale in feature
Nov. 25	Gardena, CA (100 lap midget)	Linne #99	21st

1977

Jan. 2	Ft. Wayne, IN (75 lap midget)	Caruthers #2	2nd
Jan. 16	Ft. Wayne, IN (100 lap midget)	Caruthers #2	4th
Feb. 12	Indianapolis, IN (100 lap midget)	Caruthers #2	1st
Feb. 13	Louisville, KY (100 lap midget)	Caruthers #2	6th
Feb. 20	San Jose, CA (100 lap midget)	Caruthers #2	18th
Mar. 4	Seattle, WA (100 lap midget)	Caruthers #2	7th
Mar. 6	Ontario, CA (200 mile champ)	Joe Hunt #99	10th

Mar. 12	Indianapolis, IN (100 lap midget)	Caruthers #2	3rd
Mar. 20	Salem, IN (50 lap sprint)	Bettenhausen #12	disqualified-"air foils"
Mar. 27	Phoenix, AZ (150 mile champ)	Joe Hunt #99	11th
Apr. 2	Gardena, CA (40 lap midget)	Caruthers #2	5th
Apr. 9	Salem, IN (50 lap midget)	Caruthers #2	16th
Apr. 16	Clermont, IN (40 lap sprint)	Bettenhausen #12	mech.-semi
Apr. 17	Clermont, IN (30 lap midget)	Caruthers #2	1st
Apr. 30	Trenton, N.J. (100 km mini-Indy)	Martin Piper Sales #72	11th
Apr. 30	Trenton, N.J. (200 mile champ)	Agajanian - Knievel #98	11th
May 7	Terre Haute, IN (40 lap sprint)	Moorman #42	14th
May 27	Indianapolis, IN (twin 50 lap sprint)	Moorman #42	13th - 27th
May 29	Indianapolis, IN (500 mile champ)	Agajanian - Knievel #98	16th
May 30	Salem, IN (twin 50 lap sprint)	Bettenhausen #12	failed to make feature
May 30	Salem, IN (twin 50 lap midget)	Caruthers #2	2nd - 2nd
June 1	Ft. Wayne, IN (30 lap midget)	Caruthers #2	3rd
June 5	Terre Haute, IN (40 lap sprint)	Moorman #42	4th
June 10	Hales Corner, WI (40 lap midget)	Caruthers #2	5th
June 12	Milwaukee, WI (150 mile champ)	Agajanian - Knievel #98	20th-mech.
June 15	Clermont, IN (30 lap midget)	Caruthers #2	5th
June 19	Rossburg, OH (40 lap sprint)	Moorman #42	20th
June 19	Rossburg, OH (40 lap midget)	Caruthers #2	fast time-mech.
June 26	Pocono, PA (500 mile champ)	Agajanian - Knievel #98	7th
July 2	Mosport, CAN (100 km mini-Indy)	Lathrop #37	21st
July 3	Mosport, CAN (300 km champ)	Agajanian - Knievel #98	2nd
July 4	Fairmont, MN (30 lap midget)	Caruthers #2	2nd
July 7	Hardford, SD (30 lap midget)	Caruthers #2	2nd
July 9	Morristown, MN (40 lap midget)	Brown #56	16th
July 10	New Bremen, OH (40 lap sprint)	Moorman #42	4th
July 13	Kokomo, IN (40 lap midget)	Caruthers #2	19th
July 16	Toledo, OH (40 lap sprint)	Moorman #42	5th
July 17	Irish Hills, MI (200 mile champ)	Agajanian - Knievel #98	17th
July 20	Clermont, IN (30 lap midget)	Lithgow #28	mech.-practice
July 23	Winchester, IN (40 lap sprint)	Moorman #42	failed to make feature
July 24	Winchester, IN (40 lap sprint)	Moorman #42	failed to make feature
July 30	Toledo, OH (40 lap sprint)	Moorman #42	8th
July 31	Terre Haute, IN (40 lap sprint)	Moorman #42	3rd
Aug. 3	Shererville, IN (40 lap sprint)	Moorman #42	2nd
Aug. 7	Sandusky, OH (40 lap sprint)	Moorman #42	4th
Aug. 10	Clermont, IN (30 lap midget)	Tezak #97ec	4th
Aug. 12	Rockford, IL (30 lap midget)	DeVea #4x	15th
Aug. 14	Salem, IN (40 lap sprint)	Moorman #42	16th
Aug. 20	Springfield, IL (100 mile dirt)	Armstrong #43	flipped in qualifications
Aug. 21	Milwaukee, WI (200 mile champ)	Agajanian - Knievel #98	8th
Aug. 26	Hamburg, N.Y. (40 lap sprint)	Moorman #42	1st
Aug. 28	DuQuoin, IL (100 mile champ)	Armstrong #43	2nd
Sept. 4	Ontario, CA (500 mile champ)	Agajanian - Knievel #98	17th
Sept. 5	Salem, IN (50 lap sprint)	Moorman #42	16th
Sept. 10	Indianapolis, IN (100 mile dirt)	Armstrong #43	18th
Sept. 11	Terre Haute, IN (100 lap midget)	Linne #99	3rd
Sept. 18	Rossburg, OH (40 lap sprint)	Moorman #42	flipped in semi
Oct. 15	Syracuse, N.Y. (100 mile dirt)	Haller #77	28th-mech.
Oct. 16	Winchester, IN (twin 50 lap sprint)	Bettenhausen #12	Bigelow in features

Oct. 22	Seattle, WA (100 lap midget)	Linne #93	15th
Oct. 29	Phoenix, AZ (150 mile champ)	Agajanian - Knievel #98	14th
Nov. 5	Gardena, CA (40 lap sprint)	Bettenhausen #12	7th
Nov. 12	Gardena, CA (40 lap sprint)	Bettenhausen #12	mech.
Nov. 20	Bakersfield, CA (40 lap midget)	Linne #99	7th
Nov. 24	Gardena, CA (100 lap midget)	Linne #99	failed to make feature

1978

Jan. 15	Ft. Wayne, IN (75 lap midget)	Linne #93	8th
Feb. 11	Indianapolis, IN (twin 35 lap midget)	Linne #93	failed to make feature
Feb. 12	Indianapolis, IN (100 lap midget)	Linne #93	failed to make feature
Mar. 18	Phoenix, AZ (100 km mini-Indy)	American Eagle #69	20th-engine
Mar. 18	Phoenix, AZ (150 mile champ)	Oberdofer #98	21st-engine
Mar. 26	Ontario, CA (200 mile champ)	Oberdofer #98	12th
Apr. 8	Clermont, IN (40 lap sprint)	Bettenhausen #99	20th-water hose
Apr. 9	Winchester, IN (40 lap sprint)	Bettenhausen #99	4th
Apr. 23	Trenton, N.J. (100 km mini-Indy)	American Eagle #97	3rd
Apr. 23	Trenton, N.J. (200 mile champ)	Oberdorfer #98	19th-half shaft
Apr. 29	Columbus, OH (40 lap sprint)	Bettenhausen #99	19th-accident
Apr. 30	Sandusky, OH (40 lap sprint)	Bettenhausen #99	6th
May 6	Terre Haute, IN (40 lap sprint)	Bettenhausen #99	too slow
May 21	Clermont, IN (40 lap sprint)	Bettenhausen #99	12th-piston
May 26	Indianapolis, IN (tripple 33 lap sprint)	Bettenhausen #99	18th - 28th
May 28	Indianapolis, IN (500 mile champ)	Oberdorfer #98	16th-piston
June 3	Shererville, IN (40 lap sprint)	Bettenhausen #99	fuel pump
June 4	Terre Haute, IN (40 lap sprint)	Bettenhausen #99	2nd
June 11	Mosport, CAN (100 km mini-Indy)	American Eagle #97	17th
June 11	Mosport, CAN (300 km champ)	Oberdorfer #98	6th
June 18	Milwaukee, WI (100 km mini-Indy)	American Eagle #97	4th
June 18	Milwaukee, WI (150 mile champ)	Oberdorfer #98	2nd alt.
June 25	Pocono, PA (500 mile champ)	Oberdorfer #98	29th-stalled
July 1	Syracuse, N.Y. (100 mile dirt)	King #98	2nd
July 8	Kansas City, MO (40 lap sprint)	Bettenhausen #99	mech.
July 9	Odessa, MO (40 lap sprint)	Bettenhausen #99	18th-accident
July 12	Kokomo, IN (40 lap midget)	Turner #82	rain
July 15	Toledo, OH (40 lap sprint)	Bettenhausen #99	20th-mech.
July 28	Hindsdale, IL (40 lap sprint)	Easton #88	mech.-semi
July 29	Shererville, IN (40 lap sprint)	Bettenhausen #99	17th
Aug. 6	College Station, TX (100 km mini-Indy)	American Eagle #97	22nd-oil leak
Aug. 12	Salem, IN (40 lap sprint)	Bettenhausen #99	mech.
Aug. 13	Salem, IN (50 lap sprint)	Bettenhausen #99	mech.
Aug. 18	Shererville, IN (40 lap sprint)	Moorman #42	1st
Aug. 19	Springfield, IL (100 mile champ)	King #98	1st
Aug. 20	Milwaukee, WI (100 km mini-Indy)	American Eagle #97	Bagley qual.
Aug. 20	Milwaukee, WI (200 mile champ)	Oberdorfer #98	22nd-piston
Aug. 28	Hamburg, N.Y. (40 lap sprint)	Moorman #42	2nd
Aug. 27	DuQuoin, IL (100 mile dirt)	King #98	19th-hit wall
Sept. 2	Ontario, CA (twin 100 km mini)	American Eagle #97	7th -9th
Sept. 4	Winchester, IN (twin 30 lap sprint)	Bettenhausen #99	19th - 19th
Sept. 9	Indianapolis, IN (100 mile dirt)	King #98	3rd
Sept. 10	Terre Haute, IN (100 lap midget)	Turner #82	too slow

Sept. 17	Rossburg, OH (40 lap sprint)	Easton #88	Sheldon Kinser-feature
Sept. 23	Trenton, N.J. (100 km mini-Indy)	Bertils #45	28th
Sept. 23	Trenton, N.J. (150 mile champ)	Oberdorfer #98	9th
Oct. 1	Salem, IN (40 lap sprint)	Bettenhausen #99	9th
Oct. 8	Cincinnati, OH (40 lap sprint)	Bettenhausen #99	3rd
Oct. 15	Winchester, IN (twin 50 lap sprint)	Bettenhausen #99	20th-broke axle
Oct. 28	Phoenix, AZ (100 km mini-Indy)	Bertils #45	8th
Oct. 28	Phoenix, AZ (150 mile champ)	Oberdorfer #98	21st-valve

1979

Jan. 7	Ft. Wayne, IN (75 lap midget)	Bozard #18	failed to make feature
Jan. 14	Cincinnati, OH (100 lap midget)	Bozard #18	2nd
Jan. 28	Ft. Wayne, IN (100 lap midget)	Bozard #18	failed to make feature
Feb. 10	Indianapolis, IN (twin 35 lap midget)	Bozard #18	9th-DNS
Feb. 11	Indianapolis, IN (100 lap midget)	Bozard #18	3rd
Feb. 17	Gardena, CA (15 lap sprint)	Morales #21	2nd
Feb. 18	Gardena, CA (50 lap sprint)	Morales #21	22nd-rear end
Feb. 25	Cincinnati, OH (100 lap midget)	Bozard #18	1st
Mar. 25	Ontario, CA (200 mile champ)	Armstrong #46	18th-hit wall
Apr. 8	College Station, TX (100 km mini-Indy)	Bertils #8	10th
Apr. 8	College Station, TX (200 mile champ)	Armstrong #46	2nd
Apr. 22	Winchester, IN (40 lap sprint)	Bettenhausen #99	mech.-heat
Apr. 29	Rossburg, OH (40 lap sprint)	Delrose-Holt #11	mech.-heat
Apr. 29	Rossburg, OH (40 lap midget)	Bozard #18	mech.-heat
May 5	Terre Haute, IN (40 lap sprint)	Delrose-Holt #11	failed to make feature
May 6	Terre Haute, IN (40 lap sprint)	Delrose-Holt #11	13th
May 11	Anderson, IN (40 lap midget)	Bozard #18	20th-oil pump
May 25	Indianapolis, IN (tripple 33 lap sprint)	Delrose-Holt #11	2nd - 2nd
May 26	Indianapolis, IN (50 lap midget)	Bozard #18	5th
May 26	Indianapolis, IN (100 km mini-Indy)	Bertils #8	NT-mech.
May 27	Indianapolis, IN (50 lap midget)	Bozard #18	5th
May 27	Indianapolis, IN (500 mile champ)	Oberdorfer #98	too slow
June 2	Schererville, IN (40 lap midget)	Bozard #68wc	NT-mech.
June 3	Terre Haute, IN (40 lap sprint)	Delrose-Holt #11	6th
June 10	Milwaukee, WI (150 mile champ)	Oberdorfer #98	6th
June 14	Kokomo, IN (40 lap midget)	Bozard #18	mech.-heat
June 16	Salem, IN (40 lap sprint)	Bettenhausen #99	8th
June 26	Pocono, PA (500 mile champ)	Oberdorfer #98	9th
June 30	DuQuoin, IL (50 mile midget)	Bozard #18	24th-oil pump
July 1	Dayton, OH (40 lap sprint)	Bettenhausen #99	6th
July 4	Hartford, OH (40 lap sprint)	Bettenhausen #99	7th
July 7	Schererville, IN (40 lap sprint)	Bettenhausen #99	4th
July 14	Toledo, OH (40 lap sprint)	Bettenhausen #99	4th
July 15	New Bremen, OH (40 lap sprint)	Delrose-Holt #11	18th-crash
July 21	Winchester, IN (twin 25 lap midget)	Bozard #18	6th-flipped
July 22	Winchester, IN (twin 30 lap sprint)	Bettenhausen #99	NT-power steering
July 29	College Station, TX (200 mile champ)	Armstrong #46	5th
Aug. 4	Schererville, IN (40 lap sprint)	Bettenhausen #99	NT-mech.
Aug. 5	Terre Haute, IN (40 lap sprint)	Delrose-Holt #11	2nd
Aug. 12	Milwaukee, WI (200 mile champ)	Armstrong #46	6th
Aug. 18	Springfield, IL (100 mile dirt)	Delrose-Holt #2	13th-overheat
Aug. 19	New Bremen, OH (40 lap sprint)	Delrose-Holt #11	3rd
Aug. 26	DuQuoin, IL (100 mile dirt)	Delrose-Holt #2	16th-flipped
Sept. 2	Winchester, IN (40 lap sprint)	Bettenhausen #99	NT-mech.
Sept. 3	Winchester, IN (twin 30 lap sprint)	Bettenhausen #99	Bubby Jones drives
Sept. 8	Indianapolis, IN (100 mile dirt)	Delrose-Holt #2	4th
Sept. 9	Terre Haute, IN (100 lap midget)	Bozard #18	10th
Sept. 16	Dayton, OH (40 lap sprint)	Bettenhausen #99	17th
Sept. 23	Terre Haute, IN (40 lap sprint)	Delrose-Holt #11	Tom Bigelow drives

Sept. 30	New Bremen, OH (40 lap sprint)	Delrose-Holt #11	18th
OCt. 6	Syracuse, NY (63 lap sprint)	Bettenhausen #99	36th-engine
Oct. 21	Winchester, IN (twin 50 lap sprint)	Bettenhausen #99	19th-mech.
Nov. 22	Gardena, CA (100 lap midget)	Bozard #68wc	NT-mech.

1980

Jan. 27	Phoenix, AZ (40 mile sprint)	Bettenhausen #99	20th-engine
Apr. 20	Winchester, IN (40 lap sprint)	Bettenhausen #99	5th
May 3	Terre Haute, IN (40 lap sprint)	Delrose-Holt #111	15th-accident
May 4	Terre Haute, IN (40 lap sprint	Delrose-Holt #111	12th-overheat
May 10	Clermont, IN (40 lap sprint)	Bettenhausen #99	2nd
May 25	Indianapolis, IN (500 mile champ)	Armstrong #46	3rd
May 26	Indianapolis, IN (40 lap sprint)	Delrose-Holt #111	6th
May 31	DuQuoin, IL (100 mile dirt)	Delrose-Holt #12	1st
June 8	Milwaukee, WI (150 mile champ)	Armstrong #46	12th
June 16	Cayuga, CAN (twin 50 lap sprint)	Bettenhausen #99	2nd - 12th
June 22	Pocono, PA (500 mile champ)	Armstrong #46	33rd-clutch
June 28	Schererville, IN (40 lap sprint)	Bettenhausen #99	4th
June 29	Terre Haute, IN (40 lap sprint)	Delrose-Holt #111	19th-mech.
July 12	Toledo, OH (40 lap sprint)	Bettenhausen #99	8th
July 13	Lexington, OH (250 km champ)	Armstrong #46	20th-engine
July 20	Irish Hills, MI (200 mile champ)	Armstrong #46	9th
July 25	Hinsdale, IL (40 lap sprint)	Delrose-Holt #111	6th
July 26	Rossburg, OH (40 lap sprint)	Delrose-Holt #111	3rd
Aug. 3	Watgins Glen, NY (150 mile champ)	Armstrong #46	11th
Aug. 10	Milwaukee, WI (200 mile champ)	Armstrong #46	withdrew
Aug. 19	Springfield, IL (100 mile dirt)	Delrose-Holt #12	18th-fuel pump
Aug. 23	Hartsford, OH (40 lap sprint)	Bettenhausen #99	flipped-heat
Aug. 24	DuQuoin, IL (100 mile dirt)	Delrose-Holt #12	1st
Aug. 31	Ontario, CA (500 mile champ)	Armstrong #46	31st-transmission
Sept. 1	Winchester, IN (40 lap sprint)	Leyba #8	M. Alderson drives
Sept. 6	Indianapolis, IN (100 mile dirt)	Delrose-Holt #12	1st
Sept. 14	Terre Haute, IN (100 lap midget)	Linne #96	23rd
Sept. 20	Irish Hills, MI (150 mile champ)	Armstrong #46	19th-oil cooler
Sept. 21	Terre Haute, IN (40 lap sprint)	Radar Racing #30	4th
Sept. 28	Tulsa, OK (twin 75 lap dirt)	Delrose-Holt #12	2nd - 2nd
Oct. 5	Salem IN (40 lap sprint)	Armstrong #43	3rd
Oct. 12	Rossburg, OH (twin 50 lap sprint)	Radar Racing #30	missed feature
Oct. 26	Winchester, IN (twin 50 lap sprint)	Armstrong #43	1st - 2nd
Nov. 2	Terre Haute, IN (100 lap dirt)	Delrose-Holt #121st	
Nov. 8	Phoenix, AZ (150 mile champ)	Armstrong #46	3rd

1981

Jan. 4	Ft. Wayne, IN (75 lap midget)	Northern Finance #18	mech.
Feb. 1	Phoenix, AZ (40 mile sprint)	Bettenhausen #99	2nd
Apr. 26	Rossburg, OH (100 lap dirt)	Delrose-Holt #1	Steve Chassey drives
May 2	Indianapolis, IN (60 mile dirt)	Delrose-Holt #1	3rd
May 3	Terre Haute, IN (30 lap sprint)	Delrose-Holt #5	no time
May 24	Indianapolis, IN (500 mile champ)	Hopkins #8	26th-broken rod
June 5	Kansas City, MO (30 lap sprint)	Booth #62	4th
June 6	Knoxville, IA (100 lap dirt)	Delrose-Holt #1	mech.
June 21	Pocono, PA (500 mile champ)	Vollstedt #27	27th-oil pressure
July 25	Irish Hills, MI (500 mile champ)	Rhoades #12	6th
July 26	Winchester, IN (30 lap sprint)	Bettenhausen #99	16th
Aug. 9	Terre Haute, IN (30 lap sprint)	Delrose-Holt #5	20th-mech.
Aug. 15	Springfield, IL (100 mile dirt)	Delrose-Holt #1	20th-rear end
Aug. 30	DuQuoin, IL (100 mile dirt)	Delrose-Holt #1	18th-handling

Sept. 5	Milwaukee, WI (200 mile champ)	Rhoades #12	19th-turbo
Sept. 6	Ft. Wayne, IN (30 lap sprint)	Bettenhausen #99	3rd
Sept. 7	Terre Haute, IN (30 lap sprint)	Delrose-Holt #5	21st-mech.
Sept. 9	Paragon, IN (30 lap sprint)	Delrose-Holt #5	12th
Sept. 12	Indianapolis, IN (100 mile dirt)	Delrose-Holt #14	3rd
Oct. 11	Rossburg, OH (30 lap sprint)	Bettenhausen #99	mech.
Oct. 11	Rossburg, OH (50 lap dirt)	Delrose-Holt #1	3rd

1982

Jan. 31	Phoenix, AZ (40 mile sprint)	Bettenhausen #99	21st-gearbox
May 1	Springfield, IL (100 mile dirt)	Delrose-Holt #7	18th-rear end
May 8	Indianapolis, IN (60 mile dirt)	Delrose-Holt #7	2nd
May 30	Indianapolis, IN (500 mile champ)	Hopkins #8	12th-engine
June 26	Clermont, IN (30 lap sprint)	Bettenhausen #99	2nd
June 27	Cincinnati, OH (30 lap sprint)	Bettenhausen #99	2nd
July 4	Flemington, NJ (50 mile dirt)	Delrose-Holt #7	20th-engine
July 18	Irish Hills, MI (500 mile champ)	Genesee #56	6th
Apg. 1	Milwaukee, WI (200 mile champ)	Provimi Veal #8	13th-oil pressure
Aug. 15	Pocono, PA (500 mile champ)	Genesee #56	8th
Aug. 21	Denver, CO (100 lap dirt)	Delrose-Holt #7	5th
Sept. 6	DuQuoin, IL (100 mile dirt)	Delrose-Holt #7	1st
Sept. 11	Indianapolis, IN (100 mile dirt)	Delrose-Holt #7	23rd-accident
Sept. 12	Terre Haute, IN (100 lap midget)	Sheehan lec	Kenyon subs

Racing Record of Merle Bettenhausen, 1967

Apl. 28	Lubbock, Tex. (50 lap midget)	Allard #19	11th
Apl. 29	Lubbock, Tex. (50 lap midget)	Allard #19	12th
May 29	Kokomo, Ind. (100 lap midget)	Nowicke #6	10th
June 2	Lake Geneva, Wis. (50 lap midget)	Nowicke #6	failed to finish
June 18	Louisville, KY (50 lap midget)	Nowicke #6	15th
June 22	Grand Rd., Mich. (40 lap midget)	Nowicke #6	11th
June 23	Sante Fe, Ill. (50 lap midget)	Nowicke #6	18th-spun out
July 1	S. Bend, Ind. (50 lap midget)	Nowicke #6	failed to make feature
July 4	Flat Rock, Mich. (50 lap midget)	Nowicke #6	14th
July 16	N. Bremen, Ohio (30 lap midget)	Nowicke #6	15th
July 20	Rockford, Ill. (50 lap midget)	Nowicke #6	14th
July 21	Sante Fe, Ill. (50 lap midget)	Nowicke #6	failed to make feature
July 22	Kokomo, Ind. (50 lap midget)	Nowicke #6	13th
Sept. 4	Columbus, Ohio (100 lap midget)	Nowicke #6	10th
Sept. 10	Louisville, KY (30 lap midget)	Nowicke #6	3rd
Sept. 24	Terre Haute, Ind. (50 lap midget)	Nowicke #6	— —
Oct. 1	N. Bremen, Ohio (30 lap midget twin)	Nowicke #6	1st: 18th - 2nd: 16th
Oct. 8	Knoxville, Tenn. (50 lap midget)	Nowicke #6	9th
Oct. 21	Fresno, Cal. (50 lap midget)	Nowicke #6	13th

1968

Apl. 5	Tucson, Ariz. (40 lap midget)	Nowicke #98	13th
Apl. 6	Phoenix, Ariz. (40 lap midget)	Nowicke #98	17th
June 2	Louisville, Ky (30 lap midget)	Nowicke #98	5th
June 5	Avilla, Ind. (50 lap midget)	Nowicke #98	2nd
June 18	Davenport, Iowa (40 lap midget)	Nowicke #98	14th

June 21	Sante Fe, Ill. (50 lap midget)	Loniewski #87	16th
June 29	S. Bend, Ind. (50 lap midget)	Loniewski #87	8th
July 6	Valley Park, Mo. (50 lap midget)	Loniewski #87	9th
July 14	N. Bremen, Ohio (twin 30 lap midget)	Loniewski #87	2nd: 7th
July 19	Sante Fe, Ill. (50 lap midget)	Loniewski #87	12th
July 21	Kokomo, Ind. (50 lap midget)	Loniewski #87	15th
July 27	La Grange, Ga. (40 lap midget)	Loniewski #87	4th
July 31	Knoxville, Iowa (40 lap midget)	Loniewski #87	failed to make feature
Aug. 2	Grand Rapids, Mich. (40 lap midget)	Loniewski #87	6th
Aug. 4	Terre Haute, Ind. (100 lap midget)	Loniewski #87	17th
Aug. 10	Clermont, Ind. (30 lap midget)	Loniewski #87	8th
Aug. 13	Davenport, Iowa (40 lap midget)	Loniewski #87	7th
Aug. 14	Joliet, Ill. (40 lap midget)	Loniewski #87	9th
Aug. 16	Springfield, Ill. (50 lap midget)	Loniewski #87	4th
Aug. 22	Rockford, Ill. (50 lap midget)	Loniewski #87	14th
Aug. 23	Santa Fe, Ill. (50 lap midget)	Loniewski #87	16th
Aug. 24	Valley Park, Mo. (40 lap midget)	Loniewski #87	15th
Aug. 25	Mazon, Ill. (50 lap midget)	Loniewski #87	16th
Aug. 28	Sterling, Ill. (40 lap midget)	Loniewski #87	——
Sept. 6	Hales Cor., Wis. (100 lap midget)	Loniewski #87	——
Sept. 13	Springfield, Ill. (50 lap midget)	Loniewski #87	——
Sept. 21	Clermont, Ind. (30 lap midget)	Loniewski #87	1st
Sept. 22	N. Bremen, Ohio (twin 30's midget)	Loniewski #87	1st: 8th - 2nd: 6th
Sept. 28	Granite City, Ill. (30 lap midget)	Loniewski #87	12th
Nov. 16	Phoenix, Ariz. (40 lap midget)	Loniewski #87	5th
Nov. 23	El Cajon, Cal. (50 lap midget)	Loniewski #87	14th
Nov. 28	Gardena, Cal. (150 lap midget)	Loniewski #87	7th

1969

Mrh. 8	Houston, Tex. (100 lap midget)	Linne #96	22nd
Mrh. 29	Phoenix, Ariz. (40 lap midget)	Alexander #27	3rd
May 3	Hershey, Pa. (100 lap midget)	Lockhard #69	13th
May 4	Jennerstown, Pa. (40 lap midget)	Nowicke #7	12th
May 20	Davenport, Iowa (40 lap midget)	Lockhard #69	3rd
May 23	Santa Fe, Ill. (50 lap midget)	Lockhard #69	——
May 29	Clermont, Ind. (twin 30's midgets)	Lockhard #69	1st: 5th - 2nd: 7th
May 31	Kokomo, Ind. (50 lap midget)	Lockhard #69	4th
June 5	Rockford, Ill. (50 lap midget)	Lockhard #69	10th
June 11	Avilla, Ind. (50 lap midget)	Lockhard #69	13th
June 13	Jackson, Mich. (50 lap midget)	Lockhard #69	5th
June 14	Lansing, Mich. (50 lap midget)	Lockhard #69	1st
June 17	Davenport, Iowa (40 lap midget)	Lockhard #69	2nd
June 19	Knoxville, Iowa (40 lap midget)	Lockhard #69	2nd
June 20	Springfield, Ill. (40 lap midget)	Lockhard #69	——
June 21	Valley Park, Mo. (40 lap midget)	Lockhard #69	17th
June 27	Haubstadt, Ind. (50 lap midget)	Lockhard #69	13th
June 28	Joliet, Ill. (50 lap midget)	Lockhard #69	2nd
June 29	Oxford, Ind. (50 lap midget)	Lockhard #69	2nd
July 3	Valley Park, Mo. (40 lap midget)	Lockhard #69	4th
July 4	Springfield, Ill. (40 lap midget)	Lockhard #69	Tangled with Tattersall in turn 2 of 3rd heat and both flipped
July 11	Hales Cor., Wis. (40 lap midget)	H. Turner #82	spun 1st lap
July 12	Clermont, Ind. (30 lap midget)	Lockhard #69	6th
July 13	N. Bremen, Ohio (30 lap midget)	Lockhard #69	3rd
July 16	Avilla, Ind. (50 lap midget)	Lockhard #69	5th
July 19	Valley Park, Mo. (50 lap midget)	Lockhard #69	3rd
July 20	Granite City, Ill. (40 lap midget)	Lockhard #69	6th

July 22	Davenport, Iowa (40 lap midget)	Lockhard #69	4th
July 23	Knoxville, Iowa (50 lap midget)	Lockhard #69	2nd
July 24	Minneapolis, Minn. (50 lap midget)	Lockhard #69	3rd
July 25	Santa Fe, Ill. (50 lap midget)	Lockhard #69	12th
July 27	Madison, Wis. (30 lap midget)	Lockhard #69	3rd
Aug. 2	Clermont, Ind. (30 lap midget)	Loniewski #87	failed to make feature
Aug. 3	Pocono, Pa. (twin 30's sprints)	Watson #10	1st: 9th - 2nd: ——
Aug. 6	Kaukauna, Wis. (50 lap midget)	Lockhard #69	5th
Aug. 8	Hales Cor., Wis. (50 lap midget)	Lockhard #69	2nd
Aug. 10	Terre Haute, Ind. (50 lap sprint)	Werglund #14	failed to make feature
Aug. 10	Cincinnati, Ohio (40 lap midget)	Lockhard #69	11th
Aug. 13	Terre Haute, Ind. (30 lap midget)	Lockhard #69	14th
Aug. 16	Jackson, Mich. (50 lap midget)	Lockhard #69	4th
Aug. 19	Davenport, Iowa (40 lap midget)	Lockhard #69	2nd
Aug. 20	Fairbury, Ill. (50 lap midget)	Lockhard #69	3rd
Aug. 22	Stafford Spg., Conn. (50 sprint)	Werglund #14	failed to make feature
Aug. 23	Hamburg, N.Y. (30 lap sprint)	Werglund #14	failed to make feature
Aug. 24	Rossburg, Ohio (30 lap midget)	Lockhard #69	16th
Aug. 27	Madison, Wis. (30 lap midget)	Lockhard #69	3rd
Aug. 30	DuQuoin, Ill. (twin 50's midgets)	Linne #93	1st: 6th - 2nd: 22nd
Aug. 31	Cincinnati, Ohio (30 lap sprint)	Hoffman #78	failed to make feature
Sept. 11	Jefferson City, Mo. (40 lap midget)	Lockhard #69	2nd
Sept. 12	Springfield, Ill. (50 lap midget)	Lockhard #69	5th
Sept. 13	Valley Park, Mo. (50 lap midget)	Gamester #35	failed to make feature
Sept. 14	Granite City, Ill. (30 lap midget)	Lockhard #69	8th
Sept. 19	Hales Cor., Wis. (100 lap midget)	Lockhard #69	15th
Sept. 20	Clermont, Ind. (30 lap midget)	Lockhard #69	17th
Sept. 21	Oxford, Ind. (30 lap midget)	Gamester #35	failed to make feature
Sept. 28	Terre Haute, Ind. (100 lap midget)	Lockhard #69	failed to make feature
Oct. 5	Salem, Ind. (30 lap sprint)	W & W #76	failed to make feature
Oct. 12	N. Bremen, Ohio (30 lap midget)	Lockhard #69	12th
Oct. 19	Terre Haute, Ind. (30 lap sprint)	W & W #76	7th
Oct. 22	Navasota, Tex. (40 lap midget)	Lockhard #69	18th
Oct. 25	Wichita Falls, Tex. (40 lap midget)	Lockhard #69	2nd
Oct. 26	Okl. City, Okl. (40 lap midget)	Lockhard #69	8th
Nov. 14	Phoenix, Ariz. (40 lap midget)	Lockhard #69	18th
Nov. 27	Gardena, Cal. (100 lap midget)	Lockhard #69	18th

1970

Mrh. 14	Houston, Tex. (100 lap midget)	Lockhard #69	15th
Mrh. 27	Phoenix, Ariz. (40 lap midget)	Lockhard #69	1st
Mrh. 29	Gardena, Cal. (30 lap midget)	Lockhard #69	7th
Apl. 3	Vallejo, Cal. (100 lap midget)	Lockhard #69	17th
Apl. 11	Cincinnati, Ohio (40 lap midget)	Lockhard #69	13th
Apl. 12	Dayton, Ohio (40 lap sprint)	Lockhard #69	12th
Apl. 17	Navasota, Tex. (40 lap midget)	Lockhard #69	1st
Apl. 18	Okl. City, Okl. (40 lap midget)	Lockhard #69	4th
Apl. 19	Lawton, Okl. (40 lap midget)	Lockhard #69	4th
Apl. 25	Reading, Pa. (40 lap sprint)	Lockhard #69	4th
May 2	Rossburg, Ohio (40 lap sprint)	Lockhard #69	14th
May 10	Madison, Wis. (40 lap sprint)	Lockhard #69	crashed - 3rd heat
May 18	Clermont, Ind. (40 lap sprint)	Lockhard #69	11th
May 29	Clermont, Ind. (50 lap midget)	Lockhard #69	4th
May 30	Kokomo, Ind. (50 lap midget)	Lockhard #69	13th
May 31	N. Bremen, Ohio (40 lap sprint)	Lockhard #69	14th
June 3	Joliet, Ill. (40 lap midget)	Lockhard #69	failed to make feature
June 5	Hales Cor., Wis. (50 lap midget)	Lockhard #69	failed to make feature

June 11	Jefferson City, Mo. (40 lap midget)	Lockhard #69	16th
June 13	Nazareth, Pa. (twin 45's sprints)	Lockhard #69	1st: 24th - 2nd: ——
June 17	Flamboro, Can. (100 lap midget)	Lockhard #69	15th
June 20	Kaukauna, Wis. (50 lap midget)	Lockhard #69	16th
June 21	Terre Haute, Ind. (40 lap sprint)	Lockhard #69	failed to make feature
June 26	Grand Rapids, Mich. (40 lap sprint)	Lockhard #69	8th
June 27	Toledo, Ohio (40 lap sprint)	Lockhard #69	7th
June 28	N. Bremen, Ohio (40 lap sprint)	Lockhard #69	16th - crashed into Todd Gibson
July 4	Valley Park, Mo. (40 lap midget)	Lockhard #69	6th
July 11	Wms. Grove, Pa. (40 lap sprint)	Lockhard #69	failed to make feature
July 15	Avilla, Ind. (50 lap midget)	Lockhard #69	10th
July 16	Clermont, Ind. (50 lap midget)	Lockhard #69	6th
July 17	Madison, Wis. (30 lap midget)	Lockhard #69	7th
July 19	Minneapolis, Minn. (50 lap midget)	Lockhard #69	18th
Aug. 1	Kokomo, Ind. (50 lap midget)	Weiland #84	failed to make feature
Aug. 6	Sante Fe, Ill. (50 lap midget)	Weiland #84	14th - broke axle
Aug. 9	Terre Haute, Ind. (40 lap sprint)	LeFevre #32	let Gary drive feature
Aug. 14	Hales Cor., Wis. (50 lap midget)	Jack Mucia #53	10th
Aug. 15	Rossburg, Ohio (40 lap sprint)	LeFevre #32	16th
Aug. 21	Grand Rapids, Mich. (40 lap sprint)	LeFevre #32	9th
Aug. 22	Springfield, Ill. (100 mile champ)	Boyce Holt #44	8th-91 laps-timing chain
Aug. 26	Fairbury, Ill. (40 lap midget)	H. Turner #82	4th
Aug. 29	Hamburg, N.Y. (40 lap sprint)	City-Syracuse #1	3rd
Aug. 30	Sun Prairie, Wis. (30 lap midget)	H. Turner #82	18th
Sept. 5	DuQuoin, Ill. (twin 50's midgets)	H. Turner #82	1st: 23rd - 2nd: ——
Sept. 11	Rossburg, Ohio (40 lap sprint)	Forberg #7	18th
Sept. 20	Granite City, Ill. (30 lap midget)	Sohm #90	10th
Sept. 27	Terre Haute, Ind. (100 lap midget)	Sohm #90	2nd
Oct. 4	Sacramento, Cal. (100 mile champ)	McClung Adv #46	7th
Oct. 25	Salem, Ind. (50 lap sprint)	Forberg #7	18th
Nov. 20	Phoenix, Ariz. (30 lap midget)	Schweitzer #60	9th
Nov. 21	Phoenix, Ariz. (150 mile champ)	Thermo King #71	hit wall in practice
Nov. 22	Phoenix, Ariz. (100 lap midget)	Schweitzer #60	failed to make feature
Nov. 26	Gardena, Cal. (100 lap midget)	Schweitzer #60	10th

1971

Mrh. 26	Phoenix, Ariz. (40 lap midget)	Willey #74	15th
Apl. 18	N. Bremen, Ohio (40 lap sprint)	LeFevre #32	17th-spun out
Apl. 24	Reading, Pa. (40 lap sprint)	LeFevre #32	9th
Apl. 25	Cincinnati, Ohio (40 lap midget)	Bettenhausen #16	14th
May 1	Terre Haute, Ind. (40 lap sprint)	LeFevre #32	7th
May 2	Cincinnati, Ohio (40 lap sprint)	LeFevre #32	10th
May 15	Clermont, Ind. (40 lap sprint)	LeFevre #32	13th
May 21	Santa Fe, Ill. (50 lap midget)	Stan Lee #66	4th
May 28	Clermont, Ind. (50 lap midget)	Loniewski #87	21st
June 5	Knoxville, Iowa (40 lap sprint)	LeFevre #32	14th
June 10	Cincinnati, Ohio (30 lap midget)	Lehmann #27	4th
June 11	Grand Rapids, Mich. (40 lap sprint)	LeFevre #32	crashed-2nd heat
June 17	Cincinnati, Ohio (30 lap midget)	Lehmann #27	10th
June 20	Granite City, Ill. (30 lap midget)	Lehmann #27	1st
June 24	Cincinnati, Ohio (30 lap midget)	Lehmann #27	2nd
June 25	Peotone, Ill. (50 lap midget)	Lehmann #27	18th
June 26	S. Bend, Ind. (50 lap midget)	H. Turner #82	4th
June 27	Sun Prairie, Wis. (40 lap midget)	H. Turner #82	15th
July 9	Hales Cor., Wis. (50 lap midget)	H. Turner #82	9th
July 24	DeGraf, Ohio (40 lap midget)	H. Turner #82	12th

July 25	Louisville, Ky. (50 lap midget)	H. Turner #82	5th
July 30	Peotone, Ill. (50 lap midget)	H. Turner #82	4th
Aug. 5	Santa Fe, Ill. (50 lap midget)	H. Turner #82	10th
Aug. 7	Kokomo, Ind. (50 lap midget)	H. Turner #82	6th
Aug. 13	Hales Cor., Wis. (50 lap midget)	H. Turner #82	4th
Aug. 14	Peotone, Ill. (40 lap midget)	H. Turner #82	11th
Aug. 20	Springfield, Ill. (twin 50's midgets)	H. Turner #82	1st: 6th - 2nd: 15th
Aug. 20	Springfield, Ill. (50 lap midget)	H. Turner #82	10th
Aug. 22	Springfield, Ill. (100 mile dirt)	Joe Hunt #99	7th
Aug. 27	Santa Fe, Ill. (50 lap midget)	H. Turner #82	7th
Aug. 29	Sun Prairie, Wis. (40 lap midget)	H. Turner #82	13th
Sept. 4	DuQuoin, Ill. (twin 50's midgets)	H. Turner #82	1st: 21st - 2nd: 12th
Sept. 6	DuQuoin, Ill. (100 mile dirt)	Joe Hunt #99	14th - 75 laps lost exhaust pipe
Sept. 11	Indianapolis, Ind. (100 mile dirt)	Joe Hunt #99	10th
Sept. 12	Terre Haute, Ind. (100 lap midget)	H. Turner #82	11th
Sept. 19	Rossburg, Ohio (40 lap sprint)	Thermo King #2	13th
Nov. 20	Phoenix, Ariz. (100 lap midget)	Lehmann #27	11th

1972

Mrh. 11	Houston, Tex. (100 lap midget)	Lehmann #27	6th
Mrh. 17	Phoenix, Ariz. (40 lap midget)	Bettenhausen #16	1st
Apl. 9	Winchester, Ind. (40 lap sprint)	Meskowski #17	18th-spun to miss R. West, lap one
Apl. 22	Charleston, Ill (50 lap midget)	Lehmann #27	2nd
Apl. 30	Terre Haute, Ind. (40 lap sprint)	Welch #43	14th
May 6	Cincinnati, Ohio (40 lap sprint)	Welch #43	18th
May 7	N. Bremen, Ohio (40 lap sprint)	Welch #43	11th
May 13	Clermont, Ind. (40 lap sprint)	Welch #43	17th
May	Indianapolis, Ind.	Ayr-Way Lloyds #35	practiced
May 26	Indianapolis, Ind. (twin 50's midgets)	Bettenhausen #16	1st: 39th - 2nd: 6th
May 28	Liberty, Ind. (40 lap midget)	Lehmann #27	1st
May 29	Salem, Ind. (40 lap midget)	Lehmann #27	17th
June 1	Rockford, Ill. (50 lap midget)	Lehmann #27	13th
June 10	Rossburg, Ohio (40 lap sprint)	Welch #43	3rd
June 11	Terre Haute, Ind. (40 lap sprint)	Welch #43	14th
July 4	Charleston, Ill. (40 lap midget)	Lehmann #27	14th
July 7	Hales Cor., Wis. (50 lap midget)	Lehmann #27	15th
July 9	N. Bremen, Ohio (40 lap sprint)	Meskowski #17	failed to make feature
July 16	Cambridge Jct., MI (200 mile champ)	Ayr-Way Lloyds #35	25th - 3 laps - hit fence in turn two

1973

June 16	Lost Creek, Ky. (40 lap midget)	Steed #16	18th
June 22	Rockford, Ill. (30 lap midget)	Steed #16	11th
June 23	Charleston, Ill. (50 lap midget)	Steed #16	8th
June 24	Hartford, Mich. (40 lap midget)	Steed #16	17th
July 8	Sun Prairie, Wis. (50 lap midget)	Steed #16	failed to make feature
July 13	Hartford, Ohio (40 lap sprint)	Davis #24	8th
July 14	Toledo, Ohio (40 lap sprint)	Davis #24	failed to make feature
July 19	Englewood, Col. (40 lap midget)	Steed #16	14th
July 20	Lakewood, Col. (50 lap midget)	Steed #16	13th
July 24	Provo, Utah (40 lap midget)	Steed #16	13th
July 25	Meridian, Id. (50 lap midget)	Steed #16	15th
July 29	Olympia, Wash. (50 lap midget)	Steed #16	failed to make feature

Aug. 3	Victoria B.C. (40 lap midget)	Steed #16	8th
Aug. 4	Skagit, Wash. (50 lap midget)	Shefchik #99	19th
Aug. 9	Wichita, Kan. (40 lap midget)	Steed #16	10th
Aug. 10	Hales Cor., Wis. (100 lap midget)	Steed #16	20th
Aug. 12	Sun Prairie, Wis. (50 lap midget)	Steed #16	15th
Aug. 31	Johnson City, Tenn. (40 lap midget)	Steed #16	1st
Sept. 1	Kingsport, Tenn. (40 lap midget)	Steed #16	18th
Sept. 15	Indianapolis, Ind. (100 mile dirt)	Steed #16	crankshaft-practice
Sept. 16	Rossburg, Ohio (40 lap sprint)	Davis #24	12th
Sept. 23	Terre Haute, Ind. (100 lap midget)	Steed #16	4th
Sept. 30	Kansas City, Mo. (50 lap midget)	Steed #16	3rd
Oct. 6	College St., Tex. (200 mile stock)	Chevelle #88	19th
Nov. 23	Gardena, Cal. (100 lap midget)	Steed #16	12th
Nov. 25	Phoenix, Ariz. (twin 50 lap midget)	Steed #16	1st: 3rd - 2nd: 21st

1974

Jan. 6	Ft. Wayne, Ind. (75 lap midget)	Bettenhausen #16	3rd
Jan 20	Ft. Wayne, Ind. (100 lap midget)	Bettenhausen #16	failed to make feature
Feb. 17	San Jose, Cal. (100 lap midget)	Bettenhausen #16	20th
Feb. 22	San Francisco, Cal. (100 lap midget)	Bettenhausen #16	failed to make feature
Mrh. 9	Indianapolis, Ind. (100 lap midget)	Bettenhausen #16	4th
Mrh. 29	Chula Vista, Cal. (40 lap midget)	Stan Lee #66	12th
May 5	Cincinnati, Ohio (40 lap sprint)	Davis #24	failed to make feature
May 18	Clermont, Ind. (40 lap sprint)	Davis #24	failed to make feature
May 24	Indianapolis, Ind. (twin 50's sprints)	Lehmann #23	1st: —— - 2nd: 26th
May 25	Clermont, Ind. (30 lap midget)	Bettenhausen #16	7th
June 2	Columbus, Ohio (50 lap midget)	Bettenhausen #16	9th
June 8	Clermont, Ind. (40 lap sprint)	Lehmann #23	failed to make feature
June 13	Sun Prairie, Wis. (40 lap midget)	Bettenhausen #16	10th
June 14	Santa Fe, Ill. (40 lap midget)	Bettenhausen #16	feature rained out
June 15	Springfield, Ill. (40 lap midget)	Bettenhausen #16	9th
June 16	Winchester, Ind. (twin 25's midgets)	Bettenhausen #16	1st: 6th - 2nd: 3rd
June 20	Wichita, Kan. (40 lap midget)	Bettenhausen #16	5th
June 21	Enid, Okl. (40 lap midget)	Bettenhausen #16	3rd
June 22	Kansas City, Mo. (40 lap midget)	Bettenhausen #16	3rd
June 28	Charleston, Ill. (40 lap midget)	Bettenhausen #16	11th

Racing Record of Tony Bettenhausen, Jr., 1973

Apl. 7	College Sta., Tx. (200 mile stock)	Vita Fresh Chevy #38	15th
July 8	Salem, Ind. (40 lap sprint)	Davis #24	practiced
July 29	Pocono, Pa. (500 mile stock)	Vita Fresh Chevy #38	9th
Aug. 16	Milwaukee, Wis. (150 mile stock)	Vita Fresh Chevy #38	22nd
Aug. 19	Milwaukee, Wis. (200 mile stock)	Vita Fresh Chevy #38	29th-111 laps blown engine
Oct. 6	College Sta., Tx. (200 mile stock)	Vita Fresh Chevy #38	26th-26 laps, blown engine, led laps 24

1974

Jan. 26	Riverside, Cal. (500 mile stock)	Vita Fresh Chevy #9	17th-144 laps engine failure

Feb. 17	Daytona, Fla. (500 mile stock)	Vita Fresh Chevy #9	33rd-75 laps engine failure
Feb. 24	Richmond, Va. (500 mile stock)	Vita Fresh Chevy #9	12th
Mrh. 3	Rockingham, N.C. (500 mile stock)	Vita Fresh Chevy #9	12th
Mrh. 17	Bristol, Tenn. (500 mile stock)	Vita Fresh Chevy #9	19th
Apl. 7	Darlington, S.C. (500 mile stock)	Vita Fresh Chevy #9	18th
Apl. 21	N. Wilkesboro, N.C. (400 mile stock)	Vita Fresh Chevy #9	14th
Apl. 28	Martinsville, Va. (500 mile stock)	Vita Fresh Chevy #9	29th-55 laps engine failure
May 5	Talladega, Alb. (500 mile stock)	Vita Fresh Chevy #9	30th-147 laps valve spring
May 12	Nashville, Tenn. (420 mile stock)	Vita Fresh Chevy #9	23rd-rear end
May 19	Dover, Del. (500 mile stock)	Vita Fresh Chevy #9	34th-54 laps spun
May 26	Charlotte, N.C. (600 mile stock)	Vita Fresh Chevy #9	21st
June 9	Riverside, Cal. (400 mile stock)	Vita Fresh Chevy #9	31st-21 laps valve
June 16	Cambridge Jct. Mich. (400 mile stock)	Vita Fresh Chevy #9	36th-0 laps piston
July 4	Daytona, Fla. (400 mile stock)	Ford #64	14th
July 20	Nashville, Tenn. (420 mile stock)	Vita Fresh Chevy #9	11th
July 28	Atlanta, Ga. (500 mile stock)	Vita Fresh Chevy #9	24th-200 laps engine failure
Aug. 4	Pocono, Pa. (500 mile stock)	Vita Fresh Chevy #9	27th-44 laps piston
Aug. 11	Talladega, Alb. (500 mile stock)	Vita Fresh Chevy #9	32nd-98 laps engine failure
Aug. 25	Cambridge Jct, Mich. (400 mile stock)	Vita Fresh Chevy #9	35th-57 laps crashed
Sept. 2	Darlington, S.C. (500 mile stock)	Vita Fresh Chevy #9	11th
Sept. 8	Richmond, Va. (500 mile stock)	Vita Fresh Chevy #9	7th
Sept. 15	Dover, Del (500 mile stock)	Vita Fresh Chevy #9	15th
Sept. 22	N. Wilkesboro, N.C. (400 mile stock)	Vita Fresh Chevy #9	25th-36 laps oil pressure
Sept. 29	Martinsville, Va. (500 mile stock)	Vita Fresh Chevy #9	14th-310 laps crashed
Oct. 20	Rockingham, N.C. (500 mile stock)	Chevy #40	20th

1975

May 17	Champaign, Ill. (100 lap stock)	Chevrolet #16	7th
June 1	Odessa, Mo. (150 lap stock)	Chevrolet #16	7th
June 8	Salem, Ind. (100 lap stock)	Chevrolet #16	8th
July 13	Milwaukee, Wis. (200 lap stock)	Chevrolet #16	25th
July 20	Cambridge, Jct. (200 lap stock)	Chevrolet #16	13th
Aug. 10	Columbus, Ohio (40 lap midget)	Polak #10	N/T
Aug. 20	Clermont, Ind. (30 lap midget)	Polak #10	18th
Sept. 1	St. Paul, Minn. (150 lap stock)	Chevrolet #16	12th
Sept. 21	Trenton, N.J. (150 lap stock)	Chevrolet #16	11th

1976

Apr. 11	Clermont, IN (30 lap midget)	Bettenhausen Racing Ent. #16	no time
May 19	Indianapolis, IN (30 lap midget)	B.R.E. #16	missed feature
May 29	Clermont, IN (30 lap midget)	B.R.E. #16	missed feature
June 20	Rossburg, OH (40 lap midget)	B.R.E. #16	missed feature
July 7	Kokomo, IN (40 lap midget)	B.R.E. #16	mech.
July 10	Springfield, IL (40 lap midget)	B.R.E. #16	missed feature
July 11	Schererville, IN (40 lap midget)	B.R.E. #16	11th
July 20	Huron, SD (50 lap midget)	B.R.E. #16	mech.
July 28	Terre Haute, IN (30 lap midget)	B.R.E. #16	rain
July 30	Blue Island, IL (40 lap midget)	B.R.E. #16	9th
July 31	Wilmot, WI (40 lap midget)	B.R.E. #16	7th
Aug. 1	Columbus, OH (40 lap midget)	B.R.E. #16	11th
Aug. 8	Dayton, OH (40 lap midget)	B.R.E. #16	B. Engelhart subs
Aug. 14	Trenton, NJ (34 mile midget)	B.R.E. #16	13th
Aug. 15	Trenton, NJ (34 mile midget)	B.R.E. #16	19th-spun
Aug. 18	Clermont, IN (40 lap midget)	B.R.E. #16	missed feature
Aug. 23	Erie, CO (40 lap midget)	B.R.E. #16	missed feature
Aug. 25	Meridian, ID (40 lap midget)	B.R.E. #16	14th
Aug. 27	Salt Lake, UT (100 lap midget)	B.R.E. #16	6th
Aug. 28	Salt Lake, UT (100 lap midget)	B.R.E. #16	7th
Aug. 29	Colorado Springs, CO (40 lap midget)	B.R.E. #16	6th
Sept. 3	Hinsdale, IL (40 lap midget)	B.R.E. #16	8th
Sept. 12	Terre Haute, IN (100 lap midget)	B.R.E. #16	19th
Nov. 25	Gardena, CA (100 lap midget)	B.R.E. #16	missed feature

1977

Jan. 2	Ft. Wayne, IN (75 lap midget)	M. Betten-hausen #16	missed feature
Jan. 8	Norfolk, VA (100 lap midget)	Bettenhausen #16	12th
Jan. 16	Ft. Wayne, IN (100 lap midget)	Bettenhausen #16	missed feature
Feb. 12	Indianapolis, IN (100 lap midget)	Bettenhausen #16	9th
Feb. 13	Louisville, KY (100 lap midget)	Bettenhausen #16	missed feature
Feb. 20	San Jose, CA (100 lap midget)	Bettenhausen #16	missed feature
Mar. 4	Seattle, WA (100 lap midget)	Bettenhausen #16	17th
Mar. 12	Indianapolis, IN (100 lap midget)	Bettenhausen #16	missed feature
Apr. 9	Salem, IN (50 lap midget)	Bettenhausen #16	T. Bigelow subs
Apr. 17	Clermont, IN (30 lap midget)	Bettenhausen #16	16th
Apr. 30	Cincinnati, OH (40 lap sprint)	G. Betten-hausen #12	missed feature
May 1	Oxford, IN (100 lap midget)	Bettenhausen #16	missed feature
May 7	Terre Haute, IN (40 lap sprint)	G. Betten-hausen #12	no time
May 14	Clermont, IN (40 lap sprint)	G. Betten-hausen #12	missed feature
June 10	Hales Corners, IL (40 lap midget)	Bettenhausen #16	16th
June 11	Springfield, IL (40 lap midget)	Bettenhausen #16	missed feature
July 13	Kokomo, IN (40 lap midget)	Bettenhausen #16	missed feature
July 15	Hinsdale, IL (40 lap midget)	Bettenhausen #16	11th
July 16	Springfield, IL (40 lap midget)	Bettenhausen #16	missed feature
July 20	Clermont, IN (30 lap midget)	Bettenhausen #16	16th
July 23	Winchester, IN (40 lap midget)	Bettenhausen #16	no time
Aug. 7	Sandusky, OH (40 lap sprint)	G. Betten-hausen #12	missed feature
Aug. 10	Clermont, IN (30 lap midget)	Bettenhausen #16	missed feature
Aug. 13	Paragon, IN (40 lap midget)	Bettenhausen #16	missed feature
Aug. 14	Columbus, IN (50 lap midget)	Bettenhausen #16	no time
Aug. 28	Columbus, IN (50 lap midget)	Paul Bozard #68	8th

1978

Jan. 15	Ft. Wayne, IN (75 lap midget)	T. Bettenhausen #16	missed feature
Feb. 11	Indianapolis, IN (twin 35 lap midget)	Bettenhausen #16	6th-11th
Feb. 12	Indianapolis, IN (100 lap midget)	Bettenhausen #16	3rd
Apr. 30	Clermont, IN (30 lap midget)	Bettenhausen #16	missed feature
May 5	Haubstadt, IN (40 lap midget)	Bettenhausen #16	no time
May 27	Clermont, IN (30 lap midget)	Bettenhausen #16	missed feature
June 14	Clermont, IN (30 lap midget)	Bettenhausen #16	missed feature
June 28	Angola, IN (40 lap midget)	Bettenhausen #16	missed feature
July 4	Reading, PA (40 lap midget)	Bettenhausen #16	20th
July 7	Hinsdale, IL (40 lap midget)	Bud Doty #50	missed feature
July 12	Kokomo, IN (40 lap midget)	T. Bettenhausen #16	flipped
July 14	Owosso, MI (40 lap midget)	Bettenhausen #16	missed feature
July 15	Springfield, IL (40 lap midget)	Bettenhausen #16	20th-mech.
July 19	Indianapolis, IN (40 lap midget)	Bettenhausen #16	17th
Aug. 1	Erie, CO (40 lap midget)	Bettenhausen #16	missed feature
Aug. 5	Hartford, OH (40 lap sprint)	G. Bettenhausen #99	rain
Aug. 6	Sandusky, OH (40 lap sprint)	G. Bettenhausen #99	14th
Aug. 9	Indianapolis, IN (40 lap midget)	T. Bettenhausen #16	no time
Sept. 2	Hartford, OH (40 lap sprint)	G. Bettenhausen #99	9th
Sept. 8	Paragon, IN (40 lap midget)	T. Bettenhausen #16	missed feature
Sept. 10	Terre Haute, IN (100 lap midget)	Bettenhausen #16	missed feature

1979

Feb. ?	Jackson, MS (? lap midget)	Bettenhausen #16	1st
Feb. 10	Indianapolis, IN (twin 35 lap midget)	Logan #16	missed feature
Feb. 11	Indianapolis, IN (100 lap midget)	Logan #16	missed feature
Apr. 8	College Station, TX (200 mile champ)	Shirley McElreath #26	9th
June 2	Schererville, IN (40 lap midget)	Schnieder #67	J. Weeks subs
June 10	Milwaukee, WI (150 mile champ)	Lawarre #60	9th
June 24	Pocono, PA (500 mile champ)	Lawarre #60	13th
July 29	College Station, TX (200 mile champ)	Lawarre #86	13th
Aug. 12	Milwaukee, WI (200 mile champ)	Lawarre #86	15th
Aug. 26	DuQuoin, IL (100 mile dirt)	Precision Racing #86	no time
Sept. 8	Indianapolis, IN (100 mile dirt)	Precision Racing #86	10th in consi.

1980

Jan. 6	Ft. Wayne, IN (75 lap midget)	Barnett #16	missed feature
May 25	Indianapolis, IN (500 mile champ)	Medlin #32	bumped
June 8	Milwaukee, WI (150 mile champ)	Medlin #32	too slow
June 22	Pocono, PA (500 mile champ)	Medlin #32	32nd-piston
July 13	Lexington, OH (250 km champ)	King #98	too slow

1981

May 4	Indianapolis, IN (500 mile champ)	H&R Racing #16	7th
June 7	Milwaukee, WI (150 mile champ)	H&R Racing #16	12th

June 28	Atlanta, GA (twin 125 mile champ)	H&R Racing #16	7th-11th
July 25	Irish Hills, MI (500 mile champ)	H&R Racing #16	2nd
Sept. 5	Milwaukee, WI (200 mile champ)	H&R Racing #16	14th
Sept. 20	Irish Hills, MI (150 mile champ)	H&R Racing #16	10th
Oct. 4	Watkins Glen, NY (200 mile champ)	H&R Racing #16	8th
Oct. 18	Mexico City, MX (150 mile champ)	H&R Racing #16	11th
Oct. 31	Phoenix, AZ (150 mile champ)	H&R Racing #16	19th-gearbox

1982

Mar. 28	Phoenix, AZ (150 mile champ)	Provimi-Veal #6	12th-out of fuel
May 2	Atlanta, GA (200 mile champ)	Provimi-Veal #6	19th-oil pressure
May 30	Indianapolis, IN (500 mile champ)	Provimi-Veal #16	26th-accident
June 13	Milwaukee, WI (150 mile champ)	Provimi-Veal #6	12th
July 18	Irish Hills, MI (500 mile champ)	Provimi-Veal #6	10th
Aug. 1	Milwaukee, WI (200 mile champ)	Provimi-Veal #6	20th-handling
Aug. 15	Pocono, PA (500 mile champ)	Provimi-Veal #6	5th
Aug. 22	Irish Hills, MI (400 mile stock)	Provimi Veal Buick #24	24th-engine
Aug. 29	Riverside, CA (500 km champ)	Provimi-Veal #6	18th-engine

Index

* * *

Index to Photographs

* * *

Tony Bettenhausen in 1960. [*IMS*]

27
10
PROVIMI
VEAL
8